Signs of Life in the U.S.A.

Taikā

haikā

Seventh Edition

Signs of Life in the U.S.A.

Readings on Popular Culture for Writers

Sonia Maasik
University of California, Los Angeles

Jack Solomon
California State University, Northridge

BEDFORD/ST. MARTIN'S   Boston ◆ New York

For Bedford/St. Martin's

Developmental Editor: Adam Whitehurst
Associate Production Editor: Kellan Cummings
Associate Production Supervisor: Samuel Jones
Senior Marketing Manager: Molly Parke
Editorial Assistant: Nicholas McCarthy
Copy Editor: Diana George
Photo Researcher: Susan Doheny
Permissions Manager: Kalina K. Ingham
Art Director: Lucy Krikorian
Text Design: Anna Palchik
Cover Design: Marine Bouvier Miller
Cover Photo: Liz West, *Cataloguing Color: Household*, 2009.
    Photography by Liz West.
Composition: Cenveo Publisher Services
Printing and Binding: RR Donelley and Sons

President: Joan E. Feinberg
Editorial Director: Denise B. Wydra
Editor in Chief: Karen S. Henry
Director of Development: Erica T. Appel
Director of Marketing: Karen R. Soeltz
Director of Production: Susan W. Brown
Associate Director, Editorial Production: Elise S. Kaiser
Managing Editor: Shuli Traub

Library of Congress Control Number: 2011939166

Manufactured in the United States of America.

6   5   4   3
f   e   d   c

For information, write: Bedford/St. Martin's, 75 Arlington Street, Boston, MA 02116 (617-399-4000)

ISBN: 978-0-312-64700-1

Acknowledgments

Preface for Instructors

Since the 1994 publication of the first edition of *Signs of Life in the U.S.A.*, a popular cultural revolution has taken place, a revolution that is easy to take for granted but whose profundity demands the kind of analytic attention that this book is designed to foster. That revolution, of course, involves the explosive growth of digital technology and its many uses—the world of Facebook and Google, Twitter and texting, iPads and iPhones, and every other expression of a digitally linked-up world. The information superhighway of the 1990s has become the social network, and everything from the way we interact with one another to the way we consume entertainment is changing.

But one thing hasn't changed throughout the history of this book: the ever-increasing dominance of popular culture in American life. To put this another way, American popular culture is not simply an embellishment on our lives anymore, a superficial ornament that can be put on or taken off at will. Popular culture has virtually *become* our culture, permeating almost everything we do. So if we wish to understand ourselves, we must learn to think critically about the vast panoply of what was once condescendingly regarded as "mass culture." And now that digital technology has blurred beyond recognition the line between everyday life and entertainment, work and play, with the work places of school and office becoming veritable play stations wherein students and employees alike text and tweet while updating their Facebook pages, the relevance of *Signs of Life*'s focus on popular culture has only increased.

Then and Now

The importance of understanding the role of popular culture in our lives has not always been apparent to the academic world. When the first edition of *Signs of Life* appeared, the study of popular culture was still embroiled in the "culture wars" of the late 1980s and early 1990s, a struggle for academic legitimacy in which the adherents of popular cultural studies ultimately prevailed. Since then, more and more scholars and teachers have come to recognize the importance of understanding what Michel de Certeau has called "the practice of everyday life" and the value of using popular culture as a thematic ground for educating students in critical thinking and writing. Once excluded from academic study on the basis of a naturalized distinction between "high" and "low" culture, which contemporary cultural analysis has shown to be historically contingent, popular culture has come to be an accepted part of the curriculum, widely studied in freshman composition classrooms as well as in upper-division undergraduate courses and graduate seminars.

But recognition of the importance that popular culture has assumed in our society has not been restricted to the academy. Increasingly, Americans are realizing that American culture and popular culture are virtually one and the same, and that whether we are looking at our political system, our economy, or simply our national consciousness, the power of popular culture to shape our lives is strikingly apparent. That is why, unlike most other popular cultural texts, *Signs of Life* adopts an interpretive approach — semiotics — that is explicitly designed to analyze that intersection of ideology and entertainment that we call *popular culture*. We continue to make semiotics the guiding methodology behind *Signs of Life* because semiotics helps us, and our students, avoid the common pitfalls of uncritical celebration or simple trivia swapping.

The Critical Method: Semiotics

The reception of the first six editions of this text has demonstrated that the semiotic approach to popular culture has indeed found a place in America's composition classrooms. Composition instructors have seen that students feel a certain sense of ownership toward the products of popular culture and that using popular culture as a focus can help students overcome the sometimes alienating effects of traditional academic subject matter. At the same time, the semiotic method has helped instructors teach their students how to analyze the popular cultural phenomena that they enjoy writing about and through these methods students have learned the critical thinking and writing skills that their composition classes are designed to impart.

Reflecting the broad academic interest in cultural studies, we've assumed an inclusive definition of *popular culture*. The seven chapters in *Signs of Life in the U.S.A.* embrace everything from the marketing and consumption of the products of mass production to the mythologies and contradictions that underlie the actual content of the television programs and movies that entertain us. We have chosen semiotics as our approach because it has struck us that while students enjoy assignments that ask them to look at popular cultural phenomena, they often have trouble distinguishing between an argued interpretive analysis and the simple expression of an opinion. Some textbooks, for example, suggest assignments that involve analyzing a TV show or film, but they don't always tell a student how to do that. The semiotic method provides that guidance.

As a conceptual framework, semiotics teaches students to formulate cogent, well-supported interpretations. It emphasizes the examination of assumptions and of the way language shapes our apprehension of the world. And, because semiotics focuses on how beliefs are formulated within a social and political context (rather than just judging or evaluating those beliefs), it's ideal for discussing sensitive or politically charged issues. As an approach used in literature, media studies, anthropology, art and design coursework, sociology, law, and market research (to name only some of its more prominent field applications), semiotics has a cross-disciplinary appeal that makes it ideal for a writing class of students from a variety of majors and disciplines. We recognize that semiotics has a reputation for being highly technical or theoretical; rest assured that *Signs of Life* does not require students or instructors to have a technical knowledge of semiotics. We've provided clear and accessible introductions that explain what students need to know.

We also recognize that adopting a theoretical approach may be new to some instructors, so we've designed the book to allow instructors to use semiotics with their students as much or as little as they wish. The book does not obligate instructors or students to spend a lot of time with semiotics — although we do hope you'll find the approach intriguing and provocative.

The Editorial Apparatus

With its emphasis on popular culture, *Signs of Life* should generate lively class discussion and inspire many kinds of writing and thinking activities. The general introduction provides an overall framework for the book, acquainting students with the semiotic method they can use to interpret the topics raised in each chapter. It is followed by the section "Writing about Popular Culture" that not only provides a brief introduction to this topic but also features three sample student essays that demonstrate different approaches to writing critical essays on popular cultural topics. Also included in that section are three articles that guide students in the appropriate use of the Internet as a research tool. The introduction concludes with "Conducting Research and Citing Sources," a section to help your students properly document the research they've done for their writing assignments.

Each chapter starts with a frontispiece, a provocative visual image related to the chapter's topic, and an introduction that suggests ways to "read" the topic, provides model interpretations, and links the issues raised by the reading selections. Every chapter introduction contains three types of boxed questions designed to stimulate student thinking on the topic. The Exploring the Signs questions invite students to reflect on an issue in a journal entry or other prewriting activity, while the Discussing the Signs questions trigger class activities such as debates, discussions, or small-group work. Reading the Net questions invite students to explore the chapter's topic on the Internet, both for research purposes and for texts to analyze.

Two sorts of assignments accompany each reading. The Reading the Text questions help students comprehend the selections, asking them to identify important concepts and arguments, explain key terms, and relate main ideas to one another and to the evidence presented. The Reading the Signs questions are writing and activity prompts designed to produce clear analytic thinking and strong persuasive writing; they often make connections among reading selections from different chapters. Most assignments call for analytic essays, while some invite journal responses, in-class debates, group work, or other creative activities. Complementing the readings in each chapter are images that serve as visual texts to be discussed. We also include a glossary of semiotic terms, which can serve as a ready reference to key words and concepts used in the chapter introductions. Finally, the Instructor's Manual (*Editors' Notes for Signs of Life in the U.S.A.*) provides suggestions for organizing your syllabus, encouraging student responses to the readings, and using popular culture and semiotics in the writing class.

What's New in the Seventh Edition

Popular culture evolves at a rapid pace, and the substantial revision required for the seventh edition of *Signs of Life in the U.S.A.* reflects this essential mutability. First, we have updated our readings, including over thirty new selections focusing on issues and trends that have emerged since the last edition of this book. We have also updated the exemplary topics in our introductions, which are used to model the critical assignments that follow, and have adjusted the focus of some chapters to reflect changing conditions of students' lives and the ways they consume popular culture. A new chapter, "American Makeover: Constructing Identity in the Age of Entertainment," combines the sections on multicultural and gender semiotics from earlier editions to reflect the new, more flexible approach to personal identity that contemporary students embrace.

From the beginning, *Signs of Life in the U.S.A.* has been based on the premise that in a postindustrial, McCluhanesque world, the image has come to supplant the printed word in American, and global, culture. That is yet another of the reasons we chose semiotics, which provides a rational basis for the critical analysis of images as the guiding methodology for every edition of our book. Each edition of *Signs of Life* has accordingly included images for critical analysis; the seventh edition continues this tradition. The images included in the text supplement the readings, offering a visual perspective designed to enhance the critical understanding modeled by the texts. Yet the images are not meant to replace the texts—we strongly believe that while the semiotic interpretation of images can help students hone their writing skills, it should not be a substitute for learning critical thinking through the analysis of written texts.

Even as we revise this text to reflect current trends, popular culture continues to evolve. The inevitable gap between the pace of editing and publishing, on the one hand, and the flow of popular culture, on the other, need not affect the use of popular culture in the classroom, however. The readings in the text, and the semiotic method we propose, are designed to show students how to analyze and write critical essays about any topic they choose. They can choose a topic that appeared before they were born, or they can turn to the latest box-office or prime-time hit to appear after the publication of this edition of *Signs of Life in the U.S.A.* Facebook and Twitter may be replaced by new sites within the life span of this edition (indeed, Facebook surpassed MySpace in popularity shortly after the publication of the sixth edition), but such changes are opportunities for further analysis, not obstacles. To put it another way, the practice of everyday life may itself be filled with evanescent fads and trends, but daily life is not itself a fad. As the vital texture of our lived experience, popular culture provides a stable background against which students of every generation can test their critical skills.

You Get More Digital Choices for *Signs of Life in the U.S.A.*

Signs of Life doesn't stop with a book. Online, you'll find both free and affordable premium resources to help students get even more out of the book and your course. You'll also find convenient instructor resources, such as downloadable sample syllabi, classroom activities, and even a nationwide community of teachers. To learn more about or to order any of the products below, contact your Bedford/St. Martin's sales representative, e-mail sales support (**sales_support@bfwpub.com**), or visit the Web site at **bedfordstmartins.com**.

COMPANION WEB SITE FOR SIGNS OF LIFE IN THE U.S.A.
bedfordstmartins.com/signsoflife

Send students to free and open resources, choose flexible premium resources to supplement your print text, or upgrade to an expanding collection of innovative digital content.

Free and open resources for *Signs of Life in the U.S.A.* provide students with easy-to-access reference materials, visual tutorials, and support for working with sources.

- Three free tutorials from *ix: visual exercises* by Cheryl Ball and Kristin Arola
- *TopLinks* with reliable online sources
- *The Bedford Bibliographer*: a tool for collecting source information and making a bibliography in MLA, APA, or *Chicago* styles

Assign an interactive e-book. It is almost quaint to say that the Internet is ever-present in students' lives. Perhaps it is more apt to say that social media and Web 2.0 deliver a larger percentage of the popular culture that students consume than ever before. For the first time ever, *Signs of Life in the U.S.A.* is available in an e-book format. With all the content of the print book, the ***Signs of Life in the U.S.A. e-Book*** lets students easily search, highlight, and bookmark. Instructors can customize and rearrange chapters, add and share notes, and link to quizzes and activities. Loaded with additional multimodal readings, the e-book gives students more flexible options for thinking and writing about popular culture. The ***Signs of Life in the U.S.A. e-Book*** can be purchased standalone or packaged with the print book. To order the e-book packaged with the print book, use ISBN 978-1-4576-1830-7.

Additional online readings. Even if you don't order the e-book, you can package the additional online readings with the print textbook. These video and audio clips, from such diverse organizations as NPR and The Moth storytelling series, add a new dimension to students' analysis of popular culture. For more information about the extra multimodal selections, visit the catalog page at **bedfordstmartins.com/signsoflifecatalog**.

Let students choose their format. Students can purchase *Signs of Life in the U.S.A.* in popular e-book formats for computers, tablets, and e-readers. For more details, visit **bedfordstmartins.com/ebooks**.

VideoCentral: English is a growing collection of videos for the writing class that captures real-world, academic, and student writers talking about how and why they write. *VideoCentral: English* can be packaged for free with *Signs of Life in the U.S.A.* An activation code is required. To order *VideoCentral* packaged with the print book, use ISBN 978-1-4576-1020-2.

Re:Writing Plus gathers all of Bedford/St. Martin's premium digital content for composition into one online collection. It includes hundreds of model documents, the first ever peer-review game, and *VideoCentral: English*. *Re:Writing Plus* can be purchased separately or packaged with the print book at a significant discount. An activation code is required. To order *Re:Writing Plus* packaged with *Signs of Life in the U.S.A.,* use ISBN 978-1-4576-1022-6.

I-SERIES

Add more value to your text by choosing one of the following tutorial series, free when packaged with *Signs of Life in the U.S.A.* This popular series presents multimedia tutorials in a flexible format — because there are things you can't do in a book. To learn more about package options or any of the following products, contact your Bedford/St. Martin's sales representative or visit **bedfordstmartins.com**.

ix visualizing composition 2.0 (available online) helps students put into practice key rhetorical and visual concepts. To order *ix visualizing composition* packaged with the print book, use ISBN 978-1-4576-1283-1.

i-claim: visualizing argument (available on CD-ROM) offers a new way to see argument — with six tutorials, an illustrated glossary, and over seventy multimedia arguments. To order *i-claim: visualizing argument* packaged with the print book, use ISBN 978-1-4576-1021-9.

i-cite: visualizing sources (available online as part of *Re:Writing Plus*) brings research to life through an animated introduction, four tutorials, and hands-on source practice. To order *i-cite: visualizing sources* packaged with the print book, use ISBN 978-1-4576-1023-3.

INSTRUCTOR RESOURCES

You have a lot to do in your course. Bedford/St. Martin's wants to make it easy for you to find the support you need — and to get it quickly.

The *Editors' Notes for Signs of Life in the U.S.A.* is available in PDF format and can be downloaded from **bedfordstmartins.com/signsoflife**. In addition to chapter overviews and teaching tips, the *Editors' Notes* includes sample syllabi and suggestions for classroom activities.

TeachingCentral (**bedfordstmartins.com/teachingcentral**) offers the entire list of Bedford/St. Martin's print and online professional resources in one place. You'll find landmark reference works, sourcebooks on pedagogical issues, award-winning collections, and practical advice for the classroom — all free for instructors.

Bits (**bedfordbits.com**) collects creative ideas for teaching a range of composition topics in an easily searchable blog. A community of teachers — leading scholars, authors, and editors — discuss revision, research, grammar and style, technology, peer review, and much more. Take, use, adapt, and pass around the ideas. Then, come back to the site to comment or share your own suggestion. Visit the *Signs of Life in the U.S.A.* blog, written by author Jack Solomon, featured on *Bits* at **http://blogs.bedfordstmartins.com/bits/author /solomon**.

Bedford Coursepacks allow you to easily integrate our most popular content into your own course management systems. For details, visit **bedfordstmartins.com/cms**.

Acknowledgments

The vastness of the terrain of popular culture has enabled many users of the sixth edition of this text to make valuable suggestions for the seventh edition. We have incorporated many such suggestions and thank all for their comments on our text: Danielle Bienvenue Bray, Xavier University of Louisiana; Wallace T. Cleaves, University of California, Riverside; Macklin Cowart, Gainesville State College; Judy Dragoo, South Puget Sound Community College; TJ Gerlach, Mesa State College; Lauren Gras, East Los Angeles College; Nance Hahn, Onondaga Community College; Beatty George Henson, Chaffey College; Brooke Hughes, California State University, Bakersfield; Cecile Kandl, Bucks County Community College; Terry Kruger, Central Oregon Community College; Elizabeth Luciano, Bucks County Community College; Tim Melnarik, Pasadena City College; Shawn Nichols-Boyle, Indiana University, South Bend; Christine Palumbo-DeSimone, Temple University; Bidhan Roy, California State University, Los Angeles; Sandra C. Snow, Central Michigan University; Richard G. Swartz, University of Southern Maine; Judith Tabler, Marymount University; David Venditto, Bucks County Community College; Paul Walker, Murray State University; Shannon Walters, Temple University; Rob Wilds, Columbia State Community College; Brad Windhauser, Temple University; Lara M. Zeises, University of Delaware.

We are also grateful to those reviewers who examined the book in depth: Jeffrey Andelora, Mesa Community College; Linsey Cuti, Kankakee Community College; Gareth Euridge, Tallahassee Community College; Rebecca Gerdes, Indiana University, South Bend; Robert S. Imbur, University of Toledo; Tammie M. Kennedy, University of Nebraska, Omaha; Mark Lanting, Kankakee Community College; Caesar Perkowski, Gordon College; Pamela Roeper, University of Akron — Medina County University Center; Joshua Ethan Rubin, Indiana University, South Bend; Graham R. Scott, University of California, Riverside; and Anne C. Wheeler, Boston Architectural College. If we have not included something you'd like to work on, you may still direct your students to it, using this text as a guide, not as a set of absolute prescriptions. The practice of everyday life includes the conduct of a classroom, and we want all users of the seventh edition of *Signs of Life in the U.S.A.* to feel free to pursue that practice in whatever way best suits their interests and aims.

Once again, we wish to thank heartily the people at Bedford/St. Martin's who have enabled us to make this new edition a reality, beginning with Joan Feinberg, who has now been at the helm through nine of our ten textbook projects. We especially want to thank our editor Adam Whitehurst, who brought to the seventh edition of *Signs of Life* both a fresh perspective and a storehouse of creative energy that, in the tradition of our collaboration with Bedford's editors, has left its own imprint on the book. Kellan Cummings, Sam Jones, and Shuli Traub ably guided our manuscript through the rigors of production, while Nicholas McCarthy handled the innumerable questions and details that arose during textbook development. Susan Doheny expertly researched and obtained permission for art, and Margaret Gorenstein cleared text permissions. Our thanks go as well to Diana George for her fine copyediting of this book.

Contents

"Frontier; opportunity; more. This has been the American trinity from the very start."

"Retailers don't just want to know how shoppers behave in their stores. They *have* to know."

"Everyone, from the architecture critic at the *New York Times* to kids in the hall of a Montana high school, knows what *Ralph Lauren* means."

"The extreme turbulence that hit the American economy in 2008 offers a rare window of opportunity to hit the re-set button on consumer culture as we know it."

A popular play figure for girls makes a purchase.

"Packages serve as symbols both of their contents and of a way of life."

MINETTE E. DRUMRIGHT and PATRICK E. MURPHY: *How Advertising Practitioners View Ethics: Moral Muteness, Moral Myopia, and Moral Imagination* 199

"Ethical issues did not appear to be on the radar screens of our first group of [advertising] informants."

JENNIFER L. POZNER: *Dove's "Real Beauty" Backlash* 219

"Even though Dove's 'Real Beauty' ads play to and subtly reinforce the stereotypes they claim to be exposing, it's impossible not to feel inspired by the sight of these attractive, healthy women smiling playfully at us from their places of billboard honor."

ERIC SCHLOSSER: *Kid Kustomers* 222

"The aim of most children's advertising is straightforward: Get kids to nag their parents and nag them well."

JULIA B. CORBETT: *A Faint Green Sell: Advertising and the Natural World* 227

"The values that advertising communicates about the natural world revolve around an idealized and materialized environment."

ALAN FOLJAMBE: *Car Advertising — Dominating Nature* 246

"Car companies are positioning themselves as part of, rather than a threat to, the environment."

GLORIA STEINEM: *Sex, Lies, and Advertising* 249

"What could women's magazines be like if they were as editorially free as good books?"

Portfolio of Advertisements

Go RVing

Levi's

World Wildlife Federation

Converse

Toyota Celica

Braun Series 3

ThinkB4YouSpeak.com

Chapter 3.
Video Dreams: *Television and Cultural Forms* 271

FRANCINE PROSE: *Voting Democracy off the Island: Reality TV and the Republican Ethos* 287

"The castaways vote, as we do, but it's a democracy that might have been conceived if the spirit of Machiavelli had briefly possessed the mind of Thomas Jefferson."

Signs of Life in the U.S.A.

POPULAR SIGNS

*Or, Everything You Always
Knew about American Culture
(but Nobody Asked)*

Beverly Hills, 90210 (with Vampires)

You really know that something is happening when Walmart is selling a collectible Barbie and Ken vampire set.

OK, it's the Barbie Pink Label Edward & Bella Twilight Collector Doll Bundle, to be precise, and there are also Jacob, Alice, and Victoria dolls available, at latest count. But you get the picture. To put it simply: Vampires are hot. From *True Blood* to *Twilight, The Vampire Diaries* to *The Gates*, contemporary popular culture is awash in vampire stories. And while nothing is particularly new about the popularity of supernatural tales about these immortal blood-sucking monsters, what *is* new is that vampires aren't simply monsters anymore. In fact, much of the time they aren't monsters at all, but are, rather, heroes and heroines, and very cool, very sexy ones at that.

All of this raises an important question: What is going on in our culture?

It is easy to take vampiremania for granted — after all, the vampire story has been best-selling stuff ever since Bram Stoker dusted off the old folk tales of shape-changing bat-men (related, not so coincidentally, to werewolves) and gave Count Dracula to the world. But these vampires are not the same. It's as if *Dawson's Creek* were set in Transylvania and *Nosferatu* moved to Melrose Place.

Such a shift is a **sign**, a **signifier** of a profound change in American consciousness marked by the *difference* between a vampire story whose entertainment value lies in the pursuit and destruction of a literally bloodthirsty demon and one that is essentially a romance within which vampires are the romantic leads. That today's vampire story is entertaining is self-evident (or,

1

at least, evident from its ubiquity in contemporary popular culture). The question is, why is the new version so entertaining *now*? *What* makes it entertaining? *Why* is it popular? What does that popularity reveal about us?

Asking such questions is the essence of critical thinking, which goes beyond the gathering of information to create an assessment of its significance. This book is designed to help you learn how to think and write critically, taking American popular culture as its focus. Each chapter in *Signs of Life in the U.S.A.* takes a particular facet of the kaleidoscopic panorama of American pop culture and, through readings, images, and assignments, guides you through the process that will help you answer such questions as why vampire stories have been so popular recently and help you write about your conclusions. We will return shortly in this introduction to the vampire question itself, but first it would be useful to look at just what we mean by the words "popular culture" and why it is useful, even important, to think critically about it.

From Folk to Fab

Traditionally, popular or "low" culture constituted the culture of the masses. It was set apart from "high" culture, which included such things as classical music and literature, the fine arts and philosophy, and the elite learning that was the province of the ruling classes who had the money and leisure necessary to attain it — and who were often the direct patrons of high art and its artists. Low culture, for its part, had two main sides. One side, most notoriously illustrated by the violent entertainments of the Roman Empire (such as gladiatorial contests, public executions, feeding Christians to lions) continues to be a sure crowd pleaser to this day, as demonstrated by the widespread popularity of violent, erotic, and/or vulgar entertainment (can you spell *Jackass*?). The other side, which we can call "popular" in the etymological sense of being of the people, overlaps with what we now call "folk culture." Quietly existing alongside high culture, folk culture expressed the experience and creativity of the masses in the form of ballads, agricultural festivals, fairy tales, feasts, folk art, folk music, and so on. Self-produced by amateur performers, folk culture can be best envisioned by thinking of neighbors gathering on a modest Appalachian front porch to play their guitars, banjos, dulcimers, zithers, mandolins, fiddles, and whatnot to perform, for their own entertainment, ballads and songs passed down from generation to generation.

Folk culture, of course, still exists. But for the past two hundred years it has been dwindling, with increasing rapidity, as it becomes overwhelmed by a new kind of popular culture, a commercialized culture that, while still including elements of both the folk and the vulgar traditions, represents the outcome of a certain historical evolution. This culture, the popular culture that is most familiar today and which is the topic of this book, is a commercial, for-profit culture aimed at providing entertainment to a mass

Traditional high culture: Deborah Voigt in performance at the
Metropolitan Opera in New York.

audience. Corporate rather than communal, it has transformed entertainment into a commodity to be marketed alongside all the other products in a
consumer society.

The forces that transformed the low culture of the past into contemporary popular culture arose in the industrial revolution of the late eighteenth
century and its accompanying urbanization of European and American society. Along with the rise of corporate capitalism and the advent of electronic
technologies, these historical forces shaped the emergence of the mass cultural marketplace of entertainments that we know today. To see how this
happened, let's begin with the industrial revolution.

Prior to the industrial revolution, most Europeans and Americans lived
in scattered agricultural settlements. While traveling entertainers in theatrical

troupes and circuses might come to visit the larger of these settlements, most people, especially those with little money, had little access to professional entertainment and so had to produce their own. But with the industrial revolution, masses of people who had made their living through agriculture were compelled to leave their rural communities and move to the cities where employment increasingly was to be had. Population began to concentrate in urban centers as the rural countryside emptied, leading to the development of mass societies.

With the emergence of mass society came the development of **mass culture**. For just as mass societies are governed by centralized systems of governance (consider how the huge expanse of the United States is governed by a federal government concentrated in Washington, DC), so too are mass cultures entertained by culture industries concentrated in a few locations (as the film and TV industries are concentrated in Hollywood and its immediate environs). Thanks to the invention of such technologies as the cinema, the phonograph, and the radio at the end of the nineteenth century, and of television and digital technology in the mid-to-late-twentieth century, the means to disseminate centrally produced mass entertainments to a mass society became possible. Thus, whether you live in Boston or Boise, New York or Nebraska, the entertainment you enjoy is produced in the same few locations and is the same entertainment (TV programs, movies, DVDs, what-have-you) no matter where you consume it. This growth of mass culture has been conditioned by the growth of a capitalist economic system in America. That is, it is American-style capitalism that has ensured that mass culture would develop as a for-profit industry.

To get a better idea of how the whole process unfolded, let's go back to that Appalachian front porch. Before electricity and urbanization, folks living in the backwoods of rural America needed to make their music themselves if they wanted music. They had no radios, phonographs, CD players, or iPods, or even electricity, and theaters with live performers were hard to get to and too expensive. Under such conditions, the Appalachian region developed a vibrant folk musical culture. But as people began to move to places like Pittsburgh and Detroit, where the steel and auto industries began to offer employment in the late nineteenth and early twentieth centuries, the conditions under which neighbors could produce their own music decayed, for the communal conditions under which folk culture thrives were broken down by the mass migration to the cities. At the same time, the need to produce one's own music declined as folks who once plucked their own guitars and banjos could simply turn on their radios or purchase records to listen to professional musicians perform for them. Those musicians — like Bill Monroe, who pioneered bluegrass in the 1930s as a commercial synthesis of the folk music traditions he had grown up with — were contracted by recording companies in business to turn a profit, and their music, in turn, could be heard on the radio because corporate sponsors provided the advertising that made (and still makes) commercial radio broadcasting possible.

Traditional folk culture in transition: Bill Monroe is known as the father of bluegrass music.

So what had once been an amateur, do-it-yourself activity (the production of folk music) became a professional, for-profit industry with passive consumers paying for their entertainment either through the direct purchase of a commodity (e.g., a record) or by having to listen to the advertising that encouraged them to purchase the products that sponsored their favorite radio programs. It was and still is possible, of course, to make one's own music (or, more generally, one's own entertainment), but not only is it easier and perhaps aesthetically more pleasing to listen to a professional recording, in the kind of mass consumer society in which we live, we are, in effect, constantly being trained to be the sort of passive consumers that keep the whole consumer-capitalist system going. Without that consumption, the economy might totally collapse.

This is hardly an exaggeration, for the advent of postindustrial capitalism has made popular culture all the more important with every passing year. With the American economy turning further and further away from industrial production toward the production and consumption of entertainment (including sports), entertainment has been moving from the margins of our cultural consciousness — as a mere form of play or recreation — to its center as a major buttress of our economy. A constant bombardment of advertising (which, after all, is the driving force behind the financing of Web 2.0 media, just as it was for radio and television a generation or two ago) continually prods us to consume the entertainments that our economy produces. That bombardment has been so successful that our whole cultural consciousness is changing, becoming more childlike, more concerned with play rather than with work, even while *at* work. (Tell the truth now: Do you ever text a friend or play games on your laptop during class?)

The result of the centuries-long process we have sketched above is the kind of culture we have today: one centered on entertainments and enter-tainers. From infotainment to televangelism, Christian rock to Rock the Vote, America shows signs today of an evolutionary development in which the high and low cultures of the past are melding into a cultural synthesis that could be called an *entertainment culture* — a culture, that is to say, in which all aspects of society (including politics and the traditional elite arts) are linked by a com-mon imperative to entertain.

Throw another song on the Barbie: Mattel has produced an MP3 player in the shape of the popular girls' toy.

Pop Goes the Culture

Thus, far from being a mere recreational frivolity, a leisure activity that our society could easily dispense with, popular cultural entertainment today constitutes the essential texture of our everyday lives. From the way we entertain ourselves to the goods and services that we produce and consume, we are enveloped in a popular cultural environment that we can neither do without nor escape, even if we wanted to. To see this, just try to imagine a world without the Internet, TV, movies, sports, music, shopping malls, advertising, or DVDs, MTV, or MP3s. Still, you might be surprised to find popular culture as the topic for your university composition class, because until recently the study of popular culture was largely excluded from university curricula. As institutions of a high culture that is rapidly dwindling into a sort of "museum" culture that has little to do with ordinary, everyday life, universities have been regarded as havens from, and bastions against, the popular cultural entertainments that have driven high culture from the stage. Not until the advent of cultural studies, which was first pioneered in English universities and came to the United States in the late 1980s, did the study of popular culture become a common, and accepted, topic for university study in America. But as the barrier between high and low culture, privileged and popular, continues to erode — in a world where *Romeo and Juliet* is a pop opera and string quartets have been part of the rock scene ever since the Beatles's "Yesterday," where divas like Deborah Voigt feel compelled to undergo gastric bypass surgery in order to maintain their careers in an operatic world that is demanding that its sopranos resemble Britney Spears — the study of pop culture is emerging as a mainstay of contemporary higher education.

This has been especially true in American composition classrooms, which have taken the lead in incorporating popular culture into academic study, both because of the subject's inherent interest value and because of its profound familiarity to most students. Your own expertise in popular culture means not only that you may know more about a given topic than your instructor but that you may use that knowledge as a basis for learning the critical thinking and writing skills that your composition class is charged to teach you. This book is designed to show you how to do that — how to write about American popular culture as you would write about any other academic subject.

Signs of Life in the U.S.A., then, is designed to let you exploit your knowledge of popular culture so that you may grow into a better writer about any subject. You can interpret the popularity of a TV program like *House*, for example, in the same manner as you would interpret, say, a short story, because *House*, too, constitutes a kind of **sign**. A sign is something, anything, that carries a meaning. A stop sign, for instance, means exactly what it says, "Stop when you approach this intersection," while carrying the implied message "or risk getting a ticket or into an accident." Words, too, are signs: You read them to figure out what they mean. You were trained to read such signs, but that training began so long ago that you may well take your ability to read for granted. Nevertheless, all your life you have also been encountering, and interpreting, other sorts of signs. Although you were never formally taught to read them, you know what they mean anyway. Take the way you wear your hair. When you get your hair cut, you are not simply removing hair: You are making a statement, sending a message about yourself. It's the same for both men and women. Why was your hair short last year and long this year? Aren't you saying something with the scissors? In this way, you make your hairstyle into a sign that sends a message about your identity. You are surrounded by such signs. Just look at your classmates.

The world of signs could be called a kind of **text**, the text of America's popular culture. We want you to think of *Signs of Life in the U.S.A.* as a window onto that text. What you read in this book's essays and introductions should lead you to study and analyze the world around you for yourself. Let the readings guide you to your own interpretations, your own readings, of the text of America.

In this edition of *Signs of Life in the U.S.A.*, we have chosen seven "windows" that look out onto separate, but often interrelated, segments of the American scene. In some cases, we have put some of the scenery directly into this book, as when we include actual ads in our chapter on advertising that can be directly interpreted. In other cases, where it is impossible to put something directly into a textbook, like a TV show or a movie, we have included essays that help you think about specific programs and films, and assignments that invite you to go out and interpret a TV show or movie of your own choosing. Each chapter also includes an introduction written to alert you to the kinds of signs you will find there, along with model analyses and advice on how to go about interpreting the topics that the chapter raises.

We have designed *Signs of Life in the U.S.A.* to reflect the many ways in which culture shapes our sense of reality and of ourselves, from the products that we buy to the way that culture, through such media as television and the movies, constructs our personal identities. This text thus introduces you to both the entertainment and the ideological sides of popular culture — and shows how the two sides are mutually interdependent. Indeed, one of the major lessons you can learn from this book is how to find the ideological underpinnings of some of the most apparently innocent entertainments and consumer goods.

Signs of Life in the U.S.A. accordingly begins with a chapter on "Consuming Passions," because America is a consumer culture, and so the environment within which the galaxy of popular signs functions is, more often than not, a consumerist one. This is true not only for obvious consumer products like clothes and cars but for such traditionally nonconsumer items as political candidates, who are often marketed like any other consumer product. It is difficult to find anything in contemporary America that is not affected somehow by our consumerist ethos or by consumerism's leading promoter, the advertiser. Thus, the second chapter, "Brought to You B(u)y," explores the world of advertising, for advertising provides the grease, so to speak, that lubricates the engine of America's consumer culture. Because television and film are the sources of many of our most significant cultural products, we include a chapter on each. Chapters on new media, American contradictions and conflicts, and personal identity round out our survey of everyday life.

Throughout, the book invites you to go out and select your own "texts" for analysis (an advertisement, a film, a fashion fad, a political opinion, and so on). Here's where your own experience is particularly valuable, because it has made you familiar with many different kinds of popular signs and their backgrounds, as well as with the particular popular cultural system or environment to which they belong.

The seven "windows" you will find in *Signs of Life in the U.S.A.* are all intended to reveal the common intersections of entertainment and ideology that can be found in contemporary American life. Often what seems to be simply entertainment, like a TV show, can actually be quite political, while what seems political, like health care, can be cast as entertainment as well — as in movies like *Sicko*. The point is to see that little in American life is merely entertainment; indeed, just about everything we do has a meaning, often a profound one.

The Semiotic Method

To find this meaning, to interpret and write effectively about the signs of popular culture, you need a method, and it is part of the purpose of this book to introduce such a method to you. Without a methodology for interpreting signs, writing about them could become little more than producing descriptive reviews or opinion pieces. There is nothing wrong with writing descriptions and opinions, but one of your tasks in your writing class is to learn how to write academic essays — that is, analytical essays that present theses or arguments that are well supported by evidence. The method we draw upon in this book — a method known as *semiotics* — is especially well suited for analyzing popular culture. Whether or not you're familiar with this word, you are already practicing sophisticated semiotic analyses every day of your life. Reading this page is an act of semiotic decoding (words and letters are signs that must be interpreted), but so is figuring out just what a friend means by wearing a particular shirt or dress. For a semiotician (one who practices semiotic analysis), a shirt, a haircut, a television image, anything at all, can be taken as a sign, as a message to be decoded and analyzed to discover its meaning. Every cultural activity for the semiotician leaves a trace of meaning, a kind of blip on the semiotic Richter scale, that remains for us to read, just as a geologist "reads" the earth for signs of earthquakes, volcanic activity, and other geological phenomena.

Many who hear the word *semiotics* for the first time assume that it is the name of a new, and forbidding, subject. But in truth, the study of signs is neither very new nor forbidding. Its modern form took shape in the late nineteenth and early twentieth centuries through the writings and lectures of two men. Charles Sanders Peirce (1839–1914) was an American philosopher who first coined the word *semiotics*, while Ferdinand de Saussure (1857–1913) was a Swiss linguist whose lectures became the foundation for what he called *semiology*. Without knowing of each other's work, Peirce and Saussure established the fundamental principles that modern semioticians or semiologists — the terms are essentially interchangeable — have developed into the contemporary study of semiotics.

Reduced to its simplest principles, the semiotic method carries on Saussure's argument that the meaning of a sign lies, in part, in the fact that it can be *differentiated* from any other sign within the **system**, or **code**, to which it belongs. For example, in the traffic code, being able to distinguish the difference between green, red, and amber lights is essential to understanding the meaning of a traffic signal. But that's not all there is to it, because simultaneously you have to know that the meaning of a red light is connected to the concept "stop," while a green light signals the concept "go," and an amber light means "caution." To decode these meanings correctly, you need to be able to *associate* any particular red light you see in a traffic signal with all other traffic signals featuring red lights, and any green light with all other green lights, and so on.

But what if changes are introduced into the system? Here is where Peirce's contribution comes in. For Peirce, signs are situated not only within systems or codes but also within *history* — a principle of especial importance when you are interpreting popular cultural signs, because their meanings are constantly changing. For example, in the late 1960s, the Volkswagen Beetle came to signify the freewheeling lifestyle of the youth counterculture of that era. But when Volkswagen brought it back in the late 1990s as the New Beetle, it no longer had that meaning; rather, its significance was somewhat gentrified and feminized as it became a fashionable car favored by young women.

Applying semiotics to the interpretation of popular culture was pioneered in the 1950s by the French semiologist Roland Barthes (1915–1980) in his book *Mythologies* (1957). The basic principles of semiotics had already been explored by linguists and anthropologists, but Barthes took the matter to the heart of his own contemporary France, analyzing the cultural significance of everything from professional wrestling to striptease, toys, and plastics. It was Barthes, too, who established the **political** dimensions of semiotic analysis. Often, the subject of a semiotic analysis — a movie, say, or a TV program — doesn't look political at all; it simply looks like entertainment. In our society *politics* has become something of a dirty word, and to *politicize* something seems somehow to contaminate it. So you shouldn't feel uneasy if at first it feels hard to detect a political meaning in an apparently neutral topic. You may even think that to do so is to read too much into that topic. But Barthes's point — and the point of semiotics in general — is that all social behavior is political in the sense that it reflects some subjective or group interest. Such interests are encoded in the ideologies that express the values and opinions of those who hold them. Politics, then, is just another name for the clash of ideologies that takes place in any complex society where the interests of all those who belong to it constantly compete with one another.

Take the way people responded to James Cameron's *Avatar* in 2009. Seeing in it a similarity to the 1990 Kevin Costner western *Dances with Wolves*, conservatives complained that it was an anti-corporate allegory that demonized American history and foreign policy. Also seeing a connection to *Dances with Wolves*, some liberals complained about its choice of a white male as the heroic leader of a nonwhite people who, presumably, couldn't get along without him. Either way, the Internet was filled with dueling blogs about the matter.

While not all popular cultural signs are as politically controversial as *Avatar* has been, careful analysis can often uncover some set of political values within them, although those values may be subtly concealed behind an apparently apolitical facade. Indeed, the political values that guide our social behavior are often concealed behind images that don't look political at all. But that is because we have to look beyond what a popular cultural sign **denotes**, or directly shows (in *Avatar*, a human invasion of an extraterrestrial world populated by giant blue people), to what it **connotes**, or indirectly suggests (for many viewers, *Avatar* connoted a long history of European colonization and conquest of aboriginal populations). The **denotation** of a sign is its first level of meaning, and you have to be able to understand that meaning before you can move to the next level. The **connotation** of a sign takes you to its political or cultural significance.

Consider, for example, the depiction of the "typical" American family in the classic TV sitcoms of the '50s and '60s, which denoted images of happy, docile housewives in suburban middle-class families. To most contemporary viewers, who did not look beyond their denotation, those images looked "normal" or natural at the time that they were first broadcast — the way families and women were supposed to be. The shows didn't seem at all ideological. But to a feminist semiotician, the old sitcoms were in fact highly political, because from a feminist viewpoint the happy housewives they presented were really images designed to convince women that their place was in the home, not in the workplace competing with men. Such images — or signs — did not reflect reality; they reflected, rather, the interests of a patriarchal, male-centered society. That, in effect, was their **connotation**. If you think not, then ask yourself why programs were called *Father Knows Best, Bachelor Father*, and *My Three Sons*, but not *My Three Daughters*. And why did few of the women characters have jobs or ever seem to leave the house? Of course, there was *I Love Lucy*, but wasn't Lucy a screwball whose husband, Ricky, had to rescue her from one crisis after another?

Such an interpretation reflects what the English cultural theorist Stuart Hall (b. 1932) calls an *oppositional* reading. Such a reading of a cultural text

The popular television show *Leave It to Beaver* (1957–1963) exemplified traditional family values of the 1950s.

like a sitcom challenges the "preferred reading," which would simply take the program at face value, accepting its representation of family life as normative and natural. The oppositional reading, on the other hand, proposes an interpretation that resists the normative view, seeking to uncover a political subtext. The fact that so many cultural signifiers *appear* normative and natural, as transparent images of an apolitical social reality, can make oppositional reading look "unnatural," or like "reading into" your topic a meaning that isn't there. After all, isn't a sitcom simply a trivial entertainment that distracts viewers from the concerns of everyday life? But from a semiotic perspective, everything in everyday life is potentially meaningful, a sign to be decoded, and the fact that something is entertaining is only the beginning of the matter. The next question is, "*Why* is it entertaining and what does that say about those who are entertained by it?"

Abduction and Overdetermination

You may think that a semiotic analysis resembles sociological interpretation, and indeed cultural semiotics and sociology do not significantly differ. The differences are largely methodological. Sociology tends to be highly statistical in its methodology, often working with case studies, surveys, and other quantifiable evidence. Cultural semiotics largely works by looking at broad patterns of behavior and seeking what Charles Sanders Peirce called *abductive* explanations for them. **Abduction** is the process of arriving at an interpretation by seeking the most plausible explanation for something. No one can absolutely prove a semiotic interpretation, but the more material you can bring into your systems of related and differentiated signifiers, the more convincing your movement from denotation to connotation will be.

As you build up your interpretation of a cultural signifier, you will often find that you can come up with more than one explanation for it. Is that a problem? Are you just having trouble deciding on a single argument? No, because cultural signs are usually **overdetermined**: that is to say, they can have more than one cause or explanation (another word for this is *polysemous*). This is especially true for what we consider "rich" cultural signs, ones that have had a long-standing effect on our tastes and habits. As we will see in the analysis to follow, the popularity of vampire stories is especially overdetermined, with many interpretive explanations converging. Indeed, the more causes behind a cultural phenomenon, the more popular it is likely to be.

Put more simply still, a semiotic analysis begins by posing some basic questions. Why does this thing look the way it does? Why is it saying what it says? Why am I enjoying it? In short, take nothing for granted when analyzing any image or activity.

Interpreting Popular Signs: The Modern Vampire

Situating signs within systems of *related* phenomena with which they can be associated and differentiated: This is the essential formula for interpreting popular cultural signs. Being attuned to the history that provides the background for a sign is also important. To see how this works in practice, let's return now to those vampires.

To begin with, the sheer ubiquity of contemporary vampire stories tells us that they are a piece of mass culture worth interpreting. Often that is a good place to begin when choosing a subject: with something big, because the larger the phenomenon, the more likely it is to have broad cultural significance. Widely popular phenomena also offer more evidence that you can use to support your interpretation. And with the enormous success of the *Twilight* series of books and movies, along with such television programs as *True Blood, The Vampire Diaries*, and *The Gates*, we can see plenty of indicators that something significant is going on.

So the first step when conducting a semiotic analysis is to build a **system** of related signs. The building of a system often leads to the construction of larger systems that envelop your original one (for example, the *Twilight* story belongs to the system of vampire tales, which themselves are part of the horror system, which can be related to fantasy stories, and so on), but it is best to begin with the most obviously related phenomena. So let's consider the **system** of vampire stories.

This system has a long history, going back to medieval superstitions and misunderstandings about the nature of human decomposition, as well as to legends about such historical figures as Vlad the Impaler. But the key point for our analysis is that whether we are looking at folklore, superstition, or medieval history and medicine, the vampire was always a horrific figure, a monster, a demon related to such other "living dead" ghouls as zombies (it might be noted here that J. R. R. Tolkien's Nazgûl are, in effect, vampires). Even when sexuality was part of the story (and Bram Stoker's *Dracula* [1897] is a thinly veiled saga of lechery and rape), the vampire only reproduces violence.

Now stop the presses, because already a very striking difference appears as we turn to today's vampires. We see two differences actually, because the contemporary vampire often is not a monster at all (he, or she, may be given a soul, be a "vegetarian," be a protector, and, indeed, be someone a whole lot like the ordinary people among whom he or she dwells in middle-class neighborhoods). And, equally striking, the contemporary vampire is often romantic, sexy, sympathetic, and just plain cool.

This difference within the system of associated signs is the crux of the entire matter.

A little background research will reveal that the shift began with such stories as Anne Rice's *Interview With the Vampire* (1976), which made its vampires sympathetic and sexy rather than horrific and abhorrent. This change was made even more prominent, and popular, in the *Buffy the Vampire Slayer* movie and television series, which also brought the vampire into the ordinary world of schools and suburban neighborhoods. But since there are plenty of stories about romantic, sexy, sympathetic, cool people who live in the ordinary worlds of school and suburb, we still have the question as to why it has been so popular to include vampires in such stories.

To answer this question we can look at some broader associations.

As we have seen so far, the vampire story is part of a tradition of gothic/horror storytelling that has been hybridized with teen/high school narratives and romance fiction (these last two are particularly prominent in the *Twilight* series). But the contemporary vampire also has connections to the cartoon superhero (after all, the vampire has superpowers) and to stories about aliens (like extraterrestrials, the vampire is a humanoid who isn't really human). The vampire also belongs to the fantasy tradition (it is a supernatural creature who does not belong to the real world), which has enjoyed especial popularity in recent years with the resurgence of J. R. R. Tolkien's *Lord of the Rings* and the phenomenal popularity of J. K. Rowling's *Harry Potter* stories.

Now, what do stories of this type offer to their fans? Obviously, an escape from the mundane realities of day-to-day existence. They also offer fans a chance to imagine that they, too, are like the main characters, are somehow special, not like everyone else. The appeal of not being a "Muggle," of belonging to an elite group of kids within an elite school, has been especially apparent in the *Harry Potter* stories, but it also appeared in such television series as *Heroes*, which took the old superhero story and said, in effect, "this is *you*, but you've got superpowers now that give you a ticket of admission into a really elite clique." Better yet, the contemporary vampire story says that you can easily become someone who isn't like everyone else, someone with supernatural powers and sex appeal: All you have to do is fall in love with a vampire, or get bitten by one, or, preferably, both. And he, or she, may be sitting right next to you in class!

What is more, vampires are not only immortal but ageless. In this respect, they are especially attractive in a youth-obsessed culture like our own, where plastic surgery and botox are widely employed in a futile struggle to appear always young and beautiful against the tides of time. Vampires don't need botox. How cool is that?

What is more, the immortality of vampires also makes them resemble the gods and goddesses of pagan times. It is no accident that mainstream religious groups have denounced the enormous popularity of today's vampire stories (as they have also protested the popularity of the *Harry Potter* saga), because it does reflect to a certain extent the same sort of neopaganism that has made Wicca and the Druidic revival popular today. Indeed, like the gods and goddesses of old, vampires can transform mortals into godlike immortals.

But, vampires are vampires, after all, and vampires are evil, aren't they? In the past, that was the sticking point against transforming these immortal, sexy, superhuman, and supernatural figures into vicarious heroes. But with so many other heroes already to choose from, why bother to rehabilitate vampires?

Because there are many other appeals to the modern vampire that we haven't considered yet. First, in the past (this was strikingly recognizable in Bram Stoker's *Dracula*), the vampire was very much an evil Other, a Transylvanian monster preying on English womanhood, and thus stimulating not only Stoker's audience's desire to be titillated by a thinly disguised saga of sexual license and lechery but also their xenophobic fear of "foreigners." Indeed, the whole gothic tradition in Anglo-American storytelling tended to make its monsters evil beings from non–Anglo-American places like Central Europe.

But several decades of multicultural education and enlightenment have taught that the Other is not a sinister villain and is more often than not a victim to sympathize with rather than persecute. Since vampires have long been reviled within the context of a xenophobic history, their rehabilitation in a multiculturalist era as ordinary people who have simply been misunderstood is not really a surprising development. Indeed, we see a parallel change in attitudes toward ogres (*Shrek*), extraterrestrials (*E.T.*), and the Wicked Witch of the West (*Wicked*).

And there is another, related, angle here. Like Batman and Spider-Man, the contemporary vampire (when he is a "good," "vegetarian" vampire) is very much like what Robert Ray calls an "outlaw hero" (see Ray's essay on this topic in Chapter 4 of this book). An outlaw hero is someone who serves society, but not necessarily according to the established rules or laws. Outlaw heroes play by their own rules, and ever since the revolt against conventional authority that began in the cultural revolution of the 1960s, outlaw heroes have been generally more popular than the "official heroes" whose service to society is from within the establishment. (Dirty Harry and Jack Bauer are

examples of outlaw heroes who work for the established authorities but who operate on their own, by their own standards of right and wrong.) To put this another way, the vampire (when male) can be the ultimate good "bad boy," and it is no accident that Edward in the *Twilight* series bears such a striking resemblance to James Dean, pop culture's archetypal rebel without a cause.

The romantic attractiveness of the good bad-boy vampire has certain postfeminist overtones as well. *Postfeminism* is a label for the gender politics of the era that followed the women's liberation movement of the sixties and seventies. Women's liberation challenged such traditional **gender codes** that said that women and girls should be most concerned with attracting and holding onto a man, that their role in life is to be beautiful, to marry, and to have children. But in postfeminist popular culture, what was once challenged is now resurgent. Innumerable cultural signals that a woman's role in society is to be beautiful and sexy, to love and to be loved by a powerful man, can be found today, and the current of romance fiction that can be found in the contemporary vampire story (especially in the *Twilight* series), is one such signifier.

Finally, we can point to the fact that vampires are shape changers (like the werewolves that have also been transformed, in *Twilight* and *Underworld*, into dangerously attractive lovers). Shape changers are creatures who are not tied to a single identity; they are, as it were, mixed-species. At a time when more and more people, especially young people, are rejecting the rigid categories of traditional forms of social identification, when mixed-race identities are on the rise, the shape changer has a new appeal that did not exist in the days when werewolves and vampires were monsters pure and simple.

The appeal of the vampire is thus strikingly overdetermined. A fantasy at a time when fantasy storytelling has enjoyed widespread and enduring popularity, the vampire tale at its simplest level reflects a desire to transcend the mundane realities of everyday life, offering a level of excitement and adventure that both the classroom and the cubicle lack. In the context of America's youth culture, the vampire offers immortal youth, along with a sense of being

special in a mass society where individuality is under siege. And the vampire also can make us feel endowed with special powers at a time when we feel impotent in the face of wars that we cannot win (Iraq and Afghanistan), an economy that we cannot fix, and a political system that does not seem to represent us. Disenchanted with official heroes, the vampire's audience is drawn to outlaw heroes; often dissatisfied with traditional religions, fans of the vampire are drawn to his neopagan allure. Indeed, vampires have so much going for them in the current state of American consciousness that it is little wonder that they are so popular, and there is no need at all for every single facet of their appeal to be present in any individual instance. In fact, when it comes down to it, the most important element in the vampire's appeal is probably simply erotic. If nothing else, the vampire is about sex, and so too is much of American popular culture.

The Classroom Connection

This analysis could be extended further into a discussion of the kind of world that has created an audience for the contemporary vampire story, but we will leave that for you to consider for yourself. The key point to recognize is that while the vampire craze in itself is not particularly important, what it signifies *is*, taking us from the pleasures of popular culture into the serious issues of contemporary life.

Semiotic analyses of popular culture, in essence, are not different from the more conventional interpretive analyses you will be asked to perform in your college writing career. It is in the nature of all critical thinking to make connections and mark differences in order to go beyond the surface of a text or issue toward a meaning. The skills you already have as an interpreter of the popular signs around you — of images, objects, and forms of behavior — are the same skills that you develop as a writer of critical essays that present an argued point of view and the evidence to defend it.

Because most of us tend to identify closely with our favorite popular cultural phenomena and have strong opinions about them, it can be more difficult to adopt the same sort of analytic perspective toward popular culture that we do toward, say, texts assigned in a literature class. Still, that is what you should do in a semiotic interpretation: You need to set your aesthetic or fan-related opinions aside in order to pursue an interpretive argument with evidence to support it. Note how in our interpretation of the vampire story we didn't say whether or not we like it: Our concern was with what it might mean within a larger cultural context. It is not difficult to express an aesthetic opinion or statement of personal preference, but that isn't the goal of analytic writing and critical thinking. Analytic writing requires that you martial supporting evidence, just as a lawyer needs evidence to argue a case. So by learning to write analyses of our culture, by searching for supporting evidence to underpin your interpretive take on modern life, you are also learning to write critical arguments.

"But how," you (and perhaps your instructor) may ask, "can I know that a semiotic interpretation is right?" Good question — it is commonly asked by those who fear that a semiotic analysis might read too much into a subject. But then, it can also be asked of the writer of any interpretive essay, and the answer in each case is the same. No one can absolutely *prove* the truth of an argument in the human sciences; what you do is *persuade* your audience through the use of pertinent evidence through an abductive reasoning process. In writing analyses about popular culture, that evidence comes from your knowledge of the system to which the object you are interpreting belongs. The more you know about the system, the more convincing your interpretations will be. And that is true whether you are writing about popular culture or about more traditional academic subjects.

Of Myths and Men

As we have seen, in a semiotic analysis we do not search for the meanings of things in the things themselves. Rather, we find meaning in the way we can relate things together, through association and differentiation, moving from objective denotation to culturally subjective connotation. Such a movement commonly takes us from the realm of mere facts into the world of cultural values, ideological positions that we do not always recognize *as* values. Rather, we think of them as facts or truths. But from a semiotic perspective, our values too belong to systems from which they take their meaning. Semioticians call these systems of belief *cultural mythologies*.

A cultural mythology is not some fanciful story from the past; indeed, if the word "mythology" seems confusing because of its traditional association with such stories, you may prefer to use the term "value system." Consider the value system that governs our traditional thinking about gender roles. Have you ever noticed how our society presumes that it is primarily the role of women — adult daughters — to take care of aging and infirm parents? If you want to look at the matter from a physiological perspective, it might seem that men would be better suited to the task: In a state of nature, men are physically stronger and so would seem to be the natural protectors of the aged. And yet, though our cultural mythology holds that men should protect the nuclear family, it tends to assign to women the care of extended families. It is culture that decides here, not nature.

But while cultural mythologies guide our behavior, they are subject to change. You may have already experienced a transitional phase in the myths surrounding courtship behavior. In the past, the gender myths that formed the rules of the American dating game held that it is the role of the male to initiate proceedings (he calls) and for the female to react (she waits for the call). Similarly, the rules once held that it is invariably the responsibility of the male to plan the evening and pay the tab. These rules are changing, aren't they? Can you describe the rules that now govern courtship behavior?

A cultural mythology, or value system, then, is a kind of lens that governs the way we view our world. Think of it this way: Say you were born with rose-tinted eyeglasses permanently attached over your eyes, but you didn't know they were there. Because the world would *look* rose-colored to you, you would presume that it *is* rose-colored. You wouldn't wonder whether the world might look otherwise through different lenses. But in the world there are other kinds of eyeglasses with different lenses, and reality does look different to those who wear them. Those lenses are cultural mythologies, and no culture can claim to have the one set of glasses that sees things as they really are.

The profound effect our cultural mythologies have on the way we view reality, on our most basic values, is especially apparent today when the myths of European culture are being challenged by the worldviews of the many other cultures that have taken root in American soil. European-American culture, for example, upholds a profoundly individualistic social mythology, valuing individual rights before those of the group, but traditional Chinese culture believes in the primacy of the family and the community over the individual. Maxine Hong Kingston's short story "No Name Woman" poignantly demonstrates how such opposing ideologies can collide with painful results in its tale of a Chinese woman who is more or less sacrificed to preserve the interests of her village. The story, from *The Woman Warrior: Memoirs of a Girlhood among Ghosts* (1976), tells of a young woman who gives birth to a baby too many months after her husband's departure to America — along with most of her village's other young men — for it to be her husband's child. The men, who had left in order to earn money to keep the impoverished villagers from starving, knew they might be away for years; thus, they need to be assured that their wives will remain faithful to them in their absence. The unfortunate heroine of the tale — who, to sharpen the agony, had more likely been the victim of rape than the instigator of adultery — is horribly punished by the entire village as an example to any other wives who might disturb the system.

That Kingston wrote "No Name Woman" as a self-conscious Asian American, as one whose identity fuses both Chinese and Euro-American values, reveals the fault lines between conflicting mythologies. As an Asian, Kingston understands the communal values behind the sacrifice of the No Name Woman, and her story makes sure that her Euro-American readers understand this too. But, as an American and as a feminist, she is outraged by the violation of an individual woman's rights on behalf of the group (or mob, which is as the village behaves in the story). Kingston's own sense of personal conflict in this clash of mythologies — Asian, American, and feminist — offers a striking example of the inevitable conflicts that America itself faces as it changes from a monocultural to a multicultural society.

To put this another way, from the semiotic perspective, how you interpret something is very much a product of who you are, for culture is just another name for the frames that shape our values and perceptions.

Traditionally, American education has presumed a monocultural perspective, a melting-pot view that no matter what one's cultural background, truth is culture-blind. Langston Hughes took on this assumption many years ago in his classic poem "Theme for English B," in which he observes, "I guess I'm what / I feel and see and hear," and wonders "will my page be colored" when he writes. "Being me, it will not be white," he suggests, but while the poet struggles to find what he holds in common with his white instructor, he can't suppress the differences. In essence, that is the challenge of multicultural education itself: to identify the different cultural codes that inform the mythic frameworks of the many cultures that share America while searching for what holds the whole thing together.

That meaning is not culture-blind, that it is conditioned by systems of ideology and belief that are codified differently by different cultures, is a foundational semiotic judgment. Human beings, in other words, construct their own social realities, and so who gets to do the constructing becomes very important. Every contest over a cultural code is, accordingly, a contest for power, but the contest is usually masked because the winner generally defines its mythology as the truth, as what is most natural or reasonable. Losers in the contest become objects of scorn and are quickly marginalized, declared unnatural or deviant, or even insane. The stakes are high as myth battles myth, with truth itself as the highest prize.

This does not mean that you must abandon your own beliefs when conducting a semiotic analysis, only that you cannot take them for granted and must be prepared to argue for them. We want to assure you that semiotics will not tell you what to think and believe. It *does* assume that what you believe reflects some cultural system or other and that no cultural system can claim absolute validity or superiority. The readings and chapter introductions in this book contain their own values and ideologies, and if you wish to challenge those values you can begin by exposing the myths that they may take for granted.

Thus, everything in this book reflects a political point of view. If you hold a different view, it is not enough to simply presuppose the innate superiority of your own perspective — to claim that one writer is being political while you are simply telling the truth. This may sound heretical precisely because human beings operate within cultural mythologies whose political invisibility is guaranteed by the system. No mythology, that is to say, begins by saying, "this is just a political construct or interpretation." Every mythology begins, "this is the truth." It is very difficult to imagine, from within the mythology, any alternatives. Indeed, as you read this book, you may find it upsetting to see that some traditional beliefs — such as "proper" roles of men and women — are socially constructed and not absolute. But the outlines of the mythology, the bounding (and binding) frame, best appear when challenged by another mythology, and this challenge is probably nowhere more insistent than in America, where so many of us are really "hyphenated" Americans who combine two (or more) cultural traditions in our own persons.

Getting Started

Mythology, like **culture**, is not static, and so the semiotician must always keep his or her eye on the clock, so to speak. History, time itself, is a constant factor in a constantly changing world. Since the earlier editions of this book, American popular culture has moved on. In this edition, we have tried to reflect those changes, but inevitably, further changes will occur in the time it takes for this book to appear on your class syllabus. That such changes occur is part of the excitement of the semiotic enterprise: There is always something new to consider and interpret. What does not change is the nature of semiotic interpretation: Whatever you choose to analyze in the realm of American popular culture, the semiotic approach will help you understand it.

It's your turn now. Start asking questions, pushing, probing. That's what critical thinking and writing is all about, but this time you're part of the question. Arriving at answers, conclusions, is the fun part here, but answers aren't the basis of analytic thinking: questions are. You always begin with a question, a query, a hypothesis, something to explore. If you already knew the answer, there would be no point in conducting the analysis. We leave you to it to explore the almost infinite variety of questions that the readings in this book raise. Many come equipped with their own "answers," but you may (indeed will and should) find that such answers raise further questions. To help you ask those questions, keep in mind the elemental principles of semiotics that we have just explored:

1. The meaning of a sign can be found not in itself but in its relationships (both differences and associations) with other signs within a **system**. To interpret an individual sign, then, you must determine the general system to which it belongs.
2. Things have both **denotative** meanings (what they *are as things*) and **connotative** meanings (what they *suggest as signs*); semiotics seeks to go beyond the denotative surface to the connotative significance.
3. Arriving at the connotative significance of a sign involves both **abduction** (a search for the most likely explanation or interpretation) and **overdetermination** (the multiple causes behind a cultural phenomenon).
4. What we call social "reality" is a human construct, the product of cultural **mythologies** or value systems that intervene between our minds and the world we experience. Such cultural myths reflect the values and ideological interests of their builders, not the laws of nature or logic.

Perhaps our first principle could be more succinctly phrased, "everything is connected," and our second, "don't take things at face value," while our third reminds us that a semiotic interpretation requires both logical and polysemous thinking, and our fourth might be simply summarized, "question authority." Think of them that way if it helps. Or just ask yourself, whenever you are interpreting something, "what's going on here?" In short, question *everything*. And one more reminder: Signs are like weather vanes; they point in response to invisible historical winds. We invite you now to start looking at the weather.

WRITING ABOUT POPULAR CULTURE

Throughout this book, you will find readings on popular culture that you can use as models for your own writing or as subjects to which you may respond, assignments for writing critical essays on popular culture, and advice to help you analyze a wide variety of cultural phenomena. As you approach these readings and assignments, you may find it helpful to review the following suggestions for writing critical essays — whether on popular culture or on any subject — as well as some examples of student essays written in response to assignments based on *Signs of Life in the U.S.A.* Mastering the skills summarized and exemplified here should enable you to write the kinds of papers you will be assigned through the rest of your college career.

As you prepare to write a critical essay on popular culture, remember that you are already an expert in your subject. After all, simply by actively participating in everyday life, you have accumulated a vast store of knowledge about what makes our culture tick. Just think about all you know about movies, or the thousands on thousands of ads you've seen, or even the many unwritten "rules" governing courtship behavior among your circle of friends. Your very expertise in popular culture, ironically, may create a challenge, simply because you may take your knowledge for granted. It might not seem that it can "count" as material for a college-level assignment, and it might not even occur to you to use it in an essay. To write a strong essay, you need to do more than just go along with the "flow" of your subject as you live it and, instead, consider it from a critical distance.

Using Active Reading Strategies

The first step in developing a strong essay about any topic happens well before you sit down to write: You need to make sure you understand accurately the reading selections that your instructor has assigned. You want to engage in *active* reading — that is, you want not to just get the "drift" of a passage. Skimming a selection may give you a rough idea of the author's point, but your understanding of it is also likely to be partial, superficial, or even downright wrong. And that's not a solid start to writing a good paper!

Active reading techniques can help you understand the nuances of how an author constructs his or her argument accurately and precisely. With any reading selection, it can be helpful to read at least twice: first, to gain a general sense of the author's ideas and, second, to study more specifically how those ideas are put together to form an argument. To do this, you can use some formal discovery techniques, or what are called *heuristics*. One of the most famous heuristics is the journalist's "Five *W*'s and an *H*": who, what, where, when, why and how. By asking these questions, a reporter can quickly unearth the essential details of a breaking story and draft a clear account of it. For your purposes, you can try applying the following questions to a reading selection you will be discussing in your own essay.

Active Reading Questions

- What is the *author's primary argument*? Can you identify a *thesis* statement, or is the thesis implied?
- What words or *key terms* are fundamental to that argument? If you are not familiar with the fundamental vocabulary of the selection, be sure to check a dictionary or encyclopedia for the word's meaning.
- What *evidence* does the author provide to support the argument?
- What *underlying assumptions* shape the author's position? Does the author consider alternative points of view (counterarguments)?
- What *style* and *tone* does the author adopt?
- What is the *genre* of the piece? You need to take into account what kind of writing you are responding to, for different kinds have different purposes and goals. A personal narrative, for instance, expresses the writer's experiences and beliefs, but you shouldn't expect it to present a complete argument supported by documentation.
- Who is the *intended readership* of this selection, and does it affect the author's reasoning or evidence?

As you read, write *annotations*, or notes, in your book. Doing so will help you both remember and analyze what you read. A pencil or pen is probably the best memory aid ever invented. No one, not even the most experienced and perceptive reader, remembers everything — and let's face it, not everything that you read is worth remembering. Writing annotations as you read will lead you back to important points. And annotating helps you start analyzing a reading — long before you have to start writing an essay — rather than uncritically accepting what's on the page.

Learning to read actively means *interacting* with what you read by responding. Don't just skim a selection to get the "drift": that won't work for students in college. Instead, you should question, summarize, agree with, refute what the author says. It means that you're having a kind of *conversation* with the author rather than simply listening to a lecture by an expert. Studies have shown that such interactive learning simply works better than passive learning; if you read actively, you'll gain knowledge at a higher rate and retain it longer.

There's another reason to annotate what you read: You can use the material you've identified as the starting point for your journal notes and essays; and since it doesn't take long to circle a word or jot a note in the margin, you can save a great deal of time in the long run. We suggest using a pencil or pen, not a highlighter. While using a highlighter is better than using nothing — it will at least help you identify key points — writing *words* in your book goes an important step further in helping you analyze what you read. We've seen entire pages bathed in fluorescent yellow highlighter, and that's of doubtful use in finding the important stuff. Of course, if you simply can't bring yourself to mark up your book, you can write on sticky notes instead, and put those in the margins.

So as you read, circle key words, note transitions between ideas, jot definitions of unfamiliar terms (you can likely guess their meaning from the context or look them up later), underline phrases or terms to research on a search engine such as Google, write short summaries of important points, or simply note where you're confused or lost with a question mark or a *huh?!* In fact, figuring out exactly what parts you do and don't understand is one of the best ways to tackle a difficult reading. Frequently, the confusing bits turn out to be the most interesting — and sometimes the most important. We're not suggesting that you cover your pages with notes; often a few words get the job done. Responding to what you read *as* you read will help you become a more active reader — and that will ultimately help you become a stronger writer.

Signs of Life in the U.S.A. frequently asks you to respond to a reading selection in your *journal* or *reading log*, sometimes directly and sometimes indirectly, as in suggestions that you write a letter to the author of a selection. In doing so, you're taking an important step in articulating your response to the issues and to the author's presentation of them. In asking you to keep a journal or a reading log, your instructor will probably be less concerned with your writing style than with your comprehension of assigned readings and your thoughtful responses to them. Let's say you're asked to write your response to Jessica Hagedorn's "Asian Women in Film: No Joy, No Luck" in Chapter 4. You should first think through exactly what Hagedorn is saying—what her point is—by using the questions listed and by reviewing your annotations. Then consider how you feel about her essay. If you agree with Hagedorn's contention that films perpetuate outmoded stereotypes of Asian women, why do you feel that way? Can you think of films Hagedorn does not mention that reflect the gendered patterns she observes? Or do you know of films that represent Asian female characters in alternative ways? Or say you're irritated by Hagedorn's argument: Again, why do you feel that way? What would you say to her in response? Your aim in jotting all this down is not to produce a draft of an essay. It's to play with your own ideas, see where they lead, and even just help you decide what your ideas are in the first place.

Prewriting Strategies

You'll find it useful to spend some time, before you start writing, to generate your ideas freely and openly: Your goal at this point is to develop as many ideas as possible, even ones that you might not actually use in your essay. Writing instructors call this process *prewriting*, and it's a step you should take when writing on any subject in any class, not just in your writing class. This textbook includes many suggestions for how you can develop your ideas; even if your instructor doesn't require you to use all of them, you can try them on your own.

These strategies will work when you are asked to respond to a particular reading or image. Sometimes, though, you may be asked to write about a more general subject. Often your instructor may ask you to brainstorm ideas or to freewrite in response to an issue. You can use both strategies in your journal or on your own as you start working on an essay. Brainstorming is simply amassing as many relevant (and even some irrelevant) ideas as possible. Let's say your instructor asks you to brainstorm a list of popular toys used by girls and boys in preparation for an essay about the gendered designs of children's toys. Try to list your thoughts freely, jotting down whatever comes to mind. Don't censor yourself at this point. That is, don't worry if something is really a toy or a game, or if it is used by both boys and girls, or if it really is an adult toy. Later on you can throw out ideas that don't fit. What you'll be left with is a rich list of examples that you can then study and analyze. Freewriting works much the same way and is particularly useful when you're not sure how you feel about an issue. Sit down and just start writing or typing, and don't stop until you've written for at least ten or fifteen minutes. Let your ideas wander around your subject, working associatively, following their own path. As with brainstorming, you may produce some irrelevant ideas, but you may also come to a closer understanding of how you really feel about an issue.

Sometimes your instructor may invite you to create your own topic. You might be asking yourself, "Where should I start?" Let's say you need to analyze an aspect of the film industry but can't decide on a focus. Here, the Internet might help. You could explore a search engine such as Yahoo!, specifically its Movies and Films index. There you'll find dozens of subcategories, such as History, Theory and Criticism, Cultures and Groups, and Trivia. Each of these subcategories has many sites to explore: History, for instance, includes the Archives of Early Lindy Hop as well as the Bill Douglas Centre for the History of Cinema and Popular Culture, a wonderful compendium of 25,000 books, posters, and other movie-related memorabilia. With so many sites to choose from, you're bound to find something that interests you. The Net, in effect, allows you to engage in *electronic brainstorming* and to arrive at your topic.

One cautionary note: In using the Internet to brainstorm, be sure to *evaluate the appropriateness of your sources* (see p. 69). Many sites are commercial and therefore are intended more to sell a product or image than to provide reliable information. In addition, since anyone with the technological know-how can set up a Web site, some sites (especially personal home pages) amount to little more than personal expression and need to be evaluated for their reliability, accuracy, and authenticity. Scrutinize the sites you use carefully: Is the author an authority in the field? Does the site identify the author, at least by name and e-mail address? (Be wary of fully anonymous sites.) Does the site contain interesting and relevant links? If you find an advocacy site, one that openly advances a special interest, does the site's bias interfere with the accuracy of its information? Asking such questions can help ensure that your electronic brainstorming is fruitful and productive. If you are unsure of the validity of a Web site, you might want to check with your instructor.

You can strengthen your argument as well if you know and use the history of your subject. That might sound like you have to do a lot of library research, but often you don't have to: You may already be familiar with the social and cultural history of your subject. If you know, for instance, that the baggy pants so popular among teens in the mid-1990s were a few years before ubiquitous among street-gang members, you know an important historical detail that goes a long way toward explaining their significance. Depending on your assignment, you might want to expand on your own historical knowledge and collect additional data about your topic, perhaps through surveys and interviews. If you're analyzing gendered patterns of courtship rituals, for instance, you could interview some people from different age groups, as well as both genders, to get a sense of how such patterns have evolved over time. The material you gather through such an interview will be raw data, and you'll want to do more than just "dump" the information into your essay. See this material instead as an original body of evidence that you'll sort through (you probably won't use every scrap of information), study, and interpret in its own right.

Not all prewriting activities need be solitary, of course. In fact, *Signs of Life* includes lots of suggestions that ask you to work with other students, either in your class or across campus. We suggest such *group work* because much academic work really is collaborative and collegial. When a scientist is conducting research, for instance, he or she often works with a team, may present preliminary findings to colloquia or conferences, and may call or e-mail a colleague at another school to try out some ideas. There's no reason you can't benefit from the social nature of academic thinking as well. But be aware that such in-class group work is by no means "busy work." The goal, rather, is to help you to develop and shape your understanding of the issues and your attitudes toward them. If you're asked to study how a product is packaged with three classmates, for instance, you're starting to test Thomas Hine's thesis in "What's in a Package" (Chapter 1), seeing how it applies or doesn't apply and benefiting from your peers' insights.

Let's say you're asked to present to the class a semiotic reading of a childhood toy. By discussing a favorite toy with your class, you are articulating, perhaps for the first time, what it meant (or means) to you and so are taking the first step toward writing a more formal analysis of it in an essay (especially if you receive feedback and comments from your class). Similarly, if you stage an in-class debate over whether Batman is a gay character, you're amassing a wonderful storehouse of arguments, counterarguments, and evidence to consider when you write your own essay that either supports or refutes Andy Medhurst's thesis in "Batman, Deviance, and Camp" (Chapter 3). As with other strategies to develop your ideas, you may not use directly every idea generated in conversation with your classmates, but that's okay. You should find yourself better able to sort through and articulate the ideas that you do find valuable.

Developing Strong Arguments about Popular Culture

We expect that students will write many different sorts of papers in response to the selections in this book. You may write personal experience narratives, opinion pieces, research papers, formal pro-con arguments, and many others. We'd like here to focus on writing analytic essays because the experience of analyzing popular culture may seem different from that of analyzing other subjects. Occasionally we've had students who feel reluctant to analyze popular culture because they think that analysis requires them to trash their subject, and they don't want to write a "negative" essay about what may be their favorite film or TV program. Or a few students may feel uncertain because "it's all subjective." Since most people have opinions about popular culture, they say, how can any one essay be stronger than another?

While these concerns are understandable, they needn't be an obstacle in writing a strong analytic paper — whether on popular culture or any other topic. First, we often suggest that you set aside your own personal tastes when writing an analysis. We do so not because your preferences are not important; recall that we often ask you to explore your beliefs in your journal, and we want you to be aware of your own attitudes and observations about your topic. Rather, we do so because an analysis of, say, *Avatar* is not the same as a paper that explains "why I like (or dislike) this movie." Instead, an analysis would explain how it works, what cultural beliefs and viewpoints underlie it, what its significance is, and so forth. And such a paper would not necessarily be positive or negative; it would seek to explain *how* the elements of the film work together to have a particular effect on its audience. If your instructor asks you to write a critical analysis or a critical argument, he or she is requesting neither a hit job nor a celebration of your topic.

For most of your college essays, you will probably be asked to make sure that your paper has a clear *thesis*. A thesis statement tells your reader very briefly what he or she can expect to read in the pages that follow. It lays out the argument your paper intends to make and provides a scope for that paper. If you think of your thesis as a road map that your paper will follow, you might find that it is easier to structure your paper. Additionally, a strong thesis statement will help you overcome any anxieties you might have over writing a strong analysis, because a good thesis statement, rather than offering solely a simple opinion on your topic, also explains how you came to hold that opinion. That is, it informs your readers of your thought process, which your paper will lead them through. The thesis statements in the sample papers that begin on page 36 have been annotated to help you see how they function overall in academic writing.

When your paper has a strong thesis that plots the points of your analysis, the second concern, about subjectivity, becomes less of a problem. That's because your analysis should center on a clear argument about your topic that your thesis allows your readers to anticipate. You're not simply presenting a personal opinion about it; rather, you're presenting a central insight about its significance, and you need to demonstrate it with logical, specific evidence. It's that evidence that will take your essay out of the category of being "merely subjective." You should start with your own opinion, but you will want to add to it lots of proof that shows the legitimacy of that opinion. Does that sound familiar? It should, because that's what you need to do in any analytic essay, no matter what your subject matter happens to be.

When writing about popular culture, students sometimes wonder what sort of evidence they can use to support their points. Your instructor will probably give you guidelines for each assignment, but we'll provide some suggestions here. Start with your subject itself. You'll find it's useful to view your subject — whether it's an ad, a film, or anything else — as a text that you can "read" closely. That's what you would do if you were asked to analyze a poem: You would read it carefully, studying individual words, images, rhythm, and so forth, and those details would support whatever point you wanted to make about the poem. Read your pop culture subject with the same care. If your instructor asks you to analyze a television series, you should look at the details: What actors appear in the series, and what are their roles? What "story" does the program tell about its characters and the world in which they live? Is there anything missing from this world that you would expect to find? Your answers to such questions could form the basis for the evidence that you use in your essay.

Conducting a Semiotic Analysis

In an essay focused on a semiotic analysis, you could probe more specific questions about your subject that would yield even more specific evidence and arguments. You can start with some basic questions that we ask throughout the chapter introductions in this book.

For a simple example, let's consider the popular TV series *House* (for a student essay that presents its own semiotic reading of *House*, see Laurie Boloven's "*House* Calls: And Just What Is It Saying?" on p. 43).

DENOTATION

What is a simple, literal description of your subject? You need to make sure you understand this before looking for "deeper meanings," because if you misunderstand the factual status of your subject, you will likely get derailed in your analysis. In the case of *House*, we find a story of a medical genius who, though he is his hospital's most successful diagnostician, is also rude, nasty, and practically dysfunctional in his personal life, suffering from an addiction to Vicodin and almost constant depression. The plots of *House* tend to exemplify the series' slogan, "Everyone Lies," and often depict House's patients and/or their families as liars with dark secrets that they are concealing and that House eventually uncovers. Clearly, if we were to misidentify *House* as a documentary, we'd misconstrue it as a

---

Questions for Conducting a Semiotic Analysis

- What is the **denotative** meaning of your subject? In other words, determine a factual definition of exactly what it is.
- What is your topic's **connotative** significance? To do that, situate your subject in a **system** of related signs.
- What **associated** signs belong to that system?
- What **differences** do you see in those signs?
- What **abductive** explanation do you have for your observations? What is the most likely explanation for the patterns that you see?

scathing political exposé of the U.S. medical system — but that doesn't feel right; *House* is no exposé.

CONNOTATIVE MEANINGS AND A SYSTEM OF RELATED SIGNS

If your instructor has asked you to write a semiotic analysis, you can develop evidence as well by locating your subject within a larger system. Recall that a system is the larger network of related signs to which your subject belongs and that identifying it helps to reveal the significance of your subject. This may sound hard to do, but it is through identifying a system that you can draw on your own vast knowledge of popular culture. And that may sound abstract, but it becomes very specific when applied to a particular example. In our study of *House*, we need to move from our denotative understanding of the series to its connotative significance — our analysis of the larger cultural significance and meanings of the program. To identify a system of associated signs, we should compare it with programs with which it is similar. In what genre of television programming does *House* belong? What conventions, goals, and motifs do shows in this genre share? What is the history of the genre? *House*, of course, belongs to the medical drama genre, as distinct from, say, situation comedy, even though *House* does have certain comic elements that would allow us to classify it as a medical *dramedy*. The history of TV medical drama includes such programs of the 1960s as *Dr. Kildare* and *Ben Casey, Marcus Welby M.D.* and *Quincy M.E.* in the 1970s, *St. Elsewhere* and *ER* in the 1980s and beyond, and such recent programs as *Grey's Anatomy* and *Nip/Tuck*. All of these programs can be associated with *House* and testify to the enduring popularity of the genre. (Indeed, long before television, an old joke had it that the most certain formula to follow in writing a best-seller was to write a book about Abraham Lincoln's doctor's dog.)

DIFFERENCES WITHIN THE SYSTEM

But while the associations between these television series demonstrate a popular interest in doctors and medical stories, there is still a striking difference to consider, a kind of dividing line marked by the series *St. Elsewhere*. Until *St. Elsewhere*, the character of the doctor in a medical series was that of a benevolent healer whose own personal life beyond the hospital was generally not a part of the story line (there were exceptions: Dr. Kildare once had a patient with whom he fell in love; Ben Casey had a somewhat edgy nature, and Jack Klugman's Quincy — a forensic pathologist whose mystery-solving abilities anticipate those of Gregory House — had plenty of attitude). But all in all, the physician protagonists of the earlier series maintained a general profile of almost superhuman benevolence, "official heroes," in Robert B. Ray's terms (see "The Thematic Paradigm," p. 377), caring for the innocent victims of disease.

St. Elsewhere changed that, and from *St. Elsewhere* onward (especially as developed by *ER*) the flaws in the lives and personalities of the main characters, the doctors, became much more prominent. The doctors were, in short, much more humanized — a shift in characterization that has led to the caustic, sometimes dysfunctional and law-breaking, Dr. House.

ABDUCTIVE EXPLANATIONS

At this point we are ready to start interpreting, seeking abductive explanations for the shift. We can begin with the construction of another system, this time looking at the larger context of other television genres. If we look at this system we can find a similar shift to that within the history of the medical drama in situation comedy, crime series, Westerns, and many other genres. The difference between the family sitcoms of the 1950s and '60s and those of the 1980s and beyond is well known, taking us from the happy families of the Cleavers and the Nelsons to the dysfunctional Bundys and Griffins. Similarly, it is a long way from Dick Tracy and *Dragnet*'s Joe Friday to the angst-ridden, humanized cops of *NYPD Blue*. And it is an even longer way from *The Adventures of Wild Bill Hickok* and *Gun Smoke* to *Deadwood*. Many other such differences could be mentioned, but we'll move now to our abductive interpretation.

The post–*St. Elsewhere* medical drama reflects a larger trend in American entertainment away from squeaky-clean television protagonists to more "realistically" flawed ones, where the hero definitely has feet of clay. This trend reflects a larger cultural shift whose beginning can be found in the cultural revolution of the 1960s, when American mass culture began a long process of disillusionment. After the Vietnam War and Watergate, increasingly cynical Americans were no longer predisposed to believe in absolute human perfection, preferring a more "realistic" depiction of human beings with all their flaws visible.

Thus we can now see *House* as part of a larger cultural trend, within which the once cherished, even revered, figure of the physician has been pulled off its pedestal and brought to earth along with everyone else. Heroes are heroes (after all, Gregory House is just plain smarter than anyone else around him), but they are more like ordinary folks. They misbehave, get cranky, break rules: "outlaw heroes" to the "official heroes" of the past. Even the victims of misfortune (patients in a medical drama) have been degraded, no longer appearing as the objects of our sympathy but as flawed people with dark secrets. *Everyone lies.* No one is innocent. To the disillusioned, *House*, with its all-too-human hero and cast, is an entertaining, if cynical and less-than-empathetic, vision of the way things are — or at least of the way that large numbers of viewers think they are. Doctors (and cops, and families, and cowboys, and everyone else) have warts too, and, as a sort of anti–Marcus Welby, Gregory House entertains his audience by not being afraid to show his flaws to the world.

Reading Visual Images Actively

Signs of Life in the U.S.A. includes many visual images, in many cases with accompanying questions for analysis. In analyzing images, you will develop the ability to identify specific telling details and specific evidence — a talent useful no matter what your subject matter may be. Because the semiotic method lends itself especially well to visual analysis, it is an excellent means for honing this ability. Here are some questions to consider as you look at images.

Questions for Analyzing Images

- What is the **appearance of the image**? Is it black-and-white? Color? Glossy? Consider how the form in which the image is expressed affects its message. If an image is composed of primary colors, does it look fun and lively, for instance?

- What **kind of image** is it? Is it abstract, does it represent an actual person or place, or is it a combination of the two? If there are people represented, who are they?

- Who is the intended **audience** for the image? Is it an artistic photograph or a commercial work, such as an advertisement? If it is an ad, to what kind of person is it directed? Where is the ad placed? If it is in a magazine, consider the audience for the publication.

- What **emotions** does the image convey? Overall, is it serious, sad, funny? Is that expression of emotion, in your opinion, intentional? What emotional associations do you make with the image?

- If the image includes more than one element, what is the most prominent element in the **composition**? A particular section? A logo? A section of writing? A person or group of people? A product? What do each of the parts contribute to the whole?

- How does the **layout** of the image lead your eye? Are you drawn to any specific part? What is the order in which you look at the various parts? Does any particular section immediately jump out?

- Does the image include **text**? If so, how do the image and the text relate to one another?

- Does the image call for a **response**? For instance, does it suggest that you purchase a product? If so, what claims does it make?

Let's look at a sample analysis of an advertisement using the preceding questions (see image on p. 35).

Format: Although this image is reproduced here in black and white, it originally appeared in color. The colors are muted, however, almost sepia-toned, and thus suggest an old-fashioned look.

Kind of image: This is a fairly realistic image, with a patina of rural nostalgia. A solitary woman, probably in her twenties or thirties, but perhaps older, is set against an empty natural expanse. She has a traditional hairstyle evocative of the 1950s or early 1960s and leads an old-fashioned bicycle with a wicker basket attached.

Audience: This image is an advertisement for Lee jeans. The intended audience is likely a woman in her late twenties or older. We see only the model's back, and so she is faceless. That allows the viewer to project herself into the scene, and the nostalgic look suggests that the viewer could imagine herself at a younger time in her life. Note that the product is "stretch" jeans. There's no suggestion, often made, that the jeans will enhance a woman's sexual appeal; rather, the claim is that the jeans are practical — and will fit a body beyond the teen years. Note the sensible hairstyle and shoes. For an interesting contrast you might compare this ad to one for Guess? jeans.

Emotion: The woman's body language suggests individuality and determination; she's literally "going it alone." She's neither posing for nor aware of the viewer, suggesting that "what you see is what you get." And, perhaps, she doesn't particularly care what you think.

Composition and layout: The layout of the ad is carefully designed to lead your eye: The hill slopes down from top right toward middle left, and the bike draws your eye from bottom right to mid-left, with both lines converging on the product, the jeans. For easy readability, the text is included at the top against the blank sky.

Text: The message, "The things that give a woman substance will never appear on any 'what's in/what's out' list," suggests that Lee jeans is a product for those women who aren't interested in following trends, but rather want a good, old-fashioned value — "substance," not frivolity.

Response: Lee jeans would prefer, naturally, that the viewer of the ad buy the product. She would identify with the woman wearing the jeans in the advertisement and be convinced that these practical (if not particularly cutting-edge) jeans would be a good purchase.

In sum, most fashion ads stress the friends (and often, mates) you will attract if you buy the product, but this ad presents "a road not taken," suggesting the American ideology of marching to the beat of a different drummer, the kind of old-fashioned individualism that brings to mind Robert Frost and Henry David Thoreau. The pastoral surroundings and the "old painting"

effect echo artists such as Andrew Wyeth and Norman Rockwell. All of these impressions connote lasting American values (rural, solid, middle American) that are meant to be associated with anti-trendiness and enduring qualities, such as individualism and practicality. And these impressions suggest the advertisers carefully and effectively kept the ad's semiotic messages in mind as they designed it.

Reading Essays about Popular Culture

In your writing course, it's likely that your instructor will ask you to work in groups with other students, perhaps reviewing each other's rough drafts. You'll find many benefits to this activity. Not only will you receive more feedback on your own in-progress work, but you will see other students' ideas and approaches to an assignment and develop an ability to evaluate academic writing. For the same reasons, we're including three sample student essays that satisfy assignments about popular culture. You may agree or disagree with the authors' views, and you might think you'd respond to the assigned topics differently: That's fine. We've selected these essays because they differ in style, focus, and purpose and thus suggest different approaches to their assignments — approaches that might help you as you write your own essays about popular culture. We've annotated the essays to point out argumentative, organizational, and rhetorical strategies that we found effective. As you read the essays and the annotations, ask why the authors chose these strategies and how you might incorporate some of the same strategies in your own writing.

Essay 1

In this essay, Amy Lin of UCLA argues that the Barbie doll, and all its associated products and marketing, essentially is a means for engendering a consumerist ethos in young girls who are the toy's fans. To do so, Lin relies on a range of sources, including articles in *Signs of Life in the U.S.A.*, academic and journalistic sources, and a corporate Web site that presents the panoply of Barbie products. Notice that Lin treats toysrus.com not as a source of unbiased information about the products (that would amount to taking promotional material at face value); rather, she analyzes the Web site as evidence for her larger argument about consumerism. As you read Lin's essay, study how she uses her sources and integrates them into her own discussion.

Barbie: Queen of Dolls and Consumerism

In my closet, a plastic bag contains five Barbie dolls. A card-
board box beside my nightstand holds yet another, and one more
box contains a Ken doll. Under my bed we find my Barbies' traveling
walk-in closet, equipped with a light-up vanity and fold-out chair
and desk. We also find Doctor Barbie along with the baby, sticker
band-aids, and sounding stethoscope with which she came. Under
my sister's bed are their furniture set, including sofas, loveseats,
flower vases, and a coffee table. A Tupperware container holds Ken's
pants, dress shirts, and special boots (whose spurs make patterns
when rolled in ink) in addition to Barbie's excess clothing that did
not fit in the walk-in closet. In a corner of my living room sits the
special holiday edition Barbie, outfitted in a gown, fur stole, and
holly headband.

*Amy's intro-
duction is
a visual
anecdote
that illustrates
her argument
about
consumption.*

These plastic relics prove that, as a young girl, I, like many
other females, fell into the waiting arms of the Mattel Corporation. Constantly feeding the public with newer, shinier toys, the
Barbie enterprise illustrates America's propensity for consumerism. Upon close examination, Barbie products foster materialism in
young females through both their overwhelmingly large selection
and their ability to create a financially carefree world for children,
sending the message that excessive consumption is acceptable. This
consequently perpetuates the misassumption that "the American
economy [is] an endlessly fertile continent whose boundaries never
need be reached" (Shames 81) among the American youth.

*Amy articu-
lates her
thesis and
refers to
Laurence
Shames's
article as a
context.*

Search the term "Barbie" at toysrus.com, and you will receive
286 items in return — more than enough to create a blur of pinkish-
purple as you scroll down the webpage. The Barbie enterprise clearly
embraces "the observation that 'no natural boundary seems to be
set to the efforts of man'" (Shames 78). In other words, humankind
is, in all ways, ambitious; people will keep creating, buying, and
selling with the belief that these opportunities will always be available. This perfectly describes the mentality of those behind Barbie
products, as new, but unnecessary, Barbie merchandise is put on
shelves at an exorbitant rate. At toysrus.com, for example, a variety
of four different mermaids, 11 fairies, and two "merfairies" — products
from the "Fairytopia-Mermaidia" line — find their place among
the search results (toys). Instead of inventing a more original or

*The corporate
Web site is
used not as
a source of
objective
information
but as evi-
dence to
support the
thesis.*

educational product, Mattel merges the mermaid world with the fairy world into "Fairytopia-Mermaidia," demonstrating the company's lack of innovation and care for its young consumers' development. Thus the corporation's main motivation reveals itself: profit. Another prime example found among the search results is the "Barbie: 12 Dancing Princesses Horse Carriage" (toys), a more recent product in the Barbie family. The carriage, "in its original form, . . . can seat six princess dolls but . . . can expand to hold all 12 dolls at once" (toys). The dolls, of course, do not come with it, forcing the child to buy at least one for the carriage to even be of any use. But that child will see the glorious picture of the carriage filled with all 12 dolls (which are inevitably on the box), and she will want to buy the remaining 11. In addition, the product description states that the carriage "is inspired by the upcoming DVD release, Barbie in *The 12 Dancing Princesses*" (toys). Essentially, one Mattel creation inspires another, meaning that the DVD's sole purpose is to give Mattel an excuse to create and market more useless merchandise.

Much of this, however, may have to do with branding, a strategy manufacturers utilize that ultimately results in "consumers transfer[ring] a favorable or unfavorable image from one product to others from the same brand" (Neuhaus and Taylor). In accordance with this strategy, all Barbie products must maintain a certain similarity so as not to "'confuse' potential customers . . . and thereby reduce demand for the products" (Sappington and Wernerfelt). This explains the redundancy found in much of Mattel's Barbie merchandise, since the sudden manufacturing of a radically different product could encourage the migration of consumers to another brand. But given that Barbie has become "the alpha doll" (Talbot 74) for girls in today's popular culture, young female consumers clearly associate only good things with Barbie. And who can blame them? Barbie has become a tradition handed down from mother to daughter or a rite of passage that most girls go through. In this way, excessive consumption and the effects of branding are handed down as well, as Barbie dolls are essentially their physical manifestations.

With a company as driven to produce and sell products as Mattel, consumers can expect to find increasingly ridiculous items on toy store shelves. One such product found at toysrus.com is "Barbie and Tanner" (toys), Tanner being Barbie's dog. The doll and

Amy moves to the larger marketing context.

dog come with brown pellets that function both as dog food and dog waste, a "special magnetic scooper[,] and trash can" (toys). Upon telling any post-Barbie–phase female about this product, she will surely look amazed and ask, "Are you kidding me?" Unfortunately, Tanner's movable "mouth, ears, head and tail" (toys) and "soft[,] . . . fuzzy" coat will most likely blind children to the product's absurdity, instead enchanting them into purchasing the product. Another particularly hilarious item is the "Barbie Collector Platinum Label Pink Grapefruit Obsession" (toys). The doll wears a "pink, charmeuse mermaid gown with deep pink chiffon wedges sewn into the flared skirt and adorned with deep pink bands that end in bows under the bust and at the hip" (toys). And "as a . . . special surprise, [the] doll's head is scented with the striking aroma of pink grapefruit" (toys). Finally, the doll is described as "an ideal tribute to [the] delightful [grapefruit] flavor" (toys). The consumer will find it difficult to keep a straight face as he or she reads through the description, as it essentially describes a doll dedicated to a scent. The doll's randomness shows Mattel's desperation for coming out with new products. Eager to make profit, it seems as though those behind Barbie make dolls according to whatever whim that happens to cross their minds.

> The paragraph includes a rich array of concrete, specific detail.

In the quest to make profit by spreading the consumerist mindset, Barbie products even manage to commodify culture. Nowadays, Barbie dolls come in a variety of ethnicities. Take, for example, the "Diwali Festival Doll" (toys) from the "Barbie Dolls of the World" (toys) line. Except for the traditional Indian apparel and dark hair, however, the doll could easily be mistaken for Caucasian. And what about Barbie's multiracial doll friends? They are reduced to mere accessories — disposable and only supplementary to Barbie, the truly important figure. Therefore, despite Mattel's attempts at identifying with a larger group of girls, an undeniable "aura of blondness still [clings] to the Mattel doll" (Talbot 82) because its attempts aim more toward creating a larger customer base than anything else.

> Amy develops her argument by considering the cultural and ethnic angle.

But enough of dolls. Mattel has grown so large that it can expand its products beyond Barbie's mini-world. Consumers can easily find Barbie brand tennis shoes, rain boots, slippers, bicycles, and helmets. Many of Barbie's non-doll products even reflect the various fads among America's youth, such as videogames, skateboards, scooters, guitars, and dance mats (in accordance with the popularity

> A quick, short transition moves the reader to a broader consideration of Mattel's promotion of materialism.

of the game, Dance Dance Revolution). Anne Parducci, Mattel's senior VP of Barbie Marketing, claims Mattel does this because it "want[s] to make sure . . . [it] capture[s] girls in the many ways they are spending their time now and in the future" (Edut), that it "want[s] Barbie to represent a lifestyle brand for girls, not just a brand of toys" (Edut). This phenomenon, however, can simply be seen as Mattel trying to "infiltrat[e] girls' lives everywhere they go" (Edut). Either way, Mattel's actions allow materialism to develop at an early age, especially since it makes the latest "it" items more accessible to children. Those behind Barbie figure that if children are going to buy into the latest trends anyway, they might as well buy it from Mattel.

Amy allows for a counter-argument but then refutes it.

Since Barbie products promote the attitude of keeping up with society's crazes, they create a carefree fantasy world for children, obscuring the fact that Mattel's motivation is making money. The company knows that if they enchant children, those children will in turn convince their parents to buy the products for them. The company also knows that commercials are its best opportunities to do this. One recent Mattel commercial advertises the "Let's Dance Genevieve" doll, a doll also inspired by *The 12 Dancing Princesses* DVD that interacts with its owner in three ways: the doll "can dance to music for the girl" (toys), "teach the girl dance moves by demonstrating and using speech prompts" (toys), and "follow along with the girl's dance moves using special bracelets and a shoe accessory" (toys). Girls dressed in ballerina attire give overly joyous reactions to the doll's behaviors, making the doll seem remarkably advanced when, really, the doll can only raise its arms and legs. In addition, computer graphic scenes from the movie run seamlessly into scenes of the girls playing with the doll, and one of these girls is even transposed onto a clip of the movie. This blurs the lines of reality and fantasy, encouraging young viewers to think that if they own the doll, they, too, can feel like "dancing princesses," that somehow the doll can transport its owner into a fairytale world. In actuality, young females will likely tire of the doll within weeks. The commercial even resorts to flattery, describing the doll and its owner as "two beautiful dancers." Finally, the commercial ends with inspirational lyrics, singing, "You can shine." This sort of "vaguely girl-positive" (Edut) advertising only "wrap[s] the Mattel message — buy our products now!" (Edut). Together, all these advertising elements add up to a highly desirable product among young girls.

Barbie undoubtedly increases the materialistic tendencies in children, specifically females, Barbie's target audience. After all, since "Barbie dolls need new clothes and accessories more often than boys' action figures do" (Katz), "young girls learn . . . very early" to "assume consumer roles" (Katz). Interestingly, "Barbie was an early rebel against the domesticity that dominated the lives of baby-boom mothers" (Cross 773), as she shows no "car[e] for babies or children" or "visible ties to parents" (Cross 773). But ironically, instead of "[teaching] girls to shed [such] female stereotypes" (Cross 774), Barbie simply created a new stereotype for females — the shopaholic persona — because "she prompted [young girls] to associate the freedom of being an adult with carefree consumption" (Cross 774). So the overall effect of Barbie's presence on children's lives is a rising in their expectations of material possessions. Or, in other words, Barbie products cause "catalog-induced anxiety" (Easterbrook 404), a condition that can occur "from [viewing] catalogs themselves or from other forms of public exposure of the lives of the rich or celebrated, . . . mak[ing] what a typical person possesses seem paltry, even if the person is one of the many . . . living well by objective standards" (Easterbrook 405). Given that Barbie is a fictitious character, Mattel can make her as beautiful, hip, and rich as it pleases. But what happens when little girls begin comparing their lives to that of Barbie? They think, "If Barbie gets to have such amenities, so should I." And toys like the "Barbie Hot Tub Party Bus" (target) do not help the situation. The product description reads that the bus contains "all the comforts of home like a flat screen TV, dinette table, and beds" (target). Children will inevitably expect these luxuries that, for Barbie, are merely givens in her doll utopia, causing discontent when they discover they cannot have everything they want. It may even reach the point where, "as . . . more material things become available and fail to" satisfy children, "material abundance . . . [can] have the perverse effect of instilling unhappiness — because it will never be possible to have everything that economics can create" (Easterbrook 402).

For my long forgotten Barbie dolls, as for many older females, the dream house has stopped growing. In fact, the house has been

References to Gary Cross's article buttress the essay's argument.

Amy invokes Easterbrook as she explores the long-term implications of Mattel's promotion of consumerism.

Amy signals closure by coming full circle, returning to her opening anecdote.

demolished, leaving my dolls homeless. But this does not mean that women have escaped the effects of years of Barbie-play as they have temporarily escaped the clutches of Mattel. (I say temporarily because even if the female herself has outgrown Barbie, Mattel will suck her back in through her daughters, nieces, goddaughters, and granddaughters.) Since Barbie preaches the admissibility of hyper-consumption to females at a young age, women, unsurprisingly, "engage in an estimated 80% of all consumer spending" (Katz). Women, conditioned from all those trips to the toy store looking for the perfect party dress for Barbie or the perfect convertible to take her to that party, still find themselves doing this—just on a larger scale—in shopping malls. But perhaps men's consumerism is catching up. The recent "proliferation of metrosexuals" (St. John 177) signals a rise in "straight young men whose fashion and grooming tastes have crossed over into areas once reserved for feminine con-

By consider-ing men's consumer habits and male dolls, Amy ends with a refreshing twist.

sumption" (St. John 174). Mattel, too, takes part in this phenom-enon through the "reintroduc[tion] [of] the Ken doll" (Talbot 79), which now possesses a "new metrosexual look" (Talbot). Well, one thing is certain: Mattel continues its expansive construction on Bar-bie's ever-costly dream mansion, and knows that millions of little girls will do the same.

Works Cited

Cross, Gary. "Barbie, G.I. Joe, and Play in the 1960s." Maasik and Solomon 772–78.

Easterbrook, Gregg. "The Progress Paradox." Maasik and Solomon 400–407.

Edut, Ophira. "Barbie Girls Rule?" *Bitch: Feminist Response to Pop Culture* 31 Jan. 1999: 16. Print.

Katz, Phyllis A., and Margaret Katz. "Purchasing Power: Spending for Change." *Iris* 30 Apr. 2000: 36. Print.

Maasik, Sonia, and Jack Solomon, eds. *Signs of Life in the U.S.A.: Readings on Popular Culture for Writers*. 5th ed. Boston: Bedford, 2006. Print.

Neuhaus, Colin F., and James R. Taylor. "Variables Affecting Sales of Family-Branded Products." *Journal of Marketing Research* 9.4 (1972): 419–22. Print.

Sappington, David E. M., and Birger Wernerfelt. "To Brand or Not to Brand? A Theoretical and Empirical Question." *The Journal of Business* 58.3 (1985): 279–93. Print.

Shames, Laurence. "The More Factor." Maasik and Solomon 76–82.

St. John, Warren. "Metrosexuals Come Out." Maasik and Solomon 174–77.

Talbot, Margaret. "Little Hotties: Barbie's New Rivals." *The New Yorker*. 4 Dec. 2006: 74+. Print.

Toys "R" Us. Geoffrey LLC, 2006. Web. 14 Nov. 2006.

Essay 2

Student Laurie Boloven of California State University, Northridge, wrote the following essay on the TV show *House* for a class on popular culture. In it, she uses the popular show to examine the desires of America's TV audiences. As you read her essay, notice how she enhances her analysis of *House* by locating it within the history of television medical dramas.

House Calls: And Just What Is It Saying?

If the American television viewers who tuned in to watch FOX's series premiere of *House M.D.* on November 16, 2004, anticipated another medical drama revolving around the good-natured, moral, caregiving physician dedicated to saving lives that audiences have grown to know and love, boy were they in for a big surprise. The show's hero, or anti-hero rather, possessed none of the trademark qualities traditionally associated with television medical doctors. How would American audiences react to a professionally and personally unethical, pill-popping cripple, void of compassion, class, and any and all bedside manner? Fast forward six years and seven seasons later, and you'll have your answer. But had the medical professional really evolved so substantially since the years of the founding fathers of television M.D.s? Or was the difference that, perhaps, the audience were the ones who had evolved? The continued success of the series *House M.D.* reveals the American audience's desire for realism.

Unlike the hit medical drama at the time of the series' debut, *ER*, which featured an ensemble cast and everyday emergency room life, *House* was different. *House* revolves around the unorthodox genius diagnostician Dr. Gregory House and the staff of young

Laurie poses a tentative thesis to explain House's significance.

Next she provides a brief précis of the program.

doctors who work alongside him and assist him in solving the most puzzling patient cases that come through the doors of Princeton-Plainsboro Hospital. Dr. House is a diagnostic savant and rivaled by no one in terms of skill and expertise. This is the sole reason why the hospital dean, Dr. Lisa Cuddy, and fellow doctors tolerate him and his unorthodox, unethical, and unruly behavior.

To understand fully the cultural significance of *House* we must first look at the genre to which it belongs. Medical dramas have always been popular among American TV audiences, but they haven't always looked like *House*. According to Jennifer L. McMahon, "medical dramas draw upon a deep-seated cultural interest in medicine" (17). Originating with the first authentic medical drama, *Medic*, on NBC, which aired from 1954 to 1956, the genre has remained a constant on the television airwaves. A long line of television doctors pioneered the genre and laid the foundations for the way in which America perceives its doctors. Some of Dr. House's most iconic predecessors are the title characters in *Dr. Kildare, Ben Casey*, and *Marcus Welby, M.D.* To decipher the cultural significance of the popularity of Dr. House and the series, first we must understand his television ancestors.

Laurie turns to the history of TV medical dramas.

Dr. Kildare and Ben Casey were the most prominent television doctors of the 1960s. Both aired on rival networks and each offered audiences something different. In her article "5 Old School Medical Dramas," Kara Kovalchik describes Dr. Kildare: "Richard Chamberlain starred as the young intern title character who was simultaneously trying to deal with the problems of his patients while trying to please the senior doctor (Raymond Massey). Massey, as Dr. Gillespie, told Kildare on his first day 'Our job is to keep people alive, not tell them how to live,' advice which Kildare of course ignored in every episode" (Kovalchik). "Dealing with the problems of his patients" and "trying to please the senior doctor" couldn't sound less like Dr. House. But, don't forget, television also gave us Ben Casey.

"Unlike the warm, fuzzy, compassionate Dr. Kildare, Dr. Casey was gritty, gruff, and demanding. 'What are you using for brains?!' he'd bark at nurses during surgery, and he was forever at odds with any rule or hospital official that stood between him and an experimental treatment of a patient" (Kovalchik). The Museum of Broadcast Communications' *Encyclopedia of Television* describes Dr. Casey as gruff, demanding, and decisive. "Casey did not suffer fools

lightly and apparently had unqualified respect only for the chief
of neurosurgery"(Cooper). Indeed, Dr. Casey came across like a Boy
Scout compared to Dr. House. Had Dr. Casey even dared to set foot
in Princeton-Plainsboro, Dr. House would surely have chewed him
up and spit him out. But, when compared to Dr. Kildare and the
doctors of the era, Dr. Casey was the first to defy the stereotype and
may have been the Dr. House of his day.

As with Dr. Kildare and Ben Casey, it is also hard to find many
similarities in personality between Dr. House and the reigning doctor of the 1970s, Marcus Welby. During his time on the airwaves,
Marcus Welby became the model for family practitioners (Kovalchik). Welby defines the term caregiver: He is warm, compassionate,
and becomes so invested in his patients' needs that it affects him
during and after office hours.

Unlike his television doctor predecessors, Dr. House not only
lacks compassion for patients, as well as a kind bedside manner, but
often insults them. He is uncaring, rude, and offensive. This behavior
is exemplified when Dr. House enters the hospital room of a teenager
who suffers from severe facial birth defects and an abnormal growth
protruding from his head. House's first comments are, "Wow! You
are ugly" (*House*, "Ugly"). Dr. House is not concerned with leaving
a good impression. He cares only about solving the medical puzzle,
which is to correctly diagnose the patient. Dr. House is so detached
from his patients that he'll often diagnose them without meeting
them face-to-face.

Laurie explains how Dr. House differs from his predecessors.

Dr. House not only differs socially from previous TV doctors; he
demonstrates behavioral and physical differences as well. Dr. House
possesses the astounding behavioral trait of being a pill popper. He
abuses prescription drugs, specifically Vicodin, which not only is a
habit unexpected from a health professional, but is also illegal. And,
as a fan of daytime soap operas, specifically *General Hospital*, he also
finds time to watch them during work hours. Normally, one would
not assume that a medical doctor would be entertained by a daytime
soap opera, let alone ignore job responsibilities to watch a fictitious
program. Another abnormal quality about House is that he limps
and walks with a cane. In the series' pilot episode, House divulges
to a patient that his limp is a result of an infarction in his thigh
muscle, and if it hadn't been for an incorrect diagnosis, the limp and
reoccurring pain could have been prevented ("Pilot"). Audiences are

not accustomed to seeing doctors with physical handicaps. These afore-mentioned qualities are among the many that distinguish Dr. House from the stereotypical doctor we have traditionally seen on television.

The essay's analysis shifts from doctors to patients.

Furthermore, patients are portrayed differently in "early doctor shows" and *House*. In *Marcus Welby, M.D.*, the patients are rendered as innocent, suffering victims whom Dr. Welby and his colleagues painstakingly care for. Dr. Welby makes house calls and even pops by on his days off just to check on patients because he genuinely cares for them ("Hello, Goodbye, Hello"). House, on the other hand, feels impartial to the patients. He thinks they, like everyone else, are all liars and has coined the phrase "Everybody Lies" — a reoccurring phrase and theme throughout the series. Dr. House's perceptions of patients can clearly be summed up in the following conversation he has with colleagues Dr. Foreman and Dr. Cameron in the pilot episode as they are trying to diagnose a patient based on her symptoms:

FOREMAN: Shouldn't we be speaking with the patients before we start diagnosing?

HOUSE: Is she a doctor?

FOREMAN: No, but . . .

HOUSE: Everybody lies.

CAMERON: Dr. House doesn't like dealing with patients.

FOREMAN: Isn't treating patients why we became doctors?

HOUSE: No, treating illnesses is why we became doctors, treating patients is what makes most doctors miserable.

FOREMAN: So you're trying to eliminate the humanity from the practice?

HOUSE: If we don't talk to them, they can't lie to you, and we can't lie to them. Humanity is overrated. ("Pilot")

This initial conversation between Dr. House and his team of diagnosticians illustrates the extreme differences between the portrayal of both doctors and patients. This drastic shift in patient portrayal from the early doctor dramas to *House* reveals how people within society have become more skeptical of one another through the recent decades. They tend to question not only their honesty, but also their motivation and intentions. This is a notable change from the trusting 1960s, when most people didn't even bother to lock their doors at night. The differences in the ways in which the series portray the patients reflect the wariness we, as humans, have developed for one another.

Maybe Dr. House didn't inherit many of the kind personality traits of his TV doctor forefathers, nor acquire Dr. Kildare's dashing good looks, but that isn't to say he is entirely void of all their ancestral genes. Aside from Ben Casey's temper and defiance of stereotype, Dr. House and the series carries on several other traits from the television doctor family tree. Even though Dr. Welby and Dr. House first appear to be polar opposites of one another, House resembles Welby in his astounding skill to diagnose accurately. "There wasn't much that escaped his gimlet eye. Dr. Welby could spot anything from multiple sclerosis to leprosy at fifty paces" (Kovalchik). This sounds like someone we know, and wait, did she just say leprosy? Is this not a reoccurring joke on the *House* series? Another similarity between the *House* and *Welby* series is the uncanny resemblance of both series' first episode. Separated by a span of thirty-five years, it is not by mere coincidence that both series debuted with similar patients suffering from identical symptoms. In both episodes, an elementary school teacher collapses during the instruction of her students, and in both, the diagnosing physicians, House and Welby, instinctually assume it to be a brain tumor. Over the course of each episode the stories veer in different directions, ironically with the *Welby* patient dying and the *House* patient living happily ever after, but the original similarities are hard to miss.

Here Laurie shows how Dr. House bears some similarities to his predecessors.

This surprising plot similarity leads me to conclude that *House*'s creators did not ignore the original shows that spearheaded the medical drama genre when they were developing the premise for their modern series, no matter how different the series may first appear. Fed for decades with squeaky-clean images of do-gooder doctors, the minds of American audiences had been infiltrated with the impression of the American M.D. that the television genre spawned. If it wasn't for the perceptions that these early doctors and their successors left on the minds of American viewers, *House* may have never become a hit decades later.

Over time, Americans grew to realize that most doctors were not like the ones they saw on TV. For example Dr. Welby was so beloved by Americans that both ABC and Robert Young, the actor who played Dr. Welby, "received thousands of complaints from real-life doctors who found the number of malpractice suits filed against them escalating at an alarming rate simply because they 'weren't like Marcus Welby'" (Kovalchik). This audience response demonstrated that not only did Americans *want* their real-life doctors to be like the ones on TV, they were also realizing that they *were* not.

One reason behind the success of the *House* series is that Americans couldn't be fooled forever by the fictitious, fairy-tale doctors they were accustomed to seeing. Instead, they craved something more true to real life. It wouldn't be accurate to state that all doctors are like Dr. House, but what House offers is his humanization of the doctor role. Dr. House's many flaws are what make him human and what make audiences relate to and connect with him.

Yet another of *House*'s departures from the medical drama is the character's refusal to play an "official hero." As defined in Robert B. Ray's article "The Thematic Paradigm," "the official hero, normally portrayed as a teacher, lawyer, politician, farmer, or family man, represented the American belief in collective action, and the objective legal process that superseded private notions of right and wrong" (Ray 343). A TV doctor typically fits into the category of an official hero; however, Dr. House carries out the role much more like the outlaw hero that Ray defines, "the outlaw hero stood for that part of the American imagination valuing self-determination and freedom from entanglements" (Ray 343). Not only does Dr. House break hospital rules; he also violates many codes of ethics to obtain a proper diagnosis.

The fact that television audiences enjoy watching a flawed character, especially one so severely flawed as Dr. House, indicates that our culture has become jaded about the types of people it expects to fill occupations traditionally regarded as official heroes. Americans have accepted that medical professionals, as well as other official heroes (police, firefighters, members of the military, politicians), are flawed human beings, just like the rest of the population. They are not the perfect specimens the media once portrayed them to be. The evolution of the genre reveals the significance of *House*, because it proves that audiences have come a long way in their expectations of medical professionals. Audiences have become desensitized, more tolerant, and accepting that the ideal model created by the television doctor of the 1950s and 1960s simply does not exist.

Part of the realism of the series *House* that the audience craves, then, is the show's tendency to revolve story lines around current and relevant social issues. The episode "Joy to the World," which originally aired on December 9, 2008, exemplifies this trend. The episode's main story line focuses on House and his fellow doctors as they try to determine what caused Natalie, an obese teenage girl, to collapse in the middle of a vocal performance during a high school holiday concert. As Dr. House and company try to diagnose what triggered liver failure in such a young girl, several possible theories arise and then are scrapped, as is the pattern for most episodes. After ruling out several initial speculations involving hallucinogenic drugs, alcohol abuse, a potential painkiller-induced suicide attempt, and the possibility of leukemia, the answer finally dawns on Dr. Cuddy.

While listening to Dr. House describe how it was easier for him to convince a newly engaged, supposedly abstinent couple that the woman's pregnancy was the result of a medical miracle, rather than reveal that she had cheated on her fiancé, Dr. Cuddy realizes the secret she had suspected Natalie of hiding. It occurs to Dr. Cuddy that Natalie must have recently been pregnant. She diagnoses Natalie with eclampsia, a condition that occurs in pregnant women with high blood pressure, which is possible for Natalie, because of her obesity.

Natalie had hidden her unwanted pregnancy, and when the baby was born prematurely, she left it in an abandoned building once she realized it wasn't breathing. Dr. Cuddy decides to search for the remains of the abandoned baby and is surprised to find it alive and in the care of a couple who had been squatting in the house. Upon learning the eclampsia caused permanent, fatal damage to Natalie's liver and heart, both sets of grandparents agree that it would be too painful to keep the baby. The episode concludes when Dr. Cuddy discloses that she plans to adopt the baby.

Packed with current social issues, this episode features high school bullying and its effects on students. An obese high school student, Natalie is a target for bullies at her school. The audience witnesses the bullying in the episode's opening scene when fellow choir members trick Natalie into singing alternate offensive lyrics directed at their choir teacher. Natalie feels humiliated when the other students abruptly go silent during the song, because she was duped into singing the offensive lyrics as a solo.

In another scene, she describes what it's like to be a victim of bullying to Dr. Cuddy.

CUDDY: Teenagers can be incredibly mean. I know what you're going
    through.
NATALIE: I bet you were cool. You're pretty.
CUDDY: You're pretty too.
NATALIE: I'm fat. I'm a loser. They all hate me. You know what they did
    last year? They took these photos of me for the yearbook, but it
    wasn't, it was for this Web site, making fun of me, calling me a pig.
CUDDY: Forget about them. Let's just make you better.
NATALIE: What's the point? ("Joy to the World")

Through Natalie's character and the torture she endures at
school, viewers are reminded of the harshness of school bullying
and the effects it has on students. School bullying is very relevant
today. Earlier this year several incidents received massive media
attention when the bullying became so severe it resulted in the
victims, seventh-grader Seth Walsh, from Tehachapi, California, and
freshman Tyler Clementi, from Rutgers University, committing suicide as a means of escape.

This *House* episode reminds audiences that no matter how far
we think we have evolved in regard to equality and acceptance of
others' differences, people are still being singled out because of
those differences. The episode reminds viewers of just how intolerant, judgmental, and cruel adolescents can be to one another, and
the lasting, deep scars it leaves on the victims.

Teen alcohol abuse, drug abuse, and pregnancy are also
addressed in this episode. The doctors first suspect that Natalie's sudden collapse and heart failure were brought upon by hallucinogenic
mushrooms that her bullies confessed to giving her without her
consent. Once this possible cause is ruled out, the doctors suspect a
potential overdose of painkillers found in Natalie's school locker. The
fact that the scriptwriters chose drug abuse as a potential cause of
Natalie's collapse supports the fact that if the audience easily buys
teenagers' misuse and abuse of illegal and prescription drugs as a possibility, it proves not merely that teenage drug abuse exists, but has
become so mainstream that viewers aren't shocked by it.

Similarly, after the drugs are ruled out as a potential cause,
a fellow classmate reveals that Natalie consumes a lot of alcohol,
although the episode later lets us know Natalie rarely drank any,
but rather only bought alcohol illegally as an attempt to "fit in."

The episode goes beyond simply exposing teen drug and alcohol abuse. More potently, the show presents the notion that a high school student would succumb to illegal measures just to be accepted by her fellow peers. Natalie confesses that she purchased the vodka from Simon, a popular jock at school, just to maintain a relationship with him. She reveals the lengths which adolescents will go to in order to obtain acceptance and to avoid feeling like an outcast.

Beyond the problem of bullying, teenage pregnancy also appears in this episode in the form of a cultural contradiction. In our culture, among teenagers, because of sexual messages derived from the media, it is perceived to be very cool to have sex. On the other hand, it is perceived very uncool to be a "knocked-up teenager." In Natalie's case she had been sexually active with Simon, the popular and cool high school jock. Viewers can safely assume that she probably engaged in the sex to sustain their relationship. As a result, Natalie became pregnant, and being a pregnant teenager, especially at a private school, is just not socially acceptable.

Too ashamed to tell anyone about her pregnancy, Natalie wears baggy clothes, and her physical size helps her keep her peers from knowing her secret. After going into labor early, she delivers a premature baby, and because she is still terrified at how society will perceive her, she abandons it after she thinks it has been born dead.

The extreme choices that Natalie made are results of the way our society judges teenage pregnancy, which is paradoxical, because the society casting judgment is also the same society that is "selling to preteen girls revealing tops and trousers that might have once embarrassed a prostitute," (Maasik and Solomon 483). This cultural contradiction can be defined as "America's curious dichotomy between cultural puritanism and a capitalistic tendency to exploit sexuality on behalf of corporate profits" (Maasik and Solomon 483).

Laurie ties the episode's plot details to long-standing American cultural values.

Another example in which American puritanism is showcased (and mocked) in the episode occurs when Dr. House diagnoses another patient's symptoms as side effects of her pregnancy. The patient, Whitney, has made an abstinence pact with her fiancé and acts shocked when House tells her that she is pregnant. Whitney accepts an explanation of parthenogenesis, or the medical miracle of a virgin birth, for her unexpected pregnancy rather than admitting to having cheated on her fiancé. This clearly showcases an example of America's obsession with puritanical values. Whitney prefers to accept that her pregnancy is the first case of human parthenogenesis known to science rather than admit to engaging in sexual intercourse prior to marriage.

Laurie extends her analysis by adding a briefer analysis of another episode.

Other episodes reflect these patterns. "Joy to the World" also depicts racial stereotyping. After Natalie tells Dr. Kutner and Dr. Taub that Simon dropped off her textbooks, the doctors question Simon about his motive behind this gesture and its authenticity, or rather its overcompensation for guilt. During Dr. Kutner's interrogation of Simon, Dr. Taub senses his unusual hostility toward this presumed bully. Dr. Taub incorrectly assumes, as we find out later on, that Dr. Kutner was a victim of school bullies.

KUTNER: (to SIMON) Stop lying or I'll take the drugs I found in your
    locker down to the cops, you slimy little jerk.
TAUB: (to KUTNER) This kid didn't do anything to you.
KUTNER: This isn't about me.
TAUB: Yeah, yeah, I get it. You were bullied yourself when you were
    in school. Take it easy.
KUTNER: I wasn't bullied.
TAUB: Right. The Indian foster kid whose parents were shot in front of
    him. You were clearly homecoming king. ("Joy to the World")

Dr. Taub assumes, based on Dr. Kutner's race, economic background, and his animosity toward Simon, that he, too, must have been bullied in high school. Even though Dr. Kutner denies being bullied to Dr. Taub, we don't find out the truth until the end of the episode when Kutner knocks on the door of an unfamiliar apartment building and apologizes to the short man who lives there for all the horrible stuff he did to him in high school ("Joy to the World"). It is at this moment that viewers realize that not only was Dr. Kutner not bullied in high school, but in fact he had been one of the bullies. Dr. Taub, like many people, tends to prejudge and stereotype others based on race and economic status. The episode calls America out on its habit to racially stereotype people, by showing that not only was Dr. Taub incorrect to assume that Dr. Kutner was a victim of bullying, but in fact he was the perpetrator.

It is clear to see the numerous ways in which relevant social issues are portrayed in just a single episode of the series *House*. The fact that the American television audience has supplied the *House* series with the ratings to keep it on for seven seasons to date, and sent it into syndication on numerous cable channels, reveals that America has evolved to embrace a series that is not only socially relevant to the times through its depiction of social and cultural issues, but is not afraid to accept an extremely flawed human being carrying out America's most coveted profession. Audiences' enjoyment of the series shows that Americans appreciate and are entertained when a TV character shatters the television mold that had been cast of doctors and replicated for decades. The American craving for *House* symbolizes the American craving for realism and truth.

The essay concludes not with summary but with a refined explanation of House's use of realism.

Works Cited

Cooper, John. "Ben Casey U.S. Medical Drama." *Encyclopedia of Television*. The Museum of Broadcast Communications. 2010. Web. 29 Nov. 2010.

"The Day They Stole the County General." *Ben Casey*. CBS. 26 Apr. 1965. Web. 27 Nov. 2010.

"Hello, Goodbye, Hello." *Marcus Welby, M.D.* ABC. 23 Sept. 1969. DVD-ROM. Nov. 2010.

"Joy to the World." *House M.D.* FOX. 9 Dec. 2008. Web. 28 Nov. 2010.

Kovalchik, Kara. "5 Old School Medical Dramas." *Mental Floss Magazine* 14 May 2009. Web. 21 Nov. 2010.

Maasik, Sonia, and Jack Solomon. *Signs of Life in the U.S.A.* 6th ed. Boston: Bedford, 2009. Print.

McMahon, Jennifer L. "*House* and Sartre: 'Hell Is Other People.'" House *and Philosophy*. Ed. Henry Jacoby. Hoboken: Wiley, 2009. 17. Print.

"Pilot." *House M.D.* FOX. 16 Nov. 2004. Web. 28 Nov. 2010.

Ray, Robert B. "The Thematic Paradigm." Maasik and Solomon 342–50.

"Ugly." *House M.D.* FOX. 13 Nov. 2007. DVD-ROM.

Essay 3

David Goewey wrote this essay as a student at California State University, Northridge, where it won the Oliver Evans Undergraduate Essay Prize. In it he provides a semiotic analysis of the SUV craze that proves to be an eye-opener. Goewey reveals how the sport utility vehicle is a full-fledged myth-making machine, symbolically incorporating many of America's ideological values and contradictions within its several tons of heavy metal. In so doing, he creates a comprehensive semiotic analysis.

"Careful, You May Run Out of Planet":
SUVs and the Exploitation of the American Myth

"For centuries man had fantasized about the glories of independent travel," wrote the thirteenth-century scientist and philosopher Roger Bacon. Although writing during the Middle Ages, Bacon predicted, with uncanny accuracy, that humanity "shall endow chariots with incredible speed, without the aid of any animal" (Pettifer and Turner 9). Bacon's prescient forecast conjured a vision that became a twentieth-century American fact of life: the ubiquitous automobile. By 1872, French inventor Amédée Bollée had developed steam-powered demonstration models (Flink 6), and within the next thirty-five years the United States dominated the world market for gasoline-powered automobiles (Pettifer and Turner 15). In the new century America itself — with a vast geography, scattered settlements, and relatively low population density — seemed best suited to the spread of a romanticized car culture (Flink 43). America, in short, took to the roads with relish.

David starts by explaining why the automobile developed a mythological significance in America.

The automobile quickly entered American popular culture. Tin Pan Alley devoted no fewer than six hundred songs to the pleasures of motoring (Pettifer and Turner 17). The futurist art movement, furthermore, appropriated the automobile as a specific symbol of modernity itself (Wernick 80), representative of speed, progress, and technology. As a token, the car embodied escapist fantasy (Pettifer and Turner 239), allowing the individual to conquer time and space. But it was America's unique values of freedom, individualism, and the pursuit of happiness that became manifested in the automobile—values that imbued the car with definitive mythic significance (Robertson 191).

Now, at the end of the twentieth century, the vehicle that combines the most potent mix of American mythologies is the sport utility vehicle (SUV)—passenger cars/light trucks with four-wheel drive. With sales expected to exceed one million units in 1998, the SUV is the fastest-growing segment of the automobile market (Storck 79). However, as a social phenomenon, SUVs contain both practical and mythic contradictions. For example, these vehicles are designed for rugged, off-road motoring, yet a mere 10 percent of drivers ever leave surface streets or highways (Storck 99). With their muscular styling and dominant height and weight, SUVs are almost ludicrously masculine in design, yet women account for 40 percent of sales (Storck 79). Furthermore, while SUV advertising campaigns often pose the vehicle in rural settings of woodlands or along lakesides, the SUV is anything but nature-friendly with its thirsty gasoline tank and lower emission standards (Pope 14). In short, the modern SUV represents a preeminent symbol of American popular culture.

The focus narrows to SUVs.

A semiotic analysis of the contradictions inherent in the SUV phenomenon, as well as its historical and socioeconomic significance, therefore, reveals the intriguing ironies that underscore America's predominant ideology. American culture's faddish preoccupation with the SUV may be seen as deeply embedded in a national identity. Furthermore, a close look at the SUV trend also reveals America's understanding of reality and fantasy and its conflicting attitude toward human survival and environmental protection. As a cultural signifier, the SUV both reveals and reflects the principal components of America's popular mythology.

David's thesis is that the SUV embodies fundamental American values.

The most obvious ironies are perhaps best observed in the SUV model names chosen by the manufacturers. Many vehicle names are directly evocative of America's western frontier mythology, such as the Jeep Wrangler or the Isuzu Rodeo. Others are linked to the Western European tradition of the exploration and settlement of foreign lands, such as the Ford Explorer or the Land Rover Discovery. Indeed, the GMC Yukon blends both American western imagery and the European exploratory drive and thus embodies the American notion of a frontier: remote, extremely wild, and to the average person unknown.

David first demonstrates the values embodied in SUVs by analyzing the vehicles' names.

The fascination with the American frontier, which today's automakers so effectively exploit, is directly tied to America's historical beginnings. The idea of the frontier as both sacred and menacing is a principal tenet in the nation's mythology. The first Europeans, after all, encountered a daunting wilderness. *Mayflower* passenger William Bradford described a "hideous and desolate wilderness . . . represent[ing] a wild and savage hue" (Robertson 45). The Europeans, steeped in fairy-tale traditions of the forest as the dark dwelling place of witches and cannibals, therefore considered the woods intrinsically evil (Robertson 49). The forests were godless and had to be tamed before they could be inhabitable, leveled before they could be considered usable. The Native Americans, likewise, were viewed as the personification of this savage wasteland and therefore had to be subjugated along with the wilderness to ensure the spread of civilization (Robertson 50). And the early Americans' religious convictions justified this expansion.

The notion that Americans were on a God-given mission to subdue this newfound jungle and expand Western civilization "into the limitless wilderness" (Robertson 44) became institutionalized in American mythology by the Jacksonian policy of Manifest Destiny. Americans were believed to be ordained by God to carry the noble virtues of democracy, freedom, and civilization westward across the continent (Robertson 72). This relentless expansionism, then, was suffused with religious significance and mission. The frontier was seen as the demarcation between order and disorder, between goodness and evil. To challenge the frontier, therefore, took supreme courage and zeal, and men like Daniel Boone, George Rogers Clark, and Andrew Jackson became outstanding western heroes (Robertson 80).

Corollary to this idea of an expansive frontier was the belief in the ever-abundant opportunities and riches available to whoever was brave and ambitious enough to pursue them. This idea of "more" was contingent on the belief in a limitless frontier and served as a motivating factor in the pursuit of happiness and the drive to succeed. Expansion, in a sense, became an end in itself (Shames 33–34). However, in late-twentieth-century America, the concept of more has suffered a practical setback. Diminishing economic expectations from the 1960s through the 1980s, including a shrinking productivity rate, a decrease in real earnings, and a growing national debt, all contributed to challenge the mythic notion of the frontier as fruitful with economic possibilities (Shames 34–36).

It is perhaps not coincidental, then, that the sport utility vehicle craze began in earnest in the early 1980s (Storck 79). In reaction to "the fear that the world may not be . . . big enough" (Shames 37), the decade's penchant for conspicuous consumption can be seen as a challenge to that anxiety. And the introduction of large, powerful vehicles into the mass market, with names like the Ford Bronco and the Chevy Blazer, may represent the reassertion of a courageous American defiance in response to threatened frontiers.

Furthermore, the growth of the SUV market through the 1990s, with this segment comprising 23 percent of total auto sales (Storck 79), suggests the adaptability of the SUV's mythic significance. The expanding economy of the Clinton years — based on the globalization of economic interests and the consequent resurrection of expanding frontiers — recasts the SUV as a celebratory metaphor for power and control. The SUV, in this context, represents the resurgence of the conquering American.

Another popular SUV that contains a doubly potent signifier within the manufacturer's title is the Jeep Cherokee. Considered the original SUV, the Jeep Cherokee dates all the way back to 1948. As a result, owners take a measure of purist's pride, believing their SUV is the one that started it all (Storck 41). But a closer look at this SUV's mythohistorical connections may provide the owners' pride with a deeper significance.

David provides an in-depth analysis of one vehicle's name, the Jeep Cherokee.

The Jeep Cherokee prototype — the General Purpose Vehicle, which was shortened to Jeep — was introduced during World War II in response to a U.S. Army–sponsored competition among automakers. It was first developed by the Bantam Motor Company, and the design was then completed by the Willys-Overland Company. The Ford Motor Company also assisted in the mass production of what was soon considered the "backbone of all Allied military transport" and the "crowning success of the war" (Flink 276). No doubt drawing on their heroic wartime performance, surplus military Jeeps were sold stateside and helped to introduce a market for four-wheel-drive recreational vehicles (Flink 276).

The usefulness and durability of four-wheel-drive vehicles, however, was recognized even earlier during World War I, and many automakers, including Packard, Peerless, and Nash motor companies, vied for government contracts. Manufacturers found that luxury car chassis were easily converted to 2 or 3 ton truck bodies (Flink 78) — a literal blending of automobiles and trucks that clearly prefigures the modern SUV. Along with the Jeep's victorious wartime service, then, the SUV conveys such powerful militaristic connotations as morally righteous patriotism, overwhelming industrial ingenuity and might, and the imperative conquest of evil.

An interesting link between automobility and the American frontier was provided approximately forty years earlier by a Civil War hero. On his retirement in 1903, Civil War veteran General Nelson A. Miles, who had successfully hunted Chief Joseph and the Nez Perce to ground in 1877 and to whom the Apache war leader Geronimo surrendered in 1886 (Josephy 416, 429), foresaw the military promise of motor vehicles. He urged Secretary of War Elihu Root to "replace five regiments of cavalry" with troops on bicycles and in motor vehicles (Flink 74), believing that the horse was now obsolete. General Miles's foresight was ironic in light of the Jeep Cherokee's double significance.

The Jeep Cherokee's militaristic connotations become oppressive when considering the grotesquely racist misapplication of a Native American tribal name to a motor vehicle. Although the word Cherokee is a misnomer derived from the Choctaw definition for cave dwellers and actually has no meaning in the language of those to whom it is applied, it is nevertheless used to designate at least one group of Native Americans, the United Keetoowah Band of Cherokee, in Oklahoma (Josephy 323). This original misnaming indicates the indeterminability of language, especially in the traumatic context of Native American history. And while it may be argued that such indeterminacy freely allows a manufacturer's use of the name to sell a product, the word *Cherokee* nevertheless denotes a group of people still thriving today despite oppression.

In the 1820s, despite the fierce allegiance to tradition held by many Cherokee, a large number of them succumbed to the ongoing proselytizing efforts of Moravian missionaries to become the "most acculturated of southern tribes" (Josephy 320). The Cherokee learned the English alphabet and even innovated a Cherokee alphabet based on the English model. In 1828, this led to the remarkable publication, in English and Cherokee, of a native newspaper (Josephy 320). Cherokee efforts to assimilate into what could be seen even then as a dominant culture, in other words, were vigorous.

Nevertheless, also in 1828, President Andrew Jackson undertook an aggressive campaign of ethnic cleansing against the Cherokee. Capitalizing on white racism to pass anti-Cherokee legislation, and with the discovery of gold on Cherokee territory, Jackson made physical removal of the tribe a national issue (Josephy 325). This culminated in the infamous and tragic Trail of Tears, the forced march west to Oklahoma of eighteen thousand Cherokee men, women, and children under the armed escort of General Winfield Scott and seven thousand U.S. Army troops (Josephy 331).

The manufacturers of the Jeep Cherokee clearly ignore this dismal chapter in U.S. history and instead evoke superficially positive components of a mythic American past. Drawing on traditional viewpoints of the western frontier as the border between civilization and wilderness (Robertson 92) and oblivious to the fact that the Cherokee were an enforced western tribe, the Jeep Cherokee manufacturer exploits mythic identifications of Native Americans with the fearsome and violent "imagery and logic of the frontier" (Robertson 106).

The Jeep Cherokee manufacturer also mines the symbol of the quintessential American hero, the cowboy. Pitted against the frontier, the cowboy was directly descended from the backwoodsmen and pathfinders who pioneered west to the Ohio River Valley and beyond to the Northwest Passage. As the frontier pushed on, the continent's western plains and mountains became the wilderness that was next in need of subjugation and control. The cowboy, and his close companions in the American mythic imagination of the Wild West, the U.S. Cavalry, became the defenders of civilization and the champions of progress (Robertson 161–62). As such, they symbolized law and order in a lawless land. Both the cowboy and the U.S. Cavalry were the good guys risking themselves to save civilization from the bad guys, most notably the wildly violent Indians (Robertson 162).

The Jeep Cherokee, then, is a multilayered symbol indeed. This SUV appropriates the token of a victorious American struggle over the frontier, won by American cowboys and cavalrymen, and combines it with the morally righteous conquest over evil achieved during World War II. The modern driver who slips behind the wheel of a Jeep Cherokee assumes the militaristically heroic mantle that is suffused within the vehicle's legend and manifested in the control available

A summary of the significance of the Cherokee's name.

in the "tight and precise steering, easy maneuverability . . . and taut overall feel from the firm suspension" (Storck 41). Detached from historical truths, however, the SUV's "excellent visibility all around" and "superior driving position" (Storck 41), qualities essential to success in battle, capitalize on these military/frontier connotations and at the same time sublimate factual battlefield horrors into an aggressive game of on-the-road cowboys and Indians.

The SUV, with its rugged militaristic symbolism, magnifies the traditional association of the automobile as a masculine token. Yet women account for a sizable share of the SUV market (Storck 79). This appeal, in fact, extends and amplifies a traditional relationship between women and motor vehicles. The introduction of the automobile may well have affected the scope of women's societal role more than that of men. Unlike the horse and buggy, for instance, the automobile demanded skill over physical strength to operate, and so women were offered mobility and parity that driving a team of horses denied them (Flink 162).

David shifts to the way SUVs are marketed to women.

However, middle-class women by the 1920s were still traditionally tied to the home, for the most part, although electrical household appliances had nevertheless increased leisure time. The refrigerator, for example, permitted the bulk buying of a week's worth of perishable food at one stop, leaving time for socializing or an afternoon movie matinee (Flink 164). The added spare time, combined with automobility's enhanced sense of individual freedom (Robertson 191), afforded women at least temporary escape from the confines of the home that defined their routine (Flink 163).

As the automobile helped to change women's role from that of home-based providers of food and clothing into consumers of mass-produced goods, car designers soon recognized the potential of the female market. Such comfort features as plush upholstery, heaters, and automatic transmissions were planned with women in mind (Flink 163). And advertising executives, quick to determine that women were disproportionately the nation's consumers (Marchand 66), began to target automobile ads at them. One of the most famous advertisements, for the Jordan Motor Company's Playboy automobile, began "Somewhere west of Laramie there's a broncho-busting, steer-roping girl" (Pettifer and Turner 130), clearly utilizing the familiar western imagery of freedom and control.

This relationship between women and their automobiles has grown even more complex in recent years. First, the car didn't so much redefine women's fundamental domestic role as increase the scope of its domain. Also, it is reasonable to assume that the automobile facilitated women's introduction into the workplace by easing transportation between the home and job. And yet in 1997, economic equality still eludes the American workforce: Working women earn less than 75 percent of men's average income (Jones et al. 49). A woman's job, furthermore, may include not only doing outside work but ferrying children to and from school and activities and shopping for the family. A subsequent feeling of disempowerment, then, may find relief behind the wheel of a physically powerful and symbolically potent SUV.

Advertisers evidently think so. They still acknowledge a woman's buying power and capitalize on the appeal SUVs hold for many female drivers. One current SUV advertisement aimed at women, promoting the Subaru Forester, both stresses its inherent power and rugged potential and notes the female-friendly design of this smaller vehicle. The larger photo in a two-page spread in *Time* shows the Forester kicking up a dust trail as it barrels down a dirt track. The accompanying smaller picture presents a casually dressed young woman easily tying a kayak to the SUV's roof. The ad's dominant image is a rough and careless strength. And while the woman in the ad is proportionally submissive, she is capably preparing for an exciting outdoor adventure. The double message suggests a sense of diminishment that is compensated for with images of ability, ease, and the casual transference of power.

David turns to advertising as evidence of the values manufacturers ascribe to SUVs.

Perhaps the most logical and disarming association carmakers and advertisers exploit when designing and promoting an SUV is the vehicle's connection to nature. As previously noted, implicit within the SUV's frontier imagery is a confrontational attitude toward the wilderness. Accordingly, automakers design — and advertisers sell — SUVs capable of handling the roughest terrain. And indeed, much of the appeal of SUVs is their promise of providing access to the farthest reaches of the globe. As a marketing gimmick, for instance, Land Rover cosponsors and participates in the annual Camel Trophy relay, pitting various SUVs against the jungle wilds of Borneo and South America. Besides the obvious British imperialistic connotations such a race implies, the challenge of maneuvering a

Land Rover Discovery "over garbage can sized rocks" or "through streams where the entire vehicle is submerged" (Storck 6) positions the competitor in a naturally inharmonious contest.

Advertisers take a dual approach when exploiting the adversarial relationship between SUVs and nature. In some print ads this relationship is clothed in benign natural imagery, often with a warning text. The Mitsubishi Montero Sport, for example, pictures a gleaming silver vehicle perched prominently on the rocky shoreline of a wooded lakesite. The tall stand of evergreen trees are at a safe distance; the water surface is without a ripple. The bold black headline proclaims, "It Came to Comfort Earth," and the text goes on to inform the reader that "the planet wasn't exactly designed for your comfort."

So the Montero Sport offers a wondrous solution to an uncomfortable world. The proximity of nature to the vehicle in the photo is remote, suggesting that the mere presence of the Montero Sport is enough to keep nature at bay. Furthermore, the SUV's silver color combines with the headline to imply that the Montero Sport carries an otherworldly salvation. Nature and its uncomfortability, therefore, are controlled by the SUV's omnipresence, and the driver is safe due to the vehicle's "car-like . . . civility."

The design and marketing of SUVs are based on traditional American attitudes toward nature and the wilderness. The vehicles are at the same time built for access to the natural world and yet sold by exploiting that relationship as confrontational. The SUV, in other words, makes easily available a world that is threatening to the driver and its occupants. And yet underlying these contradictions, and compounding them, is the very real impact that SUVs make on the environment.

David explores how the marketing of SUVs reflects American attitudes toward nature.

The GMC Suburban, big sister to the aforementioned GMC Yukon, asserts itself with a 42 gallon capacity fuel tank. With a curb-side weight pushing five thousand pounds and amenities like air conditioning, the Suburban's gas mileage is generously estimated at about 16 miles to the gallon (Storck 29). While the GMC Suburban is admittedly the largest SUV model on the market, poor gas mileage ratios are the norm for these vehicles. Where the Environmental Protection Agency has determined that automobiles must meet a fuel economy standard of 27.5 miles a gallon, light trucks, which include all SUVs, currently need only to clear 20.7 miles a gallon. And many don't even achieve that (Bradsher).

The world oil industry may keep billions of barrels in their inventories on any given day (Yergin 686), leading to the understandable public perception that supplies are unlimited. But fossil fuels are still a nonrenewable resource. Moreover, American gasoline use is expected to rise by 33 percent within the next fifteen years, indicating that fuel conservation is not much of an issue with consumers (Bradsher).

But perhaps the more pressing problem, and one that is directly exacerbated by the SUV craze, is the threat of global warming from the increased burning of fossil fuels. Carbon dioxide levels in the atmosphere have risen by about 25 percent in the last century and appear to coincide with a worldwide increase in the use of petroleum. Various cataclysmic effects are predicted as a result, including rising sea levels from melting ice caps, the spread of tropical diseases to normally temperate regions, and extreme weather fluctuations (McKibben 9, 18). Yet the booming SUV market belies any overwhelming concern on the part of American consumers. In fact, the vehicle's popularity in the face of such dire predictions seems the latest manifestation of an established confrontational relationship to nature.

David leads to his conclusion by considering the future implications of the SUV fad.

As the world does indeed become more dangerous, the apparent protection that SUVs afford becomes more desirable, and the need to control the uncontrollable becomes more acute. Driving a five thousand pound, resource-devouring behemoth not only justifies the impact on the environment, as a means of revenge against an enemy, but it acts as a means of celebration — the exultation of victory over the savage beast of nature. The SUV, in its design and presentation, seeks to make safely available what it can ultimately dominate; as such, it attempts to reduce the entire world to the state of a drive-through wildlife nature preserve. At the end of the twentieth century, the SUV perfectly embodies an American mythology of conquest and control.

America's love affair with the sport utility vehicle shows the abiding power of traditional beliefs. The expansion of the frontiers continues despite facts that suggest there is nowhere left to go. This joyful faith in "more" feeds on the challenge of less. Indeed, a sport utility vehicle is the triumphant representation of denial — denial of the past, the present, and the future. American mythology is continuously reinvented and thereby endures in this pop cultural symbol.

David closes by succinctly and passionately arguing that SUVs embody fundamental American values.

Works Cited

Bradsher, Keith. "Light Trucks Increase Profits but Foul Air More
Than Cars." *New York Times* 30 Nov. 1997, national ed., sec.
1:1+. Print.

Flink, James J. *The Automobile Age*. Cambridge: MIT, 1988. Print.

Jones, Barbara, Anita Blair, Barbara Ehrenreich, Arlie Russell Hoch-
schild, Jeanne Lewis, and Elizabeth Perle McKenna. "Giving
Women the Business." *Harper's* Dec. 1997: 47–58. Print.

Josephy, Alvin M., Jr. *Five Hundred Nations: An Illustrated History of
North American Indians*. New York: Knopf, 1994. Print.

Marchand, Roland. *Advertising the American Dream: Making Way for
Modernity 1920–1940*. Berkeley: University of California Press,
1985. Print.

McKibben, Bill. *The End of Nature*. New York: Anchor, 1989. Print.

Pettifer, Julian, and Nigel Turner. *Automania: Man and the Motorcar*.
Boston: Little, Brown, 1984. Print.

Pope, Carl. "Car Talks — Motown Walks." *Sierra Magazine* Mar./Apr.
1996: 14+. Print.

Robertson, James Oliver. *American Myth, American Reality*. New
York: Hill & Wang, 1980. Print.

Shames, Laurence. "The More Factor." *Signs of Life in the U.S.A.:
Readings on Popular Culture for Writers*. Ed. Sonia Maasik and
Jack Solomon. Boston: Bedford, 1994. 25–31. Print.

Storck, Bob. *Sport Utility Buyer's Guide '98*. Milwaukee: Pace,
1998. Print.

Wernick, Andrew. "Vehicles for Myth." *Signs of Life in the U.S.A.:
Readings on Popular Culture for Writers*. Ed. Sonia Maasik and
Jack Solomon. Boston: Bedford, 1994. 78–94. Print.

Yergin, Daniel. *The Prize: The Epic Quest for Oil, Money and Power*.
New York: Simon & Schuster, 1991. Print.

CONDUCTING RESEARCH AND CITING SOURCES

Your instructor may ask you to use secondary sources to support your analyses of popular culture. These sources may include a wide variety of published materials, from other essays (such as those featured in this book) to interviews you conduct to YouTube videos. When you write about popular culture, a host of sources are available to you to help lend weight to your arguments as well as help you develop fresh thinking about your topic.

The Internet age has afforded us innovative research opportunities, and with a wealth of information at your fingertips, it is up to you, the writer, to learn to determine which sources you should trust and which you should be suspicious of. As always, the library is a great place to begin. Research librarians continue to be excellent resources not only for finding sources for your papers, but for learning best practices for conducting research. It is more than likely that they are aware of resources at your disposal that you haven't considered: from academic databases like EBSCOhost to library catalogs to film and video archives.

The following selections offer additional help for conducting academically sound research online.

SCOTT JASCHIK

A Stand against Wikipedia

Increasingly, college faculty are concerned about the widespread use of Wikipedia in student research and writing. The problem, as faculty see it, is twofold. First, there is the problem of reliability. Wikipedia does strive to provide reliable information, but given the wide-open nature of the site — anyone can contribute — ensuring accuracy is not really possible. This leads to student work that simply disseminates misinformation. Second, even where Wikipedia is accurate (and it can be an accurate source of information), it is, after all, an encyclopedia, and while encyclopedic sources may be suitable for background information, students performing college-level research should seek primary sources and academic-level secondary sources that they find on their own. The following article from insidehighered.com surveys the problems with Wikipedia as a research source as seen by college faculty from a number of universities.

As Wikipedia has become more and more popular with students, some professors have become increasingly concerned about the online, reader-produced encyclopedia.

While plenty of professors have complained about the lack of accuracy or completeness of entries, and some have discouraged or tried to bar students from using it, the history department at Middlebury College is trying to take a stronger, collective stand. It voted this month to bar students from citing the Web site as a source in papers or other academic work. All faculty members will be telling students about the policy and explaining why material on Wikipedia — while convenient — may not be trustworthy. "As educators, we are in the business of reducing the dissemination of misinformation," said Don Wyatt, chair of the department. "Even though Wikipedia may have some value, particularly from the value of leading students to citable sources, it is not itself an appropriate source for citation," he said.

The department made what Wyatt termed a consensus decision on the issue after discussing problems professors were seeing as students cited incorrect information from Wikipedia in papers and on tests. In one instance, Wyatt said, a professor noticed several students offering the same incorrect information, from Wikipedia. There was some discussion in the department of trying to ban students from using Wikipedia, but Wyatt said that didn't seem appropriate. Many Wikipedia entries have good bibliographies, Wyatt said. And any absolute ban would just be ignored. "There's the issue of freedom of access," he said. "And I'm not in the business of promulgating unenforceable edicts."

Wyatt said that the department did not specify punishments for citing Wikipedia, and that the primary purpose of the policy was to educate, not to be punitive. He said he doubted that a paper would be rejected for having a single Wikipedia footnote, but that students would be told that they shouldn't do so, and that multiple violations would result in reduced grades or even a failure. "The important point that we wish to communicate to all students taking courses and submitting work in our department in the future is that they cite Wikipedia at their peril," he said. He stressed that the objection of the department to Wikipedia wasn't its online nature, but its unedited nature, and he said students need to be taught to go for quality information, not just convenience.

The frustrations of Middlebury faculty members are by no means unique.   5 Last year, Alan Liu, a professor of English at the University of California at Santa Barbara, adopted a policy that Wikipedia "is not appropriate as the primary or sole reference for anything that is central to an argument, complex, or controversial." Liu said that it was too early to tell what impact his policy is having. In explaining his rationale — which he shared with an e-mail list — he wrote that he had "just read a paper about the relation between structuralism, deconstruction, and postmodernism in which every reference was to the Wikipedia articles on those topics with no awareness that there was any need to read a primary work or even a critical work."

Wikipedia officials agree — in part — with Middlebury's history department. "That's a sensible policy," Sandra Ordonez, a spokeswoman, said in an e-mail interview. "Wikipedia is the ideal place to start your research and get a global picture of a topic; however, it is not an authoritative source. In fact, we recommend that students check the facts they find in Wikipedia against other sources. Additionally, it is generally good research practice to cite an original source when writing a paper, or completing an exam. It's usually not advisable, particularly at the university level, to cite an encyclopedia." Ordonez acknowledged that, given the collaborative nature of Wikipedia writing and editing, "there is no guarantee an article is 100 percent correct," but she said that the site is shifting its focus from growth to improving quality, and that the site is a great resource for students. "Most articles are continually being edited and improved upon, and most contributors are real lovers of knowledge who have a real desire to improve the quality of a particular article," she said.

Experts on digital media said that the Middlebury history professors' reaction was understandable and reflects growing concern among faculty members about the accuracy of what students find online. But some worry that bans on citing Wikipedia may not deal with the underlying issues.

Roy Rosenzweig, director of the Center for History and New Media at George Mason University, did an analysis of the accuracy of Wikipedia for the *Journal of American History*, and he found that in many entries, Wikipedia was as accurate as or more accurate than more traditional encyclopedias. He said that the quality of material was inconsistent, and that biographical entries were generally well done, while more thematic entries were much less so. Like Ordonez, he said the real problem is one of college students using encyclopedias when they should be using more advanced sources. "College students shouldn't be citing encyclopedias in their papers," he said. "That's not what college is about. They either should be using primary sources or serious secondary sources."

In the world of college librarians, a major topic of late has been how to guide students in the right direction for research, when Wikipedia and similar sources are so easy. Some of those who have been involved in these discussions said that the Middlebury history department's action pointed to the need for more outreach to students. Lisa Hinchliffe, head of the undergraduate library and coordinator of information literacy at the University of Illinois at Urbana-Champaign, said that earlier generations of students were in fact taught when it was appropriate (or not) to consult an encyclopedia and why for many a paper they would never even cite a popular magazine or non-scholarly work. "But it was a relatively constrained landscape," and students didn't have easy access to anything equivalent to Wikipedia, she said. "It's not that students are being lazy today. It's a much more complex environment."

When she has taught, and spotted footnotes to sources that aren't appro-   10
priate, she's considered that "a teachable moment," Hinchliffe said. She said that she would be interested to see how Middlebury professors react when they get the first violations of their policy, and said she thought there could be positive discussions about why sources are or aren't good ones. That kind of teaching, she said, is important "and can be challenging."

Steven Bell, associate librarian for research and instructional services at Temple University, said of the Middlebury approach: "I applaud the effort for wanting to direct students to good quality resources," but he said he would go about it in a different way. "I understand what their concerns are. There's no question that [on Wikipedia and similar sites] some things are great and some things are questionable. Some of the pages could be by eighth graders," he said. "But to simply say 'don't use that one' might take students in the wrong direction from the perspective of information literacy."

Students face "an ocean of information" today, much of it of poor quality, so a better approach would be to teach students how to "triangulate" a source like Wikipedia, so they could use other sources to tell whether a given entry could be trusted. "I think our goal should be to equip students with the critical thinking skills to judge."

PATTI S. CARAVELLO

Judging Quality on the Web

When you conduct research on the Internet, you'll find a dizzying range of sources, from academic journals to government Web sites, from newspapers and popular magazines to blogs, wikis, and social networking and file-sharing sites. Having a plethora of sources at hand with just the click of a mouse has been a boon to researchers in all fields. But the very democratic basis of the Internet that makes all this information so readily available creates a challenge, for it comes with no guarantees of quality control. Indeed, it is incumbent upon you, the researcher, to determine the reliability of the Web sources that you use. The following article from the UCLA Library's Web site, "Judging Quality on the Web," lists criteria that will allow you to evaluate the usefulness and reliability of Internet sources.

Even after refining a query in a search engine, a researcher often retrieves a huge number of Web sites. It is essential to know how to evaluate Web sites for the same reasons you would evaluate a periodical article or a book: *to ascertain whether you can rely on the information, to identify its inherent biases or limitations, and to see how or whether it fits into your overall research strategy.*

A good (useful, reliable) Web site:

1. Clearly states the author and/or organizational **source** of the information
   Your task:
   - Consider the qualifications, other works, and organizational affiliation of the author
   - Look up the organization which produced the Web site (if it's unfamiliar) to identify its credentials, viewpoint, or agenda
   - If the source is an E-journal, discover whether it is refereed (reviewed by scholars before it is accepted for publication)

2. Clearly states the date the material was written and the date the site was last revised
   Your task:
   - If the information is not current enough for your purposes or the date is not given, look elsewhere

3. Provides **accurate** data whose parameters are clearly defined

    Your task:

    - Compare the data found on the Web site with data found in other sources (encyclopedias, reference books, articles, etc.) for accuracy, completeness, recency
    - Ask a librarian about other important sources to check for this information

4. Provides the **type and level** of information you need

    Your task:

    - Decide whether the level of detail and comprehensiveness, the treatment of the topic (e.g., scholarly or popular), and the graphics or other features are acceptable
    - If the site does not provide the depth of coverage you need, look elsewhere

5. Keeps **bias** to a minimum, and clearly indicates point of view

    Your task:

    - Be aware that producing a Web page does not require the checking and review that publishing a scholarly book requires; you might have retrieved nothing but someone's personal opinion on the topic
    - Appealing graphics can distract you from noticing even overt bias, so heighten your skepticism and examine the evidence (source, date, accuracy, level, links)

6. Provides live **links** to related high quality Web sites

    Your task:

    - Click on several of the links provided to see if they are active (or if they give an "error" message indicating the links are not being maintained) and to see if they are useful
    - Check to see if the criteria are stated for selecting the links

7. In the case of **commercial** sites, keeps advertising separate from content, and does not let advertisers determine content

    Your task:

    - Look at the Web address: Sites that are commercial have *.com* in their addresses and might have advertising or offer to sell something. The *.com* suffix is also found in news sites (e.g., newspapers, TV networks) and personal pages (sites created by individuals who have purchased a domain name but who may or may not have a commercial or institutional affiliation)

8. Is clearly organized and **designed** for ease of use

Your task:
- Move around the page to see if its organization makes sense and it is easy to return to the top or to the sections you need
- Decide whether the graphics enhance the content or detract from it

TRIP GABRIEL

For Students in Internet Age, No Shame in Copy and Paste

The Internet is an invaluable source for information when it comes to writing about popular culture, both because of its instant accessibility and because of its ability to keep pace with the rapid turnover in popular fashions and trends in a way that print-technology publication never can. But, as is so often the case with the Internet, there is a downside to the matter. Because, as Trip Gabriel observes in this feature that originally appeared in the *New York Times*, "concepts of intellectual property, copyright, and originality are under assault in the unbridled exchange of online information" — the result is a pandemic of inadvertent, and sometimes deliberate, plagiarism. Certainly in an era of group-oriented writing — as on Wikipedia — traditional notions of individual authorship are being deconstructed, which makes it all the more important that students learn in their writing classes what the conventions for documentation are and why they are still necessary. Trip Gabriel is a longtime reporter, and former Styles editor, at the *New York Times*.

At Rhode Island College, a freshman copied and pasted from a Web site's frequently asked questions page about homelessness — and did not think he needed to credit a source in his assignment because the page did not include author information.

At DePaul University, the tip-off to one student's copying was the purple shade of several paragraphs he had lifted from the Web; when confronted by a writing tutor his professor had sent him to, he was not defensive — he just wanted to know how to change purple text to black.

And at the University of Maryland, a student reprimanded for copying from Wikipedia in a paper on the Great Depression said he thought its entries — unsigned and collectively written — did not need to be credited since they counted, essentially, as common knowledge.

Professors used to deal with plagiarism by admonishing students to give credit to others and to follow the style guide for citations, and pretty much left it at that.

But these cases — typical ones, according to writing tutors and offi- 5 cials responsible for discipline at the three schools who described the plagiarism — suggest that many students simply do not grasp that using words they did not write is a serious misdeed.

It is a disconnect that is growing in the Internet age as concepts of intellectual property, copyright and originality are under assault in the unbridled exchange of online information, say educators who study plagiarism.

Digital technology makes copying and pasting easy, of course. But that is the least of it. The Internet may also be redefining how students — who came of age with music file-sharing, Wikipedia and Web-linking — understand the concept of authorship and the singularity of any text or image.

"Now we have a whole generation of students who've grown up with information that just seems to be hanging out there in cyberspace and doesn't seem to have an author," said Teresa Fishman, director of the Center for Academic Integrity at Clemson University. "It's possible to believe this information is just out there for anyone to take."

Professors who have studied plagiarism do not try to excuse it — many are champions of academic honesty on their campuses — but rather try to understand why it is so widespread.

In surveys from 2006 to 2010 by Donald L. McCabe, a co-founder of the 10 Center for Academic Integrity and a business professor at Rutgers University, about 40 percent of 14,000 undergraduates admitted to copying a few sentences in written assignments.

Perhaps more significant, the number who believed that copying from the Web constitutes "serious cheating" is declining — to 29 percent on average in recent surveys from 34 percent earlier in the decade.

Sarah Brookover, a senior at the Rutgers campus in Camden, N.J., said many of her classmates blithely cut and paste without attribution.

"This generation has always existed in a world where media and intellectual property don't have the same gravity," said Ms. Brookover, who at 31 is older than most undergraduates. "When you're sitting at your computer, it's the same machine you've downloaded music with, possibly illegally, the same machine you streamed videos for free that showed on HBO last night."

Ms. Brookover, who works at the campus library, has pondered the differences between researching in the stacks and online. "Because you're not walking into a library, you're not physically holding the article, which takes you closer to 'this doesn't belong to me,' " she said. Online, "everything can belong to you really easily."

A University of Notre Dame anthropologist, Susan D. Blum, disturbed by   15
the high rates of reported plagiarism, set out to understand how students view authorship and the written word, or "texts" in Ms. Blum's academic language.

She conducted her ethnographic research among 234 Notre Dame undergraduates. "Today's students stand at the crossroads of a new way of conceiving texts and the people who create them and who quote them," she wrote last year in the book *My Word!: Plagiarism and College Culture,* published by Cornell University Press.

Ms. Blum argued that student writing exhibits some of the same qualities of pastiche that drive other creative endeavors today — TV shows that constantly reference other shows or rap music that samples from earlier songs.

In an interview, she said the idea of an author whose singular effort creates an original work is rooted in Enlightenment ideas of the individual. It is buttressed by the Western concept of intellectual property rights as secured by copyright law. But both traditions are being challenged.

"Our notion of authorship and originality was born, it flourished, and it may be waning," Ms. Blum said.

She contends that undergraduates are less interested in cultivating a   20
unique and authentic identity — as their 1960s counterparts were — than in trying on many different personas, which the Web enables with social networking.

"If you are not so worried about presenting yourself as absolutely unique, then it's O.K. if you say other people's words, it's O.K. if you say things you don't believe, it's O.K. if you write papers you couldn't care less about because they accomplish the task, which is turning something in and getting a grade," Ms. Blum said, voicing student attitudes. "And it's O.K. if you put words out there without getting any credit."

The notion that there might be a new model young person, who freely borrows from the vortex of information to mash up a new creative work, fueled a brief brouhaha earlier this year with Helene Hegemann, a German teenager whose best-selling novel about Berlin club life turned out to include passages lifted from others.

Instead of offering an abject apology, Ms. Hegemann insisted, "There's no such thing as originality anyway, just authenticity." A few critics rose to her defense, and the book remained a finalist for a fiction prize (but did not win).

That theory does not wash with Sarah Wilensky, a senior at Indiana University, who said that relaxing plagiarism standards "does not foster creativity, it fosters laziness."

"You're not coming up with new ideas if you're grabbing and mixing and   25
matching," said Ms. Wilensky, who took aim at Ms. Hegemann in a column in
her student newspaper headlined "Generation Plagiarism."

"It may be increasingly accepted, but there are still plenty of creative
people — authors and artists and scholars — who are doing original work,"
Ms. Wilensky said in an interview. "It's kind of an insult that that ideal
is gone, and now we're left only to make collages of the work of previous
generations."

In the view of Ms. Wilensky, whose writing skills earned her the role of
informal editor of other students' papers in her freshman dorm, plagiarism
has nothing to do with trendy academic theories.

The main reason it occurs, she said, is because students leave high school
unprepared for the intellectual rigors of college writing.

"If you're taught how to closely read sources and synthesize them into
your own original argument in middle and high school, you're not going to be
tempted to plagiarize in college, and you certainly won't do so unknowingly,"
she said.

At the University of California, Davis, of the 196 plagiarism cases referred   30
to the disciplinary office last year, a majority did not involve students ignorant
of the need to credit the writing of others.

Many times, said Donald J. Dudley, who oversees the discipline office on
the campus of 32,000, it was students who intentionally copied — knowing it
was wrong — who were "unwilling to engage the writing process."

"Writing is difficult, and doing it well takes time and practice," he said.

And then there was a case that had nothing to do with a younger generation's evolving view of authorship. A student accused of plagiarism came to
Mr. Dudley's office with her parents, and the father admitted that he was the
one responsible for the plagiarism. The wife assured Mr. Dudley that it would
not happen again.

Synthesizing and Citing Sources

One of the questions you might ask yourself as you write is, "How many
sources do I need?" Your instructor may give you guidance, but questions
of exactly when you need to employ the support of other authors is up to
you. **Synthesis** in academic writing refers to the incorporation of sources into
your writing. As you develop your arguments, you will want to look at your
sources and consider how what they say interacts with your own opinions.
Do you see any similarities between what you want to write and what your

sources say, or will you be faced with the task of discussing how your sources don't see your topic the way you do? Think of your paper as a conversation between you and your sources. As you write, ask yourself where you and your sources agree and disagree, and make sure you account for this in your paper. You might want to ask yourself the following questions:

- Have I used my sources as evidence to support any claims I'm making?
- Have I considered any counterarguments?
- Have I taken care to characterize my sources in a way that is fair and accurate?
- When I have finished my draft, have I reconsidered my thesis in light of the source material I've used? Do I need to change my thesis to reflect any new discoveries I've made?

Finally, you will want to make sure you have properly documented any sources you use in your papers. When you write an essay and use another author's work — whether you use the author's exact words or his or her ideas — you need to cite that source for your readers. In most humanities courses, writers use the system of documentation developed by the Modern Language Association (MLA). This system indicates a source in two ways: (1) notations that briefly identify the sources in the body of your essay and (2) notations that give fuller bibliographic information about the sources at the end of your essay. The notations for some commonly used types of sources are illustrated in this chapter. For documenting other sources, consult a writing handbook or Joseph Gibaldi's *MLA Handbook for Writers of Research Papers*, Seventh Edition (New York: Modern Language Association of America, 2009).

In-Text Citations

In the body of your essay, you should signal to your reader that you've used a source and indicate, in parentheses, where your reader can find the source in your list of works cited. You don't need to repeat the author's name in both your writing and in the parenthetical note.

SOURCE WITH ONE AUTHOR

Patrick Goldstein asserts that "Talk radio has pumped up the volume of our public discourse and created a whole new political language — perhaps the prevailing political language" (16).

SOURCE WITH TWO OR THREE AUTHORS

Researchers have found it difficult to study biker subcultures because, as one team describes the problem, "it was too dangerous to take issue with outlaws on their own turf" (Hooper and Moore 368).

INDIRECT SOURCE

In discussing the baby mania trend, *Time* claimed that "Career women are opting for pregnancy and they are doing it in style" (qtd. in Faludi 106).

List of Works Cited

At the end of your essay, include a list of all the sources you have cited in parenthetical notations. This list, alphabetized by author, should provide full publication information for each source; you should indicate the date you accessed any online sources.

The first line of each entry should begin flush left. Subsequent lines should be indented half an inch (or five spaces) from the left margin. Double-space the entire list, both between and within entries.

Nonelectronic Sources

BOOK BY ONE AUTHOR

Weisman, Alan. *The World without Us*. New York: Dunne, 2007. Print.

BOOK BY TWO OR MORE AUTHORS

Collins, Ronald K. L., and David M. Skover. *The Death of Discourse*. New York: Westview, 1996. Print.

(Note that only the first author's name is reversed.)

WORK IN AN ANTHOLOGY

Corbett, Julia B. "A Faint Green Sell: Advertising and the Natural World." *Signs of Life in the U.S.A.: Readings on Popular Culture for Writers*. 7th ed. Ed. Sonia Maasik and Jack Solomon. Boston: Bedford, 2012. 227–45. Print.

ARTICLE IN A WEEKLY MAGAZINE

Lacayo, Richard. "How Does '80s Art Look Now?" *Time* 28 Mar. 2005: 58+. Print.

    (A plus sign is used to indicate that the article is not printed on consecutive pages; otherwise, a page range should be given: *16–25*, for example.)

ARTICLE IN A MONTHLY MAGAZINE

Judd, Elizabeth. "After School." *Atlantic* June 2005: 118. Print.

ARTICLE IN A JOURNAL

Hooper, Columbus B., and Johnny Moore. "Women in Outlaw Motorcycle Gangs."
    Journal of Contemporary Ethnography 18.4 (1990): 363–87. Print.

PERSONAL INTERVIEW

Chese, Charlie. Personal interview. 28 Sept. 2008.

Electronic Sources

FILM OR DVD

Scott Pilgrim vs. the World. Dir. Edgar Wright. Perf. Michael Cera. Universal, 2010.
    Film.
No Country for Old Men. Dir. Ethan and Joel Coen. 2007. Buena Vista Home
    Entertainment, 2008. DVD.

TELEVISION PROGRAM

"Collateral Damage." *CSI: Miami*. Perf. David Caruso. KBAK, Bakersfield. 4 May 2009.
    Television.

SOUND RECORDING

Adams, Ryan. *Cold Roses*. Lost Highway, 2005. MP3 File.

E-MAIL

Katt, Susie. "Interpreting the Mall." Message to the author. 29 Sept. 2008. E-mail.

ARTICLE IN AN ONLINE REFERENCE BOOK

"Gender." *Britannica Online*. Encyclopaedia Britannica, 31 July 2004. Web. 30 May
2008.

(Note that the first date indicates when the information was posted; the
second indicates the date of access.)

ARTICLE IN AN ONLINE JOURNAL

Schaffer, Scott. "Disney and the Imagineering of History." *Postmodern Culture* 6.3
(1996): n. pag. Web. 12 Aug. 2008.

ARTICLE IN AN ONLINE MAGAZINE

Rosenberg, Scott. "Don't Link or I'll Sue!" *Salon* 12 Aug. 1999. Web. 13 Aug. 2008.

ONLINE BOOK

James, Henry. *The Bostonians*. London and New York, 1886. *The Henry James
Scholar's Guide to Web Sites*. Aug. 1999. Web. 13 Aug. 2009.

ONLINE POEM

Frost, Robert. "The Road Not Taken." *Mountain Interval*. New York, 1915. *Project
Bartleby Archive*. Ed. Steven van Leeuwen. Mar. 1995. Web. 13 Aug. 2011.

PROFESSIONAL WEB SITE

National Council of Teachers of English. Jan. 2008. Web. 1 May 2008.

PERSONAL HOME PAGE

Stallman, Richard. Home page. Mar. 2008. Web. 4 Mar. 2008.

POSTING TO A DISCUSSION LIST

Diaz, Joanne. "Poetic Expressions." *Conference on College Composition and Communication*. NCTE, 29 Apr. 2006. Web. 4 July 2006.

ONLINE SCHOLARLY PROJECT

Barlow, Michael, ed. *Corpus Linguistics*. Rice U, Apr. 1998. Web. 13 Aug. 2010.

WORK FROM A DATABASE SERVICE

Cullather, Nick. "The Third Race." *Diplomatic History* 33.3 (2009): 507-12. *Academic OneFile* Web. 1 May 2009.

YOUTUBE OR OTHER ONLINE VIDEO

"iTunes Version--Bed Intruder Song." UCLA Library. *YouTube*. 2010. Web. 12 Feb. 2011.

PHOTOGRAPH OR WORK OF ART

Warhol, Andy. *Black Bean*. 1968. Whitney Museum of American Art. *whitney.org*. Web. 9 May 2011.

CONSUMING PASSIONS

The Culture of American Consumption

You Are What You Buy

If you were given a blank check to purchase anything — and everything — you wanted, what would you buy? Try making a list, and then annotate that list with brief explanations for why you want each item. Do your choices say something about yourself that you want others to know? Do they project an image?

Now consider the things you do own. Make another list and annotate it, too. Why did you buy this item or that? What compromises did you have to make in choosing one item over another? How often did price or quality affect your decisions? How often did style or image? Which items were presents that reflect someone else's tastes and desires? Do the images sent by your actual possessions differ from the ones sent by your ideal ones? Why? Or why not?

Such questions are a good place to begin a semiotic analysis of American consumer culture, for every choice you make in the products you buy, from clothing to furniture to cars to electronics and beyond, is a **sign**, a signal you are sending to the world about yourself. Those aren't just a pair of shoes you're wearing: They're a statement about your identity. That's not just an iPod playlist: It's a message about your worldview.

To read the signs of American consumption, it is best to start with yourself, because you've already got an angle on the answers. But be careful and be honest. Remember, a cultural sign gets its meaning from the **system**, or **code**, in which it appears. Its significance does not lie in its usefulness but rather in its symbolism, in the image it projects, and that image is socially constructed. You didn't make it by yourself. To decode your possessions, you've got to ask what you are trying to say with them and what you want other people to think about you. And you've got to remember the difference between fashion and function.

To give you an idea of how to go about analyzing consumer objects and behavior, let's look at skinny jeans.

The Skinny on Skinny Jeans

Once again, it all begins with a **difference**: baggy vs. skinny.

For the past two decades or so, vastly oversized jeans have been the jean fashion of choice for many Americans, especially males. This fashion itself has a meaning that we need to explore in order to understand the significance of the skinny jeans fad. To find that meaning, we need to look at the system within which both baggy and skinny jeans can be associated. That system began in the nineteenth century when Levi Strauss tailored durable denim cloth into trousers for men during the California gold rush. Given such origins, those trousers, blue jeans, came to signify "work clothes," for both rural and urban men, with cowboys being the most glamorous of blue jeans wearers. By the 1950s, blue jeans, often known as dungarees, also came to signify a kind of casual wear for middle-class Americans, both male and female, that was not suitable for formal social occasions (indeed, through part of the 1960s, students were often forbidden to wear jeans to school, and jeans certainly weren't allowed in white-collar workplaces).

But during the countercultural revolution of the 1960s, American baby boomers adopted blue jeans as a kind of uniform in defiance of middle-class proscriptions, often wearing them as a sign of solidarity with the working class. Jeans became so identified with the counterculture that Charles Reich, in his popular 1970 book *The Greening of America*, argued that denim

---

Discussing the Signs of Consumer Culture

On the board, list in categories the fashion styles worn by members of the class. Be sure to note details, such as styles of shoes, jewelry, watches, or sunglasses, as well as broader trends. Then discuss what the clothing choices say about individuals. What messages are people sending about their personal identity? Do individual students agree with the class's interpretations of their clothing choices? Can any distinctions be made by gender, age, or ethnicity? Then discuss what the fashion styles worn by the whole class say: Is a group identity projected by class members?

bell-bottoms were a particular symbol of the Age of Aquarius, signifying a free and freewheeling new generation. But as happens so often in American popular culture, what was once a symbol of defiance became a simple fashion statement, and by the later 1970s, blue jeans signified little more than fashionable clothing. This opened the way for designer jeans, like Jordache and Chic, which were worn very tight by both men and women and styled to enhance their sex appeal.

At the same time, members of some punk rock and New Wave bands introduced a new jeans alternative. The album jacket art for Blondie's record *Parallel Lines* provides a good illustration: the male band members all are wearing black jeans that taper down very narrowly at the ankle. What is more, one is wearing bright red Converse sneakers, while another is wearing one black Converse sneaker and one red one. The look is boyish rather than sexy, and, as we shall see in a moment, has obvious resonances with today's skinny jeans fashion.

Meanwhile, in the 1980s extravagantly oversized, or baggy, jeans entered into denim's history as part of the hip-hop scene. Taking the place of the loose sweats popular during the break-dancing era, baggy jeans were a signifier of the evolution of rap/hip-hop toward its gangsta incarnation. Part of a uniform that included backward-facing ball caps and untied Nikes, baggy jeans were often worn "sagging" and alluded to prison wear, while at the same time functionally facilitating the concealment of weapons. The gangsta-inflected fashion system within which baggy jeans signified soon became a fashion statement itself for white American youth as they adopted (or adapted) rap/hip-hop for themselves — as when skateboarders adopted baggy jeans for their own use. This turn to oversized jeans created a fashion system that has endured for well over twenty years.

Which takes us to the present. Recently, various post-punk, indie, and emo music performers (generally categorized as "alternative") have revived the skinny jean style of such bands as Blondie. The Kings of Leon, for example, often appear in the same black jeans, narrow ties, and sport jackets that were popular in the New Wave era, but this time the style is known by a new name: "hipster." Which entails its own history.

The first self-proclaimed hipsters were the Beats. Comprising a social and aesthetic movement of the 1950s, the Beats were the predecessors of the countercultural revolution of the 1960s. Denizens of the coffeehouse sporting such fashions as black tights or capris for women and black berets and goatees for men, Beat hipsters are the grandparents of today's hipsters, who also hang out in college coffeehouses and literature departments. Adopting the "cool" pose of the Beats (along with the cigarette smoking of the pre-Surgeon General's tobacco warning era), the hipster of the new millennium continues a bohemian tradition whose more notable luminaries include the French poet Charles Baudelaire and the English dramatist Oscar Wilde.

If the skinny jeans worn by the modern hipster reflects a Beat revival grounded in a history of European bohemianism, the same jeans, as worn by such rap performers as New Boyz, signify something quite different. The fashion of choice for the dance and hip-hop routines known as "jerkin'," skinny jeans in this context belong to a code wherein their difference from baggy jeans is crucial to their significance. The fact that this difference matters is apparent in the kinds of comments that accompany New Boyz videos on YouTube. These comments aren't reprintable here. Let's just say that along with the fan responses there is a lot of hostility, denunciations of New Boyz and accusations that they are "murdering" hip-hop. Why should a simple difference between the cut of a pair of jeans evoke such emotion?

The crux of the matter goes back to those baggy jeans, which became such an enduring signifier of African American street culture. One may say that it's a question of authenticity. Baggy jeans have long been a key identifier of the gangsta rap style. Interviews with the members of New Boyz and other figures in the jerkin' scene clearly indicate that their stylistic departure from the signifiers and attitudes of gangsta rap is intentional. While they retain many of the signifiers of hip-hop through their rapping, their wearing of baseball caps (though adjusted their own way), and even wearing skinny jeans in a sagging manner, they also explicitly distinguish themselves from the gangsta subculture and speak of the "positive" attractions of such things as entrepreneurialism. Given that their skinny jeans have their origins in such white-coded fashions as punk (significantly, a hairstyle seen among jerkers is called the "frohawk") and New Wave, the proponents of this new variety of hip-hop are reversing a certain trend in American youth culture, which usually features white youth adopting and adapting the signifiers of black youth culture. This time, black youth are adapting the signifiers of white styles.

Here we find the origin of the hostile reactions to jerkin' and skinny jeans, even as the popularity of the fashion grows. For many people, baggy jeans and gangsta culture signify African American authenticity, and the departure from such symbols appears to be some sort of sellout, akin to "acting white." Indeed, one fan of skinny jeans has remarked to a reporter that he swaps his skinny jeans for baggy ones before returning home in order to avoid getting into trouble in his neighborhood.

Once again, we see how the same object, **denotatively** regarded simply *as* an object, can come to assume an array of **connotative** meanings depending upon the system, or code, in which it appears. Jerkin' jeans, while objectively identical to hipster jeans, simply do not mean the same thing. They belong to a different system, a code that, like all fashion codes, changes with time and context. To revise Magritte's famous painting "This is not a pipe," we might say, thus, of a pair of jeans: "This is a pair of jeans, but this is not *only* a pair of jeans."

Disposable Decades

When analyzing a consumer sign, you will often find yourself referring to particular decades in which certain popular fads and trends were prominent, because the decade in which a given style appears may be an essential key to the system that explains it. Have you ever wondered why American cultural trends seem to change with every decade, why it is so easy to speak of the sixties or the seventies or the eighties and immediately recognize the popular styles that dominated each decade? Have you ever looked at the style of a friend and thought, "Oh, she's so seventies"? Can you place platform shoes or bell-bottoms at the drop of a hat? A change in the calendar always seems to herald a change in style in a consuming culture. But why?

The decade-to-decade shift in America's pop cultural identity goes back a good number of years. It is still easy, for example, to distinguish F. Scott Fitzgerald's Jazz Age twenties from John Steinbeck's wrathful thirties. The fifties, an especially connotative decade, raise images of ducktail haircuts and poodle skirts, drive-in culture and Elvis, family sitcoms and white-bread innocence, while the sixties are remembered for acid rock, hippies, the student revolution, and back-to-the-land communes. We remember the seventies as a pop cultural era divided among disco, Nashville, and preppiedom, with John Travolta, truckers, and Skippy and Muffy as dominant pop icons. The boom-boom eighties gave us Wall Street glitz and the yuppie invasion. Indeed, each decade since World War I—which, not accidentally, happens to coincide roughly with the rise of modern advertising and mass production—seems to carry its own consumerist style.

It's no accident that the decade-to-decade shift in consumer styles coincides with the advent of modern advertising and mass production because

---

Exploring the Signs of Consumer Culture

"You are what you buy." In your journal, freewrite on the importance
of consumer products in your life. How do you respond to being told
your identity is equivalent to the products you buy? Do you resist the
notion? Do you recall any instances when you have felt lost without a
favorite object? How do you communicate your sense of self to others
through objects, whether clothing, books, food, home decor, electronic
goods, or something else?

---

it was mass production that created a need for constant consumer turnover
in the first place. Mass production, that is, promotes stylistic change because
with so many products being produced, a market must be created to consume
all of them, and this means constantly consuming *more*. To get consumers to
keep buying all the new stuff, you have to convince them that the stuff they
already have is passé. Why else do fashion designers completely change their
lines each year? Why else do car manufacturers annually change their color
schemes and body shapes when the previous year's model seemed good
enough? The new designs aren't simply functional improvements (though
they are marketed as such); they are inducements to go out and replace what
you already have to avoid appearing out of fashion. Just think: If you could
afford to buy any car that you want, what would it be? Would your choice a
few years ago have been the same?

Mass production, then, creates consumer societies based on the constant
production of new products that are intended to be disposed of with the next
product year. But something happened along the way to the establishment of
our consumer culture: We began to value consumption more than production.
Shoppers storm the doors as the Christmas shopping season begins earlier
and earlier every year. Listen to the economic news: Consumption, not production, is relied upon to carry America out of its economic downturns. When
Americans stop buying, our economy grinds to a halt. Consumption lies at
the center of our economic system now, constituting some two-thirds of our
economic activity, and the result has been a transformation in the very way
we view ourselves.

A Tale of Two Cities

It has not always been thus in America, however. Once, Americans prided
themselves on their productivity. In 1914, for example, the poet Carl Sandburg
boasted of a Chicago that was "Hog Butcher for the World, / Tool maker,
Stacker of Wheat, / Player with Railroads and the Nation's Freight Handler."

One wonders what Sandburg would think of the place today. From the South Side east to the industrial suburb of Gary, Indiana, Chicago's once-proud mills and factories rust in the winter wind. At the Chicago Mercantile Exchange, trade today is in commodity futures, not commodities.

Meanwhile, a few hundred miles to the northwest, Bloomington, Minnesota, buzzes with excitement. For there stands the Mall of America, a colossus of consumption so large that it contains within its walls a seven-acre Knott's Berry Farm theme park, with lots of room to spare. You can find almost anything you want in the Mall of America, but most of what you will find won't have been manufactured in America. The proud tag "Made in the USA" is an increasingly rare item.

It's a long way from Sandburg's Chicago to the Mall of America, a trip that traverses America's shift from a producer to a consumer economy. This shift is not simply economic; it is behind a cultural transformation that is shaping a new mythology within which we define ourselves, our hopes, and our desires.

Ask yourself right now what your own goals are in going to college. Do you envision a career in law, or medicine, or banking and finance? Do you want to be a teacher, an advertising executive, or a civil servant? Or maybe you are preparing for a career in an Internet-related field. If you've considered any of these career examples, you are contemplating what are known as service jobs. While essential to a society, none of them actually produces anything. If you've given thought to going into some facet of manufacturing, on the other hand, you are unusual because America offers increasingly fewer opportunities in that area and little prestige. The prestigious jobs are in law and medicine and in high-tech operations like Google, a fact that is easy to take for granted. But ask yourself: Does it have to be so?

To ask such questions is to begin to reveal the outline of a cultural mythology based on consumption rather than production. For one thing, while law and medicine require specialized training available to only a few, doctors and lawyers also make a lot of money and so are higher up on the scale of consumption. Quite simply, they can buy more than others can. It is easy to presume that this would be the case anywhere, but in the former Soviet Union physicians—many of whom were women—were relatively low on the social scale. Male engineers, on the other hand, were highly valued for their role in facilitating military production. In what was a producer rather than a consumer culture, it was the producers who roosted high on the social ladder.

To live in a consumer culture is not simply a matter of shopping, however; it is also a matter of being. For in a consumer society, you are what you consume, and the entire social and economic order is maintained by the constant encouragement to buy. The ubiquity of television and advertising in America is a direct result of this system, for these media deliver the constant stimulus to buy through avalanches of consuming images. Consider how difficult it is to escape the arm of the advertiser. You may turn off the TV, but a screen awaits you at the supermarket checkout counter, displaying incentives to spend your money. If you rush to the restroom to hide, you may find advertisements tacked to the stalls. If you log on to the Internet, ads greet you on the screen. Resistance is useless. Weren't you planning to do some shopping this weekend anyway?

When the Going Gets Tough, the Tough Go Shopping

In a cultural system where our identities are displayed in the products we buy, it accordingly behooves us to pay close attention to what we consume and why. From the cars we drive to the clothes we wear, we are enmeshed in a web of consuming images. As students, you are probably freer to choose the particular images you wish to project through the products you consume than most other demographic groups in America. This claim may sound paradoxical: After all, don't working adults have more money than starving students? Yes, generally. But the working world places severe restrictions on the choices employees can make in their clothing and grooming styles, and even automobile choice may be restricted (real estate agents, for example, can't escort their clients around town in Kia Souls). Corporate business wear, for all its variations, still revolves around a central core of necktied and dark-hued sobriety, regardless of the gender of the wearer. On campus, however, you can be pretty much whatever you want to be, which is why your own daily lives provide you with a particularly rich field of consumer signs to read and decode.

So go to it. By the time you finish reading this book, a lot will have changed. Look around. Start reading the signs.

Reading Consumer Culture on the Net

Log on to one of the many home shopping networks or auction sites. You might try the QVC (www.QVC.com), Shop at Home (www.shopathome.com), or eBay (www.ebay.com). Analyze both the products sold and the way they are marketed. Who is the target audience for the network you're studying, and what images and values are used to attract this market? How does the marketing compare with nonelectronic sales pitches, such as displays in shopping malls and magazines or TV advertising? Does the electronic medium affect your own behavior as a consumer? Does the time pressure of an electronic auction affect your behavior as a consumer? How do you account for any differences in electronic and traditional marketing strategies?

The Readings

As this chapter's lead essay, Laurence Shames's "The More Factor" provides a mythological background for the discussions of America's consuming behavior that follow. Shames takes a historical approach to American consumerism, relating our frontier history to our ever-expanding desire for more goods and services. Next, in a paired set of readings, Malcolm Gladwell reveals the elaborate measures that retail store managers take to maximize your consumption when you visit their shops, and Anne Norton follows with a semiotic analysis of shopping malls, mail-order catalogs, and the Home Shopping Network, focusing on the ways in which they construct a language of consumption tailored to specific consumer groups. Next, Mark Dery ruminates on the "undeath of the American mall" during the Great Recession. Thomas Hine's interpretation of the packaging that contains America's most commonly consumed products shows how packages constitute complex sign systems intended for consumer "readings," while Joan Kron studies the ways in which we use home furnishings to reflect our sense of personal identity. Next, Andrea Chang reports on the "shop and tell" phenomenon of teen "hauling": teenaged fashion consumers who are doing just that by posting their purchases online on such sites as YouTube. S. Craig Watkins turns to today's always turned on and tuned in world of digital entertainment, wondering if it isn't all leading to an epidemic of Continuous Partial Attention. Less enamored of conspicuous consumption, John Verdant, founder of the anti-consumption Web site verdant.net, presents the parable of "The Ables vs. the Binges," and, concerned with women's place in the world of digital technology, Tammy Oler looks at the many attempts to "make geek chic." The chapter concludes with Thomas Frank's musings on how corporate America has turned consumption into a hip signifier of inauthentic counterculturalism.

LAURENCE SHAMES
The More Factor

A bumper sticker popular in the 1980s read, "Whoever dies with the most toys wins." In this selection from *The Hunger for More: Searching for Values in an Age of Greed* (1989), Laurence Shames shows how the great American hunger for more—more toys, more land, more opportunities—is an essential part of our history and character, stemming from the frontier era when the horizon alone seemed the only limit to American desire. The author of *The Big Time: The Harvard Business School's Most Successful Class and How It Shaped America* (1986) and the holder of a Harvard M.B.A., Shames is a journalist who has contributed to such publications as *Playboy, Vanity Fair, Manhattan, inc.,* and *Esquire.* He currently is working full-time on writing fiction and screenplays, with his most recent publications including *Florida Straits* (1992), *Sunburn* (1995), *Welcome to Paradise* (1999), *The Naked Detective* (2000), and, with Peter Barton, *Not Fade Away* (2003).

1

Americans have always been optimists, and optimists have always liked to speculate. In Texas in the 1880s, the speculative instrument of choice was towns, and there is no tale more American than this.

What people would do was buy up enormous tracts of parched and vacant land, lay out a Main Street, nail together some wooden sidewalks, and start slapping up buildings. One of these buildings would be called the Grand Hotel and would have a saloon complete with swinging doors. Another might be dubbed the New Academy or the Opera House. The developers would erect a flagpole and name a church, and once the workmen had packed up and moved on, the towns would be as empty as the sky.

But no matter. The speculators, next, would hire people to pass out handbills in the Eastern and Midwestern cities, tracts limning the advantages of relocation to "the Athens of the South" or "the new plains Jerusalem." When persuasion failed, the builders might resort to bribery, paying people's moving costs and giving them houses, in exchange for nothing but a pledge to stay until a certain census was taken or a certain inspection made. Once the nose count was completed, people were free to move on, and there was in fact a contingent of folks who made their living by keeping a cabin on skids and dragging it for pay from one town to another.

The speculators' idea, of course, was to lure the railroad. If one could create a convincing semblance of a town, the railroad might come through it, and a real town would develop, making the speculators staggeringly rich. By these devices a man named Sanborn once owned Amarillo.[1]

But railroad tracks are narrow and the state of Texas is very, very wide. For every Wichita Falls or Lubbock there were a dozen College Mounds or Belchervilles,[2] bleached, unpeopled burgs that receded quietly into the dust, taking with them large amounts of speculators' money.

Still, the speculators kept right on bucking the odds and depositing empty towns in the middle of nowhere. Why did they do it? Two reasons — reasons that might be said to summarize the central fact of American economic history and that go a fair way toward explaining what is perhaps the central strand of the national character.

The first reason was simply that the possible returns were so enormous as to partake of the surreal, to create a climate in which ordinary logic and prudence did not seem to apply. In a boom like that of real estate when the railroad barreled through, long shots that might pay one hundred thousand to one seemed worth a bet.

The second reason, more pertinent here, is that there was a presumption that America would *keep* on booming — if not forever, then at least longer than it made sense to worry about. There would always be another gold rush, another Homestead Act, another oil strike. The next generation would always ferret out opportunities that would be still more lavish than any that had gone before. America *was* those opportunities. This was an article not just of faith, but of strategy. You banked on the next windfall, you staked your hopes and even your self-esteem on it, and this led to a national turn of mind that might usefully be thought of as the habit of more.

A century, maybe two centuries, before anyone had heard the term *baby boomer*, much less *yuppie*, the habit of more had been instilled as the operative truth among the economically ambitious. The habit of more seemed to suggest that there was no such thing as getting wiped out in America. A fortune lost in Texas might be recouped in Colorado. Funds frittered away on grazing land where nothing grew might flood back in as silver. There was always a second chance, or always seemed to be, in this land where growth was destiny and where expansion and purpose were the same.

The key was the frontier, not just as a matter of acreage, but as idea. Vast, varied, rough as rocks, America was the place where one never quite came to the end. Ben Franklin explained it to Europe even before the Revolutionary War had finished: America offered new chances to those "who, in their own Countries, where all the Lands [were] fully occupied . . . could never [emerge] from the poor Condition wherein they were born."[3]

---

[1] For a fuller account of railroad-related land speculation in Texas, see F. Stanley, *Story of the Texas Panhandle Railroads* (Borger, Tex.: Hess Publishing Co., 1976).

[2] T. Lindsay Baker, *Ghost Towns of Texas* (Norman, Okla.: University of Oklahoma Press, 1986).

[3] Benjamin Franklin, "Information to Those Who Would Remove to America," in *The Autobiography and Other Writings* (New York: Penguin Books, 1986), 242.

So central was this awareness of vacant space and its link to economic promise that Frederick Jackson Turner, the historian who set the tone for much of the twentieth century's understanding of the American past, would write that it was "not the constitution, but free land . . . [that] made the democratic type of society in America."[4] Good laws mattered; an accountable government mattered; ingenuity and hard work mattered. But those things were, so to speak, an overlay on the natural, geographic America that was simply *there*, and whose vast and beckoning possibilities seemed to generate the ambition and the sometimes reckless liberty that would fill it. First and foremost, it was open space that provided "the freedom of the individual to rise under conditions of social mobility."[5]

Open space generated not just ambition, but metaphor. As early as 1835, Tocqueville was extrapolating from the fact of America's emptiness to the observation that "no natural boundary seems to be set to the efforts of man."[6] Nor was any limit placed on what he might accomplish, since, in that heyday of the Protestant ethic, a person's rewards were taken to be quite strictly proportionate to his labors.

Frontier; opportunity; more. This has been the American trinity from the very start. The frontier was the backdrop and also the raw material for the streak of economic booms. The booms became the goad and also the justification for the myriad gambles and for Americans' famous optimism. The optimism, in turn, shaped the schemes and visions that were sometimes noble, sometimes appalling, always bold. The frontier, as reality and as symbol, is what has shaped the American way of doing things and the American sense of what's worth doing.

But there has been one further corollary to the legacy of the frontier, with its promise of ever-expanding opportunities: Given that the goal — a realistic goal for most of our history — was *more*, Americans have been somewhat backward in adopting values, hopes, ambitions that have to do with things *other than* more. In America, a sense of quality has lagged far behind a sense of scale. An ideal of contentment has yet to take root in soil traditionally more hospitable to an ideal of restless striving. The ethic of decency has been upstaged by the ethic of success. The concept of growth has been applied almost exclusively to things that can be measured, counted, weighed. And the hunger for those things that are unmeasurable but fine — the sorts of accomplishment that cannot be undone by circumstance or a shift in social fashion, the kind of serenity that cannot be shattered by tomorrow's headline — has gone largely unfulfilled, and even unacknowledged.

---

[4]Frederick Jackson Turner, *The Frontier in American History* (Melbourne, Fla.: Krieger, 1976 [reprint of 1920 edition]), 293.
[5]Ibid., 266.
[6]Tocqueville, *Democracy in America.*

2

If the supply of more went on forever, perhaps that wouldn't matter very much. Expansion could remain a goal unto itself, and would continue to generate a value system based on bulk rather than on nuance, on quantities of money rather than on quality of life, on "progress" itself rather than on a sense of what the progress was for. But what if, over time, there was less more to be had?

That is the essential situation of America today.

Let's keep things in proportion: The country is not running out of wealth, drive, savvy, or opportunities. We are not facing imminent ruin, and neither panic nor gloom is called for. But there have been ample indications over the past two decades that we are running out of more.

Consider productivity growth—according to many economists, the single most telling and least distortable gauge of changes in real wealth. From 1947 to 1965, productivity in the private sector (adjusted, as are all the following figures, for inflation) was advancing, on average, by an annual 3.3 percent. This means, simply, that each hour of work performed by a specimen American worker contributed 3.3 cents worth or more to every American dollar every year; whether we saved it or spent it, that increment went into a national kitty of ever-enlarging aggregate wealth. Between 1965 and 1972, however, the "more-factor" decreased to 2.4 percent a year, and from 1972 to 1977 it slipped further, to 1.6 percent. By the early 1980s, productivity growth was at a virtual standstill, crawling along at 0.2 percent for the five years ending in 1982.[7] Through the middle years of the 1980s, the numbers rebounded somewhat—but by then the gains were being neutralized by the gargantuan carrying costs on the national debt.[8]

Inevitably, this decline in the national stockpile of more held consequences for the individual wallet.[9] During the 1950s, Americans' average hourly earnings were humping ahead at a gratifying 2.5 percent each year. By the late seventies, that figure stood just where productivity growth had come to stand, at a dispiriting 0.2 cents on the dollar. By the first half of the eighties, the Reagan "recovery" notwithstanding, real hourly wages were actually moving backward—declining at an average annual rate of 0.3 percent.

Compounding the shortage of more was an unfortunate but crucial demographic fact. Real wealth was nearly ceasing to expand just at the moment

---

[7]These figures are taken from the Council of Economic Advisers, *Economic Report of the President,* February 1984, 267.

[8]For a lucid and readable account of the meaning and implications of our reservoir of red ink, see Lawrence Malkin, *The National Debt* (New York: Henry Holt and Co., 1987). Through no fault of Malkin's, many of his numbers are already obsolete, but his explanation of who owes what to whom, and what it means, remains sound and even entertaining in a bleak sort of way.

[9]The figures in this paragraph and the next are from "The Average Guy Takes It on the Chin," *New York Times,* 13 July 1986, sec. 3.

when the members of that unprecedented population bulge known as the baby boom were entering what should have been their peak years of income expansion. A working man or woman who was thirty years old in 1949 could expect to see his or her real earnings burgeon by 63 percent by age forty. In 1959, a thirty-year-old could still look forward to a gain of 49 percent by his or her fortieth birthday.

But what about the person who turned thirty in 1973? By the time that worker turned forty, his or her real earnings had shrunk by a percentage point. For all the blather about yuppies with their beach houses, BMWs, and radicchio salads, and even factoring in those isolated tens of thousands making ludicrous sums in consulting firms or on Wall Street, the fact is that between 1979 and 1983 real earnings of all Americans between the ages of twenty-five and thirty-four actually declined by 14 percent.[10] The *New York Times*, well before the stock market crash put the kibosh on eighties confidence, summed up the implications of this downturn by observing that "for millions of bread-winners, the American dream is becoming the impossible dream."[11]

Now, it is not our main purpose here to detail the ups and downs of the American economy. Our aim, rather, is to consider the effects of those ups and downs on people's goals, values, sense of their place in the world. What happens at that shadowy juncture where economic prospects meld with personal choice? What sorts of insights and adjustments are called for so that economic ups and downs can be dealt with gracefully?

Fact one in this connection is that, if America's supply of more is in fact diminishing, American values will have to shift and broaden to fill the gap where the expectation of almost automatic gains used to be. Something more durable will have to replace the fat but fragile bubble that had been getting frailer these past two decades and that finally popped — a tentative, partial pop — on October 19, 1987. A different sort of growth — ultimately, a growth in responsibility and happiness — will have to fulfill our need to believe that our possibilities are still expanding.

The transition to that new view of progress will take some fancy stepping, because, at least since the end of World War II, simple economic growth has stood, in the American psyche, as the best available substitute for the literal frontier. The economy has *been* the frontier. Instead of more space, we have had more money. Rather than measuring progress in terms of geographical expansion, we have measured it by expansion in our standard of living. Economics has become the metaphor on which we pin our hopes of open space and second chances.

The poignant part is that the literal frontier did not pass yesterday: it has not existed for a hundred years. But the frontier's promise has become so much a part of us that we have not been willing to let the concept die. We have kept the frontier mythology going by invocation, by allusion, by hype. 25

[10]See, for example, "The Year of the Yuppie," *Newsweek*, 31 December 1984, 16.
[11]"The Average Guy."

It is not a coincidence that John F. Kennedy dubbed his political program the New Frontier. It is not mere linguistic accident that makes us speak of Frontiers of Science or of psychedelic drugs as carrying one to Frontiers of Perception. We glorify fads and fashions by calling them Frontiers of Taste. Nuclear energy has been called the Last Frontier; solar energy has been called the Last Frontier. Outer space has been called the Last Frontier; the oceans have been called the Last Frontier. Even the suburbs, those blandest and least adventurous of places, have been wryly described as the crabgrass frontier.[12]

What made all these usages plausible was their being linked to the image of the American economy as an endlessly fertile continent whose boundaries never need be reached, a domain that could expand in perpetuity, a gigantic playing field that would never run out of room and on which the game would get forever bigger and more filled with action. This was the frontier that would not vanish.

It is worth noting that people in other countries (with the possible exception of that other America, Australia) do not talk about frontier this way. In Europe, and in most of Africa and Asia, "frontier" connotes, at worst, a place of barbed wire and men with rifles, and at best, a neutral junction where one changes currency while passing from one fixed system into another. Frontier, for most of the world's people, does not suggest growth, expanse, or opportunity.

For Americans, it does, and always has. This is one of the things that sets America apart from other places and makes American attitudes different from those of other people. It is why, from *Bonanza* to the Sierra Club, the notion or even the fantasy of empty horizons and untapped resources has always evoked in the American heart both passion and wistfulness. And it is why the fear that the economic frontier — our last, best version of the Wild West — may finally be passing creates in us not only money worries but also a crisis of morale and even of purpose.

3

It might seem strange to call the 1980s an era of nostalgia. The decade, after all, has been more usually described in terms of coolness, pragmatism, and a blithe innocence of history. But the eighties, unawares, were nostalgic for frontiers; and the disappointment of that nostalgia had much to do with the time's greed, narrowness, and strange want of joy. The fear that the world may not be a big enough playground for the full exercise of one's energies and yearnings, and worse, the fear that the playground is being fenced off and will no longer expand — these are real worries and they have had consequences. The eighties were an object lesson in how people play the game when there is an awful and unspoken suspicion that the game is winding down.

---

[12]With the suburbs again taking on a sort of fascination, this phrase was resurrected as the title of a 1985 book — *Crabgrass Frontier: The Suburbanization of America*, by Kenneth T. Jackson (Oxford University Press).

It was ironic that the yuppies came to be so reviled for their vaunting ambition and outsized expectations, as if they'd invented the habit of more, when in fact they'd only inherited it the way a fetus picks up an addiction in the womb. The craving was there in the national bloodstream, a remnant of the frontier, and the baby boomers, described in childhood as "the luckiest generation,"[13] found themselves, as young adults, in the melancholy position of wrestling with a two-hundred-year dependency on a drug that was now in short supply.

True, the 1980s raised the clamor for more to new heights of shrillness, insistence, and general obnoxiousness, but this, it can be argued, was in the nature of a final binge, the storm before the calm. America, though fighting the perception every inch of the way, was coming to realize that it was not a preordained part of the natural order that one should be richer every year. If it happened, that was nice. But who had started the flimsy and pernicious rumor that it was normal?

READING THE TEXT

1. Summarize in a paragraph how, according to Shames, the frontier functions as a symbol of American consciousness.

2. What connections does Shames make between America's frontier history and consumer behavior?

3. Why does Shames term the 1980s "an era of nostalgia" (para. 30)?

4. Characterize Shames's attitude toward the American desire for more. How does his tone reveal his personal views on his subject?

READING THE SIGNS

1. **CONNECTING TEXTS**   Shames asserts that Americans have been influenced by the frontier belief "that America would *keep* on booming" (para. 8). Do you feel that this belief continues to be influential into the twenty-first century? Write an essay arguing for your position. To develop your ideas, consult John Verdant's "The Ables vs. the Binges" (p. 152) and Barbara Ehrenreich's "Bright-Sided" (p. 532).

2. Shames claims that, because of the desire for more, "the ethic of decency has been upstaged by the ethic of success" (para. 14). In class, form teams and debate the validity of Shames's claim.

3. **CONNECTING TEXTS**   Read or review Joan Kron's "The Semiotics of Home Decor" (p. 128). How is Martin J. Davidson influenced by the frontier myth that Shames describes?

4. **CONNECTING TEXTS**   In an essay, argue for or refute the proposition that the "hunger for more" that Shames describes is a universal human trait, not simply American. To develop your ideas, consult Joan Kron, "The Semiotics of Home Decor" (p. 128).

[13]Thomas Hine, *Populuxe* (New York: Alfred A. Knopf, 1986), 15.

MALCOLM GLADWELL

The Science of Shopping

Ever wonder why the season's hottest new styles at stores like the Gap are usually displayed on the right at least fifteen paces in from the front entrance? It's because that's where shoppers are most likely to see them as they enter the store, gear down from the walking pace of a mall corridor, and adjust to the shop's spatial environment. Ever wonder how shop managers know this sort of thing? It's because, as Malcolm Gladwell reports here, they hire consultants like Paco Under-hill, a "retail anthropologist" and "urban geographer" whose studies (often aided by hidden cameras) of shopping behavior have become valuable guides to store managers looking for the best ways to move the goods. Does this feel just a little Orwellian? Read on. A staff writer for the *New Yorker*, in which this selection first appeared, Gladwell has also written *The Tipping Point* (2000), *Blink: The Power of Thinking without Thinking* (2005), and *Outliers: The Story of Success* (2008).

Human beings walk the way they drive, which is to say that Americans tend to keep to the right when they stroll down shopping-mall concourses or city sidewalks. This is why in a well-designed airport travellers drifting toward their gate will always find the fast-food restaurants on their left and the gift shops on their right: people will readily cross a lane of pedestrian traffic to satisfy their hunger but rarely to make an impulse buy of a T-shirt or a magazine. This is also why Paco Underhill tells his retail clients to make sure that their window displays are canted, preferably to both sides but especially to the left, so that a potential shopper approaching the store on the inside of the sidewalk—the shopper, that is, with the least impeded view of the store window—can see the display from at least twenty-five feet away.

Of course, a lot depends on how fast the potential shopper is walking. Paco, in his previous life, as an urban geographer in Manhattan, spent a great deal of time thinking about walking speeds as he listened in on the great debates of the nineteen-seventies over whether the traffic lights in midtown should be timed to facilitate the movement of cars or to facilitate the movement of pedestrians and so break up the big platoons that move down Manhattan sidewalks. He knows that the faster you walk the more your peripheral vision narrows, so you become unable to pick up visual cues as quickly as someone who is just ambling along. He knows, too, that people who walk fast take a surprising amount of time to slow down—just as it takes a good stretch of road to change gears with a stick-shift automobile. On the basis of his research, Paco estimates the human downshift period to be anywhere from twelve to twenty-five feet, so if you own a store, he says, you never want to be next door to a bank: potential shoppers speed up when they walk past a bank (since there's nothing to look at), and by the time they slow down they've walked right past your business. The downshift factor also means that when potential shoppers enter a store it's going to take them from five to fifteen paces to adjust to the light and refocus and gear down from walking speed to shopping speed—particularly if they've just had to navigate a treacherous parking lot or hurry to make the light at Fifty-seventh and Fifth.

Paco calls that area inside the door the Decompression Zone, and something he tells clients over and over again is never, ever put anything of value in that zone—not shopping baskets or tie racks or big promotional displays—because no one is going to see it. Paco believes that, as a rule of thumb, customer inter-action with any product or promotional display in the Decompression Zone will increase at least thirty percent once it's moved to the back edge of the zone, and even more if it's placed to the right, because another of the fundamental rules of how human beings shop is that upon entering a store—whether it's Nordstrom or K Mart, Tiffany or the Gap—the shopper invariably and reflexively turns to the right. Paco believes in the existence of the Invariant Right because he has actually verified it. He has put cameras in stores trained directly on the doorway, and if you go to his office, just above Union Square, where videocassettes and boxes of Super-eight film from all his work over the years are stacked in plastic Tupperware containers practically up to the ceiling, he can show you reel upon reel of grainy entryway video—customers striding in the door, downshifting, refocusing, and then, again and again, making that little half turn.

Paco Underhill is a tall man in his mid-forties, partly bald, with a neatly trimmed beard and an engaging, almost goofy manner. He wears baggy khakis and shirts open at the collar, and generally looks like the academic he might have been if he hadn't been captivated, twenty years ago, by the ideas of the urban anthropologist William Whyte. It was Whyte who pioneered the use of time-lapse photography as a tool of urban planning, putting cameras in parks and the plazas in front of office buildings in midtown Manhattan, in order to determine what distinguished a public space that worked from one that didn't. As a Columbia undergraduate, in 1974, Paco heard a lecture on Whyte's work and, he recalls, left the room "walking on air." He immediately read everything Whyte had written. He emptied his bank account to buy cameras and film and make his own home movie, about a pedestrian mall in Poughkeepsie. He took his "little exercise" to Whyte's advocacy group, the Project for Public Spaces, and was offered a job. Soon, however, it dawned on Paco that Whyte's ideas could be taken a step further—that the same techniques he used to establish why a plaza worked or didn't work could also be used to determine why a store worked or didn't work. Thus was born the field of retail anthropology, and, not long afterward, Paco founded Envirosell, which in just over fifteen years has counselled some of the most familiar names in American retailing, from Levi Strauss to Kinney, Starbucks, McDonald's, Blockbuster, Apple Computer, AT&T, and a number of upscale retailers that Paco would rather not name.

When Paco gets an assignment, he and his staff set up a series of video 5
cameras throughout the test store and then back the cameras up with Envirosell staffers — trackers, as they're known — armed with clipboards. Where the
cameras go and how many trackers Paco deploys depends on exactly what
the store wants to know about its shoppers. Typically, though, he might use six
cameras and two or three trackers, and let the study run for two or three days,
so that at the end he would have pages and pages of carefully annotated tracking sheets and anywhere from a hundred to five hundred hours of film. These
days, given the expansion of his business, he might tape fifteen thousand hours
in a year, and, given that he has been in operation since the late seventies, he
now has well over a hundred thousand hours of tape in his library.

Even in the best of times, this would be a valuable archive. But today,
with the retail business in crisis, it is a gold mine. The time per visit that
the average American spends in a shopping mall was sixty-six minutes last
year — down from seventy-two minutes in 1992 — and is the lowest number ever recorded. The amount of selling space per American shopper is
now more than double what it was in the mid-seventies, meaning that
profit margins have never been narrower, and the costs of starting a retail
business — and of failing — have never been higher. In the past few years,
countless dazzling new retailing temples have been built along Fifth and Madison Avenues — Barneys, Calvin Klein, Armani, Valentino, Banana Republic,
Prada, Chanel, NikeTown, and on and on — but it is an explosion of growth
based on no more than a hunch, a hopeful multimillion-dollar gamble that
the way to break through is to provide the shopper with spectacle and more
spectacle. "The arrogance is gone," Millard Drexler, the president and C.E.O.
of the Gap, told me. "Arrogance makes failure. Once you think you know the
answer, it's almost always over." In such a competitive environment, retailers
don't just want to know how shoppers behave in their stores. They *have* to
know. And who better to ask than Paco Underhill, who in the past decade and
a half has analyzed tens of thousands of hours of shopping videotape and, as
a result, probably knows more about the strange habits and quirks of the species *Emptor americanus* than anyone else alive?

Paco is considered the originator, for example, of what is known in the trade
as the butt-brush theory — or, as Paco calls it, more delicately, *le facteur
bousculade* — which holds that the likelihood of a woman's being converted
from a browser to a buyer is inversely proportional to the likelihood of her being
brushed on her behind while she's examining merchandise. Touch — or brush
or bump or jostle — a woman on the behind when she has stopped to look
at an item, and she will bolt. Actually, calling this a theory is something of a misnomer, because Paco doesn't offer any explanation for why women react that
way, aside from venturing that they are "more sensitive back there." It's really
an observation, based on repeated and close analysis of his videotape library,
that Paco has transformed into a retailing commandment: A women's product
that requires extensive examination should never be placed in a narrow aisle.

Paco approaches the problem of the Invariant Right the same way. Some retail thinkers see this as a subject crying out for interpretation and speculation. The design guru Joseph Weishar, for example, argues, in his magisterial *Design for Effective Selling Space*, that the Invariant Right is a function of the fact that we "absorb and digest information in the left part of the brain" and "assimilate and logically use this information in the right half," the result being that we scan the store from left to right and then fix on an object to the right "essentially at a 45 degree angle from the point that we enter." When I asked Paco about this interpretation, he shrugged, and said he thought the reason was simply that most people are right-handed. Uncovering the fundamentals of "why" is clearly not a pursuit that engages him much. He is not a theoretician but an empiricist, and for him the important thing is that in amassing his huge library of in-store time-lapse photography he has gained enough hard evidence to know how often and under what circumstances the Invariant Right is expressed and how to take advantage of it.

What Paco likes are facts. They come tumbling out when he talks, and, because he speaks with a slight hesitation—lingering over the first syllable in, for example, "re-tail" or "de-sign"—he draws you in, and you find yourself truly hanging on his words. "We have reached a historic point in American history," he told me in our very first conversation. "Men, for the first time, have begun to buy their own underwear." He then paused to let the comment sink in, so that I could absorb its implications, before he elaborated: "Which means that we have to *totally* rethink the way we sell that product." In the parlance of Hollywood scriptwriters, the best endings must be surprising and yet inevitable; and the best of Paco's pronouncements take the same shape. It would never have occurred to me to wonder about the increasingly

Sports apparel for sale at a NikeTown store in Chicago.

critical role played by touching — or, as Paco calls it, petting — clothes in the course of making the decision to buy them. But then I went to the Gap and to Banana Republic and saw people touching, and fondling and, one after another, buying shirts and sweaters laid out on big wooden tables, and what Paco told me — which was no doubt based on what he had seen on his videotapes — made perfect sense: that the reason the Gap and Banana Republic have tables is not merely that sweaters and shirts look better there, or that tables fit into the warm and relaxing residential feeling that the Gap and Banana Republic are trying to create in their stores, but that tables invite — indeed, symbolize — touching. "Where do we eat?" Paco asks. "We eat, we pick up food, on tables."

Paco produces for his clients a series of carefully detailed studies, totalling 10 forty to a hundred and fifty pages, filled with product-by-product breakdowns and bright-colored charts and graphs. In one recent case, he was asked by a major clothing retailer to analyze the first of a new chain of stores that the firm planned to open. One of the things the client wanted to know was how successful the store was in drawing people into its depths, since the chances that shoppers will buy something are directly related to how long they spend shopping, and how long they spend shopping is directly related to how deep they get pulled into the store. For this reason, a supermarket will often put dairy products on one side, meat at the back, and fresh produce on the other side, so that the typical shopper can't just do a drive-by but has to make an entire circuit of the store, and be tempted by everything the supermarket has to offer. In the case of the new clothing store, Paco found that ninety-one per-cent of all shoppers penetrated as deep as what he called Zone 4, meaning more than three-quarters of the way in, well past the accessories and shirt racks and belts in the front, and little short of the far wall, with the changing rooms and the pants stacked on shelves. Paco regarded this as an extraordi-nary figure, particularly for a long, narrow store like this one, where it is not unusual for the rate of penetration past, say, Zone 3 to be under fifty percent. But that didn't mean the store was perfect — far from it. For Paco, all kinds of questions remained.

Purchasers, for example, spent an average of eleven minutes and twenty-seven seconds in the store, nonpurchasers two minutes and thirty-six sec-onds. It wasn't that the nonpurchasers just cruised in and out: in those two minutes and thirty-six seconds, they went deep into the store and examined an average of 3.42 items. So why didn't they buy? What, exactly, happened to cause some browsers to buy and other browsers to walk out the door?

Then, there was the issue of the number of products examined. The pur-chasers were looking at an average of 4.81 items but buying only 1.33 items. Paco found this statistic deeply disturbing. As the retail market grows more cutthroat, store owners have come to realize that it's all but impossible to increase the number of customers coming in, and have concentrated instead on getting the customers they do have to buy more. Paco thinks that if you can sell someone a pair of pants you must also be able to sell that person a belt, or a pair of socks, or a pair of underpants, or even do what the Gap does so well: sell a person a complete outfit. To Paco, the figure 1.33 suggested that the store was doing something very wrong, and one day when I visited him in his office he sat me down in front of one of his many VCRs to see how he looked for the 1.33 culprit.

It should be said that sitting next to Paco is a rather strange experience. "My mother says that I'm the best-paid spy in America," he told me. He laughed, but he wasn't entirely joking. As a child, Paco had a nearly debilitating stammer, and, he says, "since I was never that comfortable talking I always relied on my eyes to understand things." That much is obvious from the first moment you meet him: Paco is one of those people who looks right at you, soaking up every nuance and detail. It isn't a hostile gaze, because Paco isn't hostile at all. He has a big smile, and he'll call you "chief" and use your first name a lot and generally act as if he knew you well. But that's the awkward thing: He has looked at you so closely that you're sure he does know you well, and you, meanwhile, hardly know him at all.

This kind of asymmetry is even more pronounced when you watch his shopping videos with him, because every movement or gesture means something to Paco—he has spent his adult life deconstructing the shopping experience—but nothing to the outsider, or, at least, not at first. Paco had to keep stopping the video to get me to see things through his eyes before I began to understand. In one sequence, for example, a camera mounted high on the wall outside the changing rooms documented a man and a woman shopping for a pair of pants for what appeared to be their daughter, a girl in her mid-teens. The tapes are soundless, but the basic steps of the shopping dance are so familiar to Paco that, once I'd grasped the general idea, he was able to provide a running commentary on what was being said and thought. There is the girl emerging from the changing room wearing her first pair. There she is glancing at her reflection in the mirror, then turning to see herself from the back. There is the mother looking on. There is the father—or, as fathers are known in the trade, the "wallet carrier"—stepping forward and pulling up the jeans. There's the girl trying on another pair. There's the primp again. The twirl. The mother. The wallet carrier. And then again, with another pair. The full sequence lasted twenty minutes, and at the end came the take-home lesson, for which Paco called in one of his colleagues, Tom Moseman, who had supervised the project.

"This is a very critical moment," Tom, a young, intense man wearing little round glasses, said, and he pulled up a chair next to mine. "She's saying, 'I don't know whether I should wear a belt.' Now here's the salesclerk. The girl says to him, 'I need a belt,' and he says, 'Take mine.' Now there he is taking her back to the full-length mirror."

A moment later, the girl returns, clearly happy with the purchase. She wants the jeans. The wallet carrier turns to her, and then gestures to the salesclerk. The wallet carrier is telling his daughter to give back the belt. The girl gives back the belt. Tom stops the tape. He's leaning forward now, a finger jabbing at the screen. Beside me, Paco is shaking his head. I don't get it—at least, not at first—and so Tom replays that last segment. The wallet carrier tells the girl to give back the belt. She gives back the belt. And then, finally, it dawns on me why this store has an average purchase number of only 1.33. "Don't you see?" Tom said. "*She wanted the belt.* A great opportunity to make an add-on sale . . . *lost!*"

Should we be afraid of Paco Underhill? One of the fundamental anxieties of the American consumer, after all, has always been that beneath the pleasure and the frivolity of the shopping experience runs an undercurrent of manipulation, and that anxiety has rarely seemed more justified than today. The practice of prying into the minds and habits of American consumers is now a multibillion-dollar business. Every time a product is pulled across a supermarket checkout scanner, information is recorded, assembled, and sold to a market-research firm for analysis. There are companies that put tiny cameras inside frozen-food cases in supermarket aisles; market-research firms that feed census data and behavioral statistics into algorithms and come out with complicated maps of the American consumer; anthropologists who sift through the garbage of carefully targeted households to analyze their true consumption patterns; and endless rounds of highly organized focus groups and questionnaire takers and phone surveyors. That some people are now tracking our every shopping move with video cameras seems in many respects the last straw: Paco's movies are, after all, creepy. They look like the surveillance videos taken during convenience-store holdups—hazy and soundless and slightly warped by the angle of the lens. When you watch them, you find yourself waiting for something bad to happen, for someone to shoplift or pull a gun on a cashier.

The more time you spend with Paco's videos, though, the less scary they seem. After an hour or so, it's no longer clear whether simply by watching people shop—and analyzing their every move—you can learn how to control them. The shopper that emerges from the videos is not pliable or manipulable. The screen shows people filtering in and out of stores, petting and moving on, abandoning their merchandise because checkout lines are too long, or leaving a store empty-handed because they couldn't fit their stroller into the aisle between two shirt racks. Paco's shoppers are fickle and headstrong, and are quite unwilling to buy anything unless conditions are perfect—unless the belt is presented at *exactly* the right moment. His theories of the butt-brush and petting and the Decompression Zone and the Invariant Right seek not to make shoppers conform to the desires of sellers but to make sellers conform to the desires of shoppers. What Paco is teaching his clients is a kind of slavish devotion to the shopper's every whim. He is teaching them humility.

READING THE TEXT

1. Summarize in your own words the ways that retailers use spatial design to affect the consumer's behavior and buying habits.

2. What is Gladwell's tone in this selection, and what does it reveal about his attitudes toward the retail industry's manipulation of customers?

3. What is the effect on the reader of Gladwell's description of Paco Underhill's background and physical appearance?

4. Why does Paco Underhill's mother say that he is "the best-paid spy in America" (para. 13)?

READING THE SIGNS

1. **CONNECTING TEXTS** Visit a local store or supermarket, and study the spatial design. How many of the design strategies that Gladwell describes do you observe, and how do they affect customers' behavior? Use your observations as the basis for an essay interpreting the store's spatial design. To develop your ideas further, consult Anne Norton's "The Signs of Shopping" (below).

2. In class, form teams and debate the proposition that the surveillance of consumers by retail anthropologists is manipulative and unethical.

3. Visit a Web site of a major retailer (such as www.abercrombieandfitch.com or www.gap.com). How is the online "store" designed to encourage consuming behavior?

4. Write an essay in response to Gladwell's question "Should we be afraid of Paco Underhill?" (para. 17).

UNDERSTANDING SHOPPING

ANNE NORTON
The Signs of Shopping

Shopping malls are more than places to shop, just as mail-order catalogs are more than simple lists of goods. Both malls and catalogs are coded systems that not only encourage us to buy but, more profoundly, help us to construct our very sense of identity, as in the J. Peterman catalog that "constructs the reader as a man of rugged outdoor interests, taste, and money." In this selection from *Republic of Signs* (1993), Anne Norton, a professor of political science at the University of Pennsylvania, analyzes the many ways in which malls, catalogs, and home shopping networks sell you what they want by telling you who you are. Norton's other books include *Alternative Americas* (1986), *Reflections on Political Identity* (1988), *Ninety-five Theses on Politics, Culture, and Method* (2003), and *Leo Strauss and the Politics of American Empire* (2004).

Shopping at the Mall

The mall has been the subject of innumerable debates. Created out of the modernist impulse for planning and the centralization of public activity, the mall has become the distinguishing sign of suburban decentralization, springing up in unplanned profusion. Intended to restore something of the lost unity of city life to the suburbs, the mall has come to export styles and strategies to stores at the urban center. Deplored by modernists, it is regarded with affection only by their postmodern foes. Ruled more by their content than by their creators' avowed intent, the once sleek futurist shells have taken on a certain aura of postmodern playfulness and popular glitz.

The mall is a favorite subject for the laments of cultural conservatives and others critical of the culture of consumption. It is indisputably the cultural locus of commodity fetishism. It has been noticed, however, by others of a less condemnatory disposition that the mall has something of the mercado, or the agora, about it. It is both a place of meeting for the young and one of the rare places where young and old go together. People of different races and classes, different occupations, different levels of education meet there. As M. Pressdee and John Fiske note, however, though the mall appears to be a public place, it is not. Neither freedom of speech nor freedom of assembly is permitted there. Those who own and manage malls restrict what comes within their confines. Controversial displays, by stores or customers or the plethora of organizations and agencies that present themselves in the open spaces of the mall, are not permitted. These seemingly public spaces conceal a pervasive private authority.

The mall exercises its thorough and discreet authority not only in the regulation of behavior but in the constitution of our visible, inaudible, public discourse. It is the source of those commodities through which we speak of our identities, our opinions, our desires. It is a focus for the discussion of style among peripheral consumers. Adolescents, particularly female adolescents, are inclined to spend a good deal of time at the mall. They spend, indeed, more time than money. They acquire not simple commodities (they may come home with many, few, or none) but a well-developed sense of the significance of those commodities. In prowling the mall they embed themselves in a lexicon of American culture. They find themselves walking through a dictionary. Stores hang a variety of identities on their racks and mannequins. Their window displays provide elaborate scenarios conveying not only what the garment is but what the garment means.

A display in the window of Polo provides an embarrassment of semiotic riches. Everyone, from the architecture critic at the *New York Times* to kids in the hall of a Montana high school, knows what *Ralph Lauren* means. The polo mallet and the saddle, horses and dogs, the broad lawns of Newport, Kennebunkport, old photographs in silver frames, the evocation of age, of ancestry and Anglophilia, of indolence and the Ivy League, evoke the upper class. Indian blankets and buffalo plaids, cowboy hats and Western saddles, evoke a past distinct from England but nevertheless determinedly Anglo. The supposedly arcane and suspect arts of deconstruction are deployed easily, effortlessly, by the readers of these cultural texts.

Walking from one window to another, observing one another, shoppers, especially the astute and observant adolescents, acquire a facility with the language of commodities. They learn not only words but a grammar. Shop windows employ elements of sarcasm and irony, strategies of inversion and allusion. They provide models of elegant, economical, florid, and prosaic expression. They teach composition.

The practice of shopping is, however, more than instructive. It has long been the occasion for women to escape the confines of their homes and enjoy the companionship of other women. The construction of woman's role as one of provision for the needs of the family legitimated her exit. It provided an occasion for women to spend long stretches of time in the company of their friends, without the presence of their husbands. They could exchange information and reflections, ask advice, and receive support. As their daughters grew, they would be brought increasingly within this circle, included in shopping trips and lunches with their mothers. These would form, reproduce, and restructure communities of taste.

The construction of identity and the enjoyment of friendship outside the presence of men was thus effected through a practice that constructed women as consumers and subjected them to the conventions of the marketplace. Insofar as they were dependent on their husbands for money, they were dependent on their husbands for the means to the construction of their identities. They could not represent themselves through commodities without the funds men provided, nor could they, without money, participate in the community of women that was realized in "going shopping." Their identities were made contingent not only on the possession of property but on the recognition of dependence.

Insofar as shopping obliges dependent women to recognize their dependence, it also opens up the possibility of subversion.[1] The housewife who shops for pleasure takes time away from her husband, her family, and her house and claims it for herself. Constantly taught that social order and her private happiness depend on intercourse between men and women, she chooses the company of women instead. She engages with women in an activity marked as feminine, and she enjoys it. When she spends money, she exercises an authority over property that law and custom may deny her. If she has no resources independent of her husband, this may be the only authority over property she is able to exercise. When she buys things her

---

[1] Nuanced and amusing accounts of shopping as subversion are provided in John Fiske's analyses of popular culture, particularly *Reading the Popular* (Boston: Unwin Hyman [now Routledge], 1989), pp. 13–42.

husband does not approve — or does not know of — she further subverts an order that leaves control over property in her husband's hands.[2]

Her choice of feminine company and a feminine pursuit may involve additional subversions. As Fiske and Pressdee recognize, shopping without buying and shopping for bargains have a subversive quality. This is revealed, in a form that gives it additional significance, when a saleswoman leans forward and tells a shopper, "Don't buy that today, it will be on sale on Thursday." Here solidarity of gender (and often of class) overcome, however partially and briefly, the imperatives of the economic order.

Shoppers who look, as most shoppers do, for bargains, and salespeople 10 who warn shoppers of impending sales, see choices between commodities as something other than the evidence and the exercise of freedom. They see covert direction and exploitation; they see the withholding of information and the manipulation of knowledge. They recognize that they are on enemy terrain and that their shopping can be, in Michel de Certeau's[3] term, a "guerrilla raid." This recognition in practice of the presence of coercion in choice challenges the liberal conflation of choice and consent.

Shopping at Home

Shopping is an activity that has overcome its geographic limits. One need no longer go to the store to shop. Direct mail catalogues, with their twenty-four-hour phone numbers for ordering, permit people to shop where and when they please. An activity that once obliged one to go out into the public sphere, with its diverse array of semiotic messages, can now be done at home. An activity that once obliged one to be in company, if not in conversation, with one's compatriots can now be conducted in solitude.

The activity of catalogue shopping, and the pursuit of individuality, are not, however, wholly solitary. The catalogues invest their commodities with vivid historical and social references. The J. Peterman catalogue, for example, constructs the reader as a man of rugged outdoor interests, taste, and money.[4] He wears "The Owner's Hat" or "Hemingway's Cap," a leather flight jacket or the classic "Horseman's Duster," and various other garments identified with the military, athletes, and European imperialism. The copy for "The Owner's Hat" naturalizes class distinctions and, covertly, racism:

[2]See R. Bowlby, *Just Looking: Consumer Culture in Dreiser, Gissing, and Zola* (London: Methuen, 1985), p. 22, for another discussion and for an example of the recommendation of this strategy by Elizabeth Cady Stanton in the 1850s.

[3]**Michel de Certeau** (1925–1986) French social scientist and semiotician who played an important role in the development of contemporary cultural studies. –Eds.

[4]I have read several of these. I cite *The J. Peterman Company Owner's Manual No. 5*, from the J. Peterman Company, 2444 Palumbo Drive, Lexington, Ky. 40509.

Some of us work on the plantation.
Some of us own the plantation.
Facts are facts.
This hat is for those who own the plantation.[5]

Gender roles are strictly delineated. The copy for a skirt captioned "Women's Legs" provides a striking instance of the construction of the gaze as male, of women as the object of the gaze:

Just when you think you see something, a shape you think you recognize, it's gone and then it begins to return and then it's gone and of course you can't take your eyes off it.

Yes, the long slow motion of women's legs. Whatever happened to those things at carnivals that blew air up into girls' skirts and you could spend hours watching.[6]

"You," of course, are male. There is also the lace blouse captioned "Mystery": "lace says yes at the same time it says no."[7] Finally, there are notes of imperialist nostalgia: the Shepherd's Hotel (Cairo) bathrobe and white pants for "the bush" and "the humid hell-holes of Bombay and Calcutta."[8]

It may no longer be unforgivable to say that the British left a few good things behind in India and in Kenya, Singapore, Borneo, etc., not the least of which was their Englishness.[9]

As Paul Smith observes, in his reading of their catalogues, the Banana Republic has also made capital out of imperial nostalgia.[10]

The communities catalogues create are reinforced by shared mailing lists. The constructed identities are reified and elaborated in an array of semiotically related catalogues. One who orders a spade or a packet of seeds will be constructed as a gardener and receive a deluge of catalogues from plant and garden companies. The companies themselves may expand their commodities to appeal to different manifestations of the identities they respond to and construct. Smith and Hawken, a company that sells gardening supplies with an emphasis on aesthetics and environmental concern, puts out a catalogue in which a group of people diverse in age and in their ethnicity wear

[5]Ibid., p. 5. The hat is also identified with the Canal Zone, "successfully bidding at Beaulieu," intimidation, and LBOs. Quite a hat. It might be argued against my reading that the J. Peterman Company also offers the "Coal Miner's Bag" and a mailbag. However, since the descriptive points of reference on color and texture and experience for these bags are such things as the leather seats of Jaguars, and driving home in a Bentley, I feel fairly confident in my reading.

[6]Ibid., p. 3. See also pp. 15 and 17 for instances of women as the object of the male gaze. The identification of the gaze with male sexuality is unambiguous here as well.

[7]Ibid., p. 17.

[8]Ibid., pp. 7, 16, 20, 21, 37, and 50.

[9]Ibid., p. 20.

[10]Paul Smith, "Visiting the Banana Republic," in *Universal Abandon?* ed. Andrew Ross for *Social Text* (Minneapolis: University of Minnesota Press, 1988), pp. 128–48.

the marketed clothes while gardening, painting, or throwing pots. Williams-Sonoma presents its catalogue not as a catalogue of things for cooking but as "A Catalog for Cooks." The catalogue speaks not to need but to the construction of identity.

The Nature Company dedicates its spring 1990 catalogue "to trees," endorses Earth Day, and continues to link itself to the Nature Conservancy through posters and a program in which you buy a tree for a forest restoration project. Here, a not-for-profit agency is itself commodified, adding to the value of the commodities offered in the catalogue.[11] In this catalogue, consumption is not merely a means for the construction and representation of the self, it is also a means for political action. Several commodities are offered as "A Few Things You Can Do" to save the earth: a string shopping bag, a solar battery recharger, a home newspaper recycler. Socially conscious shopping is a liberal practice in every sense. It construes shopping as a form of election, in which one votes for good commodities or refuses one's vote to candidates whose practices are ethically suspect. In this respect, it reveals its adherence to the same ideological presuppositions that structure television's Home Shopping Network and other cable television sales shows.

Both politically informed purchasing and television sales conflate the free market and the electoral process. Dollars are identified with votes, purchases with endorsements. Both offer those who engage in them the possibility to "talk back" to manufacturers. In television sales shows this ability to talk back is both more thoroughly elaborated and more thoroughly exploited. Like the "elections" on MTV that invite viewers to vote for their favorite video by calling a number on their telephones, they permit those who watch to respond, to speak, and to be heard by the television. Their votes, of course, cost money. On MTV, as in the stores, you can buy as much speech as you can afford. On the Home Shopping Network, the purchase of speech becomes complicated by multiple layers and inversions.

Each commodity is introduced. It is invested by the announcer with a number of desirable qualities. The value of these descriptions of the commodities is enhanced by the construction of the announcer as a mediator not only between the commodity and the consumer but between the salespeople and the consumer. The announcer is not, the format suggests, a salesperson (though of course the announcer is). He or she is an announcer, describing goods that others have offered for sale. Television claims to distinguish itself by making objects visible to the eyes, but it is largely through the ears that these commodities are constructed. The consumer, in purchasing the commodity, purchases the commodity, what the commodity signifies, and, as we say, "buys the salesperson's line." The consumer may also acquire the ability to speak on television. Each purchase is recorded and figures as a vote in a

---

[11] *The Nature Company Catalog*, The Nature Company, P.O. Box 2310, Berkeley, Calif. 94702, Spring 1990. See pp. 1–2 and order form insert between pp. 18 and 19. Note also the entailed donation to Designs for Conservation on p. 18.

rough plebiscite, confirming the desirability of the object. Although the purchase figures are announced as if they were confirming votes, it is, of course, impossible to register one's rejection of the commodity. Certain consumers get a little more (or rather less) for their money. They are invited to explain the virtue of the commodity — and their purchase — to the announcer and the audience. The process of production, of both the consumers and that which they consume, continues in this apology for consumption.

The semiotic identification of consumption as an American activity, indeed, a patriotic one, is made with crude enthusiasm on the Home Shopping Network and other video sales shows. Red, white, and blue figure prominently in set designs and borders framing the television screen. The Home Shopping Network presents its authorities in an office conspicuously adorned with a picture of the Statue of Liberty.[12] Yet the messages that the Home Shopping Network sends its customers — that you can buy as much speech as you can afford, that you are recognized by others in accordance with your capacity to consume — do much to subvert the connection between capitalism and democracy on which this semiotic identification depends.

READING THE TEXT

1. What does Norton mean when she claims that the suburban shopping mall appears to be a public place but in fact is not?
2. What is Norton's interpretation of Ralph Lauren's Polo line?
3. How is shopping a subversive activity for women, according to Norton?
4. How do mail-order catalogs create communities of shoppers, in Norton's view?
5. What are the political messages sent by the Home Shopping Network, as Norton sees them, and how are they communicated?

READING THE SIGNS

1. Visit a local shopping mall, and study the window displays, focusing on stores intended for one group of consumers (teenagers, for example, or children). Then write an essay in which you analyze how the displays convey what the stores' products "mean."
2. Bring a few product catalogs to class, and in small groups compare the kind of consumer "constructed" by the cultural images and allusions in the catalogs. Do you note any patterns associated with gender, ethnicity, or age group? Report your group's interpretations to the whole class.
3. Interview five women of different age groups about their motivations and activities when they shop in a mall. Use your results as evidence in an

---

[12]This moment from the Home Shopping Network was generously brought to my attention, on videotape, by Peter Bregman, a student in my American Studies class of fall 1988, at Princeton University.

essay in which you support, refute, or complicate Norton's assertion that shopping constitutes a subversive activity for women.

4. Watch an episode of the Home Shopping Network or a similar program, and write a semiotic analysis of the ways in which products are presented to consumers.

5. Select a single mail-order catalog, and write a detailed semiotic interpretation of the identity it constructs for its market.

6. Visit the Web site for a major chain store (for instance, www.urbanoutfitters .com), and study how it "moves" the consumer through it. How does the site induce you to consume?

MARK DERY

Dawn of the Dead Mall

Life hasn't been easy for shopping mall developers in recent years, with the Great Recession taking a big bite out of brick-and-mortar retail. That bite has been so big that a number of green-thinking architectural visionaries have been devising alternate futures for the abandoned spaces of the American shopping mall on behalf of a utopian vision for the future. Indeed, as Mark Dery writes in this essay, which first appeared in the online site for The Design Observer Group, "The extreme turbulence that hit the American economy in 2008 offers a rare window of opportunity to hit the re-set button on consumer culture as we know it — to re-tool market capitalism along greener, more socially conscious and, crucially, more profoundly satisfying lines." But be careful: The road to the post-mall Erewhon will be lined with highly distracting goodies, and reports of the death of the shopping mall may well prove to be exaggerated. The author of *The Pyrotechnic Insanitarium: American Culture on the Brink* (1999), Mark Dery is a freelance journalist and cultural critic.

Dead malls, according to Deadmalls.com, are malls whose vacancy rate has reached the tipping point; whose consumer traffic is alarmingly low; are "dated or deteriorating"; or all of the above. A May 2009 article in *The Wall Street Journal*, "Recession Turns Malls into Ghost Towns," predicts that the dead-mall bodycount "will swell to more than 100 by the end of this year." Dead malls are a sign of the times, victims of the economic plague years.

The multitiered, fully enclosed mall (as opposed to the strip mall) has been the Vatican of shiny, happy consumerism since it staked its claim on the crabgrass frontier — and the public mind — in postwar America. The nation's first enclosed shopping mall, the Southdale Center, opened its doors in Edina, outside Minneapolis, in 1956. Southdale was the brainchild of the Los Angeles–based architect (and Viennese refugee from the Anschluss) Victor Gruen. A socialist and former student of the modernist designer Peter Behrens, Gruen saw in the covered mall a Vision of Things to Come.

In his dreams, Southdale would be the nucleus of a utopian experiment in master-planned, mixed-use community, complete with housing, schools, a medical center, even a park and lake. It was all very Gropius-goes-Epcot. None of those Bauhausian fantasies came to pass, of course. (Do they ever?) On the bright side, Southdale did have a garden court with a café. And a fishpond. And brightly colored birds twittering in a 21-foot cage. Reporting on the opening, *Architectural Record* made it sound like the Platonic Ideal of Downtown — what downtown would be "if downtown weren't so noisy and dirty and chaotic." A town square in a bell jar: modern, orderly, spanking clean.

But it wasn't Gruen's *Mad Men* take on the Viennese plazas he remembered so fondly that made his Ur-mall go viral. Developers liked the way Gruen used architecture to socially engineer our patterns of consumption. His goal, he said, was to design an environment in which "shoppers will be so bedazzled by a store's surroundings that they will be drawn — unconsciously, continually — to shop." (Remember, Gruen was from Freud's Vienna, where psychoanalysis was a growth industry.)

Until Southdale, shopping centers had been "extroverted," in architectural 5 parlance: store windows faced outward, toward the parking lot, as well as inward, toward the main concourse. Southdale's display windows were visible to the mall crawler only; from the outside, it was a blank box, blind to its suburban surroundings — the proverbial "world in miniature, in which customers will find everything they need," as Walter Benjamin put it in his *Arcade Projects* description of the proto-malls of 19th-century Paris. In Gruen's galleria, shopping becomes a stage-managed experience in an unreal, hermetically sealed environment, where consumer behavior can (in theory, at least) be scientifically managed.

This innovation, together with Gruen's decision to squeeze more stores into a more walkably small space by building a multistoried structure connected by escalators, and his decision to bookend the mall with big-name "anchor" stores — magnets to attract shoppers who, with luck, would browse the smaller shops as well (a strategy James Farrell, author of *One Nation Under Goods: Malls and the Seductions of American Shopping,* calls "coopetition") — cut the die for nearly every mall in America today, which means Gruen "may well have been the most influential architect of the twentieth century" in Malcolm Gladwell's hedging estimation.

Unfortunately, Gruen made the fatal mistake — fatal for an arm-waving futurist visionary, anyway — of living long enough to see American consumer culture embrace his idea with a vengeance. In a 1978 speech, he recalled visiting one of his old malls, where he swooned in horror at "the ugliness . . .

of the land-wasting seas of parking" around it, and the soul-killing sprawl beyond.

Good thing he didn't survive to see the undeath of the American mall. Most economic commentators attribute its dire state to the epic fail of the American economy. In April of this year, one of the country's biggest mall operators — General Growth Properties, owner and/or manager of over 200 properties in 44 states — filed for bankruptcy, mortally wounded by the exodus of retail tenants.

Good riddance to bad rubbish, some say. In the comment thread to the November 12, 2008, *Newsweek* article, "Is the Mall Dead?," a reader writes, "The end of temples of consumerism and irresponsibility? Sweet. The demise of a culture of greed? No problem."

But wait, my Inner Marxist wonders: isn't that the voice of bobo privi- 10
lege talking? Teens marooned in decentered developments didn't ask to live there; for many of them, the local mall is the closest thing to a commons, be it ever so ersatz. And malls are employment engines. Sure, in many cases the jobs they generate are low-skill and low-wage, but From Each According to His Ability, etc.

"I'm fine if some malls die," says Farrell, "but it's important to remember that malls had good points too. In a world in which no-new-taxes has made most new public buildings look like pole barns, malls have provided an architecture of elegance and pleasure — they are some of the best public spaces in America. In a country of cars, malls have provided a place for the pleasures of pedestrianism, and for the see-and-be-seen people-watching that's one of the delights of the mall experience."

Still, Woodstockian dreams of getting ourselves back to the garden — demolishing every last mall and letting the amber waves of grain roll back — are popular these days: "tear them down, recycle what can be recycled . . . and turn them back into carbon-absorbing, tree-filled natural landscape, habitat for wild animals," a reader writes, on the *New York Times* site. For many, malls have come to symbolize the culture rot brought on by market capitalism: amok consumption, *Real Housewives of New Jersey* vulgarity.

Visions of taking a wrecking ball to malls everywhere are satisfyingly apocalyptic. But sending all that rebar, concrete, and Tyvek to a landfill is politically incorrect in the extreme. Already, architects, urbanists, designers and critics are thinking toward a near future in which dead malls are repurposed, redesigned, and reincarnated as greener, smarter, and more often than not more aesthetically inspiring places — seedbeds for locavore-oriented agriculture, vibrant social beehives or [fill in the huge footprint where the mall used to stand].

Brimming with evangelical zeal, New Urbanists are exhorting communities with dead malls to reverse the historical logic of Gruenization, turning malls inside-out so storefronts face the wider world and transforming them into mixed-use agglomerations of residences and retail; repurposing parking lots into civic plazas; infilling the dead zones that surround most malls with transit-accessible neighborhoods checkerboarded with public spaces (a rare commodity in sprawl developments), and weaving the streets of said neighborhoods into those of the surrounding suburbs.

The more visionary ideas sound a lot like what the cyberpunk design- 15 eratus Bruce Sterling calls "architecture fiction," somewhere between Greg Lynn and Silent Running, Teddy Cruz and Ecotopia. The San Francisco-based Stoner Meek Architecture and Urban Design, finalists in the 2003 Dead Malls competition launched by the Los Angeles Forum for Architecture and Urban Design, propose a post-sprawl take on the Vallejo Plaza in California: deconstruct the moribund mall, they advised, and reconstruct it as a shopping center-cum-ecotourist attraction, its stores squatting, half-submerged, in the nearby wetlands remediation project. For his third-place-winning entry in the Reburbia competition, Forrest Fulton wonders, in "Big Box Agriculture: A Productive Suburb," why a ghost-box grocery store can't morph "from retailer of food — food detached from processes from which it came to be — to producer of food"? The store as look-alike outlet for the trucked-in, taste-alike products of factory farming is reborn as a grocery store Alice Waters could love. The box transforms into a restaurant; a greenhouse pops out of its roof. Where the desolate parking lot once stood, a pocket farm springs up. Light poles turn into solar trees studded with photovoltaic cells. Fulton imagines "pushing a shopping cart through this suburban farm and picking your produce right from the vine, with the option to bring your harvest to the restaurant chef for preparation and eating your harvest on the spot."

Two other entrants, Evan Collins ("LivaBlox: Converting Big Box Stores to Container Homes") and Micah Winkelstein of B3 Architects ("Transforming the Big Box into a Livable Environment"), envision the radical re-use of ghost boxes as termite mounds of domestic, retail, and agricultural activity. Collins conjures Legoland stacks of brightly colored modular homes, fabricated from a recycled store and its discarded shipping containers. Where his "vacated megastore" now stands, Winkelstein sees a "behemoth structure" that is home to a mini-city of lofts, its ginormous common roof crowned with solar panels and carpeted with gardens and landscaped greens, wind turbines sprouting everywhere.

Radiant City, here we come. But Farrell spots some potholes in the road to Erewhon. Projects that resurrect dead malls "are visionary and wonderful," he says, but many of them "involve a sense of public purpose that seems absent in America just now. I would love to see malls function as a commons, with public-private purposes, addressing the environment we really live in instead of the consumer fantasyland that has been the mainstay of mall design so far."

As we cling by our hangnails to the historical precipice, with ecotastrophe on one side and econopocalypse on the other, that consumer fantasyland is an economic indulgence and an environmental obscenity we can't afford — the dead end of an economic philosophy tied to manic overdevelopment (codeword: "housing starts"), maxed-out credit cards (codeword: "consumer confidence"), and arcane financial plays that generate humongous profits for Wall Street's elite but little of real worth, in human terms. It's the last gasp of the consumer culture founded on the economic logic articulated early in the twentieth century by Earnest Elmo Calkins, who admonished his fellow advertising executives in 1932 that "consumer engineering must see to it that we use up the kind of goods we now merely use," and by the domestic theorist Christine Frederick, who observed in 1929 that "the way to break the vicious deadlock of a low standard of living is to spend freely, and even waste creatively."

The extreme turbulence that hit the American economy in 2008 offers a rare window of opportunity to hit the re-set button on consumer culture as we know it — to re-tool market capitalism along greener, more socially conscious and, crucially, more profoundly satisfying lines. Because an age of repurposing, recycling and retrofitting needn't be a Beige New World of Soviet-style austerity measures. On the contrary, while we'll likely have far fewer status totems in the near future, the quality of our experiential lives could be far richer in diversity, if we muster the political will to make them so. "The most important fact about our shopping malls," the social scientist Henry Fairlie told *The Week* magazine, "is that we do not need most of what they sell." Animated by the requisite "sense of public purpose," the post-mall, post-sprawl suburbs could be exuberantly heterogeneous Places That Do Not Suck, where food is grown closer to home, cottage industries are the norm, and the nowheresville of chain restaurants and big-box retailers and megamalls has given way to local cuisines, one-of-a-kind shops, and walkable communities with a sense of place and social cohesion.

Or we could persist in the fundamentalist faith in overproduction and hyperconsumption that has brought us to this pass. In *Dawn of the Dead* (1978), his black comedy about mindless consumption, George Romero offers a glimpse of that future, one of many possible tomorrows. Two SWAT team officers have just escaped from a ravening horde of cannibalistic zombies, into the safety of an abandoned mall. "Well, we're in, but how the hell are we gonna get back?" Suddenly, they realize no one's minding the store.

PETER: Who the hell cares?! Let's go shopping!
ROGER: Watches! Watches!
PETER: Wait a minute man, let's just get the stuff we need. I'll get a television and a radio.
ROGER: And chocolate, chocolate. Hey, how about a mink coat?

READING THE TEXT

1. How does Dery find the 1956 Southdale mall to be significant in the history of shopping mall design?

2. How do malls with an "interior" focus affect consumer behavior, according to Dery?

3. Why do some commentators relish the recent demise of many shopping malls?

4. Summarize in your own words the proposed "visionary" uses of dead malls that Dery describes. What social values do these proposed uses seem to promote?

5. What are Dery's predictions for future uses of shopping malls, and how does he support those predictions?

6. What is Dery's tone in this selection, and how does it affect your response to his ideas?

READING THE SIGNS

1. **CONNECTING TEXTS**   Adopting the perspective of Laurence Shames ("The More Factor," p. 90), analyze the plausibility of the future uses of shopping malls that Dery predicts. Do you think Shames would see the death of malls as a "rare window of opportunity to hit the re-set button on consumer culture" (para. 19) or as a blip on America's road to endless consumption? Or do you think he would have a different reading of the dead mall phenomenon?

2. **CONNECTING TEXTS**   Visit a local shopping mall, either one of the older "extroverted" (para. 5) designs or one of the insular malls of the Southdale design. Examine the way the mall directs consumer traffic and invites shoppers into stores. Use your observations to support an argument about how this particular mall's design works to encourage consumption. To develop your ideas, consult Malcolm Gladwell's "The Science of Shopping" (p. 97) and Anne Norton's "The Signs of Shopping" (p. 104).

3. In an argumentative essay, support, refute, or complicate James Farrell's assertion that attempts to repurpose dead malls may fail because they "involve a sense of public purpose that seems absent in America just now" (para. 17).

4. Visit online the Web site of an alternative mall design (check the 2003 dead malls competition or another such site), and analyze its design. Do you think it would fulfill the goal of being a "shopping center-cum-ecotourist attraction" (para. 15)? Or does the design seem unlikely to attract consumers? Why or why not?

5. Rent a DVD of *Dawn of the Dead*, or another anticonsumerist film such as *Wall-E* (2008). Analyze how shopping, and more broadly, consumerism, is represented in the film. Does consumption represent an opportunity for freedom and fantasy, or does it present consumerism more as "an environmental obscenity we can't afford" (para. 18)?

Credit Card Barbie

READING THE SIGNS

1. Why might girls enjoy playing with a Barbie who shops rather than engaging her in some other kind of activity?

2. Do you think that having Barbie use a credit card to purchase cosmetics has an effect on the girls who play with the doll? If so, what are those effects?

THOMAS HINE
What's in a Package

What's in a package? According to Thomas Hine, a great deal, perhaps even more than what is actually inside the package. From the cereal boxes you find in the supermarket to the perfume bottles sold at Tiffany's, the shape and design of the packages that contain just about every product we consume have been carefully calculated to stimulate consumption. Indeed, as Hine explains in this excerpt from *The Total Package: The Evolution and Secret Meanings of Boxes, Bottles, Cans, and Tubes* (1995), "for manufacturers, packaging is the crucial final payoff to a marketing campaign." A former architecture and design critic for the *Philadelphia Inquirer,* Hine has also published *Populuxe* (1986), on American design and culture; *Facing Tomorrow* (1991), on past and current attitudes toward the future; *The Rise and Fall of the American Teenager: A New History of the American Adolescent Experience* (1999); *I Want That! How We All Became Shoppers* (2002); and *The Great Funk: Falling Apart and Coming Together (on a Shag Rug) in the Seventies* (2007).

When you put yourself behind a shopping cart, the world changes. You become an active consumer, and you are moving through environments — the supermarket, the discount store, the warehouse club, the home center — that have been made for you.

During the thirty minutes you spend on an average trip to the supermarket, about thirty thousand different products vie to win your attention and ultimately to make you believe in their promise. When the door opens, automatically, before you, you enter an arena where your emotions and your appetites are in play, and a walk down the aisle is an exercise in self-definition. Are you a good parent, a good provider? Do you have time to do all you think you should, and would you be interested in a shortcut? Are you worried about your health and that of those you love? Do you care about the environment? Do you appreciate the finer things in life? Is your life what you would like it to be? Are you enjoying what you've accomplished? Wouldn't you really like something chocolate?

Few experiences in contemporary life offer the visual intensity of a Safeway, a Krogers, a Pathmark, or a Piggly Wiggly. No marketplace in the world — not Marrakesh or Calcutta or Hong Kong — offers so many different goods with such focused salesmanship as your neighborhood supermarket, where you're exposed to a thousand different products a minute. No wonder it's tiring to shop.

There are, however, some major differences between the supermarket and a traditional marketplace. The cacophony of a traditional market has given way to programmed, innocuous music, punctuated by enthusiastically intoned commercials. A stroll through a traditional market offers an array of sensuous aromas; if you are conscious of smelling something in a supermarket, there is a problem. The life and death matter of eating, expressed in traditional markets by the sale of vegetables with stems and roots and by hanging animal carcasses, is purged from the supermarket, where food is processed somewhere else, or at least trimmed out of sight.

But the most fundamental difference between a traditional market and 5 the places through which you push your cart is that in a modern retail setting nearly all the selling is done without people. The product is totally dissociated from the personality of any particular person selling it — with the possible exception of those who appear in its advertising. The supermarket purges sociability, which slows down sales. It allows manufacturers to control the way they present their products to the world. It replaces people with packages.

Packages are an inescapable part of modern life. They are omnipresent and invisible, deplored and ignored. During most of your waking moments, there are one or more packages within your field of vision. Packages are so ubiquitous that they slip beneath conscious notice, though many packages are designed so that people will respond to them even if they're not paying attention.

Once you begin pushing the shopping cart, it matters little whether you are in a supermarket, a discount store, or a warehouse club. The important thing is that you are among packages: expressive packages intended to engage your emotions, ingenious packages that make a product useful, informative packages that help you understand what you want and what you're getting. Historically, packages are what made self-service retailing possible, and in turn such stores increased the number and variety of items people buy. Now a world without packages is unimaginable.

Packages lead multiple lives. They preserve and protect, allowing people to make use of things that were produced far away, or a while ago. And they are potently expressive. They assure that an item arrives unspoiled, and they help those who use the item feel good about it.

We share our homes with hundreds of packages, mostly in the bathroom and kitchen, the most intimate, body-centered rooms of the house. Some packages — a perfume flacon, a ketchup bottle, a candy wrapper, a beer can — serve as permanent landmarks in people's lives that outlast homes, careers, or spouses. But packages embody change, not just in their age-old promise that their contents are new and improved, but in their attempt to respond to changing tastes and achieve new standards of convenience. Packages record changing hairstyles and changing lifestyles. Even social policy issues are reflected. Nearly unopenable tamperproof seals and other forms of closures testify to the fragility of the social contract, and the susceptibility of the great mass of people to the destructive acts of a very few. It was a mark of rising environmental consciousness when containers recently began to make a novel promise: "less packaging."

For manufacturers, packaging is the crucial final payoff to a marketing 10 campaign. Sophisticated packaging is one of the chief ways people find the confidence to buy. It can also give a powerful image to products and commodities that are in themselves characterless. In many cases, the shopper has been prepared for the shopping experience by lush, colorful print advertisements, thirty-second television minidramas, radio jingles, and coupon promotions. But the package makes the final sales pitch, seals the commitment, and gets itself placed in the shopping cart. Advertising leads consumers into temptation. Packaging is the temptation. In many cases it is what makes the product possible.

But the package is also useful to the shopper. It is a tool for simplifying and speeding decisions. Packages promise, and usually deliver, predictability. One reason you don't think about packages is that you don't need to. The candy bar, the aspirin, the baking powder, or the beer in the old familiar package may, at times, be touted as new and improved, but it will rarely be very different.

You put the package into your cart, or not, usually without really having focused on the particular product or its many alternatives. But sometimes you do examine the package. You read the label carefully, looking at what the product promises, what it contains, what it warns. You might even look at the package itself and judge whether it will, for example, reseal to keep a product fresh. You might consider how a cosmetic container will look on your dressing table, or you might think about whether someone might have tampered with it or whether it can be easily recycled. The possibility of such scrutiny is one of the things that make each detail of the package so important.

The environment through which you push your shopping cart is extraordinary because of the amount of attention that has been paid to the packages that line the shelves. Most contemporary environments are landscapes of inattention. In housing developments, malls, highways, office buildings, even furniture, design ideas are few and spread very thin. At the supermarket, each box and jar, stand-up pouch and squeeze bottle, each can and bag and tube and spray has been very carefully considered. Designers have worked and reworked the design on their computers and tested mock-ups on the store shelves. Refinements are measured in millimeters.

All sorts of retail establishments have been redefined by packaging. Drugs and cosmetics were among the earliest packaged products, and most drugstores now resemble small supermarkets. Liquor makers use packaging to add a veneer of style to the intrinsic allure of intoxication, and some sell their bottle rather than the drink. It is no accident that vodka, the most characterless of spirits, has the highest-profile packages. The local gas station sells sandwiches and soft drinks rather than tires and motor oil, and in turn, automotive products have been attractively repackaged for sales at supermarkets, warehouse clubs, and home centers.

With its thousands of images and messages, the supermarket is as visu- 15 ally dense, if not as beautiful, as a Gothic cathedral. It is as complex and as predatory as a tropical rain forest. It is more than a person can possibly take in during an ordinary half-hour shopping trip. No wonder a significant percentage of people who need to wear eyeglasses don't wear them when they're shopping, and some researchers have spoken of the trancelike state that pushing a cart through this environment induces. The paradox here is that the visual intensity that overwhelms shoppers is precisely the thing that makes the design of packages so crucial. Just because you're not looking at a package doesn't mean you don't see it. Most of the time, you see far more than a container and a label. You see a personality, an attitude toward life, perhaps even a set of beliefs.

The shopper's encounter with the product on the shelf is, however, only the beginning of the emotional life cycle of the package. The package is very important in the moment when the shopper recognizes it either as an old friend or a new temptation. Once the product is brought home, the package seems to disappear, as the quality or usefulness of the product it contains becomes paramount. But in fact, many packages are still selling even at home, enticing those who have bought them to take them out of the cupboard, the closet, or the refrigerator and consume their contents. Then once the product has been used up, and the package is empty, it becomes suddenly visible once more. This time, though, it is trash that must be discarded or recycled. This instant of disposal is the time when people are most aware of packages. It is a negative moment, like the end of a love affair, and what's left seems to be a horrid waste.

The forces driving package design are not primarily aesthetic. Market researchers have conducted surveys of consumer wants and needs, and consultants have studied photographs of families' kitchen cupboards and medicine chests to get a sense of how products are used. Test subjects have been tied into pieces of heavy apparatus that measure their eye movement, their blood pressure or body temperature, when subjected to different packages. Psychologists get people to talk about the packages in order to get a sense of their innermost feelings about what they want. Government regulators and private health and safety advocates worry over package design and try to make it truthful. Stock-market analysts worry about how companies are managing their "brand equity," that combination of perceived value and consumer loyalty that is expressed in advertising but embodied in packaging. The retailer is paying attention to the packages in order to weed out the ones that don't sell or aren't sufficiently profitable. The use of supermarket scanners generates information on the profitability of every cubic inch of the store. Space on the supermarket shelf is some of the most valuable real estate in the world, and there are always plenty of new packaged products vying for display.

Packaging performs a series of disparate tasks. It protects its contents from contamination and spoilage. It makes it easier to transport and store goods. It provides uniform measuring of contents. By allowing brands to be created and standardized, it makes advertising meaningful and large-scale distribution possible. Special kinds of packages, with dispensing caps, sprays, and other convenience features, make products more usable. Packages serve as symbols both of their contents and of a way of life. And just as they can very powerfully communicate the satisfaction a product offers, they are equally potent symbols of wastefulness once the product is gone.

Most people use dozens of packages each day and discard hundreds of them each year. The growth of mandatory recycling programs has made people increasingly aware of packages, which account in the United States for about forty-three million tons, or just under 30 percent of all refuse discarded. While forty-three million tons of stuff is hardly insignificant, repeated surveys have shown that the public perceives that far more than 30 percent — indeed, nearly all — their garbage consists of packaging. This perception creates a political problem for the packaging industry, but it also demonstrates the power of packaging. It is symbolic. It creates an emotional relationship. Bones and wasted food (thirteen million tons), grass clippings and yard waste (thirty-one million tons), or even magazines and newspapers (fourteen million tons) do not feel as wasteful as empty vessels that once contained so much promise.

Packaging is a cultural phenomenon, which means that it works differently 20 in different cultures. The United States has been a good market for packages since it was first settled and has been an important innovator of packaging technology and culture. Moreover, American packaging is part of an international culture of modernity and consumption. At its deepest level, the culture of American packaging deals with the issue of surviving among strangers in a new world. This is an emotion with which anyone who has been touched by modernity can identify. In lives buffeted by change, people seek the safety and reassurance that packaged products offer. American packaging, which has always sought to appeal to large numbers of diverse people, travels better than that of most other cultures.

But the similar appearance of supermarkets throughout the world should not be interpreted as the evidence of a single, global consumer culture. In fact, most companies that do business internationally redesign their packages for each market. This is done partly to satisfy local regulations and adapt to available products and technologies. But the principal reason is that people in different places have different expectations and make different uses of packaging.

The United States and Japan, the world's two leading industrial powers, have almost opposite approaches to packaging. Japan's is far more elaborate than America's, and it is shaped by rituals of respect and centuries-old traditions of wrapping and presentation. Packaging is explicitly recognized as an expression of culture in Japan and largely ignored in America. Japanese packaging is designed to be appreciated; American packaging is calculated to be unthinkingly accepted.

Foods that only Japanese eat—even relatively humble ones like refrigerated prepared fish cakes—have wrappings that resemble handmade paper or leaves. Even modestly priced refrigerated fish cakes have beautiful wrappings in which traditional design accommodates a scannable bar code. Such products look Japanese and are unambiguously intended to do so. Products that are foreign, such as coffee, look foreign, even to the point of having only Roman lettering and no Japanese lettering on the can. American and European companies are sometimes able to sell their packages in Japan virtually unchanged, because their foreignness is part of their selling power. But Japanese exporters hire designers in each country to repackage their products. Americans—whose culture is defined not by refinements and distinctions but by inclusiveness—want to think about the product itself, not its cultural origins.

We speak glibly about global villages and international markets, but problems with packages reveal some unexpected cultural boundaries. Why are Canadians willing to drink milk out of flexible plastic pouches that fit into reusable plastic holders, while residents of the United States are believed to be so resistant to the idea that they have not even been given the opportunity to do so? Why do Japanese consumers prefer packages that contain two tennis balls and view the standard U.S. pack of three to be cheap and undesirable? Why do Germans insist on highly detailed technical specifications on packages of videotape, while Americans don't? Why do Swedes think that blue is masculine, while the Dutch see the color as feminine? The answers lie in unquestioned habits and deep-seated imagery, a culture of containing, adorning, and understanding that no sharp marketer can change overnight.

There is probably no other field in which designs that are almost a century old—Wrigley's gum, Campbell's soup, Hershey's chocolate bar—remain in production only subtly changed and are understood to be extremely valuable corporate assets. Yet the culture of packaging, defined by what people are buying and selling every day, keeps evolving, and the role nostalgia plays is very small.

For example, the tall, glass Heinz ketchup bottle has helped define the American refrigerator skyline for most of the twentieth century (even though it is generally unnecessary to refrigerate ketchup). Moreover, it provides the tables of diners and coffee shops with a vertical accent and a token of hospitality, the same qualities projected by candles and vases of flowers in more upscale eateries. The bottle has remained a fixture of American life, even though it has always been a nuisance to pour the thick ketchup through the little hole. It seemed not to matter that you have to shake and shake the bottle, impotently, until far too much ketchup comes out in one great scarlet plop. Heinz experimented for years with wide-necked jars and other sorts of bottles, but they never caught on.

Then in 1992 a survey of consumers indicated that more Americans believed that the plastic squeeze bottle is a better package for ketchup than the glass bottle. The survey did not offer any explanations for this change of preference, which has been evolving for many years as older people for whom the tall bottle is an icon became a less important part of the sample. Could it be that the difficulty of using the tall bottle suddenly became evident to those born after 1960? Perhaps the tall bottle holds too little ketchup. There is a clear trend toward buying things in larger containers, in part because lightweight plastics have made them less costly for manufacturers to ship and easier for consumers to use. This has happened even as the number of people in an average American household has been getting smaller. But houses, like packages, have been getting larger. Culture moves in mysterious ways.

The tall ketchup bottle is still preferred by almost half of consumers, so it is not going to disappear anytime soon. And the squeeze bottle does contain visual echoes of the old bottle. It is certainly not a radical departure. In Japan, ketchup and mayonnaise are sold in cellophane-wrapped plastic bladders that would certainly send Americans into severe culture shock. Still, the tall bottle's loss of absolute authority is a significant change. And its ultimate disappearance would represent a larger change in most people's visual environment than would the razing of nearly any landmark building.

But although some package designs are pleasantly evocative of another time, and a few appear to be unchanging icons in a turbulent world, the reason they still exist is because they still work. Inertia has historically played a role in creating commercial icons. Until quite recently, it was time-consuming and expensive to make new printing plates or to vary the shape or material of a container. Now computerized graphics and rapidly developing technology in the package-manufacturing industries make a packaging change easier than in the past, and a lot cheaper to change than advertising, which seems a far more evanescent medium. There is no constituency of curators or preservationists to protect the endangered package. If a gum wrapper manages to survive nearly unchanged for ninety years, it's not because any expert has determined that it is an important cultural expression. Rather, it's because it still helps sell a lot of gum.

So far, we've been discussing packaging in its most literal sense: designed containers that protect and promote products. Such containers have served as the models for larger types of packaging, such as chain restaurants, supermarkets, theme parks, and festival marketplaces. . . . Still, it is impossible to ignore a broader conception of packaging that is one of the preoccupations of our time. This concerns the ways in which people construct and present their personalities, the ways in which ideas are presented and diffused, the ways in which political candidates are selected and public policies formulated. We must all worry about packaging ourselves and everything we do, because we believe that nobody has time to really pay attention.

Packaging strives at once to offer excitement and reassurance. It promises something newer and better, but not necessarily different. When we talk about a tourist destination, or even a presidential contender, being packaged, that's not really a metaphor. The same projection of intensified ordinariness, the same combination of titillation and reassurance, are used for laundry detergents, theme parks, and candidates alike.

The imperative to package is unavoidable in a society in which people have been encouraged to see themselves as consumers not merely of toothpaste and automobiles, but of such imponderables as lifestyle, government, and health. The marketplace of ideas is not an agora, where people haggle, posture, clash, and come to terms with one another. Rather, it has become a supermarket, where values, aspirations, dreams, and predictions are presented with great sophistication. The individual can choose to buy them, or leave them on the shelf.

In such a packaged culture, the consumer seems to be king. But people cannot be consumers all the time. If nothing else, they must do something to earn the money that allows them to consume. This, in turn, pressures people to package themselves in order to survive. The early 1990s brought economic recession and shrinking opportunities to all the countries of the developed world. Like products fighting for their space on the shelf, individuals have had to re-create, or at least represent, themselves in order to seem both desirable and safe. Moreover, many jobs have been reconceived to depersonalize individuals and to make them part of a packaged service experience.

These phenomena have their own history. For decades, people have spoken of writing resumes in order to package themselves for a specific opportunity. Thomas J. Watson Jr., longtime chairman of IBM, justified his company's famously conservative and inflexible dress code — dark suits, white shirts, and rep ties for all male employees — as "self-packaging," analogous to the celebrated product design, corporate imagery, and packaging done for the company by Elliot Noyes and Paul Rand. You can question whether IBM's employees were packaging themselves or forced into a box by their employer. Still, anyone who has ever dressed for success was doing a packaging job.

Since the 1950s, there have been discussions of packaging a candidate to 35 respond to what voters are telling the pollsters who perform the same tasks as market researchers do for soap or shampoo. More recently, such discussions have dominated American political journalism. The packaged candidate, so he and his handlers hope, projects a message that, like a Diet Pepsi, is stimulating without being threatening. Like a Weight Watchers frozen dessert bar, the candidate's contradictions must be glazed over and, ultimately, comforting. Aspects of the candidate that are confusing or viewed as extraneous are removed, just as stems and sinew are removed from packaged foods. The package is intended to protect the candidate; dirt won't stick. The candidate is uncontaminated, though at a slight remove from the consumer-voter.

People profess to be troubled by this sort of packaging. When we say a person or an experience is "packaged," we are complaining of a sense of excessive calculation and a lack of authenticity. Such a fear of unreality is at least a century old; it arose along with industrialization and rapid communication. Now that the world is more competitive, and we all believe we have less time to consider things, the craft of being instantaneously appealing has taken on more and more importance. We might say, cynically, that the person who appears "packaged" simply doesn't have good packaging.

Still, the sense of uneasiness about encountering packaged people in a packaged world is real, and it shouldn't be dismissed. Indeed, it is a theme of contemporary life, equally evident in politics, entertainment, and the supermarket. Moreover, public uneasiness about the phenomenon of packaging is compounded by confusion over a loss of iconic packages and personalities.

Producers of packaged products have probably never been as nervous as they became during the first half of the 1990s. Many of the world's most famous brands were involved in the merger mania of the 1980s, which produced debt-ridden companies that couldn't afford to wait for results either from their managers or their marketing strategies. At the same time, the feeling was that it was far too risky to produce something really new. The characteristic response was the line extension — "dry" beer, "lite" mayonnaise, "ultra" detergent. New packages have been appearing at a rapid pace, only to be changed whenever a manager gets nervous or a retailer loses patience.

The same skittishness is evident in the projection of public personalities as the clear, if synthetic, images of a few decades ago have lost their sharpness and broken into a spectrum of weaker, reflected apparitions. Marilyn Monroe, for example, had an image that was, Jayne Mansfield notwithstanding, unique and well defined. She was luscious as a Hershey's bar, shapely as a Coke bottle. But in a world where Coke can be sugar free, caffeine free, and cherry flavored (and Pepsi can be clear!), just one image isn't enough for a superstar. Madonna is available as Marilyn or as a brunette, a Catholic schoolgirl, or a bondage devotee. Who knows what brand extension will come next? Likewise, John F. Kennedy and Elvis Presley had clear, carefully projected images. But Bill Clinton is defined largely by evoking memories of both. As our commercial civilization seems to have lost the power to amuse or convince us in new and exciting ways, formerly potent packages are recycled and devalued. That has left the door open for such phenomena as generic cigarettes, President's Choice cola, and H. Ross Perot.

This cultural and personal packaging both fascinates and infuriates. There   40 is something liberating in its promise of aggressive self-creation, and something terrifying in its implication that everything must be subject to the ruthless discipline of the marketplace. People are at once passive consumers of their culture and aggressive packagers of themselves, which can be a stressful and lonely combination.

READING THE TEXT

1. How does Hine compare a supermarket with a traditional marketplace?
2. What does Hine mean when he asserts that modern retailing "replaces people with packages" (para. 5)?
3. How does packaging stimulate the desire to buy, according to Hine?
4. How do Americans' attitudes toward packaging compare with those of the Japanese, according to Hine?

READING THE SIGNS

1. Bring one product package to class, preferably with all students bringing items from the same product category (personal hygiene, say, or bottled water). In class, give a brief presentation in which you interpret your package. After all the students have presented, compare the different messages the packages send to consumers.
2. Visit a popular retail store, such as Urban Outfitters or Victoria's Secret, and study the ways the store uses packaging to create, as Hine puts it, "a personality, an attitude toward life" (para. 15). Be thorough in your observations, studying everything from the store's bags to perfume or cologne packages to clothing labels. Use your findings as evidence for an essay in which you analyze the image the store creates for itself and its customers.
3. In your journal, write an entry in which you explore your motives for purchasing a product simply because you liked the package. What did you like about the package, and how did it contribute to your sense of identity?
4. Visit a store with an explicit political theme, such as the Body Shop or Whole Foods, and write a semiotic analysis of the packaging you see in the store.
5. **CONNECTING TEXTS**   Study the packages that are visible to a visitor to your home, and write an analysis of the messages those packages might send to a visitor. To develop your ideas, consult Joan Kron's "The Semiotics of Home Decor" (p. 128).

JOAN KRON

The Semiotics of Home Decor

Just when you thought it was safe to go back into your living room, here comes Joan Kron with a reminder that your home is a signaling system just as much as your clothing is. In *Home-Psych: The Social Psychology of Home and Decoration* (1983), from which this selection is taken, Kron takes a broad look at the significance of interior decoration, showing how home design can reflect both an individual and a group identity. Ranging from a New York entrepreneur to Kwakiutl Indian chiefs, Kron further discusses how different cultures use possessions as a rich symbol system. The author of *High Tech: The Industrial Style and Source Book for the Home* (1978) and of some five hundred articles for American magazines, she is particularly interested in fashion, design, and the social psychology of consumption. Currently an editor-at-large at *Allure* magazine, Kron has also published *Lift: Wanting, Fearing, and Having a Face-Lift* (1998).

On June 7, 1979, Martin J. Davidson entered the materialism hall of fame. That morning the thirty-four-year-old New York graphic design entrepreneur went to his local newsstand and bought fifty copies of the *New York Times* expecting to read an article about himself in the Home section that would portray him as a man of taste and discrimination. Instead, his loft and his lifestyle, which he shared with singer Dawn Bennett, were given the tongue-in-cheek treatment under the headline: "When Nothing but the Best Will Do."[1]

Davidson, who spent no more money renovating his living quarters than many of the well-to-do folks whose homes are lionized in the *Times*'s Thursday and Sunday design pages — the running ethnographic record of contemporary upper-middle-class lifestyle — made the unpardonable error of telling reporter Jane Geniesse how much he had paid for his stereo system, among other things. Like many people who have not been on intimate terms with affluence for very long, Davidson is in the habit of price-tagging his possessions. His 69-cent-per-bottle bargain Perrier, his $700 Armani suits from Barney's, his $27,000 cooperative loft and its $150,000 renovation, his sixteen $350-per-section sectionals, and his $11,000 best-of-class stereo. Martin J. Davidson wants the world to know how well he's done. "I live the American dream," he told Mrs. Geniesse, which includes, "being known as one of Barney's best customers."[2]

---

[1] Jane Geniesse, "When Nothing but the Best Will Do," *New York Times*, June 7, 1979, p. C1ff.
[2] Ibid.

Davidson even wants the U.S. Census Bureau's computer to know how well he has done. He is furious, in fact, that the 1980 census form did not have a box to check for people who live in cooperatives. "If someone looks at my census form they'll think I must be at the poverty level or lower."[3] No one who read the *Times* article about Martin Davidson would surmise that.

It is hard to remember when a "design" story provoked more outrage. Letters to the editor poured in. Andy Warhol once said that in our fast-paced media world no one could count on being a celebrity for more than fifteen minutes. Martin Davidson was notorious for weeks. "All the Martin Davidsons in New York," wrote one irate reader, "will sit home listening to their $11,000 stereos, while downtown, people go to jail because they ate a meal they couldn't pay for."[4] "How can one man embody so many of the ills afflicting our society today?"[5] asked another offended reader. "Thank you for your clever spoof," wrote a third reader. "I was almost convinced that two people as crass as Martin Davidson and Dawn Bennett could exist."[6] Davidson's consumption largesse was even memorialized by Russell Baker, the *Times*'s Pulitzer Prize–winning humorist, who devoted a whole column to him: "While simultaneously consuming yesterday's newspaper," wrote Baker, "I consumed an article about one Martin Davidson, a veritable Ajax of consumption. A man who wants to consume nothing but the best and does."[7] Counting, as usual, Davidson would later tell people, "I was mentioned in the *Times* on three different days."

Davidson, a self-made man whose motto is "I'm not taking it with me   5 and while I'm here I'm going to spend every stinking penny I make," couldn't understand why the *Times* had chosen to make fun of him rather than to glorify his 4,000-square-foot loft complete with bidet, Jacuzzi, professional exercise gear, pool table, pinball machine, sauna, two black-tile bathrooms, circular white Formica cooking island, status-stuffed collections of Steiff animals, pop art (including eleven Warhols), a sound system that could weaken the building's foundations if turned up full blast, and an air-conditioning system that can turn cigarette smoke, which both Davidson and Bennett abhor, into mountain dew — a loft that has everything Martin Davidson ever wanted in a home except a swimming pool and a squash court.

"People were objecting to my lifestyle," said Davidson. "It's almost as if there were a correlation between the fact that we spend so much on ourselves and other people are starving. No one yells when someone spends $250,000 for a chest of drawers at an auction," he complained. "I just read in the paper that someone paid $650,000 for a stupid stamp. Now it'll be put away in a vault and no one will ever see it."[8]

---

[3]Author's interview with Martin Davidson.
[4]Richard Moseson, "Letters: Crossroads of Decadence and Destitution," *New York Times*, June 14, 1979, p. A28.
[5]Letter to the Editor, *New York Times*, June 14, 1979, p. C9.
[6]Letter to the Editor, ibid.
[7]Russell Baker, "Observer: Incompleat Consumer," *New York Times*, June 9, 1979, p. 25.
[8]Author's interview with Martin Davidson.

But Dawn Bennett understood what made Davidson's consumption different. "It's not very fashionable to be an overt consumer and admit it,"[9] she said.

What Are Things For?

As anyone knows who has seen a house turned inside out at a yard sale, furnishing a home entails the acquisition of more objects than there are in a spring housewares catalog. With all the time, money, and space we devote to the acquisition, arrangement, and maintenance of these household possessions, it is curious that we know so little about our relationships to our possessions.

"It is extraordinary to discover that no one knows why people want goods," wrote British anthropologist Mary Douglas in *The World of Goods*.[10] Although no proven or agreed-upon theory of possessiveness in human beings has been arrived at, social scientists are coming up with new insights on our complicated relationships to things. Whether or not it is human nature to be acquisitive, it appears that our household goods have a more meaningful place in our lives than they have been given credit for. What comes across in a wide variety of research is that things matter enormously.

Our possessions give us a sense of security and stability. They make us feel in control. And the more we control an object, the more it is a part of us. If it's *not mine*, it's *not me*.[11] It would probably make sense for everyone on the block to share a lawn mower, but then no one would have control of it. If people are reluctant to share lawn mowers, it should not surprise us that family members are not willing to share TV sets. They want their own sets so they can watch what they please. Apparently, that was why a Chicago woman, furious with her boyfriend for switching from *The Thorn Birds* to basketball, stabbed him to death with a paring knife.[12]

Besides control, we use things to compete. In the late nineteenth century the Kwakiutl Indian chiefs of the Pacific Northwest made war with possessions.[13] Their culture was built on an extravagant festival called the "potlatch,"

10

[9]Author's interview with Dawn Bennett.

[10]Mary Douglas and Baron Isherwood, *The World of Goods* (New York: Basic Books, 1979), p. 15. A number of other social scientists have mentioned in recent works the lack of attention paid to the human relationship to possessions: See Coleman and Rainwater, *Social Standing*, p. 310. The authors observed that "the role of income in providing a wide range of rewards — consumption — has not received sufficient attention from sociologists." See Carl F. Graumann, "Psychology and the World of Things," *Journal of Phenomenological Psychology*, Vol. 4, 1974–75, pp. 389–404. Graumann accused the field of sociology of being thing-blind.

[11]Lita Furby, "Possessions: Toward a Theory of Their Meaning and Function Throughout the Life Cycle," in Paul B. Baltes (ed.), *Life-Span Development and Behavior*, Vol. 1 (New York: Academic Press, 1978), pp. 297–336.

[12]"'Touch That Dial and You're Dead,'" *New York Post*, March 30, 1983, p. 5.

[13]Ruth Benedict, *Patterns of Culture* (Boston: Houghton Mifflin [1934], 1959); Frederick V. Grunfeld, "Homecoming: The Story of Cultural Outrage," *Connoisseur*, February 1983, pp. 100–106; and Lewis Hyde, *The Gift* (New York: Vintage Books, [1979, 1980], 1983), pp. 25–39.

a word that means, roughly, to flatten with gifts. It was not the possession of riches that brought prestige, it was the distribution and destruction of goods. At winter ceremonials that took years to prepare for, rival chiefs would strive to outdo one another with displays of conspicuous waste, heaping on their guests thousands of spoons and blankets, hundreds of gold and silver bracelets, their precious dance masks and coppers (large shields that were their most valuable medium of exchange), and almost impoverishing themselves in the process.

Today our means of competition is the accumulation and display of symbols of status. Perhaps in Utopia there will be no status, but in this world, every human being is a status seeker on one level or another — and a status reader. "Every member of society," said French anthropologist Claude Lévi-Strauss, "must learn to distinguish his fellow men according to their mutual social status."[14] This discrimination satisfies human needs and has definite survival value. "Status symbols provide the cue that is used in order to discover the status of others, and, from this, the way in which others are to be treated," wrote Erving Goffman in his classic paper, "Symbols of Class Status."[15] Status affects who is invited to share "bed, board, and cult,"[16] said Mary Douglas. Whom we invite to dinner affects who marries whom, which then affects who inherits what, which affects whose children get a head start.

Today what counts is what you eat (gourmet is better than greasy spoon), what you fly (private jet is better than common carrier), what sports you play (sailing is better than bowling), where you matriculate, shop, and vacation, whom you associate with, how you eat (manners count), and most important, where you live. Blue Blood Estates or Hard Scrabble zip codes as one wizard of demographics calls them. He has figured out that "people tend to roost on the same branch as birds of a feather."[17] People also use status symbols to play net worth hide-and-seek. When *Forbes* profiled the 400 richest Americans,[18] its own in-house millionaire Malcolm Forbes refused to disclose his net worth but was delighted to drop clues telling about his status entertainments — his ballooning, his Fabergé egg hunts, his châteaux, and his high lifestyle. It is up to others to translate those obviously costly perks into dollars.

A high price tag isn't the only attribute that endows an object with status. Status can accrue to something because it's scarce — a one-of-a-kind artwork or a limited edition object. The latest hard-to-get item is Steuben's $27,500 bowl etched with tulips that will be produced in an edition of five — one per year for five years. "Only one bowl will bloom this year,"[19] is the headline

[14]Edmund Leach, *Claude Lévi-Strauss* (New York: Penguin Books, 1980), p. 39.

[15]Erving Goffman, "Symbols of Class Status," *British Journal of Sociology*, Vol. 2, December 1951, pp. 294–304.

[16]Douglas and Isherwood, *World of Goods*, p. 88.

[17]Michael J. Weiss, "By Their Numbers Ye Shall Know Them," *American Way*, February 1983, pp. 102–6 ff. "You tell me someone's zip code," said Jonathan Robbin, "and I can predict what they eat, drink, drive, buy, even think."

[18]"The Forbes 400," *Forbes*, September 13, 1982, pp. 99–186.

[19]Steuben Glass advertisement, *The New Yorker*, April 4, 1983, p. 3.

on the ad for it. Status is also found in objects made from naturally scarce materials: Hawaii's rare koa wood, lapis lazuli, or moon rock. And even if an object is neither expensive nor rare, status can rub off on something if it is favored by the right people, which explains why celebrities are used to promote coffee, cars, casinos, and credit cards.

If you've been associated with an object long enough you don't even have to retain ownership. Its glory will shine on you retroactively. Perhaps that is why a member of Swiss nobility is having two copies made of each of the Old Master paintings in his collection. This way, when he turns his castle into a museum, both his children can still have, so to speak, the complete collection, mnemonics of the pictures that have been in the family for centuries. And the most potent status symbol of all is not the object per se, but the *expertise* that is cultivated over time, such as the appreciation of food, wine, design, or art.

If an object reflects a person *accurately*, it's an index of status. But *symbols* of status are not always good indices of status. They are not official proof of rank in the same way a general's stars are. So clusters of symbols are better than isolated ones. Anyone with $525 to spare can buy one yard of the tiger-patterned silk velvet that Lee Radziwill used to cover her dining chair seats.[20] But one status yard does not a princess make. A taxi driver in Los Angeles gets a superior feeling from owning the same status-initialed luggage that many of her Beverly Hills fares own. "I have the same luggage you have," she tells them. "It blows their minds," she brags. But two status valises do not a glitterati make. Misrepresenting your social status isn't a crime, just "a presumption," said Goffman. Like wearing a $69 copy of a $1,000 watch that the mail-order catalog promises will make you "look like a count or countess on a commoner's salary."[21]

"Signs of status are important ingredients of self. But they do not exhaust all the meanings of objects for people," wrote sociologists Mihaly Csikszentmihalyi and Eugene Rochberg-Halton in *The Meaning of Things: Domestic Symbols of the Self*.[22] The study on which the book was based found that people cherished household objects not for their status-giving properties but especially because they were symbols of the self and one's connections to others.

The idea that possessions are symbols of self is not new. Many people have noticed that *having* is intricately tied up with *being*. "It is clear that between what a man calls *me* and what he simply calls *mine*, the line is difficult to draw," wrote William James in 1890.[23] "Every possession is an

[15]

[20]Paige Rense, "Lee Radziwill," *Celebrity Homes* (New York: Penguin Books, 1979), pp. 172–81.

[21]*Synchronics* catalog, Hanover, Pennsylvania, Fall 1982.

[22]Mihaly Csikszentmihalyi and Eugene Rochberg-Halton, *The Meaning of Things: Domestic Symbols of the Self* (New York: Cambridge University Press, 1981), p. 18.

[23]William James, *Principles of Psychology*, Vol. 1 (New York: Macmillan, 1890), p. 291.

extension of the self," said Georg Simmel in 1900.[24] "Humans tend to integrate their selves with objects," observed psychologist Ernest Beaglehole some thirty years later.[25] Eskimos used to *lick* new acquisitions to cement the person/object relationship.[26] We stamp our visual taste on our things making the totality resemble us. Indeed, theatrical scenic designers would be out of work if Blanche DuBois's boudoir could be furnished with the same props as Hedda Gabler's.

Csikszentmihalyi and Rochberg-Halton discovered that "things are cherished not because of the material comfort they provide but for the information they convey about the owner and his or her ties to others."[27] People didn't value things for their monetary worth, either. A battered toy, a musical instrument, a homemade quilt, they said, provide more meaning than expensive appliances which the respondents had plenty of. "What's amazing is how few of these things really make a difference when you get to the level of what is important in life,"[28] said Csikszentmihalyi. All those expensive furnishings "are required just to keep up with the neighbors or to keep up with what you expect your standard of living should be."

"How else should one relate to the Joneses if not by keeping up with them," 20
asked Mary Douglas provocatively.[29] The principle of reciprocity requires people to consume at the same level as one's friends.[30] If we accept hospitality, we have to offer it in return. And that takes the right equipment and the right setting. But we need things for more than "keeping level" with our friends. We human beings are not only toolmakers but symbol makers as well, and we use our possessions in the same way we use language — the quintessential symbol — to *communicate* with one another. According to Douglas, goods make the universe "more intelligible." They are more than messages to ourselves and others, they are "the hardware and the software . . . of an information system."[31] Possessions speak a language we all understand, and we pay close attention to the inflections, vernacular, and exclamations.

---

[24]Georg Simmel, *The Philosophy of Money*, trans. Tom Bottomore and David Frisby (Boston: Routledge & Kegan Paul, 1978), p. 331.

[25]Ernest Beaglehole, *Property: A Study in Social Psychology* (New York: Macmillan, 1932).

[26]Ibid., p. 134.

[27]Csikszentmihalyi and Rochberg-Halton, p. 239.

[28]Author's interview with Mihaly Csikszentmihalyi.

[29]Douglas and Isherwood, *World of Goods*, p. 125. Also see Jean Baudrillard, *For a Critique of the Political Economy of the Sign*, trans. Charles Levin (St. Louis, MO: Telos Press, 1981), p. 81. Said Baudrillard: "No one is free to live on raw roots and fresh water. . . . The vital minimum today . . . is the standard package. Beneath this level, you are an outcast." Two classic novels on consumption are (1) Georges Perec, *Les Choses* (New York: Grove Press, [1965], 1967). (2) J. K. Huysmans, *Against the Grain (A Rebours)* (New York: Dover Publications, [1931], 1969).

[30]Douglas and Isherwood, *World of Goods*, p. 124.

[31]Ibid., p. 72.

The young husband in the film *Diner* takes his things very seriously. How could his wife be so stupid as to file the Charlie Parker records with his rock 'n' roll records, he wants to know. What's the difference, she wants to know. What's the difference? How will he find them otherwise? Every record is sacred. Different ones remind him of different times in his life. His things *take* him back. Things can also *hold* you back. Perhaps that's why Bing Crosby's widow auctioned off 14,000 of her husband's possessions — including his bed. " 'I think my father's belongings have somehow affected her progress in life,' " said one of Bing's sons.[32] And things can tell you where you stand. Different goods are used to rank occasions and our guests. Costly sets of goods, especially china and porcelain, are "pure rank markers. . . . There will always be luxuries because rank must be marked," said Douglas.[33]

One of the pleasures of goods is "sharing names."[34] We size up people by their expertise in names — sports buffs can converse endlessly about hitters' batting averages, and design buffs want to know whether you speak sponge-ware, Palladio, Dansk, or Poggenpohl. All names are not equal. We use our special knowledge of them to show solidarity and exclude people.

In fact, the social function of possessions is like the social function of food. Variations in the quality of goods define situations as well as different times of day and seasons. We could survive on a minimum daily allotment of powdered protein mix or grains and berries. But we much prefer going marketing, making choices, learning new recipes. "Next to actually eating food, what devout gastronomes seem to enjoy most is talking about it, planning menus, and remembering meals past," observed food critic Mimi Sheraton.[35] But it's not only experts who thrive on variety. Menu monotony recently drove a Carlsbad, New Mexico, man to shoot the woman he was living with. She served him green beans once too often. "Wouldn't you be mad if you had to eat green beans all the time?" he said.[36] If every meal were the same, and if everyone dressed alike and furnished alike, all meanings in the culture would be wiped out.[37]

The furnishings of a home, the style of a house, and its landscape are all part of a system — a system of symbols. And every item in the system has meaning. Some objects have personal meanings, some have social meanings which change over time. People understand this instinctively and they desire things, not from some mindless greed, but because things are necessary to communicate with. They are the vocabulary of a sign language. To be without things is to be left out of the conversation. When we are "listening" to others we may not necessarily agree with what this person or that "says" with his or her decor, or we may misunderstand what is being said; and when we are

---

[32]Maria Wilhelm, "Things Aren't Rosy in the Crosby Clan as Kathryn Sells Bing's Things (and not for a Song)," *People*, May 31, 1982, pp. 31–33.

[33]Douglas and Isherwood, *World of Goods*, p. 118.

[34]Ibid., p. 75.

[35]Mimi Sheraton, "More on Joys of Dining Past," *New York Times*, April 9, 1983, p. 48.

[36]"Green Beans Stir Bad Blood," *New York Times*, March 26, 1983, p. 6.

[37]Douglas and Isherwood, *World of Goods*, p. 66.

doing the "talking" we may not be able to express ourselves as eloquently as we would like. But where there are possessions, there is always a discourse.

And what is truly remarkable is that we are able to comprehend and manipulate all the elements in this rich symbol system as well as we do — for surely the language of the home and its decor is one of the most complex languages in the world. But because of that it is also one of the richest and most expressive means of communication.

Decor as Symbol of Self

One aspect of personalization is the big I — Identity. Making distinctions between ourselves and others. "The self can only be known by the signs it gives off in communication," said Eugene Rochberg-Halton.[38] And the language of ornament and decoration communicates particularly well. Perhaps in the future we will be known by our computer communiqués or exotic brainwaves, but until then our rock gardens, tabletop compositions, refrigerator door collages, and other design language will have to do. The Nubian family in Africa with a steamship painted over the front door to indicate that someone in the house works in shipbuilding, and the Shotte family on Long Island who make a visual pun on their name with a rifle for a nameplate, are both decorating their homes to communicate "this is where our territory begins and this is who we are."

Even the most selfless people need a minimum package of identity equipment. One of Pope John Paul I's first acts as pontiff was to send for his own bed. "He didn't like sleeping in strange beds," explained a friend.[39] It hadn't arrived from Venice when he died suddenly.

Without familiar things we feel disoriented. Our identities flicker and fade like ailing light bulbs. "Returning each night to my silent, pictureless apartment, I would look in the bathroom mirror and wonder who I was," wrote D. M. Thomas, author of *The White Hotel*, recalling the sense of detachment he felt while living in a furnished apartment during a stint as author-in-residence at a Washington, D.C., university. "I missed familiar things, familiar ground that would have confirmed my identity."[40]

Wallpaper dealers wouldn't need fifty or sixty sample books filled with assorted geometrics, supergraphics, and peach clamshells on foil backgrounds if everyone were content to have the same roses climbing their walls. Chintz wouldn't come in forty flavors from strawberry to licorice, and

[38]Eugene Rochberg-Halton, "Where Is the Self: A Semiotic and Pragmatic Theory of Self and the Environment." Paper presented at the 1980 American Sociological Meeting, New York City, 1980, p. 3.

[39]Dora Jane Hamblin, "Brief Record of a Gentle Pope," *Life*, November 1978, p. 103.

[40]D. M. Thomas, "On Literary Celebrity," *The New York Times Magazine*, June 13, 1982, pp. 24–38, citation p. 27.

Robert Kennedy Jr.'s bride Emily wouldn't have trotted him around from store to store "for ten hours" looking for a china pattern[41] if the home wasn't an elaborate symbol system — as important for the messages it sends to residents and outsiders as for the functions it serves.

In the five-year-long University of Chicago study[42] into how modern Americans relate to their things, investigators Mihaly Csikszentmihalyi and Eugene Rochberg-Halton found that we all use possessions to stand for ourselves. "I learned that things can embody self," said Rochberg-Halton. "We create environments that are extensions of ourselves, that serve to tell us who we are, and act as role models for what we can become."[43] But what we cherish and what we use to stand for ourselves, the researchers admitted, seemed to be "scripted by the culture."[44] Even though the roles of men and women are no longer so tightly circumscribed, "it is remarkable how influential sex-stereotyped goals still remain."[45] Men and women "pay attention to different things in the same environment and value the same things for different reasons," said the authors.[46] Men and children cared for action things and tools; women and grandparents cared for objects of contemplation and things that reminded them of family. It was also found that meaning systems are passed down in families from mothers to daughters — not to sons.

Only children and old people cared for a piece of furniture because it was useful. For adults, a specific piece of furniture embodied experiences and memories, or was a symbol of self or family. Photographs which had the power to arouse emotions and preserve memories meant the most to grandparents and the least to children. Stereos were most important to the younger generation, because they provide for the most human and emotional of our needs — release, escape, and venting of emotion. And since music "seems to act as a modulator of emotions," it is particularly important in adolescence "when daily swings of mood are significantly greater than in the middle years and . . . later life."[47] Television sets were cherished more by men than women, more by children than grandparents, more by grandparents than parents. Plants had greater meaning for the lower middle class, and for women, standing for values, especially nurturance and "ecological consciousness."[48] "Plateware," the term used in the study to cover all eating and

[41]"Back Home Again in Indiana Emily Black Picks Up a Freighted Name: Mrs. Robert F. Kennedy, Jr.," *People*, April 12, 1982, pp. 121–23, citation p. 123.

[42]Eugene Rochberg-Halton, "Cultural Signs and Urban Adaptation: The Meaning of Cherished Household Possessions." Ph.D. dissertation, Department of Behavioral Science, Committee on Human Development, University of Chicago, August 1979; and Mihaly Csikszentmihalyi and Eugene Rochberg-Halton, *The Meaning of Things: Domestic Symbols of the Self* (New York: Cambridge University Press, 1981).

[43]Author's interview with Eugene Rochberg-Halton.

[44]Csikszentmihalyi and Rochberg-Halton, *Meaning of Things*, p. 105.

[45]Ibid., p. 112.

[46]Ibid., p. 106.

[47]Ibid., p. 72.

[48]Ibid., p. 79.

drinking utensils, was mentioned mostly by women. Of course, "plates" are the tools of the housewife's trade. In many cultures they are the legal possession of the women of the house.

The home is such an important vehicle for the expression of identity that one anthropologist believes "built environments"—houses and settlements—were originally developed to *"identify a group*—rather than to provide shelter."[49] But in contemporary Western society, the house more often identifies a person or a family instead of a group. To put no personal stamp on a home is almost pathological in our culture. Fear of attracting attention to themselves constrains people in crime-ridden areas from personalizing, lack of commitment restrains others, and insecurity about decorating skill inhibits still others. But for most people, painting some sort of self-portrait, decoratively, is doing what comes naturally.

All communications, of course, are transactions. The identity we express is subject to interpretation by others. Will it be positive or negative? David Berkowitz, the "Son of Sam" murderer, didn't win any points when it was discovered he had drawn a circle around a hole in the wall in his apartment and written "This is where I live."[50] A person who fails to keep up appearances is stigmatized.

READING THE TEXT

1. Summarize how, according to Kron, our possessions act as signs of our identity.

2. How do our living spaces work to create group identity?

3. Why did *New York Times* readers object to the consumption habits of Martin J. Davidson?

4. In your own words, explain how possessions give one a sense of "stability" (para. 10).

READING THE SIGNS

1. In a small group, discuss the brand names of possessions that each of you owns. Then interpret the significance of each brand. What do the brands say about each of you and about the group?

2. With your class, brainstorm factors other than possessions that can communicate a person's identity. Then write an essay in which you compare the relative value of possessions to your own sense of identity with the additional factors your class brainstormed.

3. Write an essay in which you argue for or against Kron's claim that "to put no personal stamp on a home is almost pathological in our culture" (para. 32).

[49]Amos Rapoport, "Identity and Environment," in James S. Duncan (ed.), *Housing and Identity: Cross-Cultural Perspectives* (London: Croom Helm, 1981), pp. 6–35, citation p. 18.

[50]Leonard Buder, "Berkowitz Is Described as 'Quiet' and as a Loner," *New York Times*, August 12, 1977, p. 10.

4. Analyze semiotically your own apartment or a room in your house, using Kron's essay as a critical framework. How do your possessions and furnishings act as signs of your identity? Alternately, conduct such an analysis of a friend's home.

5. **CONNECTING TEXTS**   Adopting Kron's essay as a critical framework, analyze the consumption behavior of the two families profiled in John Verdant's "The Ables vs. the Binges" (p. 152).

ANDREA CHANG

Teen "Haulers" Become a Fashion Force

> When teenaged girls rush home from the shopping mall to post YouTube videos of their latest purchases, you know that digitized consumption is a force to be considered. Called "hauling," this mixture of exhibitionism and commerce has not been missed by major marketers who, as Andrea Chang reports in this feature for the *Los Angeles Times*, "have begun reaching out to haulers, giving them free merchandise in the hopes that the girls will make haul videos in which they endorse the products." Talk about "buzz": There's nothing like letting your consumers do your marketing for you with television time costing so much these days. Andrea Chang is a reporter for the *Los Angeles Times*.

When 14-year-old Bethany Mota gets back from the mall, she eagerly models her latest finds for friends and family. And for tens of thousands more on YouTube.

The rising high school sophomore from Los Banos, Calif., is a "hauler," a term for tech-savvy young fashionistas who show off their purchases, or hauls, in homemade videos that they post online. Bethany started hauling about a year ago and now has more than 48,000 YouTube subscribers who tune in to watch her show off her favorite back-to-school outfits ("you don't want to wear heels and stuff, obviously"), big-volume mascara ("this is like my new obsession") and perfumes ("summer in a bottle right here!"). "You get to connect with girls around the world, and that's what reeled me in," said the doe-eyed, fresh-faced teen, who could pass for Kim Kardashian's younger sister. "YouTube videos, they're more personal and more real than a commercial on TV."

Hauling has become an Internet phenomenon over the last year or so, fueled by a mix of exhibitionism and voyeurism. As the shop-and-tell trend has grown, so has the influence of haulers themselves, usually teen girls or young women. A successful video can garner hundreds of thousands of views, which has boosted some haulers into so-called beauty gurus with huge fan bases.

Major retailers are watching too. Several, including JCPenney and Marshalls, have begun reaching out to haulers, giving them free merchandise in the hopes that the girls will make haul videos in which they endorse the products. Others, such as Forever 21 and Urban Outfitters, are holding haul video contests and offering gift cards and other prizes for the best hauls. "The bottom line is: It's marketing for less," said Eli Portnoy, a marketing expert and chief brand strategist of the Portnoy Group. "What better way to reach your customers than from what seems to be independent voices saying 'I love these products and I love these stores'? Instead of you promoting your products, they're doing it for you."

Bethany is one of them. In June, JCPenney flew her and five other haulers 5 from around the country to Texas and gave each girl gift cards worth $1,000 to shop the department store's back-to-school selection. After the shopping spree, the girls were required to record their own haul videos, which JCPenney posted on its Web site and on Facebook and YouTube. "It's the perfect marriage of two of Gen Y's favorite things: technology and shopping," said Mike Boylson, chief marketing officer at JCPenney. "Marketers have to realize that they're truly not in control. More and more, this idea of consumers as publishers is huge."

At the heart of the trend is the girls' bubbly charm, attractive looks, and somewhat ditzy personalities. "It's real girls that like fashion, rather than experts telling people what to wear," said Audrey Kitching, a fashion writer and model from Hollywood who was one of the haulers chosen by JCPenney. "It's more organic and not somebody who's getting paid to say 'wear this' or 'wear that.' " In a recent haul video about nail polish, Bethany begins with: "Hey, guys! So, first off, please excuse the hair. It's, like, really crazy." And in her seven-minute, 33-second video about her JCPenney haul, she uses the word "cute" 27 times — as in: "I also got this really cute blue T-shirt and it has some studded rhinestones on the shoulders. I think that's so, so cute!" As often as three times a week, Bethany sets up a video camera from her Paris-themed bedroom and records herself showing off her latest purchases. It takes about a day to film and edit a video, which she posts on YouTube under the user name Macbarbie07.

Her most-watched haul — on spring and summer fashions — has attracted more than 96,000 views. To protect her safety, Bethany's parents monitor her YouTube channel and comments, watch her videos, and forbid her from giving out personal information online. Other than that, they said they don't mind their daughter posing in flirty outfits for virtual strangers. "There's never closed doors or anything like that," said her mother, Tammy Mota. "I've never been concerned. I know how careful she is, and if anything suspicious comes, or someone tries to talk to her, she'll never do it."

Critics have decried the haul sensation as an indulgent display of excess by spoiled teenagers bragging about their latest splurges. Others say haul videos help teens do what they've always done — express themselves and share shopping finds with their girlfriends — but on a global scale. Hauling is one of the fastest-growing categories on YouTube, with more than 200,000 videos, said Anna Richardson, a spokeswoman for the Web site. And making videos can be lucrative: Haulers and other users who join YouTube's "partner" program can get a cut of the profits from ads that run with their videos. Hauling is, in fact, big business. Two of the most famous haulers are Elle and Blair Fowler, sisters from Tennessee who have leveraged their celebrity status on YouTube into growing empires. The girls have been featured in *Seventeen* and *Marie Claire* magazines, appeared on "Good Morning America," and hired an agent and a publicist to help field the many requests for interviews, product reviews and appearances they receive. That has made them among the most sought-after haulers by big-name companies. Elle, 22, and Blair, 17, were recently featured in back-to-school campaigns for Marshalls and Sears, are creating a makeup collection for Los Angeles–based Nyx Cosmetics and are teaming with Forever 21 to host a haul video contest on the cheap chic retailer's Web site this month. "The brand exposure is huge," said Kirstin Nagle, marketing manager at Los Angeles–based Forever 21. "That's what makes it exciting for us."

Retail executives acknowledged that by courting haulers, they're shifting some marketing power to consumers — and to their opinions, both good and bad. "It's a two-edged sword — it works both ways," said JCPenney's Boylson. "There's nowhere to hide. You can't control what they say or do, and you really have to learn to roll with it."

These days, the department store chain has employees who monitor social media sites for comments on JCPenney's merchandise; if the opinions are overwhelmingly negative the company may take action to improve the item or stop stocking it, he said. 10

But as retailers increasingly get involved with haulers, especially as they lavish free swag and even compensation for videos, the line between a third-party review and paid advertising is becoming blurred. Some industry experts have warned that viewers could become disillusioned with haulers if they come across as shills for big-name corporations.

Bethany, for instance, has received free Rimmel cosmetics and Sigma makeup brushes, plus a hair dryer from beauty Web site Folica.com. Some of the companies gave her extra products to give to her viewers.

She said that about 90 percent of her reviews are positive but said that the vast majority of her videos are based on items she purchased on her own and that she has never accepted money from a retailer for making a video. When she does receive freebies, she discloses them under Federal Trade Commission rules.

"I don't say yes to every company because I don't want to recommend a product to my viewers if I don't believe in it," she said. "I don't want to lie to my subscribers, so I'm really honest about my reviews and stuff."

READING THE TEXT

1. According to Chang, what are the motivations behind the hauling trend, for both the haulers themselves and their audience?

2. What has been retailers' response to hauling?

3. What criticisms have been raised about hauling, according to the article?

4. In what ways has hauling become "big business" (para. 8)?

READING THE SIGNS

1. **CONNECTING TEXTS** In an essay, support, refute, or complicate the contention that hauling is "an indulgent display of excess by spoiled teenagers bragging about their latest splurges" (para. 8). To develop your ideas, consult Laurence Shames, "The More Factor" (p. 90), and Joan Kron, "The Semiotics of Home Decor" (p. 128).

2. In class, conduct a debate on whether haulers are "shills" (para. 11) for big business or, rather, innocent expressions of teenagers' enjoyment of fashion. To develop your team's argument, consult some hauling Web sites and analyze how the haulers present themselves and their acquisitions. In addition, you might interview some haulers to determine their motivations and assess their experiences.

3. **CONNECTING TEXTS** Write an essay in which you respond to the contention that haulers are simply being manipulated by marketers for "free" or almost free advertising. You can compare haulers' activities with the trend of prominently wearing brand-name clothing for the image value of the brand, or even carrying a shopping bag with a prominent store logo. To develop your ideas, consult Thomas Hine, "What's in a Package" (p. 118).

4. According to Bethany, "YouTube videos, they're more personal and more real than a commercial on TV" (para. 2). Look up some hauling or other YouTube videos and write an essay in which you compare the conventions of commercials and YouTube videos. Do you agree or disagree with Bethany? Why or why not?

S. CRAIG WATKINS

Fast Entertainment and Multitasking in an Always-On World

Thanks to digital technology, a veritable universe of entertainment is now available to us whenever and wherever we want it. S. Craig Watkins, in this excerpt from his book *The Young and the Digital* (2009), calls this cornucopia of always-on diversion "fast entertainment," focusing here on the multitasking ways of its youthful consumers. But, Watkins warns, "Like fast food, fast entertainment is easy to get, all around us, and typically cheap, but not always good for you." Something to keep in mind while studying for finals. S. Craig Watkins is a professor at the University of Texas at Austin, where he teaches in the departments of Radio-Television-Film, Sociology, and the Center for African and African American Studies. His previous books include *Hip Hop Matters* (2005) and *Representing: Hip Hop Culture and the Production of Black Cinema* (1998).

> For the younger generation of multitaskers, the great electronic din is an expected part of everyday life. And given what neuroscience and anecdotal evidence have shown us, this state of constant intentional self-distraction could well be of profound detriment to individual and cultural well-being.
> — CHRISTINE ROSEN, Senior Editor of *The New Atlantis*[1]

Laptop computers, mobile phones, and iPods deliver a vast assortment of digital media content in unprecedented speed — now! Today, we can view video clips, listen to our favorite music downloads, squeeze in a game, access user-generated content, or just about anything else in smaller and quicker doses, thus making these digital delights all-pervading and irresistible. A 2007 *Wired* magazine cover story titled "Snack Culture" celebrates the rise of what it calls bite-size entertainment and the emergent world of one-minute media. "We now devour our pop culture," writes Nancy Miller, "the same way we enjoy candy and chips — in conveniently packaged bite-size nuggets made to be munched easily with increased frequency and maximum speed."[2] *Wired* calls it snack culture. I call it fast entertainment — this ever-widening menu of media content that we can consume easily and on the go.

No matter where we are, fast entertainment is generally just a click away. I liken the efficient delivery of digital media content to another staple in the

[1]Christine Rosen, "The Myth of Multitasking," *New Atlantis* no. 20 (Spring 2008): 105–10.
[2]Nancy Miller, "Minifesto for a New Age," *Wired*, March 2007.

daily American diet: fast food. Like fast food, fast entertainment is easy to get, all around us, and typically cheap, but not always good for you.

It is hard to know which came first — our appetite for speedy entertainment or the widespread manufacturing and aggressive marketing of it. Mobile technologies are ideal platforms for delivering bite-size media easily and effectively. For much of its early life, fast entertainment was the primary domain of technology companies, Silicon Valley start-ups, and Web entrepreneurs. Known for its user-generated content, a major part of YouTube's success can also be attributed to the creation of a space that supplies an endless stream of short video clips that complement our desire to consume a lot very quickly. Yahoo! is also a favorite online destination to grab a quick video clip, music playlist, or game. Social-network sites allow users to share a wide range of content with their fellow users casually and throughout the day. Come across a funny video and send it to your Facebook friends. Discover a cool new underground hip-hop band and spread the word through MySpace. Nowhere is the hegemony of fast entertainment more evident than in the rise of Apple's iTunes Store, one of the most prolific platforms for delivering digital media content.

In his book *The Perfect Thing: How the iPod Shuffles Commerce, Culture, and Coolness, Newsweek* chief technology correspondent Steven Levy explains how the music industry insiders dismissed the idea of selling digital downloads. Apple's CEO, Steve Jobs, told Levy, "When we first approached the labels, the online music business was a disaster. Nobody had ever sold a song for ninety-nine cents. Nobody ever really sold a *song*."[3] When Apple launched the iTunes Store in 2003, the service developed a reputation for delivering digital music downloads quickly, reliably, legally, and cheaply. From day one the iTunes Store was a huge success, reportedly selling 275,000 downloads in its first eighteen hours of operation. By day five, the number of downloads reached one million. In six short years, iTunes went from being nonexistent to surpassing the retail behemoth, Walmart, to become the number one music retailer in the United States.

In 2005 the iTunes Store began offering downloads of music videos and popular television programs for the iPod. Soon after that the store expanded to include movies, podcasts, audiobooks, and games, among other things. Apple's iPhone has been an even bigger hit and distributor of fast entertainment. In just nine months iPhone users downloaded more than one billion applications, many from categories like games, music, and entertainment. Apple's iPod and iPhone made it convenient and cool to carry our entire inventory of media and entertainment in our pocket. No matter if you are at home or on the road, access to your media entertainment library is just a touch of a button away. Technology companies such as YouTube, Yahoo!, and Apple were among the first to superserve our desire to quickly and constantly consume media. After

[3]Steven Levy, *The Perfect Thing: How the iPod Shuffles Commerce, Culture, and Coolness* (New York: Simon & Schuster, 2006), 135.

realizing our desire to consume content on the go and in smaller bites, the old media guard is responding.

From the big music labels to the network television industry, the major media companies are investing, strategically and financially, in fast entertainment by offering up their own versions of bite-size media. In 2007 Sony Corporation and its production studio, Sony Pictures Television, tossed its hat in the fast entertainment ring. The studio announced that it would begin sifting through its massive inventory to produce three-to-five-minute versions of programs that once filled the thirty-minute and hour-length programming slots in the primetime schedule. Sony executives call these tiny TV episodes minisodes. According to the studio, minisodes are not clips but rather full episodes containing a discernible narrative structure consisting of a beginning, middle, and end. The initial roster of miniature programs included old television series like *Charlie's Angels*, *T.J. Hooker*, and *Starsky & Hutch*.

Sony executives characterize the minisodes as campy and fun, but the decision to produce them is a serious response to how young people enjoy their media. In many ways, the creation of three-to-five-minute episodes are influenced by a video-clip culture that is a staple in the online experiences of many young people. From Lime Wire to BitTorrent, the adoption of file-sharing platforms not only alters how the young and the digital consume media content; it also reflects a greater interest on their part to manage, share, and engage content.

One of the more intriguing paradoxes of today's digital media environment is that we consume more and less at the same time. How is this possible? The rise of YouTube, founded in February 2005 by Chad Hurley and Steve Chen, is a great illustration. They launched the video file-sharing site to empower users of social media to do with videos what they were doing with photos — create, manage, and share them with peers. You name it — music videos, sports highlights, news segments, political speeches, user-generated content, clips from television and film — and YouTube users share it. According to comScore, "Americans viewed more than 11.4 billion videos for a total duration of 558 million hours during the month of July 2008."[4] Five billion, or 44 percent, of the videos were watched on YouTube. More precisely, 91 million viewers watched a YouTube video, which averages out to about fifty-five videos per person. The average length of a video watched in July 2008: 2.9 minutes. In short, Americans watched a ton of online videos, the vast majority of them short clips. In the digital media age, more equals less.

In addition to consuming less of more, we are constantly consuming. We have evolved from a culture of instant gratification to one of constant gratification. Fast entertainment encourages an insatiable desire to be entertained no matter where we are (at work) or what we are doing (driving a car). While the scientific merits of Internet addiction are still being measured, analyzed, and assessed, one thing is undeniable: the desire for fast entertainment is widespread and voracious. We not only want our media content now, we expect it

[4]*YouTube Draws 5 Billion U.S. Online Video Views in July 2008* (Reston, VA: comScore Media Metrix, September 10, 2008), www.comscore.com/press/release.asp?press = 2444.

now. Not that long ago, consuming media on the go was a luxury. Today, it is a standard feature of daily life.

In many ways, the social- and mobile-media lifestyle represents a new ₁₀ cultural ethos and a profound shift in how we consume media — in smaller and steadier portions and on smaller and more mobile screens. Along with changing how we consume media, fast entertainment changes where we consume media. Two developments defined the post-war boom Americans experienced starting around the 1950s: a rapid increase in home ownership and a bustling consumer economy. By the 1950s Americans were furnishing their new homes with all kinds of appliances that helped to establish a more modern and socially mobile lifestyle. Beginning with the radio, the phonograph, and then the television, Americans also filled their homes with media. Over the next half century, Americans participated in a flourishing home-centered media consumer culture that redefined leisure and household life.

Not that long ago we typically left our homes to purchase a wide array of media — music, books, magazines, videocassettes, games, DVDs — and then returned home to enjoy it. Today, however, the reverse is increasingly more common. We collect content from the comfort and convenience of our home, via digital downloads and peer-to-peer networks, to take with us when we leave our home. Throughout the last two decades of the twentieth century, Americans turned their homes into what media technology professor Jorge Schement calls the wired castle. Our homes became the ultimate leisure space. But in an always-on world, any place can be a good place to grab a quick bite of entertainment.

Despite all the euphoria over iTunes, iPods, iPhones, Webisodes, minisodes, minigames, and one-minute media, is the ability to be entertained constantly and no matter where you are really a good thing?

Young people are media rich. They own music players, computers, mobile phones, TVs, and game consoles. Young people's media environment is like a kid who wakes up one day and finds himself in a candy store. Surrounded by so many tasty options, what does he do? Naturally, he devours as much of it as he can, any way that he can. And that is essentially what we are seeing young people do with media. Immersed in a world of media, they use as much of it as they can, any way that they can. Innovative as ever, the one sure way for young people to use all of the media and technology they own is to use it simultaneously. One study, for example, found that American youth report spending about six hours a day with media. If you include the simultaneous use of media, that figure grows to about eight hours a day. Communication scholars refer to this as media multitasking.

We all media multitask. As I work on this chapter, my e-mail box, music player, photo application, and several tabs on my two favorite browsers are all open on my computer screen. But the young and the digital are widely viewed as masterful multitaskers, capable of managing several technologies, screens, and conversations fluidly and simultaneously. They multitask habitually and according to many observers, they also do it instinctively.

Donald F. Roberts, a Stanford University communications professor, has   15
studied the media behaviors of children and adolescents for more than thirty
years. Roberts believes that adolescents' multitasking ways began to really take
shape as the media in their homes migrated into their bedrooms. With the use
of ethnographic techniques, time diaries, and surveys, researchers began building more nuanced portraits of the media environment in American homes in the
1970s. A 1972 study of southern California sixth graders found that 6 percent of
the sample had a television in their bedrooms.[5] Since then, the flow of media
into children's bedrooms has continued at a steady clip. In his study of media use
by youth, Roberts and his colleagues found that no matter if they were especially
young, ages two to seven, or older, ages eleven to fourteen, kids in America access
a lot of media from their bedrooms.[6]

At least a third of young children, for example, can watch television or listen
to music from their own bedroom. Similarly, three-quarters of older children
are able to watch TV or play a videogame from the comforts of their bedroom.[7]
By the year 2000, about 20 percent of older youth, ages twelve to eighteen, were
accessing computers from their bedrooms. Assessing the state of young people's
media environment by the start of the new millennium, Roberts writes, "Compared with even a few years ago, the sheer numbers of children and adolescents
possessing personal media is remarkable."[8] The movement of media into children's bedrooms creates the context for more frequent, intense, unsupervised,
and in the view of some researchers, unhealthy media behaviors.

Until recently the data on media multitasking was extremely limited. How
much do young people media multitask? According to a 2006 study by the Kaiser
Family Foundation, a lot.

The San Mateo, California–based research unit surveyed a national cross-
section of 2,032 school-age kids ages eight to eighteen. In addition, Kaiser analyzed
data from a self-selected subsample of 694 respondents who completed a seven-
day diary of their media use. Here are some of the study's findings. Children and
teenagers spend at least a quarter of their time with multiple media.[9] On a typical day, Kaiser reports, eight in ten school-age children media multitask. Predictably, young people do a lot of their multitasking when they are using a computer.
Older children, ages fourteen to eighteen, multitask more, but by the age of ten,
their desire to multitask is strong. Young multitaskers tend to use other media—
such as television or music—while on the computer. Even when using the computer is the only activity, it is common for young people to shuffle back and forth

[5]J. Lyle and H. R. Hoffman, "Children's Use of Television and Other Media," in E. A.
Rubinstein, G. A. Comstock, and J. P. Murray, eds., *Television and Social Behavior*, vol. 4, *Television in Day-to-Day Life: Patterns and Use* (Washington, DC: U.S. Government Printing Office,
1972): 129–256.

[6]Roberts and Foehr, *Kids and Media in America*, 42–48.

[7]Ibid., 42–43.

[8]Ibid., 42.

[9]For a detailed assessment of media multitasking among young people, see Foehr, *Media
Multitasking Among American Youth*.

between instant messaging, their favorite Web sites, online videos, and games, all while managing a wealth of digital content such as photos and music files.

Tweens and teens are not the only ones multitasking their media. Our surveys and in-depth conversations show that college students are avid users of multiple media too. They multitask with just about every media they use — the Internet, music, television, and books and magazines. A decisive majority, 95 percent, listen to music either most or some of the time when using the computer. Seventy-two percent of our survey respondents said they watch television most or some of the time when using a computer is their primary activity. And when television is the primary activity, 81 percent of our respondents said they use a computer either most or some of the time. That is what Justin, a twenty-one-year-old psychology major, does.

"I multitask the most with the computer and television," Justin explained.   20
When there are commercials he usually goes online. "In that gap of time, I am normally on instant messenger talking to friends."

Twenty-one-year-old Andrea, an advertising major, uses television and the Internet at the same time too. "For me, the television works as background noise and the Internet allows me to be connected at all times," she said. When she gets bored with television, her computer is never too far away. Different media require different cognitive loads. For example, the load needed to listen to music is considered less than the cognitive resources needed to read a book. One thing is consistently clear in our research: among college students, using one media almost always means interacting with other media too.

Multitasking media habits are formed relatively early and right around the time young teens begin to develop their own peer networks, media interests, and greater independence from their parents. Among the young people we met, media multitasking is widely accepted as a fact of everyday life. Johnson, a nineteen-year-old, summed up multitasking this way: "I don't really think about it. It's just something that I've always done." Twenty-two-year-old Justine's multitasking skills are at once typical and amazing. "At one time I can be banking, paying bills, checking my e-mail, Facebooking, e-mailing my parents, talking online to my friends, checking the *TV Guide* on the Internet, and researching possible graduate schools," she said. As one young woman put it when referring to her generation, "Multitasking is easy and natural for us."

She's right. Multitasking for the young and the digital is easy and it certainly appears natural. But a growing body of evidence provokes the question, is media multitasking effective? More important, is it healthy?

When we asked young people why they multitask, the response was consistent: to accomplish more things efficiently. Twenty-two-year-old Brandon said, "I would never get anything done if I did not multitask." Most of us, in fact, multitask as a way to more effectively manage our time. And yet, even as humans continue managing multiple screens, media, and tasks simultaneously, cutting-edge brain research is beginning to confirm what some say is obvious: doing several things at once actually reduces task efficiency and proficiency. There is growing evidence that multitasking may not only slow down the completion of tasks but may also impair our performance. Addressing our incessant desire to multitask in a piece that appears in the *Atlantic*, Walter Kirn writes, "The great irony of multitasking — that its overall goal, getting more done in less time, turns out to be chimerical."[10]

In 2007 a team of psychology professors working from the Human Information Processing Laboratory at Vanderbilt University conducted a series of test trials to assess the brain's capacity to perform multiple tasks. For years brain specialists have suspected that the brain contains a bottleneck function that keeps us from concentrating on two different things at once. Dr. René Marois, one of the principal investigators from the Vanderbilt lab, focuses on the neural basis of attention and information processing in the human brain. More precisely, Marois and his colleagues seek to more fully understand why humans appear unable to execute more than one mental task at a time. Using functional magnetic resonance imaging (fMRI) of the brain, Marois and his colleagues identified what doctors believe is the mechanism that prohibits humans from processing two or more things at the same time, the central bottleneck of information processing.

To determine what happens when we ask our brain to execute two tasks at the same time, the Vanderbilt researchers conducted dual-task trials.[11] In the first task participants were instructed to touch the appropriate button in response to a sound stimulus. In the second task participants were asked to select the appropriate vocal response to a visual stimulus. Compared to the complex information processing that takes place daily, each task in the trials is easy to perform. Hear a sound, push a particular button. See an image, utter a specific word. Easy, right? But the Vanderbilt team made things more interesting and challenging by varying the time interval in between these two simple tasks. In some instances participants were given 300 milliseconds in between tasks, while others were allotted more time, on average about 1560 milliseconds.

Among the test subjects with very little time in between the first and second tasks, there was a statistically significant delay in executing the second tasks. The experiments along with the brain scanning data from the fMRI provide neural evidence of what researchers call dual-task interference. That is, when we try to process two pieces of information simultaneously, a traffic jam ensues in the brain. Conversely, among the subjects allotted more time in between each task, there was no significant delay in their execution of the second task. In addition to executing the trial experiments more efficiently, the subjects with a longer interval between tasks were more likely to push

25

[10]Walter Kirn, "The Autumn of the Multitaskers," *Atlantic*, November 2007, www .theatlantic.com/doc/200711/multitasking.

[11]Paul E. Dux et al., "Isolation of a Central Bottleneck of Information Processing with Time-Resolved fMRI," *Neuron* 52 (December 21, 2006): 1109–20.

the correct button or execute the right vocal response. In short, subjects with more time in between tasks were much more efficient and proficient. Our brains, it turns out, are not wired to process dual information simultaneously. Results of the study were published in the December 2007 issue of the medical journal *Neuron*.

In the summary section of the peer-reviewed article, the Vanderbilt researchers write, "When humans attempt to perform two tasks at once, execution of the first task usually leads to postponement of the second one." The results of the trial experiments, the doctors maintain, "suggest that a neural network of frontal lobe areas acts as a central bottleneck of information processing that severely limits our ability to multitask."[12]

The significance of these findings extend well beyond medical labs and scientific journals. Multitasking has real-life implications both for our brains and our world. Think about how frequently we multitask throughout the day. In some situations multitasking — say, responding to e-mails while eating lunch — may be quite useful in managing a busy day. In other situations multitasking may be inappropriate and even fatal. That was certainly the case on September 20, 2008, when twenty-five people were killed after Metrolink III crashed head-on with an oncoming Union Pacific freight train in Chatsworth, California. It was the worst California train disaster in fifty years. An investigation revealed that, seconds before the crash, the Metrolink engineer at the helm of the train was sending and receiving text messages. Concentrating on his phone messages meant that he could not focus on his path and a series of warning signals that would have almost certainly prevented the accident.

At this point and time there are as many questions as there are answers 30 when it comes to understanding the neurological implications of multitasking. For instance, some brain specialists believe that constant multitasking may be stretching our neural capabilities beyond their outer limits and subtly changing the machinations of our brain. Studies show that certain regions of the human brain are wired to process information, whereas other regions facilitate our ability to recall information. There is growing speculation in the medical community that young multitaskers may be conditioning their brains to quickly access, manage, and process information while underdeveloping the neural ability to recall and understand the information that they find.

Popular notions of media multitasking are misleading. The person using a computer while watching television and responding to text messages on their phone actually uses one screen at a time. Multitasking involves switching one's attention back and forth from one platform to another. In reality, the issue media multitasking raises is not simultaneous media use per se, but rather the ability of humans to pay attention in an always-on, always-connected digital-media environment. Underscoring this very issue, Christine Rosen, senior editor of the *New Atlantis*, writes, "When we talk about

[12]Ibid., 1109.

multitasking, we are really talking about attention: the art of paying attention, the ability to shift our attention, and, more broadly, to exercise judgment about what objects are worthy of our attention."[13]

Now that anytime, anywhere technology and fast entertainment are pervasive parts of our cultural environment, deciding what to pay attention to is more challenging than ever. Linda Stone, a communication technology thought leader and consultant, believes that the constant efforts by humans to manage our time — a main reason we multitask — should be accompanied by an equally zealous effort to better manage our attention. In an age of multiplying screens, constant connections, and content overload, Stone, a former Apple researcher, believes that humans suffer severe lapses in attention. She even has a name for this particular state of being: continuous partial attention, or CPA. Whether or not humans are genuinely addicted to the Web is still a major source of debate, but one thing is undeniable — managing our attention in a world of anytime, anywhere technology is one of the great challenges of modern life.

Stone makes a distinction between multitasking and CPA. With multitasking, she maintains, "we are motivated by a desire to be more productive and more efficient."[14] We multitask to save time. Conversely, Stone writes, "we pay continuous partial attention in an effort NOT TO MISS ANYTHING." She adds that CPA "is an always-on, anywhere, anytime, anyplace behavior that involves an artificial sense of constant crisis. We are always in high alert when we pay continuous partial attention."[15] CPA describes a familiar yet relatively recent state of being — the constantly tethered to technology lifestyle. No matter if it's sending a text message, responding to e-mails, tagging the latest batch of pictures posted by a friend online, or downloading the latest application for your cool new phone, the digital world is a busy world. The nonstop access to content and comrades via smaller and more mobile screens keeps us on constant alert. Meanwhile, our attention stays on the move, constantly shifting from one task to the next, one conversation to the next, one screen to the next.

Whereas CPA is an increasingly normal state of being, it is not a very healthy state of being. As a result of CPA, Stone argues that "in a 24/7, always-on world, continuous partial attention used as our dominant attention mode contributes to a feeling of [being overwhelmed], over-stimulation and to a sense of being unfulfilled."[16]

Along with understanding the neurological implications of multitasking, 35 we need to understand the sociological implications too. Millions of people talking on their phones while driving make the roads less safe. Multitasking while doing homework, a common behavior these days, can contribute to

[13]Rosen, "Myth of Multitasking."
[14]http://continuouspartialattention.jot.com/WikiHome.
[15]Ibid.
[16]Ibid.

poor academic performance. For robust multitaskers like the young and the digital the stakes are even higher, the outcomes potentially more profound. As Rosen notes, "For the younger generation of multitaskers, the great electronic din" is a common aspect of life. Rosen notes, however, that "when people do their work only in the 'interstices of their mind-wandering,' with crumbs of attention rationed out among many competing tasks, their culture may gain in information, but it will surely weaken in wisdom."[17]

READING THE TEXT

1. In your own words, what do the terms "fast entertainment" and "snack culture" (para. 1) mean?

2. What does Watkins mean by saying "In the digital media age, more equals less" (para. 8)?

3. Summarize the results of the scientific studies of the brain's ability to handle multiple tasks simultaneously.

4. What does the term "continuous partial attention" mean, according to the article, and why is it "not a very healthy state of being" (paras. 32–34)?

READING THE SIGNS

1. In an essay, write your own response to Watkins's question: "Is the ability to be entertained constantly and no matter where you are really a good thing?" (para. 12).

2. In your journal, explore your own ability to multitask. For you, is multitasking "a fact of everyday life" (para. 22) that makes completing daily activities more efficient? Or do you tend to forgo multitasking, preferring to concentrate on one activity at a time? How do you explain your behavioral choices?

3. Write an argumentative essay that supports, refutes, or complicates Watkins's quote from editor Christine Rosen: "When people do their work only . . . with crumbs of attention rationed out among many competing tasks, their culture may gain in information, but it will surely weaken in wisdom" (para. 35).

4. **CONNECTING TEXTS** In an essay, discuss the extent to which University of Maryland students (see "Students Addicted to Social Media," p. 483) who participated in a research study on social media are indeed "addicted" to their electronic toys.

5. **CONNECTING TEXTS** Watkins claims that "we have evolved from a culture of instant gratification to one of constant gratification" (para. 9). Drawing upon Laurence Shames's "The More Factor" (p. 90), write an essay analyzing whether "consuming media on the go" is a twenty-first century extension of "the hunger for more."

[17]Rosen, "Myth of Multitasking."

JOHN VERDANT
The Ables vs. the Binges

In a world of conspicuous consumption, where consumerism has become the foundation for our social values and consciousness, some people are fighting back. From "freecyclers," who Dumpster dive and freely exchange unwanted goods at designated drop-off sites, to anti-consumers who take vows of nonconsumption, some Americans are seeking to escape the confines of a consumerist mythology. Web sites like verdant.net provide guidance for the anti-consumerist rebel, and in this fictional narrative of two families — the hyper-consuming Binges and the careful-consuming Ables — the editors at verdant .net provide a parable for our times. John Verdant is the founder of verdant.net, a Web site devoted to "Ideas and shared solutions for sustainable & low cost green living and economic survival."

Two families — each having the same income and basic housing situation in the same community — can be used to illustrate the negative effects of consumerism and the healthy effects of actively avoiding it. This is not a study of good and evil, merely of behavior and its consequences. One family, the Ables, makes careful decisions about their economic and social activities and thus are working for their own self-preservation. Even while spending little and saving much, they can live well and enjoy their surroundings while they strengthen their community and thus the nation. The other family, the Binges, blindly goes on its way leaving a trail of social and spiritual destruction in its wake. They consume and spend and go deeper into debt. Things just happen to them, life seems out of control, because, for them, it is.

The Able family maintains a "wish list" of things that they decide they need in their home. Often the items on the list are crossed off as a substitute is found or a different way of doing things is discovered or they just decide that the novelty is not worth the price both in money and the before-tax time needed to earn it. If a household item breaks, a repair is made. If this is not possible or a replacement is not found from alternate sources such as second-hand stores, garage sales or Craigslist, they then research the purchase of a new item.

Research means using the Internet or personal recommendations from friends. *Consumer Reports* magazine back issues are consulted at the local library. The Ables actually subscribe to the magazine in the library's name: this way they get to read it and so does the community. Advertising is a sign that the item probably is of lesser quality — otherwise, why spend money touting it?

These researched items are purchased, where possible, from local small businesses whose owners have a stake in their community, living near or in it and treating it with respect, rather than just as a "market." The items that the Ables buy may cost more short-term but pay for themselves many times over in durability and the pleasure that they provide, to say nothing of potential resale value.

Domestic and local manufacturers and food growers are favored, helping   5 to keep money in the local and national economy and assuring that the items are made under U.S. environmental regulations. Buying organic produce grown nearby assures local food security and keeps the landscape nearby in farms and ranches rather than malls or subdivisions.

When they decide on a purchase, the Ables pay the local merchants in cash unless they choose to use a credit card to get a warranty extension or to buy something unavailable locally. Paying by cash or check saves the merchant the 1.5% to 4% percentage fee they pay to the credit card company on the purchase plus the per transaction fee they have to pay their bank. Sometimes Lorna will ask them to split the savings with her on more expensive items bought for cash.

Michael Able often researches his purchases online but he never buys this way; instead he calls the vendor's 800 number or goes to the retail outlet, because no matter what the Web site says, no matter what gimmicky security software they tout, he just doesn't trust it. Besides, he enjoys talking with people, asking about the product and their working situation. A few 800 numbers recently have been answered by people in India who work for slave wages. He asks them to hold on and puts the phone down, then walks away for five minutes or so and abandons the company for good. For the same reasons no one in the family has ever used an ATM card — instead they make face to face contact with the bank tellers, who are their neighbors.

The new items the Ables buy are treated as though they have to last a lifetime. For example, metal tools are carefully oiled; instructions, warranties, and receipts are filed alphabetically in a flex folder by store name. If an item is later sold or traded, having all the paperwork enhances its value. Any item that does fail gets returned to the store where it was bought. The Ables are merciless when it comes to this. If something fails, they take it back. If they don't need the item, they take it back. If they bought too much of something, they take it back. Before they buy anything, they check to make sure that there is no restocking fee. Sears is actually a pretty good store to shop in as their Craftsman line of U.S.-made tools is returnable if they break. Because of this, it is the only large corporate store that the Ables patronize and only for garden or other tools which they often wear out and then replace for free.

The Ables treat every economic transaction as an opportunity to exercise their social convictions. They will point out to local merchants that aren't known to them why they are deliberately shopping in the local community and boycotting large stores and that they will only buy quality merchandise. Shop owners embrace these convictions and often converse with Michael or Lorna and soon become their friends. When they have no alternative but to patronize large chain stores, they will ask the employees in the checkout line how they are treated, whether they have health benefits, and if they are able to support themselves or their families. Often, other customers and sometimes nervous managers get involved in the discussion. The Ables have referred bright, pleasant people that they have met this way to several local businesses where they have become valuable employees. Once Lorna was told by an officious manager of a large national retail chain that employees were not allowed to discuss details of their employment with members of the public, and she had to stop asking questions. That's all it took for her to basically cause a riot in the checkout line. One employee quit on the spot and took off his apron, throwing it on the ground at the feet of the corporate clown manager; customers were siding with Lorna and were shouting at the manager and vowing never to come back, and other employees were giggling and hiding their smiles.

The Ables buy organic food from nearby farms and an ever-increasing   10 amount raised in their own backyard. They hang out in the garden a lot. It took a while to get the knowledge how to build up the soil and grow things in their climate, but now they have more fruit and seasonal vegetables than they can ever eat. They subscribe to a Community Agriculture Farm Service that delivers a box of in-season fresh local produce to their door. This does cost slightly more than buying cheap industrial agriculture produce from their local Safeway, but they are receiving far more nutrition and satisfaction from it and are saving on potential future medical bills stemming from the long-term effects of pesticides, herbicides, fungicides, additives, preservatives and chemicals used in packaging.

As Lorna, a Ph.D. microbiologist, puts it, "One pesticide-induced lymphoma or breast cancer will eat up the savings from a lifetime of buying cheap food."

Lorna's major contribution to family economy is that she doesn't spend a lot on buying things for herself or to change her appearance. Eating healthy food, working in the backyard, and getting enough sleep is her beauty regimen. She jumps out of bed in the morning, brushes her hair, and pins it back. Michael's contribution is that he doesn't buy all the macho toys that tempt most Americans such as the sports car or all-terrain pickup truck, the wide-screen TV, golf clubs or other closet-stuffing junk.

The Ables spend less on material things than many of their neighbors and thus can actually save money or choose to work less, which gives the family more time for leisure, interaction with each other, neighbors, and friends. They plan to live in their home for a long time, while they continually improve it, thus benefiting their community and becoming a greater part of it.

By working less, they pay fewer taxes on income. Let's rephrase this in case the significance of this evades you. Individuals in the family can choose to earn only enough reported income to reach the standard deduction and no more.

Richard Able does just this. He attends university in the Bay Area and   15
lives very comfortably in a communal housing situation where his daily
expenses for housing, utilities, and food are less than twenty dollars per day.
There is a contentment in their household. They are far less vulnerable to
economic dislocation since they have distanced themselves from relying on
the consumer economy. The only debt that they have is their mortgage, which
they refinanced when rates dropped without taking any cash out.

The Binge Family (not their real name — we live too close to them for
comfort — they might read this) watches lots of TV and lusts after the endless things advertised. But they are in luck! The Cadillac Escalade was zero
down, lots of options, but its purchase drives them even further into debt. The
DiTech cash-out mortgage that they used to buy even more stuff is a looming
monster now that the value of their house has plunged and they are in negative equity. Their trips to the NASCAR races, malls, franchise steak houses,
movie theaters, and other such things are really cutting into their credit line
and are taking more and more time out of their weekend. The parents are
getting real nervous and the stress level is building. The kids are becoming
even more psychotic as they pick up on this stress. Their house is a mess, full
of clutter and junky products that break and get thrown out.

These folks succumb to fashion and purchase on impulse without
researching prices or quality. They buy things made cheaply overseas, usually in corporate-owned high-rent department stores or malls with high
debt service and huge overhead expenses paid for by the inflated price
of the merchandise sold therein. These high prices are often masked by
expensive advertising campaigns that promote "sales" and "discounts"
designed to lure in consumers. They subscribe to a megachannel lineup of
sports, shopping, infotainment, and other cultural sewage that never seems
to satisfy.

So how do we know all this about them? What's on the curb in front of
their house on garbage day reveals a lot. You can tell by the post-sale timing
of the big store shopping bags as well as a lot of consumer electronics car-
tons and Styrofoam inserts piled by the three overflowing garbage cans. Every
year they throw out another steel Christmas tree stand with their tree instead
of reusing it and getting a discount on the tree. Or at least they used to. Now
they don't even bother with the tree. Recycling? They don't bother. Large car-
tons overflowing Styrofoam peanuts into the gutter and last year's gimmicks
get heaped up every garbage day.

You can tell by the logos on the trucks in front of their house that this
family purchases mass-consumption type services from corporate strangers, often from outside of the community. The employees are paid as close
to minimum wage as possible, often with a sales commission to give them
incentive to sell a product, no matter what its quality. Thus they have less
inclination to give customer service or know their merchandise than would
workers in a family-run or small store. Often these corporate employees are
immigrants that cannot give customer service except in Spanish.

Stores like those patronized by the Binge Family offer a sea of chang- 20
ing faces — few long-term employees. For example, a chain of furniture stores
ships its management trainees from city to city. They live in apartments and
have barely settled into a community when it's time for the next move out
of town and up the corporate ladder. One Binge Family daughter is away in
another city doing just such a rotation. Her out-of-state personalized license
plate, framed by a faded plastic sports franchise holder, makes some crude
attempt at glorifying her former telemarketing "career."

Purchases of this family are made on credit, which can add up to 29 percent or more interest to the purchase price. (We know this because they constantly complain about it to their neighbors.) When products cease to work or
fall out of favor, which happens quickly because of poor quality, often masked
by trendy design, they are sent to the landfill. Their house is the one with the
broken rebounder aerobic exerciser as well as a poorly made, TV-advertised
treadmill sitting in the backyard under the broken Home Depot special lamp:
Do they think this stuff will fix itself sitting out in the weather? Their personal junkyard is a-building. Any day now we expect to see a car on blocks
appear there.

Their self-image is dependent on what they wear, drive, and where they
spend money. And do they spend it: Convenience fees to use ATMs, T-shirts,
and knickknacks for the body, stomach, and mind are favored. Sports statistics are their intellectual fodder and sports talk or fashion gossip fills their
limited intellectual horizons. They live from day to day and rarely plan. They
keep the local branch of a national convenience market profitable with spo-
radic three-block drives to purchase small quantities of factory food and
impulse buys.

Having many things requires much time to maintain them and to justify
their existence by actively and publicly using them. Ipod Nanos, personal TVs,
health club memberships, videogames, all these things distract and remove
the members of this family from interaction and participation in home or
community life. Mrs. Binge now has the obligatory little lap dog that sits in
her lap when she drives to the mall in her color-coordinated SUV. The poor
creature howls and yaps all day long when abandoned in their side yard.

Human relationships with friends and neighbors must suffer in this environment because, after all, for them consumption is a form of aggressive competition. They are constantly showing off the latest knickknack that they have
bought. They literally go out of their way to drive by or even walk up to neighbors' fences to show off the latest thing. There is actually something kind of
childishly naïve about these folks and in a way they are fortunate — they can
march down to the mall and whip out their credit cards and buy themselves
some (temporary) happiness. No need for original thoughts or introspection
or pondering life's mysteries because there's always last night's ball game or
American Idol to talk about. It's not lack of education either: Mr. Binge has an
advanced technical degree that allows him to earn a very good salary. Mrs.
Binge laughs about how she went to college to obtain her MRS degree.

A new car, usually junky quality and a heavily advertised brand like a Pon- 25 tiac Vibe or a Jeep Whatever, is bought by a different Binge family member every year or so to temporarily resurrect their self-image. The vehicle usually is loaded with gimmicks that inflate the price and repair costs. It's inevitably dead last on the *Consumer Reports* ratings of cars. The depreciation of the car robs it of much of its value in the first year. Registration, taxes, and insurance are higher for this new vehicle than they would be for an older, simpler car. It has little trade-in value because of faddish design, and lack of durability. Mr. Binge made the big step recently of buying a brand new Cadillac Escalade. He of course picked the most impractical color that there is — jet black — guess he likes to run the air conditioner and constantly wash dust off it. Also it is a top theft target and has the worst overall insurance theft losses. I would guess that the Ables spend a third of their income on their cars.

Because of the longer hours this family must work, they often resort to saving time by eating out in fast food terminals like Panda Express, McDonald's, or Outback Steakhouses. The factory food dispensed therein is loaded with fat and chemicals. Not much money and some time are saved now, but at what price to long-term health in the future?

What of their long-term prospects and family structure? Their eldest daughter has been married twice before the age of twenty-five. Their only son changes his look like a shop window every year or so. Several years ago he was into some kind of heavy metal or such thing, greasing his hair up and sporting all manner of dime store junk that he attached to a cheap leather jacket that he would wear to the mall where he hung out in fast food places. This year, it is a different clown costume and set of different CDs and canned values that he can shop for at the mall.

Mrs. Binge is a sight to behold. She buys products for her body — lots of products. They don't necessarily improve her looks although she must think that they do. She cannot pass by a window or a mirror without looking at her reflection. Her hair is heavy with spray, she reeks of perfume, lays the makeup on to cover up the junk-food induced acne, and stinks of cigarettes. The top of her breasts must hold a special fascination for her because she is constantly looking down at them as if to reassure herself that they are still there. Manicure, pedicure, facials, waxing, God knows what plastic surgery, and the battle is still being lost because she doesn't get enough sleep, judging from the blue flickering light emanating from her bedroom window until late at night. I would venture a guess that she hasn't eaten a vegetable in the last decade, indicated by the constant refinery odor coming from their barbecue area.

Her daughter must have bought her own make-up trowel because she too now sports the Noh-theater pink-edged mask of foundation, eyeliner, and other facial goop. She's smoking too.

The Binge family does have one dubious advantage. They can seek, and 30 obtain, immediate short-term satisfaction in things and they do not have to work at self-examination or better living; "blessed are the meek for they are easily satisfied: plenty of time to watch TV, sports, and a freezer full of steaks — at least until the power goes off."

The Family Able has far more money and time to spend on themselves, the education of their children, or save than does Family Binge. They support their local community, of which they are a part, and help keep their neighbors working while they generate less waste and use less energy than the Binge Family. The Family Able eats well, is not torn by artificially created demands for more things, and makes do with less. They work together toward common goals and have profited from frugality. When energy gets expensive and scarce which family will live better?

Which family has a truly higher standard of living?

READING THE TEXT

1. In your own words, how do the Ables "strengthen their community" (para. 1)?

2. What strategies do the Ables use to be effective shoppers?

3. Characterize the Binges's attitudes toward consumer products. How do material goods contribute to the family's lifestyle?

4. What do the Ables and the Binges do for entertainment, according to Verdant, and what effect do those choices have on the environment?

5. Describe Verdant's tone and style in this selection. How does it affect your response to his stated goal of outlining consumer "behavior and its consequences" (para. 1)?

READING THE SIGNS

1. In class, discuss Verdant's presentation of the two families. To what extent could he be accused of stereotyping them? Or do you recognize some consumer habits in these families, even if they are somewhat extremely drawn?

2. Write an essay that argues for your response to Verdant's concluding question: "Which family has a truly higher standard of living?" (para. 32).

3. **CONNECTING TEXTS**   Using Joan Kron's "The Semiotics of Home Decor" (p. 128) as a critical framework, write an essay in which you analyze the meanings that material goods hold for both the Able and the Binge families.

4. As a consumer society, the United States, in part, depends on mass consumption for economic stability. Write an essay in which you analyze how the consuming habits of the Binge and the Able families work to affect the national economy.

5. **CONNECTING TEXTS**   Drawing on Laurence Shames's "The More Factor" (p. 90), analyze the Binge family's attitudes toward consumption. To what extent could they be said to be suffering from "the hunger for more"?

TAMMY OLER
Making Geek Chic

"A growing community of crafters, designers, and students are mak-ing their own fashion technology creations," Tammy Oler writes in this report for *Bitch Magazine*, "and they believe that 'tech crafting' may just be the key to getting more women and girls involved in technology." With women composing only twenty-five percent of the workforce in computer-related professions, such designers are seeking to overcome the traditional gender coding that designates technology as a male domain. Is the answer to be found in such tech-nological fashions as "Nike sneakers with sensors that wirelessly sync with an iPod or iPhone to control song selection and display workout information such as time, distance, pace, and calories burned," or in Mattel's new Barbie, who appears as a "'digital diva [who] engi-neers the perfect geek-chic look, with hot pink accessories and sleek gadgets to match?'" Or does focusing on fashion only reinforce tra-ditional gender codes after all? Oler is hoping for the best. A self-described "intrepid nerd" who "writes about film, fandom, and pop culture for a wide range of magazines and blogs," Tammy Oler is a writing consultant based in Brooklyn, New York.

Wearable technology may feel like science fiction, but it's actually becoming a reality right before our eyes. Law enforcement, the military, and the medi-cal industry have long sought ways to integrate technology with clothing to augment health and personal safety. More recently, high fashion has started swooning over the possibilities of techy dressing: The artsy Rodarte label debuted LED-embedded glowing heels at Fashion Week earlier this year and Lady Gaga recently performed in a gown with a moving skirt and headpiece that she called a "living dress." And Katy Perry made headlines when she showed up at the Metropolitan Museum's Costume Institute Gala in a light-up dress by Cute Circuit, a London-based fashion technology company.

Everyday consumers are next. Some of the efforts to bring smart clothing to market — such as the No-Contact Jacket, a "defensive jacket" developed in 2003 to protect women from street violence — aren't here yet; others, like the Nike sneakers with sensors that wirelessly sync with an iPod or iPhone to con-trol song selection and display workout information such as time, distance, pace, and calories burned, are becoming commonplace.

A growing community of crafters, designers, and students are making their own fashion technology creations — and they believe that "tech craft-ing" may just be the key to getting more women and girls involved in tech-nology. Tech crafting combines electronic circuitry with sewing or handwork to produce wearable (or "soft") technologies. Projects range from a handbag that lights up when your cell phone receives a call to "socially interactive" clothing such as a hoodie that lets you display your mood with ambient lights on the sleeve. The tech-crafting community has expanded rapidly in the past two years to include numerous blogs and Web sites dedicated to sharing projects, such as Fashioning Technology, Switch, electricfoxy, and talk2myshirt .com. Thanks to such DIY efforts, manufacturers are starting to make conductive threads and e-textile tools like the LilyPad Arduino, a microcontroller board specifically designed to be sewn into textiles and wearables, more readily available.

Syuzi Pakhchyan and Alison Lewis are two tech crafters who want to get these tools into the hands of more women and girls specifically. The pair convened a dialogue at 2010's SXSW Interactive Festival that drew a crowd of parents, educators, and industry professionals eager to use fashion technology to hook girls — who are generally less likely than boys to be urged toward computers and mechanics — into a more tech-focused future.

Pakhchyan, the creator of the online smart-crafting community SparkLab   5 and the author of *Fashioning Technology: A DIY Intro to Smart Crafting*, came face-to-face with the challenges of engaging girls with technology when she was in graduate school and teaching a robotics class for children. The class, she recalls, mostly comprised boys who "just loved building BattleBots. But none of the girls were really that interested in building BattleBots, so it became this struggle to keep them engaged. I wondered if it was purely context, because the girls at that age were actually much better programmers than the boys." Pakhchyan sees fashion and crafts that emphasize social or creative expression as critical teaching tools for girls, noting that tech craft "could become [a] context for getting them interested in electronics and computation."

Efforts to get more girls and women involved in tech are taking on a new sense of urgency these days. According to statistics compiled by the National Center for Women and Information Technology, only 18 percent of all computer science degrees earned in 2008 were earned by women, down from 37 percent in 1985. And while more than half of all professional occupations are held by women, only 25 percent of computing-related professions are — and women are executives at only 11 percent of Fortune 500 technology companies. Additionally, only a very small percentage of women working in technology professions are African American, Latina, or Asian.

As you might guess, this shortage of female representation in the technology workforce has its roots in early childhood and educational experiences. A recent report published by the Anita Borg Institute for Women and Technology, the Computer Science Teachers Association, and the University of Arizona concluded that girls turn away from science and math as early as elementary school because of limited exposure, discouragement from parents, and a lack of interest.

And mass media doesn't help. The long-established cultural attitudes about technology and gender were front and center in Verizon's notorious 2009 tough-guy ad campaign for the Droid phone. The commercial asked, "Should a phone be pretty?" and went on to emphasize the power and manliness of its phone by characterizing the competing iPhone as a "tiara-wearing, digitally clueless beauty-pageant queen." The final moments of the spot show a woman applying lipstick as a voiceover asserts that the Droid "trades hairdo for can-do."

The ad generated criticism from both technology and feminist blogs, but its central assertion about the Droid, that "It's not a princess, it's a robot," served as a useful reminder of how hardwired gender stereotypes about technology, power, and intelligence still exist in our culture.

It's this social coding of technology as default male that inspired designer 10 and producer Alison Lewis to, like Pakhchyan, embrace fashion and tech crafting as a way to get girls past the boys'-club barrier. Her book, *Switch Craft: Battery-Powered Crafts to Make and Sew*, as well as her blog, Switch, is aimed at showcasing innovative design and fashion from what she sees as a distinctly feminine, craft-inspired perspective. "Fashion and design and craft can be the right language . . . to ignite the initial spark. Once that spark has been ignited, and girls and women become interested, they're fine," she says.

Lewis has quickly become a leading voice in both the technology and fashion communities, and was named one of *Fast Company*'s Most Influential Women in Technology 2010. She asserts, "Women don't need help. There's nothing wrong with our learning capabilities. We just need to know socially that [technology] is an option, and it doesn't feel that way right now."

Tech crafting's girlcentric reframing of technology, and its message that women can have their hairdo *and* their digital can-do, was embraced by the numerous female engineers and girl geeks who got out the vote in 2009 when Mattel posted an online poll, urging users to choose Barbie's next career. As a result of their efforts, the 125th doll in the Barbie "I Can Be . . . " collection is a computer engineer. The Society of Women Engineers and the National Academy of Engineering even contributed to the development of Barbie's clothes and accessories. According to Mattel, "this digital diva engineers the perfect geek-chic look, with hot pink accessories and sleek gadgets to match."

A girlcentric approach is also the strategy used by Girlstart, an Austin-based nonprofit that offers a variety of science, math, and technology education programs in a female-friendly environment. By offering hands-on, girls-only camps and workshops, female role models, and style-conscious programs (Web Divas Club and Designer Paradise, among others), Girlstart attempts to reframe engineering as a cool and fun activity for girls interested in diverse subjects and hobbies. And many local organizations and programs that are part of the National Girls Collaborative Project, an initiative designed to foster collaboration among organizations promoting science, technology, engineering, and math (also known as STEM) careers to girls, have started to use a similar approach, offering girls-only clubs that focus on exploring technology through hobbies that girls are already engaged in.

But while tech crafting and girlcentric offerings may offer welcome alternatives to BattleBot building, they do little to ameliorate existing gender stereotypes around technology. In fact, much like Computer Engineer Barbie and her pink gadgets, they may actually reinforce a few. The downside of the tech-crafting push is that it risks ascribing women's interest in technology to the domains of fashion and craft, and may inadvertently support the gender divide at the heart of the problem it seeks to help overcome. Both Pakhchyan and Lewis assert that theirs is a pragmatic approach, one that engages girls and women who are already interested in fashion, crafting, and socializing with friends to simply add more electronic, computerized facets. Pakhchyan is quick to point out the double standard at work in the criticism that a fashion platform is limiting for girls. "[Boys] become engineers of other stuff—they don't just engineer BattleBots," she notes. "To say that girls, because they're engineering socially interactive garments, are going to grow up engineering only socially interactive garments [is inaccurate]."

In fact, it would be pretty awesome to train a generation of girls who 15 could engineer socially interactive garments. Fashion is but one type of design that is evolving to incorporate technology, which will require a change in the way that goods are developed and manufactured. Engineering and computer science will only continue to become more integral to every aspect of our lives, including the clothes we wear and the devices we carry. That's to say nothing about the way technology drives advances in the industrial and medical sectors: From a big-picture perspective, tech crafting is a promising method for developing transferable engineering and computational skills that cut across industries. As Lewis notes, "There are so many things made for us as women. [Yet] so few of us have an actual ability to control what is made for us, and have a say of how it's designed from a technological level." No doubt we need better choices than BattleBots vs. Barbies, but encouraging women to visualize themselves as innovators is definitely a step in the right direction.

READING THE TEXT

1. What does Oler mean by "techy dressing" (para. 1)?
2. Why do techy dressing proponents believe that such creations may encourage women to enter technological fields that tend to be dominated by men?
3. In class, brainstorm examples of techy dressing that are now available in the everyday consumer marketplace.

READING THE SIGNS

1. Visit the blogs and Web sites mentioned in the article that feature examples of techy dressing. In class, discuss both the potential appeal and market for such clothing. Do you think they are sufficiently broad to enable their proponents' loftier educational goals to succeed?

2. **CONNECTING TEXTS**   In class, form teams and debate whether techy dressing can indeed attract women into professions traditionally held by men on the one hand or, on the other, simply encourages women to focus their professional interests on traditionally "female" domains, namely fashion and appearance. To develop your ideas, consult Aaron Devor, "Gender Role Behaviors and Attitudes" (p. 672), and Deborah Blum, "The Gender Blur: Where Does Biology End and Society Take Over?" (p. 678).

3. Interview five or six female engineering or computer majors, and ask them their opinion about tech crafting. Do they think their interest in their majors would have been heightened if they had access to tech crafting education in high school? What were their motives for entering their chosen fields? Use your results as the basis for an essay in which you defend, refute, or modify the assumption that fashion technology can "hook girls . . . into a more tech-focused future" (para. 4).

4. What other professions can you think of that are stereotypically male or female? Choose a couple of them and write a reflective essay in which you discuss how those professions might reinforce a gender divide.

THOMAS FRANK
Commodify Your Dissent

"Sometimes You Gotta Break the Rules." "This is different. Different is good." "The Line Has Been Crossed." "Resist the Usual." If you are guessing that these defiant declarations must come from the Che Guevara/Jack Kerouac Institute of World Revolution and Extreme Hipness, you're in for a surprise, because they are actually advertising slogans for such corporations as Burger King, Arby's, Toyota, Clash Clear Malt, and Young & Rubicam. Just why huge corporations are aping the language of the Beats and the 1960s counterculture is the centerpiece of Thomas Frank's thesis that the countercultural idea has become "the official aesthetic of consumer society." Commodifying the decades-long youth habit of dissenting against corporate America, corporate America has struck back by adopting the very attitudes that once meant revolution, Frank believes, thus turning to its own capitalist uses the postures of rebellion. Indeed, when Apple can persuade you to buy a computer because its guy is just plain *cooler* than some IBM nerd, there may be no way out. Frank is the author of *Commodify Your Dissent: Salvos from the Baffler* (with Matt Weiland, 1997), from which this selection is taken; *The Conquest of Cool: Business Culture, Counterculture, and the Rise of Hip Consumerism*

(1998); *One Market Under God: Extreme Capitalism, Market Populism, and the End of Economic Democracy* (2001); *What's the Matter with Kansas?: How Conservatives Won the Heart of America* (2005); and *The Wrecking Crew: How Conservatives Rule* (2008).

The public be damned! I work for my stockholders.
—WILLIAM H. VANDERBILT, 1879

Break the rules. Stand apart. Keep your head. Go with your heart.
—TV commercial for Vanderbilt perfume, 1994

Capitalism is changing, obviously and drastically. From the moneyed pages of the *Wall Street Journal* to TV commercials for airlines and photocopiers we hear every day about the new order's globe-spanning, cyber-accumulating ways. But our notion about what's wrong with American life and how the figures responsible are to be confronted haven't changed much in thirty years. Call it, for convenience, the "countercultural idea." It holds that the paramount ailment of our society is conformity, a malady that has variously been described as over-organization, bureaucracy, homogeneity, hierarchy, logocentrism, technocracy, the Combine, the Apollonian.[1] We all know what it is and what it does. It transforms humanity into "organization man," into "the man in the gray flannel suit." It is "Moloch[2] whose mind is pure machinery," the "incomprehensible prison" that consumes "brains and imagination." It is artifice, starched shirts, tailfins, carefully mowed lawns, and always, always, the consciousness of impending nuclear destruction. It is a stiff, militaristic order that seeks to suppress instinct, to forbid sex and pleasure, to deny basic human impulses and individuality, to enforce through a rigid uniformity a meaningless plastic consumerism.

As this half of the countercultural idea originated during the 1950s, it is appropriate that the evils of conformity are most conveniently summarized with images of 1950s suburban correctness. You know, that land of sedate music, sexual repression, deference to authority, Red Scares, and smiling white people standing politely in line to go to church. Constantly appearing as a symbol of arch-backwardness in advertising and movies, it is an image we find easy to evoke.

The ways in which this system are to be resisted are equally well understood and agreed-upon. The Establishment demands homogeneity; we revolt by embracing diverse, individual lifestyles. It demands self-denial and rigid adherence to convention; we revolt through immediate gratification, instinct uninhibited, and liberation of the libido and the appetites. Few have put it more bluntly than Jerry Rubin did in 1970: "Amerika says: Don't! The yippies say: Do It!" The countercultural idea is hostile to any law and every

[1]**Apollonian**   An allusion to the god Apollo, a term for rational consciousness. –EDS.
[2]**Moloch**   An ancient idol to whom children were sacrificed, used by Allen Ginsberg as a symbol for industrial America in his poem "Howl." –EDS.

establishment. "Whenever we see a rule, we must break it," Rubin continued. "Only by breaking rules do we discover who we are." Above all rebellion consists of a sort of Nietzschean antinomianism,[3] an automatic questioning of rules, a rejection of whatever social prescriptions we've happened to inherit. Just Do It is the whole of the law.

The patron saints of the countercultural idea are, of course, the Beats, whose frenzied style and merry alienation still maintain a powerful grip on the American imagination. Even forty years after the publication of *On the Road*, the works of Kerouac, Ginsberg, and Burroughs remain the sine qua non of dissidence, the model for aspiring poets, rock stars, or indeed anyone who feels vaguely artistic or alienated. That frenzied sensibility of pure experience, life on the edge, immediate gratification, and total freedom from moral restraint, which the Beats first propounded back in those heady days when suddenly everyone could have their own TV and powerful V-8, has stuck with us through all the intervening years and become something of a permanent American style. Go to any poetry reading and you can see a string of junior Kerouacs go through the routine, upsetting cultural hierarchies by pushing themselves to the limit, straining for that gorgeous moment of original vice when Allen Ginsberg first read "Howl" in 1955 and the patriarchs of our fantasies recoiled in shock. The Gap may have since claimed Ginsberg and *USA Today* may run feature stories about the brilliance of the beloved Kerouac, but the rebel race continues today regardless, with ever-heightening shit-references calculated to scare Jesse Helms, talk about sex and smack that is supposed to bring the electricity of real life, and ever-more determined defiance of the repressive rules and mores of the American 1950s — rules and mores that by now we know only from movies.

But one hardly has to go to a poetry reading to see the countercultural 5 idea acted out. Its frenzied ecstasies have long since become an official aesthetic of consumer society, a monotheme of mass as well as adversarial culture. Turn on the TV and there it is instantly: the unending drama of consumer unbound and in search of an ever-heightened good time, the inescapable rock 'n' roll soundtrack, dreadlocks and ponytails bounding into Taco Bells, a drunken, swinging-camera epiphany of tennis shoes, outlaw soda pops, and mind-bending dandruff shampoos. Corporate America, it turns out, no longer speaks in the voice of oppressive order that it did when Ginsberg moaned in 1956 that *Time* magazine was

> always telling me about responsibility. Business-
> men are serious. Movie producers are serious.
> Everybody's serious but me.

---

[3]**Nietzschean antinomianism** An allusion to the German philosopher Friedrich Nietzsche's challenging of conventional Christian morality. –Eds.

Nobody wants you to think they're serious today, least of all Time Warner. On the contrary: the Culture Trust is now our leader in the Ginsbergian search for kicks upon kicks. Corporate America is not an oppressor but a sponsor of fun, provider of lifestyle accoutrements, facilitator of carnival, our slang-speaking partner in the quest for that ever-more apocalyptic orgasm. The countercultural idea has become capitalist orthodoxy, its hunger for transgression upon transgression now perfectly suited to an economic-cultural regime that runs on ever-faster cyclings of the new; its taste for self-fulfillment and its intolerance for the confines of tradition now permitting vast latitude in consuming practices and lifestyle experimentation.

Consumerism is no longer about "conformity" but about "difference." Advertising teaches us not in the ways of puritanical self-denial (a bizarre notion on the face of it), but in orgiastic, never-ending self-fulfillment. It counsels not rigid adherence to the tastes of the herd but vigilant and constantly updated individualism. We consume not to fit in, but to prove, on the surface at least, that we are rock 'n' roll rebels, each one of us as rule-breaking and hierarchy-defying as our heroes of the 60s, who now pitch cars, shoes, and beer. This imperative of endless difference is today the genius at the heart of American capitalism, an eternal fleeing from "sameness" that satiates our thirst for the New with such achievements of civilization as the infinite brands of identical cola, the myriad colors and irrepressible variety of the cigarette rack at 7-Eleven.

As existential rebellion has become a more or less official style of Information Age capitalism, so has the countercultural notion of a static, repressive Establishment grown hopelessly obsolete. However the basic impulses of the countercultural idea may have disturbed a nation lost in Cold War darkness, they are today in fundamental agreement with the basic tenets of Information Age business theory. . . .

Contemporary corporate fantasy imagines a world of ceaseless, turbulent change, of centers that ecstatically fail to hold, of joyous extinction for the craven gray-flannel creature of the past. Businessmen today decorate the walls of their offices not with portraits of President Eisenhower and emblems of suburban order, but with images of extreme athletic daring, with sayings about "diversity" and "empowerment" and "thinking outside the box." They theorize their world not in the bar car of the commuter train, but in weepy corporate retreats at which they beat their tom-toms and envision themselves as part of the great avant-garde tradition of edge-livers, risk-takers, and ass-kickers. Their world is a place not of sublimation and conformity, but of "leadership" and bold talk about defying the herd. And there is nothing this new enlightened species of businessman despises more than "rules" and "reason." The prominent culture-warriors of the right may believe that the counterculture was capitalism's undoing, but the antinomian businessmen

know better. "One of the t-shirt slogans of the sixties read, 'Question authority,'" the authors of *Reengineering the Corporation* write. "Process owners
might buy their reengineering team members the nineties version: 'Question
assumptions.'"

The new businessman quite naturally gravitates to the slogans and sensibility of the rebel sixties to express his understanding of the new Information World. He is led in what one magazine calls "the business revolution" by
the office-park subversives it hails as "business activists," "change agents,"
and "corporate radicals." . . . In television commercials, through which the
new American businessman presents his visions and self-understanding to
the public, perpetual revolution and the gospel of rule-breaking are the orthodoxy of the day. You only need to watch for a few minutes before you see
one of these slogans and understand the grip of antinomianism over the
corporate mind:

> Sometimes You Gotta Break the Rules — Burger King
> If You Don't Like the Rules, Change Them — WXRT-FM
> The Rules Have Changed — Dodge
> The Art of Changing — Swatch
> There's no one way to do it. — Levi's
> This is different. Different is good. — Arby's
> Just Different From the Rest — Special Export beer
> The Line Has Been Crossed: The Revolutionary New Supra — Toyota
> Resist the Usual — the slogan of both Clash Clear Malt and Young &
>   Rubicam
> Innovate Don't Imitate — Hugo Boss
> Chart Your Own Course — Navigator Cologne
> It separates you from the crowd — Vision Cologne

In most, the commercial message is driven home with the vanguard iconography of the rebel: screaming guitars, whirling cameras, and startled old timers
who, we predict, will become an increasingly indispensable prop as consumers require ever-greater assurances that, Yes! You are a rebel! Just look at how
offended they are! . . .

The structure and thinking of American business have changed enormously 10
in the years since our popular conceptions of its problems and abuses were
formulated. In the meantime the mad frothings and jolly apolitical revolt of
Beat, despite their vast popularity and insurgent air, have become powerless
against a new regime that, one suspects, few of Beat's present-day admirers
and practitioners feel any need to study or understand. Today that beautiful countercultural idea, endorsed now by everyone from the surviving Beats
to shampoo manufacturers, is more the official doctrine of corporate America than it is a program of resistance. What we understand as "dissent" does

not subvert, does not challenge, does not even question the cultural faiths of Western business. What David Rieff wrote of the revolutionary pretensions of multiculturalism is equally true of the countercultural idea: "The more one reads in academic multiculturalist journals and in business publications, and the more one contrasts the speeches of CEOs and the speeches of noted multiculturalist academics, the more one is struck by the similarities in the way they view the world." What's happened is not co-optation or appropriation, but a simple and direct confluence of interest.

READING THE TEXT

1. In your own words, define what Frank means by "countercultural idea" (para.1).

2. How does Frank explain the relationship between the countercultural idea and conformity?

3. How are the Beats early progenitors of today's countercultural ideas, according to Frank?

4. In what ways does Frank believe that modern business has co-opted the countercultural idea?

5. How do you characterize Frank's tone in this selection, and does it enhance or detract from the forcefulness of his argument?

READING THE SIGNS

1. Analyze some current advertising, either in a magazine, on the Internet, or on television, asking whether the advertisements employ the countercultural idea as a marketing ploy. Use your observations as the basis for an essay in which you assess whether that idea and the associated "iconography of the rebel" still prevail in advertising as Frank suggests.

2. In class, brainstorm a list of today's cultural rebels, either marketing characters or real people such as actors or musicians, and discuss why these rebels are considered attractive to their intended audience. Use the class discussion as a springboard for your own essay in which you analyze how the status of cultural rebels is a sign of the mood of modern American culture.

3. **CONNECTING TEXTS**   Write an essay in which you agree with, disagree with, or modify Frank's contention that marketing no longer promotes conformity but, rather, "never-ending self-fulfillment" and "constantly updated individualism" (para. 6). To develop your ideas, consult the Introduction to Chapter 6, "American Paradox."

4. Visit a youth-oriented store such as Urban Outfitters and analyze its advertising, product displays, and both exterior design and interior decor. Write an

essay in which you gauge the extent to which the store uses the iconography of the rebel as a marketing strategy.

5. Study a current magazine focused on business or on modern technology, such as *Bloomberg, Businessweek, Business* 2.0, or *Wired*. To what extent does the magazine exemplify Frank's claim that modern business eschews conformity and embraces rebellion and rule-breaking? Alternately, you might analyze some corporate Web sites, preferably several from companies in the same industry. Keep in mind that different industries may have very different corporate cultures; the values and ideals that dominate high tech, for instance, may differ dramatically from those in finance, entertainment, or social services.

"Mind if I smoke?"
"Care if I die?"
Van Wagner
VIDEO
EUROWORLD
VIDEO

BROUGHT TO YOU B(U)Y

The Signs of Advertising

Inside the Office

A woman sits inside her car in a parking lot and begins to pound the steering wheel and scream. Another woman, dressed in a business suit, fantasizes that she is riding a dolphin, while a man stands in the street, briefcase in hand, sobbing. An executive lounges with his feet propped on a spacious desk inside a luxurious office complete with an ornamental moose head mounted on the wall behind him, while another man sits in a dingy cubicle at a computer desk situated between the hind legs of the aforementioned ornamental moose. A woman receives a box of flowers delivered to her cubicle and is surrounded by her coworkers as the flowers begin to trash-talk and humiliate her. A man is hurled out the window of an office building after making an unpopular cost-cutting suggestion. Another man discusses the casual clothing policies of his office workplace as his underwear-clad coworkers parade by. The boss gets hit where it hurts when an employee throws a crystal ball in his direction thinking that by doing so he will soon be getting a raise.

All of these scenes were presented in television advertisements during Super Bowls XLIII and XLIV. And all of them point to something that is happening in American society today.

The scenes described above came from spots for CareerBuilder ("Tips"), Budweiser ("Meeting"), Monster ("Need a New Job?"), Teleflora ("Talking Flowers"), and Doritos ("Crystal Ball")—ad titles all taken from http://www.hulu .com, where you can view them for yourselves. What all of these ads share is their business-office-related themes, which is an obvious allusion to the popular situation comedy series *The Office.* Piggybacking on the success of *The*

171

Office, these ads reflect a common advertising strategy of borrowing the aura of something that is already popular and hoping that it will be transplanted to the product or service that is for sale.

The *association* between the ads and the television series indicates that there is a *system* involved here within which we can determine their larger cultural significance. Enlarging our range of reference, we can find popular cartoon strips like "Dilbert" and the movie *Office Space* (1999) — which both present a grim, if comic, vision of white-collar work in America — along with the dramatic series *Mad Men*, which not only features an office setting but uses the advertising industry itself as a site for the critique of larger social issues. We can *differentiate* this contemporary vision of office life from such office-themed entertainments from the past as *How to Succeed in Business Without Really Trying*, a 1960s musical that makes fun of the silly things that go on in white-collar work while maintaining a light-hearted attitude toward it all and concluding with a happy ending. (And with Robert Morse, the star of that 1962 production reappearing as a character in *Mad Men*, we can be confident that we are actually intended to notice the ironic connection.)

Today's office-related entertainments are neither happy nor have happy endings. Their humor, when they are comical, is based in a combination of schadenfreude (taking pleasure in the suffering or misfortunes of others) and a certain rueful satisfaction taken by watching the sorts of things that one has to endure in real working life exaggerated for the sake of comedy. This difference indicates a growing desperation on the part of America's white-collar workforce. Both the ads and the sitcoms feature horrible working conditions in which bosses and coworkers alike are cretinous fools, with only one or two characters excepted so that the audience can have someone with whom to identify. For example, in CareerBuilder's "Tips," one such fool is a nerdy nincompoop wearing nothing but a Speedo bathing suit as he jabbers on the phone next to "your" cubicle. Others include a supervisor who passes by only to insult a cubicled wage slave, along with the images of desperately unhappy workers described above.

All of the ads, of course, are meant to be funny, a sort of whistling in the dark for America's office workers, who presumably take comfort in seeing their sufferings comically presented. But there is an ironic contradiction, especially in the ads by CareerBuilder ("Tips") and Monster ("Need a New Job?") that are aimed at viewers who are looking for work. Because the message of the office-themed ads when taken as a group, as well as the office-themed TV shows they are imitating, is that office life is *universally* horrible. CareerBuilder and Monster comically show why someone would want another job, but the whole message is that no such jobs can be found. Office work is awful everywhere. All you can do is laugh at your own misery.

And that may be the most significant **semiotic** point of all. Laughter and entertainment are not good motivators for taking action against the slings and arrows of outrageous capitalism. (Think about it: What gets you moving, anger at injustice, or laughter at the ridiculous?) By keeping its white-collar victims laughing, capitalism, in effect, keeps them docile. Who do you think wins? The boss will still get the paneled walls and the mounted moose head. The office worker will still get the moose's rear end.

When Things Get Tough, the Tough Get Sentimental

By 2010, however, the reality had become that while office jobs might not be fun, it was better to have one than to be unemployed. And with so few opportunities available for any jobs, much less better ones, continuing an ad campaign based upon the premise that if you don't like your current position you should look for another one would seem to be a bit dated. That didn't faze CareerBuilder, which aired the guy-talking-about-the-casual-dress-code ad mentioned above, but it did affect Monster, which aired a very different kind of ad from the previous year's moose. But it did feature animals.

Ask yourself, what you would do if you were assigned the task of creating an ad for an online job search service in a time of high unemployment? It's no easy task. Too much humor could well backfire, causing unemployed viewers to feel insulted by the appearance that their plight is not being taken seriously. At the other extreme, too much realism could definitely be a downer: being unemployed is bad enough without having it rubbed in your face.

So Monster chose populist sentimentality, a very common appeal when things get tough in America. While a bit on the corny side, the ad made a determined effort to address the reality that many of Monster's clients are currently unemployed, while being entertaining and uplifting. The strategy chosen was cute animals. The story line of the ad featured a beaver (yes, a beaver) who fiddles country music (a traditional populist symbol) while his fellow beavers are hard at work. The beaver logs on to Monster.com in search of a violinist position. We next see the beaver move to a large city, where he plays on the streets and in subways, and finally lands an audition, which in turn lands him in something like Carnegie Hall. The final shot shows the beaver driving away in a hot-tub-equipped limo with a beaming blond on board.

By making its unemployed protagonist a cute animal, the ad put a distance between the beaver and the viewer. The viewer would be able to identify with the beaver's joblessness, but painlessly because it is, after all, only an animated beaver. At the same time, the corny rags-to-riches story is presented with a wink of ironic self-awareness, thus avoiding insulting the target audience with any unrealistic claims of what Monster can do for job seekers. Again, it's just an animated beaver. Still, the ad ends with that rags-to-riches triumph, and so an impression of extravagant success lingers after all, lending a pleasant aura to Monster that might lead the prospective job seeker to choose Monster rather than its competitors.

Discussing the Signs of Advertising

Bring to class a print ad from a newspaper, a magazine, or a commercial Web site and in small groups discuss your semiotic reading of it. Be sure to ask, "Why am I being shown this or being told that?" How do the characters in the ad function as signs? What sort of people don't appear as characters? What cultural myths are invoked in this ad? What relationship do you see between those myths and the intended audience of the publication? Which ads do your group members respond to positively and why? Which ads doesn't your group like?

The Monster beaver, in his turn, can be associated with the famous E*Trade babies, who first appeared early in 2008 in the midst of the subprime mortgage debacle that was pummeling E*Trade as well as the rest of the economy at the time. So E*Trade had an advertising dilemma similar to that of Monster.com: how to avoid insulting its target viewers by ignoring the severity of their situation, or, on the other hand, depressing them by dwelling on the dismal realities of the stock market at the time. Solution: adorable babies with adult voiceovers.

Cute babies are like cute animals: They are sentimental favorites and make people feel good. A sober conversation about the investment climate between two adult actors who had just lost their shirts in the market would not have worked at all.

And Here's the Pitch

The preceding analyses are intended to illustrate how advertisements too are **signs** of cultural desire and consciousness. Indeed, advertising is not just show and tell. In effect, it's a form of behavior modification, a psychological strategy designed not only to inform you about products but also to persuade you to buy them by making associations between the product and certain pleasurable experiences or emotions that may have nothing to do with the product at all — like sex, or a promise of social superiority, or a simple laugh. Indeed, in no other area of popular culture can we find a purer example of the deliberate movement from objective **denotation** (the pictorial image of a product that appears in an advertisement) to subjective **connotation** (the feeling that the advertiser wishes to associate with the product), thereby transforming things into *signs*.

No one knows for sure just how effective a given ad campaign might be in inducing consumer spending by turning objects into signs, but no one is

---

Exploring the Signs of Advertising

Select one of the products advertised in the "Portfolio of Advertisements" (in this chapter), and design in your journal an alternative ad for that product. Consider what different images or cast of characters you could include. What different **myths** — and thus different values — could you use to pitch this product? Then freewrite on the significance of your alternative ad. If you have any difficulty imagining an alternative image for the product, what does that say about the power of advertising to control our view of the world? What does your choice of imagery and cultural myths say about you?

---

taking any chances either, as you can see by the annual increase in advertising costs for the Super Bowl: At last count it was some $3 million for a thirty-second spot. And it is the promise of ever-increasing advertising revenues that has turned Google into the Web 2.0 darling of Wall Street. As James B. Twitchell has written, America is indeed an "ad culture," a society saturated with advertising.

With all the advertising out there, it is getting harder for advertisers to get our attention, or keep it, so they are constantly experimenting with new ways of getting us to listen. For years now, advertisers who are out to snag the youth market stage their TV ads as if they were MTV videos — complete with rapid jump-cuts, rap or rock music, and dizzying montage effects — to grab the attention of their target audience and to cause their viewers to associate the product with the pleasures of MTV. Self-conscious irony is also a popular technique as advertisers strive to overcome the ad-savvy sophistication of generations of consumers who have become skeptical of advertising ploys.

More recently, a marketing strategy known as "stealth advertising" has appeared in selected locations. For example, companies pay people to do things like sit in Starbucks and play computer games; when someone takes an interest, they talk about how cool it is and ask passersby on the street to take their photo with a really cool new camera — and by the way, they say, isn't this a really cool new camera?! The trick here is to advertise without having people actually know they're being marketed to — just what the ad doctor ordered for advertising-sick consumers.

As the years pass and the national mood shifts with the tides of history, new advertising techniques will emerge. So look around and ask yourself, as you're bombarded with advertising, "Why am I being shown *that*, or being told this?" Or cast yourself as the director of an ad, asking yourself what you would do to pitch a product; then look at what the advertiser has done. Pay attention to the way an ad's imagery is organized, its precise denotation. Every detail counts. Why are these colors used, or why is the ad in black and white? Why are cute stuffed animals chosen to pitch toilet paper? What are those people doing in that perfume commercial? Why the cowboy hat in an ad for jeans? Look too for what the ad doesn't include: Is it missing a clear view of the product itself or an ethnically diverse cast of characters? In short, when interpreting an ad, transform it into a text, going beyond what it denotes to what it connotes — to what it is trying to insinuate or say.

The Semiotic Foundation

There is perhaps no better field for semiotic analysis than advertising, for ads work characteristically by substituting signs for things, and by reading those signs you can discover the values and desires that advertisers seek to exploit. It has long been recognized that advertisements substitute images of desire for the actual products, selling images of fun, or popularity, or sheer celebrity, promising a gratifying association with the likes of Jessica Simpson if you get your next pizza from Pizza Hut. Automobile commercials, for their part, are notorious for selling not transportation but fantasies of power, prestige, and sexual potency.

Today's Special: The Home Shopping Network.

By substituting desirable images for concrete needs, modern advertising seeks to transform desire into necessity. You need food, for example, but it takes an ad campaign to convince you through attractive images that you need a Big Mac. Your job may require you to have a car, but it's an ad that persuades you that a Land Rover is necessary for your happiness. If advertising worked otherwise, it would simply present you with a functional profile of a product and let you decide whether it will do the job.

From the early twentieth century, advertisers have seen their task as the transformation of desire into necessity. In the 1920s and '30s, for example, advertisements created elaborate story lines designed to convince readers that they needed this mouthwash to attract a spouse or that caffeine-free breakfast drink to avoid trouble on the job. In such ads, products were made to appear not only desirable but absolutely necessary. Without them, your very survival as a socially competent being would be in question. Many ads still work this way, particularly "guilt" ads that prey on your insecurities and fears. Deodorants and mouthwashes still are pitched in such a fashion, playing on our fear of smelling bad in public. Can you think of any other products whose ads play on guilt or shame? Do you find them to be effective?

The Commodification of Desire

Associating a logically unrelated desire with an actual product (as in pitching beer through sexual come-ons) can be called the **commodification** of desire. In other words, desire itself becomes the product that the advertiser is selling. This marketing of desire was recognized as early as the 1950s in Vance Packard's *The Hidden Persuaders*. In that book, Packard points out how by the 1950s America was well along in its historic shift from a producing to a consuming economy. The implications for advertisers were enormous. Since the American economy was increasingly dependent on the constant growth of consumption, as discussed in the Introduction to Chapter 1, manufacturers had to find ways to convince people to consume ever more goods. So they turned to the advertising mavens on Madison Avenue, who responded with ads that persuaded consumers to replace perfectly serviceable products with "new and improved" substitutions within an overall economy of planned design obsolescence.

America's transformation from a producer to a consumer economy also explains that while advertising is a worldwide phenomenon, it is nowhere so prevalent as it is here. Open a copy of the popular French picture magazine *Paris Match*. You'll find plenty of paparazzi photos of international celebrities but almost no advertisements. Then open a copy of *Vogue*. It is essentially a catalog, where scarcely a page is without an ad. Indeed, advertisers themselves call this plethora of advertising "clutter" that they must creatively "cut through" each time they design a new ad campaign. The ubiquity of advertising in our lives points to a society in which people are constantly pushed to buy, as opposed to economies like Japan's that empha-size constant increases in production. And desire is what loosens the pocket-book strings.

While the basic logic of advertising may be similar from era to era, the content of an ad, and hence its significance, differs as popular culture changes. Looking at ads from different eras tells the tale. Advertising in the 1920s, for instance, focused especially on its market's desires for improved social status. Ads for elocution and vocabulary lessons appealed to working- and lower-middle-class consumers who were invited to fantasize that buy-ing the product or service could help them enter the middle class. Mean-while, middle-class consumers were invited to compare their enjoyment of the sponsor's product with that of the upper-class models shown hap-pily slurping this coffee or purchasing that vacuum cleaner in the ad. Of course, things haven't changed that much since the twenties. Can you think of any ads that use this strategy today? How often are glamorous celebrities called in to make you identify with their "enjoyment" of a product? Have you heard ads for vocabulary-building programs that promise you a "verbal advantage" in the corporate struggle?

One particularly amusing ad from the twenties played on America's fear of communism in the wake of the Bolshevik revolution in Russia. "Is your washroom breeding Bolsheviks?" asks a print ad from the Scott Paper Company. The ad's lengthy copy explains how it might be doing so: If your company restroom is stocked with inferior paper towels, it says, discontent will proliferate among your employees and lead to subversive activities. RCA Victor and Campbell's Soup, we are assured, are no such breeding grounds of subversion, thanks to their contracts with Scott. You, too, can fight the good fight against communism by buying Scott towels, the ad suggests. To whom do you think this ad was directed? What did they fear?

Reading Advertising on the Net

Many viewers watch the Super Bowl as much for the commercials as for the football game; indeed, the Super Bowl ads now have their own pregame public-relations hype and, in many a media outlet, their own postgame analysis and ratings. Visit *Advertising Age's* report on the most recent Super Bowl (www.adage.com), and study the ads and their commentary about them. What images and styles predominate, and what do the dominant patterns say about popular taste? What does the public's avid interest in Super Bowl ads say about the power of advertising and its role in American culture?

Populism vs. Elitism

American advertising tends to swing in a pendulum motion between the status-conscious ads that dominated the twenties and the more populist approach of decades like the seventies, when *The Waltons* was a top TV series and country music and truck-driving cowboys lent their popular appeal to Madison Avenue. This swing between elitist and populist approaches in advertising reflects a basic division within the American dream itself, a mythic promise that at once celebrates democratic equality and encourages you to rise above the crowd, to be better than anyone else. Sometimes Americans are more attracted to one side than to the other, but there is bound to be a shift back to the other side when the thrill wears off. Thus, the populist appeal of the seventies (even disco had a distinct working-class flavor: recall John Travolta's character in *Saturday Night Fever*) gave way to the elitist eighties, and advertising followed. Products such as Gallo varietal wines, once considered barely a step up from jug wine, courted an upscale market, while Michelob light beer promised its fans that they "could have it all." Status advertising was all the rage in that glitzy, go-for-the-gold decade.

The nineties brought in a different kind of advertising that was neither populist nor elitist but was characterized by a cutting, edgy humor. This humor was especially common in dot.com ads that typically addressed the sort of young, irreverent, and rather cocky souls who were the backbone of what was then called the "New Economy" and now "Web 1.0." More broadly, edgy advertising appealed to twentysomething consumers who were coveted by the marketers who made possible such youth-oriented TV networks as Fox and the WB. Raised in the *Saturday Night Live* era, such consumers were accustomed to cutting humor and particularly receptive to anything that smacked of attitude, and in the race to get their attention, advertisers followed with attitude-laden advertising.

The office ads discussed earlier indicate that this sort of advertising and attitude is still very much alive today. Look at the ads around you: What moods and desires can you detect? Are Americans drawing together, or are we splintering into niche market groups and atomizing into single units of competitive consumption? The ads will tell.

The Readings

Our selections in this chapter include interpretations and analyses of the world of advertising, as well as advertisements for you to interpret yourselves. The chapter begins with a paired set of readings by James B. Twitchell and Steve Craig on the psychology of advertising, revealing the elaborate social profiling schemes through which marketers seek to categorize and control our consuming behavior, along with the gender-coded formulae by which television advertisers seek to appeal to men or women consumers. Minette E. Drumright and Patrick E. Murphy follow with a sociological study of what advertising executives themselves think of the ethics of their profession; short answer: not much. Next, Jennifer L. Pozner lambastes the male critics of the Dove Campaign for Real Beauty, and Eric Schlosser looks at the world of children's advertising, in which kids are manipulated to manipulate their parents. Julia B. Corbett then looks at the ways in which marketers seek to cash in on the "lucrative market of 'green consumers,'" while Alan Foljambe analyzes the particular strategies of "green" automotive advertising. Gloria Steinem's insider's view of what goes on behind the scenes at women's magazines concludes the readings with an exposé of the often cozy relationships between magazine content and advertisers' desires. This chapter also includes a "Portfolio of Advertisements" for you to decode for yourself.

When You Come Home

READING THE SIGNS

1. The advertisement on page 181 tells a story. What is it? You might start with the title of the ad.

2. To whom is the ad directed? What emotions does it play on? Be sure to provide evidence for your answers. What are the "dearest possessions" the ad refers to?

3. This ad originally appeared in 1914. If you were to update it for a magazine today, what changes would you make? Why?

JAMES B. TWITCHELL

What We Are to Advertisers

Are you a "believer" or a "striver," an "achiever" or a "struggler," an "experiencer" or a "maker"? Or do you have no idea what we're talking about? If you don't, James Twitchell explains it all to you in this selection in which the psychological profiling schemes of American advertising are laid bare. For like it or not, advertisers have, or think they have, your number, and they will pitch their products according to the personality profile they have concocted for you. And the really spooky thing is that they're often right. A prolific writer on American advertising and culture, Twitchell's books include *Adcult USA: The Triumph of Advertising in American Culture* (1996), *Twenty Ads That Shook the World* (2000), *Living It Up: Our Love Affair with Luxury* (2002), *Lead Us into Temptation: The Triumph of American Materialism* (1999), from which this selection is taken, and *Branded Nation* (2004). His most recent book is *Shopping for God: How Christianity Went from in Your Heart to in Your Face* (2007).

Mass production means mass marketing, and mass marketing means the creation of mass stereotypes. Like objects on shelves, we too cluster in groups. We find meaning together. As we mature, we move from shelf to shelf, from aisle to aisle, zip code to zip code, from lifestyle to lifestyle, between what the historian Daniel Boorstin calls "consumption communities." Finally, as full-grown consumers, we stabilize in our buying, and hence meaning-making, patterns. Advertisers soon lose interest in us not just because we stop buying but because we have stopped changing brands.

The object of advertising is not just to brand parity objects but also to brand consumers as they move through these various communities. To explain his job, Rosser Reeves, the master of hard-sell advertising like the old Anacin ads, used to hold up two quarters and claim his job was to make you believe they were different, and, more importantly, that one was better than the other. Hence, at the macro level the task of advertising is to convince different sets of consumers—target groups—that the quarter they observe is somehow different in meaning and value than the same quarter seen by their across-the-tracks neighbors.

In adspeak, this is called *positioning.* "I could have positioned Dove as a detergent bar for men with dirty hands," David Ogilvy famously said, "but I chose to position it as a toilet bar for women with dry skin." Easy to say, hard to do. But if Anheuser-Busch wants to maximize its sales, the soccer mom driving the shiny Chevy Suburban must feel she drinks a different Budweiser than the roustabout in the rusted-out Chevy pickup.[1]

The study of audiences goes by any number of names: psychographics, ethnographics, macrosegmentation, to name a few, but they are all based on the ineluctable principle that birds of a feather flock together. The object of much consumer research is not to try to twist their feathers so that they will flock to your product, but to position your product in such a place that they will have to fly by it and perhaps stop to roost. After roosting, they will eventually think that this is a part of their flyway and return to it again and again.

Since different products have different meanings to different audiences, segmentation studies are crucial. Although agencies have their own systems for naming these groups and their lifestyles, the current supplier of much raw data about them is a not-for-profit organization, the Stanford Research Institute (SRI). 5

The "psychographic" system of SRI is called acronomically VALS (now VALS2 +), short for Values and Lifestyle System. Essentially this schematic is based on the common-sense view that consumers are motivated "to acquire products, services, and experiences that provide satisfaction and give shape, substance, and character to their identities" in bundles. The more "resources" (namely money, but also health, self-confidence, and energy) each group has, the more likely they will buy "products, services, and experiences" of the group they associate with. But resources are not the only determinant.

---

[1] Cigarette companies were the first to find this out in the 1930s, much to their amazement. Blindfolded smokers couldn't tell what brand they were smoking. Instead of making cigarettes with different tastes, it was easier to make different advertising claims to different audiences. Cigarettes are hardly unique. Ask beer drinkers why they prefer a particular brand and invariably they tell you: "It's the taste," "This goes down well," "This is light and refreshing," "This is rich and smooth." They will say this about a beer that has been described as their brand, but is not. Anheuser-Busch, for instance, spent three dollars per barrel in 1980 to market a barrel of beer; now they spend nine dollars. Since the cost to reach a thousand television households has doubled at the same time the audience has segmented (thanks to cable), why not go after a particular market segment by tailoring ads emphasizing, in different degrees, the Clydesdales, Ed McMahon, Beechwood aging, the red and white can, dates certifying freshness, the spotted dog, the Eagle, as well as "the crisp, clean taste." While you cannot be all things to all people, the object of advertising is to be as many things to as many segments as possible. The ultimate object is to convince as many segments as possible that "This Bud's for you" is a sincere statement.

Customers are also motivated by such ineffables as principles, status, and action. When SRI describes these various audiences they peel apart like this (I have provided them an appropriate car to show their differences):

- Actualizers: These people at the top of the pyramid are the ideal of everyone but advertisers. They have "it" already, or will soon. They are sophisticated, take-charge people interested in independence and character. They don't need new things; in fact, they already have their things. If not, they already know what "the finer things" are and won't be told. They don't need a new car, but if they do they'll read *Consumer Reports*. They do not need a hood ornament on their car.

- Fulfilled: Here are mature, satisfied, comfortable souls who support the status quo in almost every way. Often they are literally or figuratively retired. They value functionality, durability, and practicality. They drive something called a "town car," which is made by all the big three automakers.

- Believers: As the word expresses, these people support traditional codes of family, church, and community, wearing good Republican cloth coats. As consumers they are predictable, favoring American products and recognizable brands. They regularly attend church and Walmart, and they are transported there in their mid-range automobile like an Oldsmobile. Whether Oldsmobile likes it or not, they do indeed drive "your father's Oldsmobile."

Moving from principle-oriented consumers who look inside to status-driven consumers who look out to others, we find the Achievers and Strivers.

- Achievers: If consumerism has an ideal, here it is. Bingo! Wedded to their jobs as a source of duty, reward, and prestige, these are the people who not only favor the establishment but are the establishment. They like the concept of prestige. Not only are they successful, they demonstrate their success by buying such objects as prestigious cars to show it. They like hood ornaments. They see no contradiction in driving a Land Rover in Manhattan.

- Strivers: A young Striver is fine; he will possibly mature into an Achiever. But an old Striver can be nasty; he may well be bitter. Since they are unsure of themselves, they are eager to be branded as long as the brand is elevating. Money defines success and they don't have enough of it. Being a yuppie is fine as long as the prospect of upward mobility is possible. Strivers like foreign cars even if it means only leasing a BMW.

Again, moving to the right are those driven less by the outside world but by their desire to participate, to be part of a wider world.

- Experiencers: Here is life on the edge — enthusiastic, impulsive, and even reckless. Their energy finds expression in sports, social events, and "doing something." Politically and personally uncommitted, experiencers are an advertiser's dream come true as they see consumption as fulfillment and are willing to spend a high percent of their disposable income to attain it. When you wonder about who could possibly care how fast a car will accelerate from zero to sixty m.p.h., they care.

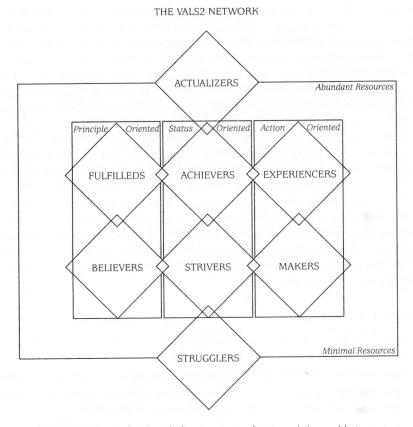

The VALS2 paradigm. Lifestyle styled: a taxonomy of taste and disposable income. (Stanford Research Institute)

- Makers: Here is the practical side of Experiencers; they like to build things and they experience the world by working on it. Conservative, suspicious, respectful, they like to do things in and to their homes, like adding a room, canning vegetables, or changing the oil in their pickup trucks.

- Strugglers: Like Actualizers, these people are outside the pale of materialism not by choice, but by low income. Strugglers are chronically poor. Their repertoire of things is limited not because they already have it all, but because they have so little. Although they clip coupons like Actualizers, theirs are from the newspaper. Their transportation is usually public, if any. They are the invisible millions.

As one might imagine, these are very fluid categories, and we may move through as many as three of them in our lifetimes. For instance, between ages 18–24 most people (61 percent) are Experiencers in desire or deed, while less than 1 percent are Fulfilled. Between ages 55 to 64, however, the Actualizers, Fulfilled, and Strugglers claim about 15 percent of the population each, while the Believers have settled out at about a fifth. The Achievers, Strivers, and Makers fill about 10 percent apiece, and the remaining 2 percent are Experiencers. The numbers can be broken down at every stage allowing for marital status, education, household size, dependent children, home owner-ship, household income, and occupation. More interesting still is the ability to accurately predict the appearance of certain goods in each grouping. SRI sells data on precisely who buys single-lens reflex cameras, who owns a laptop computer, who drinks herbal tea, who phones before five o'clock, who reads the *Reader's Digest*, and who watches *Beavis and Butthead*.

When one realizes the fabulous expense of communicating meaning for a product, the simple-mindedness of a system like VALS2+ becomes less risible. When you are spending millions of dollars for a few points of market share for your otherwise indistinguishable product, the idea that you might be able to attract the owners of socket wrenches by shifting ad content around just a bit makes sense. Once you realize that in taste tests consumers cannot tell one brand of cigarettes from another — including their own — nor distinguish such products as soap, gasoline, cola, beer, or what-have-you, it is clear that the product must be overlooked and the audience isolated and sold.

READING THE TEXT

1. What do marketers mean by "positioning" (para. 3), and why is it an impor-tant strategy to them?

2. What does the acronym VALS stand for, and what is the logic behind this system?

3. Why do marketers believe that "the product must be overlooked and the audience isolated and sold" (para. 8), according to Twitchell?

READING THE SIGNS

1. Consult the VALS2 network chart on page 185 and write a journal entry in which you place yourself on the chart. To what extent do you see yourself reflected in the VALS2 paradigm? What is your attitude toward being stereo-typed by marketers?

2. In class, discuss whether the categories of consumers defined by the VALS2 paradigm are an accurate predictor of consumer behavior. Use the discussion as the basis of an essay in which you argue for or against the proposition that stereotyping consumer lifestyles is an effective way of marketing goods and services.

3. Study the VALS2 paradigm in terms of the values it presumes. To what extent does it presume traditionally American values such as individualism? Use your analysis to formulate an argument about whether this marketing tool is an essentially American phenomenon.

4. **CONNECTING TEXTS** Using the VALS2 paradigm, analyze the shopping patterns of the two families described in John Verdant's "The Ables vs. the Binges" (p. 152). Do the families fit neatly into the paradigm, or does their behavior call for a revision of it? Use your findings as the basis of an essay in which you assess the usefulness of the paradigm.

5. **CONNECTING TEXTS** Twitchell, Eric Schlosser ("Kid Kustomers," p. 222), and Malcolm Gladwell ("The Science of Shopping," p. 97) all describe marketing research strategies. Read these selections, and write an argument that supports, opposes, or modifies the proposition that marketers have misappropriated academic research techniques for manipulative and therefore ethically questionable purposes.

CREATING CONSUMERS

STEVE CRAIG

Men's Men and Women's Women

Men and women both drink beer, but you wouldn't guess that from the television ads that pitch beer as a guy beverage and associate beer drinking with such guy things as fishing trips, bars, and babes. Conversely, both men and women can find themselves a few pounds overweight, but you wouldn't know that from the ads, which almost always feature women intended to appeal to women dieters. In this selection, Steve Craig provides a step-by-step analysis of four TV commercials, showing how advertisers carefully craft their ads to appeal, respectively, to male and female consumers. A professor in the department of radio, television, and film at the University of North Texas, Craig has written widely on television, radio history, and gender and media. His most recent book is *Out of the Dark: A History of Radio and Rural America* (2009).

Gender and the Economics of Television Advertising

The economic structure of the television industry has a direct effect on the placement and content of all television programs and commercials. Large advertisers and their agencies have evolved the pseudo-scientific method of time purchasing based on demographics, with the age and sex of the consumer generally considered to be the most important predictors of purchasing behavior. Computers make it easy to match market research on product buying patterns with audience research on television viewing habits. Experience, research, and intuition thus yield a demographic (and even psychographic) profile of the "target audience." Advertisers can then concentrate their budgets on those programs which the target audience is most likely to view. The most economical advertising buys are those in which the target audience is most concentrated (thus, the less "waste" audience the advertiser must purchase) (Barnouw, 1978; Gitlin, 1983; Jhally, 1987).

Good examples of this demographic targeting can be seen by contrasting the ads seen on daytime television, aimed at women at home, with those on weekend sports telecasts. Ads for disposable diapers are virtually never seen during a football game any more than commercials for beer are seen during soap operas. True, advertisers of some products simply wish to have their commercials seen by the largest number of consumers at the lowest cost without regard to age, sex, or other demographic descriptors, but most consider this approach far too inefficient for the majority of products.

A general rule of thumb in television advertising, then, is that daytime is the best time to reach the woman who works at home. Especially important to advertisers among this group is the young mother with children. Older women, who also make up a significant proportion of the daytime audience, are generally considered less important by many advertisers in the belief that they spend far less money on consumer goods than young mothers.

Prime time (the evening hours) is considered a good time to reach women who work away from home, but since large numbers of men are also in the audience, it can also be a good time to advertise products with wider target audiences. Weekend sports periods (and, in season, "Monday Night Football") are the only time of the week when men outnumber women in the television audience, and therefore, become the optimum time for advertising products and services aimed at men.

Gendered Television, Gendered Commercials

In his book *Television Culture* (1987, Chs. 10, 11), John Fiske discusses "gen- 5 dered television," explaining that the television industry successfully designs some programs for men and others for women. Clearly, program producers and schedulers must consider the target audience needs of their clients (the advertisers) in creating a television program line up. The gendering of programming allows the industry to provide the proper audience for advertisers by constructing shows pleasurable for the target audience to watch, and one aspect of this construction is in the gender portrayals of characters.

Fiske provides the following example:

> Women's view of masculinity, as evidenced in soap operas, differs markedly from that produced for the masculine audience. The "good" male in the daytime soaps is caring, nurturing, and verbal. He is prone to making comments like "I don't care about material wealth or professional success, all I care about is us and our relationship." He will talk about feelings and people and rarely express his masculinity in direct action. Of course, he is still decisive, he still has masculine power, but that power is given a "feminine" inflection. . . . The "macho" characteristics of goal centeredness, assertiveness, and the morality of the strongest that identify the hero in masculine television, tend here to be characteristics of the villain. (p. 186)

But if the programming manipulates gender portrayals to please the audience, then surely so must the commercials that are the programs' reason for being. My previous research (Craig, 1990) supports the argument that advertisers also structure the gender images in their commercials to match the expectations and fantasies of their intended audience. Thus, commercials portraying adult women with children were nearly four times more likely to appear during daytime soap operas than during weekend sports (p. 50). Daytime advertisers exploit the image of women as mothers to sell products to mothers. Likewise, during the weekend sports broadcasts, only 18% of the primary male characters were shown at home, while during the daytime ads, 40% of them were (p. 42). For the woman at home, men are far more likely to be portrayed as being around the house than they are in commercials aimed at men on weekends.

Gendered commercials, like gendered programs, are designed to give pleasure to the target audience, since it is the association of the product with a pleasurable experience that forms the basis for much American television advertising. Yet patriarchy conditions males and females to seek their pleasure differently. Advertisers therefore portray different images to men and women in order to exploit the different deep-seated motivations and anxieties connected to gender identity. I would now like to turn to a close analysis of four television commercials to illustrate some of these differing portrayals. Variations in how men and women are portrayed are especially apparent when comparing weekend and daytime commercials, since ads during these day parts almost completely focus on a target audience of men or women respectively.

Analysis of Four Commercials

In order to illustrate the variation of gender portrayal, I have chosen four commercials. Each was selected to provide an example of how men and women are portrayed to themselves and to the other sex. The image of men and women in commercials aired during weekend sports telecasts I call "Men's Men" and "Men's Women." The portrayals of men and women in commercials aimed at women at home during the daytime hours I call "Women's Men" and "Women's Women." Although there are certainly commercials aired during these day parts which do not fit neatly into these categories, and even a few which might be considered to be counter-stereotypical in their gender portrayals, the commercials and images I have chosen to analyze are fairly typical and were chosen to permit a closer look at the practices revealed in my earlier content analysis. Further, I acknowledge that the readings of these commercials are my own. Others may well read them differently.

Men's Men

I would first like to consider two commercials originally broadcast during 10 weekend sports and clearly aimed at men. (These and the other commercials I will discuss were broadcast on at least one of the three major networks. I recorded them for analysis during January, 1990.)

COMMERCIAL 1: ACURA INTEGRA (:30)

MUSIC: Light rock guitar music runs throughout. Tropical elements (e.g., a steel drum) are added later.

A young, white, blond, bespectacled male wearing a plain sweatshirt is shown cleaning out the interior of a car. He finds an old photograph of himself and two male companions (all are young, slender, and white) posing with a trophy-sized sailfish. He smiles. Dissolve to what appears to be a flashback of the fishing trip. The three men are now seen driving down the highway in the car (we now see that it is a new black Acura Integra) in a Florida-like landscape. We see a montage of close-ups of the three men inside the car, then a view out the car window of what looks to be the Miami skyline.

ANNOUNCER (male): "When you think about all the satisfaction you get out of going places. . . . Why would you want to take anything less . . ."

Dissolve to a silhouette shot of a young woman in a bathing suit walking along the beach at sunset.

ANNOUNCER: ". . . than America's most satisfying car?"

On this last line, the three young men are seen in silhouette knee-deep in the water at the same beach, apparently watching the woman pass. One of the men drops to his knees and throws his arms up in mock supplication. A montage of shots of the three men follows, shots of a deep-sea fishing boat intercut with shots of the first man washing the car. The montage ends with the three posing with the trophy sailfish. The screen flashes and freezes and becomes the still photo seen at the first shot of the commercial. The final shot shows a long shot of the car, freshly washed. The first man, dressed as in the first shot, gives the car a final polish and walks away. The words "Acura" and "Precision Crafted Performance" are superimposed over the final shot.

ANNOUNCER: "The Acura Integra."

This ad, which ran during a weekend sports telecast, has a number of features that makes it typical of many other commercials aimed at men. First, it is for an automobile. My previous research found that 29% of the network commercials telecast in the weekend time period were for cars and other automotive products (compared to only 1% during the daytime sample) (Craig, 1990, p. 36). In our culture, automobiles are largely the male's province, and men are seen by the automotive industry as the primary decision makers when it comes to purchases. Further, cars are frequently offered as a means of freedom (literally so in this ad), and escapism is an important component in many weekend ads (only 16% of weekend ads are set at home compared to 41% of daytime ads) (p. 43).

Second, with the exception of a brief silhouette of the woman on the beach, there are no women in this commercial. Camaraderie in all-male or nearly all-male groupings is a staple of weekend commercials, especially those for automobiles and beer. Again, my earlier research indicates that fully one-third of weekend commercials have an all-adult male cast (but only 20% of daytime commercials have an all-adult female cast) (p. 36).

The escapism and male camaraderie promised in this commercial are simply an extension of the escapism and camaraderie men enjoy when they watch (and vicariously participate in) weekend sports on television. Messner (1987) suggests that one reason for the popularity of sports with men is that it offers them a chance to escape from the growing ambiguity of masculinity in daily life.

> Both on a personal/existential level for athletes and on a symbolic/ideological level for spectators and fans, sport has become one of the "last bastions" of male power and superiority over — and separation from — the "feminization" of society. The rise of football as "America's number-one game" is likely the result of the comforting *clarity* it provides between the polarities of traditional male power, strength, and violence and the contemporary fears of social feminization. (p. 54)

The Acura commercial acts to reinforce male fantasies in an environment of clear masculinity and male domination. Men's men are frequently portrayed as men without women. The presence of women in the commercials might serve to threaten men's men with confusing uncertainty about the nature of masculinity in a sexist, but changing, society (Fiske, 1987, pp. 202–209, offers an extended psychoanalytic explanation of the absence of women in masculine television). On the other hand, the absence of women must *not* suggest homosexuality. Men's men are clearly heterosexual. To discourage any suspicions, the Acura ad portrays three (rather than two) men vacationing together.

It is also at least partly for this reason that the single quick shot in which the woman *does* appear in this commercial is important. She is nothing more than an anonymous object of desire (indeed, in silhouette, we cannot even see her face), but her presence both affirms the heterosexuality of the group while at the same time hinting that attaining sexual fulfillment will be made easier by the possession of the car. Men's men have the unchallenged freedom of a fantasized masculinity — to travel, to be free from commitment, to seek adventure.

Men's Women

COMMERCIAL 2: MILLER BEER (:30)

> We see the interior of a cheap roadside cafe. It is lit with an almost blinding sunlight streaming in the windows. A young couple sits in a far booth holding hands. A young, blond waitress is crossing the room. A silent

jukebox sits in the foreground. At first we hear only natural sounds. We cut to a close-up from a low angle from outside the cafe of male legs as they enter the cafe. The legs are clad in blue jeans and cowboy boots. As the man enters, we cut to a close-up of the blond waitress looking up to see the man. We see a close-up of the man's body as he passes the silent jukebox. As if by magic, the jukebox begins to play the rhythm and blues number "I Put a Spell on You." We see the couple that was holding hands turn in surprise. The man in the booth's face is unlit and we can see no features, but the woman is young with long blond hair. She looks surprised and pulls her hand away from the man's. We cut to an extreme close-up of the waitress's face. It is covered with sweat. As she watches the man pass, a smile appears on her face. She comes over to take the man's order. The camera takes the man's point of view.

MAN: "Miller Genuine Draft."
WAITRESS: "I was hopin' you'd say that."

We see a shot of a refrigerator door opening. The refrigerator is filled with sweating, backlit bottles of Miller beer. We then see a close-up of the man holding a bottle and opening it magically with a flick of his thumb (no opener). A montage of shots of the product amid blowing snow follows this. The sounds of a blizzard are heard.

ANNOUNCER: "Cold filtered. Never heat pasteurized. Miller Genuine Draft. For those who discover this real draft taste . . . the world is a *very* cool place."

On this last line we see close-ups of the woman in the booth and the waitress. Wind is blowing snow in their faces and they are luxuriating in the coolness. The waitress suddenly looks at the camera with shocked disappointment. We cut to an empty seat with the man's empty beer bottle rocking on the table. The music, snow, and wind end abruptly. We see the man's back as he exits the cafe. The final shot is of the waitress, elbow propped on the counter, looking after the man. The words "Tap into the Cold" are superimposed.

When women do appear in men's commercials, they seldom challenge the primary masculine fantasy. Men's women are portrayed as physically attractive, slim, and usually young and white, frequently blond, and almost always dressed in revealing clothing. Since most men's commercials are set in locations away from home, most men's women appear outside the home, and only infrequently are they portrayed as wives. There are almost always hints of sexual availability in men's women, but this is seldom played out explicitly. Although the sexual objectification of women characters in these ads is often quite subtle, my previous content analysis suggests that it is far more common in weekend than in daytime ads (Craig, 1990, p. 34). Men's women are also frequently portrayed as admirers (and at times, almost voyeurs), generally approving of some aspect of product use (the car he drives, the beer he drinks, the credit card he uses).

In these respects, the Miller ad is quite typical. What might have been a simple commercial about a man ordering and drinking a beer becomes an elaborate sexual fantasy, in many respects constructed like a porn film. The attractive, eager waitress is mystically drawn to the man who relieves her bored frustrations with an orgasmic chug-a-lug. She is "hot" while he (and the beer) is "*very* cool." But once he's satisfied, he's gone. He's too cool for conversation or commitment. We never see the man's face, but rather are invited, through the use of the point-of-view shot, to become a participant in the mystic fantasy.

There is, of course, considerable tongue-in-cheek intent in this ad. Males know that the idea of anonymous women lusting after them, eager for sex without commitment, is fantasy. But for many men, it is pleasurable fantasy, and common enough in weekend commercials. The main point is that the product has been connected, however briefly, with the pleasure of this fantasy. The physical pleasure of consuming alcohol (and specifically cold Miller beer) is tied to the pleasurable imaginings of a narrative extended beyond that which is explicitly seen.

One industry executive has explained this advertising technique. Noting the need for "an imaginary and motivating value" in ads, Nicolas (1988) argues that:

> Beyond the principle of utility, it becomes more and more important to associate a principle of pleasure to the value. The useful must be linked to the beautiful, the rational to the imaginary, the indispensable to the superfluous. . . . It is imperative that the image be seductive. (p. 7)

Although some research has documented changes in gender portrayals in [20] television advertising over the past few years (e.g., Bretl & Cantor, 1988; Ferrante, et al., 1988), such conclusions are based on across-the-schedule studies or of prime time rather than of specifically gendered day parts. While avoiding portraying women as blatant sex objects is doubtless good business in daytime or prime time, it would almost certainly inhibit male fantasies such as this one, commonly seen during weekend sports. The man's woman continues to be portrayed according to the rules of the patriarchy.

The next two commercials were originally aired during daytime soap operas. They represent Madison Avenue's portrayal of women and men designed for women.

Women's Women

COMMERCIAL 3: WEIGHT WATCHERS (:30)

> The opening shot is a quick pan from toe to head of a young, thin, white woman with dark hair. She is dressed in a revealing red bathing suit and appears to be reclining on the edge of a pool. Her head is propped up with a pillow. She is wearing sunglasses and smiling.

ANNOUNCER (woman, voice-over): "I hate diets . . . but I lost weight fast with Weight Watchers' new program."

We see the same woman sitting at a dining table in a home kitchen eating a meal. She is wearing a red dress. The camera weaves, and we briefly glimpse a man and two small children also at the table. Another close-up of the woman's body at the pool. This time the camera frames her waist.

ANNOUNCER: "And I *hate* starving myself."

We see the same family group eating pizza at a restaurant. More close-ups of the woman's body at poolside.

ANNOUNCER: "But with their new 'fast and flexible' program I don't have to."

Shot of the woman dancing with the man, followed by a montage of more shots of the family at dinner and close-ups of the woman at poolside.

ANNOUNCER: "A new food plan lets me live the way I want . . . eat with my family and friends, still have fun."

Close-up shot of balance scales. A woman's hand is moving the balance weight downward.

ANNOUNCER: "And in no time . . . *here I am!*"

Shot of the woman on the scales. She raises her hands as if in triumph. The identical shot is repeated three times.

ANNOUNCER: "Now there's only one thing I hate . . . not joining Weight Watchers sooner."

As this last line is spoken, we see a close-up of the woman at the pool. She removes her sunglasses. The man's head comes into the frame from the side and kisses her on the forehead.

This commercial portrays the woman's woman. Her need is a common one in women's commercials produced by a patriarchal society — the desire to attain and maintain her physical attractiveness. Indeed, my previous research indicates that fully 44% of the daytime ads sampled were for products relating to the body (compared with only 15% of the ads during weekend sports). In this ad, her desire for an attractive body is explicitly tied to her family. She is portrayed with a husband, small children, and a nice home. It is her husband with whom she dances and who expresses approval with a kiss. Her need for an attractive body is her need to maintain her husband's interest and maintain her family's unity and security. As Coward (1985) has written:

Most women know to their cost that appearance is perhaps the crucial way by which men form opinions of women. For that reason, feelings about self-image get mixed up with feelings about security and comfort. . . . It sometimes appears to women that the whole possibility of being loved and comforted hangs on how their appearance will be received. (p. 78)

But dieting is a difficult form of self-deprivation, and she "hates" doing it. Implicit also is her hatred of her own "overweight" body — a body that no longer measures up to the idealized woman promoted by the patriarchy (and seen in the commercial). As Coward explains:

. . . advertisements, health and beauty advice, fashion tips are effective precisely because somewhere, perhaps even subconsciously, an anxiety, rather than a pleasurable identification [with the idealized body] is awakened. (p. 80)

Weight Watchers promises to alleviate the pain of dieting at the same time it relieves (or perhaps delays) the anxiety of being "overweight." She can diet and "still have fun."

A related aspect is this ad's use of a female announcer. The copy is written in the first person, but we never see the model speaking in direct address. We get the impression that we are eavesdropping on her thoughts — being invited to identify with her — rather than hearing a sales pitch from a third person. My earlier research confirmed the findings of other content analyses that female voice-overs are relatively uncommon in commercials. My findings, however, indicated that while only 3% of the voice-overs during weekend sports were by women announcers, 16% of those during daytime were. Further, 60% of the women announcers during daytime were heard in commercials for body-related products (Craig, 1990, p. 52).

Women's Men

COMMERCIAL 4: SECRET DEODORANT (:30)

We open on a wide shot of a sailing yacht at anchor. It is sunrise and a woman is on deck. She descends into the cabin. Cut to a close-up of the woman as she enters the cabin.

WOMAN: "Four bells. Rise and shine!"

A man is seen in a bunk inside the cabin. He has just awakened. Both he and the woman are now seen to be young and white. She is thin and has bobbed hair. He is muscular and unshaven (and a Bruce Willis look-alike).

MUSIC: Fusion jazz instrumental (UNDER).
MAN (painfully): "Ohhhh . . . I can't move."
WOMAN: "Ohhhhh. I took a swim — breakfast is on — I had a shower. Now it's *your turn*."

As she says this, she crosses the cabin and places a container of Secret deodorant on a shelf above the man. The man leans up on one elbow then falls back into bed with a groan.

MAN: "Ahhh, I can't."

She pulls him back to a sitting position then sits down herself, cradling him in her arms.

WOMAN: "Come onnn. You only changed *one* sail yesterday."
MAN (playfully): "Yeah, but it was a *big* sail."

Close-up of the couple. He is now positioned in the bed sitting with his back to her. He leans his head back on her shoulder.

WOMAN: "Didn't you know sailing's a sport? You know . . . an active thing."
MAN: "I just don't get it. . . . You're so together already. . . . Um. You smell great."
WOMAN: "Must be my Secret."

She looks at the container of Secret on the shelf. The man reaches over and picks it up. Close-up of the Secret with the words "Sporty Clean Scent" visible on the container.

MAN: "Sporty clean?"
WOMAN: "It's new."
MAN: "Sounds like something I could use."
WOMAN: "Unnnnn . . . I don't think so. I got it for me."

She takes the container from him and stands up and moves away. He stands up behind her and holds her from behind.

WOMAN: "For these close quarters . . . ?"
MAN: "Well close is good."

He begins to kiss her cheek.

WOMAN: "I thought you said you couldn't move."

She turns to face him.

MAN: "I was saving my strength?"
WOMAN: "Mmmm."

We dissolve to a close-up of the product on the shelf.

ANNOUNCER (woman): "New Sporty Clean Secret. Strong enough for a man, but pH-balanced for an active woman."

This commercial portrays the woman's man. He's good looking, sensitive, romantic, and he appreciates her. What's more, they are alone in an exotic location where he proceeds to seduce her. In short, this commercial is a 30-second romance novel. She may be today's woman, be "so together," and she may be in control, but she still wants him to initiate the love-making. Her man is strong, active, and probably wealthy enough to own or rent a yacht. (Of course, a more liberated reading would have her as the owner of the yacht, or at least sharing expenses.) Yet he is also vulnerable. At first she mothers him, holding him in a Pietà-like embrace and cooing over his sore muscles. Then he catches her scent — her Secret — and the chase is on.

As in the Weight Watchers commercial, it is the woman's body that is portrayed as the source of the man's attraction, and it is only through maintaining that attraction that she can successfully negotiate the relationship. Although at one level the Secret woman is portrayed as a "new woman" — active, "sporty," self-assured, worthy of her own deodorant — she still must rely on special (even "Secret") products to make her body attractive. More to the point, she still must rely on her body to attract a man and fulfill the fantasy of security and family. After all, she is still mothering and cooking breakfast.

Once again, the product is the source of promised fantasy fulfillment — not only sexual fulfillment, but also the security of a caring relationship, one that allows her to be liberated, but not too liberated. Unlike the women of the Acura and Miller's commercials who remained anonymous objects of desire, the men of the Weight Watchers and Secret commercials are intimates who are clearly portrayed as having relationships that will exist long after the commercial is over.

Conclusion

Gender images in television commercials provide an especially intriguing field of study. The ads are carefully crafted bundles of images, frequently designed to associate the product with feelings of pleasure stemming from deep-seated fantasies and anxieties. Advertisers seem quite willing to manipulate these fantasies and exploit our anxieties, especially those concerning our gender identities, to sell products. What's more, they seem to have no compunction about capitalizing on dehumanizing gender stereotypes to seek these ends.

A threat to patriarchy is an economic threat, not only to men who may 30 fear they will have their jobs taken by women, but also in a more fundamental way. Entire industries (automotive, cosmetics, fashion) are predicated on the assumption that men and women will continue behaving according to their stereotypes. Commercials for women therefore act to reinforce patriarchy and to co-opt any reactionary ideology into it. Commercials for men need only reinforce masculinity under patriarchy and, at most, offer men help in coping with a life plagued by women of raised conscience. Betty Friedan's comments of 1963 are still valid. Those "deceptively simple, clever, outrageous ads and commercials" she wrote of are still with us. If anything, they have become more subtle and insidious. The escape from their snare is through a better understanding of gender and the role of mass culture in defining it.

WORKS CITED

Barnouw, E. (1978). *The sponsor*. New York, NY: Oxford.
Bretl, D. J., & Cantor, J. (1988). The portrayal of men and women in U.S. television commercials: A recent content analysis and trends over 15 years. *Sex Roles, 18*(9/10), 595–609.
Coward, R. (1985). *Female desires: How they are sought, bought and packaged*. New York, NY: Grove.
Craig, S. (1990, December). *A content analysis comparing gender images in network television commercials aired in daytime, evening, and weekend telecasts*. (ERIC Document Reproduction Service Number ED 329 217.)
Ferrante, C., Haynes, A., & Kingsley, S. (1988). Image of women in television advertising. *Journal of Broadcasting & Electronic Media, 32*(2), 231–237.
Fiske, J. (1987). *Television culture*. New York, NY: Methuen.
Friedan, B. (1963). *The feminine mystique*. New York, NY: Dell.
Gitlin, T. (1983). *Inside prime time*. New York, NY: Pantheon.
Jhally, S. (1987). *The codes of advertising: Fetishism and the political economy of meaning in the consumer society*. New York, NY: St. Martin's.
Messner, M. (1987). Male identity in the life course of the jock. In M. Kimmel (Ed.), *Changing men* (pp. 53–67). Newbury Park, CA: Sage.
Nicolas, P. (1988). From value to love. *Journal of Advertising Research, 28*, 7–8.

READING THE TEXT

1. How, according to John Fiske, is television programming gendered?

2. Why is male camaraderie such a common motif in "men's men" advertising, according to Craig?

3. What roles do women tend to play in the two types of commercials aimed at men? What roles do men tend to play in the two types of commercials aimed at women?

4. Why does Craig believe that "a threat to patriarchy is an economic threat" (para. 30)?

READING THE SIGNS

1. In class, discuss whether you agree with Craig's interpretations of the four commercials that he describes. If you disagree, what alternative analysis do you propose?

2. The four commercials Craig analyzes aired in 1990. View some current commercials broadcast during daytime and sports programs. Use your observations as the basis for an argument about whether the gendered patterns in advertising that Craig outlines exist today. If the patterns persist, what implications does that have for the tenacity of gender codes? If you see differences, how can you account for them?

3. Write an essay in which you support, refute, or modify Craig's belief that gendered advertising of the sort he describes is "dehumanizing" (para. 29).

4. Watch TV programs that are not overtly geared toward one gender, such as prime-time drama or network news. To what extent does the advertising that accompanies these shows fit Craig's four categories of gender portrayal? How do you account for your findings?

5. **CONNECTING TEXTS**   Enter the debate over the origins of gender identity: Is it primarily biological or largely socially constructed? Write an essay in which you advance your position; you can develop your ideas by consulting Aaron Devor's "Gender Role Behaviors and Attitudes" (p. 672), Deborah Blum's "The Gender Blur: Where Does Biology End and Society Take Over?" (p. 678), or Mariah Burton Nelson's "I Won. I'm Sorry" (p. 569).

MINETTE E. DRUMRIGHT AND PATRICK E. MURPHY

How Advertising Practitioners View Ethics: Moral Muteness, Moral Myopia, and Moral Imagination

Ever since the publication of Vance Packard's *The Hidden Persuaders* (1957), most Americans have been aware of the psychological tricks and games played by advertisers, but very little attention has been paid to what advertising personnel think of the ethics of their profession. To fill in this gap, Minette E. Drumright and Patrick E. Murphy conducted a study that included interviews with advertising professionals at twenty-nine different agencies and discovered that advertisers generally break down into two groups: those who feel that ethics is largely irrelevant to advertising, and those who "typically recognized moral issues and talked about them inside the agency with their coworkers and outside the agency with their clients and potential clients." So many informants, however, belonged to the first group that Drumright and Murphy have broken down their attitudes into categories that run the gamut from "Moral Myopia" to "Moral Imagination." Their results may well explain why you are still likely to see simulated rape scenes in fashion magazine advertising spreads. Minette E. Drumright is an associate professor in the department of advertising at the University of Texas at Austin and Patrick E. Murphy is C. R. Smith Codirector of the Institute for Ethical Business Worldwide and professor of marketing at the University of Notre Dame.

Advertising practitioners face ethical issues that are common to all professionals, but they also encounter issues related to factors unique to advertising. Despite some academic and popular discussion of ethics in advertising, ranging from its broad social consequences to consumers' perceptions of potentially objectionable ads, we know little about how advertising practitioners react to ethical issues when they arise. This paper is an attempt to address this relatively neglected area. Our focus is to examine how advertising practitioners perceive, process, and think about ethical issues. Summarizing our findings, within our sample of the advertising community, significant numbers of practitioners either do not see ethical dilemmas that arise or their vision is shortsighted. Reasons or justifications for this visual impairment can be categorized. When ethical issues are recognized, there is little communication about them. There are exceptions, however — some practitioners do see and talk about ethical issues. Finally, the type of organizational community has an impact on awareness of ethical issues and ways of dealing with them.

Findings

Generally speaking, we found two kinds of advertising practitioners with regard to ethical sensitivity, and as discussed below, generally speaking, this division was a result of where they worked. We first report our findings regarding the group that was less ethically sensitive and then contrast them with findings from the more ethically sensitive group.

We start from a normative position. We assume that ethical issues can and do arise in advertising, and that when and if they do arise, it is best if they are acknowledged and dealt with in what would be considered an ethical way. That said, we acknowledge that reasonable people can disagree over whether a particular situation poses an ethical dilemma, as well as over what the ethical response should be.

Ethical issues did not appear to be on the radar screens of our first group of informants. As one informant noted:

> Usually, ethics is something that doesn't seem to apply much. . . . You don't really think about it too much.

Even when ethical issues were noticed, they often were not discussed. As one informant put it in what was an oft-reported phenomenon:

> It's unfortunate, but it's [ethics] not a high priority. . . . This line of questioning is so interesting because it has never come up.

"Moral muteness," a term borrowed from Bird and Waters (1989), was pervasive among our first group of informants. Ethical issues did not enter into discourse at either an individual or organizational level. Bird (1996) states that people are morally mute "when they do not recognizably communicate their moral concerns in settings where such communicating would be fitting" (p. 27). When they would be expected to express themselves with respect to ethical concerns, "they either voice no moral sentiments or communicate in ways that obscure their moral beliefs and commitments" (Bird 2002, p. 16).

In addition to moral muteness, we also found what we call "moral myopia."[1] In fact, the myopia helped explain the muteness. We define moral myopia as a distortion of moral vision, ranging from shortsightedness to near blindness, which affects an individual's perception of an ethical dilemma. Moral myopia hinders moral issues from coming clearly into focus, particularly those that are not proximate, and it can be so severe that it may render a person effectively morally blind. If moral issues are not seen at all or are somehow distorted, it is highly unlikely that sound ethical decision making will occur. The most proximate issues and those most likely to be in focus were at the workaday level of the individual, which usually were intimately tied to the individual's personal self-interest (e.g., "Is anyone stealing my ideas?"). Less proximate and more likely to be affected by myopia were issues regarding advertising messages and organizational practices of agencies and clients. Least proximate and most likely to be affected by myopia were issues referred to as "advertising's unintended social consequences." Pollay (1986, p. 19) defined the unintended social consequences of advertising as "the social byproducts of the exhortations to 'buy products,'" which tend to occur at the aggregate level of society. While we found evidences of moral myopia regarding ethical issues at all three levels — that of the individual, the organization, and society — moral shortsightedness was most acute at the societal level. We see distinct similarities between moral myopia and Levitt's (1960) marketing myopia in that both involve an inability to "see" certain important issues that are a part of the larger context in which one is working.

Not only did we find moral muteness and moral myopia; we also sought to understand the underlying assumptions, perceptions, and paradigms that support them. To do so, we examined informants' responses in more depth to understand the ways they frame and think about ethical issues. The responses ranged from a rejection of the possibility of ethical concerns in advertising at all to a variety of rationalizations that largely dismissed potential ethical concerns or responsibility. Sometimes multiple rationalizations were used simultaneously by a single individual — woven into a web of supporting rationalizations. Some informants evidenced both myopia and muteness. Indeed, these problems frequently overlapped and were

---

[1] In *The Muted Conscience*, Bird (1996) described various moral shortcomings, including moral silence, moral blindness, and moral deafness. Moral myopia is similar to his notion. We simply label it a bit differently as it applies to our informants' answers. We use the term "moral" as a synonym for "ethical" to describe muteness and myopia. This interpretation is slightly different from some of the moral philosophical accounts, which define morality as more of a systemwide practice and ethics to be more individually focused (DeGeorge 1999, p. 19).

reinforcing. Nevertheless, in principle, moral muteness and moral myopia are different. It is helpful to distinguish a perspective that does not really see a problem from a perspective in which the problem is seen but avoided and not discussed.

Moral Myopia

Many of our informants had difficulty seeing ethical issues or seeing them clearly. Our assessment is that people may be affected by moral myopia in varying degrees of severity, ranging from blindness to shortsightedness. While some people fail to see the moral dimension of problems at all, others have distorted moral vision that results largely from rationalization or from an unwillingness to focus on the problem so that it is seen clearly. The rationalizations contribute to and reinforce the perceptual problem. Interestingly, these responses could be categorized. We report the categories that we heard time and again. Although usually only one informant is quoted, the quotation is representative of what others expressed.

CONSUMERS ARE SMART

> Consumers are really smart, really astute. . . . I feel like I am so unpowerful that if I were unethical in my [creative] presentation [of the advertising message] and were I to oversell, I would be found out so incredibly quickly.

We heard about a strong and unwavering faith in consumers. This faith asserted that consumers are smart and therefore cannot and will not be fooled or led astray by any unethical advertising message. Since consumers will not be misled, the advertising message does not need to be ethically evaluated. This rationalization is understandable, and is certainly not unique to advertising, but in the advertising context, it seems less persuasive. It seems somewhat surprising that people whose professional raison d'être is to create advertising that works would simultaneously assert the powerlessness of their endeavors. Some informants seemed to want to have it both ways, claiming that advertising is important, worthy, and effective in selling products, but at the same time asserting that it is also relatively powerless to mislead or have any harmful effects.

PASSING THE BUCK

> Personally I haven't thought much about this issue [negative effects of advertising], but now I think the responsibility goes back to families and the law.

Informants rationalized responsibility for the negative effects of advertising by "passing the buck." The number of potential parties to whom the buck was passed was large and included families, especially parents, peers, the media, the movies, MTV, videos, clients, the regulators, and others. Relatedly, often the buck was passed to society at large. Informants asserted that they are not creating images but merely reflecting the images that already exist in society, which is what society wants. Thus, any responsibility and/or blame should be placed on society, not on advertising. This was another iteration of the age-old debate of whether advertising creates or reflects society (Lantos 1987; Pollay 1986). As one agency president said:

> We're more sheep than we are shepherds. We follow the trends. We don't create them. We're too scared to create them; our clients are too scared to create them.

Another practitioner put it this way:

> Are you going to use an overweight, short gal with an acne problem to sell that product, or are you going to use a model with big breasts and a lot of skin? Unfortunately, that is more of a reflection of society and what society wants to see than advertisers setting out and creating this false image. . . . I think this is also what society wants to believe about itself.

One need not resolve whether advertising creates or reflects society to admit that advertising bears some responsibility. Taking an example from earlier history, advertising did not create racism, but many would say the industry contributed to it when pandering to racial stereotypes. The "sheep not shepherd" assumption enabled many advertising practitioners to avoid any responsibility for advertising's unintended consequences and for making moral judgments about them.

The buck was also passed to products and clients. The problem was 10 with the products, not with the advertising itself. Clients, not agencies, bore responsibility for the products. Advertising professionals saw themselves as scapegoats. They and their profession were unjust recipients of blame that should be directed at other parties. Because advertising is visible and salient, it is a vulnerable, convenient, and easy target. In a slight variation of this theme with a McLuhanesque twist, one practitioner explained:

> We've become the scapegoat for things we don't even create. We're so easy to find on the radar screen. . . . . We actually create something. We take the brunt of "Television is bad for you," which has become "Advertising is bad for you."

WHAT IS LEGAL IS MORAL

Related to buck passing, our informants, like many others, often equated the legal with the moral. Writers in ethics generally view the law as the "floor" — the moral minimum — but for some of our informants, if it is legal, it is ethical (Drumwright 1993; Preston 1994). A number of our informants assumed that because regulations exist and because attorneys are involved, they themselves are off the hook. As an agency president explained:

> I think this is probably one of the most ethical businesses there is. It is so regulated. Everything that we do has to go through our lawyers to make sure that it's conforming to law, and then our client's lawyers, and then we have to send it through to the networks and their lawyers. . . . It's really hard to be unethical in this business even if you wanted to.

Another senior ad agency executive framed his comments about a specific product, but his point was that the law, not ethics, should drive advertising.

> I don't feel it's ethically wrong to advertise them [cigarettes]. I don't smoke. . . . My feeling is that if they want to make it illegal, fine. But as long as it's a legal product, it should be legally sold.

The two quotes above address slightly different issues. The first is a position generally rejected as a sound basis for an ethical conclusion, that is, the contention that if it is legal, it is moral. The latter perspective is more complicated and has many adherents in advertising and beyond. Whatever one's conclusion on this matter, the potential danger is that it can buffer advertising practitioners (or any other professionals for that matter) from serious consideration of ethical issues. The worrisome thing about the perspectives exemplified by both of the quotes above is that ethical decision making is delegated to attorneys or policymakers, and it assumes that the observance of the law or regulation is sufficient. Preston (1994, p. 128) asserted that "ethics begins only where the law ends." His logic is that "the law tells you what you must do," whereas "ethics prompts you to do things even though you don't have to." As such, Preston observed that for advertisers who believed that the law was sufficient, "ethics never really starts." The "legal is moral" approach is particularly problematic given Preston's arguments that for some advertising claims, the law ends too soon. The law is often a "blunt tool"—a cumbersome and often inefficient method with which to deal with ethical issues.

THE FIRST AMENDMENT MISUNDERSTANDING

We heard frequent references to the First Amendment as a justification for not "censoring" advertising messages. For example, when an agency president was asked if he had considered developing a code of ethics for his agency and the advertising produced for their clients, he responded, "How could I? It would violate the First Amendment." He then pledged his allegiance to the First Amendment, suggested that everyone was attacking it, and expounded on the need to protect the First Amendment.

A naïve understanding, or perhaps a misunderstanding, of the First 15 Amendment was prevalent among some of our informants. The Supreme

Court has never afforded absolute protection to speech, despite Justice Hugo Black's literal interpretation that the free speech clause of the First Amendment, "Congress shall make no law," meant that Congress should absolutely make no law that would infringe speech. Moreover, it has determined that "commercial speech" does not receive all the protection of other forms of speech. That said, the commercial speech distinction is being increasingly diminished by the Court (see *Central Hudson v. Public Service Commission* and *44 Liquormart, Inc. v. Rhode Island*).

But these doctrinal issues are not the source of the naïveté to which we refer. The First Amendment prohibits government from abridging freedom of speech; it does not stand for the proposition that all speech is equally worthy and should be uttered or encouraged, or that speakers should not be condemned for the speech that they make. To the extent that informants quoted speech maxims, they only talked about a part of the story. The part they understood was that there are desirable aspects to a "marketplace of ideas" that is free from governmental control. The justification for a "marketplace of ideas" assumes that ideas that are not currently popular should not be prohibited by the government because they may contain kernels of truth. The part informants did not understand or did not remember is that the marketplace metaphor assumes that "bad" ideas are supposed to be exposed for the lies they perpetuate and the damage that they do to the truth. Once exposed, they are to be roundly condemned. Indeed, the justification for the government allowing "bad" (i.e., false, hurtful, misleading) speech to enter the marketplace is so that it can be discredited. That the government does not prosecute those who make racial slurs does not mean that racial epithets should be encouraged. In short, some of our informants misinterpreted free speech law as meaning that they were exonerated from personal and professional responsibility, or perhaps they misunderstood the First Amendment more generally. Advertising professionals, like all speakers, have a responsibility to make judgments about speech. This becomes even more the case as the Supreme Court lessens the distinction between commercial and noncommercial speech.

GOING NATIVE

Another reported phenomenon that distorts moral vision involves becoming so close to a client's business and corporate culture that one fails to recognize or ask moral questions. We refer to this as "going native." This phenomenon is often associated with anthropologists, foreign service officers, or others who become overly immersed in foreign cultures to the point that they lose their objectivity. In advertising, going native involves overidentifying with the client's perspective to the point that one loses the ability to be critical of clients and objective in assessing their behavior and advertising. One informant elaborated on her experience:

> When you've got a group of [client] R & D people telling you this [good things about the product], and the demos . . . are showing you that maybe it's not as [good] as they make it out to be, you believe [the good things]. If you're living it every day, you believe it. . . . So, when you tell the consumer about it, you find that you're stretching the truth. This [product] is your life. It becomes your life for a year. So it doesn't feel like you're doing anything wrong.

When advertising practitioners go native, it can render them less able to make critical moral judgments.

THE OSTRICH SYNDROME

Like the ostrich with its head in the sand, when out of sight, looming ethical issues were out of mind. Or as one informant succinctly put it: "Ignorance is bliss." A seasoned veteran with more than 15 years in the business admitted:

> I think that if I did a little bit more digging into a company's connections . . . then yes, I'd probably have a problem working on it.

Better not to dig. Again, this is not unique to advertising, but the hectic pace of the advertising business and the transient nature of projects made it easy to adopt this approach. A less experienced practitioner alluded to this:

> I don't have a lot of time to sit and think about if the people who make this thing are really evil. You just don't have time to do that. That's just the reality of it.

Moral Muteness

We now turn to moral muteness. Though moral myopia and moral muteness are often intertwined and reinforce one another, it is helpful conceptually to distinguish them. Moral muteness refers to individuals who recognize ethical issues but remain silent and avoid confronting them either personally or organizationally. Moral muteness occurs whenever people fail to communicate moral concerns that they genuinely feel, regardless of how the failure happens. Bird (2002, p. 34) identifies three forms of moral muteness: (1) negative expressions (e.g., not blowing the whistle on observed abuses, not questioning aspects of decisions thought to be morally debatable); (2) positive expressions (e.g., not speaking up for ideals), and (3) not holding others sufficiently accountable (e.g., not providing adequate feedback in supervisory relationships). Upon examination of our informants' responses, we identified four categories of rationalizations that help to explain muteness.

COMPARTMENTALIZATION

One approach that contributed to moral muteness was compartmentaliza- 20 tion. The classic form separates one's work life from one's personal life and convictions. The result is having one set of standards for work and another for nonwork matters. When asked about ethical issues at both the organizational and societal level, one young practitioner, a star creative talent, described the classic case of compartmentalization:

> I know that things go on. When I'm at home, all of these things sicken me, really. But when I'm here, it's different because I'm so into creatively what I'm doing, it's like a different picture.

Compartmentalization, which can occur for many reasons, is a complex phenomenon that can be driven by positive forces. The comment above illustrates how enjoyment of the work itself, particularly the creative aspect, encourages compartmentalization. Creativity was viewed by our informants as a chief virtue. Perhaps, and this is only speculation, when one is pursuing something that is good—being creative, entertaining the public, increasing wealth, furthering democracy, and so forth—it can serve to further compartmentalization.

Compartmentalization often involved separating one's personal standards from a client's business standards. A seasoned veteran demonstrated this approach:

> The [client] company is running a business. They can choose what they want to convey. . . . Therefore, if they want to put in these models who look like they're taking heroin or heroin chic or ultrathin models, then that is their right because it is their business, and they're running it the way that they want to. On a personal level, I find it very offensive.

The informant has a young daughter and expressed concern regarding the potential influence of advertising on children and their conceptions of beauty. Nonetheless, she compartmentalized those concerns, and as the above quote reveals, she did not make a moral judgment or exert influence on the client.

Two issues that some respondents viewed as raising ethical problems were cigarette advertising and advertising to young children, but these, too, were vulnerable to forms of compartmentalization. The informant quoted above illustrates compartmentalization with respect to advertising's effect on children. With respect to cigarettes, we observed a different variation of compartmentalization. Many agencies appeared to allow their employees substantial leeway in declining to work on controversial products, and a number of individuals said, "I'll refuse to work on cigarette advertising." This refrain was sounded often, especially by the more junior advertising practitioners, and it represents a sea change among advertising practitioners, who formerly flocked to the side of the cigarette companies (Rangan 1989). Often, however, informants appeared to ignore the connection between their personal position and their employers' institutional position. One senior executive did acknowledge the conflict:

> I personally never, would never, will never work on a cigarette ad. . . . I'm a hypocrite because . . . if the agency makes money, I get a bonus; part of that is cigarette money. I just won't work on it. I just feel better, but you want to know what it is? It's [expletive]. We shouldn't do cigarettes.

There were many ways to compartmentalize, but they all resulted in the same effect. They permitted informants to avoid taking responsibility for negative effects of advertising.

THE CLIENT IS ALWAYS RIGHT

> Most clients come in saying they want to have really terrific advertising. . . . I found very quickly that what they want is for us to collude with them on issues. And I never can predict what it will be. We can agree to pretend to each other that they have reached excellence in some area. . . . I'm not a hard-ass in that I have people who want to keep their jobs. . . . I collude with them. . . . I always wish that I could be very straightforward with my clients, but they don't want it. They really don't want it. It's just annoying to them.

The client-is-always-right syndrome means that informants did not want to tell clients "no" regarding ethics or anything else. This often led informants into the role of a "please-o-holic" or "yes-person" rather than that of a trusted business collaborator with an eye toward constructive advice that may be critical at times. It reinforced the perception that advertising practitioners do not have the right to pass judgment on clients. As one young practitioner explained:

> Obviously, the last thing that you want to do is to tell your client that they're wrong. You're shooting yourself in the foot if you do that.

A senior executive had this to say:

> Obviously, agencies don't like saying "No" to a client. They don't like telling a client that he or she cannot do something, whether it's time constraints or budget constraints or it just doesn't make sense.

There were repeated claims that clients did not want to be confronted with critical questioning from their advertising agencies. In response, some informants came to believe that they should not evaluate or pass judgment on their client's ethical values:

> So the last thing that you want to do is make them [the client] feel uncomfortable about what they're doing and what their beliefs are.

Along with please-o-holic tendencies, avoidance of criticism means that an 25 agency does not collaborate with the client as a full-fledged partner. It keeps an agency in a subordinate position, at times forcing it to censor what could be its most valuable contribution — its criticism, related to ethics or otherwise. It also reinforces the notion that advertising practitioners should not exercise the prerogative of making moral judgments about clients or exerting influence on them. These findings reinforce a description of advertisers, agencies, and the media as an "unholy trinity," in which all three parties abdicate ethical responsibility and behavior sinks to a low level (Murphy 1998b). Fiduciary responsibility then becomes equated with doing the client's bidding. To some degree, this tendency exists in other client-related businesses; however, it appears that advertising practitioners may have a special reluctance to assert their opinions. For example, lawyers must represent their clients' interests, but part of the job of a lawyer is to instruct clients in what is in their best interest.

ETHICS IS BAD FOR BUSINESS

Cultural disincentives discouraged talking about ethical considerations. One particularly strong disincentive was that ethics was viewed as a conservative constraint, a sentence to blandness in advertising messages. What could be worse in an industry that strives for scintillating messages that "push the edge of the envelope" and are "over the top" or "edgy"? As the chief creative officer of one agency explained:

> Unfortunately, the solution [to ethical dilemmas] is often to do even less interesting advertising that's even more acceptable to the masses by offending no one.

Another significant disincentive involved inferences that were perceived to be made regarding people who would raise such concerns. For example, there was a fear that clients or coworkers would equate one who raises ethical concerns with a lack of business acumen. The chief creative officer quoted above elaborated on the reasons that advertising practitioners do not raise ethical issues with clients:

> The reason the agency doesn't want to come in and say, "Hey, this isn't ethical," is because they would be laughed out of the office. I think that they're afraid that the client would say, "Well, if you want to run a church, run a church, but if you want to make some money, you're going to have to do it our way." . . . I think there is a fear that if they were to talk about it [ethical concerns], then all of a sudden, they are taken less seriously as a businessperson. And they are looked upon suspiciously as someone who has let their religious philosophies get in the way of their business acumen.

PANDORA'S BOX SYNDROME

Some expressed the view that raising any ethical issues must be avoided for fear of opening a Pandora's box. As a result, potentially harmful effects of advertising were simply not confronted or discussed since considering them could be too dangerous. It could lead one to becoming less effective at work or worse. The effects of opening a Pandora's box could ultimately prompt one to leave the industry. As one senior executive explained:

> When you start looking for ethical issues, they are everywhere. . . . You open up a can of worms that just goes on and on and on. . . . You could get so bogged down in wondering if what you are doing is right that you would end up not doing anything. . . . If you look and probe and focus the microscope, you finally get down to, "It's the darn system." . . . You pretty much get to the point, "Are we going to be in advertising or not?"

The Pandora's box syndrome seemed to block reflection and critical thinking. It caused some advertising practitioners to shy away from critically examining issues affecting the larger profession and its impact.

"Seeing, Talking" Advertising Practitioners

> I think that one of the things that would be helpful in terms of the advertising industry is to have more communication about marketing ethics. . . . I think it would make for smarter consumers and a smarter agency and smarter clients.

Notable exceptions emerged to our findings of myopia and muteness among advertising practitioners. There were "seeing, talking" advertising practitioners who typically recognized moral issues and talked about them inside the agency with their coworkers and outside the agency with their clients and potential clients. We now examine the themes that differentiated these individuals from others in our sample. We noted no systematic differences between the individuals in the first and second groups in terms of age, seniority level, gender, job assignment, or background. We did note a difference in the contexts in which these individuals worked. Almost without exception, the agencies in which the "seeing, talking" practitioners worked appeared to have organizational cultures and climates that encouraged moral seeing and talking. These agencies appeared to have some authentic norms regarding ethical behavior that were widely held and clearly articulated by members of the community. In addition, the agencies tended to be small, privately held agencies in one location or nearly autonomous units of large conglomerates typically in only one location. As mentioned earlier, we intentionally conducted additional interviews in agencies in which we found ethically sensitive informants to gain a better understanding of both this type of informant and the contexts in which they were working. The ways in which the "seeing, talking" advertising practitioners differed from the others in our sample can be likened to a decision-making process: recognition of the issue, communication about it, and the decision itself.

RECOGNITION

The "seeing, talking" advertising practitioners appeared to recognize moral issues readily, evidencing moral discernment and understanding. For example, one informant reported that he and a colleague had recognized an unethical practice when reviewing a potential client's past advertising and had told the potential client in no uncertain terms that they were unwilling to accept the company as a client if it wanted to continue ethically problematic work of that nature. Another agency executive explained:

> Whenever we get a sense that [a promise that can't be fulfilled] is in the back of a client's mind, we point it out, and it usually goes away.

Upon recognizing unethical behavior, one individual reported that he and his colleagues ridiculed it, refusing to take it seriously.

> If, when we're getting creative, something that's unethical comes up, we laugh more than anything else. [We say,] "We can't do that; that's ridiculous." . . .
> To me, it's almost an embarrassment to take something to a client and have them say, "We can't do that. That's unethical." The agency should have felt that way before the client did.

This is in contrast to other advertising practitioners who feared that if they brought up an ethical issue, their co-workers and clients would think that they did not have business savvy. Rather than talking of "smart consumers" who cannot be deceived, these informants talked of "smart clients," who know that being unethical is not good for business. Again, this is in contrast to other informants who refrained from confronting their clients, thereby supposedly "shooting themselves in the foot." These "seeing, talking" advertising practitioners did not conceive of their roles as merely doing their clients' bidding. Instead, their roles encompassed making judgments and asserting opinions, as would be expected of a trusted partner.

There was one notable exception to the moral seeing and speaking of these informants, which frequently tended to be a blind spot. Like our other informants with moral muteness and moral myopia, they too often failed to see or be concerned about advertising's unintended social consequences. As one said:

> I don't worry about those things. I don't believe that those are the consequences [of advertising].

Another explained:

> I do not subscribe to that theory [that advertising has unintended consequences]. I do not believe it. I think that advertising is a reflection of society. . . . Maybe nobody in this business believes this. Otherwise, we'd be lawyers.

This is in keeping with Rotzoll and Christians' (1980) finding that the advertising practitioners in their sample, whom they portrayed as ethically sensitive, "generally think in terms of the closest at hand, apparently finding something like 'consequences to society' as too amorphous and involving too many results, which are simply incalculable. Social and institutional questions, therefore, receive only meager attention" (p. 429).

Some of our informants did, however, acknowledge advertising's unintended consequences:

> I'll have to be honest. There is no question that there seems to be a growing degree of expressed interest on the part of people as to advertising's unintended consequences. I guess we always need to be mindful that the communications that we create can have a ripple effect—unintended and unmeant kinds of consequences. An example is videogames and the contribution that those kinds of messages have to promote the nation's undercurrent of aggressive or violent behavior. Yeah, I do think that we need to be mindful of that.

COMMUNICATION

The "seeing, talking" advertising practitioners professed a strong belief in the importance of overt, direct communication, and it was not unusual for these communications to have an ethical dimension. As one senior agency executive said, "People need to talk. . . . Communication is good. We talk 15 to 20 times a day." These individuals tried to be clear in communicating their ethical values as they solicited new business, and they reported instances in which they had been direct and forthright in confronting their clients and prospective clients about their values. They even used the values of potential clients as a screening criterion in accepting new business. As one individual expressed, "We do not want to work with people who are not fair as an organization." Another informant put it even more frankly:

> And we try to be very clear with our clients, from the first time that we meet them, about what we stand for. That it's about the work, and they need to be able to not just tolerate, but welcome and encourage, bone honesty. And we're going to give them our opinion, and they're not always going to like that.

These informants often spoke of agency leaders who communicated 35 the importance of ethics both through the examples that they set and clear statements of their values. More often than not, they reported that their agencies had an official statement that communicated a comprehensive, overarching vision of the kind of culture they wanted the agency to nurture. These visions were based on well thought out principles, and they often had been created by a group of individuals who had gone through "a lot of soul searching about what kind of community we were going to be." The visions typically were prominently featured in permanent displays within the agencies and communicated externally as well. The point is not that these agencies had statements or codes, but that the statements or codes appeared to articulate authentic norms of the agency communities and efforts were made to put them into action.

SAYING NO

Some advertising practitioners had the moral courage to say no to their co-workers and to their clients. For example, one agency CEO walked away from the agency's largest account when the client's COO insisted that he do something that he deemed unfair and unethical. He was widely quoted among workers in his agency as asserting, "It's OK to get fired. It's OK to resign." He not only said no, he obviously talked about it in his agency. These views were in stark contrast to prevalent sentiments described earlier that the client must be pleased at all costs. A related sentiment that these informants identified as being a part of the agency culture was, "It's OK to make mistakes." This perception enabled individuals to be straightforward about their mistakes, freeing them from the need to lie about them or cover them up.

BEYOND NORMAL VISION: MORAL IMAGINATION

At times, the "seeing, talking" advertising practitioners demonstrated what some scholars have referred to as moral imagination (e.g., Johnson 1993; Werhane 1999). Moral imagination entails being able to see and think outside the box, envisioning moral alternatives that others do not. Our research was not designed to study moral imagination, but as we studied the real problems faced by practitioners, we saw many instances of where imaginative solutions were needed. Moreover, we believe we saw some instances in which moral imagination was employed. For example, the agency CEO who walked away from his largest account when his client insisted that he do something that he considered unethical appeared to exhibit not only moral seeing and talking, but moral imagination. He readily envisioned the implications that the unethical behavior would bring about for him, for his agency, and for his client's competitors. He also knew that resigning the account, which represented more than 25% of the agency's billings, could force him to lay off a number of agency employees, but he did not succumb to thinking he had only two alternatives—act unethically, keep the account, and avoid layoffs or act ethically and lay off a number of workers. He discussed these problems openly and at length with his client and with his coworkers. Through the discussions, the CEO envisioned a resourceful way to keep from laying people off if they lost or resigned the client. When the client refused to yield, the CEO resigned the account and implemented the alternative, avoiding layoffs. Through the combined use of moral seeing, talking, and imagination, the CEO had found an acceptable and ethical solution.

The "seeing, talking" advertising practitioners appear to have mastered the various aspects of Rest's (1994, p. 23) model of four psychological components determining moral behavior: "1) moral sensitivity (interpreting the situation), 2) moral judgment (judging which action is morally right/wrong), 3) moral motivation (prioritizing moral values relative to other values), and 4) moral character (having courage, persisting, overcoming distractions, implementing skills)." When informants demonstrated moral imagination, they also exhibited an added dimension involving unique insights, inventiveness, and resourcefulness. This enabled them to generate moral alternatives that others had not seen and uniquely equipped them to engage in moral problem solving. This dimension is somewhat akin to what Levitt (1986) identified as "marketing imagination," through which marketers make "an inspired leap from the obvious to the meaningful," reconceptualize a problem, and generate an ingenious solution to it.[2]

Conclusions

The first step in solving a problem is identifying it and developing a better understanding of it. In this paper, we have identified moral muteness and moral myopia and tried to shed light on the rationalizations and communities that support or counteract them. We have also reported evidence of moral imagination and identified the characteristics of the communities in which it, along with moral seeing and talking, flourishes. We hope that the directions for future research that our study has produced will serve as a catalyst for improving the theory and practice of advertising and marketing ethics in academic and advertising communities.

REFERENCES

Advertising Age (1988), "Industry Ethics Are Alive," 59 (April 18), 88.

Aristotle (1962), *Nicomachean Ethics*, New York: Macmillan.

Arnould, Eric J., and Linda L. Price (1993), "River Magic: Extraordinary Experience and the Extended Service Encounter," *Journal of Consumer Research*, 20 (June), 24–45.

Bird, Frederick B. (1996), *The Muted Conscience: Moral Silence and the Practice of Business Ethics*, Westport, CN: Quorum Books.

———— (2002), *The Muted Conscience: Moral Silence and the Practice of Business Ethics*, rev. ed., Westport, CN: Quorum Books.

————, and James A. Waters (1989), "The Moral Muteness of Managers," *California Management Review*, 32 (Fall), 73–88.

Bishop, F. P. (1949), *The Ethics of Advertising*, Bedford Square, UK: Robert Hale.

Bonoma, Thomas V. (1985), "Case Research in Marketing: Opportunities, Problems, and a Process," *Journal of Marketing Research*, 22 (May), 199–208.

[2]The commonality between "marketing imagination" and "moral imagination" was suggested to us by George Brenkert of Georgetown University.

Braybrooke, David (1965), *Philosophical Problems of the Social Sciences*, New York: Macmillan.

Brenkert, George G. (1998), "Ethics in Advertising: The Good, the Bad, and the Church," *Journal of Public Policy and Marketing*, 17 (Fall), 325–331.

Central Hudson Gas v. Public Service Commission, 447 U.S. 557 (1980).

Chen, Amber Wenling, and Jeanne Mei-Chi Liu (1998), "Agency Practitioners' Perceptions of Professional Ethics in Taiwan," *Journal of Business Ethics*, 17 (January), 15–23.

Cunningham, Peggy H. (1999), "Ethics of Advertising," in *The Advertising Business*, John Phillip Jones, ed., Thousand Oaks, CA: Sage, 499–513.

Davis, Joel J. (1994), "Ethics in Advertising Decisionmaking: Implications for Reducing the Incidence of Deceptive Advertising," *The Journal of Consumer Affairs*, 28 (Winter), 380–402.

DeGeorge, Richard T. (1999), *Business Ethics*, 5th ed., Upper Saddle River, NJ: Prentice Hall.

Dexter, Lewis Anthony (1970), *Elite and Specialized Interviewing*, Evanston, IL: Northwestern University Press.

Dougherty, Deborah (1990), "Understanding New Markets for Products," *Strategic Management Journal*, 11 (January), 59–78.

——— (1992), "Interpretive Barriers to Successful Product Innovation in Large Firms," *Organizational Science*, 3 (May), 179–202.

Drumright, Minette E. (1993), "Ethical Issues in Advertising and Sales Promotion," in *Ethics in Marketing*, N. Craig Smith and John A. Quelch, eds., Homewood, IL: Irwin.

——— (1994), "Socially Responsible Organizational Buying: Environmental Concern as a Noneconomic Buying Criterion," *Journal of Marketing*, 58 (July), 1–19.

——— (1996), "Company Advertising with a Social Dimension: The Role of Noneconomic Criteria," *Journal of Marketing*, 60 (October), 71–88.

Dunfee, Thomas W., N. Craig Smith, and William T. Ross, Jr. (1999), "Social Contracts and Marketing Ethics," *Journal of Marketing*, 63 (July), 14–32.

Eisenhardt, Kathleen M. (1989), "Building Theory from Case Study Research," *Academy of Management Review*, 14 (October), 532–550.

Federal Trade Commission (1980), "Guides Concerning Use of Endorsements and Testimonials in Advertising," 16CFR 255, available at www.ftc.gov/bcp/guides/endorse.htm (accessed April 14, 2004).

Ferrell, O. C., Mary Zey-Ferrell, and Dean Krugman (1983), "Comparisons of Predictors of Ethical and Unethical Behaviors Among Corporate and Advertising Agency Managers," *Journal of Macromarketing*, 3 (Spring), 19–27.

Fielding, Nigel G., and Jane L. Fielding (1986), *Linking Data*, Newbury Park, CA: Sage.

Galbraith, John Kenneth (1958), *The Affluent Society*, Boston: Houghton Mifflin.

——— (1967), *The New Industrial State*, Boston: Houghton Mifflin.

Golden-Biddle, Karen, and Karen Locke (1993), "Appealing Work: An Investigation of How Ethnographic Texts Convince," *Organization Science*, 4 (November), 595–616.

Gulas, Charles S., and Kim McKeage (2000), "Extending Social Comparison: An Examination of the Unintended Consequences of Idealized Advertising Imagery," *Journal of Advertising*, 29 (Summer), 17–28.

Hartman, Edwin M. (1994), "The Commons and the Moral Organization," *Business Ethics Quarterly*, 4 (July), 253–270.

——— (1996), *Organizational Ethics and the Good Life*, New York: Oxford University Press.

Hofstede, Geert H. (1980), *Culture's Consequences: International Differences in Work-Related Values*, Beverly Hills, CA: Sage.

———— (1983), "The Cultural Relativity of Organizational Practices and Theories," *Journal of International Business Studies*, 14 (Fall), 75–89.

Hunt, Shelby D., and Lawrence B. Chonko (1987), "Ethical Problems of Advertising Agency Executives," *Journal of Advertising*, 16 (4), 16–24.

————, V. R. Wood, and Lawrence B. Chonko (1989), "Corporate Ethical Values and Organizational Commitment in Marketing," *Journal of Marketing*, 53 (July), 79–90.

Hyman, Michael R., Richard Tansley, and James W. Clark (1994), "Research on Advertising Ethics: Past, Present, and Future," *Journal of Advertising*, 23 (3), 5–15.

James, E. Lincoln, Cornelius B. Pratt, and Tommy V. Smith (1994), "Advertising Ethics: Practitioner and Student Perspectives," *Journal of Mass Media Ethics*, 9 (2), 69–83.

Johnson, Mark (1993), *Moral Imagination: Implications of Cognitive Science for Ethics*, Chicago, IL: University of Chicago Press.

King, Nigel (1994), "The Qualitative Research Interview," in *Qualitative Methods in Organizational Research: A Practical Guide*, Catherine Cassell and Gillian Symon, eds., Thousand Oaks, CA: Sage.

Kohlberg, Lawrence (1967), "Moral and Religious Education in the Public Schools: A Developmental View," in *Religion and Public Education*, Theodor R. Sizer, ed., Boston, MA: Houghton Mifflin.

———— (1971), "From Is To Ought," in *Cognitive Development and Epistemology*, Theodore Mischel, ed., New York: NY Academic Press.

———— (1984), *The Psychology of Moral Development*, San Francisco: Harper and Row.

Kover, Arthur J. (1995), "Copywriters' Implicit Theories of Communication: An Exploration," *Journal of Consumer Research*, 21 (March), 596–611.

Lantos, Geoffrey P. (1987), "Advertising: Looking Glass or Molder of the Masses?" *Journal of Public Policy and Marketing*, 6, 104–128.

LaTour, Michael S., and Tony L. Henthome (1994), "Ethical Judgments of Sexual Appeals in Print Advertising," *Journal of Advertising*, 23 (3), 81–90.

Leiser, Burton (1979), "Beyond Fraud and Deception: The Moral Uses of Advertising," in *Ethical Issues in Business*, Thomas Donaldson and Patricia Werhane, eds., Englewood Cliffs, NJ: Prentice-Hall, 59–66.

Levitt, Theodore (1960), "Marketing Myopia," *Harvard Business Review*, 38 (July/August), 45–56.

———— (1986), *The Marketing Imagination: New, Expanded Edition*, New York: NY Free Press.

44 Liquormart, Inc. v. Rhode Island, 517 U.S. 484 (1996).

Marshall, Catherine, and Gretchen B. Rossman (1989), *Designing Qualitative Research*, Newbury Park, CA: Sage.

McCracken, Grant D. (1988), *The Long Interview*, Newbury Park, CA: Sage.

Miles, Matthew B., and A. Michael Huberman (1994), *Qualitative Data Analysis*, 2nd ed., Newbury Park, CA: Sage.

Moon, Young Sook, and George R. Franke (2000), "Cultural Influences on Agency Practitioners' Ethical Perceptions: A Comparison of Korea and the U.S.," *Journal of Advertising*, 29 (Spring), 51–65.

Moriarity, Roland T. (1983), *Industrial Buying Behavior*, Lexington, MA: Lexington Books.

Murphy, Patrick E. (1998a), *Eighty Exemplary Ethics Statements*, Notre Dame, IN: University of Notre Dame Press.

———— (1998b), "Ethics in Advertising: Review, Analysis, and Suggestions," *Journal of Public Policy in Marketing*, 17 (Fall), 316–319.

Nahser, F. Byron (1997), *Learning to Read the Signs*, Woburn, MA: Butterworth-Heinemann.

Nesteruk, Jeffrey (1996), "Law, Virtue, and the Corporation," *American Business Law Journal*, 33 (Spring), 473–487.

Piaget, Jean (1965), *The Moral Development of the Child*, New York: Free Press.
Piper, Thomas R., Mary C. Gentile, and Sharon Daloz Parks (1993), *Can Ethics Be Taught?* Boston: Harvard Business School Press.
Pollay, Richard W. (1986), "The Distorted Mirror: Reflections on the Unintended Consequences of Advertising, " *Journal of Marketing*, 50 (April), 18–36.
Pontifical Council for Social Communications (1997), *Ethics in Advertising*, Vatican City: Vatican Documents.
Pratt, Cornelius B., and E. Lincoln James (1994), "Advertising Ethics: A Contextual Response Based on Classical Ethical Theory," *Journal of Business Ethics*, 13 (June), 455–568.
Preston, Ivan (1994), *The Tangled Web They Weave*, Madison: University of Wisconsin Press.
——— (1996), *The Great American Blow-Up: Puffery in Advertising and Selling*, Madison: University of Wisconsin Press.
Prosser, William (1984), *Handbook of the Law of Torts*, 5th ed., St. Paul: West.
Rangan, V. Kasturi (1989), "The Smoke Wars: The Case for and Against the Cigarette Industry," case no. 9-590-040, Boston: Harvard Business School Press.
Rest, James R. (1984), "The Major Components of Morality," in *Morality, Moral Behavior, and Moral Development*, W. Kurtines and J. Gewirtz, eds., New York: Wiley.
——— (1986), *Moral Development: Advances in Research and Theory*, New York: Praeger.
——— (1994), "Theory and Research," in *Moral Development in the Professions: Psychology and Applied Ethics*, James R. Rest and Darcia Narvaez, eds., Hillsdale, NJ: Lawrence Erlbaum.
Rotzoll, Kim B., and Clifford G. Christians (1980), "Advertising Agency Practitioners' Perceptions of Ethical Decisions," *Journalism Quarterly*, 57 (Autumn), 425–431.
Santilli, Paul (1983), "The Informative and Persuasive Functions of Advertising: A Moral Appraisal," *Journal of Business Ethics*, 2 (February), 27–33.
Schwartzman, Helen B. (1993), *Ethnography in Organizations*, Newbury Park, CA: Sage.
Solomon, Robert C. (1992), *Ethics and Excellence*, New York: Oxford University Press.
——— (1999), *A Better Way to Think About Business*, New York: Oxford University Press.
Spiggle, Susan (1994), "Analysis and Interpretation of Qualitative Data in Consumer Research," *Journal of Consumer Research*, 21 (December), 491–503.
Stern, Louis W., and Thomas L. Eovaldi (1984), *Legal Aspects of Marketing Strategy: Antitrust and Consumer Protection Issues*, Englewood Cliffs, NJ: Prentice Hall.
Strauss, Anselm L. (1990), *Qualitative Analysis for Social Scientists*, Cambridge: Cambridge University Press.
Tinkham, Spencer F., and Ruth Ann Waver-Larisay (1994), "Ethical Judgments of Political Television Commercials as Predictors of Attitude Toward the Ad," *Journal of Advertising*, 23 (September), 43–57.
Triese, Debbie, Michael F. Weigold, Jenneane Conna, and Heather Garrison (1994), "Ethics in Advertising: Ideological Correlates of Consumer Perceptions," *Journal of Advertising*, 23 (September), 59–69.
Waide, John (1987), "The Making of Self and World in Advertising," *Journal of Business Ethics*, 6 (February), 73–79.
Wallendorf, Melanie, and Merrie Brucks (1993), "Introspection in Consumer Research: Implementation and Implications," *Journal of Consumer Research*, 20 (December), 339–359.
Werhane, Patricia H. (1999), *Moral Imagination and Management Decision-Making*, New York: Oxford University Press.
Woodruff, Paul (2001), *Reverence: Renewing a Forgotten Virtue*, New York: Oxford University Press.
Workman, John P., Jr. (1993), "Marketing's Limited Role in New Product Development in One Computer System Firm," *Journal of Marketing Research*, 30 (November), 405–421.

READING THE TEXT

1. How do advertising professionals who display "moral muteness" respond to ethically problematic advertising, according to the authors?

2. In your own words, describe how advertisers rationalize their avoidance of ethical problems in their industry.

3. How do advertisers tend to construe the Constitution's First Amendment, according to the article?

4. Define in your own words the relationship between the terms "moral myopia" and "moral muteness."

5. What do Drumright and Murphy mean by advertising professionals who are "seeing, talking," and how do those people approach ethical dilemmas in their job?

6. What do the authors mean when they say that some advertising professionals display "moral imagination"?

READING THE SIGNS

1. This selection is an excerpt of an academic research article published in *The Journal of Advertising*. Study the writing style used here. How would you characterize it? How does it compare with the style of a selection published in a journalistic venue, such as Andrea Chang's "Teen 'Haulers' Become a Fashion Force" (p. 138) or Neal Gabler's "The Social Networks" (p. 355)?

2. While occasionally explicit about what would be considered "ethical" behavior in advertising, the authors' assumptions about it tend to be implicit. Read through this selection carefully, and synthesize a definition of what constitutes ethics in advertising. Share your results with the class.

3. Write an argumentative response to the comment of an advertising agency president: "We're more sheep than we are shepherds. We follow the trends. We don't create them. We're too scared to create them; our clients are too scared to create them" (para. 9). To develop your argument, consult the Introduction to this chapter.

4. **CONNECTING TEXTS** In an essay, support, refute, or complicate the authors' belief that "Advertising professionals, like all speakers, have a responsibility to make judgments about speech" (para. 16). To develop your ideas, consult selections about using sources in academic writing, and think about whether university standards should apply to the so-called real world. See Patti S. Caravello's "Judging Quality on the Web" (p. 69) and Trip Gabriel's "For Students in the Internet Age, No Shame in Copy and Paste" (p. 71).

5. In a creative essay, first consider how advertisers might define the Be Stupid jeans campaign described in the Introduction to Chapter Six, drawing upon the defenses of ethically dubious advertising practices described in this article. Then switch roles and write your own critique of that defense.

6. **CONNECTING TEXTS** In class, stage a debate about the moral implications of cigarette advertising, with one team presenting a defense of such advertising

and another opposing it on ethical grounds. Use the debate as a group brainstorming session for your own argument on this question. Alternatively, debate the ethics behind the sort of marketing to young children that Eric Schlosser describes in "Kid Kustomers" (p. 222).

JENNIFER L. POZNER
Dove's "Real Beauty" Backlash

It sounds almost like the Macy's Santa Claus advising shoppers to look for something at Gimbel's in *Miracle on 34th Street*, but there you have it: Dove's "Campaign for Real Beauty" is actually telling ordinary girls and women to feel good about themselves. And, for the most part, Jennifer L. Pozner is rather glad it is, even if the Dove ads are still aimed at selling beauty products according to the implicit philosophy that "cellulite is unsightly, women's natural aging process is shameful, and flabby thighs are flawed and must be fixed." No, what angers Pozner are the male media figures who have voiced dismay at Dove's display of women with realistic figures and faces, some of whom dare to be middle-aged. Indeed, for Pozner, it is the commentary of such men that makes the Dove campaign so necessary in the first place. Pozner is executive director of Women In Media & News, and her media criticism has appeared in many national publications.

When it comes to Madison Avenue misogyny, usually it's the ad that's objectionable (hello, *Advertising Week!*), rather than the product itself.

The opposite is true in the latest incarnation of Dove's "Campaign for Real Beauty," which poses a bevy of full-figured babes in bras and boyshorts on billboards throughout New York, Chicago, D.C., L.A., and other top urban markets . . . just in time for the rollout of their new line of "firming cremes."

If the same smiling size sixes (and eights, and tens) were hawking hair dye or shilling for soap, the campaign would be revolutionary—but despite the company's continued and commendable intent to expand notions of female beauty to include the non-skinny and non-white, Dove's attempts are profoundly limited by a product line that comes with its own underlying philosophy: cellulite is unsightly, women's natural aging process is shameful, and flabby thighs are flawed and must be fixed . . . oh, so conveniently by Dove's newest lotion.

The feel-good "women are ok at whatever size" message is hopelessly hampered by the underlying attempt to get us to spend, spend, spend to

Gina Crisanti was featured in Dove's campaign.

"correct" those pesky "problem areas" advertisers have always told us to hate about our bodies. As Salon.com's Rebecca Traister put it, the message is "love your ass but not the fat on it."

Yet even though Dove's "Real Beauty" ads play to and subtly reinforce   5 the stereotypes they claim to be exposing, it's impossible not to feel inspired by the sight of these attractive, healthy women smiling playfully at us from their places of billboard honor, their voluptuous curves all the more luscious alongside the bags-of-bones in competitors' campaigns.

Unless, of course, you're *Chicago Sun Times* columnist Richard Roeper, who reacted to Dove's "chunky women" with the sort of fear and loathing he should reserve for the cheesy Hollywood schlock he regularly "thumbs up" during his Ebert & Roeper film reviews. "I find these Dove ads a little unsettling. If I want to see plump gals baring too much skin, I'll go to Taste of Chicago, OK?," Roeper ranted, saying that while he knows he should probably praise Dove for breaking away from airbrushed, impossible-to-achieve, youth-obsessed ad imagery, he much prefers to bitch and moan. "When we're talking women in their underwear on billboards outside my living room windows, give me the fantasy babes, please. If that makes me sound superficial, shallow and sexist — well yes, I'm a man."

Unsettling? Try Roeper's implication that all men are just naturally sexist — and that a man who wears gender-based bigotry as a badge of pride has some of the most power in the media to determine which films succeed and which fail. (Remember Reoper's admission next time his thumb goes way up for a flick whose humor rarely rises above cheap gags about sperm as hair gel, or when he pans a promising movie centered around strong female characters.)

Dozens of major media outlets jumped on Roeper's comments as an excuse to run insulting headlines such as "Fab or Flab," with stories exploring the "controversy" over whether Dove's ads are, as *People* put it, "the best thing to happen to advertising since the free sample, or an eyesore of outsize proportions."

The tone of this debate turned nasty, quickly, with women's self esteem in one camp and men's fragile eyes in another as typified by a second *Sun Times* writer's comments that these "disturbing" and "frightening" women should "put on clothes (please, really)" because "ads should be about the beautiful people. They should include the unrealistic, the ideal or the unattainable look for which so many people strive." Besides, wrote Lucio Guerrero, "the only time I want to see a thigh that big is in a bucket with bread crumbs on it."

From there, print and broadcast outlets featured a stream of man-on-the-street interviews begging Madison Avenue to bring back the starvation-saturated, silicone enhanced sweeties they'd come to expect seeing on their commutes to work, echoing Guerrero's mean-spirited musings.   10

Some masked their aesthetic objections under the guise of health concerns: "At the risk of sounding politically incorrect," Bill Zwecker, the balding, paunchy, middle-aged anchor of CBS's local newscast in Chicago, weighed in on his CBS blog, "In this day and age, when we are facing a huge obesity problem in this country, we don't need to encourage anyone — women OR men — to think it's okay to be out of shape." Perhaps this line of attack would have been more convincing if the women in the ads were unhealthily overweight (they're actually smaller-sized than the average American woman), or if Zwecker was a little more *GQ* and a little less *Couch Potato Quarterly*.

Certainly, these men so quick to demonize "the Dove girls" show no understanding that those "fantasy babes" of traditional ads have a profoundly negative impact on the health of girls and women in America. Advertising has never glorified obesity (though that problem is arguably a byproduct of McDonald's, M&Ms, and other junk food ads), but the industry has equated starvation and drug addiction with women's beauty and value for decades.

The "real beauty" backlash underscores just how necessary Dove's campaign is — however hypocritical the product they're selling may be. What's "unsettling" is not that Roeper, Guerrero, and Zwecker might have to look at empowerment-infused ads targeted to female consumers — it's that men with power positions in the media still think it's acceptable to demand that women be displayed only in the hyper-objectifying images they feel is somehow their due.

Reading the Text

1. Why does Pozner believe that Dove's "Real Beauty" ads "reinforce the stereotypes they claim to be exposing" (para. 5)?

2. In Pozner's view, what is the basis of the objections that Richard Roeper and some other male commentators have to the Dove "Campaign for Real Beauty"?

3. Characterize Pozner's tone in this selection, particularly in her comments regarding male critics of Dove's ads. What effect does it have on your response to her essay?

Reading the Signs

1. In a creative journal assignment, assume the perspective of one of the Dove "Real Beauty" models and write a letter in response to Richard Roeper's complaints about the Dove ads.

2. Write an argumentative essay that validates, rejects, or complicates Pozner's claim that "the 'real beauty' backlash underscores just how necessary Dove's campaign is—however hypocritical the product they're selling may be" (para. 13).

3. Write an essay evaluating Richard Roeper's response to the Dove ad campaign. To what extent is it "unsettling" (para. 7), as Pozner sees it, or do you find it to be simply honest?

4. Write an essay arguing whether ad campaigns such as Dove's "Real Beauty" and Nike's "My Butt Is Big" are indeed revolutionary or simply a new twist on advertising's tendency to objectify women's bodies.

ERIC SCHLOSSER
Kid Kustomers

Children rarely have much money of their own to spend, but they have a great deal of "pester power," along with the "leverage" to get their parents to buy them what they want. And so, as Eric Schlosser reports in this reading, Madison Avenue has been paying a great deal of attention to "kid kustomers" in recent years, pitching them everything from toys and candy to cell phones and automobiles. With more and more working couples spending more money on their kids to compensate for spending less time with them, Schlosser suggests, we are likely to see only an increase in such advertising in the years to come. Hmmm . . . are preteen dating services next?

A correspondent for *The Atlantic*, Schlosser is the author of *Fast Food Nation* (2001), from which this selection is taken, and *Reefer Madness: Sex, Drugs, and Cheap Labor in the American Black Market* (2003). In 2006 he published, with Charles Wilson, a book for young readers titled *Chew on This: Everything You Don't Want to Know about Fast Food.*

Twenty-five years ago, only a handful of American companies directed their marketing at children — Disney, McDonald's, candy makers, toy makers, manufacturers of breakfast cereal. Today children are being targeted by phone companies, oil companies, and automobile companies as well as clothing stores and restaurant chains. The explosion in children's advertising occurred during the 1980s. Many working parents, feeling guilty about spending less time with their kids, started spending more money on them. One marketing expert has called the 1980s "the decade of the child consumer." After largely ignoring children for years, Madison Avenue began to scrutinize and pursue them. Major ad agencies now have children's divisions, and a variety of marketing firms focus solely on kids. These groups tend to have sweet-sounding names: Small Talk, Kid Connection, Kid2Kid, the Gepetto Group, Just Kids, Inc. At least three industry publications — *Youth Market Alert, Selling to Kids,* and *Marketing to Kids Report* — cover the latest ad campaigns and market research. The growth in children's advertising has been driven by efforts to increase not just current, but also future, consumption. Hoping that nostalgic childhood memories of a brand will lead to a lifetime of purchases, companies now plan "cradle-to-grave" advertising strategies. They have come to believe what Ray Kroc and Walt Disney realized long ago — a person's "brand loyalty" may begin as early as the age of two. Indeed, market research has found that children often recognize a brand logo before they can recognize their own name.

The discontinued Joe Camel ad campaign, which used a hip cartoon character to sell cigarettes, showed how easily children can be influenced by the right corporate mascot. A 1991 study published in the *Journal of the American Medical Association* found that nearly all of America's six-year-olds could identify Joe Camel, who was just as familiar to them as Mickey Mouse. Another study found that one-third of the cigarettes illegally sold to minors were Camels. More recently, a marketing firm conducted a survey in shopping malls across the country, asking children to describe their favorite TV ads. According to the CME KidCom Ad Traction Study II, released at the 1999 Kids' Marketing Conference in San Antonio, Texas, the Taco Bell commercials featuring a talking chihuahua were the most popular fast food ads. The kids in the survey also liked Pepsi and Nike commercials, but their favorite television ad was for Budweiser.

The bulk of the advertising directed at children today has an immediate goal. "It's not just getting kids to whine," one marketer explained in *Selling*

Do Frosted Flakes plus Yoda equal a "sugar-coated nag"?

to Kids, "it's giving them a specific reason to ask for the product." Years ago sociologist Vance Packard described children as "surrogate salesmen" who had to persuade other people, usually their parents, to buy what they wanted. Marketers now use different terms to explain the intended response to their ads—such as "leverage," "the nudge factor," "pester power." The aim of most children's advertising is straightforward: Get kids to nag their parents and nag them well.

James U. McNeal, a professor of marketing at Texas A&M University, is considered America's leading authority on marketing to children. In his book *Kids As Customers* (1992), McNeal provides marketers with a thorough analysis of "children's requesting styles and appeals." He classifies juvenile nagging tactics into seven major categories. A *pleading* nag is one accompanied by repetitions of words like "please" or "mom, mom, mom." A *persistent* nag involves constant requests for the coveted product and may include the phrase "I'm gonna ask just one more time." *Forceful* nags are extremely pushy and may include subtle threats, like "Well, then, I'll go and ask Dad." *Demonstrative* nags are the most high-risk, often characterized by full-blown tantrums in public places, breath-holding, tears, a refusal to leave the store. *Sugar-coated* nags promise affection in return for a purchase and may rely on seemingly heartfelt declarations like "You're the best dad in the world." *Threatening* nags are youthful forms of blackmail, vows of eternal hatred and of running away if something isn't bought. *Pity* nags claim the child will be heartbroken, teased, or socially stunted if the parent refuses to buy a certain item. "All of these appeals and styles may be used in combination," McNeal's research has discovered, "but kids tend to stick to one or two of each that proved most effective . . . for their own parents."

McNeal never advocates turning children into screaming, breath-holding ₅
monsters. He has been studying "Kid Kustomers" for more than thirty years
and believes in a more traditional marketing approach. "The key is getting
children to see a firm . . . in much the same way as [they see] mom or dad,
grandma or grandpa," McNeal argues. "Likewise, if a company can ally itself
with universal values such as patriotism, national defense, and good health, it
is likely to nurture belief in it among children."

Before trying to affect children's behavior, advertisers have to learn about
their tastes. Today's market researchers not only conduct surveys of children in shopping malls, they also organize focus groups for kids as young
as two or three. They analyze children's artwork, hire children to run focus
groups, stage slumber parties and then question children into the night. They
send cultural anthropologists into homes, stores, fast food restaurants, and
other places where kids like to gather, quietly and surreptitiously observing
the behavior of prospective customers. They study the academic literature on
child development, seeking insights from the work of theorists such as Erik
Erikson and Jean Piaget. They study the fantasy lives of young children; they
apply the findings in advertisements and product designs.

Dan S. Acuff—the president of Youth Market System Consulting and
the author of *What Kids Buy and Why* (1997)—stresses the importance of
dream research. Studies suggest that until the age of six, roughly 80 percent
of children's dreams are about animals. Rounded, soft creatures like Barney,
Disney's animated characters, and the Teletubbies therefore have an obvious
appeal to young children. The Character Lab, a division of Youth Market System Consulting, uses a proprietary technique called Character Appeal Quad-
rant Analysis to help companies develop new mascots. The technique purports
to create imaginary characters who perfectly fit the targeted age group's level
of cognitive and neurological development.

Children's clubs have for years been considered an effective means of
targeting ads and collecting demographic information; the clubs appeal to a
child's fundamental need for status and belonging. Disney's Mickey Mouse
Club, formed in 1930, was one of the trailblazers. During the 1980s and
1990s, children's clubs proliferated, as corporations used them to solicit
the names, addresses, zip codes, and personal comments of young customers. "Marketing messages sent through a club not only can be personalized,"
James McNeal advises, "they can be tailored for a certain age or geographical
group." A well-designed and well-run children's club can be extremely good
for business. According to one Burger King executive, the creation of a Burger
King Kids Club in 1991 increased the sales of children's meals as much as
300 percent.

The Internet has become another powerful tool for assembling data
about children. In 1998 a federal investigation of Web sites aimed at children found that 89 percent requested personal information from kids; only
1 percent required that children obtain parental approval before supplying
the information. A character on the McDonald's Web site told children that

Ronald McDonald was "the ultimate authority in everything." The site encouraged kids to send Ronald an e-mail revealing their favorite menu item at McDonald's, their favorite book, their favorite sports team — and their name. Fast food Web sites no longer ask children to provide personal information without first gaining parental approval; to do so is now a violation of federal law, thanks to the Children's Online Privacy Protection Act, which took effect in April of 2000.

Despite the growing importance of the Internet, television remains the 10 primary medium for children's advertising. The effects of these TV ads have long been a subject of controversy. In 1978, the Federal Trade Commission (FTC) tried to ban all television ads directed at children seven years old or younger. Many studies had found that young children often could not tell the difference between television programming and television advertising. They also could not comprehend the real purpose of commercials and trusted that advertising claims were true. Michael Pertschuk, the head of the FTC, argued that children need to be shielded from advertising that preys upon their immaturity. "They cannot protect themselves," he said, "against adults who exploit their present-mindedness."

The FTC's proposed ban was supported by the American Academy of Pediatrics, the National Congress of Parents and Teachers, the Consumers Union, and the Child Welfare League, among others. But it was attacked by the National Association of Broadcasters, the Toy Manufacturers of America, and the Association of National Advertisers. The industry groups lobbied Congress to prevent any restrictions on children's ads and sued in federal court to block Pertschuk from participating in future FTC meetings on the subject. In April of 1981, three months after the inauguration of President Ronald Reagan, an FTC staff report argued that a ban on ads aimed at children would be impractical, effectively killing the proposal. "We are delighted by the FTC's reasonable recommendation," said the head of the National Association of Broadcasters.

The Saturday-morning children's ads that caused angry debates twenty years ago now seem almost quaint. Far from being banned, TV advertising aimed at kids is now broadcast twenty-four hours a day, closed-captioned and in stereo. Nickelodeon, the Disney Channel, the Cartoon Network, and the other children's cable networks are now responsible for about 80 percent of all television viewing by kids. None of these networks existed before 1979. The typical American child now spends about twenty-one hours a week watching television — roughly one and a half months of TV every year. That does not include the time children spend in front of a screen watching videos, playing videogames, or using the computer. Outside of school, the typical American child spends more time watching television than doing any other activity except sleeping. During the course of a year, he or she watches more than thirty thousand TV commercials. Even the nation's youngest children are watching a great deal of television. About one-quarter of American children between the ages of two and five have a TV in their room.

READING THE TEXT

1. Why, according to Schlosser, did an "explosion in children's advertising" (para. 1) occur during the 1980s?
2. What is "pester power" (para. 3), and how is it used as a marketing strategy?
3. How has the Internet contributed to the expansion in advertising directed toward children, according to Schlosser?
4. What strategies does Schlosser say marketers use to determine children's tastes in products?

READING THE SIGNS

1. Watch a morning of Saturday cartoon shows on TV and make a list of all the products that are advertised. What products are directly tied in to the show? Use your observations as the basis for an essay in which you analyze the relationship between children's programming and the advertising that supports it.
2. Perform a semiotic analysis of an advertisement from any medium directed at children. What signifiers in the ad are especially addressed to children? Consider such details as the implied narrative of the ad, its characters, and their appearance, colors, music, and voice track.
3. Conduct an in-class debate over whether children's advertising should be more strictly regulated. To develop support for your team's position, watch some TV programs aimed at children and the advertising that accompanies it.
4. **CONNECTING TEXTS**   Read or reread James B. Twitchell's "What We Are to Advertisers" (p. 182) and write an essay in which you analyze whether Twitchell's assertion that "mass marketing means the creation of mass stereotypes" (para. 1) applies to child consumers.

JULIA B. CORBETT

A Faint Green Sell: Advertising and the Natural World

Though "green" marketing and advertising is not as prevalent today as it was in the 1980s and 1990s, advertisers still exploit natural imagery to move the goods. Believing, however, that "The business of advertising is fundamentally 'brown'" and that "therefore the idea of advertising being 'green' and capable of supporting environmental values is an oxymoron," Julia B. Corbett sets out to analyze and categorize the ways in which advertising exploits nature, from treating it as a commodity to presenting nature as something that exists solely for the pleasure of human beings. All these strategies, Corbett concludes, perpetuate "an anthropocentric, narcissistic relationship" with the natural world. In other words, beautiful mountain ad backgrounds do not mean that you should go out and buy an SUV. Julia B. Corbett is a professor of communication at the University of Utah.

In the 1980s, advertisers discovered the environment. When a revitalized environmental movement helped establish environmentalism as a legitimate, mainstream public goal (Luke, 1993), corporate America quickly capitalized on a lucrative market of "green consumers" (Ottman, 1993; Zinkham & Carlson, 1995). Marketers not only could create new products and services, they could also reposition existing ones to appear more environmentally friendly. What resulted was a flood of advertisements that focused on green product attributes, touting products as recyclable and biodegradable and claiming them good or safe for the environment. Increases in this genre were remarkable, with green print ads increasing 430 percent and green television ads increasing 367 percent between 1989 and 1990 (Ottman, 1993). The total number of products claiming green attributes doubled in 1990 to 11.4 percent from the previous year ("Selling green," 1991).

Virtually all of the existing research on so-called green advertising was conducted during this boom. Green advertising was defined by researchers as product ads touting environmental benefits or corporate green-image ads (Shrum, McCarty, & Lowrey, 1995; Banerjee, Gulas, & Iyer, 1995). Researchers also targeted and segmented green consumers (Ottman, 1993) and tested their motivations (Luke, 1993). Green appeals were categorized (Iyer & Banerjee, 1993; Obermiller, 1995; Schuhwerk & Lefkoff-Hagius, 1995) and consumer response to green ads analyzed (Mayer, Scammon, & Zick, 1993; Thorson, Page, & Moore, 1995).

By the late 1990s, advertisers announced the end of the green-ad boom. *Advertising Age* reported that as the country headed into the thirtieth anniversary of Earth Day, green positioning had become more than just a nonissue — it was almost an anti-issue (Neff, 2000). Marketers were launching a whole new class of disposable products from plastic storage containers to dust mops. There was a perceived decline in controversy over anti-green products such as disposable diapers, toxic batteries, and gas-guzzling SUVs (sport utility vehicles). In addition, only 5 percent of new products made claims about recyclability or recycled content, and the explosion of e-tailing added boxes, styrofoam peanuts, and air-puffed plastic bags to the waste stream. Green product ads in prime-time television, which never amounted to more than a blip, virtually disappeared by 1995, reflecting "the television tendency to get off the environmental bandwagon after it had lost its trendiness" (Shanahan & McComas, 1999, p. 108).

But Shanahan and McComas noted that their study—like virtually all research published during the green-ad boom—did not consider the most prevalent use of the environment in advertising: when nature functions as a rhetorically useful backdrop or stage. Using nature merely as a backdrop—whether in the form of wild animals, mountain vistas, or sparkling rivers—is the most common use of the natural world in advertisements. For all but the most critical message consumers, the environment blends into the background. We know that an advertisement for a car shows the vehicle outdoors and that ads for allergy medications feature flowers and "weeds." The environment per se is not for sale, but advertisers are depending on qualities and features of the non-human world (and our relationship to it) to help in the selling message. When the natural world is so depicted, it becomes a convenient, culturally relevant tool to which meanings can be attached for the purpose of selling goods and services. Although this intentional but seemingly casual use of the environment in advertising is by far the most common, it is the least studied by researchers.

Nature-as-backdrop ads also are notable for their enduring quality. 5 Although the number of ads that focus on product attributes such as "recyclable" may shift with marketing trends and political winds, nature has been used as a backdrop virtually since the dawn of advertising. The natural world was depicted in early automobile ads ("see the USA in your Chevrolet") and Hamms Beer commercials ("from the land of sky-blue water") and continues to be a prominent feature in the advertising landscape. Nature-as-backdrop ads, therefore, provide an important record of the position of the natural world in our cultural environment and, as such, deserve scrutiny.

Advertisements are a special form of discourse because they include visual signals and language fragments (either oral or written) that work together to create messages that go beyond the ability of either individually. This essay undertakes a critical analysis of the symbolic communicative discourse of advertising, viewing nature-as-backdrop ads as cultural icons of environmental values embedded in our social system. When ads present the environment with distorted, inauthentic, or exaggerated discourse, that discourse has the potential to foster inauthentic relationships to nature and influences the way we perceive our environment and its value to us.

Schudson (1989) argued that ads have special cultural power. In addition to being repetitive and ubiquitous, ads reinforce messages from primary institutions in the social system, provide dissonance to countering messages, and generally support the capitalistic structure that the advertising industry was created to support. This essay will discuss how the ad industry developed, how ads work on us, and how ads portray the natural world. It will argue, according to environmental theories such as deep ecology (Naess, 1973; Bullis, 1996), that the "green" in advertising is extremely faint by examining and developing six related concepts:

1. The business of advertising is fundamentally "brown"; therefore the idea of advertising being "green" and capable of supporting environmental values is an oxymoron.
2. Advertising commodifies the natural world and attaches material value to non-material goods, treating natural resources as private and possessible, not public and intrinsic.
3. Nature-as-backdrop ads portray an anthropocentric, narcissistic relationship to the biotic community and focus on the environment's utility and benefit to humans.
4. Advertising idealizes the natural world and presents a simplified, distorted picture of nature as sublime, simple, and unproblematic.
5. The depiction of nature in advertising disconnects and estranges us from what is valued, yet at the same time we are encouraged to reconnect through products, creating a circular consumption.
6. As a ubiquitous form of pop culture, advertising reinforces consonant messages in the social system and provides strong dissonance to oppositional or alternative messages.

The "Brown" Business of Advertising

1. The business of advertising is fundamentally "brown"; therefore, the idea of advertising being "green" and capable of supporting environmental values is an oxymoron.

Advertisements are nothing new to this century or even previous ones. There are plentiful examples in literature, including the works of Shakespeare, that peddlers have long enticed buyers by advertising (in print or orally) a good's attributes and associated meanings. After World War II, however, advertising found a firm place in the worldview of Americans. According to Luke (1993), after 1945, corporate capital, big government, and professional experts pushed practices of a throw-away affluent society onto consumers as a purposeful political strategy to sustain economic growth, forestall mass discontent, and empower scientific authority. Concern for the environment was lacking in the postwar prosperity boom, at least until the mid-1960s when Rachel Carson sounded the alarm over chemicals and the modern-day environmental movement was born (Corbett, 2001).

To help alert consumers to new mass-produced goods, a new type of show called the "soap opera" was created for the relatively recent phenomenon of television. These daytime dramas were created for the sole purpose of delivering an audience of homemakers to eager manufacturers of household products, including soap. Advertisers realized that advertising on soap operas would help to establish branding, or creating differing values for what are essentially common, interchangeable goods such as soap.

Essentially, advertising was viewed as part of the fuel that would help keep a capitalist economy burning. Capitalism is a market system that measures its success by constant growth (such as the gross national product and housing starts), a system that many environmentalists recognize as ultimately unsustainable. You might even say that advertising developed as the culture that would help solve what some economists view as the central problem of capitalism: the distribution of surplus goods (Twitchell, 1996). Schudson (1989) concluded, "Advertising is capitalism's way of saying 'I love you' to itself." In a capitalist economy, advertising is a vital handmaiden to consumption and materialism. In the words of the author of *Adcult*, Americans "are not too materialistic. We are not materialistic enough" (Twitchell, 1996, p. 11).

The development of mass media, particularly radio and television, played an important role in delivering audiences to advertisers. By the mid-1980s, half of U.S. homes had cable, and the burgeoning number of channels allowed advertisers to target more specific audience segments. Advertisers and media programmers engage in a dance to fill each other's needs, each having a vested interest in constructing certain versions of the world and not others. According to Turow (1999), "the ad industry affects not just the content of its own campaigns but the very structure and content of the rest of the media system" (p. 194). At the same time, media develop formats and tones for their outlets and programming deemed to be most acceptable to the audiences that they hope marketers find most attractive. What this means for programming is that the upscale twenty-something audience — the most appealing segment to advertisers — will find itself represented in more media outlets than older men and women to whom only a small number of highly targeted formats are aimed. According to researchers of the green marketing boom, the segments of the population most committed to the environment do not belong to this twenty-something group (Ottman, 1993).

It is precisely the ability of advertisers and media programmers to tell some stories and not others that gives these entities power. "When people read a magazine, watch a TV show, or use any other ad-sponsored medium, they are entering a world that was constructed as a result of close cooperation between advertisers and media firms" (Turow, 1999, p. 16). Because all media provide people with insights into parts of the world with which they have little direct contact, media representations of the natural world to a largely urbanized population are highly significant. They show us, over and over again, where we belong in the world and how we should treat it. Yet, representations of the natural world are crafted for the sole purpose of selling certain audiences to advertisers.

The close cooperation between advertisers and media firms is understandable given advertising's financial support of media. For newspapers and some magazines, at least 50 percent of their revenue is from advertising; ad support approaches 100 percent for much of radio and television. By some estimates, advertisers spent $27 billion on support to television, $9 billion on radio, $46 billion on daily newspapers, and about $7 billion on consumer magazines (Turow, 1999, p. 13).

Given advertising's purpose of selling audiences to advertisers, is it even 15
possible for any form of advertising — whether product ads or nature-as-
backdrop ads — to be "green"? Dadd and Carothers (1991) maintained that
a truly green economy would require all products to be audited and analyzed
from cradle to grave for their environmental effects. Effects could include the
resources used and pollution generated in the product's manufacture, energy
used to produce and transport the product, the product's role in the economic
and social health of the country of origin, investment plans of the company,
and final disposal of product.

Applying this standard at the most basic level connotes it is an oxymoron to label marginally useful or necessary products (and the ads that
promote them) as "green" or somehow good for the environment. Can an
advertisement that encourages consumption of a product (or patronage of a
company that produces the product) ever be green with a capital G? In his
attempt to reconcile a brown industry with green ideals, Kilbourne (1995)
identified three levels of green in advertisements. But even at the lowest
level (defined as ads promoting a small "techno-fix" such as biodegradabil-
ity) the message is still that "consuming is good, more is better, and the
ecological cost is minimal" (p. 15). If an ad recognizes finite resources, it
nevertheless views the environment purely as a resource, not as possessing
intrinsic, non-economic value. Kilbourne concluded that from a purely ecological position, a truly Green ad is indeed an oxymoron: "the only Green
product is the one that is not produced" (p. 16). Other researchers have
likewise tried to categorize the green in advertisements (Banerjee et al.,
1995). Adapting the deep and shallow ecology concepts of Naess (1973) to
advertisements, they concluded that very few ads were "deep" — 2 percent
of television and 9 percent of print — defined by the researchers as discussing environmental issues in depth and mentioning actions requiring more
commitment.

However, these attempts to make advertising fit a green framework
simply illustrate how ideologically opposed advertising and environmental
values are. Because advertising is the workhorse of capitalism and supports
continually increased production, it is ideologically contrary to environmentalism, which recognizes that ever-increasing growth and consumption are
inherently unsustainable. It matters not whether an ad boasts of recyclability
or quietly features pristine mountain meadows in the background; the basic
business of advertising is brown. Perhaps the only truly Green product is not
only one not produced, but also one not advertised.

Nature as Commodity

*2. Advertising commodifies the natural world and attaches material value
to non-material goods, treating natural resources as private and ownable, not
public and intrinsic.*

Have you ever viewed a single advertisement and then rushed out to buy that product? Probably not. That is not the way that advertising generally works on us, especially not for national consumer goods. Advertising scholars argue that ads cannot create, invent, or even satisfy our desires; instead, ads channel and express current desires with the hope of exploiting them.

You may disagree that ads cannot create desires, particularly if you have ever found yourself yearning for a product that six months ago you did not know existed or that you "needed." But even if ads do not greatly corrupt our immediate buying habits, they can gradually shape our values by becoming our social guides for what is important and valued. According to Benton (1995), advertising displays values and signals to people what our culture thinks is important. Advertising is not capable of inventing social values, but it does a masterful job at usurping and exploiting certain values and not others. The prominent (though not monopolistic) role of advertising in the symbolic marketplace is what gives advertising "a special cultural power" (Schudson, 1989). In the words of one scholar, "Advertising is simply one of a number of attempts to load objects with meaning . . . it is an ongoing conversation within a culture about the meaning of objects." (Twitchell, 1996, p. 13).

The rhetorical challenge for an advertiser, then, is to load one product (even though numerous similar ones exist) with sufficient meaning so that the product appears able to express a desire. The natural world is full of cultural meaning with which to associate products, thereby attaching commodity value to qualities that are impossible to own. By borrowing and adapting well-known, stereotypical portrayals of nature, advertising is able to associate water with freshness and purity and weather as fraught with danger. If, for example, an ad wants to attach the value of "safety" to one particular car, it might demonstrate the car's ability to dodge "dangerous" elements of nature, such as falling rocks. On the other hand, if the ad wants to convey a truck's durability, it could just as easily attach a very different meaning to the same resource and say the truck is "like a rock." Neither product guarantees that you can buy safety or durability; both product ads merely expressed a consumer desire for them by associating a non-material good with a material one.

Animals in particular provide cultural shorthand for advertising. Animals, as popular symbols of the nonhuman environment, are a way for advertisers to link the perceived "personality" and stereotyped cultural value of the animal to the product (Phillips, 1996). In car advertising alone, ads compare vehicles to rams, eagles, wolves, cougars, falcons, and panthers. Some ads go so far as to portray the vehicle as an animal itself. An individual needs no direct experience with untamed environs to know what an eagle or cougar represents and is valued for.

The portrayal of animals in advertising need not be authentic or realistic for us to ascertain the value they represent. In a television commercial, two raccoons are peering inside a brightly lit living room window, "singing" a song from *My Fair Lady*. As the camera moves beyond the raccoons into the living room — where it appears the residents are not home — it focuses on the rocker-recliner. The raccoons sing, "All I want is a room somewhere, far away from the cold night air. Warm hands, warm feet . . ."

In this ad, the rocker-recliner you are enticed to buy has no direct or obvious connection to the natural world, but animals are very much part of the overall persuasive message. We are able to overlook the anthropomorphized singing raccoons because we have enough shared cultural meaning about raccoons and their behavior. We can decipher that these cute, mischievous "bandits" would like to "break in" to this warm room far away from the cold night air and maybe even snooze in that rocker. The intrinsic value of raccoons as a species has been usurped and exploited to demonstrate the comfort and desirability of a certain brand of chair.

Even if the original function of advertising was to market simple products such as soap, advertising now functions to market feelings, sensations, and lifestyles. According to advertisers, the consumption of an object often has more to do with its meaning than with its actual use (Twitchell, 1996). Discrete objects — whether cold medicine or fabric softener — are easier to sell if they are associated with social and personal meaning. The purpose of an ad is not to stress that the product functions properly, but that consumption of it will cure problems (Lasch, 1978), whether loneliness, aging, or even a desire to connect with the natural world. Advertising channels our psychological needs and ambitions into consumptive behaviors (Pollay, 1989). Price (1996) concluded that the success of the store The Nature Company depends "not so much [on] what nature is as what nature means to us" (p. 189).

Take for example a series of print and television ads for a particular SUV that labeled the vehicle as "the answering machine for the call of the wild." The print version tells us that "nature calls out for us" but with the vehicle's leather-trimmed seats, "civilization's never very far away." In television versions, we see the vehicle traveling over rugged terrain (but not the woman driving it) while an answering machine plays numerous messages from a worried mother and boyfriend to the woman who has escaped into the wild.

These ads do not focus on all the ways that this vehicle is superior to all the other very similar SUVs out there. The ads give us no reason to believe that the repair record, safety rating, price, or other important product attributes are somehow superior. Instead, these ads are selling meanings and values associated with the natural world. This product will reconnect you with "the wild," which appears to be missing in your life, and it will help you escape from your troubles and relationships. A rugged environment (yet one somehow made safer and more civilized by this SUV) is portrayed as the best place to find peace and this vehicle will take you there. (An ad for a very different type of product used the same slogan in a different way: "Radio Shack is answering the call of the wild with two-way personal radios." In the ad, "renowned wildlife expert" Jim Fowler uses the radio in a remote-looking location. "No matter where the wild calls you, you'll be ready to answer.")

Some scholars insist that advertising appeals primarily to personal dissatisfactions in our lives and insecurities over the ways and pace in which we live, not to our personal needs. In doing so, ads are carriers of anxiety that serve only to alienate us further (Lasch, 1978). In the SUV ads, the driver is not portrayed as using the vehicle for personal need, but for escape from relationship problems to an environment that is depicted as being free of all problems.

The rhetorical argument of commodification leads us to believe that we can solve problems and dissatisfactions with a purchase. We buy the peace and escape — represented by the wilderness and promised by the product — even though the product is incapable of fulfilling that promise. The intent of advertising, says Pollay (1989), is to preoccupy society with material concerns and to see goods as a path to happiness and a solution to problems (which is very brown thinking). In many of the appeals of nature-as-backdrop ads, the advertisements attempt to associate material goods with nonmaterial qualities that have disappeared from many people's lives, qualities such as solitude, wilderness, lush landscapes, free-flowing water, and clean air. In a print ad for L.L. Bean, we see a man wading across calm, milky blue waters to a small sailboat in early morning light. The caption reads, "Don't mistake a street address for where you actually live." Apparently this man cannot "live" in his everyday life — which we assume takes place in a far less serene setting — but must leave it to achieve qualities it lacks. Yet another SUV ad promises, "Escape. Serenity. Relaxation." Pristine mountain vistas and sparkling waters (usually devoid of people) allow us to romanticize about a life lost or connections broken. When such adventures are tied in such a way to products, that connection materializes a way of experiencing the natural world.

Commodification of what are essentially public resources — like milky ₃₀ blue waters — encourages us to think of resources as private and possessible. Ads may invoke public values of family, friendship, and a common planet as part of their message, but these values are put to work to sell private goods, a very capitalist principle. The satisfaction derived from these goods, even those that appear inherently collective such as water, is depicted as invariably private. This encourages "the promotion of a social order in which people are encouraged to think of themselves and their private worlds" (Schudson, 1989, p. 83), a very anthropocentric and narcissistic perspective. The environment, in many respects, doesn't function well as private space.

For the Pleasure of Humans

3. Nature-as-backdrop ads portray an anthropocentric, narcissistic relationship to the biotic community and focus on the environment's utility and benefit to humans.

Another common feature in advertising appeals that utilize the natural world is self-absorption and narcissism. The word derives from Narcissus, a youth in Greek mythology who fell in love with his own reflection in a pool. The way in which advertising portrays this universal emotional type is as self-absorbed, self-righteous, and dependent on momentary pleasures of assertion. Narcissism in advertising often takes the form of outdoor adventure, as in this print ad: Two pickup trucks are parked on an expansive, rolling sand dune. In the open bed of each truck, a young man in a wet suit appears to be wind-surfing — through the manipulation of computer graphics. Water splashes around them in the air and onto the sand. The caption says the trucks are "built fun tough" and have "gallons of attitude." Of course we know this picture to be fake (although a similar juxtaposition of desert and water exists in human-made Lake Powell), but the picture tells us that these men are in it for the fun, for the adventure.

A narcissist is most concerned with pleasing himself or herself at the expense of others, and if we extend the analogy, at the expense of the environment. In terms of environmental ideology, a narcissist would be anthropocentric, believing that his or her own outdoor pleasure comes before that of other species and their needs. Ads that show people "conquering" natural elements are expressing me-first anthropocentrism. According to Lasch (1978), our culture is marked by an exaggerated form of self-awareness and mass narcissism, finely attuned (with the help of advertising) to the many demands of the narcissistic self.

Another example is a television ad that shows a young boy working through the pages of a puzzle book. He reads aloud, "Help the knight reach the castle," and with his crayon follows the winding path safely past the dragon to the castle. On the next page he reads, "Help the Jeep Wrangler reach the fishing hole." "Hmm," he says, grins, and makes a noise like a truck revving up. He draws a line straight across the puzzle book landscape, across two mountain ranges, a deep valley, and a patch of quicksand, ignoring the cleared path. As he smiles smugly, the announcer tells us that a Jeep is "more fun than you imagine."

Yet another truck commercial begins in a deserted mountain valley at 35 twilight. Next, a gigantic booted foot with a spur crashes to the ground, reverberating all in sight. We then see that the foot belongs to a cowboy the size of Paul Bunyan. The message is that the human is essentially larger than life, dominating the entire landscape and all within it, as Bunyan did. Such exaggerated domination intentionally positions humans at the top of a pyramid, instead of belonging equally to a biotic community.

Nature as Sublime

4. Nature-as-backdrop ads idealize the natural world and present a simplified, distorted picture of nature as sublime, simple, and unproblematic.

As much as ads intentionally distort reality (in images such as wind-surfing in a truck or singing raccoons), they also present reality as it should be, a reality that is worth desiring and emulating (and owning). If you have backpacked or camped, you know that slapping mosquitoes, getting dirty, getting wet, and sweating are often part of the package. Such a real outdoor experience is unlikely to be depicted in advertisements (unless the product is for something like insect repellent). Instead, ads subordinate reality to a romanticized past, present, or even future. "Real" in advertising is a cultural construct: "The makers of commercials do not want what is real but what will seem real on film. Artificial rain is better than 'God's rain' because it shows up better on film or tape" (Schudson, 1989, p. 79). Advertisers do not intend to capture life as it really is, but intend instead to portray the "ideal" life and to present as normal and everyday what are actually relatively rare moments, such as a phenomenal sunset or a mosquito-less lake.

A great many nature-as-backdrop ads present the natural world as sublime, a noble place inspiring awe and admiration. As an exercise, my students draw their interpretation of a sublime place in nature, and invariably, similar elements appear in their pictures: snow-capped mountain peaks towering above pine trees and a grassy or flower-filled meadow, through which a clear creek or river flows. Sometimes, large mammals such as deer graze in the meadow. Humans are rarely present.

According to Oravec (1996), the sublime is a literary and artistic convention that uses a prescribed form of language and pictorial elements to describe nature, and that in turn encourages a specific pattern of responses to nature. Artistically, sublime representations can include blurring, exaggeration of detail, and compositional elements such as a foreground, middle ground, and frame. Settings are frequently pastoral or wild with varying amounts of human presence. There is a self-reflexive nature to the positioning, with the observer feeling both within a scene and also outside it, viewing the scene (and reflexively, the self) from a higher or more distant (and morally outstanding) perspective.

Oravec has called the sublime the founding trope in the rhetoric of environmentalism: "Sublimity has remained a touchstone or grounding for our public conception of nature and, through nature, of the environment" (1996, p. 68). As a conventional linguistic device, the sublime represents and encodes our understanding of the natural world. Because the sublime is associated with what is "natural," "the sublime connotes an authenticity and originality that is part of its very meaning; yet like rhetoric itself, it has a longstanding reputation for exaggeration and even falsehood" (p. 69).

The sublime is as much a part of advertising as it is of the artistic and literary realms. Advertising presents the natural world as pristine, simple, and not endangered, yet depictions are always contrived and often created. What appears as real rain is artificial, what looks like a natural wildlife encounter is contrived, and what appears entirely natural was created with computer animation and digital manipulation. The artificial seamlessly approximates the real in the sublime world of advertising.

Numerous vacation advertisements depict people in sublime settings, such as thin and tan couples on pristine white sand beaches, or peacefully cruising under sunny skies amid glaciers and whales. Vacationers in this ideal-ized world never encounter anything other than perfect environmental condi-tions and enjoy these sublime locations unfettered by crowds.

A host of pharmaceutical ads likewise enlist nature backdrops as rhetoric for the sublime. One ad for an arthritis medication takes place in a pastoral setting assumed to be a park. The sun is shining, the park is empty except for the actors, there is no litter or noise, and even the dogs are exceedingly friendly and behaved. In another ad for what is presumed to be a mood-enhancer, a woman strolls slowly along a pristine, deserted beach in soft light, a contented smile on her face. In these instances, the sublime backdrop doubly represents the sublime state the person will achieve upon taking the medication. Many of these ads rely so heavily on the power of sublime mean-ing that the actual purpose of the drug is not stated, only assumed.

Other commercials depict the sublime after a product has changed prob-lematic nature into idealized nature. Numerous ads for lawn care products and allergy medications first portray nature in a state of chaos or war, needing to be tamed and brought under control. One television ad for lawn chemicals showed a small army of men and supplies descending from the sky to tame and tackle nature. Some allergy commercials depict the flowers and weeds physically attacking people. But ah, after the product is introduced, unprob-lematic and peaceful nature returns.

When humans are introduced into sublime scenes, their representation is also idealized. Just as nature is presented as reality-as-it-should-be, people are presented as-they-should-be in a limited number of social roles. There-fore, people in ads are primarily attractive, young or middle-aged, vibrant, and thin, or they are celebrities with those qualities. The environments in which they live, whether inside or outside, are also limited to idealized condi-tions; no one has dirty houses or unkempt lawns, and no one travels through dirty city streets, encounters polluted rivers, or finds abused landscapes. In the world of advertising, there are no poor people, sick people, or unattract-ive people, and sometimes there are no people at all. For example, most car ads do not show anyone actually driving the vehicle through the tinted win-dows, and you hear only the disembodied voice of the announcer. The social roles played by advertising actors are easily identifiable — the businessper-son, the grandmother, the teenager — but the actors are anonymous as indi-vidual people and portray only social roles tailored to specific demographic categories. The flat, abstract, idealized, and sometimes anonymous world of advertising "is part of a deliberate effort to connect specific products in peo-ple's imagination with certain demographic groupings or needs or occasions" (Schudson, 1989, p. 77).

Of course you recognize pieces of this idealized presentation of peo-ple and their environments, just as you recognize the utterly impossible pieces — a car parked on an inaccessible cliff or polar bears drinking Coke. We are not stupefied by a natural world that is unrealistic and idealized in advertising: in fact, we expect it.

A Natural Disconnect

5. The depiction of nature in advertising disconnects and estranges us from what is valued, and we attempt to reconnect through products, creating a circular consumption.

Some critics believe that advertising may be more powerful the less people believe it and the less it is acknowledged. According to Schudson (1989), ads do not ask to be taken literally and do not mean what they say, but "this may be the very center of their power" (p. 87). While we are being exposed to those 3,000 ads a day, we may carry an illusion of detachment and think them trivial and unimportant. According to some theories, though, it is very possible to "learn" without active involvement, a so-called sleeper effect. This myth of immunity from an ad's persuasion may do more to protect our self-respect than help us comprehend the subtleties and implications of their influence (Pollay, 1989). Although we may not think an ad speaks to us, its slogan may suddenly pop into our vocabulary — just do it, it does a body good, got milk? We may be unaware and uninvolved in front of the television, but the message of the ad may prove important at purchase time. According to Pollay (1989), advertising does more than merely stimulate wants; it plays a subtle role in changing habits.

Take the habit of drying your clothes, an activity that for many people throughout the world involves pinning clothes to a line in the backyard or between buildings. When I was a girl, I loved sliding between clean sheets dried outside on the clothesline and drinking in the smell. How do many people get that same outside-smell nowadays? They get it with detergents and fabric softeners with names like "mountain air" and "springtime fresh" or with similarly scented dryer sheets. Although perceived convenience and affordable dryers no doubt helped change our clothes-drying habits, where did we learn to associate the smell of outdoors with purchased products? Advertising.

The message in these product ads is that the artificial smell is some- 50 how easier or superior or even just equivalent to the real smell in the natural world. It not only commodifies something of value from the natural world, it gradually disconnects us from that thing of value. The more successfully ads teach us to associate natural qualities such as fresh air with products, the more disconnected we become from what was originally valued. The more estranged from the original thing of value, the more we may attempt to reconnect through products that promise an easy replacement. When we become so estranged from the natural world that we attempt to reconnect through products, a circular consumptive pattern is created — which supports the capitalist economy that advertising was created to support. If advertising tells us that non-saleable qualities of the outdoors such as fresh air and natural smells are easy to bring inside, need we worry about the condition of the real world?

Just as advertising can change habits, it can help create rituals and taboos. A good example of a taboo largely created by advertising is litter. Through national advertising campaigns begun decades ago, litter was labeled as an environmental no-no. While cleaning up litter makes for a visually appealing environment, the automobiles from which the trash is generally tossed cause far more environmental harm than almost all types of litter.

Advertising also works to create rituals. A ritual is created when we make inert, prosaic objects meaningful and give them symbolic significance. Mistletoe means little to us as a parasitic evergreen, but it is loaded with significance as a holiday ritual about kissing. Whales mean more to us as communicative, spiritual symbols of the deep than for their inherent value and place in ocean ecosystems. Price (1996) concluded that Native American fetishes and baskets, which have been ritualized by nonnative populations (and appropriated by advertising), "associate nature nearly interchangeably with indigenous peoples" (1996, p. 189). In a similar way, once a species or animal has been so ritualized, it precludes a more complete and accurate knowing of it and disconnects us.

Advertising, directly and subtly, idealizes and materializes a way of experiencing the world, including the natural world. It promotes products as the simple solutions to complex dilemmas by tapping into our dissatisfactions and desires. If you feel disconnected to the natural world, you can "solve" that with mountain-scented laundry products, bear fetishes, and whale audiotapes, but these purchases only increase the estrangement. If you need to escape modern life yet want to feel safe and civilized while doing so, you can simply solve that by taking a rugged SUV into the wilderness.

Yet environmental dilemmas are anything but simple, and wilderness is a good example. A print ad features a four-wheel-drive car crossing a sparkling, boulder-strewn stream and announces, "Coming soon to a wilderness near you." In this idealized portrayal, there is no mud being stirred up from the bottom of the stream, no dirt of any kind on the car, and of course, there is no visible driver. But in addition, "wilderness" is a rare commodity that rarely exists "near you," and by its very definition, includes few people and even fewer developed signs of people. In wilderness with a capital W, cars and all motorized equipment are forbidden. Setting aside an area as wilderness involves contentious negotiations and land-use trade-offs. But whether formally designated or not, experiencing wilderness is not the simple matter of materialization and driving a certain kind of car.

Another example of advertising portraying a complex environmental issue as simple and uncomplicated is the depiction of water. We see it babbling down brooks in beverage commercials, refreshing someone in a soap commercial, quenching thirst in ads for water filters and bottled water. Pure, clean, healthy — but simple? More than half the world's rivers are drying up or are polluted. Agricultural chemicals have seeped into many U.S. underground aquifers. Oil, gas, and a host of herbicides and pesticides wash off streets and lawns into waterways. Political and legal fights are waged over dams, diversions, and water rights. A host of bacterial contaminants have threatened water supplies and public health in major U.S. cities, and traces of antibiotics and other prescription drugs have been detected in some municipal water supplies. Clean water is definitely not a simple environmental issue.

Advertising Does Not Stand Alone

6. As a ubiquitous form of popular culture, advertising reinforces consonant messages in the social system and provides strong dissonance to oppositional or alternative messages.

For any societal element to wield power, it must exist in concert with other social institutions in a way that is mutually reinforcing. Advertising is layered on top of other cultural elements and bound up with other institutions, from entertainment and popular culture to corporate America and manufacturing. Each element is heteroglossic, continually leaking into other sectors, with advertising slogans showing up in both casual conversation and political speeches. The very ubiquitousness of advertising — extending beyond regular media buys to include placing products in movies, sponsoring sporting events, and the full-length infomercial — ensures its power and influence in numerous places and institutions.

For an example of this interwoven character of advertising and consumption with other elements of society, consider plastics recycling. We routinely see ads touting how certain products are recyclable or made from recycled items. Currently, the plastics industry is running an advertising campaign that reminds us of all the wonderful ways that plastic contributes to our lives. That means that multiple corporate public relations departments and public relations agencies are involved in getting mileage from the recycling issue. Public relations and advertising personnel have regular contact with media people in both the advertising and editorial sides, and the boundaries between news and advertising functions are becoming increasingly blurred (Stauber & Rampton, 1995). Meanwhile, giant corporate conglomerates have become the norm, putting journalists under the same corporate roof as advertisers and the very companies they attempt to scrutinize. For example, if a television station is owned by General Electric and is also receiving thousands of dollars in revenue from an ad campaign about the value of plastics, there is dissonance — whether acknowledged or not — for those TV reporters covering a story about environmental impacts and energy used to recycle plastic.

The hallowed halls of education are not immune from commercial messages, including those about plastic. Captive youngsters are a tempting market: more than 43 million kids attend schools and even elementary-age children exert tremendous spending power, about $15 billion a year (McNeal, 1994). Ads cover school buses, book covers, and scoreboards, and corporate flags fly next to school flags. The Polystyrene Packaging Council, like other corporations, has supplied "supplemental educational materials" free of charge to K–12 classrooms. Their "Plastics and the Environment" lesson teaches that plastics are great and easily recycled, even though most plastics are not recyclable for lack of markets. Consumers Union evaluated this lesson as "highly commercial and incomplete with strong bias . . . [T]he disadvantages of plastics . . . are not covered" (Zillions, 1995, p. 46). Another critic noted that when teachers use such materials, "American students are introduced to environmental issues as they use materials supplied by corporations who pollute the soil, air, and water" (Molnar, 1995, p. 70).

Beyond communication and education, legal sectors also get involved in 60 advertising claims about recycled and recyclable plastic, and politicians know it is wise to support recycling as a generalized issue. Some municipalities sponsor curbside pick-up programs for plastic, and trash haulers and manufacturers run businesses dependent on recycling plastics. Recycling plastics not only creates new business opportunities, it also is philosophically consistent with a capitalist economy that is based on ever-increasing consumption. After all, the message of recycling is not to reduce or avoid consumption but essentially to consume something again. According to one critic in *Harper's*, oftentimes the new product created from recycled plastics is "the perfect metaphor for everything that's wrong with the idea of recycling plastics. It's ugly as sin, the world doesn't need it, and it's disposable" (Gutin, 1992, p. 56).

The vested interest of so many powerful social institutions makes it that much harder to separate the influence of one from another — such as advertising from news media — and to effect significant social change. It also makes the ubiquitous, repetitive messages of advertising reinforced and in a sense replicated, free of charge. Individuals or groups with oppositional messages about plastics would have to contend with what seems a united front about the place, if not the value, of plastic.

Working Together

Obviously, the six concepts presented here work in concert. Here is one filial example of an ad that considers them together.

First, the visual of this television ad: A waterfall flows over the driver's seat of a car and a tiny kayaker (in relation to the size of the car seat) spills down the face of the falls. The scene quickly shifts to the kayaker (full-sized now and paddling away from us) amid glaciers. The next scene takes us into the car's back cargo area — still covered with water — and two orca whales breach in front of the kayaker, who pauses mid-stroke. (In all of these shots, we have never seen the kayaker's face; when he paddles away, his head is covered in a fur-lined parka that looks "native.") The next shot is a close-up of a paddle dipping into water shimmering with the colors of sunset and above the words "Discover Chevy Tahoe." The last scene shows the unoccupied vehicle parked on the edge of a stream in front of snow-covered mountain peaks. The accompanying audio includes Native American-sounding drum beats and a mixed chorus singing a chant-like, non-English song. Over this music, we hear the voice of a male announcer who quotes a passage from John Muir about how a person needs silence to get into the heart of the wilderness away from dust, hotels, baggage, and chatter.

The meanings that these elements convey to us are multiple. Peace, serenity, at-oneness with nature, and a return to a simple yet sublime "native" existence are part of the promise of this vehicle. Native drums, whales, glaciers, paddling through still waters, and even the deep ecologist Muir are powerful, idealized, and ritualized symbols that are employed to market a feeling and a sensation. The seamless juxtaposition of scene both inside and outside the vehicle conveys that nature is transported effortlessly for you to experience these things directly, without leaving the safety and luxury of your car. The vehicle is the commodity to aid your escape to this sublime place, a place depicted as real yet entirely contrived, with kayakers spilling over car seats. The entire promise is one of self-gratification, helping the driver/kayaker travel to this idealized wilderness. Yet, if you truly want to heed John Muir's advice, silence is needed to get into the heart of the wilderness, not a noisy car. Hence if you buy into (pun intended) the vehicle being the solution (and not existing instead in your own life or soul) the result is further estrangement from the very thing desired and valued. Advertising, as a primary support system for a capitalist economy, can only transfer meaning and express latent desires — not deliver on any of these promises.

REFERENCES

Banerjee, S., Gulas, C. S., & Iyer, E. (1995). Shades of green: A multidimensional analysis of environmental advertising. *Journal of Advertising, 24*, 21–32.

Benton, L. M. (1995). Selling the natural or selling out? Exploring environmental merchandising. *Environmental Ethics, 17*, 3–22.

Bullis, C. (1996). Retalking environmental discourses from a feminist perspective: The radical potential of ecofeminism. In J. G. Cantrill & C. L. Oravec (Eds.), *The symbolic earth: Discourse and our creation of the environment* (pp. 123–148). Lexington, KY: University Press of Kentucky.

Corbett, J. B. (2001). Women, scientists, agitators: Magazine portrayal of Rachel Carson and Theo Colborn. *Journal of Communication, 51*, 720–749.

Dadd, D. L., & Carothers, A. (1991). A bill of goods? Green consuming in perspective. In C. Plant & J. Plant (Eds.), *Green business: Hope or hoax?* Philadelphia, PA: New Society Publishers (pp. 11–29).

Fink, E. (1990). Biodegradable diapers are not enough in days like these: A critique of commodity environmentalism. *EcoSocialist Review, 4*.

Gutin, J. (1992, March–April). Plastics-a-go-go. *Harper's, 17*, 56–59.

Iyer, E. & Banerjee, B. (1993). Anatomy of green advertising. *Advances in Consumer Research, 20*, 484–501.

Kilbourne, W. E. (1995). Green advertising: Salvation or oxymoron? *Journal of Advertising, 24*, 7–20.

Lasch, C. (1978). *The culture of narcissism.* New York, NY: W. W. Norton.

Luke, T. W. (1993). Green consumerism: Ecology and the ruse of recycling. In J. Bennett & W. Chaloupka (Eds.), *In the nature of things: Languages, politics and the environment* (pp. 154–172). Minneapolis, MN: University of Minnesota Press.

Mayer, R. N., Scammon, D. L., & Zick, C. D. (1993). Poisoning the well: Do environmental claims strain consumer credulity? *Advances in Consumer Research, 20*, 698–703.

McNeal, J. U. (1994, February 7). Billions at stake in growing kids market. *Discount Store News, 41*.

Molnar, A. (1995). Schooled for profit. *Educational Leadership, 53*, 70–71.

Naess, A. (1973). The shallow and the deep, long-range ecology movement: A summary. *Inquiry, 16*, 95–100.

Neff, J. (2000, April 10) It's not trendy being green. *Advertising Age, 16*.

Obermiller, C. (1995). The baby is sick/the baby is well: A test of environmental communication appeals. *Journal of Advertising, 24*, 55–70.

Oravec, C. L. (1996). To stand outside oneself: The sublime in the discourse of natural scenery. In J. G. Cantrill & C. L. Oravec (Eds.), *The symbolic earth: Discourse and our creation of the environnment* (pp. 58–75). Lexington, KY: University Press of Kentucky.

Ottman, J. A. (1993). *Green marketing: Challenges and opportunities for the new marketing age.* Lincolnwood, IL: NTC Business Books.

Phillips, B. J. (1996). Advertising and the cultural meaning of animals. *Advances in Consumer Research, 23*, 354–360.

Pollay, R. W. (1989). The distorted mirror: Reflections on the unintended consequences of advertising. In R. Hovland & G. B. Wilcox (Eds.), *Advertising in society* (pp. 437–476). Lincolnwood, IL: NTC Business Books.

Price, J. (1996). Looking for nature at the mall: A field guide to the Nature Company. In W. Cronon (Ed.), *Uncommon ground: Rethinking the human place in nature*, (pp. 186–203). New York, NY: W.W. Norton.

Schudson, M. (1989). Advertising as capitalist realism. In R. Hovland & G. B. Wilcox (Eds.), *Advertising in society* (pp. 73–98). Lincolnwood, IL: NTC Business Books.

Schuhwerk, M. E., & Lefkoff-Hagius, R. (1995). Green or non-green? Does type of appeal matter when advertising a green product? *Journal of Advertising, 24*, 45–54.

Selling green. (1991, October). *Consumer Reports, 56*, 687–692.

Shanahan, J., & McComas, K. (1999). *Nature stories: Depictions of the environment and their effects.* Cresskill, NJ: Hampton Press.

Shrum, L. J., McCarty, J. A., & Lowrey, T. M. (1995). Buyer characteristics of the green consumer and their implications for advertising strategy. *Journal of Advertising, 24*, 71–82.

Stauber, J., & Rampton, S. (1995). *Toxic sludge is good for you! Lies, damn lies, and the public relations industry.* Monroe, ME: Common Courage Press.

Thorson, E., Page, T., & Moore, J. (1995). Consumer response to four categories of "green" television commercials. *Advances in Consumer Research, 22*, 243–250.

Turow, J. (1999). *Breaking up America: Advertisers and the new media world.* Chicago, IL: University of Chicago Press.

Twitchell, J. B. (1996). *Adcult USA: The triumph of advertising in American culture.* New York, NY: Columbia University Press.

Zillions: For Kids from Consumer Reports (1995). *Captive kids: Commercial pressures on kids at school.* New York, NY: Consumers Union Education Services.
Zinkham, G. M. & Carlson, L. (1995). Green advertising and the reluctant consumer. *Journal of Advertising, 24,* 1–6.

READING THE TEXT

1. Define in your own words "nature-as-backdrop" ads.

2. How, according to Corbett, did advertising become "part of the fuel that would help keep a capitalist economy burning" (para. 11)?

3. Why does Corbett say that "commodification of what are essentially public resources — like milky blue waters — encourages us to think of resources as private and possessible" (para. 30)? Why does she think such commodification is problematic?

4. In your own words, define the term "sublime."

5. How can some ads using nature as a backdrop be considered to reflect our narcissism?

6. Why does Corbett have concerns regarding ad campaigns for plastics recycling?

READING THE SIGNS

1. In an essay, write your own argument in response to Corbett's speculative question: "is it even possible for any form of advertising — whether product ads or nature-as-backdrop ads — to be 'green'?" (para. 15).

2. Study some travel magazines, focusing on the advertising. To what extent is nature presented as "sublime" or as a backdrop? Use your observations to demonstrate, refute, or complicate the contention that presenting nature as "unproblematic" can have a dangerous effect on our environmental consciousness.

3. Select a single ad that uses nature as a backdrop, and conduct an in-depth analysis of it. As a critical framework, use the six reasons advertising can be "faint" that Corbett outlines on pages 229–42.

4. **CONNECTING TEXTS** Adopting the perspective of Laurence Shames ("The More Factor," p. 90), write an essay in which you argue whether the "faint green" advertising Corbett describes is an expression of the American desire for "more."

5. Corbett asserts that "attempts to make advertising fit a green framework simply illustrate how ideologically opposed advertising and environmental values are" (para. 17). In class, form teams and debate this assertion. Use the debate as a jumping-off point for your own essay in which you explore your own response.

6. Study advertisements for oil, plastics, or chemical companies. Do they use nature as a backdrop, as Corbett describes, or is nature presented in a different way? Use your observations to describe and critique the techniques such companies use to present a positive public image.

7. **CONNECTING TEXTS** As an alternative, do the same with automobile advertising. To develop your ideas, consult Alan Foljambe, "Car Advertising — Dominating Nature" (p. 246) and David Goewey, "'Careful, You May Run Out of Planet'" (p. 54).

ALAN FOLJAMBE

Car Advertising — Dominating Nature

With increasing pressure, literally, to clean up their act, automobile manufacturers are turning to advertising strategies whereby, in Alan Foljambe's words, "Vehicles in car ads exist within a natural world that is completely unaffected by their presence. Mountains, clean air, and fragile desert landscapes surround the cars in pristine splendor." Either that, or the vehicle is shown trampling through (and usually up) some back road location, promising "fun, excitement, and self-fulfillment, with no consideration given to environmental issues." But these ads sell cars. Alan Foljambe is a freelance writer and art historian who writes for such sites as suite101.com, where this reading originally appeared.

Through visual and linguistic techniques of persuasion, flattery, veiled threat, humor, or inspiration, automotive advertisers attempt to associate their products with conditions or qualities that are desirable to the consumer. In a world of increasingly pressing ecological problems, many of which are caused or exacerbated by cars, automotive manufacturers are utilizing green advertising in an attempt to convince the public of the essentially benign effect of cars on planetary systems.

Car Marketing Goes Green

Car companies are positioning themselves as part of, rather than a threat to, the environment. In their advertisements, cars are presented not only as harmless tools of travel and recreation, but as totems of individual freedom and interaction with the natural world.

Subhabrata Banerjee identifies two types of "green" in automotive advertising: deep green, or alleviation ads, characterized by an appeal to the consumer's concern with nature and a presentation of the car as low-impact and kind to the earth, and shallow green, or domination ads, characterized by the use of nature as an inspiring backdrop with no substance, and typified by images of "tough trucks" dominating the landscape.

Domination advertising is only "green" in the sense that images of nature are used. Julia Corbett writes that this is "the most prevalent use of the environment in advertising: when nature functions as a rhetorically useful backdrop or stage (Corbett, *Enviropop*, 2002)." Nature is presented as threatening rather than threatened, unpredictable, and something to be commanded by tough trucks and heavy equipment. By juxtaposing the vehicle with enormous and apparently timeless landscapes, advertisers attempt to confer the qualities of the landscape onto the car.

Appealing to Privilege

In a typical Land Rover ad, the vehicle sits surrounded by desert rock 5
formations, the sun slanting in from the left into a dry riverbed with no apparent means of access. The vehicle's ability to access remote locales highlights its power. A connection is made in this advertisement between inaccessible landscapes and the elite nature of exclusive sectors of society. In the terminology of John Urry, the vehicle is the subject of a "romantic" as opposed to a "collective" gaze: "In the former, the emphasis is upon solitude, privacy, and a personal, semi-spiritual relationship with the object of the gaze."

While in the real world, the car serves as a vehicle, in the advertisement it is an icon of individual worth. It represents the unique and privileged position of the buyer. The text below the image reads "Gaining admittance isn't merely about having the right connections." The end of the text, where the Land Rover's $55,500 price tag is referred to as "a small price for admission," removes all doubt as to what market sector is being sought in this ad. The vehicle sits alone in the landscape just as the consumer sits alone at the top of the socio-economic pyramid.

Denial of Ecological Impact

Vehicles in car ads exist within a natural world that is completely unaffected by their presence. Mountains, clean air, and fragile desert landscapes surround the cars in pristine splendor. The message is that one can use these vehicles, on or off road, without concern for the environment, because they don't do any harm. While this is never stated in words, the visual imagery is far more subtle and effective than a slogan. The rich, perfectly lit contours of the natural landscape surround these vehicles in a loving way, naturalizing and welcoming them.

Utilizing viewers' nostalgic desire for an unblemished world, advertisers associate cars, paradoxically but convincingly within the context of the ad, with a pristine nonhuman environment. The choice of desert over other landscapes in car advertising is not random. Richard Olsen writes that "the desert is a frequent setting in SUV ads. This taps into long-standing connections between the desert and purification or spirituality . . ." It is an ideal setting for self-denial that may lead to spiritual epiphanies (Olsen, *Enviropop*, 2002).

When the vehicles in dominance ads are not sitting in unblemished perfection, they are roaring effortlessly up impossible grades. In a typical ad, a Toyota truck is zooming up a near-vertical dirt track, its driver obscured behind tinted windows, dramatic puffs of dirt in the air behind it but not a speck on the truck itself. Emblazoned across the image are the words "when your life path is more like a trajectory."

The focus here is on fun, excitement, and self-fulfillment, with no consideration given to environmental issues. The direction of the vehicle is always up, never down, an expression of the cultural belief that privileges verticality, power, and progress. Nature is presented as a fun, yet easily defeated, challenge to technology, while technology is portrayed as an extension of the self: powerful, in control, and dominant. 10

BIBLIOGRAPHY

Banerjee, Subhabrata, Charles S. Gulas, and Easwar Iyer. "Shades of Green: A Multidimensional Analysis of Environmental Advertising." *Journal of Advertising* 24, no. 2 (1995), p. 21–32.

Crawshaw, Carol, and John Urry. *"Tourism and the Photographic Eye."* In *Touring Cultures: Transformations of Travel and Theory*, edited by Rojek and Urry, 176–95. London: Routledge, 1997.

Greenpeace. *The Environmental Impact of the Car: A Greenpeace Report*. Washington, D.C.: Greenpeace, 1992.

Meister, Mark, and Phyllis M. Japp, eds. *Enviropop: Studies in Environmental Rhetoric and Popular Culture*. Westport, CT: Praeger, 2002.

READING THE TEXT

1. In your own words, describe the positive values that car manufacturers associate with their vehicles.

2. What are the differences between "deep green" and "shallow green" ads, according to Foljambe?

3. Define in your own words a "collective" and a "romantic" gaze.

READING THE SIGNS

1. Study a magazine such as *Car and Driver* and, focusing on ads that present vehicles in outdoor settings, analyze the ads' use of the natural environment as a "scene." Do deep green or shallow green techniques dominate? Do the ads use other strategies? If so, what shade of green would you apply to them?

2. Look at advertising that promotes alternative-fuel vehicles, such as the Prius, Volt, or Leaf. Do these ads use either the deep or shallow green strategies? If not, what promotional techniques do they use, and what shade of green would you apply to them?

3. **CONNECTING TEXTS** Given that cars contribute to ecological problems, write an essay that either defends or attacks green ads. To develop your ideas, consult

Minette E. Drumright and Patrick E. Murphy, "How Advertising Practitioners View Ethics: Moral Muteness, Moral Myopia, and Moral Imagination" (p. 199).

4. In the wake of the 2010 BP oil rig disaster in the Gulf Coast, we saw an increase in green advertising for products other than cars. In small groups, collect a range of such ads (you could visit your college library and survey popular magazines from the latter half of 2010). In what ways do such ads associate an environmental message with their products? Do you find these ads to be informative, on the one hand, or opportunistic on the other?

GLORIA STEINEM
Sex, Lies, and Advertising

One of the best-known icons of the women's movement, Gloria Steinem has been a leader in transforming the image of women in America. As a cofounder of *Ms.* magazine, in which this selection first appeared, Steinem has provided a forum for women's voices for more than thirty years, but as her article explains, it has not been easy to keep this forum going. A commercial publication requires commercials, and the needs of advertisers do not always mesh nicely with the goals of a magazine like *Ms.* Steinem ruefully reveals the compromises *Ms.* magazine had to make over the years to satisfy its advertising clients, compromises that came to an end only when *Ms.* ceased to take ads. Steinem's publications include *Revolution from Within* (1992), a personal exploration of the power of self-esteem; *Moving beyond Words* (1994); *Outrageous Acts and Everyday Rebellions* (2nd ed., 1995), and *Doing Sixty & Seventy* (2006). Currently a consulting editor for *Ms.*, Steinem continues to combine her passion for writing and activism as an unflagging voice in American feminism.

Goodbye to cigarette ads where poems should be.
Goodbye to celebrity covers and too little space.
Goodbye to cleaning up language so *Ms.* advertisers won't be boycotted
    by the Moral Majority.
In fact, goodbye to advertisers *and* the Moral Majority.
Goodbye to short articles and short thinking.
Goodbye to "post-feminism" from people who never say "post-
    democracy."

Goodbye to national boundaries and hello to the world.
Welcome to the magazine of the post-patriarchal age.
The turn of the century is *our turn!*

That was my celebratory mood in the summer of 1990 when I finished the original version of the exposé you are about to read. I felt as if I'd been released from a personal, portable Bastille. At least I'd put on paper the ad policies that had been punishing *Ms.* for all the years of its nonconforming life and still were turning more conventional media, especially (but not only) those directed at women, into a dumping ground for fluff.

Those goodbyes were part of a letter inviting readers to try a new, ad-free version of *Ms.* and were also a homage to "Goodbye to All That," a witty and lethal essay in which Robin Morgan bade farewell to the pre-feminist male Left of twenty years before. It seemed the right tone for the birth of a brand-new, reader-supported, more international form of *Ms.*, which Robin was heading as editor-in-chief, and I was serving as consulting editor. Besides, I had a very personal kind of mantra running through my head: *I'll never have to sell another ad as long as I live.*

So I sent the letter off, watched the premiere issue containing my exposé go to press, and then began to have second thoughts: Were ad policies too much of an "inside" concern? Did women readers already know that magazines directed at them were filled with editorial extensions of ads — and not care? Had this deceptive system been in place too long for anyone to have faith in changing it? In other words: Would anybody give a damn?

After almost four years of listening to responses and watching the ripples spread out from this pebble cast upon the waters, I can tell you that, yes, readers do care; and no, most of them were not aware of advertising's control over the words and images around it. Though most people in the publishing industry think this is a practice too deeply embedded ever to be uprooted, a lot of readers are willing to give it a try — even though that's likely to mean paying more for their publications. In any case, as they point out, understanding the nitty-gritty of ad influence has two immediate uses. It strengthens healthy skepticism about what we read, and it keeps us from assuming that other women must want this glamorous, saccharine, unrealistic stuff.

Perhaps that's the worst punishment ad influence has inflicted upon us. It's made us feel contemptuous of other women. We know we don't need those endless little editorial diagrams of where to put our lipstick or blush — we don't identify with all those airbrushed photos of skeletal women with everything about them credited, *even their perfume* (can you imagine a man's photo airbrushed to perfection, with his shaving lotion credited?) — but we assume there must be women out there somewhere who *do* love it; otherwise, why would it be there?

Well, many don't. Given the sameness of women's magazines resulting from the demands made by makers of women's products that advertise in all of them, we probably don't know yet what a wide variety of women readers want. In any case, we do know it's the advertisers who are determining what women are getting now.

The first wave of response to this exposé came not from readers but from writers and editors for other women's magazines. They phoned to say the pall cast by anticipated or real advertising demands was even more widespread than rebellious *Ms.* had been allowed to know. They told me how brave I was to "burn my bridges" (no critic of advertising would ever be hired as an editor of any of the women's magazines, they said) and generally treated me as if I'd written about organized crime instead of practices that may be unethical but are perfectly legal. After making me promise not to use their names, they offered enough additional horror stories to fill a book, a movie, and maybe a television series. Here is a typical one: when the freelance author of an article on moisturizers observed in print that such products might be less necessary for young women — whose skin tends to be not dry but oily — the article's editor was called on the carpet and denounced by her bosses as "anti-moisturizer." Or how about this: the film critic for a women's magazine asked its top editor, a woman who makes millions for her parent company, whether movies could finally be reviewed critically, since she had so much clout. No, said the editor; if you can't praise a movie, just don't include it; otherwise we'll jeopardize our movie ads. This may sound like surrealism in everyday life, or like our grandmothers advising, "If you can't say something

Gloria Steinem (left) and Patricia Carbine cofounded *Ms.* magazine.

nice, don't say anything," but such are the forces that control much of our information.

I got few negative responses from insiders, but the ones I did get were bitter. Two editors at women's magazines felt I had demeaned them by writing the article. They loved their work, they said, and didn't feel restricted by ads at all. So I would like to make clear in advance that my purpose was and is to change the system, not to blame the people struggling within it. As someone who has written for most women's magazines, I know that many editors work hard to get worthwhile articles into the few pages left over after providing all the "complementary copy" (that is, articles related to and supportive of advertised products). I also know there are editors who sincerely want exactly what the advertisers want, which is why they're so good at their jobs. Nonetheless, criticizing this ad-dominant system is no different from criticizing male-dominant marriage. Both institutions make some people happy, and both seem free as long as your wishes happen to fall within their traditional boundaries. But just as making more equal marital laws alleviates the suffering of many, breaking the link between editorial and advertising will help all media become more honest and diverse.

A second wave of reaction came from advertising executives who were asked to respond by reporters. They attributed all problems to *Ms.* We must have been too controversial or otherwise inappropriate for ads. I saw no stories that asked the next questions: Why had non-women's companies from Johnson & Johnson to IBM found our "controversial" pages fine for their ads? Why did desirable and otherwise unreachable customers read something so "inappropriate"? What were ad policies doing to *other* women's media? To continue my marriage parallel, however, I should note that these executives seemed only mildly annoyed. Just as many women are more dependent than men on the institution of marriage and so are more threatened and angry when it's questioned, editors of women's magazines tended to be more upset than advertisers when questioned about their alliance. . . .

Then came the third wave—reader letters which were smart, thought- 10 ful, innovative, and numbered in the hundreds. Their dominant themes were anger and relief: relief because those vast uncritical oceans of food/fashion/beauty articles in other women's magazines weren't necessarily what women wanted after all, and also relief because *Ms.* wasn't going to take ads anymore, even those that were accompanied by fewer editorial demands; anger because consumer information, diverse articles, essays, fiction, and poetry could have used the space instead of all those oceans of articles about ad categories that had taken up most of women's magazines for years. . . .

Last and most rewarding was the response that started in the fall. Teachers of journalism, advertising, communications, women's studies, and other contemporary courses asked permission to reprint the exposé as a supplementary text. That's another reason why I've restored cuts, updated information, and added new examples—including this introduction. Getting subversive ideas into classrooms could change the next generation running the media.

The following pages are mostly about women's magazines, but that doesn't mean other media are immune.

Sex, Lies, and Advertising

Toward the end of the 1980s, when glasnost was beginning and *Ms.* magazine seemed to be ending, I was invited to a press lunch for a Soviet official. He entertained us with anecdotes about the new problems of democracy in his country; for instance, local Communist leaders who were being criticized by their own media for the first time, and were angry.

"So I'll have to ask my American friends," he finished pointedly, "how more subtly to control the press."

In the silence that followed, I said: "Advertising."   15

The reporters laughed, but later one of them took me aside angrily: How dare I suggest that freedom of the press was limited in this country? How dare I imply that *his* newsmagazine could be influenced by ads?

I explained that I wasn't trying to lay blame, but to point out advertising's media-wide influence. We can all recite examples of "soft" cover stories that newsmagazines use to sell ads, and self-censorship in articles that should have taken advertised products to task for, say, safety or pollution. Even television news goes "soft" in ratings wars, and other TV shows don't get on the air without advertiser support. But I really had been thinking about women's magazines. There, it isn't just a little content that's designed to attract ads; it's almost all of it. That's why advertisers—not readers—had always been the problem for *Ms.* As the only women's magazine that didn't offer what the ad world euphemistically describes as "supportive editorial atmosphere" or "complementary copy" (for instance, articles that praise food/fashion/beauty subjects in order to "support" and "complement" food/fashion/beauty ads), *Ms.* could never attract enough ads to break even.

"Oh, *women*'s magazines," the journalist said with contempt. "Everybody knows they're catalogs—but who cares? They have nothing to do with journalism."

I can't tell you how many times I've had this argument since I started writing for magazines in the early 1960s, and especially since the current women's movement began. Except as moneymaking machines—"cash cows," as they are so elegantly called in the trade—women's magazines are usually placed beyond the realm of serious consideration. Though societal changes being forged by women have been called more far-reaching than the industrial revolution by such nonfeminist sources as the *Wall Street Journal*—and though women's magazine editors often try hard to reflect these changes in the few pages left after all the ad-related subjects are covered—the magazines serving the female half of this country are still far below the journalistic and ethical standards of news and general-interest counterparts. Most depressing of all, this fact is so taken for granted that it doesn't even rate as an exposé.

For instance: If *Time* and *Newsweek*, in order to get automotive and GM ads, had to lavish editorial praise on cars and credit photographs in which newsmakers were driving, say, a Buick from General Motors, there would be a scandal — maybe even a criminal investigation. When women's magazines from *Seventeen* to *Lear's* publish articles lavishing praise on beauty and fashion products, and credit in text, the cover, and other supposedly editorial photographs a particular makeup from Revlon or a dress from Calvin Klein because those companies also advertise, it's just business as usual.

When *Ms.* began, we didn't consider *not* taking ads. The most important reason was to keep the price of a feminist magazine low enough for most women to afford. But the second and almost equal reason was to provide a forum where women and advertisers could talk to each other and experiment with nonstereotyped, informative, imaginative ads. After all, advertising was (and is) as potent a source of information in this country as news or TV or movies. It's where we get not only a big part of our information but also images that shape our dreams.

We decided to proceed in two stages. First, we would convince makers of "people products" that their ads should be placed in a women's magazine: cars, credit cards, insurance, sound equipment, financial services — everything that's used by both men and women but was then advertised only to men. Since those advertisers were accustomed to the division between editorial pages and ads that news and general-interest magazines at least try to maintain, such products would allow our editorial content to be free and diverse. Furthermore, if *Ms.* could prove that women were important purchasers of "people products," just as men were, those advertisers would support other women's magazines, too, and subsidize some pages for articles about something other than the hothouse worlds of food/fashion/beauty. Only in the second phase would we add examples of the best ads for whatever traditional "women's products" (clothes, shampoo, fragrance, food, and so on) that subscriber surveys showed *Ms.* readers actually used. But we would ask those advertisers to come in *without* the usual quid pro quo of editorial features praising their product area; that is, the dreaded "complementary copy."

From the beginning, we knew the second step might be even harder than the first. Clothing advertisers like to be surrounded by editorial fashion spreads (preferably ones that credit their particular labels and designers); food advertisers have always expected women's magazines to publish recipes and articles on entertaining (preferably ones that require their products); and shampoo, fragrance, and beauty products in general insist on positive editorial coverage of beauty aids — a "beauty atmosphere," as they put it — plus photo credits for particular products and nothing too depressing; no bad news. That's why women's magazines look the way they do: saccharine, smiley-faced, and product-heavy, with even serious articles presented in a slick and sanitized way.

But if *Ms.* could break this link between ads and editorial content, then we should add "women's products" too. For one thing, publishing ads only for gender-neutral products would give the impression that women have to become "like men" in order to succeed (an impression that *Ms.* ad pages sometimes *did* give when we were still in the first stage). For another, presenting a full circle of products that readers actually need and use would allow us to select the best examples of each category and keep ads from being lost in a sea of similar products. By being part of this realistic but unprecedented mix, products formerly advertised only to men would reach a growth market of women, and good ads for women's products would have a new visibility.

Given the intelligence and leadership of *Ms.* readers, both kinds of products would have unique access to a universe of smart consultants whose response would help them create more effective ads for other media too. Aside from the advertisers themselves, there's nobody who cares as much about the imagery in advertising as those who find themselves stereotyped or rendered invisible by it. And they often have great suggestions for making it better.

As you can see, we had all our energy, optimism, and arguments in good working order.

I thought at the time that our main problem would be getting ads with good "creative," as the imagery and text are collectively known. That was where the women's movement had been focusing its efforts, for instance, the National Organization for Women's awards to the best ads, and its "Barefoot and Pregnant" awards for the worst. Needless to say, there were plenty of candidates for the second group. Carmakers were still draping blondes in evening gowns over the hoods like ornaments that could be bought with the car (thus also making clear that car ads weren't directed at women). Even in ads for products that only women used, the authority figures were almost always male, and voice-overs for women's products on television were usually male too. Sadistic, he-man campaigns were winning industry praise; for example, *Advertising Age* hailed the infamous Silva Thin cigarette theme, "How to Get a Woman's Attention: Ignore Her," as "brilliant." Even in medical journals, ads for tranquilizers showed depressed housewives standing next to piles of dirty dishes and promised to get them back to work. As for women's magazines, they seemed to have few guidelines; at least none that excluded even the ads for the fraudulent breast-enlargement or thigh-thinning products for which their back pages were famous.

Obviously, *Ms.* would have to avoid such offensive imagery and seek out the best ads, but this didn't seem impossible. The *New Yorker* had been screening ads for aesthetic reasons for years, a practice that advertisers accepted at the time. *Ebony* and *Essence* were asking for ads with positive black images, and though their struggle was hard, their requests weren't seen as unreasonable. . . .

Let me take you through some of our experiences — greatly condensed, but just as they happened. In fact, if you poured water on any one of these, it would become a novel:

- Cheered on by early support from Volkswagen and one or two other car 30 companies, we finally scrape together time and money to put on a major reception in Detroit. U.S. carmakers firmly believe that women choose the upholstery color, not the car, but we are armed with statistics and reader mail to prove the contrary: A car is an important purchase for women, one that is such a symbol of mobility and freedom that many women will spend a greater percentage of income for a car than will counterpart men.

But almost nobody comes. We are left with many pounds of shrimp on the table, and quite a lot of egg on our face. Assuming this near-total boycott is partly because there was a baseball pennant play-off the same day, we blame ourselves for not foreseeing the problem. Executives go out of their way to explain that they wouldn't have come anyway. It's a dramatic beginning for ten years of knocking on resistant or hostile doors, presenting endless documentation of women as car buyers, and hiring a full-time saleswoman in Detroit — all necessary before *Ms.* gets any real results.

This long saga has a semi-happy ending: Foreign carmakers understood better than Detroit that women buy cars, and advertised in *Ms.*; also years of research on the women's market plus door-knocking began to pay off. Eventually, cars became one of our top sources of ad revenue. Even Detroit began to take the women's market seriously enough to put car ads in other women's magazines too, thus freeing a few more of their pages from the food/fashion/beauty hothouse.

But long after figures showed that a third, even half, of many car models were being bought by women, U.S. makers continued to be uncomfortable addressing female buyers. Unlike many foreign carmakers, Detroit never quite learned the secret of creating intelligent ads that exclude no one and then placing them in media that overcome past exclusion. Just as an African American reader may feel more invited by a resort that placed an ad in *Ebony* or *Essence*, even though the same ad appeared in *Newsweek*, women of all races may need to see ads for cars, computers, and other historically "masculine" products in media that are clearly directed at them. Once inclusive ads are well placed, however, there's interest and even gratitude from women. *Ms.* readers were so delighted to be addressed as intelligent consumers by a routine Honda ad with text about rack-and-pinion steering, for example, that they sent fan mail. But even now, Detroit continues to ask: "Should we make special ads for women?" That's probably one reason why foreign cars still have a greater share of the women's market in the United States than of the men's.

- In the *Ms.* Gazette, we do a brief report on a congressional hearing into coal tar derivatives used in hair dyes that are absorbed through the skin and may be carcinogenic. This seems like news of importance: Newspapers and newsmagazines are reporting it too. But Clairol, a Bristol-Myers subsidiary that makes dozens of products, a few of which have just come into our pages as ads *without* the usual quid pro quo of articles on hair and beauty, is outraged. Not at newspapers or newsmagazines, just at us. It's bad enough that *Ms.* is the only women's magazine refusing to provide "supportive editorial" praising beauty products, but to criticize one of their product categories on top of it, however generically or even accurately — well, *that* is going too far.

We offer to publish a letter from Clairol telling its side of the story. In an 35 excess of solicitousness, we even put this letter in the Gazette, not in Letters to the Editors, where it belongs. Eventually, Clairol even changes its hair-coloring formula, apparently in response to those same hearings. But in spite of surveys that show *Ms.* readers to be active women who use more of almost everything Clairol makes than do the readers of other women's magazines, *Ms.* gets almost no ads for those dozens of products for the rest of its natural life.

• Women of color read *Ms.* in disproportionate numbers. This is a source of pride to *Ms.* staffers, who are also more racially representative than the editors of other women's magazines (which may include some beautiful black models but almost no black decisionmakers; Pat Carbine hired the first black editor at *McCall's*, but she left when Pat did). Nonetheless, the reality of *Ms.*'s staff and readership is obscured by ads filled with enough white women to make the casual reader assume *Ms.* is directed at only one part of the population, no matter what the editorial content is.

In fact, those few ads we are able to get that feature women of color — for instance, one made by Max Factor for *Essence* and *Ebony* that Linda Wachner gives us while she is president of Max Factor — are greeted with praise and relief by white readers, too, and make us feel that more inclusive ads should win out in the long run. But there are pathetically few such images. Advertising "creative" also excludes women who are not young, not thin, not conventionally pretty, well-to-do, able-bodied, or heterosexual — which is a hell of a lot of women.

• Our intrepid saleswomen set out early to attract ads for the product category known as consumer electronics: sound equipment, computers, calculators, VCRs, and the like. We know that *Ms.* readers are determined to be part of this technological revolution, not to be left out as women have been in the past. We also know from surveys that readers are buying this kind of stuff in numbers as high as those of readers of magazines like *Playboy* and the "male 18 to 34" market, prime targets of the industry. Moreover, unlike traditional women's products that our readers buy but don't want to read articles about, these are subjects they like to see demystified in our pages. There actually *is* a supportive editorial atmosphere.

"But women don't understand technology," say ad and electronics executives at the end of our presentations. "Maybe not," we respond, "but neither do men — and we all buy it."

"If women *do* buy it," counter the decisionmakers, "it's because they're 40
asking their husbands and boyfriends what to buy first." We produce letters
from *Ms.* readers saying how turned off they are when salesmen say things
like "Let me know when your husband can come in."

Then the argument turns to why there aren't more women's names sent
back on warranties (those much-contested certificates promising repair or
replacement if anything goes wrong). We explain that the husband's name
may be on the warranty, even if the wife made the purchase. But it's also
true that women are experienced enough as consumers to know that such
promises are valid only if the item is returned in its original box at midnight
in Hong Kong. Sure enough, when we check out hair dryers, curling irons,
and other stuff women clearly buy, women don't return those warranties very
often either. It isn't the women who are the problem, it's the meaningless
warranties.

After several years of this, we get a few ads from companies like JVC
and Pioneer for compact sound systems — on the grounds that women can
understand compacts, but not sophisticated components. Harry Elias, vice
president of JVC, is actually trying to convince his Japanese bosses that
there is something called a woman's market. At his invitation, I find myself
speaking at trade shows in Chicago and Las Vegas trying to persuade JVC
dealers that electronics showrooms don't have to be locker rooms. But as
becomes apparent, however, the trade shows are part of the problem. In
Las Vegas, the only women working at technology displays are seminude
models serving champagne. In Chicago, the big attraction is Marilyn Cham-
bers, a porn star who followed Linda Lovelace of *Deep Throat* fame as Chuck
Traynor's captive and/or employee, whose pornographic movies are being
used to demonstrate VCRs.

In the end, we get ads for a car stereo now and then, but no VCRs; a
welcome breakthrough of some IBM personal computers, but no Apple or no
Japanese-made ones. Furthermore, we notice that *Working Woman* and *Savvy*,
which are focused on office work, don't benefit as much as they should from
ads for office equipment either. . . .

• Then there is the great toy train adventure. Because *Ms.* gets letters from
little girls who love toy trains and ask our help in changing ads and box-top
photos that show only little boys, we try to talk to Lionel and to get their ads.
It turns out that Lionel executives *have* been concerned about little girls. They
made a pink train and couldn't understand why it didn't sell.

Eventually, Lionel bows to this consumer pressure by switching to a photo- 45
graph of a boy *and* a girl — but only on some box tops. If trains are associated
with little girls, Lionel executives believe, they will be devalued in the eyes of
little boys. Needless to say, *Ms.* gets no train ads. If even 20 percent of little
girls wanted trains, they would be a huge growth market, but this remains
unexplored. In the many toy stores where displays are still gender divided,
the "soft" stuff, even modeling clay, stays on the girls' side, while the "hard"

stuff, especially rockets and trains, is displayed for boys — thus depriving both. By 1986, Lionel is put up for sale.

We don't have much luck with other kinds of toys either. A *Ms.* department, Stories for Free Children, edited by Letty Cottin Pogrebin, makes us one of the very few magazines with a regular feature for children. A larger proportion of *Ms.* readers have preschool children than do the readers of any other women's magazine. Nonetheless, the industry can't seem to believe that feminists care about children — much less have them.

• When *Ms.* began, the staff decided not to accept ads for feminine hygiene sprays and cigarettes on the same basis: They are damaging to many women's health but carry no appropriate warnings. We don't think we should tell our readers what to do — if marijuana were legal, for instance, we would carry ads for it along with those for beer and wine — but we should provide facts so readers can decide for themselves. Since we've received letters saying that feminine sprays actually kill cockroaches and take the rust off metal, we give up on those. But antismoking groups have been pressuring for health warnings on cigarette ads as well as packages, so we decide we will accept advertising if the tobacco industry complies.

Philip Morris is among the first to do so. One of its brands, Virginia Slims, is also sponsoring women's tennis tournaments and women's public opinion polls that are historic "firsts." On the other hand, the Virginia Slims theme, "You've come a long way, baby," has more than a "baby" problem. It gives the impression that for women, smoking is a sign of progress.

We explain to the Philip Morris people that this slogan won't do well in our pages. They are convinced that its success with *some* women means it will work with *all* women. No amount of saying that we, like men, are a segmented market, that we don't all think alike, does any good. Finally, we agree to publish a small ad for a Virginia Slims calendar as a test, and to abide by the response of our readers.

The letters from readers are both critical and smart. For instance: Would 50 you show a photo of a black man picking cotton next to one of an African American man in a Cardin suit, and symbolize progress from slavery to civil rights by smoking? Of course not. So why do it for women? But instead of honoring test results, the executives seem angry to have been proved wrong. We refuse Virginia Slims ads, thus annoying tennis players like Billie Jean King as well as incurring a new level of wrath: Philip Morris takes away ads for *all* its many products, costing *Ms.* about $250,000 in the first year. After five years, the damage is so great we can no longer keep track.

Occasionally, a new set of Philip Morris executives listens to *Ms.* saleswomen, or laughs when Pat Carbine points out that even Nixon got pardoned. I also appeal directly to the chairman of the board, who agrees it is unfair, sends me to another executive — and *he* says no. Because we won't take Virginia Slims, not one other Philip Morris product returns to our pages for the next sixteen years.

Gradually, we also realize our naïveté in thinking we could refuse all cigarette ads, with or without a health warning. They became a disproportionate source of revenue for print media the moment television banned them,
and few magazines can compete or survive without them; certainly not *Ms.*,
which lacks the support of so many other categories. Though cigarette ads
actually inhibit editorial freedom less than ads for food, fashion, and the
like — cigarette companies want only to be distant from coverage on the dangers of smoking, and don't require affirmative praise or photo credits of their
product — it is still a growing source of sorrow that they are there at all. By the
1980s, when statistics show that women's rate of lung cancer is approaching
men's, the necessity of taking cigarette ads has become a kind of prison.

Though I never manage to feel kindly toward groups that protest our ads
and pay no attention to magazines and newspapers that can turn them down
and still keep their doors open — and though *Ms.* continues to publish new
facts about smoking, such as its dangers during pregnancy — I long for the
demise of the whole tobacco-related industry. . . .

• General Mills, Pillsbury, Carnation, Del Monte, Dole, Kraft, Stouffer, Hor-
mel, Nabisco: You name the food giant, we try to get its ads. But no matter
how desirable the *Ms.* readership, our lack of editorial recipes and traditional
homemaking articles proves lethal.

We explain that women flooding into the paid labor force have changed   55
the way this country eats; certainly, the boom in convenience foods proves
that. We also explain that placing food ads *only* next to recipes and how-to-
entertain articles is actually a negative for many women. It associates food
with work — in a way that says only women have to cook — or with guilt over
not cooking and entertaining. Why not advertise food in diverse media that
don't always include recipes (thus reaching more men, who have become a
third of all supermarket shoppers anyway) and add the recipe interest with
specialty magazines like *Gourmet* (a third of whose readers are men)?

These arguments elicit intellectual interest but no ads. No advertising
executive wants to be the first to say to a powerful client, "Guess what, I *didn't*
get you complementary copy." Except for an occasional hard-won ad for
instant coffee, diet drinks, yogurt, or such extras as avocados and almonds,
the whole category of food, a mainstay of the publishing industry, remains
unavailable to us. Period. . . .

• By the end of 1986, magazine production costs have skyrocketed and
postal rates have increased 400 percent. Ad income is flat for the whole
magazine industry. The result is more competition, with other magazines
offering such "extras" as free golf trips for advertisers or programs for "sampling" their products at parties and other events arranged by the magazine
for desirable consumers. We try to compete with the latter by "sampling" at
what we certainly have enough of: movement benefits. Thus, little fragrance
bottles turn up next to the dinner plates of California women lawyers (who
are delighted), or wine samples lower the costs at a reception for political

women. A good organizing tactic comes out of this. We hold feminist seminars in shopping centers. They may be to the women's movement what churches were to the civil rights movement in the South—that is, *where people are*. Anyway, shopping center seminars are a great success. Too great. We have to stop doing them in Bloomingdale's up and down the East Coast, because meeting space in the stores is too limited, and too many women are left lined up outside stores. We go on giving out fancy little liquor bottles at store openings, which makes the advertisers happy—but not us.

Mostly, however, we can't compete in this game of "value-added" (the code word for giving the advertisers extras in return for their ads). Neither can many of the other independent magazines. Deep-pocketed corporate parents can offer such extras as reduced rates for ad schedules in a group of magazines, free tie-in spots on radio stations they also own, or vacation junkets on corporate planes.

Meanwhile, higher costs and lowered income have caused the *Ms.* 60/40 preponderance of edit over ads—something we promised to readers—to become 50/50: still a lot better than most women's magazines' goals of 30/70, but not good enough. Children's stories, most poetry, and some fiction are casualties of reduced space. In order to get variety into more limited pages, the length (and sometimes the depth) of articles suffers. Though we don't solicit or accept ads that would look like a parody in our pages, we get so worn down that some slip through. Moreover, we always have the problem of working just as hard to get a single ad as another magazine might for a whole year's schedule of ads.

Still, readers keep right on performing miracles. Though we haven't been 60 able to afford a subscription mailing in two years, they maintain our guaranteed circulation of 450,000 by word of mouth. Some of them also help to make up the advertising deficit by giving *Ms.* a birthday present of $15 on its fifteenth anniversary, or contributing $1,000 for a lifetime subscription—even those who can ill afford it.

What's almost as angering as these struggles, however, is the way the media report them. Our financial problems are attributed to lack of reader interest, not an advertising double standard. In the Reagan–Bush era, when "feminism-is-dead" becomes one key on the typewriter, our problems are used to prepare a grave for the whole movement. Clearly, the myth that advertisers go where the readers are—thus, if we had readers, we would have advertisers—is deeply embedded. Even industry reporters rarely mention the editorial demands made by ads for women's products, and if they do, they assume advertisers must be right and *Ms.* must be wrong; we must be too controversial, outrageous, even scatalogical to support. In fact, there's nothing in our pages that couldn't be published in *Time, Esquire,* or *Rolling Stone*—providing those magazines devoted major space to women—but the media myth often wins out. Though comparable magazines our size (say, *Vanity Fair* or the *Atlantic*) are losing more money in a single year than *Ms.* has lost in sixteen years, *Ms.* is held to a different standard. No matter how much never-to-be-recovered cash is poured into starting a magazine or keeping it going, appearances seem to be all that matter. (Which is why we haven't been able to explain our fragile state in public. Nothing causes ad flight like the smell of nonsuccess.)

My healthy response is anger, but my not-so-healthy one is depression, worry, and an obsession with finding one more rescue. There is hardly a night when I don't wake up with sweaty palms and pounding heart, scared that we won't be able to pay the printer or the post office; scared most of all that closing our doors will be blamed on a lack of readers and thus the movement, instead of the real cause. ("Feminism couldn't even support one magazine," I can hear them saying.)

We're all being flattened by a velvet steamroller. The only difference is that at *Ms.*, we keep standing up again.

Do you think, as I once did, that advertisers make decisions based on rational and uniform criteria? Well, think again. There is clearly a double standard. The same food companies that insist on recipes in women's magazines place ads in *People* where there are no recipes. Cosmetics companies support the *New Yorker*, which has no regular beauty columns, and newspaper pages that have no "beauty atmosphere."

Meanwhile, advertisers' control over the editorial content of women's magazines has become so institutionalized that it is sometimes written into "insertion orders" or dictated to ad salespeople as official policy — whether by the agency, the client, or both. The following are orders given to women's magazines effective in 1990. Try to imagine them being applied to *Time* or *Newsweek*.

- Dow's Cleaning Products stipulated that ads for its Vivid and Spray 'n' Wash products should be adjacent to "children or fashion editorial"; ads for Bathroom Cleaner should be next to "home furnishing/family" features; with similar requirements for other brands. "If a magazine fails for ½ the brands or more," the Dow order warned, "it will be omitted from further consideration."

- Bristol-Myers, the parent of Clairol, Windex, Drano, Bufferin, and much more, stipulated that ads be placed next to "a full page of compatible editorial."

- S. C. Johnson & Son, makers of Johnson Wax, lawn and laundry products, insect sprays, hair sprays, and so on, insisted that its ads *"should not be opposite extremely controversial features or material antithetical to the nature/copy of the advertised product."* (Italics theirs.)

- Maidenform, manufacturer of bras and other women's apparel, left a blank for the particular product and stated in its instructions: "The creative concept of the _____ campaign, and the very nature of the product itself, appeal to the positive emotions of the reader/consumer. Therefore, it is imperative that all editorial adjacencies reflect that same positive tone. The editorial must not be negative in content or lend itself contrary to the _____ product imagery/message (e.g., *editorial relating to illness, disillusionment, large size fashion, etc.*)." (Italics mine.)

- The De Beers diamond company, a big seller of engagement rings, pro- 70 hibited magazines from placing its ads with "adjacencies to hard news or anti-love/romance themed editorial."

- Kraft/General Foods, a giant with many brands, sent this message with an Instant Pudding ad: "urgently request upbeat parent/child activity editorial, mandatory positioning requirements — opposite full page of positive editorial — right hand page essential for creative — minimum 6 page competitive separation (i.e., all sugar based or sugar free gelatins, puddings, mousses, creames [sic] and pie filling) — Do not back with clippable material. Avoid: controversial/negative topics and any narrow targeted subjects."

- An American Tobacco Company order for a Misty Slims ad noted that the U.S. government warning must be included, but also that there must be: "no adjacency to editorial relating to health, medicine, religion, or death."

- Lorillard's Newport cigarette ad came with similar instructions, plus: "Please be aware that the Nicotine Patch products are competitors. The minimum six page separation is required."

Quite apart from anything else, you can imagine the logistical nightmare this creates when putting a women's magazine together, but the greatest casualty is editorial freedom. Though the ratio of advertising to editorial pages in women's magazines is only about 5 percent more than in *Time* or *Newsweek*, that nothing-to-read feeling comes from all the supposedly editorial pages that are extensions of ads. To find out what we're really getting when we pay our money, I picked up a variety of women's magazines for February 1994, and counted the number of pages in each one (even including table of contents, letters to the editors, horoscopes, and the like) that were not ads and/or copy complementary to ads. Then I compared that number to the total pages. Out of 184 pages, *McCall's* had 49 that were nonad or ad-related. Of 202, *Elle* gave readers 48. *Seventeen* provided its young readers with only 51 nonad or ad-related pages out of 226. *Vogue* had 62 out of 292. *Mirabella* offered readers 45 pages out of a total of 158. *Good Housekeeping* came out on top, though only at about a third, with 60 out of 176 pages. *Martha Stewart Living* offered the least. Even counting her letter to readers, a page devoted to her personal calendar, and another one to a turnip, only 7 out of 136 pages had no ads, products, or product mentions. . . .

Within the supposedly editorial text itself, praise for advertisers' products 75 has become so ritualized that fields like "beauty writing" have been invented.

One of its practitioners explained to me seriously that "It's a difficult art. How many new adjectives can you find? How much greater can you make a lipstick sound? The FDA restricts what companies can say on labels, but we create illusion. And ad agencies are on the phone all the time pushing you to get their product in. A lot of them keep the business based on how many editorial clippings they produce every month. The worst are products [whose manufacturers have] their own name involved. It's all ego."

Often, editorial becomes one giant ad. An issue of *Lear's* featured an elegant woman executive on the cover. On the contents page, we learn she is wearing Guerlain makeup and Samsara, a new fragrance by Guerlain. Inside, there just happen to be full-page ads for Samsara, plus a Guerlain antiwrinkle skin cream. In the article about the cover subject, we discover she is Guerlain's director of public relations and is responsible for launching, you guessed it, the new Samsara. . . .

When the *Columbia Journalism Review* cited this example in one of the few articles to include women's magazines in a critique of ad influence, Frances Lear, editor of *Lear's*, was quoted at first saying this was a mistake, and then shifting to the defense that "this kind of thing is done all the time."

She's right. Here's an example with a few more turns of the screw. Martha Stewart, *Family Circle's* contributing editor, was also "lifestyle and entertaining consultant" for Kmart, the retail chain, which helped to underwrite the renovation of Stewart's country house, using Kmart products; *Family Circle* covered the process in three articles not marked as ads; Kmart bought $4 million worth of ad pages in *Family Circle*, including "advertorials" to introduce a line of Martha Stewart products to be distributed by Kmart; and finally, the "advertorials," which at least are marked and only *look* like editorial pages, were reproduced and distributed in Kmart stores, thus publicizing *Family Circle* (owned by the New York Times Company, which would be unlikely to do this kind of thing in its own news pages) to Kmart customers. This was so lucrative that Martha Stewart now has her own magazine, *Martha Stewart Living* (owned by Time Warner), complete with a television version. Both offer a happy world of cooking, entertaining, and decorating in which nothing critical or negative ever seems to happen.

I don't mean to be a spoilsport, but there are many articles we're very unlikely to get from that or any other women's magazine dependent on food ads. According to Senator Howard Metzenbaum of Ohio, more than half of the chickens we eat (from ConAgra, Tyson, Perdue, and other companies) are contaminated with dangerous bacteria; yet labels haven't yet begun to tell us to scrub the meat and everything it touches — which is our best chance of not getting sick. Nor are we likely to learn about the frequent working conditions of this mostly female work force, standing in water, cutting chickens apart with such repetitive speed that carpal tunnel syndrome is an occupational hazard. Then there's Dole Food, often cited as a company that keeps women in low-level jobs and a target of a lawsuit by Costa Rican workers who were sterilized by contact with pesticides used by Dole — even though

Dole must have known these pesticides had been banned in the United States.

The consumerist reporting we're missing sometimes sounds familiar. 80 Remember the *Ms.* episode with Clairol and the article about potential carcinogens in hair dye? Well, a similar saga took place with L'Oréal and *Mademoiselle* in 1992, according to an editor at Condé Nast. Now, editors there are supposed to warn publishers of any criticism in advance, a requirement that might well have a chilling effect.

Other penalties are increasing. As older readers will remember, women's magazines used to be a place where new young poets and short story writers could be published. Now, that's very rare. It isn't that advertisers of women's products dislike poetry or fiction, it's just that they pay to be adjacent to articles and features more directly compatible with their products.

Sometimes, advertisers invade editorial pages — literally — by plunging odd-shaped ads into the text, no matter how that increases the difficulty of reading. When Ellen Levine was editor of *Woman's Day*, for instance, a magazine originally founded by a supermarket chain, she admitted, "The day the copy had to rag around a chicken leg was not a happy one."

The question of ad positioning is also decided by important advertisers, a rule that's ignored at a magazine's peril. When Revlon wasn't given the place of the first beauty ad in one Hearst magazine, for instance, it pulled its ads from *all* Hearst magazines. In 1990 Ruth Whitney, editor in chief of *Glamour*, attributed some of this pushiness to "ad agencies wanting to prove to a client that they've squeezed the last drop of blood out of a magazine." She was also "sick and tired of hearing that women's magazines are controlled by cigarette ads." Relatively speaking, she was right. To be as controlling as most advertisers of women's products, tobacco companies would have to demand articles in flat-out praise of smoking, and editorial photos of models smoking a credited brand. As it is, they ask only to be forewarned so they don't advertise in the same issue with an article about the dangers of smoking. But for a magazine like *Essence*, the only national magazine for African American women, even taking them out of one issue may be financially difficult, because other advertisers might neglect its readers. In 1993, a group called Women and Girls Against Tobacco, funded by the California Department of Health Services, prepared an ad headlined "Cigarettes Made Them History." It pictured three black singers — Mary Wells, Eddie Kendricks, and Sarah Vaughan — who died of tobacco-related diseases. *Essence* president Clarence Smith didn't turn the ad down, but he didn't accept it either. When I talked with him in 1994, he said with pain, "the black female market just isn't considered at parity with the white female market; there are too many other categories we don't get." That's in spite of the fact that *Essence* does all the traditional food-fashion-beauty editorial expected by advertisers. According to California statistics, African American women are more addicted to smoking than the female population at large, with all the attendant health problems.

Alexandra Penney, editor of *Self* magazine, feels she has been able to include smoking facts in health articles by warning cigarette advertisers in advance (though smoking is still being advertised in this fitness magazine). On the other hand, up to this writing in 1994, no advertiser has been willing to appear opposite a single-page feature called "Outrage," which is reserved for important controversies, and is very popular with readers. Another women's magazine publisher told me that to this day Campbell's Soup refuses to advertise because of an article that unfavorably compared the nutritional value of canned food to that of fresh food — fifteen years ago.

I don't mean to imply that the editors I quote here share my objections to   85
ad demands and/or expectations. Many assume that the women's magazines at which they work have to be the way they are. Others are justifiably proud of getting an independent article in under the advertising radar, for instance, articles on family violence in *Family Circle* or a series on child sexual abuse and the family courts in *McCall's*. A few insist they would publish exactly the same editorial, even if there were no ads. But it's also true that it's hard to be honest while you're still in the job. "Most of the pressure came in the form of direct product mentions," explained Sey Chassler, who was editor in chief of *Redbook* from the sixties to the eighties and is now out of the game. "We got threats from the big guys, the Revlons, blackmail threats. They wouldn't run ads unless we credited them."

What could women's magazines be like if they were as editorially free as good books? as realistic as the best newspaper articles? as creative as poetry and films? as diverse as women's lives? What if we as women — who are psychic immigrants in a public world rarely constructed by or for us — had the same kind of watchful, smart, supportive publications on our side that other immigrant groups have often had?

We'll find out only if we take the media directed at us seriously. If readers were to act in concert in large numbers for a few years to change the traditional practices of *all* women's magazines and the marketing of *all* women's products, we could do it. After all, they depend on our consumer dollars — money we now are more likely to control. If we include all the shopping we do for families and spouses, women make 85 percent of purchases at point of sale. You and I could:

- refuse to buy products whose ads have clearly dictated their surroundings, and write to tell the manufacturers why;
- write to editors and publishers (with copies to advertisers) to tell them that we're willing to pay *more* for magazines with editorial independence, but will *not* continue to pay for those that are editorial extensions of ads;
- write to advertisers (with copies to editors and publishers) to tell them that we want fiction, political reporting, consumer reporting, strong opinion, humor, and health coverage that doesn't pull punches, praising them when their ads support this, and criticizing them when they don't;

- put as much energy and protest into breaking advertising's control over what's around it as we put into changing the images within it or protesting harmful products like cigarettes;

- support only those women's magazines and products that take us seriously as readers and consumers;

- investigate new laws and regulations to support freedom from advertising influence. The Center for the Study of Commercialism, a group founded in 1990 to educate and advocate against "ubiquitous product marketing," recommends whistle-blower laws that protect any members of the media who disclose advertiser and other commercial conflicts of interest, laws that require advertiser influence to be disclosed, Federal Trade Commission involvement, and denial of income tax exemptions for advertising that isn't clearly identified—as well as conferences, citizen watchdog groups, and a national clearinghouse where examples of private censorship can be reported.

Those of us in the magazine world can also use this carrot-and-stick technique. The stick: If magazines were a regulated medium like television, the editorial quid pro quo demanded by advertising would be against the rules of the FCC, and payola and extortion would be penalized. As it is, there are potential illegalities to pursue. For example: A magazine's postal rates are determined by the ratio of ad pages to editorial pages, with the ads being charged at a higher rate than the editorial. Counting up all the pages that are *really* ads could make an interesting legal action. There could be consumer fraud cases lurking in subscriptions that are solicited for a magazine but deliver a catalog.

The carrot is just as important. In twenty years, for instance, I've found no independent, nonproprietary research showing that an ad for, say, fragrance is any more effective placed next to an article about fragrance than it would be when placed next to a good piece of fiction or reporting. As we've seen, there are studies showing that the greatest factor in determining an ad's effectiveness is the credibility and independence of its surroundings. An airtight wall between ads and edit would also shield corporations and agencies from pressures from both ends of the political spectrum and from dozens of pressure groups. Editors would be the only ones responsible for editorial content—which is exactly as it should be.

Unfortunately, few agencies or clients hear such arguments. Editors often 90 maintain the artificial purity of refusing to talk to the people who actually control their lives. Instead, advertisers see salespeople who know little about editorial, are trained in business as usual, and are usually paid on commission. To take on special controversy editors might also band together. That happened once when all the major women's magazines did articles in the same month on the Equal Rights Amendment. It could happen again—and regularly.

Meanwhile, we seem to have a system in which everybody is losing. The reader loses diversity, strong opinion, honest information, access to the arts, and much more. The editor loses pride of work, independence, and freedom from worry about what brand names or other critical words some sincere freelancer is going to come up with. The advertiser loses credibility right along with the ad's surroundings, and gets more and more lost in a sea of similar ads and interchangeable media.

But that's also the good news. Because where there is mutual interest, there is the beginning of change.

If you need one more motive for making it, consider the impact of U.S. media on the rest of the world. The ad policies we tolerate here are invading the lives of women in other cultures — through both the content of U.S. media and the ad practices of multinational corporations imposed on other countries. Look at our women's magazines. Is this what we want to export?

Should *Ms.* have started out with no advertising in the first place? The odd thing is that, in retrospect, I think the struggle was worth it. For all those years, dozens of feminist organizers disguised as *Ms.* ad saleswomen took their courage, research, slide shows, humor, ingenuity, and fresh point of view into every advertising agency, client office, and lion's den in cities where advertising is sold. Not only were sixteen years of *Ms.* sustained in this way, with all the changeful words on those thousands of pages, but some of the advertising industry was affected in its imagery, its practices, and its understanding of the female half of the country. Those dozens of women themselves were affected, for they learned the art of changing a structure from both within and without, and are now rising in crucial publishing positions where women have never been. *Ms.* also helped to open nontraditional categories of ads for women's magazines, thus giving them a little more freedom — not to mention making their changes look reasonable by comparison.

But the world of advertising has a way of reminding us how far there is 95 to go.

Three years ago, as I was finishing this exposé in its first version, I got a call from a writer for *Elle*. She was doing an article on where women parted their hair: Why, she wanted to know, did I part mine in the middle?

It was all so familiar. I could imagine this writer trying to make something out of a nothing assignment. A long-suffering editor laboring to think of new ways to attract ads for shampoo, conditioner, hairdryers, and the like. Readers assuming that other women must want this stuff.

As I was working on this version, I got a letter from Revlon of the sort we disregarded when we took ads. Now, I could appreciate it as a reminder of how much we had to disregard:

> We are delighted to confirm that Lauren Hutton is now under contract to Revlon.

We are very much in favor of her appearing in as much editorial as possible, but it's important that your publication avoid any mention of competitive color cosmetics, beauty treatment, hair care or sun care products in editorial or editorial credits in which she appears.

We would be very appreciative if all concerned are made aware of this.

I could imagine the whole chain of women — Lauren Hutton, preferring to be in the Africa that is her passion; the ad executive who signed the letter, only doing her job; the millions of women readers who would see the resulting artificial images; all of us missing sources of information, insight, creativity, humor, anger, investigation, poetry, confession, outrage, learning, and perhaps most important, a sense of connection to each other; and a gloriously diverse world being flattened by a velvet steamroller.

I ask you: Can't we do better than this?   100

READING THE TEXT

1. What does Steinem mean by "complementary copy" (para. 17) and "advertorials" (para. 78)?

2. Summarize the relationship Steinem sees between editorial content and advertising in women's magazines.

3. In Steinem's view, what messages about gender roles does complementary copy send readers of women's magazines?

4. What is the history of response to this article since its initial publication in 1990, according to Steinem?

READING THE SIGNS

1. Steinem asserts that virtually all content in women's magazines is a disguised form of advertising. Test her hypothesis in a detailed analysis of a single issue of a magazine such as *Cosmopolitan*, *Vogue*, or *Elle*. Do you find instances of complementary copy and advertorials? How do you react as a potential reader of such a magazine?

2. Explore whether Steinem's argument holds for men's magazines such as *Maxim* or *GQ*. If you identify differences, how might they be based on different assumptions about gender roles?

3. Have each member of the class bring in a favorite magazine. In small groups, study the relationship between ads and articles. What magazines have the most complementary copy? How can you account for your findings?

4. In your journal, explore whether you believe advertisers infringe on the freedom of the press.

Your Way
HEALTH
Vitameatavegamin
VITAMEATAVEGAMIN
FOR HEALTH

VIDEO DREAMS
Television and Cultural Forms

From Symbols to Icons

In **semiotic** terms, the ubiquity of televised or digitized images in our lives represents a shift from one kind of **sign system** to another. As Marshall McLuhan pointed out some fifty years ago in *The Gutenberg Galaxy* (1962), Western culture since the fifteenth century defined itself around the printed word — the linear text that reads from left to right and top to bottom. The printed word, in the terminology of the American founder of semiotics, Charles Sanders Peirce, is a **symbolic sign**, one whose meaning is entirely arbitrary or conventional. A symbolic sign means what it does because those who use it have decided so. Words don't look like what they mean. Their significance is entirely abstract.

Not so with a visual image, which does resemble its object and is not entirely arbitrary. Although a photograph is not literally the thing it depicts and may reflect a good deal of staging and manipulation by the photographer, we often respond to it as if it were an innocent reflection of the world. Peirce called such signs "icons," referring by this term to any sign that resembles what it means. The way you interpret an **icon**, then, differs from the way you interpret a symbol or word. The interpretation of words involves your cognitive capabilities; the interpretation and reception of icons are far more sensuous, more a matter of vision than cognition. The shift from a civilization governed by the paradigm of the book to one dominated by the image accordingly involves a shift in the way we "read" our world, as the symbolic field of the printed page yields to the iconic field of the screen.

The shift from a symbolic, or word-centered, world to an iconic universe filled with visual images carries profound cultural implications. Such implications are not necessarily negative. The accessibility of digital technology, for example, has created opportunities for personal expression that have never before existed. It is difficult to publish a paper-and-ink book, but easy to post to YouTube. The rapid transmissibility of images speeds up communication and can bond groups of linguistically and culturally diverse people together.

At the same time, video images may be used to stimulate political action. Indeed, while many critics of TV deplore the passivity of its viewers, the medium is not inherently passive. Look at it this way: TV has a visceral power that print does not. Words abstractly describe things; television shows concrete images. Dramatic television images of drowning polar bears, for example, have recently helped awaken people to the effects of global warming and climate change. Images, in short, have the potential to awaken the apathetic as written texts cannot.

But there is a price to be paid for the modes of perception that the iconic world of TV stimulates. For while one can read visual images actively and cognitively (which, of course, is the whole point of this book), and one *can* be moved to action by an image, the sheer visibility of icons tempts one to receive them uncritically and passively. Icons look so much like the realities they refer to that it is easy to forget that icons, too, are signs: images that people can construct to carry ideological meanings. Just think of all those iconic images of the classic fifties-era sitcoms. *Leave It to Beaver*, *Father Knows Best*, *The Adventures of Ozzie & Harriet*, and so on, established an American mythology of an idyllic era by the sheer persuasiveness of their images. In fact, the 1950s were not such idyllic years. Along with the McCarthyite hysteria of the Cold War and the looming specter of nuclear war and contamination from open-air nuclear testing, there were economic downturns; the Korean War; and a growing sense that American life was becoming sterile, conformist, and materialistic — though it wasn't until the sixties that this uneasiness broke into the open. Few fathers in the fifties had the kind of leisure that the sitcom dads had, and the feminist resurgence in the sixties demonstrated that not all women were satisfied with the housewifely roles assigned them in every screenplay. And yet, those constructed images of white middle-class contentment and security have become so real in the American imagination that they can be called on in quite concrete ways, as when political candidates refer to them as "evidence" of a lost world of "family values" that they promise to restore.

Mixing Media: Writing about Television

Writing about television is nothing new in American education. Even before the advent of cultural studies and semiotics, it was a common assignment in American classrooms, so this chapter's topic might be quite familiar to you. Indeed, in high school you may have been asked to write about a favorite TV program, perhaps in a summary-writing exercise, a descriptive essay, or an opinion piece on why such-and-such a program is your favorite show. But here you will be asked to write semiotic interpretations of television, a somewhat different task from expressing an opinion about how entertaining a program is. In interpreting TV, you still need to rely on your skills in description and summary, because you need to describe the show for your reader, but your purpose will be to go beyond these writing tasks toward the construction of interpretive arguments about the cultural significance of your topic.

Television offers an especially rich field of possible writing topics, ranging from a historical analysis of a whole category, or genre, of TV programming (such as the sitcom, detective show, medical drama), or of a general trend, to an interpretation of a single episode. Whatever approach to television you are taking, you will probably need to do some research. No one can be expected to know in advance about all of the television programs that can be associated with, and differentiated from (both from the past and from the present) any particular show that you are analyzing, so you should plan to find reliable sources to help you contextualize whatever program you are interpreting.

We have already provided a model for interpreting a particular television genre in our analysis of the medical drama *House* in the "Writing about Popular Culture" section of this book, but let's look now at a recent television trend to see how the fundamental concepts behind a television program can bear cultural significance.

Extreme Lifestyles

Breaking Bad, Weeds, The Gates, Big Love, Dexter, The Sopranos.

Although quite different in many respects, these current and recent television programs have something fundamental in common: They all feature ordinary people with ordinary families and ordinary lives — except that they are also drug dealers, vampires, serial killers, polygamists, or mobsters.

That's a lot different from the programming of the fifties, sixties, and seventies, where sitcoms and dramas featuring ordinary families (*Leave It To Beaver, Father Knows Best, The Dick Van Dyke Show, All in the Family, Happy Days, The Waltons*, etc., etc.) that were, well, ordinary. As always in a semiotic analysis of popular culture, it is this difference within the system that signals that something is going on in America that is worth interpreting.

A little research reveals a history consisting of a lot of situation comedies, which generally focus on a middle-class family living in the suburbs, though programs like *The Jeffersons* in the 1970s and *The Bill Cosby Show* in the 1980s signaled, through their differences from the pattern, the mainstreaming of the civil rights movement. Some family-based dramas from the past also include *The Brady Bunch, Little House on the Prairie,* and *Dallas. Dallas* was significant in the way that it featured an upper-class family, challenging the general television convention of presenting working-class (*All in the*

Family, The Waltons) or, much more commonly, middle-class families, thus heralding the emergence of a widespread cultural fascination with upper-class glitter and wealth in the 1980s (*Falcon Crest, Knot's Landing, Wall Street,* etc.). The working-class sitcoms of the 1970s—*All in the Family, Laverne & Shirley*—were similarly significant, but in the other direction, signifying a populist turn in the 1970s that was also reflected in the rise of country music, the short-lived "truckers" fad, and shows like *The Dukes of Hazzard.*

Dallas also departed from the conventions of family television by making the show's featured family, the Ewings, strikingly dysfunctional and unhappy (*Bonanza*'s Cartwrights were upper-class in their way, but they were a loyal, happy family). Dysfunctional families began to dominate American family sit-coms by the end of the 1980s, with the success of *Married with Children, The Simpsons,* and the innumerable unhappy-family sitcoms of the 1990s all sig-nifying a reaction, in an era of high divorce rates, against what had come to be perceived as earlier sitcoms' unrealistic portrayal of family life.

As we look at shows like *Breaking Bad, Weeds, The Gates, Big Love, Dexter,* and *The Sopranos* we find something strikingly different, however. The differ-ence lies in the fact that while the families in these shows are presented as being as much like their audiences as possible, their lives are not in the least ordinary. *The Gates* works on the conceit that a vampire family can live in a suburb and be, almost, like everyone else, and thus is really a pure fantasy; but the Mafia family in *The Sopranos,* the polygamist family of *Big Love,* the killer-killing serial killer in *Dexter,* and the drug-dealing characters of *Weeds* and *Breaking Bad,* are, if not impossible or fantastic, unlikely and atypical. They are living what could be called "extreme lifestyles." So, what could the popularity of such shows signify?

As always, our interpretation must be **overdetermined**—that is, there is no single explanation and we need to look at various possibilities. Let's start with *Breaking Bad* and *Weeds.* Both feature once-middle-class protagonists who have been driven by economic desperation into lives of crime. When we consider the way that the American economy crashed into recession in the decade in which these shows appeared, we can see how they might resonate with middle-class audiences who, fearing for their own economic futures, may be entertained by viewing the desperate measures taken by people with whom they can identify. Indeed, they may enjoy a certain catharsis in seeing others struggling in worse situations than their own.

It is significant to note that *The Waltons* also featured a family in tough economic times (the show is situated in the era of the Great Depression), but what was appealing about that show was the way that the Waltons all main-tained their fundamental decency in tough times, how they held onto their values when under pressure. So, while part of the popularity of programs like *Breaking Bad* and *Weeds* lies in the way that their audiences can identify with their characters' desperation, that cannot explain it all.

And, after all, *The Gates, Big Love,* and *The Sopranos* are not about eco-nomic desperation; instead, they are about unusual (or impossible) twists upon ordinary life. We can easily explain *The Gates* as an attempt to cash in on the vampire craze (see the general Introduction of this book for a fuller interpretation of that), but it is striking that the show's creators have emphasized the otherwise upper-middle-class *normalcy* of its characters. The same is true for *Big Love*. Polygamy is illegal in America, and it is not ordinarily practiced in this country, especially not in typical suburban neighborhoods. So what is striking about the show is not so much its basic concept (it is a show about polygamy) but the way that it tries to present its polygamous protagonists as ordinary people like you and me. We see the same pattern in *The Sopranos*. Most Americans aren't mob bosses, but what drew many people (especially women viewers) to the series was less its depiction of the violence of life in the Mafia than the ordinary problems faced within the Soprano family — raising their children, school matters, conflicts with relatives. Like *Big Love*, *The Sopranos* successfully normalized the abnormal.

Given that *Breaking Bad* and *Weeds* do something like this too, we can **abductively** propose that part of the significance of these extreme-lifestyle family programs lies both in a general relaxation of social attitudes toward crime (one way or another, the protagonists of all these shows are criminals, but rather than judging them, their fans identify with them) and in a general *boredom* with ordinary life in contemporary America. The same audiences who made *The Office* a hit (with its searingly comic depiction of the banalities of life in the white-collar cubicle) can also be fantasizing about a life that is more exciting, more on the edge than the lives they actually lead. And, if nothing else, the lives led by the superficially ordinary people in *Breaking Bad*, *Weeds, The Gates, Big Love, Dexter,* and *The Sopranos* are certainly exciting and on the edge.

The Kids Aren't All Right

Another program that could be introduced into the **system** of extreme-lifestyle family programming is the popular "dramedy" *Desperate Housewives*, a show that we can use now to demonstrate a semiotic interpretation of a single episode of a television series.

The interpretation of a television episode is much like interpreting a short story. You should consider every potentially significant detail in the episode and subject it to a close reading. As with all semiotic analyses, your first step when preparing to analyze a TV program is to suspend your aesthetic opinions — that is, whether you like a show or not. What you are working toward is a critical analysis, what you think a program's underlying cultural significance may be. This process also differs from describing what you think the show's explicit message is. Many programs have clearly presented messages, or morals, but what you are looking for is the message beyond the message, so to speak; the implicit, often contradictory, signals the show is sending.

Discussing the Signs of Television

In class, choose a current television program, and have the entire class watch one episode (either watch the episode as "homework" or ask someone to record it and then watch it in class). Interpret the episode semiotically. What values and cultural myths does the show project? What do the commercials broadcast during the show say about the presumed audience for it? Go beyond the episode's surface appeal or "message" to look at the particular images it uses to tell its story, always asking, "What is this program *really* saying?"

A clear example of this type of double message can be found in "My Heart Belongs to Daddy" (Episode 204 of *Desperate Housewives*). This episode concluded with a voice-over from the show's ghostly narrator, Mary Alice, intoning about the good things that happen when families have good fathers and the bad things that happen when they don't, and it appeared to be the explicit moral of a story packed with family dysfunctionality due to absent fathers. But a closer look at the details reveals a powerful undercurrent of meaning that the explicit moral does not state.

You may find a recap of "My Heart Belongs to Daddy" on the show's official Web site at http://abc.go.com/shows/desperate-housewives/episode-guide/my-heart-belongs-to-daddy/25140. Given the soap-operatic nature of a dramedy like *Desperate Housewives* — the way that any individual episode is intertwined with past episodes and never achieves closure in itself — you should research the backstory of a series of this kind before attempting an analysis, as we did prior to our own analysis. But rather than attempting to summarize here the highly involved situation in which this particular episode is entwined, we shall treat it as a largely stand-alone story, focusing on three different subplots featuring the behavior of young boys.

These subplots center on the characters of Lynette, Susan, and Bree. Lynette has recently returned to her job in the corporate world because her husband lost *his* job, and she is unhappy about missing time with her young son Parker. Unmarried Susan, for her part, is pursuing a romantic relationship with Mike, who happens to be the secret father of Zach, a homicidal teenaged runaway. Zach is looking for Paul, who is his presumptive father and has gone missing for reasons of his own. Meanwhile, widow Bree is dating George, and her son Andrew highly resents the relationship since it is so soon after his father's death.

Got all that? Fans of the show will be aware of the excessively complicated story line that has taken the series to this point, but this will do for our purposes.

Let's begin with Lynette. She isn't simply unhappy; she is driven to tears by Parker's behavior in response to her absence. He has invented an "imaginary friend" whom he calls Mrs. Mulberry and who is embodied in a black umbrella (obviously inspired by *Mary Poppins*) that he carries with him everywhere and insists on sleeping with. When his mother comes in to kiss him goodnight, Parker rejects her while expressing his deep affection for Mrs. Mulberry. The situation could make us very sympathetic for a young child who is going through severe separation anxiety, but he is really nasty about the whole matter. Not only does he callously reject Lynette's sincere attempts to connect with him, but he uses the umbrella to assault his teacher at school, an event that leads to Lynette's having to meet with the school principal.

Lynette surreptitiously tosses the umbrella into the trash, but the next morning the trash collector accidentally drops the umbrella in the street. When Lynette comes out shortly thereafter to take Parker (who is protesting that he can't leave until he finds Mrs. Mulberry) to school, she tells him that Mrs. Mulberry has gone on to help another child, but at this moment they both see the umbrella lying in the street. An expression of joy crosses Parker's face, soon to be replaced by one of horror when a car drives by and flattens the umbrella. Lynette looks relieved, as Parker finally turns to his mother for comfort. She's gotten him back, and she's back in control.

Meanwhile Bree has invited George over for dinner, and Andrew, trying to disgust George and drive him away from his mother, starts telling him about the noises his mother makes during sex. Bree, who is in the kitchen, doesn't hear this, and when George erupts in anger, he is the one who looks bad to Bree as Andrew smirkingly looks on. The audience, however, can see very clearly that Bree is being duped.

George gets his revenge at a swim meet, carefully planning things so that just at the beginning of Andrew's race, Andrew will look up into the stands to see Bree rapturously kissing George. Andrew jumps out of the pool, runs into the stands, and begins to slug George. Bree erupts at Andrew, to George's great satisfaction. Andrew is subsequently packed off to a camp for troublesome children, and his mother is firmly in control at the end of the episode.

Finally, Susan, who has located the missing Zach, is on the verge of helping him find his "father," Paul, when Zach brings up his continuing romantic feelings for Susan's daughter, Julia. A homicidal near-maniac with a track record of threatening people with guns, Zach is not exactly any mother's idea of a good suitor for her daughter. Susan changes her mind about helping Zach and instead tricks him into leaving the state. As with Parker's shock and Andrew's comeuppance, the situation is presented in such a manner that the audience's sympathy is likely to be with the woman, not the boy. Susan skillfully controls the situation.

To determine a semiotic significance for these details, one needs to keep in mind the program's target audience and what is likely to entertain that audience. Remember, commercial television exists to entertain, and analyzing what makes it entertaining is what leads us to its significance. In the case of *Desperate Housewives*, the target audience predominantly consists of women, often mothers, who can especially identify with the parenting difficulties of the women depicted in the program. An episode packed with conflicts with misbehaving boys who have taken control of various situations but who all get a comeuppance in the end points to an existing frustration in the mothers who enjoy the show. The entertainment value lies in the catharsis such viewers may feel in seeing the boys "punished." Note that none of the boys suffers any physical harm (mothers would not be entertained by *that*); the punishment lies in a restoration of maternal power: In each case the boy's comeuppance leaves the woman in control after she had lost her authority for a while. Evidently, a significant number of American women are feeling such desperation, or the scriptwriters would not have exploited it to write the story. Commercial TV exists to attract its audience, not repel it, and *Desperate Housewives* is not a show for young boys.

This episode of *Desperate Housewives* thus sends a signal beyond the explicit message. Recall that the explicit message is, in effect, patriarchal, a declaration of the need for good and strong fathers. But the underlying message, somewhat contradictorily, is matriarchal, presenting the cathartic triumph of women over young males. The potentially subversive significance of this counter-message is masked by Mary Alice's voice-over, which makes the episode appear completely conventional and thus avoids the sort of controversy that could sink a prime-time series. But it is that unconventional, subtle counter-signal in the plot that may account for much of the success of *Desperate Housewives*, an indicator that there are a good many desperate women eager to see their frustrations sympathetically dramatized and addressed.

The Flow

Whatever show you choose to analyze, remember why it is on TV in the first place: Television, whether network or cable, is there to make money. It is a major part of our consumer culture, and most of what appears on TV is there because advertisers who want to reach their intended markets sponsor it. The shows that command the highest share of viewers, accordingly, command the highest advertising rates. Producers are anxious to have their viewers emotionally connect with their programs — and a main strategy for encouraging this connection involves satisfying viewer fantasies. This is especially striking in teen-address shows that feature fashion-model-glamorous actors (often in their twenties) playing adolescents in the awkward years, but it is also true for adult-address shows, which invite their viewers to identify with high-status professionals like doctors (*ER*) and lawyers (*The Practice*). Identifying with their favorite characters, viewers — or so television sponsors hope — will identify with the products they see advertised on the shows. And buy them.

For this reason, the advertising that accompanies the show is one of the most revealing features in a television program analysis. By paying attention to the ads, you can learn much about the intended audience. Ask yourself, then, why is the nightly news so often sponsored by over-the-counter pain-killers? Why is daytime TV, especially in the morning, typically accompanied by ads for vocational training schools? Why are youth-oriented prime-time shows filled with fast-food commercials, while family programs have a lot of car ads?

Your analysis of a single episode of a television program can also use-fully include a survey of where the show fits within what cultural studies pioneer Raymond Williams called the "flow" of an evening's TV schedule. Flow refers to the sequence of TV programs and advertisements, from, say, the five o'clock news, through the pre–prime-time 7:00 to 8:00 slot, through prime time and on through to the 11:00 news and the late-night talk shows. What precedes your program? What follows? Can you determine the strategy behind your show's scheduling?

Niche Marketing

The proliferation of cable channels in recent years has worked its own changes in the content of the television viewing experience, as it has fostered a more finely targeted programming schedule that focuses on narrowly defined audiences, from nature lovers to home shoppers. This is referred to as "niche marketing," and television today is far more divided into special niches than it was in the early days. For this reason, today's Nielsen leaders, which have been designed to appeal to special niche markets, don't get nearly the numbers that 1960s hits like *The Beverly Hillbillies* enjoyed. They don't need to. Producers now target the most desirable audiences — that is, those who are perceived as commanding the most disposable income. Thus,

---

Exploring the Signs of Television: Viewing Habits

In your journal, explore your television viewing habits and how the way you have watched TV has changed over time. When and why do you usually watch television? Have you transitioned from watching shows with your family or friends to watching them alone on a computer? Do you watch shows when they are broadcast, or do you watch them via Netflix, Hulu, or DVR on your own time? Do you think of watching television as a social activity? If so, write about how the diverse options for watching television have complicated this notion. If not, what place does watching television occupy in your life?

most prime-time television is aimed at middle-class to upper-middle-class viewers between the ages of eighteen and forty-nine, with the upper-end age figure dropping to as low as twenty-nine or thirty on the Fox network.

The fine-tuning of audiences, then, simply reflects a fine-tuning of marketing: Specially defined audiences can be targeted for specially defined marketing campaigns. In this sense, cable TV repeats the same history as that of traditional commercial television, which became a medium primarily for the pitching of goods and services. But the proliferation of channels bears the potential to upset television's commercial monopoly. When NBC, CBS, ABC, and their affiliates ruled the airways, programming decisions for an entire nation were made by a small group of executives. Aside from the Nielsen ratings, viewers had little chance to let programmers know what they wanted to see. While certainly no revolution has occurred in the wake of cable, there has been some movement toward more audience participation in what gets broadcast.

Reality Bites

One kind of programming that you simply cannot miss anymore in the evening's flow is reality TV (RTV). With its relatively low production costs and lack of superstar salary demands, reality TV has been a producer's dream come true from the first, but audiences, especially in the coveted eighteen- to thirty-year-old market niche, have absolutely adored it. Despite its popularity, RTV is not without its critics, and there is certainly something about the genre that begs for cultural analysis. Let's conduct one here.

As with any semiotic analysis, a little history is helpful. One might say that reality television began in 1948 with Allen Funt's *Candid Camera*, which featured the filming of real people (who didn't know that they were on camera, unlike today's reality contestants) as they reacted to annoying situations concocted by the show's creators. The show's attraction lay in the humor viewers could enjoy in watching other people get into minor jams. There is a name for this kind of humor that comes from psychoanalytic theory: schadenfreude, or taking pleasure in the misfortunes of others, as when we laugh at someone slipping on a banana peel. And we shall see that this early appeal from the history of reality TV is very much a part of the current popularity of the genre.

After *Candid Camera* came the 1970s' PBS series *An American Family*. In this program a camera crew moved in with a suburban family named the Louds and filmed them in their day-to-day lives. The Louds were not contestants and there were no prizes to be won. The program was conceived as an experiment in cinema verité to see if it was possible for television to be authentically realistic. The experiment was a bit of a failure, however, as the Loud family members began to act out for the camera. The result was the eventual dissolution of the Louds as a family unit and a general sense of unease about such experiments.

The next, and probably most crucial step, was when MTV in effect revived the concept behind *An American Family* and launched *The Real World* in 1992. Like *An American Family*, *The Real World* attempts to be realistic, with its constant camera recording of the lives of a group of people living together in the same house. Unlike *An American Family*, however, *The Real World* is a fantasy that caters to young adult viewers, who can imagine themselves living in glamorous circumstances and vicariously enjoy the experience of becoming instant TV stars. (A similar dynamic is at work in the more recent *Jersey Shore*.) That there is a certain tampering with reality in *The Real World*, a deliberate selection of participants based upon their appearance and how they can be cast into often-contrived romances as well as antagonisms, constitutes a contradiction that differentiates *The Real World* from *An American Family* and leads us to the dawning of the reality revolution.

The astounding success of the inaugural versions of *Who Wants to Marry a Multi-Millionaire?* and *Survivor* established reality TV's full coming-of-age. In both programs we can see strong traces of what made their pioneering predecessors popular. But through their introduction of a game show element, complete with contestants competing for huge cash prizes, a whole new dimension was added with new layers of significance in an even more overdetermined fashion.

Those reality programs that include a game show dimension offer their viewers the vicarious chance to imagine themselves as being in the shoes of the contestants (after all, anyone in principle can get on a game show) and winning lots of money. There is an element of schadenfreude here as well, if one takes pleasure in watching the losers in game show competitions. But by adding the real-life element of actual marriage to the mix, *Who Wants to Marry a Multi-Millionaire?* (and its descendants) have brought a whole new dimension of humiliation to the genre. For while it's one thing to be caught on camera during the emotional upheaval of competing for large cash prizes, it is quite another to be in an erotic competition, and lose, with millions watching you.

Shows like *Who Wants to Marry a Multi-Millionaire?* and all its progeny (*The Bachelor*, *The Bachelorette*, *Age of Love*, and so on and so forth) have their origins, in part, in the system of television programming that began with *The Dating Game* in the 1960s and the many dating programs that followed in its wake. But *The Dating Game* tried to reduce the inherent humiliation factor in such competitions through a split-screen effect that allowed the audience to see a single contestant, say, on the left, and three other contestants on the right, who would be concealed from the one on the left. That contestant would ask questions of the three concealed contestants (men if the questioner was a woman, women if it was a man) and pick one for a date. This sort of nicety looks rather quaint today in the aftermath of another pioneering RTV program, *Temptation Island*, a show that made the sexual humiliation of its protagonists the main attraction, along with voyeuristic sexual titillation.

Thus, in *Temptation Island* voyeurism linked up with schadenfreude in a formula that is now common on sex-themed RTV programs.

Survivor, for its part, combines a game show element with an action-adventure theme that invites viewers to imagine themselves in exciting outdoor situations that are exaggerated versions of the sort of adventure-safari vacations that had become very popular in the 1990s and continue to be so today. With people spending $75,000 and upward to be guided to the top of Mount Everest, a show like *Survivor* is very much a reflection of the fantasies of its viewers. Indeed, it presents the ultimate fantasy of enjoying an extreme vacation and becoming a television star overnight, as contestants reemerge in civilization on the talk-show circuit and in milk commercials.

Survivor also includes elements of voyeurism and schadenfreude in its formula for success, as viewers can watch the weekly humiliation of contestants struggling to stay in the game, while ogling the younger female contestants in their often skimpy attire. But it adds yet another dimension to the mix by inviting viewers to identify with some contestants and to despise others (though the creators of the show deny this, there is evidence that contestants are directed to play out specified roles). One need only look at the weekly Internet commentary to see just how much the ordinary folk on *Survivor* can be hated, and the experience of watching contestants be voted off the show brings in a dimension of outright sadism as viewers take pleasure in the disappointments of the contestants they dislike.

While game shows usually feature some sort of competition among the contestants, the *Survivor* series takes such competition to a new level by compelling its contestants to engage in backstabbing conspiracies as they claw their way toward a million-dollar payoff. (The 2006 season even introduced an element of racial conflict by forming tribes according to race.) It isn't enough for tribe to compete against tribe; there has to be intratribal backbiting and betrayal as well. Such a subtext constitutes a kind of grotesque parody of American capitalism itself, in which the cutthroat competition of the workplace is moved to the wilderness. Not to miss out on a good thing, RTV soon brought it all back to the office with *The Apprentice*, a show that makes capitalist competition its major theme, while echoing the talent show elements of *American Idol*. Indeed, so successful was the formula that *The Apprentice* would be joined for a while by *My Big Fat Obnoxious Boss*, which really turned the evils of life under capitalism into schadenfreude-laden entertainment.

Voyeurism. Schadenfreude. Sadism. Dog-eat-dog capitalist competitiveness. Conspicuous consumption. RTV's formula seems to appeal to some of the most primitive and socially disruptive of human instincts, violating taboos in the name of profits (for an example of *real* taboo tweaking, consider the *Jackass* franchise). Indeed, in the aftermath of an actual injury suffered by one of the *Survivor: Outback* contestants (he was burned by a fire), commentators wondered whether future installments would have to include the death of a contestant to satisfy their viewers' ever-greater desires for mayhem. But while there has been no such event (to date), reality TV continues to grow, covering every imaginable possible topic (spouse swapping, anyone?). Combining disdain with desire, RTV invites viewers to fantasize that they too can effortlessly become celebrities, or rich, or beautiful, while sneering at those who, by being contestants or characters on such shows, actually pursue the fantasy. We've come a long way from the "I'm OK. You're OK" era. Today, it's more like "I'm not OK. You're an idiot."

Real Populists of the U.S.A.

Among the more recent varieties of reality television are those programs that focus on fundamentally working-class occupations (*America's Toughest Jobs, Ice Road Truckers, Deadliest Catch*) or, in a return to the premise of *An American Family*, shows that follow the lives of ordinary families (*Jon & Kate Plus 8, The Real Housewives of Orange County, Real Housewives of . . .* wherever). Such programs combine elements of documentary filmmaking with the voyeuristic appeal of so much else within RTV, but the emphasis on the ordinariness of its characters, the claim that you are being shown what life is like for either working-class or middle-class people who could be you, introduces yet another layer of significance that might best be explained in relation to the contradictory **mythologies** of American populism and elitism that we also explore in Chapter 6, "American Paradox."

America's populist tradition celebrates the common citizen, the ordinary man or woman on the street, "Joe Sixpack." These are the heroes of our democratic tradition and institutions. But at the same time, the American dream stimulates us to seek to rise above the level of common life, to seek an elite status among the stars. Reality television programs like *Jon & Kate Plus 8* and

Reading about TV and Community on the Net

The Internet has given rise to a number of popular sites for TV criticism and community discussion, including *Television without Pity*. Using a search engine, find a forum devoted to your favorite TV show and take notes on how the community of fans interacts. What about the show you've chosen most interests fans? What topics are most popular, or most contested? Does the conversation stick to television, or does it veer into discussions of users' personal lives? Are you drawn to participate? Using the forum as a microcosm, reflect on how television might be considered a social adhesive. How do the fans of TV shows use the Web to bond over the show and with each other?

America's Toughest Jobs mediate that contradiction by making stars out of common folk. Viewers are invited to identify with the ordinary people in the shows while at the same time fantasize that they too can become TV stars if only some RTV producers knocked on their door (a striking variation on this theme occurred in 2010 when former Jet Blue flight attendant Steven Slater was offered his own reality program after his famous on-the-job meltdown).

Such a combination of contraries (celebrating ordinariness while making elite TV stars out of ordinary people) is a striking reflection of what it means to live in an entertainment culture. In such a culture, the ultimate achievement is to join the pantheon of entertainment celebrities. Shows like *American Idol*, which is essentially a mass cultural talent show, not only allow ordinary people to audition directly for stardom, they also invite viewers to engage in a kind of parody of democracy by allowing them to join the elite panel of celebrity judges in voting for who, in the end, will be vaulted out of the realm of commonality into the stratosphere of celebrity. And even when the audience itself cannot vote on the outcome, shows like *Project Runway* offer the fantasy of being a behind-the-scenes insider in the creation of the next flavor-of-the-month star fashion designer.

Thus, in an era when many Americans are feeling ever more disenfranchised and powerless, reality television offers a fantasy of opportunity and empowerment, even as the off-screen reality presents an ever-widening gap between the stars and those who can't dance with them.

All the News That's Fit to Jeer

News programming is a sort of "reality TV" too, but traditionally its purpose has been to present actual realities to an informed citizenry. It has long been recognized that the news has never presented a simple, unbiased window on the world, but with the rise of infotainment programming, a large segment of the news has simply stopped even trying to pretend that it is presenting an objective view. In a shift that parallels the deconstruction of the line between high and low culture, television news broadcasts are increasingly being compelled to compete with such entertainment-based news "sources" as Comedy Central's *The Daily Show*, as "anchors" like Jon Stewart and Stephen Colbert (not to mention Bill O'Reilly, Rush Limbaugh, and Glenn Beck) take the once-hallowed places of such network anchors as Walter Cronkite and Dan Rather. With younger viewers avoiding traditional network news broadcasts, the "news" is being transformed to be more like the sources such viewers prefer. For their part, by bringing in anchors like Katie Couric, the traditional networks are struggling to make the news more entertaining, sexier, and edgier in order to compete, thus undermining the old distinction between information and entertainment that TV news once relied upon.

This movement toward a world of infotainment can be regarded from two different perspectives. On the one hand, it can be argued that young

Stephen Colbert.

viewers have never been drawn to the network news and that the popularity of comedic news sources simply means that today's younger viewers are both savvier than viewers of their generation in the past and better informed because their attraction to shows like *The Daily Show* keeps them abreast of current events. A further argument for this position could be made by expanding the system in which we analyze the rise of infotainment to include the political and cultural implications of such programs as *The Simpsons* and *South Park*, both of which regularly address, and skewer, contemporary political and cultural issues, weighing in on current controversies with a directness and daring that the conventional news never approaches. From such a perspective, it could be argued that thanks to making the news entertaining, television is raising a remarkably sophisticated, news-savvy generation of Americans.

Without dismissing such a position, it is nevertheless possible to offer a counterargument. That is, when there was still a clear distinction between entertainers whose material was based on current politics — like Mort Sahl and Mark Russell — and news broadcasters — like Walter Cronkite — the subject matter of the news could be taken more seriously and thus have a greater effect on viewers. For the fundamental nature of entertainment is precisely that it is not serious; it is a distraction from the grim realities of everyday life. We seek entertainment to escape reality, not engage with it. Thus, if our source of information about reality is packaged as entertainment, we are less likely to be actively affected by it and to get involved in the issues presented to us. Laughter is a great catharsis, a release of energy, but when we laugh at the grimly real problems of our day, we are all the less likely to expend that energy on doing anything about them.

So, whether we are watching *The Daily Show* or *South Park*, enjoying the points that such programs may be scoring against the political targets that we like to see attacked, our very enjoyment may be disempowering after all, allowing jeering to replace acting and laughter to replace outrage.

The Readings

We begin the readings in this chapter with Francine Prose's provocative analysis of reality TV, arguing that the ruthless Machiavellian behavior we can watch every night on such shows as *Survivor* and *The Apprentice* is really no different from — in fact, is a reflection of — the behavior of America's corporate and political leadership. James Harold follows with a philosophical meditation on the guilty pleasures of *The Sopranos*. Carl Matheson then looks at *The Simpsons* — one of TV's longest-running institutions — and explores what happens when self-conscious irony overrides just about everything else. In a paired set of readings, Stephen Garrett analyzes the proliferation of television anti-heroes—badly behaving characters like Don Draper and Peter Griffin— in an era of moral ambiguity, as Natasha Simons unravels the political significance of *Mad Men*, a show that looks different depending upon your own ideology. Next, Rita Koganzon deconstructs *Glee*, finding traces of both camp and anti-camp attitudes within its contradictory plot lines, followed by Andy Medhurst's gleeful exploration of television's *Batman*, perhaps the campiest TV series of all time. Jaime J. Weinman then reports on the Fox network's ideologically motivated attempt to take on Comedy Central. Drake Bennett's surprising essay on television soap operas argues that viewers all over the world learn how *not* to behave by watching them, while Neal Gabler suggests that having contributed to the atomization of American society, "TV has learned how to compensate for the increasing alienation it seems to induce" by filling its schedule with shows filled with "flocks" of friends and family relationships. Roland Laird concludes the chapter with an essay on *The Boondocks* and its place in cultural history.

FRANCINE PROSE

Voting Democracy off the Island: Reality TV and the Republican Ethos

It is an essential semiotic principle that, one way or another, every-thing connects up in a society. In this provocative analysis of the underlying ideology of reality television (RTV), Francine Prose dis-covers what may seem a surprising connection between the RTV craze and current trends in American politics. When millions of Americans tune in to watch Donald Trump dump, one by one, the frantic contenders for a dazzling corporate job, or cheer as the quasi-democracies of *Survivor* vote each other out until only one "winner" is left, we can see the Social Darwinism that seems to guide, as Prose argues, the current crop of national leaders at work. The author of sixteen books of fiction — including *Hunters and Gatherers* (1996), *Guided Tours of Hell: Novellas* (1997), and *Goldengrove* (2008) — and five nonfiction books — including the best-selling *Reading Like a Writer* (2006) — Prose is a contributing editor at *Harper's* and a writer on art for the *Wall Street Journal*. This article originally appeared in *Harper's* in 2004.

Not even Melana can believe it's real. As the "former NFL cheerleader and beauty queen looking to fall in love with the perfect guy" swans a bit dazedly through the Palm Springs mansion in which she will soon undertake the task of selecting Mr. Right from among sixteen eligible bachelors, she coos about the thrill of living a "dream come true."

It's the premiere episode of NBC's *Average Joe*, one of the extremely popular and profitable "reality-based" television shows that, in recent years, have proliferated to claim a significant share of major-network prime time. Featuring ordinary people who have agreed to be filmed in dangerous, challenging, or embarrassing situations in return for the prom-ise of money, romance, or fame, these offerings range from *Who Wants to Marry a Millionaire?* to *Who Wants to Marry My Dad?*, from long-run hits such as *Survivor* and *The Real World* to the short-lived *Are You Hot?* and *Boy Meets Boy*.

The title *Average Joe* has evidently alerted Melana to the possibility that her bachelor pool may not be stocked with the same species of dazzling hunks, those walking miracles of body sculpting, cosmetic dentistry, and hair-gel expertise who courted *The Bachelorette*. Clearly, she's expecting to meet the more routinely, unself-consciously attractive sort of guy one might spot on the street or at the water cooler.

But, as frequently happens, the audience is privy to an essential truth — or, in the argot of reality programming, a "reveal" — concealed from the hapless participants. Now, as the cameras whisk us to the bachelors' quarters, we instantly get the visual joke that is, even by the standards of reality TV, sadistic.

The men about to compete for Melana's affections are not merely Joe 5 Well Below Average but Joe Out of the Question. Several are obese; others have tics, dermatological or dental problems, or are short, bespectacled, balding, stooped. Racial and cultural diversity is provided by a diminutive "university professor" from Zimbabwe with a penchant for intellectual boasting and grave fashion miscalculations.

Although the sight of Melana's suitors is intended to amuse and titillate rather than to touch us, it would (to paraphrase Dickens amid this Dickensian crowd) take a heart of stone not to be moved by the moment when the men take a look at one another and realize that their inclusion in this confraternity of nerds is probably not a mistake.

Meanwhile, night has fallen on the desert, and the lovely Melana, all dressed up and as starry-eyed as a kid on Christmas morning, comes out to meet the guys. A white limousine pulls up. A male model emerges, and Melana's face brightens, only to darken seconds later when he announces that, sadly, he is not one of her bachelors.

The white limo carries the tease away. Presently a bus arrives.

The bus doors open. They send the fat guys out first. And by the time a half-dozen sorry specimens are lined up, grinning their hearts out, even Melana gets it. Her shock and dismay are genuine. The men cannot help but notice. "This is *bad*," she whispers, and we can read her lips. "Someone's messing with my head."

What lends the scene its special poignancy is that Melana knows, as do 10 we, that what has befallen her is not some cruel accident of fate. Rather, she has brought misfortune on herself. In filling out the questionnaire that led to her being selected as the heroine of *Average Joe*, she indicated that "a good personality" mattered more to her than did appearance. And in doing so, she violated one of the cardinal rules, a basic article of faith, one of the values that this new version of reality pumps out, hour after hour, night after night, into the culture. Had Melana watched more reality-based TV, she would have learned that surface beauty (preferably in concert with a strong manipulative instinct, a cunning ability to play the game, and vast quantities of money) is all that counts. Melana has transgressed. And now, as we sit back and watch, she is about to be punished.

If this — a dash of casual brutality, a soupçon of voyeurism — is your recipe for entertainment, it's a taste you can satisfy, in the privacy of your living room, nearly every evening. In fact, unless you own one of those televisions that allow you to watch two programs at once, you may be forced to make some hard choices.

Landing the big one: a scene from the début of the RTV hit *Survivor*.

On a typical night — Thanksgiving Eve, November 26, 2003 — you could, at eight, watch a contestant on CBS's *Survivor: Pearl Islands* secure himself some sympathy by misleading his fellow tribe members into thinking that his grandmother has just died. But witnessing the "biggest lie ever told on *Survivor*" would mean missing the episode of NBC's *Queer Eye for the Straight Guy* in which a quintet of homosexual fashion and lifestyle advisers convince a balding lawyer to lose his unflattering hairpiece. At nine, you could shop along with ABC's Trista for *Trista and Ryan's Wedding*, an account of the big-ticket ceremony that would solemnize the love affair spawned, as America watched, on *The Bachelorette*. And at ten, on *Extreme Makeover*, the most literally invasive series so far, two lucky souls (chosen from more than 10,000 applicants) have their lives transformed by plastic surgery. On this night a man whose 200-pound weight loss has left him looking like a shar-pei, and a rather pretty grade-school teacher — who believes that she is only a rhinoplasty and a chin implant away from rivaling her beautiful sisters — will go under the knife.

In the event that three hours of watching your fellow humans suffer and squirm and endure surgical procedures has left you feeling uneasy about how you have spent your time, or what you have found amusing, you can be reassured — as are the network executives, it would seem — by the fact that you are not alone. In January 2003 the premiere of Fox Network's *Joe Millionaire*, in which a construction worker courted women tricked into believing that he possessed a vast personal fortune, attracted 18.6 million viewers; 40 million tuned in for its conclusion. *American Idol*, the talent show that asks fans to vote for their favorite contestants by telephone, received 110 million calls in its first season and 15.5 million calls during the final show alone. By contrast, the most popular national news program — NBC's *Nightly News* — averages around 11 million viewers per night.

Like Melana, network accountants were quick to see reality shows as a dream come true. For although production values and costs have risen, reality-based programs are still relatively cheap to produce, mostly because they avoid the expense of hiring actors whose salary demands can rise astronomically if the show becomes a hit. One consequence is that television actors have seen a radical reduction in the number and range of available roles.

Despite the fact that journalists periodically hail the death of reality TV, it 15 has proved remarkably long-lived. MTV's *The Real World*, which sends seven attractive young strangers to spend six months turning their luxury housing into a petri dish of sexual, racial, and interpersonal tension, has been running since 1992. Now in its eighth season, *Survivor* has airlifted a succession of warring "tribes" from the Amazon to the jungles of Thailand. During the week of November 17–23, 2003, the only shows more popular than *Survivor: Pearl Islands* (which drew 19.9 million viewers) were *CSI, ER,* and *Friends.*

On aesthetic grounds alone, it's arguable that reality-based shows are no better or worse than *CSI, ER,* and *Friends.* But the most obvious difference is the most crucial one. Fans of *Friends* understand that they are watching a sitcom, cast with celebrity actors. Watching *Survivor* and *The Real World,* they believe that they are observing *real* men and women.

Viewers do, of course, realize that some of what they're seeing has been instigated or exacerbated by the show's producers. Yet the fact is that viewers *are* watching people who, regardless of their career ambitions or masochistic exhibitionism, are amateurs who may have been chosen *for* their fragility and instability. Many of the "Average Joes" could never get hired as character actors. And observing their response to stress and humiliation generates a gladiatorial, bread-and-circus atmosphere that simply does not exist when we see movie stars in scrubs sail a gurney down the halls of *ER.*

Reality-based TV, then, is not a scripted fiction but an improvisation, an apparently instructive improvisation that doles out consistent and frequently reinforced lessons about human nature and, yes, reality. These programs also generate a jittery, adrenalized buzz that produces a paradoxically tranquilized numbness in which our defenses relax and leave us more receptive to the "information" we are receiving. For this reason alone, even those who take pride in never looking at TV, except for the occasional peek at PBS, might want to tune in and see what reality their fellow citizens have been witnessing.

What might future anthropologists (or, for that matter, contemporary TV-addicted children and adults) conclude about our world if these programs constituted their primary source of information? The most obvious lesson to be drawn from reality TV, the single philosophical pole around which everything else revolves, is that the laws of natural selection are even more brutal, inflexible, and *sensible* than one might suppose from reading *Origin of Species.* Reality is a Darwinian battlefield on which only the fittest survive, and it's not merely logical but admirable to marshal all our skills and resources to succeed in a struggle that only one person can win.

Compelling its testy, frequently neurotic castaways to operate as if they 20
were several rungs down the evolutionary ladder, grubbing roots and berries
and forced to earn such basic necessities as blankets by performing acrobatic
stunts, *Survivor* is the prototype. The show urges its participants to labor for
their tribe but always, ultimately, for themselves. Because at the end of the
day — in this case, the final episode — only one person will walk away with a
million dollars. And in case we lose sight of first principles, the show's motto,
which appears in its logo, is "Outwit. Outplay. Outlast."

Survivor is the younger American cousin of the 1997 Swedish *Expedition
Robinson*, a title judged too literary for the U.S. market. It's probably just as well
that the series wasn't called *Expedition Robinson*. *Robinson Crusoe* and *Swiss
Family Robinson* extol the virtues and advantages of fellowship and cooperation,
whereas on *Survivor* such considerations are useful only to a point. *Survivor*
could be Defoe's masterpiece rewritten by Ayn Rand. And for all its Darwinian trappings, the series offers a skewed view of the *purpose* of the struggle for
dominance. Propagating the species is the last thing on these people's minds.

And so the steps that lead toward that goal aren't determined by physical
combat or brilliant displays of plumage. Rather, contestants are eliminated by
a democratic process; every few days, tribe members vote on which of their
fellows will be forced to leave the island. As we watch, the loser trudges across
a rope bridge or rock ledge and off to a dismal future without a million dollars.

Observant readers may already have noted that the guiding principles to
which I've alluded — flinty individualism, the vision of a zero-sum society in
which no one can win unless someone else loses, the conviction that altruism and compassion are signs of folly and weakness, the exaltation of solitary striving above the illusory benefits of cooperative mutual aid, the belief
that certain circumstances justify secrecy and deception, the invocation of a
reviled common enemy to solidify group loyalty — are the exact same themes
that underlie the rhetoric we have been hearing and continue to hear from
the Republican Congress and our current administration.

Of course, no sensible person would imagine that Donald Rumsfeld is sitting down with the producers of reality-based TV to discuss the possibility that
watching the contestants sweat and strain to bring civilization to the jungle
will help us accept the sacrifices we have been and are still being asked to
make in Iraq. On the other hand, there is the unsettling precedent set by
Profiles from the Front Line, a series that aired around the time of the war in
Iraq and was produced for ABC Entertainment by Jerry Bruckheimer, whose
credits include *Black Hawk Down*.

According to an advance release from the network,   25

the Pentagon and the Department of Defense lent their full support and
cooperation to this unique production. . . . As America prepares for a
possible war with Iraq, the country continues to wage a perilous war on
terrorism. ABC will transport viewers to actual battlefields in Central Asia
with a six-episode series that will feature actual footage of the elite U.S.

Special Operations forces apprehending possible terrorists, as well as compelling, personal stories of the U.S. military men and women who bear the burden and risks of this fighting.

Indeed, ABC News complained that—in order to film the soldiers arresting a "big-time" Taliban leader, disarming rockets, providing medical care to Afghan civilians, capturing fuel-truck hijackers, and accepting the love and gratitude of the Afghan people—the show's producers were being granted a level of access to the troops that Pentagon officials denied the network's actual reporters.

But even when the collaboration between the military, the government, and the entertainment industry is not nearly so overt, these shows continue to transmit a perpetual, low-frequency hum of agitprop. The ethics (if one can call them that) and the ideals that permeate these programs at once reflect and reinforce the basest, most mindless, and ruthless aspects of the current political zeitgeist. If the interests of the corporate culture that controls our television stations are at heart the same as those that fund and support lobbyists and politicians, it stands to reason that—when network executives do meet to determine what is appropriate, entertaining, profitable, what people want and need to see—they are unlikely to flinch at portraying stylized versions of the same behavior we read about in the press, or can observe on the Senate floor.

If reality TV does turn out to be not only the present but also the future of prime-time television, it seems more than likely that a steady, high-intake, long-term diet of *Survivor* and *The Bachelorette* will subtly, or not so subtly, affect the views and values of the audiences that tune in week after week. Watching a nightly Darwinian free-for-all cannot help but have a desensitizing effect. Once you've absorbed and assimilated the idea that civility is, at best, a frill, you may find yourself less inclined to suppress an eruption of road rage or the urge to ridicule the homely Average Joe who dares to approach a pretty girl. If the lesson of reality TV is that anyone will do anything for money, that every human interaction necessarily involves the swift, calculated formation and dissolution of dishonest, amoral alliances, it seems naïve to be appalled by the fact that our government has been robbing us to pay off its supporters in the pharmaceutical industry and among the corporations profiting from the rebuilding of Iraq. After you've seen a "real person" lie about his grandmother's death, you may be slightly less shocked to learn that our leaders failed to come clean about the weapons of mass destruction.

After all, it's the way the world works; it's how people behave. We can't have witnessed all that reality without having figured that out by now. How foolish it would be to object to the billing practices of companies such as Halliburton, or to the evidence that our government has been working behind the scenes to dismantle the social security system and to increase (in the guise of reducing) what the elderly will have to pay for health care. *Everybody* acts like that, given half the chance. And we all admire a winner, regardless of how the game was won.

Which is the message we get, and are meant to be getting, every time a bachelor outsmarts his rivals, every time the castaways vote a contender off the island and inch one rung up the ladder. Indeed, those weekly tribal councils at which the voting occurs, held in a cavern or cave decorated to evoke the palm-fringed exotica of the tiki lounge or the Bugs Bunny cartoon, are arguably the most disturbing and pernicious moments in the reality-TV lineup. They're a travesty of democracy so painfully familiar, so much like what our political reality is actually becoming, that it's far more unnerving than watching Donald Trump brutally fire each week's losers, or ugly single guys made to feel even more unattractive than they are.

The castaways vote, as we do, but it's a democracy that might have 30 been conceived if the spirit of Machiavelli had briefly possessed the mind of Thomas Jefferson; indeed, the reasons behind the survivors' ballots might puzzle our Founding Fathers. Because this fun-house version of the electoral process seeks to dismantle civilization rather than to improve it, the goal is neither a common good nor the furthering of life, liberty, or the pursuit of happiness. It's a parody of democracy, robbed of its heart and soul, a democracy in which everyone always votes, for himself.

READING THE TEXT

1. What explanations does Prose provide for the recent dramatic increase in the number of reality TV programs?

2. How does Prose contrast reality TV with other sorts of programming, such as sitcoms and dramas?

3. Summarize in your own words the guiding social and philosophical principles that underlie reality television.

4. What is the relationship that Prose sees between reality TV and Republican politics?

5. What effect does Prose believe a long-term diet of reality TV will have on the American consciousness?

READING THE SIGNS

1. In an argumentative essay, support, refute, or modify Prose's proposition that the guiding principles that underlie reality TV are the same that shaped the policies of the George W. Bush administration.

2. Interview several fans of reality TV about their attraction to such programs. Do they like all reality TV shows, or do they discriminate among them? If the latter, what is their pattern of preference? Then use your findings as the basis of an argumentative essay about why this genre has developed such a large following in early twenty-first-century America.

3. Read or reread the Introduction to this chapter, and write an essay in which you analyze whether the appeal of the episode of *Average Joe* that Prose describes is based on schadenfreude. Alternately, watch another current RTV

program, particularly one that is based on voting contestants out of a competition, and conduct the same sort of analysis.

4. In class, brainstorm responses to Prose's question, "What might future anthropologists . . . conclude about our world if [reality] programs constituted their primary source of information?" (para. 19). Then write an essay in which you propose your own response to this question.

5. Write an essay in which you support, challenge, or complicate Prose's claim that the contestant voting ritual that occurs on many reality TV programs is "a parody of democracy, robbed of its heart and soul, a democracy in which everyone always votes, for himself" (para. 30). To develop your ideas, you might consider the appearance of Bristol Palin as a competitor in the 2010 season of *Dancing with the Stars*, given that both supporters and opponents of her mother, Sarah Palin, accused the other side of stacking the audience's voting deck.

"You're Fired."

Reading the Signs

1. What is *The Apprentice*? To what does "You're Fired" refer? Provide reasons why this expression has become a popular catchphrase.

2. What is the purpose of this banner? What does it promote? Is it, in your opinion, effective?

JAMES HAROLD

A Moral Never-Never Land: Identifying with Tony Soprano

> Tony Soprano kills people. He breaks their legs and threatens to cas-
> trate them. Yet, somehow, James Harold likes Tony Soprano. He
> knows this might seem odd, and he wonders whether there is any-
> thing morally wrong with it. Since Harold is also a philosopher, he
> is well equipped to reflect on the matter, as he does in this philo-
> sophical exploration, which first appeared in *The Sopranos and Phi-
> losophy* (2004), of the moral effect of *The Sopranos*. Arguing that *The
> Sopranos* offers a multifaceted view of gangster life that combines
> both sympathetic and repulsive elements, Harold concludes that it
> is indeed beneficial for such a TV show to stimulate viewers to think
> deeply about the nature of good and evil. An associate professor of
> philosophy at Mount Holyoke College, Harold has published essays in
> the *Journal of Aesthetics and Art Criticism, Philosophical Investigations,*
> and the *British Journal of Aesthetics.*

I like Tony Soprano; I can't help it. I like him despite the fact that I recognize
that he's a vicious and dangerous criminal. I don't particularly *want* to like
him, and I certainly don't think I would like him if he were a real person who
lived down the street from me. If he were really my neighbor, I think I'd feel
for him what the Cusamanos do: a mixture of fear, fascination, and disgust.
Nonetheless, recognizing that he is fictional, I like him. I find myself sympathizing with him: when he is depressed, I pity him; when he is wronged, I
feel anger toward those who have betrayed him; and when he is successful, I
share in his happiness. I want him to do well. I root for him to defeat his opponents, and, at the end of Season Four, for him to win back his wife Carmela.

Is there anything *morally* wrong with caring about Tony Soprano in this
way? If Tony Soprano were a real person, then most people would agree that
liking him is at least a little bit morally unsavory. This is Charmaine Bucco's
opinion, for example, especially with regard to her husband Artie's friendship with Tony, and it's also the view of most of the other non-Mafia related
characters on the show, such as Dr. Melfi's friends and family, the Cusamanos, and so on. But Tony Soprano isn't real — he's fictional, and I know that
even if the Cusamanos don't. So what could be wrong with my liking Tony
Soprano, given that I know that *The Sopranos* is a work of fiction?

From time to time, as political winds change, politicians, including, for
example, Tipper Gore, Joseph Lieberman, and Bob Dole, have weighed in
against various artworks in popular culture on the grounds that these artworks
are morally dangerous. *The Sopranos* has attracted its fair share of this kind

Dr. Melfi and Tony Soprano.

of criticism. Usually these criticisms are answered by proponents of freedom of expression, and the discussion turns to censorship and the necessity of toleration and diversity of viewpoints. What often gets left behind in these debates is the crucial issue of whether or not there really is any reason to think that a series like *The Sopranos* can be morally corrupting. It is often unclear exactly how artworks like *The Sopranos* are supposed to be bad for us. One of the things that worries some of us is that television shows like *The Sopranos* make very bad people seem, well, likeable.

When Is Art Dangerous?

The first Western philosopher to worry seriously about the moral effects of fiction on its audience was Plato. Plato worried about the way that the dramatic poets like Homer played on the emotions of audience members in ways that could be dangerous and manipulative. Poetry, Plato believed, evokes strong emotion in ways that could undermine social stability. In Plato's time, a dramatic poem like *The Odyssey* would be read aloud or sung in a public performance, and so poetry, for Plato, is more like theater for us. An ideal society, Plato thought, would be governed by principles of reason, and our willingness to follow through on these rational principles could be weakened by desires arising from strong emotion — the province of poetry. Poetry was supposed to be dangerous because it can lead us to sympathize with fictional characters, and thus the feelings of the fictional characters come to infect the audience. Plato wrote:

> When even the best of us hear Homer or one of the other tragedians imitating one of the heroes sorrowing and making a long lamenting speech or singing and beating his breast, you know that we enjoy it, give ourselves up to following it, sympathize with the hero, take his sufferings seriously, and praise as a good poet the one who affects us most in this way.[1]

In the end, the feelings of the audience and the feelings of the character are the same, and the audience may feel pity, or grief, even when it's not appropriate to do so. Further, we may carry these inappropriate emotions home with us, and they can become part of our character, and affect the way we act. Plato recognized how strongly we can feel about poetry, and the power that this passion can have: sympathetic attention to art, he said, "nurtures and waters them and establishes them as rulers in us."[2] These passions can become so strong that we can no longer control them in our everyday lives. Plato's example is of a man who enjoys comic plays and who then comes to act like a buffoon at home; but someone who enjoyed a show like *The Sopranos* could well be possessed by more dangerous emotions, like rage, revenge, or contempt for ordinary people. If you are inclined to think that Plato's arguments don't apply to modern audiences, consider the following quote, taken from a fan Web site discussion of "University," which speaks to just this kind of worry.

> When my boyfriend and I watch *The Sopranos*, he gets so caught up, you would think it was happening to him. This gentle man, who wouldn't harm a fly. It's strange phenomena [*sic*], and not unlike soap addicts who confuse TV with reality.[3]

In the nineteenth century, Leo Tolstoy expressed similar concerns about art (including much of his own writing) in his book *What Is Art?* Tolstoy had undergone a deep religious experience late in his life, and he came to believe that most art was morally corrupt. Like Plato, he held that art evoked strong emotions in its audience, and he believed that many such emotions are, in his view, morally corrupting. Only art motivated by true Christian feeling, according to Tolstoy, could be morally acceptable. Tolstoy therefore rejected virtually all art, except popular Christian peasant art, which, he believed, conveyed only simple Christian love. Other artworks transmitted corrupt feelings to their audiences — feelings of unjust pride or

---

[1] Plato, *Republic* (605c–d), translated by G. M. A. Grube and C. D. C. Reeve (Indianapolis: Hackett, 1992).
[2] Plato, 606d.
[3] http://www.the-sopranos.com/db/ep32_review.htm. The post was anonymous.

lust, for example.[4] These feelings make people worse morally, because the feelings are selfish, and they alienate people from one another.

Plato and Tolstoy are separated by thousands of years, but their views share certain features in common: they both hold that art corrupts its audience by playing on emotion; they both hold that some art is worse than others in doing so; they believe that the emotional impact of art is great enough to influence how we act and what kind of people we become, so that art can make us bad people; they were both particularly critical of the most popular artists of their day. There is little doubt that both of them would have disapproved of *The Sopranos*. Should we, like Plato and Tolstoy, be worried that we might be infected by watching *The Sopranos*, and caring about the immoral protagonists?

Plato and Tolstoy have their present-day counterparts, too. Some cognitive scientists believe that when we watch a television show like *The Sopranos*, we simulate the feelings of the characters portrayed on-screen. That is, we use our own minds to imitate what we imagine is going on in the minds of characters, and we feel an emotion that is in some ways like the emotion that the character feels. This emotion can then affect us in a number of ways. We sometimes call this "sympathizing" or "identifying" with a character onscreen. Though in many cases we are able to separate the character's emotion from our own feelings, sometimes our imaginings of the fictional character's emotions infect and affect our own.[5]

Tony Soprano does this himself in "Proshai, Livushka." After the death of his mother, Tony watches his favorite film, *Public Enemy*. In this movie, Jimmy Cagney's character is a gangster with a gentle, loving mother. As Tony watches, he sympathizes with the Cagney character, and imagines having a loving, trusting relationship with his mother. This makes him smile, at first, and then cry, as he compares this imagined mother-son relationship with his own experience. We understand why Tony is so deeply affected by this film, because we can also be affected by works of fiction. Tony is moved by identifying with the Cagney character, and we are moved by identifying with Tony.

A key feature of this view is that we pick out a character to identify with, and we focus on that person's feelings and emotions. It is this character that we identify with; he or she is the one that we know the best, and often, he or she is the one that we like the most. In the case of *The Sopranos*, despite a large, strong ensemble cast, the primary character with whom audiences identify is Tony himself. This is how I come to care about Tony, and why I feel relief when he is successful, even when his "success" consists in murder, as when he strangles the mob informant Febby Petrulio in "College."

[4]One important difference between Plato and Tolstoy is that Tolstoy thought that the feelings transmitted were the feelings of the artist or author, whereas Plato thought that they were the feelings of the character.

[5]This phenomenon is discussed by Robert Gordon in his "Sympathy, Simulation, and the Impartial Spectator," in *Mind and Morals: Essays on Ethics and Cognitive Science*, edited by Larry May, Marilyn Friedman, and Andy Clark (Boston: MIT Press, 1996), pp. 165–80.

The problem with this sympathetic identification is that sometimes the character with whom we identify has thoughts and feelings which are morally reprehensible, and by identifying with that character, we risk being infected by these vicious sentiments. We might start to think that Tony's views about violence and vengeance are reasonable, or we might come to share his propensity for anger, jealousy, rage, and suspicion. If imagining these feelings leads us to share them (even to a small extent), then liking Tony could make a person morally worse.

Why *The Sopranos*?

There are so many works of popular art that feature gangsters — not to mention other kinds of vicious people — as protagonists that it hardly seems fair to pick on *The Sopranos*. *The Godfather Parts I*, *II*, and *III*, *Goodfellas*, *Carlito's Way*, *Scarface*, *Casino*, and *Public Enemy* are just a few examples of films that feature gangsters as main characters. (Most of these movies are referenced and discussed by the characters in *The Sopranos*, especially by Silvio Dante, who loves to imitate Al Pacino's character from *The Godfather*.) But *The Sopranos* distinguishes itself from these other works in three ways. First, *The Sopranos* is an ongoing television series, not a two-hour movie. As of this writing, four seasons comprising fifty-two episodes have been shown, and at least two more seasons are planned. That will make more than three *days* worth of material if one were to sit down and watch them all back-to-back. By contrast, all the films of the *Godfather* series, taken together, would take fewer than ten hours to watch. So loyal viewers of *The Sopranos* spend a long time with these characters, getting to know much more about them, and potentially, to care much more about them than viewers ever could with a film character. Not surprisingly, we are more deeply affected by characters we spend more time with and get to know better, and we get to spend a lot of time with Tony and friends.

Second, the gangsters in *The Sopranos*, especially Tony, are portrayed in deeply psychological and often quite intimate ways. We often get to see Tony's dreams (occasionally we see other characters' dreams, such as Christopher's and Dr. Melfi's, but not often). Through Tony's sessions with Dr. Melfi, we get to know Tony's feelings much better than we could otherwise. In those sessions, we get to understand his childhood (through flashbacks), his hopes and concerns, and his fears. We get a very strong picture of Tony as a complete human being. The character himself is a rich and complex one. In addition to being a gangster (with all that implies) we also learn that Tony tries, in his own way, to be a good father and husband, that he cares deeply about his children and wants them to do well. We learn that he loves his friends deeply, even those (like Big Pussy) that he ends up killing. He has a strong sense of responsibility, and when he says he will do something, he feels bound to do it. Despite (perhaps because of) his evil, vicious qualities,

Tony has some good features, as well. Tony Soprano is a more fully developed character than any other fictional gangster ever created, and we get to know him intimately.

Third, *The Sopranos* strives for verisimilitude. It does not have the ironic stylishness of *Goodfellas*, nor is it an idealized period piece like *The Godfather*. With one major exception — the number of gang killings[6] — the show is strikingly realistic. Virtually every element, including the psychoanalysis, the New Jersey settings, the language used by the characters, Tony and Carmela's family dynamics, the FBI surveillance techniques, and the mob structure and organization is very close to what is found in the real world. The show is set in our own time and many of the phenomena that the characters deal with — for example, Prozac, 9/11, Attention Deficit Disorder, coaches sexually assaulting student athletes, the competitiveness of college acceptance, teen drug use — are phenomena that we deal with as well. The characters on *The Sopranos* are aware of the fictional portrayals of gangsters and they discuss these. In "Christopher," Carmela and her friends attend a lecture about the portrayal of Italian-American women as mob wives; Dr. Melfi's ex-husband Richard complains over and over again about the stereotyped portrayal of Italian-Americans in gangster films. The psychiatrist who Tony consults when Dr. Melfi won't see him makes a reference to the Robert DeNiro comedy *Analyze This*. *The Sopranos* thus continues the tradition of gangster fictions, but in a deeper, more reflective way than most do: Like us, the characters on *The Sopranos* know that these other stories are fictional.

All of these features conspire to make Tony Soprano a very sympathetic character. When Plato says, "We enjoy it, give ourselves up to following it, sympathize with the hero, take his sufferings seriously," the hero he describes could be Tony. But sympathizing with Tony is not like sympathizing with Artie Bucco; Tony is a terribly vicious and violent man. Tony personally commits five murders that we see on-screen: he strangles Febby Petrulio in "College"; he shoots one of Junior's hired killers in "I Dream of Jeanie Cusamano" (this one, at least, is self-defense); in "From Where to Eternity," he kills Matt Bevilaqua with Big Pussy; and then he, Paulie, and Silvio turn around and shoot Big Pussy in "Funhouse"; finally, he kills Ralph Cifaretto in "Whoever Did This." On top of these five, he orders many, many other killings which are carried out by other members of his gang (some shown on-screen and some off). He loses his temper continually, administering beatings to girlfriends (Irina, Gloria) and business associates (Mikey Palmice, Georgie the bartender, Ralphie Cifaretto, Assemblyman Zellman). He doesn't ever hit Dr. Melfi, but he comes quite close. On top of his propensity for personal violence, we have his virulent racism and homophobia, his profiting from corruption, gambling, drugs, and other enterprises that presumably ruin the lives

---

[6]One fan Web site counts thirty-nine deaths over the first four seasons (http://www.the-sopranos.com/db/bodycount.htm). The number of killings on the show far exceeds the number in real life for similar mobs.

of people we never see on-screen. There is no doubt that Tony Soprano is evil, vicious, and morally bankrupt. Yet we like him.

Is It Morally Wrong to Watch *The Sopranos*?

The Sopranos leads its audience to identify with a terrible person. Is it then wrong to watch the show? Could identifying with Tony make us worse people too? In the end, I doubt it. There are a number of reasons why *The Sopranos* as a whole does more than just make bad people look good. First, although Tony Soprano is the main character on the show, some of the main characters of *The Sopranos* who are quite sympathetic are not gangsters and are pretty good people, particularly Dr. Melfi and Meadow Soprano. Many other characters, if not good, at least suffer pangs of conscience for the evil they do (or the evil men they love), and they try to do good from time to time: Carmela, Artie Bucco,[7] and Adriana, for example. These characters struggle continually with their moral positions, and their complicity in the crimes being committed all around them. Even some thoroughly bad characters like Christopher and Paulie are forced from time to time to reflect on the moral consequences of what they do ("From Where to Eternity").

But the primary moral center of the show, which serves to balance out 15 the immoral facets of these attractive characters, is Jennifer Melfi's psychiatrist's office. It is here that the viewer is most often led to identify not just with Tony, but with his victims, and to see Tony's life in a richer, more morally sophisticated way. In a long-running series like *The Sopranos*, we see things from more than just one point of view. Tony's psychoanalysis sessions with Dr. Melfi afford us an opportunity to see Tony from the outside as well as from the inside, and to remind us of the self-deception and flimsy justifications that Tony uses in order to continue his life of crime and violence. Tony likes to compare himself to a soldier at war, or a "captain of industry," but he doesn't convince anyone with these analogies (perhaps not even himself). Dr. Melfi's facial expressions make clear her contempt for these facile attempts at justification.

Consider the episode entitled "House Arrest." In this episode, on the advice of his lawyer, Tony has decided to distance himself from criminal activity and spend his time with his legitimate businesses. He grows increasingly restless and agitated; he develops a serious rash; he becomes irritable and frustrated, and he complains of this to Dr. Melfi. Dr. Melfi asks him: "Do you know why a shark keeps moving? . . . There's a psychological condition

---

[7]Artie is a very interesting character, morally speaking. For the most part, he is not involved in Tony's activities. Artie did have a brief fling with loan sharking in season four, but it didn't work out, and he wasn't really up to the nasty side of it. But he does indirectly profit from Tony's business, and he keeps silent about some of his wrongdoings.

known as alexithymia,[8] common in certain personalities. The individual craves almost ceaseless action, which enables them to avoid acknowledging the abhorrent things they do." When Tony asks what happens when such people are forced to stop and reflect, she answers, "They have time to think about their behavior. How what they do affects other people. About feelings of emptiness and self-loathing, haunting them since childhood. And they crash." Tony gets her point, but he chooses to respond to this lesson not by reflecting, but by returning to Satriale's with the other mobsters and getting back into action — thus, the shark gets back in motion rather than think about the ethical consequences of how he lives.

Jennifer Melfi continually reminds us as an audience of the dangers of seeing things exclusively from Tony's point of view, and her character provides an alternative point of view on Tony's life and actions. When she complains to her psychiatrist, Elliot Kupferberg, that she is in a "moral never-never land" with Tony Soprano, "Not wanting to judge but to treat," we know exactly how she feels ("From Where to Eternity"). Dr. Melfi, and sometimes other characters such as the Buccos, Meadow, or even Carmela, provide us with an alternative moral center that allows us to see Tony and his actions from the outside, and they remind us of the moral consequences of what Tony does. After Dr. Melfi's rapist goes free, she realizes that she could tell Tony about her rapist, and be revenged on him, but she does not do so ("Employee of the Month"). During this sequence, we sympathize with Melfi, and her moral choice, not with Tony. The finale of the second season ("Funhouse") concludes with one of the few montage sequences ever used in the series.[9] We see alternating shots of the Soprano family celebrating Meadow's graduation, and various shots of the criminal activities that will be paying Meadow's tuition. By juxtaposing these two scenes, the producers of *The Sopranos* remind us that what we like about Tony cannot be separated from the evil he does.

The problem with Plato's and Tolstoy's moral criticism of art is that their emotional theories of artistic identification are simplistic. We do not just take on one character or one point of view, and we do not respond emotionally in only one way. *The Sopranos* provides us with many different ways of seeing the life of a gangster, and it also invites us to feel in a variety of ways about it. Sometimes the show does make Tony and his crew look quite sympathetic;

---

[8]Alexithymia, strictly speaking, is somewhat different than Jennifer Melfi's account of it here. Ordinarily, alexithymia refers to a condition wherein the patient has difficulty in recognizing her or his own emotions. Melfi is describing how alexithymia manifests itself in sociopathic personalities like Tony's.

[9]The second season has more of these moments of moral reflection and serious moral examination than any other season: from the very beginning of the season, when Dr. Melfi has to decide whether she has a moral responsibility to take Tony back as a patient, to this final sequence, the characters and the creators grapple with right and wrong in a very direct way. None of the other seasons has as much sustained, direct attention to morality.

but it also provides us with other perspectives, and permits us, if we try, to formulate a complex and sophisticated personal moral response to gangster life, and not merely to imitate Tony.

This does not mean that Plato's and Tolstoy's concerns about art should be dismissed lightly. They are right that artworks can affect us deeply, and sometimes cause audiences to identify with immoral characters. But whether or not these artworks are morally corrupting depends on other factors as well. Television shows like *The Sopranos* which provide multiple moral perspectives on evil characters, and which offer room for moral reflection, might even be good for us, rather than evil.

READING THE TEXT

1. Explain in your own words why Plato and Tolstoy believed that art could be "dangerous" (para. 4).

2. How, according to Harold, does the depiction of the mob in *The Sopranos* compare with other cinematic portrayals of gangsters?

3. Why does Harold believe that Dr. Melfi is the "moral center" (para. 15) of the program?

4. In class, discuss the effect of Harold's first-person opener, "I like Tony Soprano; I can't help it" (para. 1). Why do you think he begins with this confession?

READING THE SIGNS

1. Write an essay supporting, opposing, or modifying Harold's contention that *The Sopranos* has a moral center and that it is Dr. Melfi.

2. Watch an episode of *The Sopranos*, and assess the validity of Harold's claim that programs like it "might even be good for us, rather than evil" (para. 19).

3. **CONNECTING TEXTS** Read or reread Vivian Sobchack's "The Postmorbid Condition" (p. 430), and write an essay in which you argue whether or not *The Sopranos* displays the trend toward "carelessness toward violence" that Sobchack believes dominates contemporary cinema.

4. Compare and contrast *The Sopranos* with one of the gangster films that Harold lists in paragraph 10. How is the mob represented in each work, and what does that representation suggest about the values and interests of the era in which it was created?

5. **CONNECTING TEXTS** Read or reread Robert B. Ray's "The Thematic Paradigm" (p. 377), and write an essay in which you argue whether Tony Soprano can be considered a hero. If so, what kind of hero is he? If not, why not?

CARL MATHESON

The Simpsons, *Hyper-Irony, and the Meaning of Life*

Don't have a cow or anything, but most comedy, as Carl Matheson points out in this analysis of *The Simpsons*, which first appeared in *The Simpsons and Philosophy* (2001), is based in cruelty. And while Matheson doesn't "mean to argue that the makers of *The Simpsons* intended the show primarily as a theater of cruelty," he does "imagine that they did." At any rate, Matheson suggests, the pervasive irony that makes the program funny should serve as a warning to anyone who believes that this ever-popular cartoon sitcom is a warm endorser of family values. Carl Matheson is a professor in, and chair of, the department of philosophy at the University of Manitoba. He has published essays in the *British Journal of Aesthetics*, the *Journal of Aesthetics and Art Criticism,* and *Philosophy and Literature.*

DISAFFECTED YOUTH #1: Here comes that cannonball guy. He's cool.
DISAFFECTED YOUTH #2: Are you being sarcastic, dude?
DISAFFECTED YOUTH #1: I don't even know anymore.
— "Homerpalooza," Season 7

What separates the comedies that were shown on television fifty, forty, or even twenty-five years ago from those of today? First, we may notice technological differences, the difference between black-and-white and color, the difference between film stock (or even kinescope) and video. Then there are the numerous social differences. For instance, the myth of the universal traditional two-parent family is not as secure as it was in the 1950s and 1960s, and the comedies of the different eras reflect changes in its status — although even early comedies of the widow/widower happy fifties, sixties, and seventies were full of nontraditional families, such as are found in *The Partridge Family, The Ghost and Mrs. Muir, Julia, The Jerry van Dyke Show, Family Affair, The Courtship of Eddie's Father, The Andy Griffith Show, The Brady Bunch, Bachelor Father*, and *My Little Margie*. Also, one may note the ways in which issues such as race have received different treatments over the decades.

But I would like to concentrate on a deeper transformation: today's comedies, at least most of them, are funny in different ways from those of decades past. In both texture and substance the comedy of *The Simpsons* and *Seinfeld* is worlds apart from the comedy of *Leave It to Beaver* and *The Jack Benny Show*, and is even vastly different from much more recent comedies, such as *MASH* and *Maude*. First, today's comedies tend to be highly *quotational*: many of today's comedies essentially depend on the device of referring to or quoting other works of popular culture. Second, they are *hyper-ironic*: the flavor of humor offered by today's comedies is colder, based less on a shared sense of humanity than on a sense of world-weary cleverer-than-thouness. In this essay I would like to explore the way in which *The Simpsons* uses both quotationalism and hyper-ironism and relate these devices to currents in the contemporary history of ideas.

Quotationalism

Television comedy has never completely foregone the pleasure of using pop culture as a straight man. However, early instances of quotation tended to be opportunistic; they did not comprise the substance of the genre. Hence, in sketch comedy, one would find occasional references to popular culture in *Wayne and Shuster* and *Johnny Carson*, but these references were really treated as just one more source of material. The roots of quotationalism as a main source of material can be found in the early seventies with the two vision-ary comedies, *Mary Hartman Mary Hartman*, which lampooned soap operas by being an ongoing soap opera, and *Fernwood 2Night*, which, as a small-budget talk show, took on small-budget talk shows. Quotationalism then came much more to the attention of the general public between the mid-seventies and early eighties through *Saturday Night Live*, *Late Night with David Letterman*, and *SCTV*. Given the mimical abilities of its cast and its need for weekly mate-rial, the chief comedic device of *SNL* was parody — of genres (the nightly news, television debates), of particular television shows (*I Love Lucy*, *Star Trek*) and of movies (*Star Wars*). The type of quotationalism employed by Letterman was more abstract and less based on particular shows. Influenced by the much ear-lier absurdism of such hosts as Dave Garroway, Letterman immediately took the formulas of television and cinema beyond their logical conclusions (*The Equalizer Guy*, chimp cam, and spokesperson Larry "Bud" Melman).

However, it was *SCTV* that gathered together the various strains of quota-tionalism and synthesized them into a deeper, more complex, and more mys-terious whole. Like *Mary Hartman*, and unlike *SNL*, it was an ongoing series with recurring characters such as Johnny Larue, Lola Heatherton, and Bobby Bittman. However, unlike *Mary Hartman*, the ongoing series was about the workings of a television station. *SCTV* was a television show about the pro-cess of television. Through the years, the models upon which characters like Heatherton and Bittman were based vanished somewhat into the background, as Heatherton and Bittman started to breathe on their own, and therefore, came to occupy a shadowy space between real (fictional) characters and simu-lacra. Furthermore, *SCTV*'s world came to intersect the real world as some of the archetypes portrayed (such as Jerry Lewis) were people in real life. Thus, *SCTV* eventually produced and depended upon patterns of inter-textuality and cross-referencing that were much more thoroughgoing and subtle than those of any program that preceded it.

The Simpsons was born, therefore, just as the use of quotationalism was 5 maturing. However, *The Simpsons* was not the same sort of show as *SNL* and *SCTV*. One major difference, of course, was that *The Simpsons* was animated while the others were (largely) not, but this difference does not greatly affect the relevant potential for quotationalism — although it may be easier to draw the bridge of the U.S.S. *Enterprise* than to rebuild it and re-enlist the entire original cast of *Star Trek*. The main difference is that as an ostensibly ongoing family comedy, *The Simpsons* was both plot and character driven, where the other shows, even those that contained ongoing characters, were largely sketch driven. Furthermore, unlike *Mary Hartman Mary Hartman*, which existed to parody soap operas, *The Simpsons* did not have the raison d'être of parodying the family-based comedies of which it was an instance. The problem then was this: How does one transform an essentially non-quotational format into an essentially quotational show?

The answer to the above question lies in the form of quotationalism employed by *The Simpsons*. By way of contrast, let me outline what it was definitively not. Take, for instance, a *Wayne and Shuster* parody of Wilde's *The Picture of Dorian Gray*. In the parody, instead of Gray's sins being reflected in an artwork, while he remains pure and young in appearance, the effects of Gray's overeating are reflected in the artwork, while he remains thin. The situation's permissions and combinations are squeezed and coaxed to produce the relevant gags and ensuing yuks. End of story. Here the quotationalism is very direct; it is the source both of the story line and of the supposedly humorous contrast between the skit and the original novel. Now, compare this linear and one-dimensional use of quotation for the purposes of parody with the pattern of quotation used in a very short passage from an episode from *The Simpsons* entitled "A Streetcar Named Marge." In the episode, Marge is playing Blanche Dubois opposite Ned Flanders's Stanley in *Streetcar!*, her community theatre's musical version of the Tennessee Williams play. In need of day care for little Maggie, she sends Maggie to the Ayn Rand School for Tots, which is run by the director's sister. Headmistress Sinclair, a strict disciplinarian and believer in infant self-reliance, confiscates all of the tots' pacifiers which causes an enraged Maggie to lead her classmates in a highly organized reclamation mission, during which the theme from *The Great Escape* plays in the background. Having re-acquired the pacifiers the group sits, arrayed in rows, making little sucking sounds, so that when Homer arrives to pick up Maggie, he is confronted with a scene from Hitchcock's *The Birds*.

The first thing that one can say about these quotations is that they are very funny. . . . To see that these quotations are funny just watch the show again. Second, we note that these quotations are not used for the purpose of parody.[1]

---

[1] I don't mean to say that *The Simpsons* does not make use of parody. The episode currently under discussion contains a brilliant parody of Broadway adaptations, from its title to the show-stopping tune "A Stranger Is Just a Friend You Haven't Met!"

Rather, they are allusions, designed to provide unspoken metaphorical elaboration and commentary about what is going on in the scene. The allusion to Ayn Rand underscores the ideology and personal rigidity of Headmistress Sinclair. The theme music from *The Great Escape* stresses the determination of Maggie and her cohort. The allusion to *The Birds* communicates the threat of the hive-mind posed by many small beings working as one. By going outside of the text via these nearly instantaneous references, *The Simpsons* manages to convey a great deal of extra information extremely economically. Third, the most impressive feature of this pattern of allusion is its pace and density, where this feature has grown more common as the series has matured. Early episodes, for instance the one in which Bart saws the head off the town's statue of Jebediah Springfield, are surprisingly free of quotation. Later episodes derive much of their manic comic energy from their rapid-fire sequence of allusions. This density of allusion is perhaps what sets *The Simpsons* most apart from any show that has preceded it.

However, the extent to which *The Simpsons* depends on other elements of pop culture is not without cost. Just as those readers who are unfamiliar with Frazer's *Golden Bough* will be hindered in their attempt to understand Eliot's "The Waste Land," and just as many modern-day readers will be baffled by many of the Biblical and classical allusions that play important roles in the history of literature, many of today's viewers won't fully understand much of what goes on in *The Simpsons* due to an unfamiliarity with the popular culture that forms the basis for the show's references. Having missed the references, these people may interpret *The Simpsons* as nothing more than a slightly off-base family comedy populated with characters who are neither very bright nor very interesting. From these propositions they will probably derive the theorem that the show is neither substantial nor funny, and also the lemma that the people who like the show are deficient in taste, intelligence, or standards of personal mental hygiene. However, not only do the detractors of the show miss a great deal of its humor, they also fail to realize that its pattern of quotations is an absolutely essential vehicle for developing character and for setting a tone. And, since these people are usually not huge fans of popular culture to begin with, they will be reluctant to admit that they are missing something significant. Oh well. It is difficult to explain color to a blind man, especially if he won't listen. On the other hand, those who enjoy connecting the quotational dots will enjoy their task all the more for its exclusivity. There is no joke like an in-joke: The fact that many people don't get *The Simpsons* might very well make the show both funnier and better to those who do.

Hyper-Ironism and the Moral Agenda

Without the smart-ass, comedy itself would be impossible. Whether one subscribes, as I do, to the thesis that all comedy is fundamentally cruel, or merely to the relatively spineless position that only the vast majority of comedy is fundamentally cruel, one has to admit that comedy has always relied upon the joys to be derived from making fun of others. However, usually the cruelty has been employed for a positive social purpose. In the sanctimonious *MASH*, Hawkeye and the gang were simply joking to "dull the pain of a world gone mad," and the butts of their jokes, such as Major Frank Burns, symbolized threats to the liberal values that the show perpetually attempted to reinforce in the souls of its late-twentieth-century viewers. In *Leave It to Beaver*, the link between humor and the instillation of family values is didactically obvious. A very few shows, most notably *Seinfeld*, totally eschewed a moral agenda.[2] *Seinfeld*'s ability to maintain a devoted audience in spite of a cast of shallow and petty characters engaged in equally petty and shallow acts is miraculous. So, as I approach *The Simpsons*, I would like to resolve the following questions. Does *The Simpsons* use its humor to promote a moral agenda? Does it use its humor to promote the claim that there is no justifiable moral agenda? Or, does it stay out of the moral agenda game altogether?

These are tricky questions, because data can be found to affirm each 10 of them. To support the claim that *The Simpsons* promotes a moral agenda, one usually need look no further than Lisa and Marge. Just consider Lisa's speeches in favor of integrity, freedom from censorship, or any variety of touchy-feely social causes, and you will come away with the opinion that *The Simpsons* is just another liberal show underneath a somewhat thin but tasty crust of nastiness. One can even expect Bart to show humanity when it counts, as when, at military school, he defies sexist peer pressure to cheer Lisa on in her attempt to complete an obstacle course. The show also seems to engage in self-righteous condemnation of various institutional soft targets. The political system of Springfield is corrupt, its police chief lazy and self-serving, and its Reverend Lovejoy ineffectual at best. Property developers stage a fake religious miracle in order to promote the opening of a mall. Mr. Burns tries to increase business at the power plant by blocking out the sun. Taken together, these examples seem to advocate a moral position of caring at the level of the individual, one which favors the family over any institution.

However, one can find examples from the show that seem to be denied accommodation within any plausible moral stance. In one episode, Frank Grimes (who hates being called "Grimey") is a constantly unappreciated model worker, while Homer is a much beloved careless slacker. Eventually, Grimes breaks down and decides to act just like Homer Simpson. While "acting like Homer" Grimes touches a transformer and is killed instantly. During the funeral oration by Reverend Lovejoy (for "Gri-yuh-mee, as he liked to be called") a snoozing Homer shouts out "Change the channel, Marge!" The rest of the service breaks into spontaneous and appreciative laughter, with Lenny saying "That's our Homer!" End of episode. In another episode, Homer

---

[2]For a different view, see Robert A. Epperson, "Seinfeld and the Moral Life," in William Irwin, ed., *Seinfeld and Philosophy: A Book about Everything and Nothing* (Chicago: Open Court, 2000), pp. 163–74.

is unintentionally responsible for the death of Maude Flanders, Ned's wife. In the crowd at a football game, Homer is eager to catch a T-shirt being shot from little launchers on the field. Just as one is shot his way, he bends over to pick up a peanut. The T-shirt sails over him and hits the devout Maude, knocking her out of the stands to her death. These episodes are difficult to locate on a moral map; they certainly do not conform to the standard trajectory of virtue rewarded.

Given that we have various data, some of which lead us toward and others away from the claim that *The Simpsons* is committed to caring, liberal family values, what should we conclude? Before attempting to reach a conclusion, I would like to go beyond details from various episodes of the show to introduce another form of possibly relevant evidence. Perhaps, we can better resolve the issue of *The Simpsons*' moral commitments by examining the way it relates to current intellectual trends. The reader should be warned that, although I think that my comments on the current state of the history of ideas are more or less accurate, they are greatly oversimplified. In particular, the positions that I will outline are by no means unanimously accepted.

Let's start with painting. The influential critic Clement Greenberg held that the goal of all painting was to work with flatness as the nature of its medium and he reconstructed the history of painting so that it was seen to culminate in the dissolution of pictorial three-dimensional space and the acceptance of total flatness by the painters of the mid-twentieth century. Painters were taken to be like scientific researchers whose work furthered the progress of their medium, where the idea of artistic progress was to be taken as literally as that of scientific progress. Because they were fundamentally unjustifiable and because they put painters into a straitjacket, Greenberg's positions gradually lost their hold, and no other well-supported candidates for the essence of painting could be found to take their place. As a result painting (and the other arts) entered a phase that the philosopher of art Arthur Danto has called "the end of art." By this Danto did not mean that art could no longer be produced, but rather that art could no longer be subsumed under a history of progress toward some given end.[3] By the end of the 1970s, many painters had turned to earlier, more representational styles, and their paintings were as much commentaries on movements from the past, like expressionism, and about the current vacuum in the history of art, as they were about their subject matter. Instead of being about the essence of painting, much of painting came to be about the history of painting. Similar events unfolded in the other artistic media as architects, filmmakers, and writers returned to the history of their disciplines.

However, painting was not the only area in which long-held convictions concerning the nature and inevitability of progress were aggressively challenged. Science, the very icon of progressiveness, was under attack from a number of quarters. Kuhn held (depending on which interpreter of him you

[3]See Arthur Danto, *After the End of Art* (Princeton: Princeton University Press, 1996).

agree with) either that there was no such thing as scientific progress, or that if there was, there were no rules for determining what progress and scientific rationality were. Feyerabend argued that people who held substantially different theories couldn't even understand what each other was saying, and hence that there was no hope of a rational consensus; instead he extolled the anarchistic virtues of "anything goes." Early sociological workers in the field of science studies tried to show that, instead of being an inspirational narrative of the disinterested pursuit of truth, the history of science was essentially a story of office-politics writ large, because every transition in the history of science could be explained by appeal to the personal interests and allegiances of the participants.[4] And, of course, the idea of philosophical progress has continued to be challenged. Writing on Derrida, the American philosopher Richard Rorty argues that anything like *the* philosophical truth is either unattainable, non-existent, or uninteresting, that philosophy itself is a literary genre, and that philosophers should reconstrue themselves as writers who elaborate and re-interpret the writings of other philosophers. In other words, Rorty's version of Derrida recommends that philosophers view themselves as historically aware participants in a conversation, as opposed to quasi-scientific researchers.[5] Derrida himself favored a method known as deconstruction, which was popular several years ago, and which consisted of a highly technical method for undercutting texts by revealing hidden contradictions and unconscious ulterior motives. Rorty questions whether, given Derrida's take on the possibility of philosophical progress, deconstruction could be used only for negative purposes, that is, whether it could be used for anything more than making philosophical fun of other writings.

Let me repeat that these claims about the nature of art, science, and philosophy are highly controversial. However, all that I need for my purposes is the relatively uncontroversial claim that views such as these are now in circulation to an unprecedented extent. We are surrounded by a pervasive crisis of authority, be it artistic, scientific or philosophical, religious or moral, in a way that previous generations weren't. Now, as we slowly come back to earth and *The Simpsons*, we should ask this: If the crisis I described were as pervasive as I believe it to be, how might it be reflected generally in popular culture, and specifically in comedy?

We have already discussed one phenomenon that may be viewed as a consequence of the crisis of authority. When faced with the death of the idea of progress in their field, thinkers and artists have often turned to a reconsideration of the history of their discipline. Hence artists turn to art history, architects to the history of design, and so on. The motivation for this turn is

---

[4]Thomas Kuhn, *The Structure of Scientific Revolutions*, second edition (Chicago: University of Chicago Press, 1970). Paul Feyerabend, *Against Method* (London: NLB, 1975). For a lively debate on the limits of the sociology of knowledge, see James Robert Brown (ed.), *Scientific Rationality: The Sociological Turn* (Dordrecht: Reidel, 1984).

[5]Richard Rorty, "Philosophy as a Kind of Writing," pp. 90–109 in *Consequences of Pragmatism* (Minneapolis: University of Minnesota Press, 1982).

natural; once one has given up on the idea that the past is merely the infe-rior pathway to a better today and a still better tomorrow, one may try to approach the past on its own terms as an equal partner. Additionally, if the topic of progress is off the list of things to talk about, an awareness of history may be one of the few things left to fill the disciplinary conversational void. Hence, one may think that quotationalism is a natural offshoot of the crisis of authority, and that the prevalence of quotationalism in *The Simpsons* results from that crisis.

The idea that quotationalism in *The Simpsons* is the result of "something in the air" is confirmed by the stunning everpresence of historical appropria-tion throughout popular culture. Cars like the new Volkswagen Beetle and the PT Cruiser quote bygone days, and factories simply can't make enough of them. In architecture, New Urbanist housing developments try to re-create the feel of small towns of decades ago, and they have proven so popular that only the very wealthy can buy homes in them. The musical world is a hodge-podge of quotations of styles, where often the original music being quoted is simply sampled and re-processed.

To be fair, not every instance of historical quotationalism should be seen as the result of some widespread crisis of authority. For instance, the New Urbanist movement in architecture was a direct response to a perceived ero-sion of community caused by the deadening combination of economically segregated suburbs and faceless shopping malls; the movement used history in order to make the world a better place for people to live with other people. Hence the degree of quotationalism in *The Simpsons* could point toward a crisis in authority, but it could also stem from a strategy for making the world better, like the New Urbanism, or it could merely be a fashion accessory, like retro-khaki at the Gap.

No, if we want to plumb the depths of *The Simpsons*' connection with the crisis in authority we will have to look to something else, and it is at this point that I return to the original question of this section: Does *The Simpsons* use its humor to promote a moral agenda? My answer is this: *The Simpsons* does not promote anything, because its humor works by putting forward positions only in order to undercut them. Furthermore, this process of undercutting runs so deeply that we cannot regard the show as merely cynical; it manages to undercut its cynicism too. This constant process of undercutting is what I mean by "hyper-ironism."

To see what I mean, consider "Scenes from the Class Struggle in Spring- 20 field," an episode from the show's seventh season. In this episode Marge buys a Coco Chanel suit for $90 at the Outlet Mall. While wearing the suit, she runs into an old high-school classmate. Seeing the designer suit and tak-ing Marge to be one of her kind, the classmate invites Marge to the posh Springfield Glen Country Club. Awed by the gentility at the Club, and in spite of sniping from club members that she always wears the same suit, Marge becomes bent on social climbing. Initially alienated, Homer and Lisa fall in love with the club for its golf course and stables. However, just as they are about to be inducted into the club, Marge realizes that her newfound obses-sion with social standing has taken precedence over her family. Thinking that the club also probably doesn't want them anyway, she and the family walk away. However, unbeknownst to the Simpsons, the club has prepared a lavish welcome party for them, and is terribly put out that they haven't arrived — Mr. Burns even "pickled the figs for the cake" himself.

At first glance, this episode may seem like another case of the show's reaffirmation of family values: after all, Marge chooses family over status. Furthermore, what could be more hollow than status among a bunch of shal-low inhuman snobs? However, the people in the club turn out to be inclusive and fairly affectionate, from golfer Tom Kite who gives Homer advice on his swing despite that fact that Homer has stolen his golf clubs — and shoes — to Mr. Burns, who thanks Homer for exposing his dishonesty at golf. The jaded cynicism that seems to pervade the club is gradually shown to be a mere conversational trope; the club is prepared to welcome the working-class Simpsons with open arms — or has it realized yet that they are working class? Further complicating matters are Marge's reasons for walking away. First, there is the false dilemma between caring for her family and being welcomed by the club. Why should one choice exclude the other? Second is her belief that the Simpsons just don't belong to such a club. This belief seems to be based on a classism that the club itself doesn't have. This episode leaves no stable ground upon which the viewer can rest. It feints at the sanctity of family val-ues and swerves closely to class determinism, but it doesn't stay anywhere. Furthermore, upon reflection, none of the "solutions" that it momentarily holds is satisfactory. In its own way, this episode is as cruel and cold-blooded as the Grimey episode. However, where the Grimey episode wears its heart-lessness upon its sleeve, this episode conjures up illusions of satisfactory heart-warming resolution only to undercut them immediately. In my view, it stands as a paradigm of the real *Simpsons.*

I think that, given a crisis of authority, hyper-ironism is the most suit-able form of comedy. Recall that many painters and architects turned to a consideration of the history of painting and architecture once they gave up on the idea of a fundamental trans-historical goal for their media. Recall also that once Rorty's version of Derrida became convinced of the non-existence of transcendent philosophical truth, he reconstructed philosophy as an his-torically aware conversation which largely consisted of the deconstruction of past works. One way of looking at all of these transitions is that, with the abandonment of *knowledge* came the cult of *knowingness.* That is, even if there is no ultimate truth (or method for arriving at it) I can still show that I understand the intellectual rules by which you operate better than you do. I can show my superiority over you by demonstrating my awareness of what makes you tick. In the end, none of our positions is ultimately superior, but I can at least show myself to be in a superior position for now on the shift-ing sands of the game we are currently playing. Hyper-irony is the comedic instantiation of the cult of knowingness. Given the crisis of authority, there are no higher purposes to which comedy can be put, such as moral instruction, theological revelation, or showing how the world is. However, comedy can be used to attack anybody at all who thinks that he or she has any sort of handle on the answer to any major question, not to replace the object of the attack with a better way of looking at things, but merely for the pleasure of the attack, or perhaps for the sense of momentary superiority mentioned earlier. *The Simpsons* revels in the attack. It treats nearly everything as a target, every stereotypical character, every foible, and every institution. It plays games of one-upmanship with its audience members by challenging them to identify the avalanche of allusions it throws down to them. And, as "Scenes from the Class Struggle in Springfield" illustrates, it refrains from taking a position of its own.

However, to be fair to those who believe *The Simpsons* takes a stable moral stance, there are episodes that seem not to undercut themselves at all. Consider, for instance, the previously mentioned episode in which Bart helps Lisa at military school. In that episode, many things are ridiculed, but the fundamental goodness of the relationship between Bart and Lisa is left unquestioned. In another episode, when Lisa discovers that Jebediah Springfield, the legendary town founder, was a sham, she refrains from announcing her finding to the town when she notices the social value of the myth of Jebediah Springfield. And, of course, we must mention the episode in which jazzman Bleeding Gums Murphy dies, which truly deserves the Simpsonian epithet "worst episode ever." This episode combines an uncritical sentimentality with a naïve adoration of art-making, and tops everything off with some unintentionally horrible pseudo-jazz which would serve better as the theme music for a cable-access talk show. Lisa's song "Jazzman" simultaneously embodies all three of these faults, and must count as the worst moment of the worst episode ever. Given these episodes and others like them, which occur too frequently to be dismissed as blips, we are still left with the conflicting data with which we started. . . . Is *The Simpsons* hyper-ironic or not? One could argue that the hyper-ironism is a trendy fashion accessory, irony from the Gap, which does not reflect the ethos of the show. Another critically well-received program, *Buffy the Vampire Slayer* is as strongly committed to a black and white distinction between right and wrong as only teenagers can be. Its dependence on wisecracks and subversive irony is only skin deep. Underneath the surface, one will find angst-ridden teens fighting a solemn battle against evil demons who want to destroy the world. Perhaps, one could argue, beneath the surface irony of *The Simpsons* one will find a strong commitment to family values.

I would like to argue that Simpsonian hyper-ironism is not a mask for an underlying moral commitment. Here are three reasons, the first two of which are plausible but probably insufficient. First, *The Simpsons* does not consist of a single episode, but of over two hundred episodes spread out over more than ten seasons. There is good reason to think that apparent resolutions in one episode are usually undercut by others.[6] In other words, we are cued to respond ironically to one episode, given the cues provided by many other episodes. However, one could argue that this inter-episodic undercutting is itself undercut by the show's frequent use of happy family endings.

Second, as a self-consciously hip show, *The Simpsons* can be taken to be 25 aware of and to embrace what is current. Family values are hardly trendy, so there is little reason to believe that *The Simpsons* would adopt them whole-heartedly. However, this is weak confirmation at best. As a trendy show, *The Simpsons* could merely flirt with hyper-irony without fully adopting it. After all, it is hardly hyper-ironic to pledge allegiance to any flag, including the flag of hyper-ironism. Also, in addition to being a self-consciously hip show, it is also a show that must live within the constraints of prime-time American network television. One could argue that these constraints would force *The Simpsons* toward a commitment to some sort of palatable moral stance. Therefore, we cannot infer that the show is hyper-ironic from the lone premise that it is self-consciously hip.

The third and strongest reason for a pervasive hyper-ironism and against the claim that *The Simpsons* takes a stand in favor of family values is based on the perception that the comedic energy of the show dips significantly whenever moral closure or didacticism rise above the surface (as in the Bleeding Gums Murphy episodes). Unlike *Buffy the Vampire Slayer*, *The Simpsons* is fundamentally a comedy. *Buffy* can get away with dropping its ironic stance, because it is an adventure focused on the timeless battle between good and evil. *The Simpsons* has nowhere else to go when it stops being funny. Thus, it's very funny when it celebrates physical cruelty in any given *Itchy and Scratchy Show*. It's very funny when it ridicules Krusty and the marketing geniuses who broadcast *Itchy and Scratchy*. It's banal, flat, and not funny when it tries to deal seriously with the issue of censorship arising from *Itchy and Scratchy*. The lifeblood of *The Simpsons*, and its astonishing achievement, is the pace of cruelty and ridicule that it has managed to sustain for over a decade. The prevalence of quotationalism helps to sustain this pace, because the show can look beyond itself for a constant stream of targets. When the target-shooting slows down for a wholesome message or a heart-warming family moment, the program slows to an embarrassing crawl with nary a quiver from the laugh-meter.

I don't mean to argue that the makers of *The Simpsons* intended the show primarily as a theater of cruelty, although I imagine that they did. Rather, I want to argue that, as a comedy, its goal is to be funny, and we should read it in a way that maximizes its capability to be funny. When we interpret it as a wacky but earnest endorsement of family values, we read it in a way that hamstrings its comedic potential. When we read it as a show built upon the twin pillars of misanthropic humor and oh-so-clever intellectual one-upmanship, we maximize its comedic potential by paying attention to the

[6]Thanks to my colleague and co-contributor, Jason Holt, for first suggesting this to me.

features of the show that make us laugh. We also provide a vital function for the degree of quotationalism in the show, and as a bonus, we tie the show into a dominant trend of thought in the twentieth century.

But, if the heart-warming family moments don't contribute to the show's comedic potential, why are they there at all? One possible explanation is that they are simply mistakes; they were meant to be funny but they aren't. This hypothesis is implausible. Another is that the show is not exclusively a comedy, but rather a family comedy — something wholesome and not very funny that the whole family can pretend to enjoy. This is equally implausible. Alternatively, we can try to look for a function for the heart-warming moments. I think there is such a function. For the sake of argument, suppose that the engine driving *The Simpsons* is fueled by cruelty and one-upmanship. Its viewers, although appreciative of its humor, might not want to come back week after week to such a bleak message, especially if the message is centered on a family with children. *Seinfeld* never really offered any hope; its heart was as cold as ice. However, *Seinfeld* was about disaffected adults. A similarly bleak show containing children would resemble the parody of a sitcom in Oliver Stone's *Natural Born Killers*, in which Rodney Dangerfield plays an alcoholic child-abuser. Over the years, such a series would lose a grip on its viewers, to say the least. I think that the thirty seconds or so of apparent redemption in each episode of *The Simpsons* is there mainly to allow us to soldier on for twenty-one and a half minutes of maniacal cruelty at the beginning of the next episode. In other words, the heart-warming family moments help *The Simpsons* to live on as a series. The comedy does not exist for the sake of a message; the occasional illusion of a positive message exists to enable us to tolerate more comedy. Philosophers and critics have often talked of the paradox of horror and the paradox of tragedy. Why do we eagerly seek out art forms that arouse unpleasant emotions in us like pity, sadness, and fear? I think that, for at least certain forms of comedy, there is an equally important paradox of comedy. Why do we seek out art that makes us laugh at the plight of unfortunate people in a world without redemption? The laughter here seems to come at a high price. *The Simpsons*' use of heart-warming family endings should be seen as its attempt to paper over the paradox of comedy that it exemplifies so well.

I hope to have shown that quotationalism and hyper-ironism are prevalent, inter-dependent, and jointly responsible for the way in which the humor in *The Simpsons* works. The picture I have painted of *The Simpsons* is a bleak one, because I have characterized its humor as negative, a humor of cruelty and condescension — but really funny cruelty and condescension. I have left out a very important part of the picture however. *The Simpsons*, consisting of a not-as-bright version of the Freudian id for a father, a sociopathic son, a prissy daughter, and a fairly dull but innocuous mother, is a family whose members love each other. And, we love them. Despite the fact that the show strips away any semblance of value, despite the fact that week after week it offers us little comfort, it still manages to convey the raw power of the irrational (or nonrational) love of human beings for other human beings, and it makes us play along by loving these flickering bits of paint on celluloid who live in a flickering hollow world. Now *that's* comedy entertainment.

READING THE TEXT

1. Write an outline of Matheson's essay, being sure to note how Matheson establishes differences and similarities in relation to other pop culture phenomena. Compare your outline with those produced by the rest of the class.

2. Explain in your own words what Matheson means by "quotationalism" and "hyper-ironism" (para. 2).

3. What does Matheson mean by "historical appropriation" (para. 17)?

4. Matheson outlines recent intellectual trends in the study of art, science, and philosophy. What are those trends, and what relationship does Matheson find between them and a TV program such as *The Simpsons*?

5. What connection does Matheson see between the "crisis of authority" (para. 15) and hyper-irony?

READING THE SIGNS

1. Write an argumentative essay that supports, challenges, or complicates Matheson's position that "heart-warming family moments" appear in *The Simpsons* "mainly to allow us to soldier on for twenty-one and a half minutes of maniacal cruelty" (para. 28).

2. In class, brainstorm other TV shows and films that are hyper-ironic and use the list as the basis for an essay of your own in which you argue whether their popularity is a barometer of the current cultural mood in America or whether it is an aberration.

3. Watch an episode of *The Simpsons* and analyze the extent to which it supports Matheson's belief that, rather than promoting a moral stance, the show "does not promote anything" (para. 19).

4. Visit a Web site devoted to *The Simpsons*, such as www.thesimpsons.com, and study the comments fans make about the program. To what extent do your observations support Matheson's belief that "those who enjoy connecting the quotational dots will enjoy their task all the more for its exclusivity" (para. 8)?

5. Compare and contrast the humor in *The Simpsons* with that of another TV show such as *Family Guy*. Do the shows appeal to different audiences, and if so, why?

STEPHEN GARRETT

Why We Love TV's Anti-heroes

From Tony Soprano to Don Draper, Vic Mackey to Dexter, recent television programming has been filled with anti-heroes: dramatic protagonists who can be downright evil and yet elicit the sympathy of their audiences. Believing, in good semiotic style, that TV drama is "a barometer of sorts to the age that gives birth to it," Stephen Garrett accordingly asks, "What has happened to the world to provoke this wholesale reworking of hero DNA?" Comparing today's anti-heroes to the entertainment heroes of the mid-twentieth century, when evil could be clearly identified with such "baddies as the Nazis," Garrett abductively concludes that the modern anti-hero reflects a much more morally ambiguous world. Not only that, but moral certainty, Garrett suggests, has become "boring," and there is no going back to the days when Superman could unambiguously fight for truth, justice, and the American way. Audiences prefer Dexter. Stephen Garrett is a television and film producer who was recently an Oxford University News International Visiting Professor of Broadcast Media (2009–2010). This reading is an excerpt from one of his lectures delivered during that appointment.

Who are your TV heroes and heroines? Which, if you could have another life, would you want to be? George Clooney's maverick doctor in *ER*, Martin Sheen's heart-on-sleeve president in *The West Wing*, or Richard Armitage's intense and unpredictable agent in *Spooks*, produced by my company, Kudos? They are all pretty much on the side of the angels. But what about another breed of role model from TV drama series? How many of us want to be James Gandolfini's murderous racketeer in *The Sopranos*, Michael Chiklis's bent detective in *The Shield*, Glenn Close's ruthless lawyer in *Damages* or Philip Glenister's homophobic and misogynist Gene Hunt in *Life on Mars*? Can they even properly be described as heroes at all? And whatever they are, why do we love them so?

The word hero or heroic is routinely abused in the news, in sports reports and in conversation. A tabloid nonentity battles against drug addiction; a young substitute comes on and scores a winning goal in a crunch football match; someone gets me a ticket for a sell-out concert. The "H" word greets them all. In his book *The Hero With a Thousand Faces* the American mythologist Joseph Campbell defined one as someone who "towers in stature . . . a boon bringer . . . a personage of not only local but world historical moment," and much more besides. How well do the heroes of TV drama conform to this archetype?

I believe TV drama to be a barometer of sorts to the age that gives birth to it. The heroes of today are radically different from those of two or three decades ago. They have evolved to represent a radically changed world. Look no farther than that family man Tony Soprano who, in one famous episode, while taking his daughter on a tour of possible future colleges, calmly murders a former partner in crime. Or *The Shield's* Vic Mackey, who equally calmly shot a fellow cop — someone Mackey knew was gathering evidence against him — in the first episode of the series and spent the remaining five series covering it up. Or the cops in *The Wire*, whose morality is at times indistinguishable from that of the criminals they are pursuing. Or the self-interested "doctors" in *Nip/Tuck* whose livelihoods are predicated not on saving lives but on exploiting vanity. *Mad Men's* Don Draper plays fast and loose with the truth in his professional life and then goes home and lies to his loved ones. But men want to be him and women . . . well, they just want him. *Nurse Jackie*, starring Edie Falco, features a heavily medicated, dysfunctional nurse as its lead character. *Family Guy's* patriarch is the gleefully brash and offensive Peter Griffin.

So what has happened to the world to provoke this wholesale reworking of hero DNA? Until fairly recently there was in operation a morally clear universe. There were never better baddies than the Nazis, and the causes, as well as the purposes, of the Second World War were crystal clear. There was an almost archetypically monstrous enemy, we were unequivocally the good guys. But now we're fighting wars — Iraq, Afghanistan, Israel/Palestine, the War on Terror — where it's far less clear who the enemy is, indeed whether there is an enemy at all, or even that we are the good guys. In fact, since 1945, most conflicts have had at least an element of moral ambiguity built into them: Is it any wonder we have become somewhat confused, that the clarity of old when separating good from bad, right from wrong, is now at best murky — and that, as a result, our sense of what a hero might be has undergone something of a sea change? Linked to this crisis of confidence, too, faith in individual democratic processes and democratically elected leaders has been fading fast.

The twenty-first-century anti-hero is, correspondingly, taking over TV. It is 5 most evident in the changing hue of police shows. On both sides of the Atlantic (*Z Cars, Morse* here; *Columbo, Hawaii Five-O* there), the police were unequivocally heroes — morally upright, untainted by even the whiff of corruption, and it went without saying that their own position and notions of absolute justice were as one. In their world, crime never paid, the system always worked, and justice was never evaded. Nor did anyone even "take it into their own hands." It was clear who the criminals were and they got their just deserts.

Other mainstream successes tended to the medical. Hospital shows such as *Casualty* or *Holby City* here and *ER* and *Grey's Anatomy* in the United States have a black-and-white view of their protagonists: gorgeous doctors who just want to save lives. There was, too, a commensurate predictability of outcome (bar the occasional bad apple, armed with a syringe or evidence-destroying box of matches). And then came *The Sopranos*. What heroic qualities does this violent, foul-mouthed, murdering, philandering mob boss possess? Yet Tony Soprano is a profoundly twenty-first-century creature. He hit the zeitgeist. He's a businessman, an entrepreneur. And he's in therapy. He's troubled by his bad behavior, conflicted. And, weirdly, that excuses a great deal. When *The Sopranos* launched at the end of the twentieth century, that made him a hero of our time. But is Tony the end of the line or the first in an emerging order, the crime boss as increasingly legitimate entrepreneur?

There is a ruthlessness about big business that often seems not so very far removed from the psychopathy of the sort of criminal embodied by *The Sopranos*. Some of Tony's business ventures are quintessentially twenty-first century. Waste management, his front, may have something of the Victorian about it, but when he sets up new income streams through property deals or fake Internet companies he is not so much the war lord of old as the innovative and commercially savvy businessman of the here and now. The casting of Michael Chiklis as Vic Mackey was every bit as inspired as that of James Gandolfini for Tony Soprano. Just as audiences were able to connect with Tony because he was a family guy, so audiences connected with Vic because he was demonstrably good at his job, a great cop. Our empathy for him is every bit as troubling as our empathy for Tony. Vic did, after all, murder a colleague. For the audience it sets up a tension for the rest of the series. If he can do that is there anything he isn't capable of? As in all good drama, this moment triggers a journey for Vic.

The Wire's anti-hero, the cop McNulty, and its anti-villain, the murderer D'Angelo both, in the words of the author Anthony Walton, "rage in various ways against the strictures of the hierarchies in which they find themselves, but both lack any real power to effect change."

"Both," he continues, "are ultimately horrified by the changes they do effect, the trail of wreckage and bodies in their wake." It is in this way that they win our sympathy, even our empathy. These are not classic good guy/bad guy divisions. The moral compass is spinning on its axis. Both *24* and *House* have at their core men behaving badly. Jack Bauer of *24* is as much torturer as tortured, in body and soul. Yet we excuse him. And Hugh Laurie's Gregory House, the misanthropic drug addict at the heart of the show, should be unforgiveable, but instead is universally adored and admired.

A recent article in *Newsweek* bore the headline: "Too Much of a Bad Thing." [10] It argued that because it appears that no one on TV can be truly good or evil anymore, we're suffering from what it called "an anti-hero overload." It's not just drama but comedy, too, from *The Office* to *Curb Your Enthusiasm*. "It's starting to seem as if bad guys are the only good guys," *Newsweek* continued.

In Britain there is a complex mix of heroes or anti-heroes, especially in the shows that Kudos has produced. At the gentler end there are the Robin

Hood-like con-men from *Hustle*. We love them because they steal from people worse than themselves, though it's hard to dispute the fact that they are bad people who thieve for a living. If caught they'd go down for a very long time indeed. Then there's Gene Hunt, adored by the viewing public, in spite of being a racist, misogynistic bigot who is, well, unequivocally bent. And finally, our *Spooks*, MI5 agents who in the name of some higher moral calling of their own imagining have cheerfully engaged in torture, extraordinary rendition, and treason. Yet, episode in, episode out, they remain heroes for their huge audiences.

There's no going back. I believe the classic heroes of old are no longer fit for purpose and never will be again. As *The Wire*'s creator David Simon wrote recently: "We are bored with good and evil. We renounce the theme. With the exception of saints and sociopaths, few in this world are anything but a confused and corrupted combination of personal motivations, most of them selfish, some of them hilarious."

We see this every day in our politicians, our business leaders, our sports stars, and our tabloid darlings. There are no more heroes, only — at best — anti-heroes. That is the way of the world.

READING THE TEXT

1. Summarize in your own words the traditional definition of "hero" that Garrett assumes.
2. What are the reasons that the TV protagonists whom Garrett mentions do not seem heroic in his view?
3. What does Garrett mean by the term "anti-hero"?
4. What is Garrett's explanation for the proliferation of anti-heroes on television?

READING THE SIGNS

1. In class, discuss Garrett's contention that a main cause of the redefinition of TV heroism is today's sense of "moral ambiguity" in real-life social and political conflicts. Use the class discussion as a springboard for your own essay in which you assess Garrett's contention, arguing for your own explanations if they diverge from the author's.
2. Garrett claims that earlier police shows such as *Columbo* and *Hawaii Five-O* portrayed traditional heroes whose characters are at odds with today's representation of police. Watch an episode of one of these programs, and compare it with an episode of a recent cop show such as *The Shield* or *The Wire*. Analyze the heroic status of the protagonists in each, and use your observations to support, refute, or complicate Garrett's assumption that there has been "a wholesale reworking of hero DNA" (para. 4).
3. **CONNECTING TEXTS** Compare and contrast James Harold's explanation for the appeal of *The Sopranos* ("A Moral Never-Never Land: Identifying with Tony Soprano," p. 296) with Garrett's. Which do you find more convincing, and why?

4. **CONNECTING TEXTS** Read or reread Robert B. Ray's "The Thematic Paradigm" (p. 377), focusing on his definitions of "hero" and "outlaw hero." Write an essay in which you assess the relationship between Ray's notion of heroes and Garrett's. To what extent do you think that Garrett is simply replicating Ray's notion, with different terms? Or do you think that Garrett has identified a new category of hero that has emerged since Ray published his essay in 1985?

5. Write an essay demonstrating, disputing, or complicating *Newsweek*'s claim that "It's starting to seem as if bad guys are the only good guys" (qtd. in para. 10). Be sure to base your argument on your analysis of specific television programs.

DECONSTRUCTING HEROES

NATASHA SIMONS
Mad Men *and the Paradox of the Past*

Mad Men, a dramatic re-creation of early 1960s America, when the country was poised upon the brink of a cultural revolution but had not quite tipped over yet, is a deeply ambiguous television series. Does it represent an exposé of the bad old days of rampant sexual harassment in the workplace and casual racism, when everyone smoked too much and men called all the shots? Or does the show's appeal lie in nostalgia for a bygone era on the other side of a vast cultural divide? As Natasha Simons observes in this article that originally appeared in the *National Review*, it depends upon who is viewing it. Thus, as Simons notes, "Conservatives and liberals just can't help but see *Mad Men* differently: the former with apprehension, the latter with anticipation." That is, "'For unreflective liberals, *Mad Men* is only temporarily tragic. It has a happy ending. Deliverance from all this sexism and repression and cigarette smoke draws nigh'"; while for conservatives, the show is simply a cheap shot. Even the show's creator, Matthew Weiner seems divided, Simons claims. Basically a liberal, Weiner likes his main character, Don Draper, too much to make it clear just which side he's on. Such is the stuff of which pop culture paradoxes are made. Natasha Simons is assistant to the editor of the *National Review*.

Mad Men is a show about an unbending generation on the cusp of dissolution; Matthew Weiner, the show's head writer, has often said that the majority of America in the early '60s was still, by and large, living in the domestic '50s. Weiner, a baby boomer, has a conflicted relationship with this time period. Because it is the generation of his parents, he wants to explore it and pore over it; because it's the generation that, through Weiner's specific political prism, reflects a hypocritical façade, he'd like it to form a gangway for the liberation to come. This ambivalence creates a divide in the audience's responses to the show, which tend to fall along political lines.

Conservatives and liberals just can't help but see *Mad Men* differently: the former with apprehension, the latter with anticipation. The show inspires a certain self-satisfaction in the type of viewers who would observe each instance of sexism, racism, and general prejudice as just more foundation for an interpretation many critics have arrived at: "The show explains why the '60s had to happen." Rod Dreher says, "For unreflective liberals, *Mad Men* is only temporarily tragic. It has a happy ending. Deliverance from all this sexism and repression and cigarette smoke draws nigh."

The show, and in particular, the third season, is shot through with references to that impending deliverance. Don Draper says, "New York City is decaying." Paul Kinsey says, "This city has no memory." The World's Fair in New York, given passing lip service on the show, turned out to be a bust, the old-money business class's last hurrah at corralling an innocent kind of fun already beset by the counterculture. Its slogan? "Man in a Shrinking Globe in an Expanding Universe." That's not only a pointed assessment of modern fear, but a wonderful précis of the theme of *Mad Men*. And it's difficult to ignore the ambitious allusions to the prototypical decayed society of ancient Rome, which made a few cameos in the past season. Don's daughter, Sally, reads to her grandfather the beginning of a passage from *The History of the Decline and Fall of the Roman Empire:* "The Praetorian bands, whose licentious fury was the first symptom and cause of the decline of the Roman empire . . ."

The Praetorian guards, of course, were a specially chosen group of soldiers who abused their imperial power over Rome. *Mad Men* depicts a group of men who have great influence over what they consider their particular citizenry — consumers — and their particular emperor — consumerism. By cataloging this group's "licentious" excesses (imbibing during the workday, hiring prostitutes on the company dime, etc.), general indifference to the burgeoning youth counterculture (think: Bertram Cooper's horror at Kennedy's lack of hat), and miring themselves in the past (Roger Sterling's unfortunate minstrel show in "My Old Kentucky Home"), Weiner, consciously or unconsciously, is demonstrating the ways in which America's Old Guard is leading the '50s generation to its end by stubbornly refusing to go forward. Weiner has remarked of that generation of people, "[They were saying,] 'We don't want to be that way. We'd rather fail.'"

Clearly, Don Draper is the starring figure of this collapse. He is the Man in 5 the Grey Flannel Suit, an Ayn Rand–ian allegory of a stoic firmly in the past. He is the prototype '50s representative male, confident in his role without, and in turmoil within. Don is member of a dying breed who wants to play by the old business rules, and he can barely conceive of the ways in which advertising is inexorably moving (unlike, say, fellow ad man Pete Campbell). He is a relic waiting to be phased out.

But Weiner's flaw is that he loves Don Draper too much to make him that relic, as intended — he is clearly not going to leave Don in the past, if season-four promotional posters are any indication. So the show attempts to imbue him with the sympathy of the audience, despite his stodgy '50s limits — which leads to all sorts of annoying contradictions. Don looks down on Roger for the blackface, yet behaves dismissively toward his own black servant; Don assaults his mistress in a bathroom and demands women not speak to him "like that," despite facilitating his former secretary Peggy's surge upward through the ranks; Don lectures his wife about being a good parent even as he picks up strangers in his car and recklessly partakes of some unidentified drugs. These frustrating contradictions can't simply be chalked up to mere nuance of human character, either; it seems clear that Weiner started out by using Don as an emblem of the '50s, defining him in opposition to the '60s to come.

Which brings us again to the main political schism for viewers of this show: Conservatives and liberals cannot see the inevitability of the '60s the same way. The hedonism, the "licentious fury" set up in these soldiers of such terrible, soul-destroying consumerism, is about to give way to the tortured emoting of Frank O'Hara and reggae-inspired coffee commercials, both of which have been featured in the past few seasons. But conservatives understand that the hedonism is only just beginning. The Me Generation is about to swing into full effect, after which we lose both the unrepentant ambition and charming earnestness of the American Dream — a phrase never to be uttered without a small smirk again.

True, the keeping-up-with-the-Joneses mentality was unsustainable, simply because of the practical problem of the single income that families were expected to fulfill the traditional iteration of the American Dream on. And, often, the unwavering values of the '50s resulted in an outwardly homogenous appearance that left many marginalized parties gasping for air. But the '60s, with their relentless concentration on the self and self-expression, shaped individualistic tendencies in consumers that brought them out of the follow-the-leader consumption of the '50s into a gluttonous consumption merely for selfish purposes. So which is better? And is that really the redemption the show hopes to establish, and what liberal viewers gaze backward and clutch the edges of their seats in anticipation of?

Weiner's chosen narrative posits that our present is much better than the '50s zeitgeist he portrays, but the essential paradox is that he portrays it with so much love and tenderness that it is sometimes impossible to pull out the theme of generational decay. The audience is caught between a mislaid nostalgia for the often sexist and bigoted environment and an equally mislaid moral desire to see it all disappear. As Benjamin Schwarz pointed out in the *Atlantic*, the show invites us to "indulge in a most unlovely — because wholly unearned — smugness."

Mad Men has lost its way a bit; Weiner, wrapped up in adoring his main   10 character and the intricacies of a period he wants to evaporate, has fallen into a quicksand trap, not wanting to move on, despite his obvious political loyalties to the '60s generation. Critics remarked that the pace of *Mad Men* has recently slowed to a ponderous crawl, perhaps to allow Weiner time to languish a while. But he is definitely plunging forward now, having commented in an interview that "It's got to be something different. . . . Life is change." Here's hoping that the fourth season marks that change with the same ambivalence we've seen prior, which would prove Weiner is interested in portraying history with a fair hand. Falling into a rote '60s nostalgia would be wholly unwelcome for a show that has come to be known for its nuance.

READING THE TEXT

1. What significance for *Mad Men* does Simons see in scriptwriter Matthew Weiner's status as a baby boomer?

2. Summarize in your own words the ways in which conservatives and liberals interpret *Mad Men*, according to Simons.

3. What does Simons mean when she says that *Mad Men* character Don Draper "is the Man in the Grey Flannel Suit" (para. 5).

4. In class, discuss whether Simons is presenting an objective analysis of *Mad Men*, as you would want to do in an academic essay, or whether she betrays a bias favoring or opposing the program. Use the discussion of objectivity as a guide when you write your own essay on the program.

READING THE SIGNS

1. Simons claims that conservatives and liberals interpret *Mad Men* in diametrically opposed ways. Interview at least ten viewers of the program, preferably half who identify as conservative and half who identify as liberal, asking them about their reading of and reaction to it. Use your results to assess the validity of Simons's claim.

2. Write an essay in which you support, refute, or modify Simons's claim that *Mad Men*'s "audience is caught between a mislaid nostalgia for the often sexist and bigoted environment and an equally mislaid moral desire to see it all disappear" (para. 9).

3. Read Sloan Wilson's novel *The Man in the Grey Flannel Suit* (1955). To what extent does *Mad Men* reflect the discontented business culture depicted in that novel, as Simons asserts? Alternately, read Vance Packard's *The Hidden Persuaders* (1957). Do you find that book to reflect the advertising industry's practices as they are depicted in *Mad Men*?

4. **CONNECTING TEXTS** Analyze a current episode of *Mad Men* semiotically, focusing on the depiction of nonwhite characters. To what extent do you find those depictions to be realistic or stereotypical? To develop your analysis, consult Michael Omi's "In Living Color: Race and American Culture" (p. 625).

5. **CONNECTING TEXTS** Many critics of *Mad Men* focus on the show's depiction of female characters. Drawing on Aaron Devor's "Gender Role Behaviors and Attitudes" (p. 672), write an essay in which you analyze the prevailing mythology of gender roles as the program presents them.

RITA KOGANZON

All Camped Out: How "Glee" Became a Preachy After-School Special

Everybody in *Glee* seems to be messed up: "They are all damaged people who have made Bad Life Decisions," or so Rita Koganzon observes in this critique of Fox's surprise hit. But that isn't the problem; the problem, Koganzon argues, is that *Glee* is essentially schizophrenic. On the one hand, "For adults, *Glee* is a classic campy satire (set to music) about manipulative women who use the strictures of monogamous relationships, lies, sex, and babies to keep men under their thumbs," but on the other, "it intends a different, more sincere message for its younger viewers, and it can't quite keep the two aims distinct." This sort of conflict is not at all uncommon in American entertainment, making a sensitivity to contradiction an essential element in semiotic interpretations. Koganzon is an associate editor of *Doublethink Online*, where this article first appeared.

Glee, Fox's hot new musical comedy, is set in a small town in western Ohio, and that is the source of everyone's woes. Viewers should, of course, know better than to ask what specifically is wrong with small towns in western Ohio. What *isn't* wrong with them? They're bleak, boring, intolerant dead-end streets. The inhabitants of such places love football, marry their high school sweethearts, carry their teenage pregnancies to term, and while away their adult lives as assistant managers at "Sheets 'N Things," or, worse yet, as high school Spanish teachers. The only thing for thinking people to look forward to in these prisons is finally escaping them for someplace where their talents will finally be appreciated and Glenn Beck won't be blaring from the living room. And such thinking people, sometimes embodied as TV critics, have found in *Glee*'s cloying combination of underdog elitism and progressive cynicism a ballad that speaks right to their hearts.

These are the tired and tiresome tropes on which *Glee* is built, and the show reveals its elitism early on. In the pilot episode, Finn (Cory Monteith), the popular captain of the football team with a secret singing talent, joins the Glee Club, much to the derision of his teammates. When they demand that he stop hanging out with the club's loser members, he retorts, "We're all losers! Everyone in this school. Everyone in this town. Out of all the kids who graduate, maybe half will go to college, and maybe two will leave the state to do it." Going out of state for college — that is the kind of success that *Glee* affirms. One might recall that Ohio is home to at least a dozen respectable colleges, but that would be completely beside the point. College here is not about education — it's about status. The narrow, dull, cowardly person — the "loser" — stays home for school, but the person who rejects parochial attachments and renounces the small-mindedness of his neighbors in order to pursue prestige far and wide, this is the kind of person who is an example to us all.

The only problem with this view is that small-town Ohio seems, despite the repeated insistence of *Glee*'s characters, like a pretty exciting place. The school's arts program is incredible even by wealthy suburban standards; it can apparently afford a full band and multiple costume changes for each of the club's performances; a short-lived male a capella group becomes an improbable hit; and it takes hardly any convincing to get that popular archetype of hypermasculinity, the football team, to recruit a flamboyantly gay kicker and perform a dance to "Single Ladies" on the field — to the wild applause of the entire town.

Glee is not the only show that has found itself trapped between the conflicting imperatives of deriding the narrowness of small towns, and creating an interesting plot within its self-imposed constraints. *Buffy the Vampire*

Slayer also featured a miraculously expanding small town whose only landmark was a single all-ages club in the show's first season, but was discovered to be home to an entire University of California campus by its fourth.

But *Buffy* took a different view of its setting — its stifling narrowness was   5
only a matter of perception. The show's antsy adolescent cast felt it more acutely at the beginning, but the real culprit was their own teenage ennui and the oppressiveness of high school social life, which would have pained them in equal measure had they grown up in nearby Los Angeles. In reality, Sunnydale was very nearly the center of the world, located as it was over the Hellmouth, out of which regularly emerged demons who threatened apocalypse, and the town seemed to grow as the characters discovered their place in it. Everyone in *Buffy* thought they wanted nothing more than to get out of Sunnydale, but all of them ended up staying out of a sense of obligation and attachment (and, obviously, the exigencies of plot continuity).

Such charity toward rootedness is hardly to be found in *Glee*, at least so far. Western Ohio is not only suffocating to the teenage members of the Glee Club, but also to the adults around them, who are, except for their age, almost indistinguishable from the students. They are all damaged people who have made Bad Life Decisions — the club's coach Will Schuester (Matthew Morrison) impetuously married his high school sweetheart before realizing she's a manipulative harpy (Jessalyn Gilsig); the OCD guidance counselor (Jayma Mays) agrees to marry the fungus-infested football coach in an effort to forget her crush on the married Mr. Schuester; the cheerleading coach (Jane Lynch) uses her fiendishness to mask the pain of romantic rejection. For adults, this is a satire on soap opera, but what is soap opera for adults is didactic after-school special for its younger audience. (The show's popularity among kids is attested by its three nominations this year for the Teen Choice Awards.)

Indeed, one episode features the high school re-enrollment of a washed-up alcoholic former Glee Club star (Kristin Chenoweth) who behaves even more childishly than the students, plying them with alcohol and pornography. The premise is uncannily reminiscent of Amy Sedaris's old late-night show, *Strangers with Candy*, which was straightforwardly and unapologetically camp. *Glee* is in large part camp as well, which is what underwrites its mockery of "small town values," its stylized, overdrawn characters (the cheerleaders and athletes spend so much time in their uniforms that they become their uniforms, a throwback to MTV's excellent '90s caricature of adolescence, *Daria*), and its over-the-top flamboyance. But it is a confused brand of camp, trying at once to send sincere messages to kids and to wink at adults.

The show's main contradictions grow out of the pregnancy of the head cheerleader, Quinn (Dianna Agron), girlfriend of — you guessed it — the quarterback of the football team, Finn. The catch is that this is Small Town America, so the school's most popular couple is also its biggest proponent of chastity, and heads up the most popular club — the celibacy club. In the

second episode, we get a glimpse of a club meeting in which the whole ruse is exposed as a female conspiracy to sexually manipulate and shame the males — "It's all about the teasing, not about the pleasing" is the girls' motto.

It's all good campy fun until Rachel (Lea Michele), the self-important Glee Club diva and speechifying representative of Real Adolescence, turns to the celibates and offers this bizarrely placed PSA: "Did you know that most studies have demonstrated that celibacy doesn't work in high school? Our hormones are driving us too crazy to abstain. . . . The only way to deal with teen sexuality is to be prepared!" Ostensibly this is aimed at the youthful audience, who are presumed to have missed the writers' comic wink about the real motives behind abstinence education because they still need to be told the facts of life. But the facts of life according to the writers are preposterous—sex is likened to an unprovoked natural disaster, say, an asteroid falling straight out of the sky. If the ideal of television sophistication is to tell two different stories in the same show — the sincere, PC kids' tale of peer pressure and puberty, and the devilish adult mockery of such high school tropes — *Glee* manages only to find the untenable middle ground between the two — the sincere mockery of high school loserdom. And so we learn that the purpose of contraception is to thwart the evil schemes of women, who are always looking to impute paternity to the nearest patsy.

Since *Glee* wants to show up abstinence, Quinn must fall victim to that 10
ubiquitous scourge of '80s after-school specials — the unplanned teen pregnancy. She tells Finn he's the father although they've never had "complete
sex" because she prefers him to the real father, Finn's good-for-nothing best
friend and teammate, Puck (Mark Salling). The last stand of Small Town Values comes when Quinn refuses to consider an abortion, a decision we're supposed to believe is not only disadvantageous, but positively immoral. "I don't
agree with the choice you're making, but you're gonna need Glee. You have
seven months of your youth left; you should enjoy it," Rachel tells her.

But here camp gets in over its head. Susan Sontag, in her classic essay
on the genre, wrote that, "It goes without saying that the Camp sensibility
is disengaged, depoliticized — or at least apolitical." Camp can fuse the wife-
swapping soap opera and preachy after-school special into a playful stylized
musical, but it can't also presume to teach anything about love or childbear-
ing, or even sex ed. It can't skewer touchy issues like disability (the cheerleading coach counts up the Glee Club's members as "five and a half — one's a
cripple") and then subject its audience to straight-faced treacle in a Very Special Episode informing us that disabled people have feelings too.

For adults, *Glee* is a classic campy satire (set to music) about manipulative women who use the strictures of monogamous relationships, lies, sex,
and babies to keep men under their thumbs. But it intends a different, more
sincere message for its younger viewers, and it can't quite keep the two aims
distinct. The result is condescension and muddle. The *New York Post*'s Robert George has criticized the show's portrayal of women, claiming it sends
"the message that the devious gender will use every trick to lure and trap its
mate." George is wrong to think the show is serious, but he's hardly to blame
for confusing the sincere and satirical, the moralizing and the cynical.

Perhaps the most emblematic moment of *Glee*'s identity confusion came
after the touchy-feely disability episode aired, when the show's co-creator
Ryan Murphy told the *Los Angeles Times* that, "This episode is the turning
point for the show . . . Writing this made me feel the responsibility of showing the truth of the pain that outcasts go through . . . If anything else, I hope
kids who are that age can see that episode and maybe realize how hard it is
for some people that they make fun of or tease." And, with that, Wednesday
evenings on Fox have become home to reruns of *The Facts of Life* with a few
snappy musical numbers.

READING THE TEXT

1. Koganzon begins her selection by echoing what she considers to be common
   clichés about Ohio propagated by *Glee*. How does her initial paragraph affect
   your response to the rest of her article? Did you initially think she was voicing
   her own beliefs?

2. Summarize in your own words the reasons Koganzon feels that *Glee* is
   "elitist."

3. How does *Buffy the Vampire Slayer* differ from *Glee* in its depiction of small-town life, in Koganzon's view?

4. How do adults and teens "read" *Glee* differently, according to Koganzon?

5. Define in your own words what Koganzon means by "camp."

READING THE SIGNS

1. Watch an episode of *Glee*, and write an essay in which you support, refute, or complicate Koganzon's claim that the program is "trying at once to send sincere messages to kids and to wink at adults" (para. 7). To develop your evidence, you might interview adult and teens fans of the show to learn their take on it.

2. **CONNECTING TEXTS**   Adopt the perspective of Andy Medhurst ("Batman, Deviance, and Camp," below), and critique Koganzon's claim that *Glee* is imbued with camp humor, albeit "a confused brand of camp" (para. 7).

3. **CONNECTING TEXTS**   Read or reread David Denby's "High-School Confidential: Notes on Teen Movies" (p. 424). Write an essay analyzing the extent to which *Glee* replicates the stereotypical teen roles that Denby describes as common in cinema or whether it rings changes on those roles. Be sure to base your argument on a detailed analysis of at least one episode of *Glee*.

4. Koganzon mentions that *Glee* has been criticized for its depiction of female characters as "devious" (para. 12). In an essay, write your own analysis of the gender roles presented in the program, focusing on one or two particular episodes.

5. Compare and contrast *Glee* with one of the several Disney *High School Musical* films. Do the films exhibit the same use of campy satire that the TV program does? What role, if any, does music play in the two? If you find significant differences, try to explain them, keeping in mind the public image that the Disney company tries to maintain.

ANDY MEDHURST

Batman, Deviance, and Camp

Have you ever wondered what happened to Robin in the recent Batman movies? In this analysis of the history of Batman, excerpted from *The Many Lives of the Batman* (1991), Andy Medhurst explains why Robin had to disappear. Arguing that Batman has been "re-heterosexualized" in the wake of the insinuatingly homoerotic TV series of the 1960s, Medhurst indicts the homophobia of Batfans whose "Bat-Platonic Ideal of how Batman should really be" holds no place for the "camped crusader." Medhurst teaches media studies, popular culture, and lesbian and gay studies at the University of Sussex, England. He is the author of *A National Joke: Popular Comedy and English Cultural Identities* (2004, 2007). He has also coedited, with Sally Munt, *Lesbian and Gay Studies: A Critical Introduction* (1997), and, with Joanne Lacey, *The Representation Reader* (2004).

Only someone ignorant of the fundamentals of psychiatry and of the psychopathology of sex can fail to realize a subtle atmosphere of homoeroticism which pervades the adventure of the mature "Batman" and his young friend "Robin."

— Fredric Wertham[1]

It's embarrassing to be solemn and treatise-like about Camp. One runs the risk of having, oneself, produced a very inferior piece of Camp.

— Susan Sontag[2]

I'm not sure how qualified I am to write this essay. Batman hasn't been particularly important in my life since I was seven years old. Back then he was crucial, paramount, unmissable as I sat twice weekly to watch the latest episode on TV. Pure pleasure, except for the annoying fact that my parents didn't seem to appreciate the thrills on offer. Worse than that, they actually laughed. How could anyone laugh when the Dynamic Duo were about to be turned into Frostie Freezies (pineapple for the Caped Crusader, lime for his chum) by the evil Mr. Freeze?

Batman and I drifted apart after those early days. Every now and then I'd see a repeated episode and I soon began to understand and share that once infuriating parental hilarity, but this aside I hardly thought about the man in the cape at all. I knew about the subculture of comic freaks, and the new and alarmingly pretentious phrase "graphic novel" made itself known to me, but I still regarded (with the confidence of distant ignorance) such texts as violent, macho, adolescent and, well, silly.

That's when the warning bells rang. The word "silly" reeks of the complacent condescension that has at various times been bestowed on all the cultural forms that matter most to me (Hollywood musicals, British melodramas, pop music, soap operas), so what right had I to apply it to someone else's part of the popular cultural playground? I had to rethink my disdain, and 1989 has been a very good year in which to do so, because in terms of popular culture 1989 has been the Year of the Bat.

This essay, then, is not written by a devotee of Batman, someone steeped in every last twist of the mythology. I come to these texts as an interested

[1] Fredric Wertham, *Seduction of the Innocent* (London: Museum Press, 1955), p. 190.
[2] Susan Sontag, "Notes on Camp," in *A Susan Sontag Reader* (Harmondsworth: Penguin Books), p. 106.

outsider, armed with a particular perspective. That perspective is homosexuality, and what I want to try and do here is to offer a gay reading of the whole Bat-business. It has no pretension to definitiveness, I don't presume to speak for all gay people everywhere. I'm male, white, British, thirty years old (at the time of writing) and all of those factors need to be taken into account. Nonetheless, I'd argue that Batman is especially interesting to gay audiences for three reasons.

Firstly, he was one of the first fictional characters to be attacked on the 5 grounds of presumed homosexuality, by Fredric Wertham in his book *Seduction of the Innocent*. Secondly, the 1960s TV series was and remains a touchstone of camp (a banal attempt to define the meaning of camp might well start with "like the sixties' *Batman* series"). Thirdly, as a recurring hero figure for the last fifty years, Batman merits analysis as a notably successful construction of masculinity.

Nightmare on Psychiatry Street: Freddy's Obsession

Seduction of the Innocent is an extraordinary book. It is a gripping, flamboyant melodrama masquerading as social psychology. Fredric Wertham is, like Senator McCarthy,[3] like Batman, a crusader, a man with a mission, an evangelist. He wants to save the youth of America from its own worst impulses, from its id, from comic books. His attack on comic books is founded on an astonishingly crude stimulus-and-response model of reading, in which the child (the child, for Wertham, seems an unusually innocent, blank slate waiting to be written on) reads, absorbs, and feels compelled to copy, if only in fantasy terms, the content of the comics. It is a model, in other words, which takes for granted extreme audience passivity.

This is not the place to go into a detailed refutation of Wertham's work, besides which such a refutation has already been done in Martin Barker's excellent *A Haunt of Fears*.[4] The central point of audience passivity needs stressing, however, because it is crucial to the celebrated passage where Wertham points his shrill, witch-hunting finger at the Dynamic Duo and cries "queer."

Such language is not present on the page, of course, but in some ways *Seduction of the Innocent* (a film title crying out for either D. W. Griffith or Cecil B. DeMille) would be easier to stomach if it were. Instead, Wertham writes with anguished concern about the potential harm that Batman might do to vulnerable children, innocents who might be turned into deviants. He employs

---

[3]**Senator McCarthy** United States Senator Joseph R. McCarthy (1908–1957), who in the 1950s hunted and persecuted suspected Communists and Communist sympathizers.–Eds.

[4]Martin Barker, *A Haunt of Fears* (London: Pluto Press, 1984).

what was then conventional psychiatric wisdom about the idea of homosexuality as a "phase":

> Many pre-adolescent boys pass through a phase of disdain for girls. Some comic books tend to fix that attitude and instill the idea that girls are only good for being banged around or used as decoys. A homoerotic attitude is also suggested by the presentation of masculine, bad, witch-like or violent women. In such comics women are depicted in a definitely anti-erotic light, while the young male heroes have pronounced erotic overtones. The muscular male supertype, whose primary sex characteristics are usually well emphasized, is in the setting of certain stories the object of homoerotic sexual curiosity and stimulation.[5]

The implications of this are breathtaking. Homosexuality, for Wertham, is synonymous with misogyny. Men love other men because they hate women. The sight of women being "banged around" is liable to appeal to repressed homoerotic desires (this, I think, would be news to the thousands of women who are systematically physically abused by heterosexual men). Women who do not conform to existing stereotypes of femininity are another incitement to homosexuality.

Having mapped out his terms of reference, Wertham goes on to peel the lid from Wayne Manor: 10

> Sometimes Batman ends up in bed injured and young Robin is shown sitting next to him. At home they lead an idyllic life. They are Bruce Wayne and "Dick" Grayson. Bruce Wayne is described as a "socialite" and the official relationship is that Dick is Bruce's ward. They live in sumptuous quarters, with beautiful flowers in large vases, and have a butler, Alfred. Batman is sometimes shown in a dressing gown. . . . It is like a wish dream of two homosexuals living together. Sometimes they are shown on a couch, Bruce reclining and Dick sitting next to him, jacket off, collar open, and his hand on his friend's arm.[6]

So, Wertham's assumptions of homosexuality are fabricated out of his interpretation of certain visual signs. To avoid being thought queer by Wertham, Bruce and Dick should have done the following: Never show concern if the other is hurt, live in a shack, only have ugly flowers in small vases, call the butler "Chip" or "Joe" if you have to have one at all, never share a couch, keep your collar buttoned up, keep your jacket on, and never, ever wear a dressing gown. After all, didn't Noël Coward[7] wear a dressing gown?

---

[5]Wertham, p. 188.
[6]Wertham, p. 190.
[7]**Noël Coward** (1899–1973) British playwright, actor, and composer known for witty, sophisticated comedies.–EDS.

Wertham is easy to mock, but the identification of homosexuals through dress codes has a long history.[8] Moreover, such codes originate as semiotic systems adopted by gay people themselves, as a way of signalling the otherwise invisible fact of sexual preference. There is a difference, though, between sporting the secret symbols of a subculture if you form part of that subculture and the elephantine spot-the-homo routine that Wertham performs.

Bat-fans have always responded angrily to Wertham's accusation. One calls it "one of the most incredible charges . . . unfounded rumours . . . sly sneers"[9] and the general response has been to reassert the masculinity of the two heroes, mixed with a little indignation: "If they had been actual men they could have won a libel suit."[10] This seems to me not only to miss the point, but also to *reinforce* Wertham's homophobia—it is only possible to win a libel suit over an "accusation" of homosexuality in a culture where homosexuality is deemed categorically inferior to heterosexuality.

Thus the rush to "protect" Batman and Robin from Wertham is simply the other side to the coin of his bigotry. It may reject Wertham, cast him in the role of dirty-minded old man, but its view of homosexuality is identical. Mark Cotta Vaz thus describes the imputed homosexual relationship as "licentious" while claiming that in fact Bruce Wayne "regularly squired the most beautiful women in Gotham City and presumably had a healthy sex life."[11] Licentious versus healthy—Dr. Wertham himself could not have bettered this homophobic opposition.

Despite the passions aroused on both sides (or rather the two facets of the same side), there is something comic at the heart of this dispute. It is, simply, that Bruce and Dick are *not* real people but fictional constructions, and hence to squabble over their "real" sex life is to take things a little too far. What is at stake here is the question of reading, of what readers do with the raw material that they are given. Readers are at liberty to construct whatever fantasy lives they like with the characters of the fiction they read (within the limits of generic and narrative credibility, that is). This returns us to the unfortunate patients of Dr. Wertham:

> One young homosexual during psychotherapy brought us a copy of *Detective* comic, with a Batman story. He pointed out a picture of "The Home of Bruce and Dick," a house beautifully landscaped, warmly lighted and showing the devoted pair side by side, looking out a picture window. When he was eight this boy had realized from fantasies about

---

[8]See, for example, the newspaper stories on "how to spot" homosexuals printed in Britain in the fifties and sixties, and discussed in Jeffrey Weeks, *Coming Out: Homosexual Politics in Britain* (London: Quartet, 1979).

[9]Phrases taken from Chapters 5 and 6 of Mark Cotta Vaz, *Tales of the Dark Knight: Batman's First Fifty Years* (London: Futura, 1989).

[10]Les Daniels, *Comix: A History of Comic Books in America* (New York: Bonanza Books, 1971), p. 87.

[11]Cotta Vaz, pp. 47 and 53.

comic book pictures that he was aroused by men. At the age of ten or eleven, "I found my liking, my sexual desires, in comic books. I think I put myself in the position of Robin. I did want to have relations with Batman . . . I remember the first time I came across the page mentioning the 'secret batcave.' The thought of Batman and Robin living together and possibly having sex relations came to my mind. . . ."[12]

Wertham quotes this to shock us, to impel us to tear the pages of *Detective* away before little Tommy grows up and moves to Greenwich Village, but reading it as a gay man today I find it rather moving and also highly recognizable.

What this anonymous gay man did was to practice that form of bricolage[13] which Richard Dyer has identified as a characteristic reading strategy of gay audiences.[14] Denied even the remotest possibility of supportive images of homosexuality within the dominant heterosexual culture, gay people have had to fashion what we could out of the imageries of dominance, to snatch illicit meanings from the fabric of normality, to undertake a corrupt decoding for the purposes of satisfying marginalized desires.[15] This may not be as necessary as it once was, given the greater visibility of gay representations, but it is still an important practice. Wertham's patient evokes in me an admiration, that in a period of American history even more homophobic than most, there he was, raiding the citadels of masculinity, weaving fantasies of oppositional desire. What effect the dread Wertham had on him is hard to predict, but I profoundly hope that he wasn't "cured."

It wasn't only Batman who was subjected to Dr. Doom's bizarre ideas about human sexuality. Hence:

> The homosexual connotation of the Wonder Woman type of story is psychologically unmistakable. . . . For boys, Wonder Woman is a frightening image. For girls she is a morbid ideal. Where Batman is anti-feminine, the attractive Wonder Woman and her counterparts are definitely anti-masculine. Wonder Woman has her own female following. . . . Her followers are the "Holiday girls," i.e. the holiday girls, the gay party girls, the gay girls.[16]

Just how much elision can be covered with one "i.e."? Wertham's view of homosexuality is not, at least, inconsistent. Strong, admirable women will turn little girls into dykes — such a heroine can only be seen as a "morbid ideal."

---

[12]Wertham, p. 192

[13]**bricolage** A new object created by reassembling bits and pieces of other objects; here, gay-identified readings produced from classic texts.–EDS.

[14]Richard Dyer, ed., *Gays and Film*, 2nd edition (New York: Zoetrope, 1984), p. 1.

[15]See Richard Dyer, "Judy Garland and Gay Men," in Dyer, *Heavenly Bodies* (London: BFI, 1987), and Claire Whitaker, "Hollywood Transformed: Interviews with Lesbian Viewers," in Peter Steven, ed., *Jump Cut: Hollywood, Politics and Counter-Cinema* (Toronto: Between the Lines, 1985).

[16]Wertham, pp. 192–93.

Crazed as Wertham's ideas were, their effectiveness is not in doubt. The mid-fifties saw a moral panic about the assumed dangers of comic books. In the United States companies were driven out of business, careers wrecked, and the Comics Code introduced. This had distinct shades of the Hays Code[17] that had been brought in to clamp down on Hollywood in the 1930s, and under its jurisdiction comics opted for the bland, the safe, and the reactionary. In Britain there was government legislation to prohibit the importing of American comics, as the comics panic slotted neatly into a whole series of anxieties about the effects on British youth of American popular culture.[18]

And in all of this, what happened to Batman? He turned into Fred Mac- 20 Murray from *My Three Sons.* He lost any remaining edge of the shadowy vigilante of his earliest years, and became an upholder of the most stifling small-town American values. Batwoman and Batgirl appeared (June Allyson and Bat-Gidget) to take away any lingering doubts about the Dynamic Duo's sex lives. A 1963 story called "The Great Clayface-Joker Feud" has some especially choice examples of the new, squeaky-clean sexuality of the assembled Bats.

Batgirl says to Robin, "I can hardly wait to get into my Batgirl costume again! Won't it be terrific if we could go on a crime case together like the last time? (sigh)." Robin replies, "It sure would, Betty (sigh)." The elder Bats look on approvingly. Batgirl is Batwoman's niece — to make her a daughter would have implied that Batwoman had had (gulp) sexual intercourse, and that would never do. This is the era of Troy Donohue and Pat Boone,[19] and Batman as ever serves as a cultural thermometer, taking the temperature of the times.

The Clayface/Joker business is wrapped up (the villains of this period are wacky conjurors, nothing more, with no menace or violence about them) and the episode concludes with another tableau of terrifying heterosexual contentment. "Oh Robin," simpers Batgirl, "I'm afraid you'll just have to hold me! I'm still so shaky after fighting Clayface . . . and you're so strong!" Robin: "Gosh Batgirl, it was swell of you to calm me down when I was worried about Batman tackling Clayface alone." (One feels a distinct Wertham influence here: If Robin shows concern about Batman, wheel on a supportive female, the very opposite of a "morbid ideal," to minister in a suitably self-effacing way.) Batwoman here seizes her chance and tackles Batman: "You look worried about Clayface, Batman . . . so why don't you follow Robin's example and let me soothe you?" Batman can only reply "Gulp."

[17]**Hays Code** The 1930 Motion Picture Production Code, which described in detail what was morally acceptable in films.–EDS.

[18]See Barker.

[19]**Troy Donohue and Pat Boone** Clean-cut, all-American-boy stars from the 1950s and 1960s.–EDS.

Gulp indeed. While it's easy simply to laugh at strips like these, knowing as we do the way in which such straight-faced material would be mercilessly shredded by the sixties' TV series, they do reveal the retreat into coziness forced on comics by the Wertham onslaught and its repercussions. There no doubt were still subversive readers of *Batman*, erasing Batgirl on her every preposterous appearance and reworking the Duo's capers to leave some room for homoerotic speculation, but such a reading would have had to work so much harder than before. The *Batman* of this era was such a closed text, so immune to polysemic interpretation, that its interest today is only as a symptom — or, more productively, as camp. "The Great Clayface-Joker Feud" may have been published in 1963, but in every other respect it is a fifties' text. If the 1960s began for the world in general with the Beatles, the 1960s for Batman began with the TV series in 1966. If the Caped Crusader had been all but Werthamed out of existence, he was about to be camped back into life.

The Camped Crusader and the Boys Wondered

Trying to define "camp" is like attempting to sit in the corner of a circular room. It can't be done, which only adds to the quixotic appeal of the attempt. Try these:

> To be camp is to present oneself as being committed to the marginal with a commitment greater than the marginal merits.[20]
>
> Camp sees everything in quotation marks. It's not a lamp but a "lamp"; not a woman but a "woman." . . . It is the farthest extension, in sensibility, of the metaphor of life as theatre.[21]
>
> Camp is . . . a way of poking fun at the whole cosmology of restrictive sex roles and sexual identifications which our society uses to oppress its women and repress its men.[22]
>
> Camp was and is a way for gay men to re-imagine the world around them . . . by exaggerating, stylizing and remaking what is usually thought to be average or normal.[23]
>
> Camp was a prison for an illegal minority; now it is a holiday for consenting adults.[24]

All true, in their way, but all inadequate. The problem with camp is that [25] it is primarily an experiential rather than an analytical discourse. Camp is a set of attitudes, a gallery of snapshots, an inventory of postures, a modus vivendi, a shop-full of frocks, an arch of eyebrows, a great big pink butterfly

---

[20]Mark Booth, *Camp* (London: Quartet, 1983), p. 18.

[21]Sontag, p. 109.

[22]Jack Babuscio, "Camp and the Gay Sensibility," in Dyer, ed., *Gays and Film*, p. 46.

[23]Michael Bronski, *Culture Clash: The Making of Gay Sensibility* (Boston: South End Press), p. 42.

[24]Philip Core, *Camp: The Lie That Tells the Truth* (London: Plexus), p. 7.

that just won't be pinned down. Camp is primarily an adjective, occasionally a verb, but never anything as prosaic, as earthbound, as a noun.

Yet if I propose to use this adjective as a way of describing one or more of the guises of Batman, I need to arrive at some sort of working definition. So, for the purposes of this analysis, I intend the term "camp" to refer to a playful, knowing, self-reflexive theatricality. *Batman*, the sixties' TV series, was nothing if not knowing. It employed the codes of camp in an unusually public and heavily signaled way. This makes it different from those people or texts who are taken up by camp audiences without ever consciously putting camp into practice. The difference may be very briefly spelled out by reference to Hollywood films. If *Mildred Pierce*[25] and *The Letter*[26] were taken up *as* camp, teased by primarily gay male audiences into yielding meaning not intended by their makers, then *Whatever Happened to Baby Jane?*[27] is a piece of self-conscious camp, capitalizing on certain attitudinal and stylistic tendencies known to exist in audiences. *Baby Jane* is also, significantly, a 1960s' film, and the 1960s were the decade in which camp swished out of the ghetto and up into the scarcely prepared mainstream.

A number of key events and texts reinforced this. Susan Sontag wrote her *Notes on Camp*, which remains the starting point for researchers even now. Pop Art[28] was in vogue (and in *Vogue*) and whatever the more elevated claims of Lichtenstein,[29] Warhol,[30] and the rest, their artworks were on one level a new inflection of camp. The growing intellectual respectability of pop music displayed very clearly that the old barriers that once rigidly separated high and low culture were no longer in force. The James Bond films, and even more so their successors like *Modesty Blaise*, popularized a dry, self-mocking wit that makes up one part of the multifaceted diamond of camp. And on television there were *The Avengers*, *The Man from U.N.C.L.E.*, *Thunderbirds*, and *Batman*.

To quote the inevitable Sontag, "The whole point of Camp is to dethrone the serious. . . . More precisely, Camp involves a new, more complex relation to 'the serious.' One can be serious about the frivolous, frivolous about the serious."[31]

---

[25]*Mildred Pierce* 1945 murder mystery film that traces the fortunes of a homemaker who breaks with her husband.–Eds.

[26]*The Letter* 1940 murder movie whose ending was changed to satisfy moral standards of the time.–Eds.

[27]*Whatever Happened to Baby Jane?* Macabre 1962 film about a former child movie star living in an old Hollywood mansion.–Eds.

[28]**Pop Art** Art movement, begun in the 1950s, that borrowed images and symbols from popular culture, particularly from commercial products and mass media, as a critique of traditional fine art.–Eds.

[29]**Lichtenstein** Roy Lichtenstein (1923–1997), American artist at the center of the Pop Art movement, best known for melodramatic comic book scenes.–Eds.

[30]**Warhol** Andy Warhol (1930?–1987), pioneering Pop artist known for reproducing stereotyped images of famous people, such as Marilyn Monroe, and of commercial products, such as Campbell's Soup cans.–Eds.

[31]Sontag, p. 116.

The problem with Batman in those terms is that there was never anything truly serious to begin with (unless one swallows that whole portentous Dark Knight charade, more of which in the next section). Batman in its comic book form had, unwittingly, always been camp — it was serious (the tone, the moral homilies) about the frivolous (a man in a stupid suit). He was camp in the way that classic Hollywood was camp, but what the sixties' TV series and film did was to overlay this "innocent" camp with a thick layer of ironic distance, the self-mockery version of camp. And given the long associations of camp with the homosexual male subculture, Batman was a particular gift on the grounds of his relationship with Robin. As George Melly put it, "The real Batman series were beautiful because of their unselfconscious absurdity. The remakes, too, at first worked on a double level. Over the absorbed children's heads we winked and nudged, but in the end what were we laughing at? The fact they didn't know that Batman had it off with Robin."[32]

It was as if Wertham's fears were being vindicated at last, but his 1950s' bigot's anguish had been supplanted by a self-consciously hip 1960s' playfulness. What adult audiences laughed at in the sixties' *Batman* was a camped-up version of the fifties they had just left behind.

Batman's lessons in good citizenship ("We'd like to feel that our efforts may help every youngster to grow up into an honest, useful citizen"[33]) were another part of the character ripe for ridiculing deconstruction — "Let's go, Robin, we've set another youth on the road to a brighter tomorrow" (the episode "It's How You Play the Game"). Everything the Adam West Batman said was a parody of seriousness, and how could it be otherwise? How could anyone take genuinely seriously the words of a man dressed like that?

The Batman/Robin relationship is never referred to directly; more fun can be had by presenting it "straight," in other words, screamingly camp. Wertham's reading of the Dubious Duo had been so extensively aired as to pass into the general consciousness (in George Melly's words, "We all knew Robin and Batman were pouves"[34]), it was part of the fabric of *Batman*, and the makers of the TV series proceeded accordingly.

Consider the Duo's encounter with Marsha, Queen of Diamonds. The threat she embodies is nothing less than heterosexuality itself, the deadliest threat to the domestic bliss of the Bat-couple. She is even about to marry Batman before Alfred intervenes to save the day. He and Batman flee the church, but have to do so in the already decorated Batmobile, festooned with wedding paraphernalia including a large "Just Married" sign. "We'll have to drive it as it is," says Batman, while somewhere in the audience

[32]George Melly, *Revolt into Style: The Pop Arts in the 50s and 60s* (Oxford: Oxford University Press, 1989 [first published 1970]), p. 193.

[33]"The Batman Says," *Batman #3* (1940), quoted in Cotta Vaz, p. 15.

[34]Melly, p. 192.

a Dr. Wertham takes feverish notes. Robin, Commissioner Gordon, and Chief O'Hara have all been drugged with Marsha's "Cupid Dart," but it is of course the Boy Wonder who Batman saves first. The dart, he tells Robin, "contains some secret ingredient by which your sense and your will were affected," and it isn't hard to read that ingredient as heterosexual desire, since its result, seen in the previous episode, was to turn Robin into Marsha's slobbering slave.

We can tell with relief now, though, as Robin is "back in fighting form" (with impeccable timing, Batman clasps Robin's shoulder on the word "fighting"). Marsha has one last attempt to destroy the duo, but naturally she fails. The female temptress, the seductress, the enchantress must be vanquished. None of this is in the least subtle (Marsha's cat, for example, is called Circe) but this type of mass-market camp can't afford the luxury of subtlety. The threat of heterosexuality is similarly mobilized in the 1966 feature film, where it is Bruce Wayne's infatuation with Kitka (Catwoman in disguise) that causes all manner of problems.

A more interesting employment of camp comes in the episodes where the Duo battle the Black Widow, played by Tallulah Bankhead. The major camp coup here, of course, is the casting. Bankhead was one of the supreme icons of camp, one of its goddesses: "Too intelligent not to be self-conscious, too ambitious to bother about her self-consciousness, too insecure ever to be content, but too arrogant ever to admit insecurity, Tallulah personified camp."[35]

A heady claim, but perhaps justified, because the Black Widow episodes are, against stiff competition, the campiest slices of *Batman* of them all. The stories about Bankhead are legendary — the time when on finding no toilet paper in her cubicle she slipped a ten dollar bill under the partition and asked the woman next door for two fives, or her whispered remark to a priest conducting a particularly elaborate service and swinging a censor of smoking incense, "Darling, I love the drag, but your purse is on fire" — and casting her in *Batman* was the final demonstration of the series' commitment to camp.

The plot is unremarkable, the usual Bat-shenanigans; the pleasure lies in the detail. Details like the elderly Bankhead crammed into her Super-Villainess costume, or like the way in which (through a plot detail I won't go into) she impersonates Robin, so we see Burt Ward miming to Bankhead's voice, giving the unforgettable image of Robin flirting with burly traffic cops. Best of all, and Bankhead isn't even in this scene but the thrill of having her involved clearly spurred the writer to new heights of camp, Batman has to sing a song to break free of the Black Widow's spell. Does he choose to sing "God Bless America"? Nothing so rugged. He clutches a flower to his Bat chest and sings Gilbert and Sullivan's "I'm Just a Little Buttercup." It is this single image, more than any other, that prevents me from taking the post–Adam West Dark Knight at all seriously.

[35]Core, p. 25.

The fundamental camp trick which the series pulls is to make the comics speak. What was acceptable on the page, in speech balloons, stands revealed as ridiculous once given audible voice. The famous visualized sound effects (URKKK! KA-SPLOOSH!) that are for many the fondest memory of the series work along similar lines. Camp often makes its point by transposing the codes of one cultural form into the inappropriate codes of another. It thrives on mischievous incongruity.

The incongruities, the absurdities, the sheer ludicrousness of Batman were brought out so well by the sixties' version that for some audiences there will never be another credible approach. I have to include myself here. I've recently read widely in postsixties Bat-lore, and I can appreciate what the writers and artists are trying to do, but my Batman will always be Adam West. It's impossible to be somber or pompous about Batman because if you try the ghost of West will come Bat-climbing into your mind, fortune cookie wisdom on his lips and keen young Dick by his side. It's significant, I think, that the letters I received . . . began "Dear Bat-Contributor."[36] Writers preparing chapters about James Joyce or Ingmar Bergman do not, I suspect, receive analogous greetings. To deny the large camp component of Batman is to blind oneself to one of the richest parts of his history.

Is There Bat-Life after Bat-Camp?

The international success of the Adam West incarnation left Batman high 40 and dry. The camping around had been fun while it lasted, but it hadn't lasted very long. Most camp humor has a relatively short life span, new targets are always needed, and the camp aspect of Batman had been squeezed dry. The mass public had moved on to other heroes, other genres, other acres of merchandising, but there was still a hard Bat-core of fans to satisfy. Where could the Bat go next? Clearly there was no possibility of returning to the caped Eisenhower, the benevolent patriarch of the 1950s. That option had been well and truly closed down by the TV show. Batman needed to be given his dignity back, and this entailed a return to his roots.

This, in any case, is the official version. For the unreconstructed devotee of the Batman (that is, people who insist on giving him the definite article before the name), the West years had been hell — a tricksy travesty, an effeminizing of the cowled avenger. There's a scene in *Midnight Cowboy* where Dustin Hoffman tells Jon Voight that the only audience liable to be receptive to his cowboy clothes are gay men looking for rough trade. Voight is appalled — "You mean to tell me John Wayne was a fag?" (quoted, roughly, from memory). This outrage, this horror at shattered illusions, comes close to

[36]This essay originally appeared in an anthology, *The Many Lives of the Batman: Critical Approaches to a Superhero and His Media.*–EDS.

encapsulating the loathing and dread the campy Batman has received from the old guard of Gotham City and the younger born-again Bat-fans.

So what has happened since the 1960s has been the painstaking reheterosexualization of Batman. I apologize for coining such a clumsy word, but no other quite gets the sense that I mean. This strategy has worked, too, for large audiences, reaching its peak with the 1989 film. To watch this and then come home to see a video of the 1966 movie is to grasp how complete the transformation has been. What I want to do in this section is to trace some of the crucial moments in that change, written from the standpoint of someone still unashamedly committed to Bat-camp.

If one wants to take Batman as a Real Man, the biggest stumbling block has always been Robin. There have been disingenuous claims that "Batman and Robin had a blood-brother closeness. Theirs was a spiritual intimacy forged from the stress of countless battles fought side by side"[37] (one can imagine what Tallulah Bankhead might say to *that*), but we know otherwise. The Wertham lobby and the acolytes of camp alike have ensured that any Batman/Robin relationship is guaranteed to bring on the sniggers. Besides which, in the late 1960s, Robin was getting to be a big boy, too big for any shreds of credibility to attach themselves to all that father-son smokescreen. So in 1969 Dick Grayson was packed off to college and the Bat was solitary once more.

This was a shrewd move. It's impossible to conceive of the recent, obsessive, sturm-und-drang Batman with a chirpy little Robin getting in the way.[38] A text of the disturbing power of *The Killing Joke*[39] could not have functioned with Robin to rupture the grim dualism of its Batman/Joker struggle. There was, however, a post–Dick Robin, but he was killed off by fans in that infamous telephone poll.[40]

It's intriguing to speculate how much latent (or blatant) homophobia lay 45 behind that vote. Did the fans decide to kill off Jason Todd so as to redeem Batman for unproblematic heterosexuality? Impossible to say. There are other factors to take into account, such as Jason's apparent failure to live up to the expectations of what a Robin should be like. The sequence of issues in which Jason/Robin died, *A Death in the Family*, is worth looking at in some detail, however, in order to see whether the camp connotations of Bruce and Dick had been fully purged.

[37]Cotta Vaz, p. 53.

[38]A female Robin is introduced in the *Dark Knight Returns* series, which, while raising interesting questions about the sexuality of Batman, which I don't here have the space to address, seems significant in that the Dark Knight cannot run the risk of reader speculation that a traditionally male Robin might provoke.

[39]*The Killing Joke* Graphic novel by Alan Moore, Brian Bolland, and John Higgins (New York: DC Comics, 1988).–Eds.

[40]telephone poll In a 1988 issue of the *Batman* comic, a "post–Dick Robin," Jason Todd, was badly injured in an explosion, and readers were allowed to phone the publisher to vote on whether he should be allowed to survive.–Eds.

The depressing answer is that they had. This is very much the Batman of the 1980s, his endless feud with the Joker this time uneasily stretched over a framework involving the Middle East and Ethiopia. Little to be camp about there, though the presence of the Joker guarantees a quota of sick jokes. The sickest of all is the introduction of the Ayatollah Khomeini, a real and important political figure, into this fantasy world of THUNK! and THER-ACKK! and grown men dressed as bats. (As someone who lived in the part of England from which Reagan's planes took off on their murderous mission to bomb Libya, I fail to see the humor in this cartoon version of American foreign policy: It's too near the real thing.)

Jason dies at the Joker's hands because he becomes involved in a search for his own origins, a clear parallel to Batman's endless returns to *his* Oedipal scenario. Families, in the Bat-mythology, are dark and troubled things, one more reason why the introduction of the fifties versions of Batwoman and Batgirl seemed so inappropriate. This applies only to real, biological families, though; the true familial bond is between Batman and Robin, hence the title of these issues. Whether one chooses to read Robin as Batman's ward (official version), son (approved fantasy), or lover (forbidden fantasy), the sense of loss at his death is bound to be devastating. Batman finds Robin's body and, in the time-honored tradition of Hollywood cinema, is at least able to give him a loving embrace. Good guys hug their dead buddies, only queers smooch when still alive.

If the word "camp" is applied at all to the eighties' Batman, it is a label for the Joker. This sly displacement is the cleverest method yet devised of preserving Bat-heterosexuality. The play that the texts regularly make with the concept of Batman and the Joker as mirror images now takes a new twist. The Joker is Batman's "bad twin," and part of that badness is, increasingly, an implied homosexuality. This is certainly present in the 1989 film, a generally glum and portentous affair except for Jack Nicholson's Joker, a characterization enacted with venomous camp. The only moment when this dour film comes to life is when the Joker and his gang raid the Art Gallery, spraying the paintings and generally camping up a storm.

The film strives and strains to make us forget the Adam West Batman, to the point of giving us Vicki Vale as Bruce Wayne's lover, and certainly Michael Keaton's existential agonizing (variations on the theme of why-did-I-have-to-be-a-Bat) is a world away from West's gleeful subversion of truth, justice, and the American Way. This is the same species of Batman celebrated by Frank Miller: "If your only memory of Batman is that of Adam West and Burt Ward exchanging camped-out quips while clobbering slumming guest-stars Vincent Price and Cesar Romero, I hope this book will come as a surprise. . . . For me, Batman was never funny. . . ."[41]

The most recent linkage of the Joker with homosexuality comes in 50 *Arkham Asylum*, the darkest image of the Bat-world yet. Here the Joker has

---

[41] Frank Miller, "Introduction," *Batman: Year One* (London: Titan, 1988).

become a parody of a screaming queen, calling Batman "honey pie," given to exclamations like "oooh!" (one of the oldest homophobic clichés in the book), and pinching Batman's behind with the advice, "Loosen up, tight ass." He also, having no doubt read his Wertham, follows the pinching by asking, "What's the matter? Have I touched a nerve? How is the Boy Wonder? Started shaving yet?" The Bat-response is unequivocal: "Take your filthy hands off me. . . . Filthy degenerate!"

Arkham Asylum is a highly complex reworking of certain key aspects of the mythology, of which the sexual tension between Batman and the Joker is only one small part. Nonetheless the Joker's question "Have I touched a nerve?" seems a crucial one, as revealed by the homophobic ferocity of Batman's reply. After all, the dominant cultural construction of gay men at the end of the 1980s is as plague carriers, and the word "degenerate" is not far removed from some of the labels affixed to us in the age of AIDS.

Batman: Is He or Isn't He?

The one constant factor through all of the transformations of Batman has been the devotion of his admirers. They will defend him against what they see as negative interpretations, and they carry around in their heads a kind of essence of batness, a Bat-Platonic Ideal of how Batman should really be. The Titan Books reissue of key comics from the 1970s each carry a preface by a noted fan, and most of them contain claims such as "This, I feel, is Batman as he was meant to be."[42]

Where a negative construction is specifically targeted, no prizes for guessing which one it is: "you . . . are probably also fond of the TV show he appeared in. But then maybe you prefer Elvis Presley's Vegas years or the later Jerry Lewis movies over their early stuff . . . for me, the definitive Batman was then and always will be the one portrayed in these pages."[43]

The sixties' TV show remains anathema to the serious Bat-fan precisely because it heaps ridicule on the very notion of a serious Batman. *Batman* the series revealed the man in the cape as a pompous fool, an embodiment of superseded ethics, and a closet queen. As Marsha, Queen of Diamonds, put it, "Oh Batman, darling, you're so divinely square." Perhaps the enormous success of the 1989 film will help to advance the cause of the rival Bat-archetype, the grim, vengeful Dark Knight whose heterosexuality is rarely called into question (his humorlessness, fondness for violence, and obsessive monomania seem to me exemplary qualities for a heterosexual man). The answer, surely, is that they needn't be mutually exclusive.

[42]Kim Newman, "Introduction," *Batman: The Demon Awakes* (London: Titan, 1989).
[43]Jonathan Ross, "Introduction," *Batman: Vow from the Grave* (London: Titan, 1989).

If I might be permitted a rather camp comparison, each generation ⁵⁵
has its definitive Hamlet, so why not the same for Batman? I'm prepared
to admit the validity, for some people, of the swooping eighties' vigilante,
so why are they so concerned to trash my sixties' camped crusader? Why
do they insist so vehemently that Adam West was a faggy aberration, a
blot on the otherwise impeccably butch Bat-landscape? What *are* they
trying to hide?

If I had a suspicious frame of mind, I might think that they were protesting too much, that maybe Dr. Wertham was on to something when he targeted these narratives as incitements to homosexual fantasy. And if I want
Batman to be gay, then, for me, he is. After all, outside of the minds of his
writers and readers, he doesn't really exist.

READING THE TEXT

1. Summarize the objections Fredric Wertham makes to Batman in *Seduction of
    the Innocent*.

2. In a paragraph, write your own explanation of what Medhurst means by
    "camp."

3. What evidence does Medhurst supply to demonstrate that Batman is a gay
    character?

4. Explain what Medhurst means by his closing comment: "And if I want Bat-
    man to be gay, then, for me, he is. After all, outside of the minds of his writ-
    ers and readers, he doesn't really exist" (para. 56).

READING THE SIGNS

1. Do you agree with Medhurst's argument that the Batman and Robin duo
    are really a covert homosexual couple? Write an essay supporting or chal-
    lenging Medhurst's position, being sure to study his evidence closely. You
    might visit your school's media library to find file tapes of old *Batman*
    shows, or read contemporary reviews of *Batman*, to gather evidence for
    your essay.

2. Read Fredric Wertham's *Seduction of the Innocent*. Then write your own cri-
    tique of Wertham's attack on Batman.

3. Buy a few issues of the current *Batman* comic book and write an essay in
    which you explain Batman's current sexual orientation.

4. Visit your college library and obtain a copy of Susan Sontag's "Notes on
    Camp" (included in Sontag's collections *Against Interpretation* and *A Susan
    Sontag Reader*). How would Sontag interpret the character of Batman?

JAIME J. WEINMAN

Fox News Attempts to Get Funny

In the summer of 2007, *The Daily Show* sent a correspondent to Iraq, which isn't especially funny, but it is paradoxical because at the same time the Fox News network debuted a couple of news shows intended to compete with *The Daily Show* by adopting its comedic style, though delivered from the opposite end of the ideological spectrum. Jaime J. Weinman's media report on Fox's new strategy highlights a profound new media phenomenon: the fact that youthful viewers are overwhelmingly choosing overtly entertainment-based sources for news information, thus further blurring the traditional distinctions between objective reporting and propaganda, as well as between entertainment and reality. Indeed, as one conservative columnist has noted, the stakes are high when no one can afford to ignore "a crowd that will, in short order, be influencing our nation after you take the big dirt nap, conservative mom and dad." Jaime J. Weinman writes on popular culture for such journals as *Macleans* and *Salon.com*.

Why are the producers of Fox News so desperate to be funny? This past month, the conservative cable news channel added two shows that attempt to make fun of liberals, instead of just calling them traitors the way Fox News' regular anchors do. You don't see CNN trying to come up with a comedy show, but then Fox News' new programming ventures may be more about a political movement than news — or, for that matter, comedy.

The 1/2 Hour News Hour, Fox's answer to *The Daily Show*, comes from Joel Surnow, creator of the comedy-challenged hit *24*. The first episode included a guest appearance by Surnow's friend Rush Limbaugh and comparisons between Barack Obama and Oprah. If that's not enough liberal-bashing comedy for you, Fox News has also come up with a late-night talk show called *Red Eye*, starring former *Maxim UK* editor Greg Gutfeld. Gutfeld, who once called liberals "patriotic terrorists," tried to prove how cutting-edge *Red Eye* was by informing his co-panelists that Fox News was allowing him to say the word "douche."

An article by Doug Giles, a columnist for the conservative site Townhall .com, may provide a clue about why Fox News is trying to get hilarious. Giles warned his ideological comrades that they would lose the culture wars unless they learned to make viewers laugh. Pointing out that demographic trends strongly favor consumers of Comedy Central, he wrote: "Blowing off this bunch that's not listening to conservative talk radio, watching Bill [O'Reilly], or logging on to Townhall.com is to dis a crowd that will, in short order, be

347

influencing our nation after you take the big dirt nap, conservative mom and dad."

This isn't just about trying to fill up some time on a 24-hour news channel. With the popularity of liberal-leaning humor among young people, and the liberal-Democratic tilt of young voters in the 2006 mid-term elections, conservatives are worried that the future belongs to people who have been brought up to think that tax cuts and preventive war are for dorks. Fox News, a network formed to assist the conservative movement, found itself faced with a choice: Find the funny, or watch its movement slip into irrelevance.

Will the combination of humor and Republican party boosting ever take off? Gavin McNett, a writer for the liberal humor blog Sadlyno.com, doesn't think so. He says today's conservatives have a "hermetic, self-referential world view" that leads them to mistake talking points for jokes. "Referencing one of their common shibboleths often serves the purpose that humor would serve," he continues. "There has to be an element of surprise in humor — and conservatives hate surprise. It's just how they're wired." 5

Sure enough, most of the jokes on *The 1/2 Hour News Hour* aren't really jokes at all: They're Fox News segments with a laugh track. A typical remark from the pilot episode is that Democratic National Committee chairman Howard Dean is mentally ill and "getting the medical attention he has so desperately needed." We're expected to laugh not because there was any amusing spin on the talking point, but just because we agree. Anyone who doesn't already agree will be flipping the channel to a real comedy show.

But contrary to what McNett says, there have always been successful right-leaning comedians and comedy writers; today's most prominent examples are Trey Parker and Matt Stone, the creators of *South Park*. Their episodes carry titles like "Die, Hippie, Die!" and make fun of environmentalists, hybrid cars, and liberal atheist Richard Dawkins. A typical episode of *South Park* produces more laughter at the expense of liberal sacred cows than anything Fox News can come up with.

The difference is that Parker and Stone are not party men; like liberal comics, they have a political philosophy that they incorporate into their work. Much of today's conservative movement, on the other hand, is based on partisan politics: Fox News or Townhall.com are unofficial organs of the Republican party. It's hard to be an effective comedian while being an advocate for a party, any party: Al Franken hasn't been particularly funny since he stopped being a political satirist and became a Democratic candidate for the Senate.

But Fox News will keep trying to entice young viewers with *The 1/2 Hour News Hour*'s mental illness jokes. As Doug Giles wrote, if conservatives can't crack wise, they may lose "our ideological battle with the secularists who whiz on traditional American values."

That's comedy gold right there. 10

READING THE TEXT

1. Summarize in your own words Weinman's answer to his opening question, "Why are the producers of Fox News so desperate to be funny?" (para. 1).

2. What is the nature of the humor that dominates Fox News and *Red Eye*, and what is Weinman's assessment of that humor?

3. Why does Weinman say that "it's hard to be an effective comedian while being an advocate for a party, any party" (para. 8)?

READING THE SIGNS

1. In your journal, reflect on your own consumption of news. What are your principal sources of news, and why? What sort of news do you pay attention to and what sort do you ignore? What are the implications of your habits and tastes?

2. In class, form teams and debate whether programs like Fox's *The 1/2 Hour News Hour* and *The Daily Show* represent an advance in news programming because their style is attractive to a demographic group — young people — that tends not to watch news, or whether they are a dangerous assault on traditional journalistic values of objectivity and fairness. To prepare your team's position, be sure to study segments of both traditional news shows and the more comedic news shows Weinman describes.

3. Compare and contrast a conservative news program with one that has a more liberal slant, focusing not only on the humor but on the content and style of presentation as well.

4. **CONNECTING TEXTS** In class, brainstorm media — news shows, TV programs, films — that most students agree are humorous. Analyze the results and write your own essay proposing your definition of what constitutes humor for young people today. To develop your ideas, consult the Introduction to this chapter and Carl Matheson's "*The Simpsons*, Hyper-Irony, and the Meaning of Life" (p. 305).

DRAKE BENNETT

Guiding Lights: How Soap Operas Can Save the World

Given all the promiscuity, adultery, and just plain messing around in the average soap opera, you would think that the soaps would be a bad influence on human behavior. But as Drake Bennett reports in this article that originally appeared in Boston.com, all over the world audiences are using soap operas as models of how *not* to behave. From India — where girls and women appear to be given more rights in villages where soaps are watched — to Brazil — where birth rates have fallen thanks to television "novelas" — TV soaps have actually been a progressive influence. Even in America, "health tips tucked into soaps have greater sticking power than with just about any other mode of transmission." So maybe being addicted to TV soaps shouldn't be such a *guilty* pleasure after all. Drake Bennett is a staff writer for the Ideas section of the *Boston Globe*.

On most measures of the strength of a community's social fabric, the town of Oakdale would score poorly. There's the high divorce rate and appallingly low incidence of marital fidelity; the off-the-charts frequency of assault, murder, rape, and arson; the overlapping epidemics of kidnapping, identity theft, fraud, and wedding-day bridal abandonment. And there is a local justice system seemingly bent on imprisoning the innocent, leaving it up to intrepid family members and lovers to bring the truth to light. Thankfully, no one lives in Oakdale, no one real. It is the fictional town where *As the World Turns*, America's longest-running current soap opera, has tumultuously unfolded for over half a century (this season will be its last). And while the Gomorrhic dysfunction of places like the fictionalized Oakdale, Ill., or Port Charles, N.Y. (*General Hospital*) or Pine Valley, Pa. (*All My Children*) is what makes them so entertaining to their loyal fans, few would describe these as places where people live exemplary lives. Soap operas, after all, are entertainment at its least believable and least nutritious.

The possibility, therefore, that people might be modeling themselves after characters on soaps might seem both farfetched and frightening. A spate of recent research, however, suggests that, all over the world, that's exactly what's happening. What's more, we should be happy about it.

Soaps, it turns out, are shaping behavior in ways that are subtle, profound and, from the standpoint of global development experts, positive. A team of economists credits Brazilian TV "novelas" for helping to dramatically lower a fertility rate that in 1960 was above six births per woman. Others have found that in India — where soaps dominate the airwaves — villages where people watch more TV give more responsibilities and rights to women and girls. Researchers in Rwanda have found that radio soap operas there can help defuse the country's dangerous ethnic tensions. Turkish soap operas have set off a public debate about women's roles in the Middle East. And research in the United States has found that health tips tucked into soaps have greater sticking power than with just about any other mode of transmission. In a surprising number of ways, soap operas are improving lives around the world.

"The evidence we have from these academic studies is that quite often [viewers] take away different attitudes toward things like how many children they want, what is acceptable behavior for a husband toward his wife, what is the breakdown in a household of responsibilities over things like finances, should we be sending girls to school," says Charles Kenny, an economist at the World Bank who has written about global television habits, and the author of a forthcoming book on development. "All of these seem to be generated by watching some soap operas."

Intrigued and buoyed by findings like these, researchers and public 5 health and international aid organizations are looking at how to design soaps that might more effectively spread information and change attitudes about everything from tribal tensions to HIV to petty corruption. Lurid though they are, the denizens of the world's Oakdales may have something important to teach us.

For years, experts on Brazil struggled with a riddle: Throughout the second half of the 20th century, the number of babies being born to Brazilian mothers dropped far faster than traditional explanations suggest they should have, from 6.3 in 1960 to 2.3 in 2000. This was widely seen as a good thing — fewer children per family meant more resources per child, and it eased the entry of young women into the workforce and political life.

The question was why it had happened. Whereas China, for example, had resorted to a strict one-child policy to accomplish a similar reduction, Brazil's government had been deeply resistant to measures to lower birth rates.

A few years ago, reading anthropological research, Eliana La Ferrara, a developmental economist at Italy's Bocconi University, noticed accounts from poor Brazilian women about how they decided how many children to have. One of the reasons caught her attention: They said they wanted their families to be more like the smaller (and wealthier) families they saw on Brazil's popular soap operas.

If it seems unlikely that soap operas could have this much influence, consider that in Brazil, serial television dramas are a national obsession: the most popular have big budgets, far better writing and production values than American soaps, and can draw upward of 80 million viewers in a nation of 190 million. Marquee soccer matches are scheduled so that they don't overlap with the prime-time novelas.

La Ferrara, along with Alberto Chong and Suzanne Duryea of the Inter- 10 American Development Bank, set out to see whether novelas did indeed help drive this large demographic change. The researchers used historical data, tracing the entry of Rede Globo — the network that creates the majority of Brazilian novelas — into different regional markets and matching that up with census data on births.

What they found was that, in region after region, when Rede Globo and its novelas arrived, births went down. And the researchers found another change, too: In those same regions, the children who were born were disproportionately named after characters on novelas. Young potential parents weren't just watching television, they were watching novelas, and identifying strongly with the characters. For all of their contrivances, the novelas work as entertainment, La Ferrara points out, because their viewers see the characters as members of their own familiar, actual lives, and that makes behaviors from the shows contagious with their viewers.

"You put something in a show and it's as if people were talking to their friends, they tend to be a little more inclined to see these things as part of life as opposed to a message or teaching or whatever," La Ferrara says.

The effect was not overwhelming, La Ferrara emphasizes, but it was significant. More educated women generally have fewer children than less educated women, and she calculates the novela effect as comparable to giving a woman two extra years of education.

Researchers have found a similar effect on the other side of the world, in rural India. Two economists, Emily Oster at the University of Chicago and Robert Jensen at UCLA, looked at surveys on a range of social attitudes in five Indian states from 2001 to 2003, a time of rapid expansion in access to cable TV. As with Brazil's Rede Globo, Oster and Jensen found that the spread of cable brought down the fertility rate, but they found other changes as well: Women with cable access were less approving of the idea that a husband could justifiably beat his wife, and reported having more autonomy and more of a role in household financial matters. Their daughters were more likely to be enrolled in school.

And while the study didn't look specifically at what viewers watched, Oster points out that soap operas are overwhelmingly the most popular programming on Indian television. As in Brazil, they tend to portray lives that are urban and upper-middle class, in which the female characters often work outside the house and manage their own affairs—lives that, to many Indian women, are becoming something to aspire to. 15

"There are differences between urban and rural areas in India in their attitudes toward women," Oster says, "and our estimates suggest that giving people TV in rural areas moves them between 50 and 70 percent of the way from rural to urban attitudes."

Oster and La Ferrara both readily concede that their work only measures a tiny sliver of the potential changes in attitudes and behavior that soap opera viewers might exhibit—and that not all of those other changes might be healthy ones. Soap operas and novelas are full of all sorts of louche, antisocial behavior, even on the part of the heroes: a dangerous susceptibility to erotic impulses, a predilection for vigilante justice, an openness to being fooled, at least initially, by villainous suitors and step-parents. There's no research to determine whether viewers are in some small way absorbing these tendencies, as well.

And not everyone might see the changes the researchers recorded as positive. For example, in Brazil, exposure to Rede Globo and its novelas seemed to lead to an increase in the divorce rate among viewers. For women who might previously have stayed in an abusive relationship, that can be a good thing. But policymakers and scholars concerned about family stability aren't likely to see higher divorce rates as an encouraging sign.

It's no surprise that the behavioral impact of soap operas can be ambiguous. The shows are created to entertain, and to do so shamelessly. But activists, sometimes with the aid of media scholars and psychologists, are beginning to look at ways to focus the power of soaps, using them to deliver more specific messages.

To mitigate ethnic tension and fight corruption in Africa, the conflict- 20
resolution organization Search for Common Ground has created a soap opera franchise called *The Team* about the trials of an ethnically and religiously diverse professional soccer club. Locally produced versions in Kenya, Côte d'Ivoire, and Morocco have proved popular—nearly a quarter of Moroccans watch it. The BBC World Service has, since the mid-1990s, broadcast a radio soap opera in Afghanistan called *New Home, New Life*. A huge hit, the serial narrative about village life introduced Afghan audiences to the concept of the cliffhanger ending—Afghans were originally frustrated that the installments ended right when things were getting most interesting—and is used to deliver practical information about everything from animal husbandry and landmine safety to civics.

Here in the United States, the Centers for Disease Control and Prevention, working with an organization called Hollywood, Health & Society, helped *The Bold and the Beautiful*—a soap opera about a family and its fashion empire—craft a story line about HIV. The CDC wanted to reach minority women, who make up a disproportionately large segment of both soap opera viewers and new HIV infections. In a study HH&S commissioned afterward, those episodes, which included a public service announcement near the end listing the number of the national AIDS hotline, were found to have triggered more hotline calls than any other television public information campaign that year.

Still, hard data on the efficacy of such so-called "edutainment" is thin. One of the exceptions is work that Elizabeth Levy Paluck, a psychologist at Princeton University, has done on the Rwandan radio soap opera *New Dawn*. Created and broadcast by a Rwandan nongovernmental organization, it's a story of star-crossed lovers from feuding tribes. The particulars—a land shortage, government favoritism of one tribe over the other, building resentment among the less favored—work as a parable of the nation's historic Hutu–Tutsi fissures without explicitly mentioning them. The Romeo-and-Juliet tale ends not with soliloquies and double suicide, though, but with the young lovers starting a youth peace movement to agitate against the authorities.

Paluck found that the show did change listeners' beliefs, but not in all the ways it hoped to. Listeners didn't change their views on the roots of mass violence, for example, nor did they come around to the idea, emphasized in the show, that bystanders were complicit in violent acts if they did nothing.

But the show did seem to change people's understanding of social norms. In particular, it seemed to get them to see political dissent and intergroup marriage as more acceptable. Essentially, Paluck suggests, because characters on the show defended an idea, listeners were more likely to think members of their own community did, too.

To Paluck, this finding is heartening. It's social norms more than personal 25
beliefs that drive group behavior, she points out, and in Rwanda in particular

changing those — rather than trying to change individual minds — may be the key to preventing tensions from breaking out into violence.

"You're going to do what's acceptable in a certain situation, even if it's not what you think," she says.

It remains to be seen, though, how healthy soap operas can be made before they lose their hold on viewers. Different audiences have different demands, of course, but the reason soaps "work" — the reason they become so entwined in people's lives — isn't because they promise self-improvement, but something like its opposite. They promise indulgence: the taste of vicarious debasement, the mindless escape from real-world concerns and responsibilities. The world's edutainers should probably keep that in mind. Even when soaps are doing good, they need to feel a little bad.

READING THE TEXT

1. Why do you think Bennett begins by outlining the dysfunctionality of Oakdale, the fictional town in *As the World Turns*?

2. Summarize in your own words the reasons Bennett gives to explain why "soap operas are improving lives around the world" (para. 3).

3. Why might fictional television have an educational effect that traditional means of instruction may not have, according to this article?

4. In several places, Bennett admits that "the behavioral impact of soap operas can be ambiguous" (para. 19). In what ways does this admission affect the persuasiveness of his overall argument?

READING THE SIGNS

1. In class, brainstorm soap opera plots and characters, then discuss the extent to which they can be considered "edutainment." Use your observations as the basis of your own essay in which you assess the educational value, or lack thereof, of American soap operas.

2. Most of the evidence that Bennett presents for the educational benefit of soap operas involves female viewers. In an essay, explain why you think this pattern is the case. To develop your ideas, interview both male and female TV fans about their tastes in programming.

3. **CONNECTING TEXTS** In "The Social Networks" (p. 355), Neal Gabler critiques the presentation of friendship in current TV programming, while Bennett argues that watching ordinary characters' domestic lives and relationships can be beneficial. In an essay, argue which view of TV programming seems more persuasive to you, basing your argument on your reading of particular soap operas and friend-heavy shows. Be sure to take into account the differences between the two types of programs.

4. Bennett says that "activists, sometimes with the aid of media scholars and psychologists, are beginning to look at ways to focus the power of soaps, using them to deliver more specific messages" (para. 19). In class, brainstorm ways American soap operas could effectively achieve both entertainment

and didactic goals. Then step back and evaluate your suggestions: Do you believe that soap operas can be deliberately made "healthy" without losing "their hold on viewers" (para. 27)?

5. Most of the soap operas that researchers believe can influence viewers' behavior are not American. Research the place that soaps have in foreign TV broadcasting, focusing on the nations Bennett mentions. Use your findings as evidence in which you assess the applicability of researchers' conclusions to American TV audiences. What differences or similarities are there?

NEAL GABLER
The Social Networks

Remember *Friends*, that sprightly comedy in which no one ever seemed to be alone? Or *Sex and the City*, wherein busy Manhattan professional women always seemed to have time to share a glass of water and some lettuce? Indeed, wherever you look on television today, Neal Gabler notes in this essay that originally appeared in the *Los Angeles Times*, you are certain to see "lots of folks spending the better part of their day surrounded by their friends and family in happy conviviality." Yet oddly enough, this sort of programming is appearing "at a time when it is increasingly difficult to find this kind of deep social interaction anyplace but on TV." Clearly, Gabler suggests, television is providing some sort of compensation for the social atomization that it itself has contributed to, and thus, all the simulated conviviality, while being a pleasant "dream," is "pure wish fulfillment," indeed, rather "phony," and, perhaps, sad. The author of *An Empire of Their Own: How the Jews Invented Hollywood* (1989), *Winchell: Gossip, Power and the Culture of Celebrity* (1994), *Life the Movie: How Entertainment Conquered Reality* (1998), and *Walt Disney: The Triumph of the American Imagination* (2006), Gabler is a well-known analyst and historian of American cinema and popular culture.

With the new television season upon us, here are a few things you are virtually certain to see again and again and again: lots of folks spending the better part of their day surrounded by their friends and family in happy conviviality; folks wandering into the unlocked apartments and homes of friends, family, and neighbors at any time of the day or night as if this were the most natural thing in the world; friends and family sitting down and having lots of tearful heart-to-hearts; Little League games, school assemblies and dance recitals, all attended by, you guessed it, scads of friends and family.

You're going to be seeing these scenes repeatedly because the basic unit of television is not the lone individual or the partnership or even the nuclear family. The basic unit of television is the flock — be it the extended family of brothers and sisters, grandfathers and grandmothers, nieces, nephews, and cousins, or the extended circle of friends, and, rest assured, it is always a circle. On television friends never come in pairs; they invariably congregate in groups of three or more.

That television has become quite possibly the primary purveyor in American life of friendship and of the extended family is no recent blip. Over the last twenty years, beginning with *Seinfeld* and moving on through *Friends, Sex and the City* and more recently to *Desperate Housewives, Glee, The Big Bang Theory, How I Met Your Mother, Cougartown,* and at least a half-dozen other shows, including this season's newbies *Raising Hope* and *Better with You*, television has become a kind of friendship machine dispensing groups of people in constant and intimate contact with one another, sitting around in living rooms, restaurants, and coffee shops, sharing everything all the time. You might even say that friendship has become the basic theme of television, certainly of broadcast television, though cable has its own friendship orgies like *Men of a Certain Age, My Boys,* and *It's Always Sunny in Philadelphia*. Friendship is what television is about.

What makes this so remarkable is that it has been happening at a time when it is increasingly difficult to find this kind of deep social interaction anyplace but on TV. Nearly a decade ago, Harvard professor Robert Putnam observed in his classic *Bowling Alone* that Americans had become more and more disconnected from one another and from their society. As Putnam put it, "For the first two-thirds of the twentieth century a powerful tide bore Americans into ever deeper engagement in the life of their communities, but a few decades ago — silently, without warning — that tide reversed and we were overtaken by a treacherous current." It was a current that pulled Americans apart.

Moreover, the current that Putnam observed has, according to more ⁵ recent studies, only intensified in the last decade. One study found that Americans had one-third fewer nonfamily confidants than they had twenty years earlier, and 25 percent had no one in whom to confide whatsoever. Another study of 3,000 Americans found that on average they had only four close social contacts, but these included family members like one's own spouse. This decline in real friendships may account in part for the dramatic rise of virtual friendships like those on social-networking sites where being "friended" is less a sign of personal engagement than a quantitative measure of how many people your life has brushed and how many names you can collect, but this is friendship lite. Facebook, in fact, only underscores how much traditional friendship — friendship in which you meet, talk, and share — has become an anachronism and how much being "friended" is an ironic term.

Among the reasons Putnam cited for the increasing atomization in American life were economic pressures and anxieties; women entering the workplace in full-time employment by necessity and thus disengaging from their friends and neighbors; metropolitan sprawl, which meant more time spent commuting, greater social segregation, and the disruption of community boundaries; and last but by no means least, the rise of television itself, especially its splintering influence on later generations who have grown up addicted to the tube. It is no secret that watching television is not exactly a communal activity. Rather, we often use it to fill a communal void. But instead of bringing comfort, it seems only to remind us of our alienation. In Putnam's view, based on several studies, "TV is apparently especially attractive for people who feel unhappy, particularly when there is nothing else to do."

It's not that we prefer television to human contact. The laugh track attests that most people don't really want to be alone in front of their TV sets. They want to be part of a larger community. Yet another study indicates that TV provides a sort of simulacrum of community because the relationship between the TV viewer and the people he or she watches on the screen competes with and even substitutes for physical encounters with real people. It is Facebook with hundreds of "friends" but without any actual contact with any of them, only the virtual contact of watching.

But what none of these theories of television has noticed is that TV has learned how to compensate for the increasing alienation it seems to induce. And it compensates not by letting us kill time with "friends" on-screen but by providing us with those nonstop fantasies of friendship, which clearly give us a vicarious pleasure. Watch *Seinfeld* or *Friends* or *Sex and the City* or *Community* or *Men of a Certain Age* — the list is endless — and you'll see people who not only are never ever alone but people whose relationships are basically smooth, painless, uninhibited and deeply, deeply intimate — the kind of friendships we may have had in college but that most of us can only dream about now. How many adults do you know who manage to hang out with their friends every single day for hour after hour?

Or watch the incomparable *Modern Family* or *Brothers and Sisters* or *Parenthood* and you'll see big, happy family gatherings with lots of bonhomie and jokes and an outpouring of love. On the last there seems to be a huge extended family dinner every other night where most families would be lucky to have one such get-together each year at Thanksgiving. And don't forget those school assemblies, already mentioned, which everyone in the family takes off work to attend en masse or the weekend birthday parties where attendance is also compulsory.

One feels a little churlish pointing out how phony most of this intimacy 10 is. After all, these shows, even one as observant as *Modern Family*, aren't about realism. They aren't about the genuine emotional underpinnings of friendship or family, and they certainly aren't about the rough course that almost every relationship, be it with a friend or family member, takes — the inevitable squabbles, the sometimes long and even permanent ruptures, the obtuseness, the selfishness, the reprioritization, the expectations of reciprocity, the drifting apart, the agonizing sense of loneliness even within the flock. These shows are pure wish fulfillment. They offer us friends and family at one's beck and call but without any of the hassles. It is friendship as we want it to be.

For the fact is that we miss the friendships we no longer have, and we know that Facebook or e-mails cannot possibly compensate for the loss. So we sit in front of our television sets and enjoy the dream of friendship instead: a dream where we need never be alone, where there are a group of people who would do anything for us, and where everyone seems to understand us to our very core, just like Jerry and George, Chandler and Joey, Carrie and her girls, or the members of the McKinley High glee club. It is a powerful dream, and it is one that may now be the primary pleasure of television.

READING THE TEXT

1. Summarize in your own words what Gabler means by saying "The basic unit of television is the flock" (para. 2).
2. How does Robert Putnam's research on friendship in America inform Gabler's argument?
3. Why does Gabler say that "being 'friended' is an ironic term" (para. 5)?
4. How does Gabler use concession to strengthen his argument?
5. In your own words, explain what Gabler means by "simulacrum of community" (para. 7)?

READING THE SIGNS

1. Write an argumentative essay in which you assess the validity of Gabler's claim that "instead of bringing comfort, [television] seems only to remind us of our alienation" (para. 6). To support your argument, you might interview friends or acquaintances about their reasons for watching television.
2. In an essay, analyze an episode of one of the friend-heavy TV programs that Gabler mentions, such as *Desperate Housewives, Glee,* or *Modern Family*. To what extent does it confirm Gabler's assertion that "These shows are pure wish fulfillment" (para. 10)?
3. **CONNECTING TEXTS**   Write an essay in which you support, oppose, or complicate Gabler's belief that Facebook offers "friendship lite" (para. 5). To develop your ideas, read or reread "Students Addicted to Social Media" (p. 483) and Ian Daly, "Virtual Popularity Isn't Cool — It's Pathetic" (p. 480).
4. **CONNECTING TEXTS**   Read or reread Barbara Ehrenreich's "Bright-Sided" (p. 532), and write an essay in which you explore whether Americans' tendency toward sunny optimism contributes to television's unrealistic portrayal of friendships. Be sure to base your argument on an analysis of specific TV programs.

ROLAND LAIRD

The Boondocks: *Carrying On the Tradition of Subversive Black Comedy*

The Boondocks may be an acquired taste. Indeed, as Roland Laird writes in this historical analysis of the "minstrel" tradition in which the animated series can be situated, "some viewers may be offended by the self-loathing ruminations of *The Boondocks*' 'Uncle Ruckus'." But for Laird, "When I see a black character like Uncle Ruckus spouting the most anti-black sentiments ever shown on TV I laugh, but it challenges me to think about the various strains of self-hatred that are present in my community; some obvious, some not so much." *The Boondocks*, in short, is subversive comedy, Laird argues, subverting destructive behavior, both black and white. Roland Laird is the founder and CEO of Posro Media and the author of *Still I Rise: A Graphic History of African Americans* (2009).

Earlier this summer when one of my friends defiantly proclaimed that she doesn't like *The Boondocks* cartoon because it's too "minstrel-like," I almost told her how Spike Lee–ish her statement was. Instead, I held my tongue, took a deep breath, and said that although *The Boondocks* (as well as much of American ensemble comedy) may indeed have a structural indebtedness to minstrelsy, it follows in the tradition of the best subversive comedy.

Historically speaking, the American minstrel show began with Dan Emmett's Virginia Minstrels in 1843. Though there were earlier white performers that entertained audiences in blackface, Emmett and his crew were the first to dress all of its performers in blackface and as abolitionist sentiment gained steam in some parts of America, the minstrel show with its primary themes being depictions of enslaved blacks being happy and contented with their lot in life, became a popular way to maintain the status quo in the minds of many Americans. Over time these shows developed a catalog of stock characters to do their bidding. Though individual minstrel shows could point to dozens of different characters, they were all derived from seven stock characters: the Tom, the Coon, the Mulatto, the Mammy, the Buck, the Wench, and the Pickaninny.

As these characters became more deeply embedded in the American psyche, the first attempt at comically subverting them on a national stage began with black entertainers Bert Williams and George Walker. Though Williams and Walker were steeped in minstrel tradition — having performed with minstrel shows early in their careers — they felt contempt for the stereotypical roles they played, and as their careers progressed, Walker and Williams began

359

to move away from the minstrel stereotypes by introducing African themes and characters into American shows.

They first did this with the 1903 release of *In Dahomey*, a musical comedy about black people who find a pot of gold, use the money to move back to Africa and after overcoming some plot twists, are crowned royalty. For *In Dahomey* Williams and Walker teamed with Will Marion Cook, Jesse Ship, and poet/lyricist Paul Laurence Dunbar. *In Dahomey*, though hardly searing social commentary, was subversive on two levels: 1) it was the first musical to open on Broadway written and performed entirely by African Americans and 2) it used humor and dialect to positively depict the life of a black man in Africa, in contrast to that of a black man in America. This can be seen in the following lyrics:

> Evah dahkey is a King.
> Royalty is jes' de ting.
> If yo' social life is a bungle,
> Jes' you go back to the jungle,
> And remember dat you daddy was a king.
> White fo'k's what's got dahkey servants,
> Try and get dem everything.
> You must never speak insulting.
> You may be talking to a king.

Though the dialect is humorously stereotypical and simplistic, the message that life in Africa was better than life in America and that black people had a humanity that was worthy of respect came through loud and clear to those willing to look past the "darky" trappings. In 1903, this was truly a subversive message.   5

Unfortunately, Walker suffered from bad health and died in 1911, and though Williams persevered and went on to headline the Ziegfield follies, he died in 1922. With the deaths of both men, the subversive black comedic spirit was dealt a blow.

As the twentieth century progressed the stock minstrel stereotypes continued to be adopted by the next forms of American mass entertainment: the motion picture and radio.

In radio, the most famous use of these characters was the *Amos' n' Andy* program which began broadcasting in 1928. Motion pictures didn't base entire productions on the stock minstrel characters, but instead populated many of their comedies and dramas with minstrel-influenced stereotypes, with characters like Stephin Fetchit, Sleep N Eat, Buckwheat, and Butterfly, to name a few.

However, in the midst of this stereotypcial barrage on radio and film, there was one noteworthy act of subversive black comedy in book form: George Schuyler's 1931 novel, *Black No More*.

Often credited as the first work of black science fiction, Schuyler's novel   10 was a caustic satire about race relations in America. Rather than attempt to offset the minstrel stereotypes that had formed over the previous 100 years, Schuyler took America's race phobia head on by creating a character, Dr. Junius Crookman, who believes he's solved Amercia's race problem by inventing a process that removes the pigment from black people's dark skin, and for all intents and purposes turns them "white."

As a masterful work of satire, Schuyler's book is timeless and a must read for anybody who likes an intelligent laugh; however, it would be nearly thirty years before another comparably satirical voice emerged. That voice belonged to Dick Gregory.

Though a standup comedian, in many ways, Gregory's ascension was similar to Walker and Williams in that Gregory's core audience, like Walker and Williams', consisted of both black and white people. Being a product of the Civil Rights movement, these audiences responded favorably to Gregory's unique use of humor to highlight the hypocrisies and inconsistencies of American race relations. For example, in one of his early routines, Gregory made the statement, "People wonder how, with so many inferior jobs, black people afford so many Cadillacs? Well racial segregation buys us Cadillacs. I can't join no country club, so that's $500 saved right there. You know I'm not going to take my family to Florida this winter, so that's $1,500 saved there. If I walk out of here and get hit by a bus, I'm not going to the best hospital where they charge $2,500, I'm going to City Hospital where it's free. Figure it out: $500 + $1,500 + $2,500, that's $4,500 I can walk into General Motors, and get whatever I want."

Also, like Schuyler, Gregory was not afraid to direct his humor at black people. In one routine, he said, "I support the NAACP, I'm a member, but do you realize that if this country was integrated tomorrow, all those cats would be out of a job?"

Such social critique may seem tepid by today's standards, but fifty years ago, it was radical, and opened the doors for more satirical and subversively humorous racially charged commentary. Comedians like Richard Pryor, Franklin Ajaye, and Bill Cosby expanded on Gregory's wit and commentary by creating new subversive characters like Mudbone, Bumpy Woods, and Fat Albert. Mudbone was Pryor's creation, an older, foul-mouthed wino who spoke wisely, though profanely. Simply put, he was an answer to the "coon" and "tom" characters of minstrel days.

Ajaye's Bumpy Woods motif was the minstrel "buck" reconceived as 15 the politicized black man who, rather than lust after white women, protected and loved black women, albeit humorously. Finally, Cosby's Albert character was the most subversive of the bunch, because not only did Albert enable Cosby to humorously recount his childhood in his standup routine, but it also served as an answer to the pickaninny minstrel character. Once Fat Albert became an animated series, it too served as a sophisticated response to the racist *Looney Tunes* characters that were part of the company's catalog.

The collective work of each of these men created a tradition for even more subversive black comedic talents that came along later. It is this tradition, rather than the minstrel tradition, that shows like *In Living Color* of the '90s, *Chappelle's Show* of the early '00s, and the currently running, afore-mentioned *The Boondocks* owes its greatest debt.

Boondocks creator Aaron Magruder and *In Living Color* creator Keenan Ivory Wayans may or may not have heard of George Walker or Bert Williams, but when either show makes use of elaborately constructed musical and dance routines, their craftmanship and authenticity pays homage to the stage work of Walker and Williams.

Similarly, some viewers may be offended by the self-loathing rumina-tions of *The Boondocks*' "Uncle Ruckus" or the *Chappelle's Show*'s "blind black Klansman," but those comedic depictions are strongly influenced by charac-ters in Schuyler's *Black No More* as well as Pryor's Mudbone.

It's true that much of the disdain for *The Boondocks* comes from its pro-pensity for profanity, not least its use of the "n" word, but even those linguis-tic choices are part of the subversive black comedic tradition, and not the minstrel tradition. It was Gregory who wrote a book in 1964 entitled *Nigger* and Pryor who recorded the album *That Nigger's Crazy*. This is not to say that that the "n" word is a positive aspect to the subversive tradition, but merely to posit the usage in the proper place.

When my friend accused *The Boondocks* of minstrelsy, she didn't mean 20 it wasn't funny, she just thought it funny for the wrong reasons. Her con-cern is that *The Boondocks* perpetuates a negative imagery of black people and undermines the work of more socially conscious black artists. I'd argue that this type of humor in fact cleverly subverts the status quo. When I see a black character like Uncle Ruckus spouting the most anti-black sentiments ever shown on TV I laugh, but it challenges me to think about the various strains of self-hatred that are present in my community; some obvious, some not so much.

In a similar vein, when Martin Luther King is mysteriously brought back to life in an episode of *The Boondocks*, only to see self-destructive behavior going on in our communities, I realize that there is still institutional and indi-vidual racism in America despite King's progress, but that doesn't explain away the very real, ongoing self-destructive behavior among some African Americans, as this episode depicts.

This ability to sharply comment on race and society while at the same time poking fun at black and white people is part and parcel of the subversive comic tradition. Whether one thinks *The Boondocks* is a master of subversive humor or not is a matter of taste; but surely it hasn't done the tradition any disservice.

READING THE TEXT

1. How did the early minstrel shows differ from the 1903 release of *In Dahomey*, according to Laird, and what does he see as the significance of that difference?

2. What is your own response to the lyrics from *In Dahomey* that Laird quotes? Compare your response with those of your classmates.

3. How does Laird interpret the cultural contributions of artists such as George Schuyler and Dick Gregory?

4. What evidence does the author present to support his contention that *The Boondocks* should not be seen as part of the minstrel tradition?

READING THE SIGNS

1. **CONNECTING TEXTS** Read George Schuyler's 1931 novel *Black No More*. Write a semiotic analysis of its depiction of race relations. To develop your ideas, consult Michael Omi's "In Living Color: Race and American Culture" (p. 625).

2. Analyze the character Fat Albert in *Fat Albert and the Cosby Kids* and write an essay in which you take on Laird's claim that Albert "was the most subversive" black character of his time (para. 15). Do you see Albert as subversive, and why? If not, why not? Alternatively, conduct a similar analysis of the character in the 2004 film *Fat Albert*. Does the latter version of the character retain any of the subversive traits that Laird sees in his earlier incarnation?

3. Read at least two weeks' of *The Boondocks* comics, or watch an episode of the program, and write an essay in which you support, refute, or modify Laird's claim that it "cleverly subverts the status quo" (para. 20).

4. Watch an episode of a television program such as *House of Payne* or *Meet the Browns*. In an essay, analyze the extent to which it fits the description of "subversive" art that Laird proposes?

5. **CONNECTING TEXTS** In his discussion of *The Simpsons* (p. 305), Carl Matheson describes one version of subversive humor. In an analytic essay, adopt Matheson's views as a critical frame and analyze an episode of *The Boondocks*. To what extent does *The Boondocks* exhibit the sort of hyper-ironic humor that Matheson describes? If you see divergences, how do you explain them?

THE HOLLYWOOD SIGN

The Culture of American Film

The Culture Industry

Moviemakers have been providing America, and world audiences, with entertainments that have both reflected and shaped audience desires for more than a century. Long before the advent of TV, movies were providing their viewers with the glamour, romance, and sheer excitement that modern life seems to deny. So effective have movies been in molding audience desire that such early culture critics as Theodor Adorno and Max Horkheimer[1] have accused them of being part of a vast, Hollywood-centered "culture industry" whose products have successfully distracted their audiences from the inequities of modern life, and so have effectively maintained the social status quo under capitalism by drawing everyone's attention away from it.

More recent analysts, however, are far less pessimistic. Indeed, for many cultural studies "populists," films, along with the rest of popular culture, can represent a kind of mass resistance to the political dominance — or what is often called the *hegemony* — of the social and economic powers-that-be. For such critics, films can provide utopian visions of a better world, stimulating their viewers to imagine how their society might be improved, and so, perhaps, inspiring them to go out and do something about it.

Whether you believe that films distract us from the real world or inspire us to imagine a better one, their central place in contemporary American culture demands interpretation, for their impact goes well beyond the movie theater

---

[1]**Theodor Adorno** (1903–1969) and **Max Horkheimer** (1895–1973) authored *Dialectic of Enlightenment* (1947), a book whose analyses included a scathing indictment of the culture industry. — EDS.

or video screen. Far from being mere entertainments, movies constitute a profound part of our everyday lives, with every film festival and award becoming major news, and each major release becoming the talk of the country, splashed across the entire terrain of American media from newspapers to television to the Internet. Just think of the pressure you feel to be able to discuss the latest film sensation among your friends. Consider how, if you decide to save a few bucks and wait for the DVD release, you can lose face and be seriously on the social outs. No, there is nothing frivolous about the movies. You've been watching them all your life: Now's the time to start thinking about them **semiotically**.

Interpreting the Signs of American Film

Interpreting a movie or a group of movies is not unlike interpreting a television program or group of programs. Here too you must suspend your personal feelings or aesthetic judgments about your subject. As with any semiotic analysis, your goal is to interpret the cultural significance of your topic, not to give it a thumbs up or a thumbs down. Thus, you may find it more rewarding to interpret those films that promise to be culturally meaningful rather than simply choosing your favorite flick. Determining whether a movie is culturally meaningful in the prewriting stage, of course, may be a hit-or-miss affair; you may find that your first choice does not present any particularly interesting grounds for interpretation. That's why it can be helpful to consider reasons a particular movie is special, such as enormous popularity or widespread critical attention. Of course, cult favorites, while often lacking in critical or popular attention, can also be **signs** pointing toward their more self-selected audiences and so are perfectly good candidates for analysis. Academy Award candidates are also reliable as cultural signs.

Your interpretation of a movie or group of movies should begin with a construction of the *system* in which it belongs — that is, those movies, past and present, with which it can be *associated*. While tracing those associations, be on the lookout for striking *differences* from what is otherwise like what you are analyzing because those differences are what often reveal the significance of your subject.

Discussing the Signs of Film

In any given year, one film may dominate the Hollywood box office, becoming a blockbuster that captures that public's cinematic imagination. In class, discuss which film would be your choice as this year's top hit. Then analyze the film semiotically. Why has *this* film so successfully appealed to so many moviegoers?

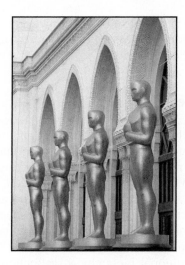

A row of Oscar statues. Oscar award–winning films are often good subjects for semiotic analysis.

Archetypes are useful features for film analysis as well. An archetype is anything that has been repeated in storytelling from ancient times to the present. There are character archetypes, such as the wise old man, which include such figures as Yoda and Gandalf, and plot archetypes, as in the heroic quest, which is the archetypal backbone of films like *The Lord of the Rings* trilogy. All those male buddy films — from *Butch Cassidy and the Sundance Kid* to *Lethal Weapon* to *Men in Black* — hark back to archetypal male bonding stories as old as *The Epic of Gilgamesh* (from the third millennium B.C.) and the *Iliad*, while Cruella de Vil from *101 Dalmatians* is sister to the Wicked Witch of the West, Snow White's evil stepmother, and every other witch or crone dreamed up by the patriarchal imagination. All those sea monsters, from Jonah's "whale" to Moby Dick to the great white shark in *Jaws*, are part of the same archetypal phylum, and every time a movie hero struggles to return home after a long journey — Dorothy to Kansas, Lassie to Timmy — a story as old as Exodus and the *Odyssey* is retold.

Hollywood is well aware of the enduring appeal of archetypes (see Linda Seger's selection in this chapter for a how-to description of archetypal script writing), and director George Lucas's reliance on the work of anthropologist Joseph Campbell in his creation of the *Star Wars* saga is widely known. But it is not always the case that either creators or consumers are consciously aware of the archetypes before them. Part of a culture's collective unconscious, archetypal stories can send messages that their audiences only subliminally understand. A heavy dosage of male-bonding films in a given Hollywood season, for instance, can send the unspoken cultural message that a man can't really make friends with a woman and that women are simply the sexual reward for manly men. Similarly, too many witches in a given Hollywood season can send the antifeminist message that there are too many bitches (think of *Fatal Attraction* and *Basic Instinct*).

Repetition with a Difference

Just as movies frequently repeat ancient archetypal character and plot types, they also may refer to other movies and modern cultural artifacts in what is referred to as a **postmodern** manner. Postmodernism is, in effect, both a historical period and an attitude. As a historical period, postmodernism refers to the culture that has emerged in the wake of the advent of mass media, one obsessed with electronic imagery and the products of mass culture. As an attitude, postmodernism rejects the values of the past, not in favor of new values but instead to ironize value systems as such. Thus, in the postmodern worldview, our traditional hierarchical distinctions valuing high culture over low culture, say, or creativity over imitation, tend to get flattened out. What was once viewed in terms of an oppositional hierarchy (origination is opposed to emulation and is superior to it) is reconceived and deconstructed. Postmodern artists, accordingly, tend to reproduce, with an ironic or parodic twist, already existing cultural images in their work, especially if they can be drawn from mass culture and mass society — as Roy Lichtenstein's cartoon canvasses parody popular cartoon books and Andy Warhol's tomato soup cans repeat the familiar labels of the Campbell Soup Company — thus mixing high culture and mass culture in a new, nonoppositional, relation.

To put this another way, the postmodern worldview holds that it is no longer possible or desirable to create new images; rather, one surveys the vast range of available images that mass culture has to offer, and repeats them, but with a difference. Postmodern filmmakers accordingly allude to existing films in their work, as in the final scene of Tim Burton's *Batman*, which directly alludes to Alfred Hitchcock's *Vertigo*, or Oliver Stone's and Quentin Tarantino's *Natural Born Killers*, which recalls *Bonnie and Clyde*. Such allusions to, and repetitions of, existing cultural images in postmodern cinema are called

---

Exploring the Signs of Film

In your journal, list your favorite movies. Then consider your list: What does it say about you? What **cultural myths** do the movies tend to reflect, and why do you think those myths appeal to you? What signs particularly appeal to your emotions? What sort of stories about human life do you most respond to?

double-coding, because of the way that the postmodern artifact simultaneously refers to existing cultural **codes** and recasts them in new contexts. The
conclusion of *Batman*, for example, while echoing *Vertigo's* climactic scene,
differs dramatically in its significance, turning from Hitchcock's tragedy to
Burton's quasi-farce.

Movies as Metaphors

Sometimes movies can also be seen as metaphors for larger cultural concerns. Consider the grade-B horror flicks of the 1950s, such as the original
Godzilla. If we study only its plot, we would see little more than a cheesy
horror story featuring a reptilian monster that is an archetypal kin of the
dragons in medieval literature. But Godzilla was no mere dragon transported
to the modern world. The dragons that populated the world of medieval storytelling were themselves often used as metaphors for the satanic serpent
in the Garden of Eden, but Godzilla was a wholly different sort of metaphor.
Created by Japanese filmmakers, Godzilla was originally a metaphor for the
nuclear era. A female mutant creation of nuclear poisoning, Godzilla rose
over her Japanese audiences like a mushroom cloud, symbolizing the potential for future mushroom clouds both in Japan and around the world in the
Cold War era.

For their part, American filmmakers in the 1950s had their own metaphors for the nuclear era. Whenever some "blob" threatened to consume New
York or some especially toxic slime escaped from a laboratory, the suggestion
that science — especially nuclear science — was threatening to destroy the
world filled the theater along with the popcorn fumes. And if it wasn't science
that was the threat, Cold War filmmakers could scare us with Communists, as
films like *Invasion of the Body Snatchers* metaphorically suggested through its

Reading Film on the Net

Most major films now released in the United States receive their own
Web sites. You can find them listed in print ads for the film (check
your local newspaper). Select a current film, find the Web address,
log on, and analyze the film's site semiotically. What images are used
to attract your interest in the film? What interactive strategies, if any,
are used to increase your commitment to the film? If you've seen the
movie, how does the Net presentation of it compare with your experience viewing it either in a theater or on video? Alternatively, analyze
the posters designed to attract attention to a particular film; a useful
resource is the Movie Poster Page (www.musicman.com/mp/mp.html).

depiction of a town in which everyone looked the same but had really been taken over by aliens. "Beware of your neighbors," the movie seemed to warn, "they could be Communists."

In such ways, an entire film can be a kind of metaphor, but you can find many smaller metaphors at work in the details of a movie as well. Early filmmakers, for example, used to put a tablecloth on the table in dining scenes to signify that the characters at the table were good, decent people (you can find such a metaphor in Charlie Chaplin's *The Kid*, where an impoverished tramp who can't afford socks or a bathrobe still has a nice tablecloth on the breakfast table). Sometimes a director's metaphors have a broad political significance, as at the end of the Rock Hudson/James Dean/Elizabeth Taylor classic *Giant*, where the parting shot presents a tableau of a white baby goat standing next to a black baby goat, which is juxtaposed with the image of a white baby standing in a crib side by side with a brown baby. Since the human babies are both the grandchildren of the film's protagonist (one of whose sons has married a Mexican woman, the other an Anglo), the goats are added to underscore metaphorically (if rather heavy-handedly) the message of racial reconciliation that the director wanted to send.

Reading a film, then, is much like reading a novel. Both are texts filled with intentional and unintentional signs, metaphors, and archetypes, and both are cultural signifiers. The major difference is in their medium of expression. Literary texts are cast entirely in written words; films combine verbal language, visual imagery, and sound effects. Thus, we perceive literary and cinematic texts differently, for the written sign is perceived in a linear fashion that relies on one's cognitive and imaginative powers, while a film primarily targets the senses: one sees and hears (and sometimes even smells!). That film is such a sensory experience often conceals its textuality. One is tempted to sit back and go with the flow, to say that it's only entertainment and doesn't have to "mean" anything at all. But even the most cartoonish cinematic entertainment can harbor a rather profound cultural significance. To see how, let's look at another *Batman*.

Batman: The Dark Knight

We can begin with a movie poster.

One of the posters used to advertise *Batman: The Dark Knight* (2008) featured the familiar figure of Batman, in full regalia, standing in front of a high-rise office building whose upper floors are on fire. This image would be immediately recognizable to American audiences as alluding to the September 11 attacks on the World Trade Center and is a key signifier of what was different about this late entry into the long history of Batman movies and television shows. As always, this difference is crucial to understanding the cultural significance of the film.

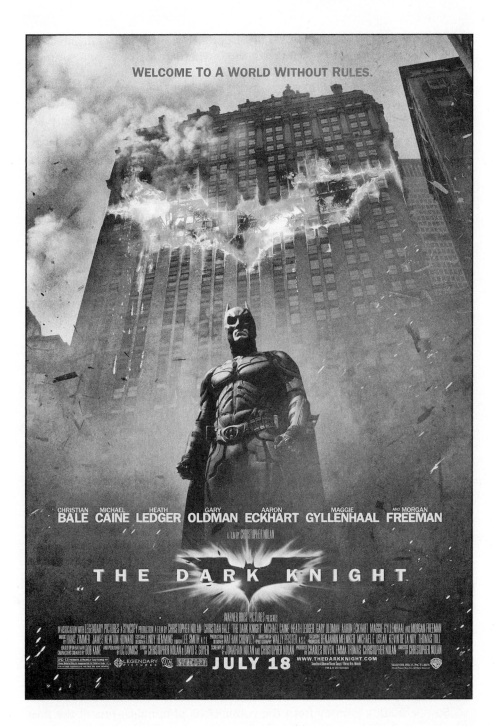

Heath Ledger's Joker provides an especially good figure with which to start. In the early days of the Batman saga, when Batman was still simply a comic book hero for children, the Joker was one of a group of villains who were little more than what Andy Medhurst has called "wacky conjurors." Like Burgess Meredith's Penguin in the 1960s *Batman* television series, the Joker was as much clown as criminal, not really very frightening and mostly out for a fast buck. Ledger's Joker belongs to this system and thus can be associated with all the other Jokers and villains within it. But we can see a striking difference. This Joker is no clown; he is an out-of-control homicidal maniac, and although he robs banks, he most certainly is not motivated by a desire for money. Something else is going on.

Ledger's Joker, of course, was not pulled out of a hat. Before Ledger there was Jack Nicholson, and before Nicholson there was *Arkham Asylum*. That graphic novel introduced a far more disturbing Joker into the system, a psychopath rather than a mere criminal. Jack Nicholson's Joker in Tim Burton's *Batman* surely displayed some of the maniacal energy of the *Arkham* Joker, and he was far more violent and sadistic than any Joker in the past. Still, Nicholson's Joker was motivated by desires that his audience could understand: He wanted money, he wanted power, and he wanted revenge. We see him ruthlessly taking over the organized crime syndicate in Gotham City because he wants to be at its head. His war with Batman is fueled by an earlier duel with the Caped Crusader that left him disfigured for life. We may not be on his side, but we can understand him.

And we can also laugh with him. His epic attack on the art gallery is just plain funny, and his ability to run rings around everyone in Gotham City, especially the news media, make Nicholson's Joker something like a standup comedian — a murderous comedian, but a comedian all the same.

Heath Ledger's Joker is no comedian. He is never funny. Much more importantly, he does not seem to have any motives for his actions. He doesn't want power, as is evident from the fact that while he makes war on the mob, he does not attempt to build his own organization. Rather, he continually murders his own subordinates, along with the mob leaders whose organization he is taking over. And he doesn't want money, which is dramatically symbolized by his setting fire to a huge pile of cash atop which sits the mob's accountant. He doesn't really seem to want revenge (even his indications that he was cruelly raised — suggesting thereby a possible revenge motive emerging from his childhood — are undercut by later speeches that make it clear that he will say just about anything, no matter how untrue). And he doesn't want sex (Nicholson's Joker had a girlfriend, though she was horribly abused; Ledger's Joker is completely unattached). Basically, all he wants to do is create mayhem and make people suffer as much as possible.

So it is quite a journey from the comic book criminal-clowns of the past to Ledger's Joker. The semiotic question is: What does this journey mean?

The key change here is one of ever-increasing violence. When we look at popular culture more generally, we can find innumerable instances of

Jack Nicholson (left) and Heath Ledger (right) had vastly different takes on *Batman* arch-villain the Joker.

ever-more-violent entertainment with which the Batman saga can be associated. Consider the difference between the horror films of the 1950s and today's splatter films, or even between Hitchcock's *Psycho* and Van Sant's. And then there's Dexter, who manages to out-Hannibal Hannibal Lecter. From all the signs, not only do today's audiences want increased violence, but they don't want much to be left to the imagination. The more gruesome, the better. What is more, audiences are attracted to representations of emotional as well as physical torture, as seen in such movies as *Hostel*, parts 1 and 2, and the *Saw* franchise, as well as in the way that Ledger's Joker emotionally tortures his victims, such as the civilians on a ferryboat who are forced to choose between the destruction of their boat or that of one carrying a group of criminals evacuated from a prison.

Does this mean that people are more violent today than in the past or more evil? No, not really. Violence has always been a staple of low cultural entertainment (indeed, for the ancient Romans, violent entertainment was literally violent and not merely a simulation). But Americans have traditionally chosen to restrict the level of violence that they allow in their entertainments. The famous Hays Code of the 1930s, for example, represented a self-imposed censorship by the film industry, restricting not only the sexual content of movies but its violent content as well. But with the passing of the years those restrictions have been considerably loosened. Why?

As always, the answer is **overdetermined**. Part of it lies in an increasing sophistication in American audiences who will no longer accept as realistic a highly toned-down representation of violence. In the TV Westerns of the 1950s, for example, when a man was shot at close range by a .45 caliber bullet, audiences were satisfied with a small spot of blood where the bullet went in. Now they want to see what a .45 caliber bullet really does at close range.

But there is another explanation as well. Remember, history shows that the appeal of violent entertainment is universal, which implies that at any time there will be an audience for it. Until relatively recently, American values held that such a desire should not be satisfied, that extremely violent entertainment should not be allowed in a civilized society. So what changed?

Here we can look at one of those primary contradictions in American culture that we will explore more fully in Chapter 6 of this book: the contradiction between America's "spiritual" and "materialistic" characteristics. Our spiritual side says that it is better for the spirit to repress our violent proclivities. But our materialistic side sees that there is a lot of money to be made precisely by catering to those ancient desires. The fact that we can find the materialistic calculation overriding the spiritual principle throughout contemporary popular culture is a striking sign of the power of modern capitalism over our culture.

And yet, there is still more. Let's return to the movie poster for *Batman: The Dark Knight*. That poster, as we have seen, was immediately evocative of one of the most violent days in American history; with such violence (and more) to be found in the real world, it should not be surprising to find a demand for its realistic representation in our entertainment. Here the difference between Nicholson's and Ledger's Jokers comes back into play, for Ledger's Joker is very much a reflection of the terroristic violence of our times. Simply stated, Ledger's Joker is a terrorist, and as such he raises an important question that is very explicitly presented in the movie: Namely, how can a society fight terrorism without becoming terroristic itself?

Batman: The Dark Knight both reflects and addresses this larger cultural dilemma by dramatizing the choices that civilized societies must make when battling enemies who do not seem to respect any limits. Thus, while Batman is willing to break some rules to fight the Joker, he is not willing to kill him when he has him at his mercy (the Joker even anticipates this as he dares Batman to kill him and so become like the Joker himself). Reflecting the dilemma that Americans face when confronted by shadowy organizations like al-Qaeda, *Batman: The Dark Knight* was ultimately a profoundly **political** film which raised questions about the conduct of the entire war on terror.

The fact that *Batman: The Dark Knight* contains both "official" and "outlaw" heroes, however, strongly indicates that it did not intend to subvert that war. As Robert B. Ray argues in "The Thematic Paradigm" (included in this chapter), an official hero is someone who serves and protects society from within its institutions. As the district attorney of Gotham City, Harvey Dent is just such a hero. His courageous war on the mob differentiates him from the bumbling and/or corrupt officials in Tim Burton's *Batman*, a difference that reflects the general rehabilitation of official heroes in the wake of the 9/11 terror attacks (such television series as the *CSI* franchise, *Criminal Minds*, and any show featuring sympathetic cops, FBI agents, or any other branch of law enforcement are all signifiers of this return to the official hero in popular culture). The fact that Harvey Dent is eventually corrupted to become Two Face does not really contradict this because the audience can see that he has a very strong motive for going "bad," and he is only after those who have hurt him (which much ameliorates his change). What is more, we see plenty of other officials in the movie who are innocent victims of the Joker (for example, the chief of police and a judge), and, in the end, it is Batman who decides that the people of Gotham City *need* an official hero, and so conspires to conceal the truth about Harvey Dent/Two Face and take all the blame for Two Face's deeds upon himself so that the people will not become overwhelmed with despair and disillusionment.

Batman himself is what Ray calls an "outlaw hero," someone who may serve and protect society, but only on his or her own terms, even if this means breaking the law. Batman is a pure outlaw hero, in that he has no official connection with law enforcement, while figures like Dirty Harry and Jack Bauer (of *24*) are outlaw heroes who work for official law enforcement institutions. Outlaw heroes have been steadily gaining precedence over official heroes in American popular culture ever since the cultural revolution of the 1960s, which dethroned most if not all of America's traditional official heroes and replaced them with a variety of outlaw heroes. It was this shift that vaulted Batman over Superman in the 1980s as America's favorite cartoon superhero.

Thus, it is significant that in *Batman: The Dark Knight* the official hero Harvey Dent and the outlaw hero Batman symbolically become one when Harvey Dent declares during a press conference that *he* is Batman in order to cover for Batman, with whom he is in alliance. This symbolic union of official and outlaw hero is especially significant in the post–9/11 era, a time when Americans have turned once more to official heroes like police, firefighters, Homeland Security personnel, and soldiers, while not abandoning the outlaw heroes of the cultural revolution.

Thus, the evidence is that *Batman: The Dark Knight* does not represent a metaphoric challenge to the war on terror. By making heroes of both sides (Dark Knight *and* D.A.) in the war with the Joker, the movie presents the moral challenges of such a war, giving the last word, so to speak, to the outlaw hero who is willing to sacrifice himself in order to keep that war going. It's all rather sentimental and not very realistic, but as a popular expression of American angst and desire in an era of unprecedented conflict, this *Batman* is no mere entertainment; it is a sign of a society desperately in need of cathartic reassurance in times that can often seem apocalyptic.

The Readings

Robert B. Ray's analysis of the "official hero" and "outlaw hero" as they appear in both American history and cinema begins this chapter, followed by Linda Seger's how-to guide for the creation of the kind of archetypal characters that made *Star Wars* one of the most popular movies of all time. In a paired set of readings, Jessica Hagedorn surveys a tradition of American filmmaking in which Asian women are stereotyped as either tragic or trivial, while Hirsh Sawhney takes on the sort of stereotyping of India in *Slumdog Millionaire* that lets Western viewers off the hook when it comes to Indian poverty. Matt Zoller Seitz follows with a critical exposé of movieland's "'Magical Negro': a saintly African American character who acts as a mentor to a questing white hero." Mitu Sengupta then surveys the critical reception of *Avatar*, a film that stirred political antipathy from both the left and the right even as it became the box-office champion of all time. Next Bob Samuels provocatively argues that *Inception* is really a kind of allegory of the way that popular culture takes hold of our consciousness, as Michael Parenti takes a social-class-based approach to the codes of American cinema, noting the caste biases inherent in such popular hits as *Pretty Woman*. David Denby's "High-School Confidential" explains why generations of teenagers flock to all those jocks-and-cheerleaders-versus-the-nerds movies, and Vivian C. Sobchack follows with an unflinching analysis of screen violence, then and now. Finally, Umberto Eco, the father of cinematic semiotics, concludes the chapter with his classic analysis of *Casablanca*.

ROBERT B. RAY
The Thematic Paradigm

Usually we consider movies to be merely entertainment, but as Robert Ray demonstrates in this selection from his book *A Certain Tendency of the Hollywood Cinema* (1985), American films have long reflected fundamental patterns and contradictions in our society's myths and values. Whether in real life or on the silver screen, Ray explains, Americans have always been ambivalent about the value of civilization, celebrating it through official heroes like George Washington and Jimmy Stewart, while at the same time questioning it through outlaw heroes like Davy Crockett and Jesse James. Especially when presented together in the same film, these two hero types help mediate America's ambivalence, providing a mythic solution. Ray's analyses show how the movies are rich sources for cultural interpretation; they provide a framework for decoding movies as different as *Lethal Weapon* and *Malcolm X*. Ray is a professor and director of film and media studies at the University of Florida at Gainesville. His publications include *The Avant Garde Finds Andy Hardy* (1995), *How a Film Theory Got Lost and Other Mysteries in Cultural Studies* (2001), and, most recently, *The ABCs of Classic Hollywood* (2008).

The dominant tradition of American cinema consistently found ways to overcome dichotomies. Often, the movies' reconciliatory pattern concentrated on a single character magically embodying diametrically opposite traits. A sensitive violinist was also a tough boxer (*Golden Boy*); a boxer was a gentle man who cared for pigeons (*On the Waterfront*). A gangster became a coward because he was brave (*Angels with Dirty Faces*); a soldier became brave because he was a coward (*Lives of a Bengal Lancer*). A war hero was a former pacifist (*Sergeant York*); a pacifist was a former war hero (*Billy Jack*). The ideal was a kind of inclusiveness that would permit all decisions to be undertaken with the knowledge that the alternative was equally available. The attractiveness of Destry's refusal to use guns (*Destry Rides Again*) depended on the tacit understanding that he could shoot with the best of them, Katharine Hepburn's and Claudette Colbert's revolts against conventionality (*Holiday, It Happened One Night*) on their status as aristocrats.

Such two-sided characters seemed particularly designed to appeal to a collective American imagination steeped in myths of inclusiveness. Indeed, in creating such characters, classic Hollywood had connected with what Erik Erikson has described as the fundamental American psychological pattern:

> The functioning American, as the heir of a history of extreme con-
> trasts and abrupt changes, bases his final ego identity on some tenta-
> tive combination of dynamic polarities such as migratory and sedentary,
> individualistic and standardized, competitive and co-operative, pious and
> free-thinking, responsible and cynical, etc. . . .
>
> To leave his choices open, the American, on the whole, lives with two
> sets of "truths."[1]

The movies traded on one opposition in particular, American culture's
traditional dichotomy of individual and community that had generated the
most significant pair of competing myths: the outlaw hero and the official
hero.[2] Embodied in the adventurer, explorer, gunfighter, wanderer, and
loner, the outlaw hero stood for that part of the American imagination valuing self-determination and freedom from entanglements. By contrast, the
official hero, normally portrayed as a teacher, lawyer, politician, farmer, or
family man, represented the American belief in collective action, and the
objective legal process that superseded private notions of right and wrong.
While the outlaw hero found incarnations in the mythic figures of Davy
Crockett, Jesse James, Huck Finn, and all of Leslie Fiedler's "Good Bad
Boys" and Daniel Boorstin's "ring-tailed roarers," the official hero developed
around legends associated with Washington, Jefferson, Lincoln, Lee, and
other "Good Good Boys."

An extraordinary amount of the traditional American mythology
adopted by Classic Hollywood derived from the variations worked by American ideology around this opposition of natural man versus civilized man.
To the extent that these variations constituted the main tendency of American literature and legends, Hollywood, in relying on this mythology, committed itself to becoming what Robert Bresson has called "the Cinema."[3] A
brief description of the competing values associated with this outlaw hero–
official hero opposition will begin to suggest its pervasiveness in traditional
American culture.

1. *Aging:* The attractiveness of the outlaw hero's childishness and pro- 5
pensity to whims, tantrums, and emotional decisions derived from America's cult of childhood. Fiedler observed that American literature celebrated
"the notion that a mere falling short of adulthood is a guarantee of insight
and even innocence." From Huck to Holden Caulfield, children in American
literature were privileged, existing beyond society's confining rules. Often,

---

[1] Erik H. Erikson, *Childhood and Society* (New York: Norton, 1963), p. 286.

[2] Leading discussions of the individual–community polarity in American culture can be
found in *The Contrapuntal Civilization: Essays Toward a New Understanding of the American
Experience*, ed. Michael Kammen (New York: Crowell, 1971). The most prominent analyses
of American literature's use of this opposition remain Leslie A. Fiedler's *Love and Death in the
American Novel* (New York: Stein and Day, 1966) and A. N. Kaul's *The American Vision* (New
Haven: Yale University Press, 1963).

[3] Robert Bresson, *Notes on Cinematography*, trans. Jonathan Griffin (New York: Urizen
Books, 1977), p. 12.

The "outlaw hero," Davy Crockett, portrayed by Fess Parker.

they set the plot in motion (e.g., *Intruder in the Dust*, *To Kill a Mockingbird*), acting for the adults encumbered by daily affairs. As Fiedler also pointed out, this image of childhood "has impinged upon adult life itself, has become a 'career' like everything else in America,"[4] generating stories like *On the Road* or *Easy Rider* in which adults try desperately to postpone responsibilities by clinging to adolescent lifestyles.

While the outlaw heroes represented a flight from maturity, the official heroes embodied the best attributes of adulthood: sound reasoning and judgment, wisdom and sympathy based on experience. Franklin's *Autobiography* and *Poor Richard's Almanack* constituted this opposing tradition's basic texts, persuasive enough to appeal even to outsiders (*The Great Gatsby*). Despite the legends surrounding Franklin and the other Founding Fathers, however, the scarcity of mature heroes in American literature and mythology indicated American ideology's fundamental preference for youth, a quality that came to be associated with the country itself. Indeed, American stories often distorted the stock figure of the Wise Old Man, portraying him as mad (Ahab), useless (Rip Van Winkle), or evil (the Godfather).

[4]Leslie A. Fiedler, *No! In Thunder* (New York: Stein and Day, 1972), pp. 253, 275.

2. *Society and Women*: The outlaw hero's distrust of civilization, typically represented by women and marriage, constituted a stock motif in American mythology. In his *Studies in Classic American Literature*, D. H. Lawrence detected the recurring pattern of flight, observing that the Founding Fathers had come to America "largely to get *away*. . . . Away from what? In the long run, away from themselves. Away from everything."[5] Sometimes, these heroes undertook this flight alone (Thoreau, *Catcher in the Rye*); more often, they joined ranks with other men: Huck with Jim, Ishmael with Queequeg, Jake Barnes with Bill Gorton. Women were avoided as representing the very entanglements this tradition sought to escape: society, the "settled life," confining responsibilities. The outlaw hero sought only uncompromising relationships, involving either a "bad" woman (whose morals deprived her of all rights to entangling domesticity) or other males (who themselves remained independent). Even the "bad" woman posed a threat, since marriage often uncovered the clinging "good" girl underneath. Typically, therefore, American stories avoided this problem by killing off the "bad" woman before the marriage could transpire (*Destry Rides Again*, *The Big Heat*, *The Far Country*). Subsequently, within the all-male group, women became taboo, except as the objects of lust.

The exceptional extent of American outlaw legends suggests an ideological anxiety about civilized life. Often, that anxiety took shape as a romanticizing of the dispossessed, as in the Beat Generation's cult of the bum, or the characters of Huck and "Thoreau," who worked to remain idle, unemployed, and unattached. A passage from Jerzy Kosinski's *Steps* demonstrated the extreme modern version of this romanticizing:

> I envied those [the poor and the criminals] who lived here and seemed so free, having nothing to regret and nothing to look forward to. In the world of birth certificates, medical examinations, punch cards, and computers, in the world of telephone books, passports, bank accounts, insurance plans, wills, credit cards, pensions, mortgages and loans, they lived unattached.[6]

In contrast to the outlaw heroes, the official heroes were preeminently worldly, comfortable in society, and willing to undertake even those public duties demanding personal sacrifice. Political figures, particularly Washington and Lincoln, provided the principal examples of this tradition, but images of family also persisted in popular literature from *Little Women* to *Life with Father* and *Cheaper by the Dozen*. The most crucial figure in this tradition, however, was Horatio Alger, whose heroes' ambition provided the complement to Huck's disinterest. Alger's characters subscribed fully to the codes

[5]D. H. Lawrence, *Studies in Classic American Literature* (New York: Viking/Compass, 1961), p. 3. See also Fiedler's *Love and Death in the American Novel* and Sam Bluefarb's *The Escape Motif in the American Novel: Mark Twain to Richard Wright* (Columbus: Ohio State University Press, 1972).
[6]Jerzy Kosinski, *Steps* (New York: Random House, 1968), p. 133.

of civilization, devoting themselves to proper dress, manners, and behavior, and the attainment of the very things despised by the opposing tradition: the settled life and respectability.[7]

3. *Politics and the Law*: Writing about "The Philosophical Approach of the Americans," Tocqueville noted "a general distaste for accepting any man's word as proof of anything." That distaste took shape as a traditional distrust of politics as collective activity, and of ideology as that activity's rationale. Such a disavowal of ideology was, of course, itself ideological, a tactic for discouraging systematic political intervention in a nineteenth-century America whose political and economic power remained in the hands of a privileged few. Tocqueville himself noted the results of this mythology of individualism which "disposes each citizen to isolate himself from the mass of his fellows and withdraw into the circle of family and friends; with this little society formed to his taste, he gladly leaves the greater society to look after itself."[8]

This hostility toward political solutions manifested itself further in an ambivalence about the law. The outlaw mythology portrayed the law, the sum of society's standards, as a collective, impersonal ideology imposed on the individual from without. Thus, the law represented the very thing this mythology sought to avoid. In its place, this tradition offered a natural law discovered intuitively by each man. As Tocqueville observed, Americans wanted "To escape from imposed systems . . . to seek by themselves and in themselves for the only reason for things . . . in most mental operations each American relies on individual effort and judgment" (p. 429). This sense of the law's inadequacy to needs detectable only by the heart generated a rich tradition of legends celebrating legal defiance in the name of some "natural" standard: Thoreau went to jail rather than pay taxes, Huck helped Jim (legally a slave) to escape, Billy the Kid murdered the sheriff's posse that had ambushed his boss, Hester Prynne resisted the community's sexual mores. This mythology transformed all outlaws into Robin Hoods, who "correct" socially unjust laws (Jesse James, Bonnie and Clyde, John Wesley Harding). Furthermore, by customarily portraying the law as the tool of villains (who used it to revoke mining claims, foreclose on mortgages, and disallow election results—all on legal technicalities), this mythology betrayed a profound pessimism about the individual's access to the legal system.

If the outlaw hero's motto was "I don't know what the law says, but I do know what's right and wrong," the official hero's was "We are a nation of laws,

---

[7]See John G. Cawelti, *Apostles of the Self-Made Man: Changing Concepts of Success in America* (Chicago: University of Chicago Press, 1965), pp. 101–23.

[8]Alexis de Tocqueville, *Democracy in America*, ed. J. P. Mayer, trans. George Lawrence (Garden City, N.Y.: Anchor/Doubleday, 1969), pp. 430, 506. Irving Howe has confirmed Tocqueville's point, observing that Americans "make the suspicion of ideology into something approaching a national creed." *Politics and the Novel* (New York: Avon, 1970), p. 337.

not of men," or "No man can place himself above the law." To the outlaw hero's insistence on private standards of right and wrong, the official hero offered the admonition, "You cannot take the law into your own hands." Often, these official heroes were lawyers or politicians, at times (as with Washington and Lincoln), even the executors of the legal system itself. The values accompanying such heroes modified the assurance of Crockett's advice, "Be sure you're right, then go ahead."

In sum, the values associated with these two different sets of heroes contrasted markedly. Clearly, too, each tradition had its good and bad points. If the extreme individualism of the outlaw hero always verged on selfishness, the respectability of the official hero always threatened to involve either blandness or repression. If the outlaw tradition promised adventure and freedom, it also offered danger and loneliness. If the official tradition promised safety and comfort, it also offered entanglements and boredom.

The evident contradiction between these heroes provoked Daniel Boorstin's observation that "Never did a more incongruous pair than Davy Crockett and George Washington live together in a national Valhalla." And yet, as Boorstin admits, "both Crockett and Washington were popular heroes, and both emerged into legendary fame during the first half of the nineteenth century."[9]

The parallel existence of these two contradictory traditions evinced the 15 general pattern of American mythology: the denial of the necessity for choice. In fact, this mythology often portrayed situations requiring decision as temporary aberrations from American life's normal course. By discouraging commitment to any single set of values, this mythology fostered an ideology of improvisation, individualism, and ad hoc solutions for problems depicted as crises. American writers have repeatedly attempted to justify this mythology in terms of material sources. Hence, Irving Howe's "explanation":

> It is when men no longer feel that they have adequate choices in their styles of life, when they conclude that there are no longer possibilities of honorable maneuver and compromise, when they decide that the time has come for "ultimate" social loyalties and political decisions — it is then that ideology begins to flourish. Ideology reflects a hardening of commitment, the freezing of opinion into system. . . . The uniqueness of our history, the freshness of our land, the plenitude of our resources — all these have made possible, and rendered plausible, a style of political improvisation and intellectual free-wheeling.[10]

Despite such an account's pretext of objectivity, its language betrays an acceptance of the mythology it purports to describe: "honorable maneuver and compromise," "hardening," "freezing," "uniqueness," "freshness," and "plenitude" are all assumptive words from an ideology that denies its own

---

[9]Daniel J. Boorstin, *The Americans: The National Experience* (New York: Random House, 1965), p. 337.
[10]*Politics and the Novel*, p. 164.

status. Furthermore, even granting the legitimacy of the historians' authenticating causes, we are left with a persisting mythology increasingly discredited by historical developments. (In fact, such invalidation began in the early nineteenth century, and perhaps even before.)

The American mythology's refusal to choose between its two heroes went beyond the normal reconciliatory function attributed to myth by Lévi-Strauss. For the American tradition not only overcame binary oppositions; it systematically mythologized the certainty of being able to do so. Part of this process involved blurring the lines between the two sets of heroes. First, legends often brought the solemn official heroes back down to earth, providing the sober Washington with the cherry tree, the prudent Franklin with illegitimate children, and even the upright Jefferson with a slave mistress. On the other side, stories modified the outlaw hero's most potentially damaging quality, his tendency to selfish isolationism, by demonstrating that, however reluctantly, he would act for causes beyond himself. Thus, Huck grudgingly helped Jim escape, and Davy Crockett left the woods for three terms in Congress before dying in the Alamo for Texas independence. In this blurring process, Lincoln, a composite of opposing traits, emerged as the great American figure. His status as president made him an ex officio official hero. But his Western origins, melancholy solitude, and unaided decision-making all qualified him as a member of the other side. Finally, his ambivalent attitude toward the law played the most crucial role in his complex legend. As the chief executive, he inevitably stood for the principle that "we are a nation of laws and not men"; as the Great Emancipator, on the other hand, he provided the prime example of taking the law into one's own hands in the name of some higher standard.

Classic Hollywood's gallery of composite heroes (boxing musicians, rebellious aristocrats, pacifist soldiers) clearly derived from this mythology's rejection of final choices, a tendency whose traces Erikson detected in American psychology:

> The process of American identity formation seems to support an individual's ego identity as long as he can preserve a certain element of deliberate tentativeness of autonomous choice. The individual must be able to convince himself that the next step is up to him and that no matter where he is staying or going he always had the choice of leaving or turning in the opposite direction if he chooses to do so. In this country the migrant does not want to be told to move on, nor the sedentary man to stay where he is; for the life style (and the family history) of each contains the opposite element as a potential alternative which he wishes to consider his most private and individual decision.[11]

The reconciliatory pattern found its most typical incarnation, however, in one particular narrative: the story of the private man attempting to keep from

---

[11]*Childhood and Society*, p. 286.

being drawn into action on any but his own terms. In this story, the reluctant hero's ultimate willingness to help the community satisfied the official values. But by portraying this aid as demanding only a temporary involvement, the story preserved the values of individualism as well.

Like the contrasting heroes' epitomization of basic American dichotomies, the reluctant hero story provided a locus for displacement. Its most famous version, for example, *Adventures of Huckleberry Finn*, offered a typically individualistic solution to the nation's unresolved racial and sectional anxieties, thereby helping to forestall more systematic governmental measures. In adopting this story, Classic Hollywood retained its censoring power, using it, for example, in *Casablanca* to conceal the realistic threats to American self-determination posed by World War II.

Because the reluctant hero story was clearly the basis of the Western, American literature's repeated use of it prompted Leslie Fiedler to call the classic American novels "disguised westerns."[12] In the movies, too, this story appeared in every genre: in Westerns, of course (with *Shane* its most schematic articulation), but also in gangster movies (*Angels with Dirty Faces*, *Key Largo*), musicals (*Swing Time*), detective stories (*The Thin Man*), war films (*Air Force*), screwball comedy (*The Philadelphia Story*), "problem pictures" (*On the Waterfront*), and even science fiction (the Han Solo character in *Star Wars*). *Gone with the Wind*, in fact, had two selfish heroes who came around at the last moment, Scarlett (taking care of Melanie) and Rhett (running the Union blockade), incompatible only because they were so much alike. The natural culmination of this pattern, perfected by Hollywood in the 1930s and early 1940s, was *Casablanca*. Its version of the outlaw hero–official hero struggle (Rick versus Laszlo) proved stunningly effective, its resolution (their collaboration on the war effort) the prototypical Hollywood ending.

The reluctant hero story's tendency to minimize the official hero's role (by making him dependent on the outsider's intervention) suggested an imbalance basic to the American mythology: Despite the existence of both heroes, the national ideology clearly preferred the outlaw. This ideology strove to make that figure's origins seem spontaneous, concealing the calculated, commercial efforts behind the mythologizing of typical examples like Billy the Kid and Davy Crockett. Its willingness, on the other hand, to allow the official hero's traces to show enables Daniel Boorstin to observe of one such myth, "There were elements of spontaneity, of course, in the Washington legend, too, but it was, for the most part, a self-conscious product."[13]

The apparent spontaneity of the outlaw heroes assured their popularity. By contrast, the official values had to rely on a rational allegiance that often wavered. These heroes' different statuses accounted for a structure fundamental to American literature, and assumed by Classic Hollywood: a split between the moral center and the interest center of a story. Thus, while the typical

20

---

[12]*Love and Death in the American Novel*, p. 355.
[13]*The Americans: The National Experience*, p. 337.

Western contained warnings against violence as a solution, taking the law into one's own hands, and moral isolationism, it simultaneously glamorized the outlaw hero's intense self-possession and willingness to use force to settle what the law could not. In other circumstances, Ishmael's evenhanded philosophy paled beside Ahab's moral vehemence, consciously recognizable as destructive.

D. H. Lawrence called this split the profound "duplicity" at the heart of nineteenth-century American fiction, charging that the classic novels evinced "a tight mental allegiance to a morality which all [the author's] passion goes to destroy." Certainly, too, this "duplicity" involved the mythology's pattern of obscuring the necessity for choosing between contrasting values. Richard Chase has put the matter less pejoratively in an account that applies equally to the American cinema:

> The American novel tends to rest in contradictions and among extreme ranges of experience. When it attempts to resolve contradictions, it does so in oblique, morally equivocal ways. As a general rule it does so either in melodramatic actions or in pastoral idylls, although intermixed with both one may find the stirring instabilities of "American humor."[14]

Or, in other words, when faced with a difficult choice, American stories resolved it either simplistically (by refusing to acknowledge that a choice is necessary), sentimentally (by blurring the differences between the two sides), or by laughing the whole thing off.

READING THE TEXT

1. What are the two basic hero types that Ray describes in American cinema?
2. How do these two hero types relate to America's "psychological pattern" (para. 2)?
3. Explain why, according to Ray, the outlaw hero typically mistrusts women.

READING THE SIGNS

1. **CONNECTING TEXTS** Read Andy Medhurst's "Batman, Deviance, and Camp" (p. 331) and write an essay that defines what sort of hero Batman is, according to Ray's schema.
2. What sort of hero is Rooster Cogburn in *True Grit*? Write an essay in which you apply Ray's categories of hero to the Bridges character, supporting your argument with specific references to the film.
3. In class, brainstorm on the blackboard official and outlaw heroes you've seen in movies. Then categorize these heroes according to characteristics they share (such as race, gender, profession, or social class). What patterns emerge in your categories, and what is the significance of those patterns?

[14]Richard Chase, *The American Novel and Its Tradition* (Garden City, N.Y.: Anchor/Doubleday, 1957), p. 1.

4. Ray focuses on film, but his categories of hero can be used as a critical frame-work to analyze other media, including television. What kind of heroes are the heroes in the program *Heroes*? Alternately, consider a character such as Dexter Morgan in *Dexter*. How might he fit Ray's definitions of hero?

5. Cartoon television series like *The Simpsons* and *South Park* feature characters that don't readily fit Ray's categories of hero. Invent a third type of hero to accommodate such characters.

6. A third type of character that has been popular in recent years is the out-and-out outlaw, someone who breaks the law without any regard for society, like Tony Soprano and Hannibal Lecter, as well as numerous other gangsters, hit men, and cops gone bad. Write a paper identifying a number of such charac-ters and construct a semiotic argument explaining their appeal to contempo-rary audiences.

7. In class, brainstorm a list of female heroes from film and television. Then try to categorize them according to Ray's article. Do the characters easily fit the categories Ray mentions, or do they seem mismatches? Do you feel a need to create an additional category? If so, what would it be?

LINDA SEGER

Creating the Myth

To be a successful screenwriter, Linda Seger suggests in this selec-tion from *Making a Good Script Great* (1987), you've got to know your archetypes. Seger reveals the secret behind the success of such Hol-lywood creations as *Star Wars'* Luke Skywalker and tells you how you can create such heroes yourself. In this how-to approach to the cinema, Seger echoes the more academic judgments of such semioti-cians of film as Umberto Eco — the road to popular success in mass culture is paved with cultural myths and clichés. A script consultant and author who has given professional seminars on filmmaking around the world, Seger has also published *Creating Unforgettable Characters* (1990) and *When Women Call the Shots: The Developing Power and Influence of Women in Television and Film* (1996).

All of us have similar experiences. We share in the life journey of growth, development, and transformation. We live the same stories, whether they involve the search for a perfect mate, coming home, the search for fulfill-ment, going after an ideal, achieving the dream, or hunting for a precious treasure. Whatever our culture, there are universal stories that form the basis for all our particular stories. The trappings might be different, the twists and turns that create suspense might change from culture to culture, the particular characters may take different forms, but underneath it all, it's the same story, drawn from the same experiences.

Many of the most successful films are based on these universal stories. They deal with the basic journey we take in life. We identify with the heroes because we were once heroic (descriptive) or because we wish we could do what the hero does (prescriptive). When Joan Wilder finds the jewel and saves her sister, or James Bond saves the world, or Shane saves the family from the evil ranchers, we identify with the character, and subconsciously recognize the story as having some connection with our own lives. It's the same story as the fairy tales about getting the three golden hairs from the devil, or finding the treasure and winning the princess. And it's not all that different a story from the caveman killing the woolly beast or the Roman slave gaining his freedom through skill and courage. These are our stories—personally and collectively—and the most successful films contain these universal experiences.

Some of these stories are "search" stories. They address our desire to find some kind of rare and wonderful treasure. This might include the search for outer values such as job, relationship, or success; or for inner values such as respect, security, self-expression, love, or home. But it's all a similar search.

Some of these stories are "hero" stories. They come from our own experiences of overcoming adversity, as well as our desire to do great and special acts. We root for the hero and celebrate when he or she achieves the goal because we know that the hero's journey is in many ways similar to our own.

We call these stories *myths*. Myths are the common stories at the root 5 of our universal existence. They're found in all cultures and in all literature, ranging from the Greek myths to fairy tales, legends, and stories drawn from all of the world's religions.

A myth is a story that is "more than true." Many stories are true because one person, somewhere, at some time, lived it. It is based on fact. But a myth is more than true because it is lived by all of us, at some level. It's a story that connects and speaks to us all.

Some myths are true stories that attain mythic significance because the people involved seem larger than life, and seem to live their lives more intensely than common folk. Martin Luther King, Jr., Gandhi, Sir Edmund Hillary, and Lord Mountbatten personify the types of journeys we identify with, because we've taken similar journeys—even if only in a very small way.

Other myths revolve around make-believe characters who might capsulize for us the sum total of many of our journeys. Some of these make-believe characters might seem similar to the characters we meet in our dreams. Or they might be a composite of types of characters we've met.

In both cases, the myth is the "story beneath the story." It's the universal pattern that shows us that Gandhi's journey toward independence and Sir

Edmund Hillary's journey to the top of Mount Everest contain many of the same dramatic beats. And these beats are the same beats that Rambo takes to set free the MIAs, that Indiana Jones takes to find the Lost Ark, and that Luke Skywalker takes to defeat the Evil Empire.

In *Hero with a Thousand Faces*, Joseph Campbell traces the elements that form the hero myth. In their own work with myth, writer Chris Vogler and seminar leader Thomas Schlesinger have applied this criteria to *Star Wars*. The myth within the story helps explain why millions went to see this film again and again.

The hero myth has specific story beats that occur in all hero stories. They show who the hero is, what the hero needs, and how the story and character interact in order to create a transformation. The journey toward heroism is a process. This universal process forms the spine of all the particular stories, such as the *Star Wars* trilogy.

The Hero Myth

1. In most hero stories, the hero is introduced in ordinary surroundings, in a mundane world, doing mundane things. Generally, the hero begins as a non-hero; innocent, young, simple, or humble. In *Star Wars*, the first time we see Luke Skywalker, he's unhappy about having to do his chores, which consist of picking out some new droids for work. He wants to go out and have fun. He wants to leave his planet and go to the Academy, but he's stuck. This is the setup of most myths. This is how we meet the hero before the call to adventure.

2. Then something new enters the hero's life. It's a catalyst that sets the story into motion. It might be a telephone call, as in *Romancing the Stone*, or

Star Wars, 1977.

the German attack in *The African Queen*, or the holograph of Princess Leia in *Star Wars*. Whatever form it takes, it's a new ingredient that pushes the hero into an extraordinary adventure. With this call, the stakes are established, and a problem is introduced that demands a solution.

3. Many times, however, the hero doesn't want to leave. He or she is a reluctant hero, afraid of the unknown, uncertain, perhaps, if he or she is up to the challenge. In *Star Wars*, Luke receives a double call to adventure. First, from Princess Leia in the holograph, and then through Obi-Wan Kenobi, who says he needs Luke's help. But Luke is not ready to go. He returns home, only to find that the Imperial Stormtroopers have burned his farmhouse and slaughtered his family. Now he is personally motivated, ready to enter into the adventure.

4. In any journey, the hero usually receives help, and the help often comes 15 from unusual sources. In many fairy tales, an old woman, a dwarf, a witch, or a wizard helps the hero. The hero achieves the goal because of this help, and because the hero is receptive to what this person has to give.

There are a number of fairy tales where the first and second son are sent to complete a task, but they ignore the helpers, often scorning them. Many times they are severely punished for their lack of humility and unwillingness to accept help. Then the third son, the hero, comes along. He receives the help, accomplishes the task, and often wins the princess.

In *Star Wars*, Obi-Wan Kenobi is a perfect example of the "helper" character. He is a kind of mentor to Luke, one who teaches him the Way of the Force and whose teachings continue even after his death. This mentor character appears in most hero stories. He is the person who has special knowledge, special information, and special skills. This might be the prospector in *The Treasure of the Sierra Madre*, or the psychiatrist in *Ordinary People*, or Quint in *Jaws*, who knows all about sharks, or the Good Witch of the North who gives Dorothy the ruby slippers in *The Wizard of Oz*. In *Star Wars*, Obi-Wan gives Luke the light saber that was the special weapon of the Jedi Knight. With this, Luke is ready to move forward and do his training and meet adventure.

5. The hero is now ready to move into the special world where he or she will change from the ordinary into the extraordinary. This starts the hero's transformation, and sets up the obstacles that must be surmounted to reach the goal. Usually, this happens at the first Turning Point of the story, and leads into Act Two development. In *Star Wars*, Obi-Wan and Luke search for a pilot to take them to the planet of Alderaan, so that Obi-Wan can deliver the plans to Princess Leia's father. These plans are essential to the survival of the Rebel Forces. With this action, the adventure is ready to begin.

6. Now begin all the tests and obstacles necessary to overcome the enemy and accomplish the hero's goals. In fairy tales, this often means getting past witches, outwitting the devil, avoiding robbers, or confronting evil. In Homer's *Odyssey*, it means blinding the Cyclops, escaping from the island of the Lotus-Eaters, resisting the temptation of the singing Sirens, and surviving a shipwreck. In *Star Wars*, innumerable adventures confront Luke. He and

his cohorts must run to the *Millennium Falcon*, narrowly escaping the Storm-troopers before jumping into hyperspace. They must make it through the meteor shower after Alderaan has been destroyed. They must evade capture on the Death Star, rescue the Princess, and even survive a garbage crusher.

7. At some point in the story, the hero often hits rock bottom. He often 20 has a "death experience," leading to a type of rebirth. In *Star Wars*, Luke seems to have died when the serpent in the garbage-masher pulls him under, but he's saved just in time to ask R2D2 to stop the masher before they're crushed. This is often the "black moment" at the second turning point, the point when the worst is confronted, and the action now moves toward the exciting conclusion.

8. Now, the hero seizes the sword and takes possession of the treasure. He is now in charge, but he still has not completed the journey. Here Luke has the Princess and the plans, but the final confrontation is yet to begin. This starts the third-act escape scene, leading to the final climax.

9. The road back is often the chase scene. In many fairy tales, this is the point where the devil chases the hero and the hero has the last obstacles to overcome before really being free and safe. His challenge is to take what he has learned and integrate it into his daily life. He *must* return to renew the mundane world. In *Star Wars*, Darth Vader is in hot pursuit, planning to blow up the Rebel Planet.

10. Since every hero story is essentially a transformation story, we need to see the hero changed at the end, resurrected into a new type of life. He must face the final ordeal before being "reborn" as the hero, proving his courage and becoming transformed. This is the point, in many fairy tales, where the Miller's Son becomes the Prince or the King and marries the Princess. In *Star Wars*, Luke has survived, becoming quite a different person from the innocent young man he was in Act One.

At this point, the hero returns and is reintegrated into his society. In *Star Wars*, Luke has destroyed the Death Star, and he receives his great reward.

This is the classic "Hero Story." We might call this example a *mission* or *task* 25 *myth*, where the person has to complete a task, but the task itself is not the real treasure. The real reward for Luke is the love of the Princess and the safe, new world he had helped create.

A myth can have many variations. We see variations on this myth in James Bond films (although they lack much of the depth because the hero is not transformed), and in *The African Queen*, where Rose and Allnutt must blow up the *Louisa*, or in *Places in the Heart*, where Edna overcomes obstacles to achieve family stability.

The *treasure myth* is another variation on this theme, as seen in *Romancing the Stone*. In this story, Joan receives a map and a phone call which forces her into the adventure. She is helped by an American birdcatcher and a Mexican pickup-truck driver. She overcomes the obstacles of snakes, the jungle, waterfalls, shootouts, and finally receives the treasure, along with the "prince."

Whether the hero's journey is for a treasure or to complete a task, the elements remain the same. The humble, reluctant hero is called to an adventure. The hero is helped by a variety of unique characters. S/he must overcome a series of obstacles that transform him or her in the process, and then face the final challenge that draws on inner and outer resources.

The Healing Myth

Although the hero myth is the most popular story, many myths involve healing. In these stories, some character is "broken" and must leave home to become whole again.

The universal experience behind these healing stories is our psychological 30 need for rejuvenation, for balance. The journey of the hero into exile is not all that different from the weekend in Palm Springs, or the trip to Hawaii to get away from it all, or lying still in a hospital bed for some weeks to heal. In all cases, something is out of balance and the mythic journey moves toward wholeness.

Being broken can take several forms. It can be physical, emotional, or psychological. Usually, it's all three. In the process of being exiled or hiding out in the forest, the desert, or even the Amish farm in *Witness*, the person becomes whole, balanced, and receptive to love. Love in these stories is both a healing force and a reward.

Think of John Book in *Witness*. In Act One, we see a frenetic, insensitive man, afraid of commitment, critical and unreceptive to the feminine influences in his life. John is suffering from an "inner wound" which he doesn't know about. When he receives an "outer wound" from a gunshot, it forces him into exile, which begins his process of transformation.

At the beginning of Act Two, we see John delirious and close to death. This is a movement into the unconscious, a movement from the rational, active police life of Act One into a mysterious, feminine, more intuitive world. Since John's "inner problem" is the lack of balance with his feminine side, this delirium begins the process of transformation.

Later in Act Two, we see John beginning to change. He moves from his highly independent lifestyle toward the collective, communal life of his Amish hosts. John now gets up early to milk the cows and to assist with the chores. He uses his carpentry skills to help with the barn building and to complete the birdhouse. Gradually, he begins to develop relationships with Rachel and her son, Samuel. John's life slows down and he becomes more receptive, learning important lessons about love. In Act Three, John finally sees that the feminine is worth saving, and throws down his gun to save Rachel's life. A few beats later, when he has the opportunity to kill Paul, he chooses a nonviolent response instead. Although John doesn't "win" the Princess, he has nevertheless "won" love and wholeness. By the end of the film, we can see that the John Book of Act Three is a different kind of person from the John Book of Act One. He has a different kind of comradeship with his fellow police officers, he's more relaxed, and we can sense that somehow, this experience has formed a more integrated John Book.

Combination Myths

Many stories are combinations of several different myths. Think of *Ghost-* 35 *busters*, a simple and rather outrageous comedy about three men saving the city of New York from ghosts. Now think of the story of "Pandora's Box." It's about the woman who let loose all manner of evil upon the earth by opening a box she was told not to touch. In *Ghostbusters*, the EPA man is a Pandora figure. By shutting off the power to the containment center, he inadvertently unleashes all the ghosts upon New York City. Combine the story of "Pandora's Box" with a hero story, and notice that we have our three heroes battling the Marshmallow Man. One of them also "gets the Princess" when Dr. Peter Venkman finally receives the affections of Dana Barrett. By looking at these combinations, it is apparent that even *Ghostbusters* is more than "just a comedy."

Tootsie is a type of reworking of many Shakespearean stories where a woman has to dress as a man in order to accomplish a certain task. These Shakespearean stories are reminiscent of many fairy tales where the hero becomes invisible or takes on another persona, or wears a specific disguise to hide his or her real qualities. In the stories of "The Twelve Dancing Princesses" or "The Man in the Bearskin," disguise is necessary to achieve a goal. Combine these elements with the transformation themes of the hero myth where a hero (such as Michael) must overcome many obstacles to his success as an actor and a human being. It's not difficult to understand why the *Tootsie* story hooks us.

Archetypes

A myth includes certain characters that we see in many stories. These characters are called *archetypes*. They can be thought of as the original "pattern" or "character type" that will be found on the hero's journey. Archetypes take many forms, but they tend to fall within specific categories.

Earlier, we discussed some of the helpers who give advice to help the hero — such as the *wise old man* who possesses special knowledge and often serves as a mentor to the hero.

The female counterpart of the wise old man is the *good mother*. Whereas the wise old man has superior knowledge, the good mother is known for her nurturing qualities, and for her intuition. This figure often gives the hero particular objects to help on the journey. It might be a protective amulet, or the ruby slippers that Dorothy receives in *The Wizard of Oz* from the Good

Witch of the North. Sometimes in fairy tales it's a cloak to make the person invisible, or ordinary objects that become extraordinary, as in "The Girl of Courage," an Afghan fairy tale about a maiden who receives a comb, a whetstone, and a mirror to help defeat the devil.

Many myths contain a *shadow figure*. This is a character who is the 40 opposite of the hero. Sometimes this figure helps the hero on the journey; other times this figure opposes the hero. The shadow figure can be the negative side of the hero which could be the dark and hostile brother in "Cain and Abel," the stepsisters in "Cinderella," or the Robber Girl in "The Snow Queen." The shadow figure can also help the hero, as the whore with the heart of gold who saves the hero's life, or provides balance to his idealization of woman.

Many myths contain *animal archetypes* that can be positive or negative figures. In "St. George and the Dragon," the dragon is the negative force which is a violent and ravaging animal, not unlike the shark in *Jaws*. But in many stories, animals help the hero. Sometimes there are talking donkeys, or a dolphin which saves the hero, or magical horses or dogs.

The *trickster* is a mischievous archetypical figure who is always causing chaos, disturbing the peace, and generally being an anarchist. The trickster uses wit and cunning to achieve his or her ends. Sometimes the trickster is a harmless prankster or a "bad boy" who is funny and enjoyable. More often, the trickster is a con man, as in *The Sting*, or the devil, as in *The Exorcist*, who demanded all the skills of the priest to outwit him. The "Till Eulenspiegel" stories revolve around the trickster, as do the Spanish picaresque novels. Even the tales of Tom Sawyer have a trickster motif. In all countries, there are stories that revolve around this figure, whose job it is to outwit.

"Mythic" Problems and Solutions

We all grew up with myths. Most of us heard or read fairy tales when we were young. Some of us may have read Bible stories, or stories from other religions or other cultures. These stories are part of us. And the best way to work with them is to let them come out naturally as you write the script.

Of course, some filmmakers are better at this than others. George Lucas and Steven Spielberg have a strong sense of myth and incorporate it into their films. They both have spoken about their love of the stories from childhood, and of their desire to bring these types of stories to audiences. Their stories create some of the same sense of wonder and excitement as myths. Many of the necessary psychological beats are part of their stories, deepening the story beyond the ordinary action-adventure.

Myths bring depth to a hero story. If a filmmaker is thinking only about 45 the action and excitement of a story, audiences might fail to connect with the hero's journey. But if the basic beats of the hero's journey are evident, a film will often inexplicably draw audiences, in spite of critics' responses to the film.

Take *Rambo*, for instance. Why was this violent, simple story so popular with audiences? I don't think it was because everyone agreed with its politics. I do think Sylvester Stallone is a master at incorporating the American myth into his filmmaking. That doesn't mean it's done consciously. Somehow he is naturally in sync with the myth, and the myth becomes integrated into his stories.

Clint Eastwood also does hero stories, and gives us the adventure of the myth and the transformation of the myth. . . . Eastwood's films have given more attention to the transformation of the hero, and have been receiving more serious critical attention as a result.

All of these filmmakers — Lucas, Spielberg, Stallone, and Eastwood — dramatize the hero myth in their own particular ways. And all of them prove that myths are marketable.

Application

It is an important part of the writer's or producer's work to continually find opportunities for deepening the themes within a script. Finding the myth beneath the modern story is part of that process.

To find these myths, it's not a bad idea to reread some of Grimm's fairy   50
tales or fairy tales from around the world to begin to get acquainted with various myths. You'll start to see patterns and elements that connect with our own human experience.

Also, read Joseph Campbell and Greek mythology. If you're interested in Jungian psychology, you'll find many rich resources within a number of books on the subject. Since Jungian psychology deals with archetypes, you'll find many new characters to draw on for your own work.

With all of these resources to incorporate, it's important to remember that the myth is not a story to force upon a script. It's more a pattern which you can bring out in your own stories when they seem to be heading in the direction of a myth.

As you work, ask yourself:

Do I have a myth working in my script? If so, what beats am I using
   of the hero's journey? Which ones seem to be missing?
Am I missing characters? Do I need a mentor type? A wise old man?
   A wizard? Would one of these characters help dimensionalize the
   hero's journey?
Could I create new emotional dimensions to the myth by starting my
   character as reluctant, naïve, simple, or decidedly "unheroic"?
Does my character get transformed in the process of the journey?

Have I used a strong three-act structure to support the myth, using the first turning point to move into the adventure and the second turning point to create a dark moment, or a reversal, or even a "near-death" experience?

Don't be afraid to create variations on the myth, but don't start with the myth itself. Let the myth grow naturally from your story. Developing myths are part of the rewriting process. If you begin with the myth, you'll find your writing becomes rigid, uncreative, and predictable. Working with the myth in the rewriting process will deepen your script, giving it new life as you find the story within the story.

READING THE TEXT

1. How does Seger define the "hero myth" (para. 4)?
2. In your own words, explain what Seger means by "the healing myth" (para. 29).
3. What is an "archetype" (para. 37) in film?

READING THE SIGNS

1. Seger is writing to aspiring screenwriters. How does her status as an industry insider affect her description of heroic archetypes?
2. **CONNECTING TEXTS** Focusing on gender issues, compare Seger's formulation of heroes with Robert B. Ray's in "The Thematic Paradigm" (p. 377). To what extent do Seger and Ray adequately explain the role of women — and men — in movies?
3. **CONNECTING TEXTS** Review Michael Parenti's "Class and Virtue" (p. 421) and write an essay identifying the myths behind the modern stories *Pretty Woman* (1991) or *Juno* (2007).
4. Rent a DVD of *Titanic* or a segment of the *Lord of the Rings* trilogy, and write an essay in which you explain the myths and archetypal characters the film includes. How might archetypal and mythic patterns explain the film's success?
5. Seger recommends that aspiring screenwriters read Grimms' fairy tales for inspiration. You can find them online. Read some of Grimms' tales, and then write an argument assessing the suitability of such tales as inspiration for films today.
6. What myths about social class, race, and gender do you see in *Forrest Gump*? Brainstorm these myths in class, and then use your list of myths to write an essay in which you explain why the film has developed such a loyal fan base.

JESSICA HAGEDORN

Asian Women in Film: No Joy, No Luck

Why do movies always seem to portray Asian women as tragic victims of history and fate? Jessica Hagedorn asks in this essay, which originally appeared in *Ms.* Even such movies as *The Joy Luck Club*, based on Amy Tan's breakthrough novel that elevated Asian American fiction to best-seller status, reinforce old stereotypes of the powerlessness of Asian and Asian American women. A screenwriter and novelist, Hagedorn calls for a different kind of storytelling that would show Asian women as powerful controllers of their own destinies. Hagedorn's publications include the novels *Dogeaters* (1990), *The Gangster of Love* (1996), and *Dream Jungle* (2003); *Danger and Beauty* (1993), a collection of poems; *Charlie Chan Is Dead: An Anthology of Contemporary Asian American Fiction* (1993); and *Fresh Kill* (1994), a screenplay.

Pearl of the Orient. Whore. Geisha. Concubine. Whore. Hostess. Bar Girl. Mama-san. Whore. China Doll. Tokyo Rose. Whore. Butterfly. Whore. Miss Saigon. Whore. Dragon Lady. Lotus Blossom. Gook. Whore. Yellow Peril. Whore. Bangkok Bombshell. Whore. Hospitality Girl. Whore. Comfort Woman. Whore. Savage. Whore. Sultry. Whore. Faceless. Whore. Porcelain. Whore. Demure. Whore. Virgin. Whore. Mute. Whore. Model Minority. Whore. Victim. Whore. Woman Warrior. Whore. Mail-Order Bride. Whore. Mother. Wife. Lover. Daughter. Sister.

As I was growing up in the Philippines in the 1950s, my fertile imagination was colonized by thoroughly American fantasies. Yellowface variations on the exotic erotic loomed larger than life on the silver screen. I was mystified and enthralled by Hollywood's skewed representations of Asian women: sleek, evil goddesses with slanted eyes and cunning ways, or smiling, sarong-clad South Seas "maidens" with undulating hips, kinky black hair, and white skin darkened by makeup. Hardly any of the "Asian" characters were played by Asians. White actors like Sidney Toler and Warner Oland played "inscrutable Oriental detective" Charlie Chan with taped eyelids and a singsong, chop suey accent. Jennifer Jones was a Eurasian doctor swept up in a doomed "interracial romance" in *Love Is a Many Splendored Thing*. In my mother's youth, white actor Luise Rainer played the central role of the Patient Chinese Wife in the 1937 film adaptation of Pearl Buck's novel *The Good Earth*. Back then, not many thought to ask why; they were all too busy being grateful to see anyone in the movies remotely like themselves.

Cut to 1960: *The World of Suzie Wong*, another tragic East/West affair. I am now old enough to be impressed. Sexy, sassy Suzie (played by Nancy

Kwan) works out of a bar patronized by white sailors, but doesn't seem bothered by any of it. For a hardworking girl turning nightly tricks to support her baby, she manages to parade an astonishing wardrobe in damn near every scene, down to matching handbags and shoes. The sailors are also strictly Hollywood, sanitized and not too menacing. Suzie and all the other prostitutes in this movie are cute, giggling, dancing sex machines with hearts of gold. William Holden plays an earnest, rather prim, Nice Guy painter seeking inspiration in The Other. Of course, Suzie falls madly in love with him. Typically, she tells him, "I not important," and "I'll be with you until you say — Suzie, go away." She also thinks being beaten by a man is a sign of true passion and is terribly disappointed when Mr. Nice Guy refuses to show his true feelings.

Next in Kwan's short-lived but memorable career was the kitschy 1961 musical *Flower Drum Song*, which, like *Suzie Wong*, is a thoroughly American commercial product. The female roles are typical of Hollywood musicals of the times: women are basically airheads, subservient to men. Kwan's counterpart is the Good Chinese Girl, played by Miyoshi Umeki, who was better playing the Loyal Japanese Girl in that other classic Hollywood tale of forbidden love, *Sayonara*. Remember? Umeki was so loyal, she committed double suicide with actor Red Buttons. I instinctively hated *Sayonara* when I first saw it as a child; now I understand why. Contrived tragic resolutions were the only way Hollywood got past the censors in those days. With one or two exceptions, somebody in these movies always had to die to pay for breaking racial and sexual taboos.

Until the recent onslaught of films by both Asian and Asian American filmmakers, Asian Pacific women have generally been perceived by Hollywood with a mixture of fascination, fear, and contempt. Most Hollywood movies either trivialize or exoticize us as people of color and as women. Our intelligence is underestimated, our humanity overlooked, and our diverse cultures treated as interchangeable. If we are "good," we are childlike, submissive, silent, and eager for sex (see France Nuyen's glowing performance as Liat in the film version of *South Pacific*) or else we are tragic victim types (see *Casualties of War*, Brian De Palma's graphic 1989 drama set in Vietnam). And if we are not silent, suffering doormats, we are demonized dragon ladies — cunning, deceitful, sexual provocateurs. Give me the demonic any day — Anna May Wong as a villain slithering around in a slinky gown is at least gratifying to watch, neither servile nor passive. And she steals the show from Marlene Dietrich in Josef von Sternberg's *Shanghai Express*. From the 1920s through the 1930s, Wong was our only female "star." But even she was trapped in limited roles, in what filmmaker Renee Tajima has called the dragon lady/lotus blossom dichotomy.

Cut to 1985: There is a scene toward the end of the terribly dishonest but weirdly compelling Michael Cimino movie *Year of the Dragon* (cowritten by Oliver Stone) that is one of my favorite twisted movie moments of all time. If you ask a lot of my friends who've seen that movie (especially if they're Asian), it's one of their favorites too. The setting is a crowded Chinatown nightclub. There are two very young and very tough Jade Cobra gang girls in a shoot-out with Mickey Rourke, in the role of a demented Polish American cop who, in spite of being Mr. Ugly in the flesh — an arrogant, misogynistic bully devoid of any charm — wins the "good" Asian American anchorwoman in the film's absurd and implausible ending. This is a movie with an actual disclaimer as its lead-in, covering its ass in advance in response to anticipated complaints about "stereotypes."

My pleasure in the hard-edged power of the Chinatown gang girls in *Year of the Dragon* is my small revenge, the answer to all those Suzie Wong "I want to be your slave" female characters. The Jade Cobra girls are mere background to the white male foreground/focus of Cimino's movie. But long after the movie has faded into video-rental heaven, the Jade Cobra girls remain defiant, fabulous images in my memory, flaunting tight metallic dresses and spiky cock's-comb hairdos streaked electric red and blue.

Mickey Rourke looks down with world-weary pity at the unnamed Jade Cobra girl (Doreen Chan) he's just shot who lies sprawled and bleeding on the street: "You look like you're gonna die, beautiful."

JADE COBRA GIRL: "Oh yeah? [blood gushing from her mouth] I'm proud of it."

ROURKE: "You are? You got anything you wanna tell me before you go, sweetheart?"

JADE COBRA GIRL: "Yeah. [pause] Fuck you."

Cut to 1993: I've been told that like many New Yorkers, I watch movies with the right side of my brain on perpetual overdrive. I admit to being grouchy and overcritical, suspicious of sentiment, and cynical. When a critic

Anna May Wong.

Michelle Yeoh, *Tomorrow Never Dies*, 1997.

like Richard Corliss of *Time* magazine gushes about *The Joy Luck Club* being "a fourfold *Terms of Endearment*," my gut instinct is to run the other way. I resent being told how to feel. I went to see the 1993 eight-handkerchief movie version of Amy Tan's bestseller with a group that included my ten-year-old daughter. I was caught between the sincere desire to be swept up by the turbulent mother-daughter sagas and my own stubborn resistance to being so obviously manipulated by the filmmakers. With every flashback came tragedy. The music soared; the voice-overs were solemn or wistful; tears, tears, and more tears flowed on-screen. Daughters were reverent; mothers carried dark secrets.

I was elated by the grandness and strength of the four mothers and the luminous actors who portrayed them, but I was uneasy with the passivity of the Asian American daughters. They seemed to exist solely as receptors for their mothers' amazing life stories. It's almost as if by assimilating so easily into American society, they had lost all sense of self.

In spite of my resistance, my eyes watered as the desperate mother 10 played by Kieu Chinh was forced to abandon her twin baby girls on a country road in war-torn China. (Kieu Chinh resembles my own mother and her twin sister, who suffered through the brutal Japanese occupation of the Philippines.) So far in this movie, an infant son had been deliberately drowned, a mother played by the gravely beautiful France Nuyen had gone catatonic with grief, a concubine had cut her flesh open to save her dying mother, an insecure daughter had been oppressed by her boorish Asian American husband, another insecure daughter had been left by her white husband, and so on. . . . The overall effect was numbing as far as I'm concerned, but a man sitting two rows in front of us broke down sobbing. A Chinese Filipino writer even more grouchy than me later complained, "Must ethnicity only be equated with suffering?"

Because change has been slow, *The Joy Luck Club* carries a lot of cultural baggage. It is a big-budget story about Chinese American women, directed by a Chinese American man, cowritten and coproduced by Chinese American women. That's a lot to be thankful for. And its box office success proves that an immigrant narrative told from female perspectives can have mass appeal. But my cynical side tells me that its success might mean only one thing in Hollywood: more weepy epics about Asian American mother-daughter relationships will be planned.

That the film finally got made was significant. By Hollywood standards (think white male; think money, money, money), a movie about Asian Americans even when adapted from a bestseller was a risky proposition. When I asked a producer I know about the film's rumored delays, he simply said, "It's still an *Asian* movie," surprised I had even asked. Equally interesting was director Wayne Wang's initial reluctance to be involved in the project; he told the *New York Times*, "I didn't want to do another Chinese movie."

Maybe he shouldn't have worried so much. After all, according to the media, the nineties are the decade of "Pacific Overtures" and East Asian chic. Madonna, the pop queen of shameless appropriation, cultivated Japanese high-tech style with her music video "Rain," while Janet Jackson faked kitschy orientalia in hers, titled "If." Critical attention was paid to movies from China, Japan, and Vietnam. But that didn't mean an honest appraisal of women's lives. Even on the art house circuit, filmmakers who should know better took the easy way out. Takehiro Nakajima's 1992 film *Okoge* presents one of the more original film roles for women in recent years. In Japanese, "okoge" means the crust of rice that sticks to the bottom of the rice pot; in pejorative slang, it means fag hag. The way "okoge" is used in the film seems a reappropriation of the term; the portrait Nakajima creates of Sayoko, the so-called fag hag, is clearly an affectionate one. Sayoko is a quirky, self-assured woman in contemporary Tokyo who does voice-overs for cartoons, has a thing for Frida Kahlo paintings, and is drawn to a gentle young gay man named Goh. But the other women's roles are disappointing, stereotypical "hysterical females" and the movie itself turns conventional halfway through. Sayoko sacrifices herself to a macho brute Goh desires, who rapes her as images of Frida Kahlo paintings and her beloved Goh rising from the ocean flash before her. She gives birth to a baby boy and endures a terrible life of poverty with the abusive rapist. This sudden change from spunky survivor to helpless, victimized woman is baffling. Whatever happened to her job? Or that arty little apartment of hers? Didn't her Frida Kahlo obsession teach her anything?

Then there was Tiana Thi Thanh Nga's *From Hollywood to Hanoi*, a self-serving but fascinating documentary. Born in Vietnam to a privileged family that included an uncle who was defense minister in the Thieu government and an idolized father who served as press minister, Nga (a.k.a. Tiana) spent her adolescence in California. A former actor in martial arts movies and fitness teacher ("Karaticize with Tiana"), the vivacious Tiana decided to make a record of her journey back to Vietnam.

From Hollywood to Hanoi is at times unintentionally very funny. Tiana 15 includes a quick scene of herself dancing with a white man at the Metropole hotel in Hanoi, and breathlessly announces: "That's me doing the tango with Oliver Stone!" Then she listens sympathetically to a horrifying account of the My Lai massacre by one of its few female survivors. In another scene, Tiana cheerfully addresses a food vendor on the streets of Hanoi: "Your hairdo is so pretty." The unimpressed, poker-faced woman gives a brusque, deadpan reply: "You want to eat, or what?" Sometimes it is hard to tell the difference between Tiana Thi Thanh Nga and her Hollywood persona: The real Tiana still seems to be playing one of her B-movie roles, which are mainly fun because they're fantasy. The time was certainly right to explore postwar Vietnam from a Vietnamese woman's perspective; it's too bad this film was done by a Valley Girl.

Nineteen ninety-three also brought Tran Anh Hung's *The Scent of Green Papaya*, a different kind of Vietnamese memento — this is a look back at the peaceful, lush country of the director's childhood memories. The film opens in Saigon, in 1951. A willowy ten-year-old girl named Mui comes to work for a troubled family headed by a melancholy musician and his kind, stoic wife. The men of this bourgeois household are idle, pampered types who take naps while the women do all the work. Mui is male fantasy: She is a devoted servant, enduring acts of cruel mischief with patience and dignity; as an adult, she barely speaks. She scrubs floors, shines shoes, and cooks with loving care and never a complaint. When she is sent off to work for another wealthy musician, she ends up being impregnated by him. The movie ends as the camera closes in on Mui's contented face. Languid and precious, *The Scent of Green Papaya* is visually haunting, but it suffers from the director's colonial fantasy of women as docile, domestic creatures. Steeped in highbrow nostalgia, it's the arty Vietnamese version of *My Fair Lady* with the wealthy musician as Professor Higgins, teaching Mui to read and write.

And then there is Ang Lee's tepid 1993 hit, *The Wedding Banquet* — a clever culture-clash farce in which traditional Chinese values collide with contemporary American sexual mores. The somewhat formulaic plot goes like this: Wai-Tung, a yuppie landlord, lives with his white lover, Simon, in a chic Manhattan brownstone. Wai-Tung is an only child and his aging parents in Taiwan long for a grandchild to continue the family legacy. Enter Wei-Wei, an artist who lives in a grungy loft owned by Wai-Tung. She slugs tequila straight from the bottle as she paints and flirts boldly with her young, uptight landlord, who brushes her off. "It's my fate. I am always attracted to handsome gay men," she mutters. After this setup, the movie goes downhill, all edges blurred in a cozy nest of happy endings. In a refrain of Sayoko's plight in *Okoge*, a pregnant, suddenly complacent Wei-Wei gives in to family pressures — and never gets her life back.

> "It takes a man to know what it is to be a real woman."
> — SONG LILING in *M. Butterfly*

Ironically, two gender-bending films in which men play men playing women reveal more about the mythology of the prized Asian woman and the superficial trappings of gender than most movies that star real women. The slow-moving *M. Butterfly* presents the ultimate object of Western male desire as the spy/opera diva Song Liling, a Suzie Wong/Lotus Blossom played by actor John Lone with a five o'clock shadow and bobbing Adam's apple. The best and most profound of these forays into cross-dressing is the spectacular melodrama *Farewell My Concubine*, directed by Chen Kaige. Banned in China, *Farewell My Concubine* shared the prize for Best Film at the 1993 Cannes Film Festival with Jane Campion's *The Piano*. Sweeping through fifty years of tumultuous history in China, the story revolves around the lives of two male Beijing Opera stars and the woman who marries one of them. The three characters make an unforgettable triangle, struggling over love, art, friendship, and politics against the bloody backdrop of cultural upheaval. They are as capable of casually betraying each other as they are of selfless, heroic acts. The androgynous Dieyi, doomed to play the same female role of concubine over and over again, is portrayed with great vulnerability, wit, and grace by male Hong Kong pop star Leslie Cheung. Dieyi competes with the prostitute Juxian (Gong Li) for the love of his childhood protector and fellow opera star, Duan Xiaolou (Zhang Fengyi).

Cheung's highly stylized performance as the classic concubine-ready-to-die-for-love in the opera within the movie is all about female artifice. His side-long glances, restrained passion, languid stance, small steps, and delicate, refined gestures say everything about what is considered desirable in Asian women — and are the antithesis of the feisty, outspoken woman played by Gong Li. The characters of Dieyi and Juxian both see suffering as part and parcel of love and life. Juxian matter-of-factly says to Duan Xiaolou before he agrees to marry her: "I'm used to hardship. If you take me in, I'll wait on you hand and foot. If you tire of me, I'll . . . kill myself. No big deal." It's an echo of Suzie Wong's servility, but the context is new. Even with her back to the wall, Juxian is not helpless or whiny. She attempts to manipulate a man while admitting to the harsh reality that is her life.

Dieyi and Juxian are the two sides of the truth of women's lives in most [20] Asian countries. Juxian in particular — wife and ex-prostitute — could be seen as a thankless and stereotypical role. But like the characters Gong Li has played in Chinese director Zhang Yimou's films, *Red Sorghum*, *Raise the Red Lantern*, and especially *The Story of Qiu Ju*, Juxian is tough, obstinate, sensual, clever, oafish, beautiful, infuriating, cowardly, heroic, and banal. Above all, she is resilient. Gong Li is one of the few Asian Pacific actors whose roles have been drawn with intelligence, honesty, and depth. Nevertheless, the characters she plays are limited by the possibilities that exist for real women in China.

"Let's face it. Women still don't mean shit in China," my friend Meeling reminds me. What she says so bluntly about her culture rings painfully true, but in less obvious fashion for me. In the Philippines, infant girls aren't drowned, nor were their feet bound to make them more desirable. But sons were and are cherished. To this day, men of the bourgeois class are coddled and prized, much like the spoiled men of the elite household in *The Scent of Green Papaya*. We do not have a geisha tradition like Japan, but physical beauty is overtreasured. Our daughters are protected virgins or primed as potential beauty queens. And many of us have bought into the image of the white man as our handsome savior: G.I. Joe.

Buzz magazine recently featured an article entitled "Asian Women/L.A. Men," a report on a popular hangout that caters to white men's fantasies of nubile Thai women. The lines between movies and real life are blurred. Male screenwriters and cinematographers flock to this bar-restaurant, where the waitresses are eager to "audition" for roles. Many of these men have been to Bangkok while working on film crews for Vietnam War movies. They've come back to L.A., but for them, the movie never ends. In this particular fantasy the boys play G.I. Joe on a rescue mission in the urban jungle, saving the whore from herself. "A scene has developed here, a kind of R-rated *Cheers*," author Alan Rifkin writes. "The waitresses audition for sitcoms. The customers date the waitresses or just keep score."

Colonization of the imagination is a two-way street. And being enshrined on a pedestal as someone's Pearl of the Orient fantasy doesn't seem so demeaning, at first; who wouldn't want to be worshipped? Perhaps that's why Asian women are the ultimate wet dream in most Hollywood movies; it's no secret how well we've been taught to play the role, to take care of our men. In Hollywood vehicles, we are objects of desire or derision; we exist to provide sex, color, and texture in what is essentially a white man's world. It is akin to what Toni Morrison calls "the Africanist presence" in literature. She writes: "Just as entertainers, through or by association with blackface, could render permissible topics that otherwise would have been taboo, so American writers were able to employ an imagined Africanist persona to articulate and imaginatively act out the forbidden in American culture." The same analogy could be made for the often titillating presence of Asian women in movies made by white men.

Movies are still the most seductive and powerful of artistic mediums, manipulating us with ease by a powerful combination of sound and image. In many ways, as females and Asians, as audiences or performers, we have learned to settle for less — to accept the fact that we are either decorative, invisible, or one-dimensional. When there are characters who look like us represented in a movie, we have also learned to view between the lines, or to add what is missing. For many of us, this way of watching has always been a necessity. We fill in the gaps. If a female character is presented as a mute, willowy beauty, we convince ourselves she is an ancestral ghost—so smart she doesn't have to speak at all. If she is a whore with a heart of gold, we claim her as a tough feminist icon. If she is a sexless, sanitized, boring nerd, we embrace her as a role model for our daughters, rather than the tragic whore. And if she is presented as an utterly devoted saint suffering nobly in silence, we lie and say she is just like our mothers. Larger than life. Magical and insidious. A movie is never just a movie, after all.

READING THE TEXT

1. Summarize in your own words Hagedorn's view of the traditional images of Asian women as presented in American film.

2. What is the chronology of Asian women in film that Hagedorn presents, and why do you think she gives us a historical overview?

3. Why does Hagedorn say that the film *The Joy Luck Club* "carries a lot of cultural baggage" (para. 11)?

4. What sort of images of Asian women does Hagedorn imply that she would prefer to see?

READING THE SIGNS

1. Watch *The Joy Luck Club* and write an essay in which you support, refute, or modify Hagedorn's interpretation of the film. Alternately, view another film featuring Asian characters, such as *Balls of Fury* or *Rising Sun*, and use Hagedorn's article as a critical framework for analyzing the film's representation of Asian characters.

2. **CONNECTING TEXTS** In class, form teams and debate the proposition that Hollywood writers and directors have a social responsibility to avoid stereotyping ethnic characters. To develop your team's arguments, brainstorm films that depict various ethnicities, and then discuss whether the portrayals are damaging or benign. You might also consult Michael Omi's "In Living Color: Race and American Culture" (p. 625).

3. Study a magazine that targets Asian American readers, such as *Hyphen* or *Yolk*. Then write an essay in which you analyze whether Asian women in the magazine fit the stereotypes that Hagedorn describes, keeping in mind the magazine's intended readership (businessmen, twenty-somethings of both sexes, and so forth).

4. **CONNECTING TEXTS** Watch one of the gender-bending films Hagedorn mentions (such as *M. Butterfly*), and write your own analysis of the gender roles portrayed in the film. To develop your ideas, consult Aaron Devor's "Gender Role Behaviors and Attitudes" (p. 672).

HIRSH SAWHNEY
An Idiot's Guide to India

India's rise as an economic power has attracted an increasing amount of popular cultural attention in the West, and *Slumdog Millionaire*, which won eight Oscars in 2009, including Best Picture, is a powerful signifier of this trend. But as Hirsh Sawhney suggests in his review of the movie, that doesn't mean that Western filmmakers will automatically get it right when making movies about India. Exploiting the old clichés about Indian poverty and corruption, Sawhney argues, *Slumdog Millionaire* only made Western audiences feel good about what the West can do for India, without exploring the less entertaining details concerning how the West has contributed to India's problems. It's all simply "India for idiots, if you will," Sawhney scathingly remarks. A good many Indian critics didn't like the movie either. Hirsh Sawhney, a native Indian, is currently an adjunct professor at the City University of New York.

When India's call centers and booming economy began to grab headlines, writers and filmmakers attempted to woo Western audiences with tales from the subcontinent. Some of these works were nuanced and sophisticated, like Richie Mehta's recent film *Amal* or Suketu Mehta's best-selling book *Maximum City*. But many of them were designed to cash in on the India craze and provide digestible titbits about the country's culture and history to Western audiences — India for idiots, if you will.

Danny Boyle's *Slumdog Millionaire*, the runaway favorite for the best picture Oscar tomorrow night, is precisely one of these simplistic texts. It contains a smattering of all the major Indian hot buttons: call centers, religious riots, urban development, sex workers, the Taj Mahal — and, of course, slums.

The film, which traces the life of Jamal Malik from the devastatingly poor streets of Mumbai to his deliverance on the TV game show *Who Wants to Be a Millionaire*, has elicited some furious reactions in India. Many have pointed out that the slum children Boyle used as actors weren't fairly compensated for their performances. A group of protestors in the city of Patna burned *Slumdog* posters and ransacked a theater where the film was being screened, claiming that film's depiction of slum dwellers was a "violation of human rights." Some Indian commentators insinuated that the movie has been successful in the West because it uses "poverty porn" to "titillate foreign audiences."

At the other end of the spectrum, *Slumdog*'s admirers assert that those who whine about the film are guilty of "patriotic indignation" and lack "genuine anger and concern" about India's horrific poverty. Fans not only find the film upbeat, colorful, and entertaining, they also applaud the fact that it sheds light on the state of slums. The Indian romance novelist Shobhaa De claimed that it has taken an outsider like Boyle "to go fearlessly into 'No Man's Land' and hold up a mirror to our sordid society. . . . "

Yes, Boyle deserves a pat on the back for diving into Mumbai's entrails   5 and drawing attention to its poverty. But it's a mistake to label him original for shedding light on India's underbelly. Before him, scores of filmmakers — from the iconic Guru Dutt to today's Madhu Bhandarkar — have decried inequity and portrayed India honestly, warts and all. The legendary Raj Kapoor even employed a mixture of fantasy and realism that pre-dates Boyle's masala formula for cinematic success.

But it's also clear that Boyle's version of the third world, complete with fetidness and depravity, is particularly gratifying to our U.K. and U.S. sensibilities. Why? Because it grossly oversimplifies poverty and our relationship with it.

After watching the film, viewers are left to infer that slums are horrid, rancid places because of beggar masters, Hindu zealots, and Muslim gangs. Of course these forces play their role in perpetuating misery. But in reality, slums are an international problem caused by an intricate set of entities: corrupt government officials, gargantuan multinational corporations, and suspect IMF structural adjustment programs.

Playing it safe, Boyle doesn't implicate any of these entities. As a result, his movie does allow us to believe that we have been responsible global citizens by engaging with the intensity of third world slums. We in the audience even feel genuine sympathy for destitution. But at no point do we have to forsake the delusion that abject poverty and inequity are strictly foreign things for which we share no culpability.

In fact, far from spreading the blame for global poverty, Boyle's film actually suggests that the West is the solution to India's problems. Protagonist Jamal only escapes his ceaseless cycle of squalor and crime once he makes it into the orderly, democratic world of a British call center. This call center, in turn, delivers him to his fateful redemption on *Millionaire*. The subtext is clear: Things are really bad in urban India but healthy servings of Western values are just what the doctor — and the Academy judges — ordered.

Of course, many relish this action-packed fairy tale. It reinforces the   10 notion that our policies and mindsets are righteous and can rid the world of its troubles. Stories that perpetuate this myth are especially appealing right now. In the wake of a grave economic collapse and a wretched, unending war, we have to begin the painful process of questioning the integrity of our way of life. A movie like *Slumdog* allows us to put that off for a few more minutes.

READING THE TEXT

1. Explain the significance of the article's title. What tone does it set for the article?

2. What does Sawhney mean by "major Indian hot buttons" (para. 2)?

3. Summarize in your own words the responses that supporters and detractors of *Slumdog Millionaire* had to the film's portrayal of Indian slums.

4. What does Sawhney mean by referring to director Danny Boyles's "masala formula for cinematic success" (para. 5)?

5. Why does the author consider *Slumdog Millionaire* a feel-good movie?

READING THE SIGNS

1. In class, brainstorm images of India that come to mind. Then compare them with Sawhney's list of "major Indian hot buttons" (para. 2). How does the class account for any similarities or differences in the two lists?

2. **CONNECTING TEXTS**   Adopt the perspective of Michael Omi's "In Living Color: Race and American Culture" (p. 625). How would Omi characterize the depiction of India in *Slumdog Millionaire*? To what extent does the film fit Omi's categories of overt or inferential racism?

3. Write an essay in which you support, oppose, or complicate the contention that Western (or, more precisely, American) popular culture is responsible for the "redemption" that viewers of *Slumdog Millionaire* feel.

4. Interview three to five friends or acquaintances who have seen *Slumdog Millionaire*. Use your findings as the basis of an essay in which you assess Sawhney's claim that the film "grossly oversimplifies poverty and our relationship with it" (para. 6).

5. Watch *Gandhi*, which won the 1982 Academy Award for Best Picture of the Year. In an essay, analyze its representation of India generally and the country's poverty more specifically. To what extent does it allow viewers to feel engaged by third world problems and thus feel redeemed simply by watching the film? Or does *Gandhi* avoid being a "masala formula for cinematic success" (para. 5) as Sawhney accuses *Slumdog Millionaire* of being?

MATT ZOLLER SEITZ

The Offensive Movie Cliché That Won't Die

You've seen a satirical portrayal of him on *The Simpsons*, in the guise of Bleeding Gums Murphy, and he has appeared quite seriously in such movies as *The Legend of Bagger Vance, The Green Mile* and *Legendary*. He's the "Magical Negro": "a saintly African American character who acts as a mentor to a questing white hero" in many recent movies. First identified as such by Spike Lee, as Matt Zoller Seitz observes in this critique of the character, the "Magical Negro" has his roots in such figures as Uncle Remus and Bill "Bojangles" Robinson, and his persistence in American popular culture can be read as a signifier of a larger cultural negotiation in which, Seitz argues, white America, finding itself no longer in complete control of the cultural and political agenda, is trying to strike a "deal." Matt Zoller Seitz is a freelance critic and film editor and the founder of the online publication *The House Next Door*.

"You always know the right things to say," says Cal Chetley (Devon Graye), the high school wrestler hero of *Legendary*, in conversation with Harry "Red" Newman (Danny Glover), a local fisherman.

The hero seems bewildered and delighted as he says this. He's about to compete in an important match, reeling from melodramatic blows. When Harry shows up out of nowhere to give Cal a pep talk, the stage is set for a *Rocky*-style, go-the-distance ending. But if Cal had thought about Harry in terms of pop culture stereotypes, he could have answered his own implied question: *How come you're always there when I need you, even though I barely know you?* Harry seems to stand apart from the rest of the community, even though he's a familiar and beloved part of it. The only character who speaks to Harry directly is Cal, and their conversations are always about Cal and his well-being. He's such the benevolent guardian angel figure that the cynical viewer half-expects him to be revealed as a figment of Cal's imagination.

He's not imaginary. He's a "Magical Negro": a saintly African American character who acts as a mentor to a questing white hero, who seems to be disconnected from the community that he adores so much, and who often seems to have an uncanny ability to say and do exactly what needs to be said or done in order to keep the story chugging along in the hero's favor.

We have Spike Lee to thank for popularizing this politically incorrect but very useful term. Lee used it in a 2001 appearance at college campuses. He was blasting a then-recent wave of such characters, played by the likes of Cuba Gooding Jr., in *What Dreams May Come* (a spirit guide helping Robin Williams rescue his wife from Hell), Will Smith in *The Legend of Bagger Vance* (a sherpa-on-the-green, mentoring Matt Damon's golfer), Laurence Fishburne in *The Matrix* (Obi-Wan to Keanu Reeves' Luke Skywalker), and Michael Clarke Duncan in *The Green Mile* (a gentle giant on death row whose touch heals white folks' illnesses).

The word choice is deliberately anachronistic — "negro" started to fall out 5 of fashion about forty years ago. But that's why it's so devastating. The word "negro" was a transitional word that fell between the white-comforting "colored" and the more militantly self-determined and oppositional "black." It asked for dignity and autonomy without going that extra step asserting that it existed anyway, with or without white America's approval. "Negro" fits the sorts of characters that incensed Lee. Even though the movies take pains to insist that the African American character is as much a flesh-and-blood person as the white hero, the relationship is that of a master and servant. And not a *real* servant, either: one that really, truly lives to serve, has no life to

A scene from *The Green Mile*.

speak of beyond his service to Da Man, and never seems to trouble himself with doubts about the cause to which he's devoting his time and energy. "How is it that black people have these powers but they use them for the benefit of white people?" Lee asked sarcastically.

The Magical Negro character (or as Lee called him, the "super-duper magical negro") wasn't invented in the 1990s. He's been around for at least a hundred years, accumulating enough examples (from Uncle Remus in *Song of the South* through the clock-keeper played by Bill Cobbs in *The Hudsucker Proxy*) to merit snarky lists, an entry in the urban dictionary, and a detailed Wikipedia page (turns out Stephen King's fiction has been a Magical Negro factory). The term gained an even wider audience when a candidate to chair the Republican National Committee mailed out a song titled "Barack the Magic

Negro," with lyrics to the tune of the Peter, Paul and Mary hit. Outraged liberals focused on the surface racism encoded in the song title, ignoring the possibility that the song, however lead-footed in its humor, was rooted in something real.

What got lost in the flap over the song was the phrase's relevance to Obama's candidacy: There was (among Democrats, at least) a widespread sense that replacing George W. Bush with the Illinois senator would send a definitive signal that everything was different now, that it was time to rebuild, repair, rejuvenate, and move forward, not just toward a post-Bush society, but a post-racial one. It was an absurd hope, one that Obama himself seemed to resist endorsing at first, only to relent and begin publicly playing up his pioneer status as the first not-entirely-Caucasian man to pursue and then win the Democratic presidential nomination. Frequent *Salon* commenter David Ehrenstein tackled this subject in a memorable 2007 *Los Angeles Times* piece that called Obama a "magic negro" almost a year before that RNC ditty appeared. Likening Obama to a spiritual descendant of the noble, kindhearted, often sexless black men portrayed by pioneering leading man Sidney Poitier, he wrote, "Like a comic-book superhero, Obama is there to help, out of the sheer goodness of a heart we need not know or understand. For as with all Magic Negroes, the less real he seems, the more desirable he becomes."

Suffice to say Obama's election triggered a paroxysm of paranoia, insecurity, and rage in roughly half the population (maybe more, if polls on immigration and the Park51 project are to be believed). These flare-ups of privilege (wherein an almost entirely white sector of the populace descended from once-despised immigrants embraces the idea that "we" have to protect or reclaim "our" country from "them") cast retrospective light on the Magical Negro resurgence, which flowered in earnest during the last Democratic administration and has been going full-steam ever since.

Between demographers' projections of a twenty-first-century majority-minority swap, Clinton's unprecedented (un-presidented?) comfort with African American culture (which he made official during the 1992 campaign, in an effective bit of pandering stagecraft, by playing sax on *The Arsenio Hall Show*), and hip-hop's supplanting rock as the country's unofficial national soundtrack, there was a sense, even in the pre-Internet era, that the white man either wasn't in control anymore or soon wouldn't be. Whitey was just going to have to deal.

Things haven't played out quite so simply, of course. In every aspect of quality of life that can be measured, nonwhite folks have always tended to be worse off than whites. That hasn't changed in the aughts, and the recession/depression has hit black men especially hard.

Looking back over the last twenty years worth of cultural and demographic unrest, the M. N. phenomenon seems a form of psychological jujitsu—one that takes a subject that some white folks find unpleasant or even troubling to ponder (justifiably resentful black people's status in a country that, fifty years after the start of the modern civil rights struggle, is still run by, and mostly for, whites) and turns it into a source of gentle reassurance. Do "they" hate us? Oh, no! In fact, deep down they want "us" to succeed, and are happy to help "us" succeed, as long as we listen well and are polite. That's why Whoopi Goldberg put her life on hold to help Demi Moore get in touch with her dead boyfriend in *Ghost,* and Jennifer Hudson lived to serve Sarah Jessica Parker in the first *Sex and the City* movie. And it's why Danny Glover's character — one of but a few black men in an otherwise white town — takes such a keen interest in the life of a bantamweight high school wrestler who has apparently lived in the same town with Harry his entire life and recognizes him as a local eccentric, yet never bothered to get to know him before now.

People that enjoyed *Legendary* may say I'm being unfair to Harry, that there's more to him than Magical Negro-hood. And yes, it's true, at the end — spoiler alert! — we're told that he's not just a gravel-voiced sweetheart who likes to hang out by the local creek, catching fish and dispensing words of wisdom. He's actually quite influential — not *literally* magical, but nevertheless demi-godlike in his influence over the town and its history. But the specifics of Harry's character don't refute the label; quite the contrary. The revelation of Harry's influence is a nifty trick, one that's common in nearly all movies featuring nonwhite mentor/sidekick/deus ex machina characters. It seems appealing enough in the abstract. But it's weak soup when you look at such a character's role in the totality of the story.

Danny Glover, arguably one of cinema's most versatile and likable character actors, gets to play something close to God (he even narrates the story and turns out to have had a hand in three generations of local lives). But he doesn't get a good scene with anybody but the hero, doesn't get even the intimation of a private life, and barely speaks to anyone in the town that supposedly adores and respects him. Like the clock-tender in *The Hudsucker Proxy,* the HIV-stricken painter/saint from *In America,* and Ben Vereen's characters in *Pippin* and *All That Jazz,* Harry's aura of omnipotence is compensation for being shut out of the movie. It's a screenwriter's distraction that obscures the character's detachment from the heart of the narrative — and the character's essentially decorative nature. Like the hot-tempered black police captain who demands the maverick white detective's badge and the stern black woman judge who dresses down the kooky but irresponsible white heroine and warns her to get her life together, the Magical Negro is a glorified walk-on role, a narrative device with a pulse. The M. N. doesn't really drive the story, but is a glorified hood ornament attached to the end of a car that's being driven by white society, vigorously turning a little steering wheel that's not attached to anything.

Which might be a harsh but accurate metaphor for our current president, come to think of it.

READING THE TEXT

1. In your own words, define the term "Magical Negro" (para. 3). Why is it considered "anachronistic"?

2. What evidence does Seitz offer to suggest that the Danny Glover character in *Legendary* is a Magical Negro?

3. Why did some commentators dub Barack Obama, who is not a cinematic character, a Magical Negro during the 2008 presidential race?

4. Characterize Seitz's tone in this selection. In what ways does it affect your response to his argument?

READING THE SIGNS

1. **CONNECTING TEXTS**   Write your own interpretation of the representation of African American characters in *Legendary, Ghost, Sex in the City, All That Jazz,* or another film that Seitz refers to. To develop your ideas, consult Michael Omi, "In Living Color: Race and American Culture" (p. 625). To what extent do the characters in the film you've selected display traits of "overt" or "inferential" racism, as Omi describes those concepts?

2. **CONNECTING TEXTS**   Both the "Magical Negro" and the "White Messiah" (see Mitu Sengupta, "Race Relations Light Years from Earth," below) are exaggerated, outsized versions of racial stereotypes. In class, compare and contrast these stereotypes. What underlying myths regarding racial difference do they display?

3. Seitz attributes the recurrence of the Magical Negro stereotype, in part, to concern about changing demographics whereby Caucasians would no longer be the dominant ethnic group in America. Considering today's political landscape, what signs do you see that support or complicate this explanation? Be sure to consider both national voting patterns and movements like the Tea Party.

4. Seitz comments parenthetically that "Stephen King's fiction has been a Magical Negro factory" (para. 6). Read at least one King novel that includes African American characters. Write an essay in which you support, refute, or modify this assertion.

5. Seitz is critical of the Magical Negro stereotype, but it has been argued that this particular representation of African Americans is a positive response to accusations that this group too often has been portrayed with overtly negative, often violent stereotypes. Write an essay in which you evaluate this argument, taking care to base your claims on an analysis of specific films and characters.

MITU SENGUPTA

Race Relations Light Years from Earth

On its way to shattering just about every box-office record in the book, James Cameron's *Avatar* also generated an enormous amount of political buzz. Conservative reviewers found in the film a critical allegory of Western capitalism and imperialism, which they resented. Liberal critics found in this reprise of the fundamental theme of *Dances with Wolves* yet another movie featuring a white savior who leads a nonwhite aboriginal people to victory over their white oppressors, which *they* resented. Sympathetic to the liberal view but wanting to be fair to the movie, Mitu Sengupta finds a certain "departure from the 'White Messiah' narrative" in *Avatar*. For one thing, the Na'vi don't really need Jake, their white "savior," and for another, he ends up ceasing to be white, joining the Na'vi entirely. But alas, by making Jake white, at least at first, "Cameron delivers his anti-modernity, pro-indigeneity, and deep-ecology parable through the most advanced of cinematic technologies and the body of a handsome white man." And thus, Sengupta concludes, "the racism charges stick." Mitu Sengupta is a professor in the Department of Politics and Public Administration at Ryerson University and writes widely on global political and popular cultural topics.

Avatar is a racist film. Or at least this has been the persistent allegation ever since its release in December 2009.

Annalee Newitz, editor in chief at io9.com was among the first to label it "white guilt fantasy," another story where the "white characters realize that they are complicit in a system which is destroying aliens, AKA people of color, and become leaders of the people they once oppressed."

David Brooks of the *New York Times* went further, calling it "a racial fantasy par excellence" which "rests on the stereotype that white people are rationalist and technocratic while colonial victims are spiritual and athletic, and that nonwhites need the White Messiah to lead their crusades."

Should the "White Messiah" accusation be taken seriously? I am not alone in wanting to dismiss if not ridicule all this fuss over the politics of a silly and predictable Hollywood movie (visually enchanting though it admittedly is). That is until I begin to think of just how many Hollywood films have shown various peoples of color (minorities, colonial subjects, the Third World poor) struggle against various social ills (poverty, authoritarianism, imperialism) only to be swiftly arrogated by white men (and, from time to time, white women).

Other than being infuriatingly patronizing, such misguided cinematic 5 altruism is dangerous: It reinforces pernicious stereotypes of the ethnic "other" as disorderly, meek, and stupid, only to undermine the hard-won voice of marginalized peoples of color and justify their continued marginalization.

Arguably, the more popular the film, the more the potential for harm. *Avatar*, now the highest grossing movie of all time and multiple Oscar nominee, may prove a particularly weighty addition to this irritating genre.

The examples are many: Brooks names *The Last Samurai, Dances with Wolves, A Man Called Horse,* and *At Play in the Fields of the Lord*. One can add to this inventory *Red Corner, City of Joy*, and David Lean's multiple Academy Award–winning epic, *Lawrence of Arabia*, widely considered to be the classic of all "White Messiah" films.

Lawrence, an officer in the British army, appropriates the dress as well as the struggle of Bedouin tribes in their fight against Turkish aggression and British imperialism. Lean's anti-imperialist message, if there is one at all, is fully submerged by his consuming interest in the persona of Lawrence (played by Peter O'Toole in the prime of his youth).

Besides being sinfully handsome, Lawrence is brilliant, just, and brave; resolute in his determination to "give freedom" to the "Arabs." Though unaccustomed to guerrilla warfare and Arabia's harsh terrain, he takes extraordinary risks, like charging fearlessly through the dreaded Nefud desert. Here he rushes into storms of bullets.

At first glance, *Avatar* is nothing more than the extraterrestrial version of   10 this tired "white guilt fantasy."

It is 2154. Jake Sully, a former U.S. Marine, is sent to Pandora to befriend its indigenous population, the Na'vi, so that his current employer, an American mining corporation, can more easily access the planet's rich stores of Unobtanium, a mineral with "exotic properties" worth "twenty million a kilo."

"Killing the indigenous looks bad," Jake is told. "Find a carrot to get them to move, or it's going to have to be all stick."

Throughout the film, Cameron is clear about whom the Na'vi represent. They are repeatedly referred to as "indigenous," "aboriginal," and "savages,"

A promotional advertisement for *Avatar*.

and the lead Na'vi characters are played by Black or Aboriginal actors (Zoe Saldana, Laz Alonso, and Wes Studi).

Jake (played by Sam Worthington) plunges into the Na'vi's midst as an "avatar," but soon comes to neglect his mission, falling "in love with the forest, the people," and predictably, with Neytiri, a Na'vi chief's daughter. Neytiri teaches Jake her people's ways because she senses in him a "strong heart"—a good investment, it turns out, as Jake's "strong heart" guides him to oppose the corporation, and its hawkish security chief, Colonel Quaritch, who later accuses Jake of "betraying his race."

Though Jake describes himself as "just another dumb grunt," we learn that he is extraordinary well beyond his "strong heart." He quickly adapts to Pandora's "savage terrain and fierce creatures," and to Na'vi society, learning their language with enviable speed and matching their physical prowess.

Jake is also a skilled military strategist and negotiator. He inspires the various Na'vi clans to join forces against the "sky people," and even subdues the fierce Toruk, a giant bird-like creature that only five Na'vi have ever managed to tame.

Jake prances through the last quarter of the film with fist thrust in the air, showering the Na'vi with stirring calls to action, swooping down on Quaritch's troops on the newly obedient Toruk, and basking in the warmth of Neytiri's devotion: "I was afraid for my people," she coos. "I am no longer afraid." In an early version of the *Avatar* script, Jake becomes the leader of Neytiri's clan.

Despite the many eye-rolling moments, in the end *Avatar* doesn't neatly follow the expected narrative.

In "White Messiah" films, the natives' world, even when romanticized, is marked as clearly inferior. In *Lawrence of Arabia*, the "Arabs" have rather barbaric ideas of justice, and it is evident they'll have trouble managing on their own once Lawrence is extricated from their midst. The native, though noble, is backward; wanting in various aspects of "civilization."

Not so much in *Avatar*. For one thing, the Na'vi's lush habitat is profoundly more beautiful than the humans' "dying world." We are told that this "strange, bewitching place" with a "dreamlike landscape reminiscent of a Magritte painting" represents "hope for our race, for our planet, and future of all living things."

The Na'vi's pantheism, community solidarity, and oneness with nature (the "symbiotic relationship between all things Pandoran") are celebrated wholeheartedly, while the American way of life—now associated with corporate greed, ruthless individualism, and misappropriated science—is squarely and unambiguously condemned.

The U.S. Marines, give or take a few, are depicted as a warmongering and boorish horde (yes, the real Marines are upset about the film, too!). They kill thoughtlessly and hurl demeaning jeers at the disabled, wheelchair-bound Jake ("meals on wheels"). Toward the end of the film, any thought that the Na'vi are "savages" seems utterly preposterous.

It's clear that the Na'vi need nothing from Jake's ilk, not their promise of "development"—"medicine, education, and roads"—or their "light beer and shopping channels" or military technology. The Na'vi may lack the coarse firepower of American bombs and guns, but they have "arrows dipped in a neurotoxin that can stop your heart in one minute." In fact, it is with these instruments of precision that Neytiri ultimately kills Quaritch. Yes, it is *she* who saves Jake.

Finally, in a fundamental departure from the "White Messiah" narrative, Jake "goes native" in a total, self-incinerating way. The Na'vi perform a ritual that permanently transforms Jake's human body into his alien avatar.

So *Avatar* is a curious film: It follows the "White Messiah" model faithfully,   25 but then ruptures it at critical moments.

I'm hesitant to subject *Avatar* to prolonged philosophical analysis — after all, Hollywood movies are known for being inconsistent. Yet the film's hybrid narrative is not without significance. It reflects how multiculturalism, environmentalism, feminism, and indigenous struggles have shifted conversations about culture and imperialism while leaving every economic fundamental unchanged.

Indigenous movements, in particular, have issued powerful critiques of imperialism, condemning not only the cruel mechanics of colonial rule, but also their devastating cultural impact via the reification of science, rationalism, and industrialization. The demands of indigenous movements stretch beyond inclusion and space in dominant "white" cultures to equal regard for difference, marked as this may be by oral traditions of knowledge, communitarian political structures, and spiritual systems based in ancestor worship.

How remarkable that the radical multiculturalism of indigenous struggles is reproduced in *Avatar*, a thoroughly mainstream production. No wonder that Evo Morales, Bolivia's first fully indigenous head of state, has praised the film for its "profound show of resistance to capitalism and the struggle for the defense of nature."

Morales's pithy tribute left me wondering if behind the racism allegation lie deeper anxieties about the film's glib indictment of modern notions of progress, including monotheism. *Telegraph* blogger Will Heaven — who wrote a scathing review of *Avatar*'s "racist subtext" in December — recently defended a Vatican spokesman's concern that *Avatar* will turn environmentalism into a "new divinity." Heaven declared: "He's right to be worried."

Perhaps if Cameron had foregone the economic logic of casting Worthing-   30 ton in the lead, he would have made a ridiculously subversive film, one worthy of all the fuss.

But the point is that he didn't. And as the possibilities of genuine dissent unravel into a confusing carnival of their co-optation, the racism charges stick.

Cameron delivers his anti-modernity, pro-indigeneity, and deep-ecology parable through the most advanced of cinematic technologies and the body of a handsome white man.

We get to revel in our equal regard for Na'vi culture from the safest distance possible — 4.4 light years from Earth to be precise — while adjusting our 3-D glasses and munching on overpriced popcorn. Cameron has it both ways, knowing that we do, too.

READING THE TEXT

1. Why do some critics of *Avatar* consider the film to be racist, according to Sengupta?
2. What does the term "White Messiah" refer to?
3. How does the film characterize the Na'vi, in Sengupta's view?
4. What does Sengupta mean by referring to the Na'vi's "pantheism" (para. 21)?
5. In your own words, how have indigenous movements voiced a critique of imperialism?

READING THE SIGNS

1. Write your own analysis of racial identity in *Avatar*. To what extent do you agree with Sengupta's conclusion that "the racism charges stick" (para. 31)?
2. **CONNECTING TEXTS**   Read or reread Robert B. Ray's "The Thematic Paradigm" (p. 377). In an essay, analyze the character of Jake Sully. What sort of hero is he, according to Ray's description of cinematic heroes?
3. Write an essay defending, refuting, or complicating the contention that 3-D effects and advanced technological tricks work to distract viewers from the racism implicit in *Avatar*.
4. Watch *Dances with Wolves* or one of the other films that Sengupta describes as containing a "White Messiah" character. To what extent does the film you've selected demonstrate or contradict this charge?
5. Some conservative viewers have criticized *Avatar* because it can be seen as an allegorical condemnation of American capitalism. In an essay, respond to this criticism, using your own analysis of specific scenes in the movie to support your argument.

BOB SAMUELS

Inception *as Deception*

Like *The Matrix*, *Inception* is a science fiction thriller that explores the technology of absolute mind control. But while science fiction stories are conventionally set in some far away place and/or time, Bob Samuels asks in this movie review that first appeared in *The Huffington Post*, "isn't this the central trick of contemporary culture and capitalism? Doesn't advertising get us to desire things and then makes us think that these desires come from our own free will?" In other words, *Inception* is really an allegory of modern American life,

Samuels suggests, but it distracts us from this "depressing" truth by presenting itself as just an entertaining fiction that "we do not have to take . . . seriously." Confusing us even as it entertains us, *Inception* only reproduces the nightmare it seeks to expose. Bob Samuels is the author of many books, including *New Media, Cultural Studies, and Critical Theory after Postmodernity* (2009), *Teaching the Rhetoric of Resistance: The Popular Holocaust and Social Change in a Post 9/11 World* (2007), and *Hitchcock's Bi-Textuality: Lacan, Feminisms, and Queer Theory* (1997). Samuels is a lecturer in the UCLA Writing Programs.

Within the plot of *Inception*, the big question concerns how can you implant an idea into another person's head so that the person receiving the idea actually thinks it comes from his or her own intention. While the film depicts this form of mind control as a futuristic mystery, we must ask, isn't this the central trick of contemporary culture and capitalism? Doesn't advertising get us to desire things and then make us think that these desires come from our own free will?

In other words, what appears to be a cutting-edge manipulation in the film is the central mechanism shaping our culture. In fact, one of the biggest illusions sold in popular culture is the illusion of individual control.

Since people want to believe that they are in control of their destiny, they must convince themselves that external desires are actually internally derived. Within the context of *Inception*, the ideas implanted into people are called viruses, and we are told on several occasions that once an idea enters someone's mind, it continues to spread and replicate. However, the film also stresses that people will defend against viral ideas, and so the implanters of the viruses have to find a way to trick the mind into thinking that the parasite is the product of the receiver's own intention.

Once again, we can see this science fiction storyline as simply mystifying the way everyday pop culture works. Fashion and hot news items enter our brains from outside, and they circulate and spread through our thoughts. Likewise, the World Wide Web can be seen as a giant shared external brain prone to viruses and the viral media.

Perhaps the most important way to understand a film like *Inception* is 5 to realize that it reflects important aspects of our lives in a distorted and fictionalized way. In other words, we are confronted with some depressing truths, but since it is just a fiction, we do not have to take those truths seriously. For instance, the movie may allow us to see how we are being manipulated by advertising into thinking that we desire the objects they want to sell us, but this critical insight is undermined by the fictional nature of its presentation. Like so many other contemporary productions, everything that is criticized in the film is also repeated in the making of the movie. Thus, as we are shown the destructive results of living in a fantasy world, we are watching a fantasy.

One of the central plots of the story is that the main character (played by Leonardo DiCaprio) is responsible for his wife's suicide because he implanted in her unconscious the idea that they are trapped in a fake world. Since the wife wants to escape her dream, she decides to kill herself. After his wife's death, the main character feels horrible guilt, and decides to re-enter his unconscious so that he can rejoin his wife who now only exists as a memory. At first, the message appears to be the standard movie message that we should not mistake fantasy for reality, and we must learn to accept our lives as they are. Thus, the wife killed herself because she failed to realize that she was living in a fantasy-dream world, and by the end of the film, the husband, our hero, also realizes that he must give up his fantasies, memories, and guilt by affirming the reality of his actual family.

This common message of favoring reality over fantasy is portrayed ironically in a fantasy film about fantasies. Call it contradiction or hypocrisy, but once again we find the media attacking the media as it produces more media about media. Like a parasitic virus that cannot stop replicating and circulating, pop culture resembles the implanted ideas, which are the real subject of the film.

However, the reason why we cannot stop the viral spread of media memes is not because we fight them off with an army of internal defense mechanisms; rather, the media viruses are always implanted with their own protective defenses. In other words, while the film wants to pretend that our minds are populated by self-controlled defenses, these defenses are actually produced and disarmed by the viral media itself.

The media not only want us to believe that all of our desires come from our own intentions, but we are also told that all of our defenses are derived from our efforts at self-preservation. The reality is actually the opposite: our desires and defenses come from the external media. We are back to where *The Matrix* left us. When Neo asks Trinity what it means that all of his memories have been implanted by the matrix (the media), he also wants to know what is left of his individuality. In response, Trinity tells him that the matrix cannot tell him who he is. Yet, if all of our desires and memories are media messages, hasn't the matrix (as the media) defined us?

Like *The Matrix, Inception* plays on the idea of a shared dream, which 10 we can read as another metaphor for film itself. But what these films may be pointing to unintentionally is the idea that our world has entered into a third space where there is no clear difference between fact and reality.

This means that virtual reality represents something that is both real and fake at the same time. Like *The Matrix*, this film appears to approach this truth, but then turns back on itself and holds a mirror up to its own mirror. In *The Matrix*, they create a simulation of the virtual reality, and as the sequels progress, there is the idea that we are always in another virtual version of a virtual reality.

Likewise, with *Inception* we are told that we are in a dream that is in a dream that is in another dream, and the result is that by the end of the film, no one knows if we are in reality or still in a dream, but perhaps this is a very truthful way of seeing our contemporary world.

The danger of new media is not so much whether the content is corrupting or enlightening; the problem is that it eats away at all of our fundamental oppositions between truth and reality, technology and nature, self and other, and memory and perception. We are so saturated with media representations that we can no longer distinguish fact from fiction. As the film argues, people dream so they can wake up, but what happens if we can only live in fiction?

READING THE TEXT

1. In your own words, explain what Samuels means by saying that "what appears to be a cutting-edge manipulation in [*Inception*] is the central mechanism shaping our culture. In fact, one of the biggest illusions sold in popular culture is the illusion of individual control" (para. 2).

2. How does the plot of *Inception* support Samuels's claim that, in this film, "we find the media attacking the media as it produces more media about media" (para. 7)?

3. What does Samuels mean by saying that "we cannot stop the viral spread of media memes . . . because . . . the media viruses are always implanted with their own protective defenses" (para. 8)?

READING THE SIGNS

1. Many TV programs (such as *Lost* and *Heroes*) and films present indecipherable plots, switching flashbacks with flashforwards, for instance, in a way that skewers conventional narrative structure. In your journal, describe your response to these sorts of plots. If you are a fan, what is their appeal? If you dislike them, why does the blurring of imaginary and real and of chronology not appeal to you?

2. **CONNECTING TEXTS**   Samuels claims that "the movie may allow us to see how we are being manipulated by advertising into thinking that we desire the objects they want to sell us, but this critical insight is undermined by the fictional nature of its presentation" (para. 5). In a critical essay, support, refute, or complicate this claim, basing your argument on an analysis of specific ad campaigns. To develop your ideas, consult Thomas Frank, "Commodify Your Dissent" (p. 163), and the Introduction to Chapter 6, "American Paradox: Culture, Conflict, and Contradiction in the U.S.A." (p. 513).

3. Write your own analysis of the film *Inception*. To what extent does that movie simultaneously dismiss and reinforce conventional media values? Alternatively, write your own analysis of *The Matrix* as a precursor to *Inception*.

4. Write a reflective essay commenting on Samuels's concluding thought that "The danger of new media is not so much whether the content is corrupting or enlightening; the problem is that it eats away at all of our fundamental oppositions between truth and reality, technology and nature, self and other, and memory and perception" (para. 13).

MICHAEL PARENTI
Class and Virtue

In 1993, a movie called *Indecent Proposal* presented a story in which a billionaire offers a newly poor middle-class woman a million dollars if she'll sleep with him for one night. In Michael Parenti's terms, what was really indecent about the movie was the way it showed the woman falling in love with the billionaire, thus making a romance out of a class outrage. But the movie could get away with it, partly because Hollywood has always conditioned audiences to root for the ruling classes and to ignore the inequities of class privilege. In this selection from *Make-Believe Media: The Politics of Entertainment* (1992), Parenti argues that Hollywood has long been in the business of representing the interests of the ruling classes. Whether it is forgiving the classist behavior in *Pretty Woman* or glamorizing the lives of the wealthy, Hollywood makes sure its audiences leave the theater thinking you can't be too rich. Parenti is a writer who lectures widely at university campuses around the country. His publications include *Power and the Powerless* (1978), *Inventing Reality: The Politics of the News Media* (1986), *Against Empire* (1995), *Dirty Truths* (1996), *America Besieged* (1998), *The Culture Struggle* (2006), *Democracy for the Few* (2007), and *God and His Demons* (2010).

Class and Virtue

The entertainment media present working people not only as unlettered and uncouth but also as less desirable and less moral than other people. Conversely, virtue is more likely to be ascribed to those characters whose speech and appearance are soundly middle- or upper-middle class.

Even a simple adventure story like *Treasure Island* (1934, 1950, 1972) manifests this implicit class perspective. There are two groups of acquisitive persons searching for a lost treasure. One, headed by a squire, has money enough to hire a ship and crew. The other, led by the rascal Long John Silver, has no money — so they sign up as part of the crew. The narrative implicitly assumes from the beginning that the squire has a moral claim to the treasure, while Long John Silver's gang does not. After all, it is the squire who puts up the venture capital for the ship. Having no investment in the undertaking other than their labor, Long John and his men, by definition, will be "stealing" the treasure, while the squire will be "discovering" it.

To be sure, there are other differences. Long John's men are cutthroats. The squire is not. Yet, one wonders if the difference between a bad pirate and a good squire is itself not preeminently a matter of having the right amount of disposable income. The squire is no less acquisitive than the conspirators.

He just does with money what they must achieve with cutlasses. The squire and his associates dress in fine clothes, speak an educated diction, and drink brandy. Long John and his men dress slovenly, speak in guttural accents, and drink rum. From these indications alone, the viewer knows who are the good guys and who are the bad. Virtue is visually measured by one's approximation to proper class appearances.

Sometimes class contrasts are juxtaposed within one person, as in *The Three Faces of Eve* (1957), a movie about a woman who suffers from multiple personalities. When we first meet Eve (Joanne Woodward), she is a disturbed, strongly repressed, puritanically religious person, who speaks with a rural, poor-Southern accent. Her second personality is that of a wild, flirtatious woman who also speaks with a rural, poor-Southern accent. After much treatment by her psychiatrist, she is cured of these schizoid personalities and emerges with a healthy third one, the real Eve, a poised, self-possessed, pleasant woman. What is intriguing is that she now speaks with a cultivated, affluent, Smith College accent, free of any low-income regionalism or ruralism, much like Joanne Woodward herself. This transformation in class style and speech is used to indicate mental health without any awareness of the class bias thusly expressed.

Mental health is also the question in *A Woman under the Influence* (1974), 5 the story of a disturbed woman who is married to a hard-hat husband. He cannot handle — and inadvertently contributes to — her emotional deterioration. She is victimized by a spouse who is nothing more than an insensitive, working-class bull in a china shop. One comes away convinced that every unstable woman needs a kinder, gentler, and above all, more *middle-class* hubby if she wishes to avoid a mental crack-up.

Class prototypes abound in the 1980s television series *The A-Team*. In each episode, a Vietnam-era commando unit helps an underdog, be it a Latino immigrant or a disabled veteran, by vanquishing some menacing force such as organized crime, a business competitor, or corrupt government officials. As always with the make-believe media, the A-Team does good work on an individualized rather than collectively organized basis, helping particular victims by thwarting particular villains. The A-Team's leaders are two white males of privileged background. The lowest ranking members of the team, who do none of the thinking nor the leading, are working-class palookas. They show they are good with their hands, both by punching out the bad guys and by doing the maintenance work on the team's flying vehicles and cars. One of them, "B.A." (bad ass), played by the African American Mr. T., is visceral, tough, and purposely bad-mannered toward those he doesn't like. He projects an image of crudeness and ignorance and is associated with the physical side of things. In sum, the team has a brain (the intelligent white leaders) and a body with its simpler physical functions (the working-class characters), a hierarchy that corresponds to the social structure itself.[1]

[1]Gina Marchetti, "Class, Ideology and Commercial Television: An Analysis of *The A-Team,*" *Journal of Film and Video* 39, Spring 1987, pp. 19–28.

Sometimes class bigotry is interwoven with gender bigotry, as in *Pretty Woman* (1990). A dreamboat millionaire corporate raider finds himself all alone for an extended stay in Hollywood (his girlfriend is unwilling to join him), so he quickly recruits a beautiful prostitute as his playmate of the month. She is paid three thousand dollars a week to wait around his super-posh hotel penthouse ready to perform the usual services and accompany him to business dinners at top restaurants. As prostitution goes, it is a dream gig. But there is one cloud on the horizon. She is low-class. She doesn't know which fork to use at those CEO power feasts, and she's bothersomely fidgety, wears tacky clothes, chews gum, and, y'know, doesn't talk so good. But with some tips from the hotel manager, she proves to be a veritable Eliza Doolittle in her class metamorphosis. She dresses in proper attire, sticks the gum away forever, and starts picking the right utensils at dinner. She also figures out how to speak a little more like Joanne Woodward without the benefit of a multiple personality syndrome, and she develops the capacity to sit in a poised, wordless, empty-headed fashion, every inch the expensive female ornament.

She is still a prostitute but a classy one. It is enough of a distinction for the handsome young corporate raider. Having liked her because she was charmingly cheap, he now loves her all the more because she has real polish and is a more suitable companion. So suitable that he decides to do the right thing by her: set her up in an apartment so he can make regular visits at regular prices. But now she wants the better things in life, like marriage, a nice house, and, above all, a different occupation, one that would allow her to use less of herself. She is furious at him for treating her like, well, a prostitute. She decides to give up her profession and get a high school diploma so that she might make a better life for herself — perhaps as a filing clerk or receptionist or some other of the entry-level jobs awaiting young women with high school diplomas.[2]

After the usual girl-breaks-off-with-boy scenes, the millionaire prince returns. It seems he can't concentrate on making money without her. He even abandons his cutthroat schemes and enters into a less lucrative but supposedly more productive, caring business venture with a struggling old-time entrepreneur. The bad capitalist is transformed into a good capitalist. He then carries off his ex-prostitute for a lifetime of bliss. The moral is a familiar one, updated for post-Reagan yuppiedom: A woman can escape from economic and gender exploitation by winning the love and career advantages offered by a rich male. Sexual allure goes only so far unless it develops a material base and becomes a class act.[3]

READING THE TEXT

1. According to Parenti, what characteristics are typically attributed to working-class and upper-class film characters?

---

[2]See the excellent review by Lydia Sargent, *Z Magazine*, April 1990, pp. 43–45.
[3]Ibid.

2. How does Parenti see the relationship between "class bigotry" and "gender bigotry" (para. 7) in *Pretty Woman*?

3. What relationship does Parenti see between mental health and class values in films?

READING THE SIGNS

1. Rent a DVD of *Wall Street, Unstoppable*, or *The Fighter*, and analyze the class issues that the movie raises. Alternatively, watch an episode of *The Apprentice*, and perform the same sort of analysis.

2. Do you agree with Parenti's interpretation of *Pretty Woman*? Write an argumentative essay in which you defend, challenge, or complicate his reading of the film.

3. **CONNECTING TEXTS**   Read or reread Aaron Devor's "Gender Role Behaviors and Attitudes" (p. 672). How would Devor explain the gender bigotry that Parenti finds in *Pretty Woman*?

4. Rent the 1954 film *On the Waterfront* and watch it with your class. How are labor unions and working-class characters portrayed in that film? Does the film display the class bigotry that Parenti describes?

5. **CONNECTING TEXTS**   Read Michael Omi's "In Living Color: Race and American Culture" (p. 625). Then write an essay in which you create a category of cinematic racial bigotry that corresponds to Parenti's two categories of class and gender bigotry. What films have you seen that illustrate your new category?

DAVID DENBY

High-School Confidential: Notes on Teen Movies

Face it: High school for most of us is one extended nightmare, a long-playing drama starring cheerleaders and football players who sneer at the mere mortals who must endure their haughty reign. So it's little wonder that, as David Denby argues in this *New Yorker* essay from 1999, teen movies so often feature loathsome cheerleaders and football stars who, one way or another, get theirs in this ever-popular movie genre. Indeed, Denby asks, "Who can doubt where Hollywood's twitchy, near-sighted writers and directors ranked—or feared they ranked—on the high-school totem pole?" Nerds at the bottom, where else, like the millions of suffering kids who flock to their films. A staff writer and film critic for the *New Yorker*, Denby is the author of *The Great Books: My Adventures with Homer, Rousseau, Woolf, and Other Indestructible Writers of the Western World* (1996), *American Sucker* (2003), and *Snark: It's Mean, It's Personal, and It's Ruining Our Conversation* (2009).

The most hated young woman in America is a blonde—well, sometimes a redhead or a brunette, but usually a blonde. She has big hair flipped into a swirl of gold at one side of her face or arrayed in a sultry mane, like the magnificent pile of a forties movie star. She's tall and slender, with a waist as supple as a willow, but she's dressed in awful, spangled taste: her outfits could have been put together by warring catalogues. And she has a mouth on her, a low, slatternly tongue that devastates other kids with such insults as "You're vapor, you're Spam!" and "Do I look like Mother Teresa? If I did, I probably wouldn't mind talking to the geek squad." She has two or three friends exactly like her, and together they dominate their realm—the American high school as it appears in recent teen movies. They are like wicked princesses, who enjoy the misery of their subjects. Her coronation, of course, is the senior prom, when she expects to be voted "most popular" by her class. But, though she may be popular, she is certainly not liked, so her power is something of a mystery. She is beautiful and rich, yet in the end she is preëminent because . . . she is preëminent, a position she works to maintain with Joan Crawford-like tenacity. Everyone is afraid of her; that's why she's popular.

She has a male counterpart. He's usually a football player, muscular but dumb, with a face like a beer mug and only two ways of speaking—in a conspiratorial whisper, to a friend; or in a drill sergeant's sudden bellow. If her weapon is the snub, his is the lame but infuriating prank—the can of Sprite emptied into a knapsack, or something sticky, creamy, or adhesive deposited in a locker. Sprawling and dull in class, he comes alive in the halls and in the cafeteria. He hurls people against lockers; he spits, pours, and sprays; he has a projectile relationship with food. As the crown prince, he claims the best-looking girl for himself, though in a perverse display of power he may invite an outsider or an awkward girl—a "dog"—to the prom, setting her up for some special humiliation. When we first see him, he is riding high, and virtually the entire school colludes in his tyranny. No authority figure—no teacher or administrator—dares correct him.

Thus the villains of the recent high-school movies. Not every American teen movie has these two characters, and not every social queen or jock shares all the attributes I've mentioned. (Occasionally, a handsome, dark-haired athlete can be converted to sweetness and light.) But as genre figures these two types are hugely familiar; that is, they are a common memory, a collective trauma, or at least a social and erotic fantasy. Such movies of the past year [1999] as *Disturbing Behavior*, *She's All That*, *Ten Things I Hate about You*, and *Never Been Kissed* depend on them as stock figures. And they may have been figures in the minds of the Littleton shooters, Eric Harris and Dylan Klebold, who imagined they were living in a school like the one in so many of these movies—a poisonous system of status, snobbery, and exclusion.

Do genre films reflect reality? Or are they merely a set of conventions that refer to other films? Obviously, they wouldn't survive if they didn't provide emotional satisfaction to the people who make them and to the audiences who watch them. A half century ago, we didn't need to see ten Westerns a year in order to learn that the West got settled. We needed to see it settled ten times a year in order to provide ourselves with the emotional gratifications of righteous violence. By drawing his gun only when he was provoked, and in the service of the good, the classic Western hero transformed the gross tangibles of the expansionist drive (land, cattle, gold) into a principle of moral order. The gangster, by contrast, is a figure of chaos, a modern, urban person, and in the critic Robert Warshow's formulation he functions as a discordant element in an American society devoted to a compulsively "positive" outlook. When the gangster dies, he cleanses viewers of their own negative feelings.

High-school movies are also full of unease and odd, mixed-up emotions. They may be flimsy in conception; they may be shot in lollipop colors, garlanded with mediocre pop scores, and cast with goofy young actors trying to make an impression. Yet this most commercial and frivolous of genres harbors a grievance against the world. It's a very specific grievance, quite different from the restless anger of such fifties adolescent-rebellion movies as *The Wild One*, in which someone asks Marlon Brando's biker "What are you rebelling against?" and the biker replies "What have you got?" The fifties teen outlaw was against anything that adults considered sacred. But no movie teenager now revolts against adult authority, for the simple reason that adults have no authority. Teachers are rarely more than a minimal, exasperated presence, administrators get turned into a joke, and parents are either absent or distantly benevolent. It's a teen world, bounded by school, mall, and car, with occasional moments set in the fast-food outlets where the kids work, or in the kids' upstairs bedrooms, with their pinups and rack stereo systems. The enemy is not authority; the enemy is other teens and the social system that they impose on one another.

The bad feeling in these movies may strike grownups as peculiar. After all, from a distance American kids appear to be having it easy these days. The teen audience is facing a healthy job market; at home, their parents are stuffing the den with computers and the garage with a bulky SUV. But most teens aren't thinking about the future job market. Lost in the eternal swoon of late adolescence, they're thinking about their identity, their friends, and their clothes. Adolescence is the present-tense moment in American life. Identity and status are fluid: abrupt, devastating reversals are always possible. (In a teen movie, a guy who swallows a bucket of cafeteria coleslaw can make himself a hero in an instant.) In these movies, accordingly, the senior prom is the equivalent of the shoot-out at the O.K. Corral; it's the moment when one's worth as a human being is settled at last. In the rather pedestrian new comedy *Never Been Kissed*, Drew Barrymore, as a twenty-five-year-old newspaper reporter, goes back to high school pretending to be a student, and immediately falls into her old, humiliating pattern of trying to impress the good-looking rich kids. Helplessly, she pushes for approval, and even gets herself chosen prom queen before finally coming to her senses. She finds it nearly impossible to let go.

Genre films dramatize not what happens but how things feel — the emotional coloring of memory. They fix subjectivity into fable. At actual schools, there is no unitary system of status; there are many groups to be a part of, many places to excel (or fail to excel), many avenues of escape and self-definition. And often the movies, too, revel in the arcana of high-school cliques. In last summer's *Disturbing Behavior*, a veteran student lays out the cafeteria ethnography for a newcomer: Motorheads, Blue Ribbons, Skaters, Micro-geeks ("drug of choice: Stephen Hawking's *A Brief History of Time* and a cup of jasmine tea on Saturday night"). Subjectively, though, the social system in *Disturbing Behavior* (a high-school version of *The Stepford Wives*) and in the other movies still feels coercive and claustrophobic: humiliation is the most vivid emotion of youth, so in memory it becomes the norm.

The movies try to turn the tables. The kids who cannot be the beautiful ones, or make out with them, or avoid being insulted by them — these are the heroes of the teen movies, the third in the trio of character types. The female outsider is usually an intellectual or an artist. (She scribbles in a diary, she draws or paints.) Physically awkward, she walks like a seal crossing a beach, and is prone to drop her books and dither in terror when she stands before a handsome boy. Her clothes, which ignore mall fashion, scandalize the social queens. Like them, she has a tongue, but she's tart and grammatical, tending toward feminist pungency and precise diction. She may mask her sense of vulnerability with sarcasm or with Plathian rue (she's stuck in the bell jar), but even when she lashes out she can't hide her craving for acceptance.

The male outsider, her friend, is usually a mass of stuttering or giggling sexual gloom: he wears shapeless clothes; he has an undeveloped body, either stringy or shrimpy; he's sometimes a Jew (in these movies, still the generic outsider). He's also brilliant, but in a morose, preoccupied way that suggests masturbatory absorption in some arcane system of knowledge. In a few special cases, the outsider is not a loser but a disengaged hipster, either saintly or satanic. (Christian Slater has played this role a couple of times.) This outsider wears black and keeps his hair long, and he knows how to please women. He sees through everything, so he's ironic by temperament and genuinely indifferent to the opinion of others — a natural aristocrat, who transcends the school's contemptible status system. There are whimsical variations on the outsider figure, too. In the recent *Rushmore*, an obnoxious teen hero, Max Fischer (Jason Schwartzman), runs the entire school: he can't pass his courses but he's a dynamo at extracurricular activities, with a knack for staging extraordinary events. He's a con man, a fund-raiser, an entrepreneur — in other words, a contemporary artist.

In fact, the entire genre, which combines self-pity and ultimate vindica- 10 tion, might be called "Portrait of the Filmmaker as a Young Nerd." Who can doubt where Hollywood's twitchy, nearsighted writers and directors ranked — or feared they ranked — on the high-school totem pole? They are still angry, though occasionally the target of their resentment goes beyond the jocks and cheerleaders of their youth. Consider this anomaly: the young actors and models on the covers of half the magazines published in this country, the shirtless men with chests like burnished shields, the girls smiling, glowing, tweezed, full-lipped, full-breasted (but not too full), and with skin so honeyed that it seems lacquered — these are the physical ideals embodied by the villains of the teen movies. The social queens and jocks, using their looks to dominate others, represent an American barbarism of beauty. Isn't it possible that the detestation of them in teen movies is a veiled strike at the entire abs-hair advertising culture, with its unobtainable glories of perfection? A critic of consumerism might even see a spark of revolt in these movies. But only a spark.

My guess is that these films arise from remembered hurts which then get recast in symbolic form. For instance, a surprising number of the outsider heroes have no mother. Mom has died or run off with another man; her child, only half loved, is ill equipped for the emotional pressures of school. The motherless child, of course, is a shrewd commercial ploy that makes a direct appeal to the members of the audience, many of whom may feel like outsiders, too, and unloved, or not loved enough, or victims of some prejudice or exclusion. But the motherless child also has powers, and will someday be a success, an artist, a screenwriter. It's the wound and the bow all over again, in cargo pants.

As the female nerd attracts the attention of the handsomest boy in the senior class, the teen movie turns into a myth of social reversal — a Cinderella fantasy. Initially, his interest in her may be part of a stunt or a trick: he is leading her on, perhaps at the urging of his queenly girlfriend. But his gaze lights her up, and we see how attractive she really is. Will she fulfill the eternal American fantasy that you can vault up the class system by removing your specs? She wants her prince, and by degrees she wins him over, not just with her looks but with her superior nature, her essential goodness. In the male version of the Cinderella trip, a few years go by, and a pale little nerd (we see him at a reunion) has become rich. All that poking around with chemicals paid off. Max Fischer, of *Rushmore*, can't miss being richer than Warhol.

So the teen movie is wildly ambivalent. It may attack the consumerist ethos that produces winners and losers, but in the end it confirms what it is attacking. The girls need the seal of approval conferred by the converted jocks; the nerds need money and a girl. Perhaps it's no surprise that the outsiders can be validated only by the people who ostracized them. But let's not be too schematic: the outsider who joins the system also modifies it, opens it up to the creative power of social mobility, makes it bend and laugh, and perhaps this turn of events is not so different from the way things work in the real world, where merit and achievement stand a good chance of trumping appearance. The irony of the Littleton shootings is that Klebold and Harris, who were both proficient computer heads, seemed to have forgotten how the plot turns out. If they had held on for a few years they might have been working at a hip software company, or have started their own business, while the jocks who oppressed them would probably have wound up selling insurance or used cars. That's the one unquestionable social truth the teen movies reflect: geeks rule.

There is, of course, a menacing subgenre, in which the desire for revenge turns bloody. Thirty-one years ago, Lindsay Anderson's semi-surrealistic *If . . .* was set in an oppressive, class-ridden English boarding school, where a group of rebellious students drive the school population out into a courtyard and open fire on them with machine guns. In Brian De Palma's 1976 masterpiece *Carrie*, the pale, repressed heroine, played by Sissy Spacek, is courted at last by a handsome boy but gets violated — doused with pig's blood — just as she is named prom queen. Stunned but far from powerless, Carrie uses her telekinetic powers to set the room afire and burn down the school. *Carrie* is the primal school movie, so wildly lurid and funny that it exploded the clichés of the genre before the genre was quite set: The heroine may be a wrathful avenger, but the movie, based on a Stephen King book, was clearly a grinning-gargoyle fantasy. So, at first, was *Heathers*, in which Christian Slater's satanic outsider turns out to be a true devil. He and his girlfriend (played by a very young Winona Ryder) begin gleefully knocking off the rich, nasty girls and the jocks, in ways so patently absurd that their revenge seems a mere wicked dream. I think it's unlikely that these movies had a direct effect on the actions of the Littleton shooters, but the two boys would surely have recognized the emotional world of *Heathers* and *Disturbing Behavior* as their own. It's a place where feelings of victimization join fantasy, and you experience the social élites as so powerful that you must either become them or kill them.

But enough. It's possible to make teen movies that go beyond these fixed 15 polarities — insider and outsider, blond-bitch queen and hunch-shouldered nerd. In Amy Heckerling's 1995 comedy *Clueless*, the big blonde played by Alicia Silverstone is a Rodeo Drive clotheshorse who is nonetheless possessed of extraordinary virtue. Freely dispensing advice and help, she's almost ironically good — a designing goddess with a cell phone. The movie offers a sun-shiny satire of Beverly Hills affluence, which it sees as both absurdly swollen and generous in spirit. The most original of the teen comedies, *Clueless* casts away self-pity. So does *Romy and Michele's High School Reunion* (1997), in which two gabby, lovable friends, played by Mira Sorvino and Lisa Kudrow, review the banalities of their high-school experience so knowingly that they might be criticizing the teen-movie genre itself. And easily the best American film of the year so far is Alexander Payne's *Election*, a high-school movie that inhabits a different aesthetic and moral world altogether from the rest of these pictures. *Election* shreds everyone's fantasies and illusions in a vision of high school that is bleak but supremely just. The movie's villain, an overachieving girl (Reese Witherspoon) who runs for class president, turns out to be its covert heroine, or, at least, its most poignant character. A cross between Pat and Dick Nixon, she's a lower-middle-class striver who works like crazy and never wins anyone's love. Even when she's on top, she feels excluded. Her loneliness is produced not by malicious cliques but by her own implacable will, a condition of the spirit that may be as comical and tragic as it is mysterious. *Election* escapes all the clichés; it graduates into art.

READING THE TEXT

1. Describe in your own words the stereotypical male and female villains common in teen movies.

2. What does Denby mean by the comment, "Adolescence is the present-tense moment in American life" (para. 6)?

3. What sort of characters are typically the heroes in teen films, in Denby's view?

4. In what ways does a Cinderella fantasy influence teen films?

5. What is the "menacing subgenre" (para. 14) of teen movies?

READING THE SIGNS

1. Using Denby's description of stock character types in teen movies as your critical framework, analyze the characters in a teen TV program, such as *Friday Night Lights* or *One Tree Hill*. Do you see the same conventions at work? How do you account for any differences you might see?

2. In class, brainstorm a list of current teen films. Then, using the list as evidence, write an essay in which you assess the validity of Denby's claim: "The enemy [in teen films] is not authority; the enemy is other teens and the social system that they impose on one another" (para. 5).

3. Rent a video or DVD of *American Beauty*, and write an essay in which you argue whether it can be categorized as a teen film, at least as Denby defines the genre.

4. **CONNECTING TEXTS**   Denby asks, "Do genre films reflect reality? Or are they merely a set of conventions that refer to other films?" (para. 4). Write an essay in which you propose your own response to these questions, using as evidence your high school experience and specific teen films. In addition, you can consider as evidence teen-based TV programs such as *Glee*. To develop your ideas, consult Rita Koganzon, "All Camped Out: How 'Glee' Became a Preachy After-School Special" (p. 326).

VIVIAN C. SOBCHACK

The Postmorbid Condition

When *Bonnie and Clyde* shuddered to a spectacular conclusion with the slow-motion machine-gunning of its main characters, the point was that in a society plagued by random and senseless violence Hollywood had a responsibility to make some kind of meaning out of it. But when Quentin Tarantino uses senseless violence for comic effect, the point, Vivian C. Sobchack argues in this essay originally published in *Screening Violence*, is that there is no point at all, or rather, that the human body has lost its meaning in contemporary life and has become little more than a machine whose destruction is on a par with an exploding automobile. Offering a profound and disturbing explanation for the popularity of movies like *Pulp Fiction* and *Natural Born Killers*, Sobchack reveals the forces behind the dehumanization of Hollywood violence. A professor and associate dean in the School of Theater, Film, and Television at UCLA, Sobchack is the author of *Screening Space: The American Science Fiction Film* (1987), *Address of the Eye: A Phenomenology of Film Experience* (1991), *The Persistence of History: Cinema, Television, and the Modern Event* (1995), *Meta-Morphing: Visual Transformation and the Culture of Quick-Change* (1999), and *Carnal Thoughts: Embodiment and Moving Image Culture* (2004).

In an essay I wrote twenty-five years ago, I argued that screen violence in American films of the late 1960s and early 1970s was new and formally different from earlier "classical" Hollywood representations of violence. This new interest in violence and its new formal treatment not only literally satisfied an intensified cultural desire for "close-up" knowledge about the material fragility of bodies, but also — and more important — made increasingly senseless violence in the "civil" sphere sensible and meaningful by stylizing and aestheticizing it, thus bringing intelligibility and order to both the individual and social body's increasingly random and chaotic destruction. Indeed, I argued that random and senseless violence was elevated to meaning in these then "new" movies, its "transcendence" achieved not only by being up there on the screen, but also through long lingering gazes at carnage and ballets of slow motion that conferred on violence a benediction and the grace of a cinematic "caress."

Today, most American films have more interest in the presence of violence than in its meaning. There are very few attempts to confer order or perform a benediction upon the random and senseless death, the body riddled with bullets, the laying waste of human flesh. (The application of such order, benediction, and transcendental purpose is, perhaps, one of the explicit achievements of Steven Spielberg's high-tech but emotionally anachronistic *Saving Private Ryan*, and it is no accident that its context is a morally intelligible World War II.) Indeed, in today's films (and whatever happened started happening sometime in the 1980s), there is no transcendence of "senseless" violence: It just *is*. Thus, the camera no longer caresses it or transforms it into something with more significance than its given instance. Instead of caressing violence, the cinema has become increasingly *careless* about it: either merely nonchalant or deeply lacking in care. Unlike medical melodramas, those films that describe violent bodily destruction evoke no tears in the face of mortality and evidence no concern for the fragility of flesh. Samuel L. Jackson's violent role and religious monologues in Quentin Tarantino's *Pulp Fiction* notwithstanding, we see no grace or benediction attached to violence. Indeed, its very intensity seems diminished: We need noise and constant stimulation and quantity to make up for a lack of significant meaning.

Perhaps this change in attitude and treatment of violence is a function of our increasingly *technologized* view of the body and flesh. We see this view dramatized outside the theater in the practices and fantasies of "maintenance" and "repair" represented by the "fitness center" and cosmetic surgery. Inside the theater, we see it dramatized in the "special effects" allowed by new technological developments and in an increasingly hyperbolic and quantified treatment of violence and bodily damage that is as much about "more" as it is about violence. It seems to me that this quantitative move to "more" in relation to violence — more blood, more gore, more characters (they're really not people) blown up or blown away — began with the contemporary horror film, with "slasher" and "splatter" films that hyperbolized violence and its victims in terms of quantity rather than through exaggerations of form. Furthermore, unlike in the "New Hollywood" films of the late 1960s and 1970s (here one thinks of Peckinpah or Penn), excessive violence in these "low" genre films, while eliciting screams, also elicited laughter, too much becoming, indeed, "too much": incredible, a "gross-out," so "outrageous" and "over the top" that ironic reflexivity set in (for both films and audiences) and the mounting gore and dead bodies became expected — and funny. (Here *Scream* and its sequel are recent examples.)

This heightened sense of reflexivity and irony that emerges from quantities of violence, from "more," is not necessarily progressive nor does it lead to a "moral" agenda or a critique of violence. (By virtue of its excesses and its emphasis on quantity and despite his intention, Oliver Stone's *Natural Born Killers* is quite ambiguous in this regard.) Indeed, in its present moment, this heightened reflexivity and irony merely leads to a heightened sense of representation: that is, care for the film as experience and text, perhaps, but a lack of any real concern for the bodies blown away (or up) upon the screen. In recent "splatter" films, in Tarantino films like *Reservoir Dogs* and *Pulp Fiction*, and in quite a number of action thrillers, bodies are more carelessly *squandered* than carefully stylized. Except, of course, insofar as excess, and hyperbole, itself constitutes stylization. Thus, most of the violence we see on-screen today suggests Grand Guignol rather than Jacobean tragedy. However, in our current cultural moment, tiredly described as "postmodern" but filled with new forms of violence like "road rage," the exaggeration and escalating quantification of violence and gore are a great deal less transgressive than they were — and a great deal more absurd. Thus, Tarantino has said on various occasions that he doesn't take violence "very seriously" and describes it as "funny" and "outrageous."

This hyperbolic escalation and quantification of violence also has become quite common to the action picture and thriller, where the body count only exceeds the number of explosions and neither matters very much to anyone: here violence and the laying waste of bodies seems more "naturalized": that is, it regularly functions to fill up screen space and time in lieu of narrative complexity, and to make the central character look good by "virtue" of his mere survival (see, for example, *Payback*). Again, there seems no moral agenda or critique of violence here — only wisecracks and devaluation uttered out of the sides of a Bruce Willis–type mouth. Indeed, here is the careless violence and laconic commentary of comic books (where the panels crackle with zaps and bullets and explosions and the body count is all that counts).

On a more progressive note, I suppose it is possible to see this new excessive and careless treatment of violence on-screen as a satiric form of what Russian literary theorist Mikhail Bakhtin has called "grotesque realism." That is, excessive representations of the body and its messier aspects might be read as containing critical and liberatory potential — this, not only because certain social taboos are broken, but also because these excessive representations of the grotesquerie of being embodied are less "allegorical" and fantastic than they are exaggerations of concrete conditions in the culture of which they are a part. In this regard, and particularly relevant to "indie" crime dramas and the action thriller (a good deal of it science-fictional), much has been written recently about the "crisis of the body" and a related "crisis of masculinity." Both of these crises are no longer of the *Bonnie and Clyde* or *Wild Bunch* variety: They are far too much inflected and informed by *technological* concerns and confusions and a new sense of the body as a technology, altered by technology, enabled by technology, and disabled by technology. Indeed, along with the Fordist assembly line and its increasing production of bodies consumed as they are violently "wasted" on the screen, comes the production of bodies as both technological *subjects* and *subjected to* technology: enhanced and extended, but also extinguished by Uzis, bombs, whatever the latest in firepower. Thus, we might argue, the excessive violence we see on the screen, the carelessness and devaluation of mere human flesh, is both a recognition of the high-tech, powerful, and uncontrollable subjects we (men, mostly) have become through technology — and an expression of the increasing frustration and rage at what seems a lack of agency and effectiveness as we have become increasingly controlled by and subject to technology.

This new quantification of and carelessness toward violence on the screen also points to other aspects of our contemporary cultural context. We have come both a long way and not so far from the assassins, serial killers, and madmen who made their mass presence visibly felt in the late 1960s and early 1970s. They, like the bodies wasted on the screen, have proliferated at an increasingly faster and decreasingly surprising rate. They and the violence that accompanies them are now a common, omnipresent phenomenon of daily life — so much so that, to an unprecedented degree, we are resigned to living with them in what has become an increasingly uncivil society. "Senseless" and "random" violence pervades our lives and

John Travolta and Samuel L. Jackson are buddies and professional killers in *Pulp Fiction*, which takes a cartoonish approach to graphic violence, using a character's exploding head as the basis for an extended comic sketch.

is barely remarkable or specific any longer — and while "road rage" and little children killed by stray bullets of gang bangers do elicit a moral *frisson*, for the most part we live in and suspect the absence of a moral context in this decade of extreme relativism. Violence, like "shit," happens — worth merely a bumper sticker nod that reconciles it with a general sense of helplessness (rather than despair).

No longer elevated through balletic treatment or narrative purpose, violence on the screen is sensed — indeed, appreciated — as senseless. But then so is life under the extremity of such technologized and uncivil conditions. Indeed, what has been called the "postmodern condition" might be more accurately thought of as the "postmorbid condition." There's a kind of meta-sensibility at work here: life, death, and the movies are a "joke" or an "illusion" and everyone's in on it. Violence on the screen and in the culture is not related to a moral context, but to a proliferation of images, texts, and spectacle. And, given that we cannot contain or stop this careless proliferation, violence and death both on the street and in *Pulp Fiction* become reduced to the practical — and solvable — problem of cleanup.

Pain, too, drops out of the picture. The spasmodic twitching that ends *Bonnie and Clyde* has become truly lifeless. The bodies now subjected to violence are just "dummies": multiple surfaces devoid of subjectivity and gravity, "straw men," if you will. "Wasting" them doesn't mean much. Hence, the power (both appealing and off-putting) of those few films that remind us that bodily damage hurts, that violently wasting lives has grave consequences. Hence, the immense popularity of *Saving Private Ryan*, a movie in which the massive quantity of graphic physical damage and the violent "squandering" of bodies and lives is "redeemed" to social purpose and meaning, its sense-lessness made sensible by its (re)insertion in a clearly defined (and clearly past) moral context. Hence, also, the popular neglect of *Beloved* or *Affliction*, movies in which violence is represented "close up" as singularly felt: graphi-cally linked to bodily pain and its destruction of subjectivity. In these films, violence is not dramatized quantitatively or technologically and thus becomes extremely difficult to watch: that is, even though an image, understood by one's own flesh as *real*.

I am not sure how to end this particular postmortem on my original essay. I still can't watch the eyeball being slit in *Un Chien Andalou*. But, as with *Straw Dogs* and *The French Connection*, I could and did watch all the vio-lence in *Pulp Fiction*. Nonetheless, there's been a qualitative change as well as a quantitative one: While I watched those earlier violent films compulsively, with some real need to know what they showed me, I watch the excesses of the current ones casually, aware they won't show me anything real that I don't already know.

READING THE TEXT

1. What was Sobchack's argument in the essay on-screen violence that she wrote now thirty years ago?

2. How does contemporary screen violence differ from that of the sixties and seventies, according to Sobchack?

3. What does Sobchack mean by referring to "our increasingly *technologized* view of the body" (para. 3)?

4. In what ways do irony and satire contribute to the desensitizing of contem-porary audiences in the face of extreme screen violence, according to Sob-chack?

READING THE SIGNS

1. Media violence has long been one of the most controversial issues in cultural politics. Referring to a selection of current violent films, write an essay argu-ing for or against the proposition that screen violence desensitizes viewers to the realities of violence.

2. Write an argumentative essay in which you support, refute, or modify Sob-chack's claim that films such as *Beloved* failed to attract audiences because, unlike most violent films, they depict pain and violence as "real" (para. 9). To develop support for your position, interview acquaintances who watched such a film and those who chose to avoid it. Alternatively, perform the same sort analysis of a film that is emotionally challenging for viewers, such as *Precious*.

3. In class, stage a debate on the proposition that the film industry should restrict its depictions of violence.

4. Watch *127 Hours, Kick-Ass, Predators*, or another violent film. To what extent does the film illustrate Sobchack's view that "we need noise and constant stimulation and quantity to make up for a lack of significant meaning" (para. 2)?

5. Watch *Boyz N the Hood* and analyze it semiotically. Use your observations as evidence for an essay in which you argue whether the film's violence is desensitizing, as Sobchack argues is the case for most contemporary films, or whether it strikes the viewer as "real." How does the film's genre — gangster film — affect your interpretation of the violence?

6. In class, discuss the reasons many moviegoers find violence to be entertaining. What does the prevalence of violence in films say about modern American cultural values?

Reservoir Dogs

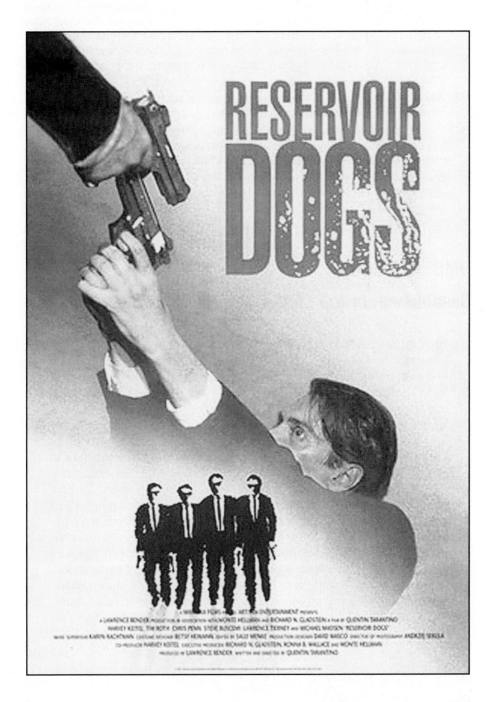

READING THE SIGNS

1. Based on the *Reservoir Dogs* poster, how would you characterize the subject matter of this film? Does the poster make you want to see the film? Why or why not? What is the effect of including one figure with part of his face obscured and the other with only his arm visible? What does the image of the four men at the bottom suggest? How do you interpret the splattering on the letters of the title?

2. Who, in your opinion, is the intended audience for this film? Why? What elements in this poster appeal to that intended audience?

3. A version of this poster includes the caption, "Four perfect killers. One perfect crime. Now all they have to fear is each other." In your opinion, is the ad more or less effective with this added text? Why or why not?

4. If you haven't seen *Reservoir Dogs*, view it (though be warned that parts are quite violent). How well does this poster represent the film? If you had to design your own poster for this movie, what would it look like?

UMBERTO ECO

Casablanca, *or the Clichés Are Having a Ball*

Next to Roland Barthes, Umberto Eco has probably been the most influential mid-twentieth-century figure in semiotics. Most widely known for his best-selling novels—*The Name of the Rose* (trans. 1983) and *Foucault's Pendulum* (trans. 1989), Eco has been a leading scholar in the revival of the theories of Charles Sanders Peirce, which he has explored in many books and essays, most notably his sweeping study *A Theory of Semiotics* (1976). An avid analyst of popular culture as well as technical semiotics, Eco turns his gaze in this selection to one of the most beloved movies in American history to reveal how and why it succeeds as it does. In short, for Eco, the secret to the success of *Casablanca* lies in its exploitation of just about every cultural myth and cliché in the book. From its paradigmatic opposition between official hero Victor Laszlo and outlaw hero Rick, to its presentation of a clear struggle between absolute good and evil, *Casablanca* satisfies every mythological expectation. Umberto Eco is President of the Scuola Superiore di Studi Umanistici at the University of Bologna. Eco's *Travels in Hyperreality* (trans. 1986) is a good place to start to discover Eco's semiotic views on American popular culture.

When people in their fifties sit down before their television sets for a rerun of *Casablanca*, it is an ordinary matter of nostalgia. However, when the film is shown in American universities, the boys and girls greet each scene and canonical line of dialogue ("Round up the usual suspects," "Was that cannon fire, or is it my heart pounding?" — or even every time that Bogey says "kid") with ovations usually reserved for football games. And I have seen the youthful audience in an Italian art cinema react in the same way. What then is the fascination of *Casablanca*?

The question is a legitimate one, for aesthetically speaking (or by any strict critical standards), *Casablanca* is a very mediocre film. It is a comic strip, a hotch-potch, low on psychological credibility, and with little continuity in its dramatic effects. And we know the reason for this: The film was made up as the shooting went along, and it was not until the last moment that the director and script writer knew whether Ilsa would leave with Victor or with Rick. So all those moments of inspired direction that wring bursts of applause for their unexpected boldness actually represent decisions taken out of desperation. What then accounts for the success of this chain of accidents, a film that even today, seen for a second, third, or fourth time, draws forth the applause reserved for the operatic aria we love to hear repeated, or the enthusiasm we accord to an exciting discovery? There is a cast of formidable hams. But that is not enough.

Here are the romantic lovers — he bitter, she tender — but both have been seen to better advantage. And *Casablanca* is not *Stagecoach*, another film periodically revived. *Stagecoach* is a masterpiece in every respect. Every element is in its proper place, the characters are consistent from one moment to the next, and the plot (this too is important) comes from Maupassant — at least the first part of it. And so? So one is tempted to read *Casablanca* the way T. S. Eliot reread *Hamlet*. He attributed its fascination not to its being a successful work (actually he considered it one of Shakespeare's less fortunate plays) but to something quite the opposite: *Hamlet* was the result of an unsuccessful fusion of several earlier Hamlets, one in which the theme was revenge (with madness as only a stratagem), and another whose theme was the crisis brought on by the mother's sin, with the consequent discrepancy between Hamlet's nervous excitation and the vagueness and implausibility of Gertrude's crime. So critics and public alike find *Hamlet* beautiful because it is interesting, and believe it to be interesting because it is beautiful.

On a smaller scale, the same thing happened to *Casablanca*. Forced to improvise a plot, the authors mixed in a little of everything, and everything they chose came from a repertoire of the tried and true. When the choice of the tried and true is limited, the result is a trite or mass-produced film, or simply kitsch. But when the tried and true repertoire is used wholesale, the result is an architecture like Gaudí's Sagrada Familia in Barcelona. There is a sense of dizziness, a stroke of brilliance.

But now let us forget how the film was made and see what it has to show us. It opens in a place already magical in itself — Morocco, the Exotic — and begins with a hint of Arab music that fades into "La Marseillaise." Then as we enter Rick's Place we hear Gershwin. Africa, France, America. At once a tangle of Eternal Archetypes comes into play. These are situations that have presided over stories throughout the ages. But usually to make a good story a single archetypal situation is enough. More than enough. Unhappy Love, for example, or Flight. But *Casablanca* is not satisfied with that: It uses them all. The city is the setting for a Passage, the passage to the Promised Land (or a Northwest Passage if you like). But to make the passage one must submit to a test, the Wait ("they wait and wait and wait," says the off-screen voice at the beginning). The passage from the waiting room to the Promised Land requires a Magic Key, the visa. It is around the winning of this Key that passions are unleashed. Money (which appears at various points, usually in the form of the Fatal Game, roulette) would seem to be the means for obtaining the Key. But eventually we discover that the Key can be obtained only through a Gift — the gift of the visa, but also the gift Rick makes of his Desire by sacrificing himself. For this is also the story of a round of Desires, only two of which are satisfied: that of Victor Laszlo, the purest of heroes, and that of the Bulgarian couple. All those whose passions are impure fail.

Thus, we have another archetype: the Triumph of Purity. The impure do not reach the Promised Land; we lose sight of them before that. But they do achieve purity through sacrifice — and this means Redemption. Rick is redeemed and so is the French police captain. We come to realize that underneath it all there are two Promised Lands: One is America (though for many it is a false goal), and the other is the Resistance — the Holy War. That is where Victor has come from, and that is where Rick and the captain are going, to join de Gaulle. And if the recurring symbol of the airplane seems every so often to emphasize the flight to America, the Cross of Lorraine, which appears only once, anticipates the other symbolic gesture of the captain, when at the end he throws away the bottle of Vichy water as the plane is leaving. On the other hand the myth of sacrifice runs through the whole film: Ilsa's sacrifice in Paris when she abandons the man she loves to return to the wounded hero, the Bulgarian bride's sacrifice when she is ready to yield herself to help her husband, Victor's sacrifice when he is prepared to let Ilsa go with Rick so long as she is saved.

Into this orgy of sacrificial archetypes (accompanied by the Faithful Servant theme in the relationship of Bogey and the black man Dooley Wilson) is inserted the theme of Unhappy Love: unhappy for Rick, who loves Ilsa and cannot have her; unhappy for Ilsa, who loves Rick and cannot leave with him;

unhappy for Victor, who understands that he has not really kept Ilsa. The interplay of unhappy loves produces various twists and turns: In the beginning Rick is unhappy because he does not understand why Ilsa leaves him; then Victor is unhappy because he does not understand why Ilsa is attracted to Rick; finally Ilsa is unhappy because she does not understand why Rick makes her leave with her husband. These three unhappy (or Impossible) loves take the form of a Triangle. But in the archetypal love-triangle there is a Betrayed Husband and a Victorious Lover. Here instead both men are betrayed and suffer a loss, but, in this defeat (and over and above it) an additional element plays a part, so subtly that one is hardly aware of it. It is that, quite subliminally, a hint of male or Socratic love is established. Rick admires Victor, Victor is ambiguously attracted to Rick, and it almost seems at a certain point as if each of the two were playing out the duel of sacrifice in order to please the other. In any case, as in Rousseau's *Confessions*, the woman places herself as Intermediary between the two men. She herself is not a bearer of positive values; only the men are.

Against the background of these intertwined ambiguities, the characters are stock figures, either all good or all bad. Victor plays a double role, as an agent of ambiguity in the love story, and an agent of clarity in the political intrigue—he is Beauty against the Nazi Beast. This theme of Civilization against Barbarism becomes entangled with the others, and to the melancholy of an Odyssean Return is added the warlike daring of an *Iliad* on open ground.

Surrounding this dance of eternal myths, we see the historical myths, or rather the myths of the movies, duly served up again. Bogart himself embodies at least three: the Ambiguous Adventurer, compounded of cynicism and generosity; the Lovelorn Ascetic; and at the same time the Redeemed Drunkard (he has to be made a drunkard so that all of a sudden he can be redeemed, while he was already an ascetic, disappointed in love). Ingrid Bergman is the Enigmatic Woman, or *Femme Fatale*. Then such myths as: They're Playing Our Song; the Last Day in Paris; America, Africa, Lisbon as a Free Port; and the Border Station or Last Outpost on the Edge of the Desert. There is the Foreign Legion (each character has a different nationality and a different story to tell), and finally there is the Grand Hotel (people coming and going). Rick's Place is a magic circle where everything can (and does) happen: love, death, pursuit, espionage, games of chance, seductions, music, patriotism. (The theatrical origin of the plot, and its poverty of means, led to an admirable condensation of events in a single setting.) This place is *Hong Kong, Macao, I'Enfer du Jeu*, an anticipation of Lisbon, and even *Showboat*.

But precisely because *all* the archetypes are here, precisely because 10 *Casablanca* cites countless other films, and each actor repeats a part played on other occasions, the resonance of intertextuality plays upon the spectator. *Casablanca* brings with it, like a trail of perfume, other situations that the viewer brings to bear on it quite readily, taking them without realizing it from films that only appeared later, such as *To Have and Have Not*, where Bogart actually plays a Hemingway hero, while here in *Casablanca* he already attracts Hemingwayesque connotations by the simple fact that Rick, so we are told, fought in Spain (and, like Malraux, helped the Chinese Revolution). Peter Lorre drags in reminiscences of Fritz Lang; Conrad Veidt envelops his German officer in a faint aroma of *The Cabinet of Dr. Caligari* — he is not a ruthless, technological Nazi, but a nocturnal and diabolical Caesar.

Thus *Casablanca* is not just one film. It is many films, an anthology. Made haphazardly, it probably made itself, if not actually against the will of its authors and actors, then at least beyond their control. And this is the reason it works, in spite of aesthetic theories and theories of filmmaking. For in it there unfolds with almost telluric[1] force the power of Narrative in its natural state, without Art intervening to discipline it. And so we can accept it when characters change mood, morality, and psychology from one moment to the next, when conspirators cough to interrupt the conversation if a spy is approaching, when whores weep at the sound of "La Marseillaise." When all the archetypes burst in shamelessly, we reach Homeric depths. Two clichés make us laugh. A hundred clichés move us. For we sense dimly that the clichés are talking *among themselves*, and celebrating a reunion. Just as the height of pain may encounter sensual pleasure, and the height of perversion border on mystical energy, so, too, the height of banality allows us to catch a glimpse of the sublime. Something has spoken in place of the director. If nothing else, it is a phenomenon worthy of awe.

READING THE TEXT

1. What evidence does Eco provide to support his contention that *Casablanca* is a "mediocre" (para. 2) film?

2. In your own words, how does Eco explain *Casablanca*'s success?

3. What does Eco mean by saying that *Casablanca* is an "anthology" (para. 11) with a "resonance of intertextuality" (para. 10)?

4. Prepare a list of the archetypes that Eco finds in *Casablanca*.

READING THE SIGNS

1. Watch *Casablanca*, and write an essay in which you propose your own response to Eco's question "What then is the fascination of *Casablanca*?" (para. 1).

---

[1]**telluric** Arising from the earth or soil — EDS.

2. **CONNECTING TEXTS**   Review Linda Seger's "Creating the Myth" (p. 386). How can her discussion of archetypes and "search" films extend and complicate Eco's analysis of *Casablanca*?

3. **CONNECTING TEXTS**   Read Robert B. Ray's "The Thematic Paradigm" (p. 377), and write an essay in which you evaluate whether *Casablanca*'s Rick is a hero and, if so, what type.

4. Adopting Eco's notion of intertextuality, analyze another film that is packed with cinematic allusions, such as *Pulp Fiction*.

TIME

PERSON OF THE YEAR

You.

Yes, you. You control the Information Age.
Welcome to your world.

YOU-TOPIAN DREAMS

Semiotics and the New Media

Whose Space?

The first chat rooms were rather primitive places. Austere, you might say, with no images, music, or decoration of any kind, just plain text boxes where ghostly words materialized as if from out of nowhere. Visiting such places was a bit of an adventure, a pioneering voyage into cyberspace and the uncharted expanses of the electronic frontier.

Things are a lot more cozy now in the world of online social networking. Homelike. In fact, if you happen to have a Facebook account — and the odds are overwhelming that you do — you may spend as much time there with your family and friends as you do with them in person.

All of this raises a number of interesting questions. First, is your personal space on the Internet a private or a public place, a space that completely belongs to you or only appears to through some illusion on the World Wide Web? Second, who really controls the worlds of online social networking: The individuals who create their own networks and content or the corporations that own the sites in which they do so? And finally, what does all this online socializing portend for the future?

Let's start with the first question. When you are online socializing with others, are you "inside" or "outside," at home in your private territory or out on the streets in some sort of vast cybermall?

The paradoxical answer is that you are both inside *and* outside. On the one hand, you can set up and visit your Facebook, MySpace, Twitter, or what-have-you page within the confines of your home, but on the other hand, these are public sites on the Internet that anyone can visit at any time. Your page not only does not belong to you but others can access it and make comments within it or show it to other people without your knowledge — surprise intrusions that have occurred even to those who thought that their Facebook settings were private and confidential.

This inside/outside, public/private space challenges all of the traditional rules that govern three-dimensional space, codes that define the way we move and that tell us, quite literally, where we may and may not go and what we may do when we get there. Consider an ordinary street, a clearly marked outside or public space. You may walk down it, but you need to stick to the side (or sidewalk if there is one), and it's best to stay to the right to avoid oncoming foot traffic. If there are private houses on the street, you may approach the front door, but you're not supposed to cut through the yard, and you're certainly not allowed to enter without permission. You may enter the public space of a store, shopping center, or post office, but you might need to pay to enter a museum, and you need to pass through a security checkpoint if you are entering a courthouse or an airline terminal.

Now consider your own physical personal space: There, you set the rules. You determine who enters it and what can be done there. You might actually write out the rules that govern your space (as in posting a NO SMOKING sign), but those rules are more likely enforced if you are personally present. Indeed, the most basic personal space rule of all is that no unauthorized person should be in it when you are absent.

The spaces of everyday life, both public and private, are, in short, packed with complex codes that we violate or ignore at our peril. These codes all originate in the way that human beings define their territories. A *territory* is a space that has been given meaning through having been claimed by an individual or group of individuals. Unclaimed, unmarked space is socially meaningless, but put up a building or a fence, and the uncircumscribed landscape becomes a bounded territory, a human habitat with its own rules for permitted and unpermitted behavior. Anyone unaware of those rules can't survive for long in human society.

But what sort of territory is a social networking site, and what rules govern it? In a sense, it is a place where its users are all hosts and guests simultaneously, with the rules being accordingly quite confusing. A host is hospitable; a guest is polite and follows the host's guidance. But with no one on the Net being entirely host or entirely guest, things can easily go wrong. You don't insult people in their own homes, but online flaming occurs all too often and has inspired a whole vocabulary for the "trolls" who break the rules of good netiquette. Indeed, many sites and forums where people socialize and communicate are described as being like the Wild West — a wide-open place known for its lack of clear rules of conduct and the way in which it challenges traditional conceptions of social space. The result has been a blurring of the traditional lines between the uses of public and private space and, with that, much confusion about how to behave in the essentially public arena of online communication. Just read responses people make in the feedback or

---

Exploring the Signs of Web 2.0

If you have a MySpace or Facebook page, describe it in your journal and discuss why you designed it as you did. What signs did you choose to communicate your identity, and why? Did you deliberately avoid including some signs? If so, why? If you chose to avoid having such a page, why?

---

comments sections of popular Web sites like YouTube.com. Certainly the old rules about public courtesy no longer seem to obtain.

It's All Over Now, Baudrillard

Let's look now at our second question: Who is really in control of the new media? Traditionally, the mass media have been structured in a top-down manner, with corporate elites providing passive consumers with the news, entertainments, and products that they consume, along with the advertisements that promote them. But now the top-down news has turned into a bottom-up conversation in which anyone can become a pundit, while newspapers and online news sites invite input from their readers. Broadband Internet access has turned video creativity over to the masses in such a way that you no longer have to be a famous director or producer to present your own television shows or films to a wide audience, and you don't have to be an authorized critic to respond, with YouTube and related sites offering unlimited opportunity to critique what you find there. In short, what was once a passive and vicarious media experience for the mass of consumers is now active and participatory.

Another way of putting this is that our relationship with the mass media until now has been more or less a one-way street. Those with the power to control the media (TV networks, radio stations, movie studios, newspaper owners, corporate sponsors with advertising dollars to spend) have broadcast their signals to us (TV and radio programs, films, newspapers, and ads), and we have passively received them, without being able to answer back. The late semiologist and sociologist Jean Baudrillard (1929–2007) regarded this situation as being one of the essential conditions of postmodern times and used it as a basis for his analyses of contemporary society. But with so much of the mass media now actively eliciting responses from their audiences, and with consumers of the mass media able to take control of their own media consumption through such technologies as TiVo, the iPod, and the Internet—indeed, now an ordinary news story can be remixed into a number one iTunes hit (as happened via YouTube in what came to be known as the "Bed Intruder Song" in 2010) — it certainly appears that something post-postmodern is emerging beyond Baudrillard's perceptions.

Going Viral

The reversal of the traditional channels of communication made possible by the new media is especially striking when it comes to the way that the news is broadcast today. Available 24/7 and constantly being updated, the news is not something we simply receive; our own contributions can help create it. This happens when what in the past might have been an obscure news story goes viral — that is, is rebroadcast endlessly through e-mails, blogs, tweets, texts, and so on. A good example of this happened in 2010, when a conservative blogger named Andrew Breitbart got hold of a video clip of a speech by an African American USDA employee named Shirley Sherrod, who instantly became famous when Breitbart clipped out one portion of the speech and posted it on his blog. In Breitbart's clip, Sherrod seemed to be speaking about a time when she refused to help a white farmer on the basis of his race. That post was picked up and rebroadcast so widely and so quickly that within a few hours Sherrod was ordered to resign. At the time few people, if any, checked to see whether Sherrod's remarks were being taken in the proper context, and when a video of the full speech was brought to light, it turned out that Sherrod's anecdote was meant to illustrate a time when she overcame her own racial prejudices. In fact, she had helped the white farmer. By the next day she was getting public apologies from the White House and new job offers from the USDA.

This was not supposed to occur in the days when professional news organizations controlled the airwaves: Stories were supposed to be checked and vetted before their release to prevent what happened to Sherrod. But that kind of control no longer exists when anyone can post just about anything online, and whatever is posted can be disseminated worldwide within minutes, not only becoming news but shaping it as well.

In an even larger incident in 2010, an online site called WikiLeaks released a cache of some 91,000 classified documents that it called the "Afghan War Diary." As intended, this release went viral and within hours the White House and the Pentagon were engulfed in a public relations nightmare that threatened the whole conduct of the war in Afghanistan. A potent strike against the war, the document release also endangered the lives of the troops serving there. One might say that the Drudge Report, which began as a personal blog and has since become a leading source of news and information to political elites and ordinary citizens alike, is what really tipped the balance of media power in the era of interactive media. But power entails its own responsibilities, and it remains to be seen whether a sense of responsibility will return to the newly unfenced spaces of the electronic frontier.

Top Down Meets Bottom Up

Whether the new two-way avenues of mass communication will result in any substantive, post-Baudrillardian changes in American society is a question whose answer is still uncertain, however. On the one hand, the new media are definitely opening up channels for democratic communication and expression that previously did not exist. Indeed, you may have felt empowered by the opportunity to display your own creative work and political opinions to a mass audience thanks to new media technologies. But the very fact that the corporate elites are gobbling up the democratic vistas of the Internet for their own profit-making purposes suggests that it all may end up being an illusion of change in what is still a mass consumer society.

And so we have a paradox: Top down meets bottom up in a situation that is at once democratic and hierarchical, your space and corporate space. The democratic, user-generated spaces of the Internet are simultaneously revolutionary and business as usual. Users create their own content and actively build their own virtual spaces, but they do so on sites that are owned by huge corporations and that are maintained for profit. In the famous 1984 Super Bowl commercial that introduced the Macintosh, Apple Computer promised that the future was going to belong to the people, not to rigid, profit-seeking corporate powers. Web 1.0 and Web 2.0 were both built, in large part, by people who believed in this vision of a sort of anti-corporate utopia. But when you are in the coils of a cultural **mythology**, it is very difficult to get out.

Thus in a mass consumer society, even entirely grassroots phenomena can be appropriated by corporate elites if they become popular enough. Accordingly, it did not take long for the top-down component of society to recognize the potential profits to be made in interactive media. Rupert Murdoch's purchase of MySpace, Google's acquisition of YouTube, and Facebook's sharing of personal information with marketers are not acts of charity. With so many people visiting such sites, the revenue potential from marketing and advertising is enormous, and Web 2.0 capitalism has been quick to recognize the parallel between freely provided commercial television and freely provided Web sites where the users create their own content.

So, is Web 2.0 the portal to a new society, or just another way to make money? Is it the harbinger of a new social consciousness, or the same old hypercapitalist scramble in a glittering new package?

All Media, All the Time

Whatever the socioeconomic implications of the new media may turn out to be, there is no question that they are altering the way we interact with each other, and perhaps altering consciousness as well. With the explosive growth of Facebook in recent years, adults have joined what was at first largely a youth movement, as social networking has become a daily way of life for

Discussing the Signs of Web 2.0

Critics of online social networking sites have expressed concern that excessive online networking will diminish participants' ability to social- ize normally in face-to-face environments. In class, discuss the legiti- macy of this concern, drawing upon your personal experiences with social networking.

literally hundreds of millions of people around the globe. And this takes us to our third question: What effects upon human consciousness might this elec- tronic form of social interaction have?

Consider the vital difference between the social space of an online net- working site like Facebook and the traditional sites where people gather to socialize. While it is an obvious difference, it bears close attention: While online socializing may supplement face-to-face encounters, it can be con- ducted in complete isolation as well. No one else need be present for you to interact with others. This is also true of socializing by telephone, letters, and e-mail, of course, but social networking sites greatly magnify the paradoxi- cal experience of being in a crowded space, while alone, online. Even more paradoxical is the now common phenomenon of individuals being intensely engaged on Facebook, while simultaneously receiving and sending text mes- sages or tweeting, even as they are physically in the presence of others, com- municating with distant friends and family rather than with those around them. Does this sound familiar?

Precisely why so many people appear to prefer digitally mediated commu- nication to face-to-face interaction is a question whose answer is not entirely understood. Emerging evidence suggests that there is an addictive quality to the new media, with experiments showing that people who are deprived of their communications devices suffer symptoms not at all dissimilar to narcotic withdrawal. But that doesn't answer the question as to what attracts people to their digital "fixes" in the first place.

One attraction, especially for the many adult users who helped Facebook eclipse MySpace as *the* go-to destination on the social web, is not only the prospect of maintaining 24/7 contact with one's friends and family but also the exciting possibility of a blast from the past at any moment, a message out of the blue from someone one knew in childhood or perhaps even loved in early adulthood. Such re-encounters of a virtual kind can be an exciting break in the humdrum routine of everyday life, a sudden high that can indeed be addictive.

Another attraction has been the prospect of virtual popularity that Face- book offers, often to people who were not popular in their schooldays. Let's face it: From grade school to high school, social life can be ruthless, and only a fortunate few ever experience having more friends than they can handle or even want. Facebook, on the other hand, is like a giant campus where just about anyone can load up on "friends." And though there is something more than a little artificial about the matter, many people take a good deal of pride in the number of friends they accumulate and can get quite competitive about it.

It really isn't possible to adumbrate all of the features that make digital media addictive, but one definitely merits further exploration: this is the *control* that digital communication gives. You can choose which messages (text or phone) to answer, and in which order. You can also choose which friends you want to interact with on your Facebook page, whenever you want, and you are empowered to decide whom you accept as a friend. And sites like Facebook and MySpace also enable you to control exactly the way you appear to others, even to be a star.

Web 2 Lets U Be U

After all, your MySpace page can be your personal public relations center. There you can present yourself much as *People* presents celebrities, complete with the details of your latest romance or, if you happen to be in a band, your latest CD. YouTube, for its part, lets you be your own auteur, a budding Woody Allen who both directs and stars in your own productions. And in some cases, you can make yourself a real star, of sorts, if your YouTube creation is a hit and is spun out from computer to computer in a viral explosion of shared content. And you can even build a rabid fanbase by posting your own online music videos. Hey, it worked for Justin Bieber.

A casual survey of the videos posted to YouTube alone reveals the enormous appeal of Web-based self-expression to a generation that has been raised in an entertainment culture within which media fame and celebrity have been presented as being among life's highest goals — if not *the* highest goal. Though most contributors will never see more than a smattering of responses to their videos, the fact remains that anyone can at least make a bid for glory on YouTube, and everyone has the chance to communicate with a worldwide audience.

In this sense, Web 2.0 bears a striking resemblance to reality television (indeed, YouTube has its roots in *America's Funniest Home Videos*), for in RTV, too, ordinary people can be transformed into overnight celebrities. But there is a crucial difference in that you don't have to audition for anything on the Internet and you can be your own impresario. No one need ever see you in person; no casting director stands in your way; no one can judge you except on the precise terms that you establish yourself. And all this is possible because of the profoundly different nature of self-presentation on the Internet. Indeed, one could call it a **proxemic** revolution.

Proxemics, a field loosely related to semiotics, is the study of the ways in which we communicate with others in face-to-face situations, including such factors as body language, facial expression, and tone of voice. But because body language, facial expression, and tone of voice are absent on the Internet, social interaction on the Web requires a very different approach. The visual cues of face-to-face interaction are so important to us in ordinary communication that we often simulate such cues online with photographs and videos of ourselves, MP3s, and, more simply, with emoticons, creating a whole new kind of communication.

The fact that we can control exactly what information we present to others while online offers us a freedom — even a fantasy freedom — to be whatever we want to be with others: more attractive, better natured, just plain more cool than we may really be. Virtual worlds like *Second Life* and *SimCity* demonstrate this freedom clearly, with an unusual proportion of participants looking awfully glamorous. This, too, is an important phenomenon to consider in our interpretation of the cultural significance of social networking sites.

So consider for a moment traditional media involving video images and projection screens. Television, film, and advertising have always broadcast images of beautiful people living more romantic or adventurous lives than most people, in reality, can ever experience. This dream machine has provided generations of viewers with vicarious images of fantasy lives, and, through advertising, has promised the accomplishment of such lives if you only purchase the advertised product. But the enthusiasm with which hundreds of millions of people from around the world have embraced the opportunities that interactive media have offered — from role-playing games like *World of Warcraft* to simulated reality sites like *Second Life* — demonstrates a craving to actually live the sort of lives that the traditional media have, either directly or indirectly, indicated that we *should* be living.

This is, paradoxically, why so many game-playing and world-building sites strive to be more and more realistic, for if the fantasy is to be truly effective, it

---

Reading Web 2.0 on the Net

YouTube allows users to create their own "television" content, yet the site is filled with content taken from other sources, such as television clips, concert footage, and the like. Conduct a survey of YouTube content to estimate the ratio of user-created content to postings of professional performers. Analyze and interpret your results semiotically. What are the implications of your findings for the bottom-up versus top-down debate over Web 2.0 "democracy"?

must feel real. Indeed, such virtual worlds as The Sims enable you not only to imagine your own life as you'd like to live it but to rehearse it — that is, building a simulated life, under the conditions of a game that can be played and replayed with ever-improving skill until you get everything just right — offering the ultimate fantasy of control. Because while real life is a messy affair, whose beginning and end we have little control over and whose middle can be played through only once without correction or second chance, simulated life fixes all that. Online, we can, in effect, play God with our own lives.

You-Topian Communities, or Not?

Perhaps this ability to control our online lives in ways that real life forbids accounts for the almost utopian feel of many online communities. A utopia — from the Greek *ou* (no)-*topos* (place) — is an idealized vision of a perfected world, a world almost always set in some unattainable future. And with the real world becoming increasingly dystopian (or anti-utopian), plagued by social and political alienation, the virtual communities of the Net can be particularly attractive. Indeed, as the traditional village-based neighborhoods of the pre-industrial era break down in the face of rampant urbanization (and are further disrupted by the geographical instabilities impelled by the modern job market), Web 2.0 technology offers a virtual village experience whose vast popularity attests to a deep desire for community in an alienated world. After all, one of the common reasons for joining Facebook or LinkedIn is "getting back in touch," and there has never been anything quite like the world of online social networking for reestablishing contacts with long-lost friends and family.

If you have ever participated in an online community, even one that was not originally designed to be a community at all (like the astronomy and bird-watching forums that the authors of this book participate in), then you are likely to have experienced the surprisingly warm friendships that can spring up among people whose only connections are cybernetic. Commonly, these online friendships lead to actual face-to-face meetings wherein the participants can be pleasantly surprised by just how much their friends are like their online personas. Sometimes such meetings lead to lifelong friendships, even romances and marriages.

And online communication offers something more, something unique in our human history: The ability to transcend the hierarchical arrangements that plague ordinary social activity. Celebrities and fans can share the same space, as can politicians and citizens. You can have loads of friends without going through the snotty rigamaroles of school or office politics and popularity polls. You don't have to be able to call your own press conference to tweet your daily activities to the rest of the world. And you don't need to have an administrative assistant to screen those with whom you wish to communicate.

In a democratic and individualistic society like America's, this is pretty heady stuff. But is there a price to pay? It's too soon to tell. But some emerging signs suggest that people who have grown up in the era of digital technology are losing the ability to engage fully in unmediated forms of experience. Are you sitting with your friends and yet texting with someone who isn't there? Do you find it necessary to broadcast on the Net everything you are doing today in order to feel complete? Did you include the whole world on your last vacation? And do you have difficulty empathizing with those immediately around you, preferring virtual people to actual? There is some evidence that this is becoming the case for those who have spent their entire lives with the new media. After all, while being able to control your interactions with others has its obvious attractions, it is not conducive to learning empathy. One way or another, it is a good time to start asking yourself what the digital revolution is all about, not just consuming the new media but analyzing them.

The Readings

Henry Jenkins begins the chapter with an analysis of that emerging phenomenon that he calls "convergence culture," a world where old media and new come together to connect people in ways that they have never been connected before. Steven Johnson and Brian Williams follow with a paired set of opinion pieces on the democratic vistas of the Web 2.0 world: One's for it and the other isn't so sure. Next, danah boyd reveals the surprising racial coding that separates rival social networking sites Facebook and MySpace, while Ian Daly meditates on the personal implications of online "friending," especially for men on Facebook, whom he sees as acting like teenaged girls. A press release from the University of Maryland's Newsdesk follows, reporting on a study by the International Center for Media and the Public Agenda that concludes "that most college students are not just unwilling, but functionally unable to be without their media links to the world." Confessing to a certain level of addiction himself, Zach Waggoner next offers a theoretical analysis of the complex play of identities that are involved in digital role-playing games, as A. B. Harris calls for a more mature, less adolescent, profile for online gamers. And Jonathan Rauch concludes the chapter with a report on how the Tea Party has made use of online technology in its rise to political power.

HENRY JENKINS

Convergence Culture

You're watching *American Idol* and a text message comes in informing you that AmericanIdolWatch.com reports that the guy who sings like Alvin the Chipmunk is outpolling your favorite contestant, so you log in to check the report and then phone in your vote to *American Idol* before "Alvin" can move on to the next level. Though it may seem pretty routine to you, your movement from television screen, to text-messaging, to the Internet, to cell phone constitutes a newly emerging mixture of old and new media that Henry Jenkins calls "convergence culture." In this selection from his book of the same title, Jenkins describes the new multi–mixed media and their possible effects on society and human consciousness. A self-avowed fan of the new media, Jenkins is the founder of MIT's Comparative Media Studies Program, and he is currently the provost's professor of communication, journalism, and cinematic arts at the University of Southern California. He is the author of numerous books, including *Textual Poachers: Television Fans and Participatory Culture* (1998), *Convergence Culture: Where Old and New Media Collide* (2006), and *The Wow Climax: Tracing the Emotional Impact of Popular Culture* (2007).

Worship at the Altar of Convergence
— Slogan, the New Orleans Media Experience (2003)

The story circulated in the fall of 2001: Dino Ignacio, a Filipino-American high school student created a Photoshop collage of *Sesame Street*'s (1970) Bert interacting with terrorist leader Osama Bin Laden as part of a series of "Bert is Evil" images he posted on his homepage. Others depicted Bert as a Klansman, cavorting with Adolph Hitler, dressed as the Unabomber, or having sex with Pamela Anderson. It was all in good fun.

In the wake of September 11, a Bangladesh-based publisher scanned the Web for Bin Laden images to print on anti-American signs, posters, and T-shirts. *Sesame Street* is available in Pakistan in a localized format; the Arab world, thus, had no exposure to Bert and Ernie. The publisher may not have recognized Bert, but he must have thought the image was a good likeness of the al-Qaeda leader. The image ended up in a collage of similar images that was printed on thousands of posters and distributed across the Middle East.

CNN reporters recorded the unlikely sight of a mob of angry protestors marching through the streets chanting anti-American slogans and waving signs depicting Bert and Bin Laden (Fig. 1). Representatives from the

FIGURE 1   Ignacio's collage surprisingly appeared in CNN coverage of anti-American protests following September 11.

Children's Television Workshop, creators of the *Sesame Street* series, spotted the CNN footage and threatened to take legal action: "We're outraged that our characters would be used in this unfortunate and distasteful manner. The people responsible for this should be ashamed of themselves. We are exploring all legal options to stop this abuse and any similar abuses in the future." It was not altogether clear whom they planned to sic their intellectual property attorneys on — the young man who had initially appropriated their images, or the terrorist supporters who deployed them. Coming full circle, amused fans produced a number of new sites, linking various *Sesame Street* characters with terrorists.

From his bedroom, Ignacio sparked an international controversy. His images crisscrossed the world, sometimes on the backs of commercial media, sometimes via grassroots media. And, in the end, he inspired his own cult following. As the publicity grew, Ignacio became more concerned and ultimately decided to dismantle his site: "I feel this has gotten too close to reality. . . . 'Bert Is Evil' and its following has always been contained and distanced from big media. This issue throws it out in the open."[1] Welcome to convergence culture, where old and new media collide, where grassroots and corporate media intersect, where the power of the media producer and the power of the media consumer interact in unpredictable ways. . . .

By convergence, I mean the flow of content across multiple media platforms, the cooperation between multiple media industries, and the migratory   5

---

[1]Josh Grossberg, "The Bert-Bin Laden Connection?" E Online, October 10, 2001, http://www.eonline.com/News/Items/0,1,8950,00.html. For a different perspective on Bert and Bin Laden, see Roy Rosenzweig, "Scarcity or Abundance? Preserving the Past in a Digital Era," *American Historical Review* 108 (June 2003).

behavior of media audiences who will go almost anywhere in search of the kinds of entertainment experiences they want. Convergence is a word that manages to describe technological, industrial, cultural, and social changes depending on who's speaking and what they think they are talking about. . . .

In the world of media convergence, every important story gets told, every brand gets sold, and every consumer gets courted across multiple media platforms. Think about the circuits that the Bert Is Evil images traveled — from *Sesame Street* through Photoshop to the World Wide Web, from Ignacio's bedroom to a print shop in Bangladesh, from the posters held up by anti-American protestors that are captured by CNN and into the living rooms of people around the world. Some of its circulation depended on corporate strategies, such as the localization of *Sesame Street* or the global coverage of CNN. Some of its circulation depended on tactics of grassroots appropriation, whether in North America or in the Middle East.

This circulation of media content — across different media systems, competing media economies, and national borders — depends heavily on consumers' active participation. I . . . argue here against the idea that convergence should be understood primarily as a technological process bringing together multiple media functions within the same devices. Instead, convergence represents a cultural shift as consumers are encouraged to seek out new information and make connections among dispersed media content. . . .

The term, *participatory culture*, contrasts with older notions of passive media spectatorship. Rather than talking about media producers and consumers as occupying separate roles, we might now see them as participants who interact with each other according to a new set of rules that none of us fully understands. Not all participants are created equal. Corporations — and even individuals within corporate media — still exert greater power than any individual consumer or even the aggregate of consumers. And some consumers have greater abilities to participate in this emerging culture than others.

Convergence does not occur through media appliances, however sophisticated they may become. Convergence occurs within the brains of individual consumers and through their social interactions with others. Each of us constructs our own personal mythology from bits and fragments of information extracted from the media flow and transformed into resources through which we make sense of our everyday lives. Because there is more information on any given topic than anyone can store in their head, there is an added incentive for us to talk among ourselves about the media we consume. This conversation creates buzz that is increasingly valued by the media industry. Consumption has become a collective process — and that's what [I mean] by *collective intelligence*, a term coined by French cybertheorist Pierre Lévy. None of us can know everything; each of us knows something; and we can put the pieces together if we pool our resources and combine our skills. Collective intelligence can be seen as an alternative source of media power. We are learning how to use that power through our day-to-day interactions within convergence culture. Right now, we are mostly using this collective power through our recreational life, but soon we will be deploying those skills for more "serious" purposes. . . .

Convergence Talk

Another snapshot of convergence culture at work: In December 2004, a hotly [10] anticipated Bollywood film, *Rok Sako To Rok Lo* (2004), was screened in its entirety to movie buffs in Delhi, Bangalore, Hyderabad, Mumbai, and other parts of India through EDGE-enabled mobile phones with live video streaming facility. This is believed to be the first time that a feature film had been fully accessible via mobile phones.[2]

Over the past several years, many of us have watched as cell phones have become increasingly central to the release strategies of commercial motion pictures around the world, as amateur and professional cell phone movies have competed for prizes in international film festivals, as mobile users have been able to listen in to major concerts, as Japanese novelists serialize their work via instant messenger, and as game players have used mobile devices to compete in augmented and alternative reality games. Some functions will take root; others will fail.

Call me old-fashioned. The other week I wanted to buy a cell phone — you know, to make phone calls. I didn't want a video camera, a still camera, a Web access device, an MP3 player, or a game system. I also wasn't interested in something that could show me movie previews, would have customizable ring tones, or would allow me to read novels. I didn't want the electronic equivalent of a Swiss army knife. When the phone rings, I don't want to have to figure out which button to push. I just wanted a phone. The sales clerks sneered at me; they laughed at me behind my back. I was told by company after mobile company that they don't make single-function phones anymore. Nobody wants them. This was a powerful demonstration of how central mobiles have become to the process of media convergence.

You've probably been hearing a lot about convergence lately. You are going to be hearing even more.

The media industries are undergoing another paradigm shift. It happens from time to time. In the 1990s, rhetoric about a coming digital revolution contained an implicit and often explicit assumption that new media were going to push aside old media, that the Internet was going to displace broadcasting, and that all of this would enable consumers to more easily access media content that was personally meaningful to them. A best-seller in 1990, Nicholas Negroponte's *Being Digital* drew a sharp contrast between "passive old media"

---

[2]"RSTRL to Premier on Cell Phone," IndiaFM News Bureau, December 6, 2004, http://www.indiafm.com/scoop/04/dec/0612rstrlcell/index.shtml.

FIGURE 2   Microsoft Corp. researchers Larry Zitnick, *left*, and Richard Hughes demonstrate "Lincoln," Windows Mobile 5 mobile phone technology that lets users take a cellphone photo of a DVD cover and then receive Amazon.com reviews and other multimedia content relating to the DVD back on their phones.

and "interactive new media," predicting the collapse of broadcast networks in favor of an era of narrowcasting and niche media on demand: "What will happen to broadcast television over the next five years is so phenomenal that it's difficult to comprehend."[3] At one point, he suggests that no government regulation will be necessary to shatter the media conglomerates: "The monolithic empires of mass media are dissolving into an array of cottage industries. . . . Media barons of today will be grasping to hold onto their centralized empires tomorrow. . . . The combined forces of technology and human nature will ultimately take a stronger hand in plurality than any laws Congress can invent."[4] Sometimes, the new media companies spoke about convergence, but by this term, they seemed to mean that old media would be absorbed fully and completely into the orbit of the emerging technologies. George Gilder, another digital revolutionary, dismissed such claims: "The computer industry is converging with the television industry in the same sense that the automobile converged with the horse, the TV converged with the nickelodeon, the word-processing program converged with the typewriter, the CAD program converged with the drafting board, and digital desktop publishing

[3]Nicholas Negroponte, *Being Digital* (New York: Alfred A. Knopf, 1995), p. 54.
[4]Ibid., pp. 57–58.

converged with the linotype machine and the letterpress."[5] For Gilder, the computer had come not to transform mass culture but to destroy it.

The popping of the dot-com bubble threw cold water on this talk of a digital revolution. Now, convergence has reemerged as an important reference point as old and new media companies try to imagine the future of the entertainment industry. If the digital revolution paradigm presumed that new media would displace old media, the emerging convergence paradigm assumes that old and new media will interact in even more complex ways. The digital revolution paradigm claimed that new media were going to change everything. After the dot-com crash, the tendency was to imagine that new media had changed nothing. As with so many things about the current media environment, the truth lay somewhere in between. More and more, industry leaders are returning to convergence as a way of making sense of a moment of disorienting change. Convergence is, in that sense, an old concept taking on new meanings. . . .

The Prophet of Convergence

If *Wired* magazine declared Marshall McLuhan the patron saint of the digital revolution, we might well describe the late MIT political scientist Ithiel de Sola Pool as the prophet of media convergence. Pool's *Technologies of Freedom* (1983) was probably the first book to lay out the concept of convergence as a force of change within the media industries:

> A process called the "convergence of modes" is blurring the lines between media, even between point-to-point communications, such as the post, telephone and telegraph, and mass communications, such as the press, radio, and television. A single physical means — be it wires, cables or airwaves — may carry services that in the past were provided in separate ways. Conversely, a service that was provided in the past by any one medium — be it broadcasting, the press, or telephony — can now be provided in several different physical ways. So the one-to-one relationship that used to exist between a medium and its use is eroding.[6]

Some people today talk about divergence rather than convergence, but Pool understood that they were two sides of the same phenomenon.

"Once upon a time," Pool explained, "companies that published newspapers, magazines, and books did very little else; their involvement with other media was slight."[7] Each medium had its own distinctive functions

---

[5]George Gilder, "Afterword: The Computer Juggernaut: Life after *Life after Television*," added to the 1994 edition of *Life after Television: The Coming Transformation of Media and American Life* (New York: W. W. Norton), p. 189. The book was originally published in 1990.

[6]Ithiel de Sola Pool, *Technologies of Freedom: On Free Speech in an Electronic Age* (Cambridge, Mass.: Harvard University Press, 1983), p. 23.

[7]Ibid.

and markets, and each was regulated under different regimes, depending on whether its character was centralized or decentralized, marked by scarcity or plentitude, dominated by news or entertainment, and owned by governmental or private interests. Pool felt that these differences were largely the product of political choices and preserved through habit rather than any essential characteristic of the various technologies. But he did see some communications technologies as supporting more diversity and a greater degree of participation than others: "Freedom is fostered when the means of communication are dispersed, decentralized, and easily available, as are printing presses or microcomputers. Central control is more likely when the means of communication are concentrated, monopolized, and scarce, as are great networks."[8]

Several forces, however, have begun breaking down the walls separating these different media. New media technologies enabled the same content to flow through many different channels and assume many different forms at the point of reception. Pool was describing what Nicholas Negroponte calls the transformation of "atoms into bytes" or digitization.[9] At the same time, new patterns of cross-media ownership that began in the mid-1980s, during what we can now see as the first phase of a longer process of media concentration, were making it more desirable for companies to distribute content across the various channels rather than within a single media platform. Digitization set the conditions for convergence; corporate conglomerates created its imperative.

Much writing about the so-called digital revolution presumed that the outcome of technological change was more or less inevitable. Pool, on the other hand, predicted a period of prolonged transition, during which the various media systems competed and collaborated, searching for the stability that would always elude them: "Convergence does not mean ultimate stability or unity. It operates as a constant force for unification but always in dynamic tension with change. . . . There is no immutable law of growing convergence; the process of change is more complicated than that."[10]

As Pool predicted, we are in an age of media transition, one marked by   20 tactical decisions and unintended consequences, mixed signals and competing interests, and most of all, unclear directions and unpredictable outcomes.[11] Two decades later, I find myself reexamining some of the core questions Pool raised — about how we maintain the potential of participatory culture in the wake of growing media concentration, about whether the changes brought about by convergence open new opportunities for expression or expand

---

[8]Ibid., p. 5.

[9]Negroponte, *Being Digital*.

[10]Pool, *Technologies of Freedom*, pp. 53–54.

[11]For a fuller discussion of the concept of media in transition, see David Thorburn and Henry Jenkins, "Towards an Aesthetics of Transition," in David Thorburn and Henry Jenkins (eds.), *Rethinking Media Change: The Aesthetics of Transition* (Cambridge, Mass.: MIT Press, 2003).

the power of big media. Pool was interested in the impact of convergence on political culture; I am more interested in its impact on popular culture, but the lines between the two have now blurred.

It is beyond my abilities to describe or fully document all of the changes that are occurring. My aim is more modest. I want to describe some of the ways that convergence thinking is reshaping American popular culture and, in particular, the ways it is impacting the relationship between media audiences, producers, and content. Although this chapter will outline the big picture (insofar as any of us can see it clearly yet), subsequent chapters will examine these changes through a series of case studies focused on specific media franchises and their audiences. My goal is to help ordinary people grasp how convergence is impacting the media they consume and, at the same time, to help industry leaders and policymakers understand consumer perspectives on these changes. This has been challenging because everything seems to be changing at once and there is no vantage point that takes me above the fray. Rather than trying to write from an objective vantage point, I describe what this process looks like from various localized perspectives—advertising executives struggling to reach a changing market, creative artists discovering new ways to tell stories, educators tapping informal learning communities, activists deploying new resources to shape the political future, religious groups contesting the quality of their cultural environs, and, of course, various fan communities who are early adopters and creative users of emerging media.

I can't claim to be a neutral observer in any of this. For one thing, I am not simply a consumer of many of these media products; I am also an active fan. The world of media fandom has been a central theme of my work for almost two decades—an interest that emerges from my own participation within various fan communities as much as it does from my intellectual interests as a media scholar. During that time, I have watched fans move from the invisible margins of popular culture and into the center of current thinking about media production and consumption. For another, through my role as director of the MIT Comparative Media Studies Program, I have been an active participant in discussions among industry insiders and policymakers; I have consulted with some of the companies discussed; my earlier writings on fan communities and participatory culture have been embraced by business schools and are starting to have some modest impact on the way media companies are relating to their consumers; many of the creative artists and media executives I interviewed are people I would consider friends. At a time when the roles between producers and consumers are shifting, my job allows me to move among different vantage points. Yet, readers should also keep in mind that my engagement with fans and producers alike necessarily colors what I say. My goal here is to document conflicting perspectives on media change rather than to critique them. I don't think we can meaningfully critique convergence until it is more fully understood; yet if the public doesn't get some insights into the discussions that are taking place, they will have little to no input into decisions that will dramatically change their relationship to media.

The Black Box Fallacy

Almost a decade ago, science fiction writer Bruce Sterling established what he calls the Dead Media Project. As his Web site (http://www.deadmedia.org) explains, "The centralized, dinosaurian one-to-many media that roared and trampled through the twentieth century are poorly adapted to the postmodern technological environment."[12] Anticipating that some of these "dinosaurs" were heading to the tar pits, he constructed a shrine to "the media that have died on the barbed wire of technological change." His collection is astounding, including relics like "the phenakistoscope, the telharmonium, the Edison wax cylinder, the stereopticon, . . . various species of magic lantern."[13]

Yet, history teaches us that old media never die — and they don't even necessarily fade away. What dies are simply the tools we use to access media content — the 8-track, the Beta tape. These are what media scholars call *delivery technologies*. Most of what Sterling's project lists falls under this category. Delivery technologies become obsolete and get replaced; media, on the other hand, evolve. Recorded sound is the medium. CDs, MP3 files, and 8-track cassettes are delivery technologies.

To define media, let's turn to historian Lisa Gitelman, who offers a model   25 of media that works on two levels: on the first, a medium is a technology that enables communication; on the second, a medium is a set of associated "protocols" or social and cultural practices that have grown up around that technology.[14] Delivery systems are simply and only technologies; media are also cultural systems. Delivery technologies come and go all the time, but media persist as layers within an ever more complicated information and entertainment stratum.

A medium's content may shift (as occurred when television displaced radio as a storytelling medium, freeing radio to become the primary showcase for rock and roll), its audience may change (as occurs when comics move from a mainstream medium in the 1950s to a niche medium today), and its social status may rise or fall (as occurs when theater moves from a popular form to an elite one), but once a medium establishes itself as satisfying some core human demand, it continues to function within the larger system of communication options. Once recorded sound becomes a possibility, we have continued to develop new and improved means of recording and playing back sounds. Printed words did not kill spoken words. Cinema did not kill theater. Television did not kill radio.[15] Each old medium was forced to coexist with

[12]Bruce Sterling, "The Dead Media Project: A Modest Proposal and a Public Appeal," http://www.deadmedia.org/modest-proposal.html.

[13]Ibid.

[14]Lisa Gitelman, "Introduction: Media as Historical Subjects," in *Always Already New: Media, History and the Data of Culture* (Cambridge, Mass.: MIT Press, 2006).

[15]For a useful discussion of the recurring idea that new media kill off old media, see Priscilla Coit Murphy, "Books Are Dead, Long Live Books," in David Thorburn and Henry Jenkins (eds.), *Rethinking Media Change: The Aesthetics of Transition* (Cambridge, Mass.: MIT Press, 2003).

the emerging media. That's why convergence seems more plausible as a way of understanding the past several decades of media change than the old digital revolution paradigm had. Old media are not being displaced. Rather, their functions and status are shifted by the introduction of new technologies.

The implications of this distinction between media and delivery systems become clearer as Gitelman elaborates on what she means by "protocols." She writes: "Protocols express a huge variety of social, economic, and material relationships. So telephony includes the salutation 'Hello?' (for English speakers, at least) and includes the monthly billing cycle and includes the wires and cables that materially connect our phones. Cinema includes everything from the sprocket holes that run along the sides of film to the widely shared sense of being able to wait and see 'films' at home on video. And protocols are far from static."[16] I have less to say about the technological dimensions of media change than about the shifts in the protocols by which we are producing and consuming media.

Much contemporary discourse about convergence starts and ends with what I call the Black Box Fallacy. Sooner or later, the argument goes, all media content is going to flow through a single black box into our living rooms (or, in the mobile scenario, through black boxes we carry around with us everywhere we go). If folks could just figure out which black box will reign supreme, then everyone can make reasonable investments for the future. Part of what makes the black box concept a fallacy is that it reduces media change to technological change and strips aside the cultural levels we are considering here.

I don't know about you, but in my living room, I am seeing more and more black boxes. There are my VCR, my digital cable box, my DVD player, my digital recorder, my sound system, and my two game systems, not to mention a huge mound of videotapes, DVDs and CDs, game cartridges and controllers, sitting atop, laying alongside, toppling over the edge of my television system. (I would definitely qualify as an early adopter, but most American homes now have, or soon will have, their own pile of black boxes.) The perpetual tangle of cords that stands between me and my "home entertainment" center reflects the degree of incompatibility and dysfunction that exists between the various media technologies. And many of my MIT students are lugging around multiple black boxes — their laptops, their cells, their iPods, their Game Boys, their BlackBerrys, you name it.

As Cheskin Research explained in a 2002 report, "The old idea of con- 30
vergence was that all devices would converge into one central device that did everything for you (à la the universal remote). What we are now seeing is the hardware diverging while the content converges. Your e-mail needs and expectations are different whether you're at home, work, school, commuting, the airport, etc., and these different devices are designed to suit your needs for accessing content depending on where you are — your situated

[16]Gitelman, "Introduction."

context."[17] This pull toward more specialized media appliances coexists with a push toward more generic devices. We can see the proliferation of black boxes as symptomatic of a moment of convergence: because no one is sure what kinds of functions should be combined, we are forced to buy a range of specialized and incompatible appliances. On the other end of the spectrum, we may also be forced to deal with an escalation of functions within the same media appliance, functions that decrease the ability of that appliance to serve its original function, and so I can't get a cell phone that is just a phone.

Media convergence is more than simply a technological shift. Convergence alters the relationship between existing technologies, industries, markets, genres, and audiences. Convergence alters the logic by which media industries operate and by which media consumers process news and entertainment. Keep this in mind: convergence refers to a process, not an endpoint. There will be no single black box that controls the flow of media into our homes. Thanks to the proliferation of channels and the portability of new computing and telecommunications technologies, we are entering an era where media will be everywhere. Convergence isn't something that is going to happen one day when we have enough bandwidth or figure out the correct configuration of appliances. Ready or not, we are already living within a convergence culture.

Our cell phones are not simply telecommunications devices; they also allow us to play games, download information from the Internet, and take and send photographs or text messages. Increasingly they allow us to watch previews of new films, download installments of serialized novels, or attend concerts from remote locations. All of this is already happening in northern Europe and Asia. Any of these functions can also be performed using other media appliances. You can listen to the Dixie Chicks through your DVD player, your car radio, your Walkman, your iPod, a Web radio station, or a music cable channel.

Fueling this technological convergence is a shift in patterns of media ownership. Whereas old Hollywood focused on cinema, the new media conglomerates have controlling interests across the entire entertainment industry. Warner Bros. produces film, television, popular music, computer games, Web sites, toys, amusement park rides, books, newspapers, magazines, and comics.

In turn, media convergence impacts the way we consume media. A teenager doing homework may juggle four or five windows, scan the Web, listen to and download MP3 files, chat with friends, word-process a paper, and respond to e-mail, shifting rapidly among tasks. And fans of a popular television series may sample dialogue, summarize episodes, debate subtexts, create original fan fiction, record their own soundtracks, make their own movies—and distribute all of this worldwide via the Internet.

[17]Cheskin Research, "Designing Digital Experiences for Youth," *Market Insights Series*, Fall 2002, pp. 8–9.

Convergence is taking place within the same appliances, within the same 35
franchise, within the same company, within the brain of the consumer, and
within the same fandom. Convergence involves both a change in the way
media are produced and a change in the way media are consumed.

The Cultural Logic of Media Convergence

Another snapshot of the future: Anthropologist Mizuko Ito has documented
the growing pace of mobile communications among Japanese youth, describing young couples who remain in constant contact with each other throughout the day, thanks to their access to various mobile technologies.[18] They
wake up together, work together, eat together, and go to bed together even
though they live miles apart and may have face-to-face contact only a few
times a month. We might call it telecocooning.

Convergence doesn't just involve commercially produced materials and
services traveling along well-regulated and predictable circuits. It doesn't just
involve the mobile companies getting together with the film companies to
decide when and where we watch a newly released film. It also occurs when
people take media in their own hands. Entertainment content isn't the only
thing that flows across multiple media platforms. Our lives, relationships,
memories, fantasies, desires also flow across media channels. Being a lover
or a mommy or a teacher occurs on multiple platforms.[19] Sometimes we tuck
our kids into bed at night and other times we Instant Message them from the
other side of the globe.

And yet another snapshot: Intoxicated students at a local high school use
their cell phones spontaneously to produce their own soft-core porn movie
involving topless cheerleaders making out in the locker room. Within hours,
the movie is circulating across the school, being downloaded by students and
teachers alike, and watched between classes on personal media devices.

When people take media into their own hands, the results can be wonderfully creative; they can also be bad news for all involved.

For the foreseeable future, convergence will be a kind of kludge—a jerry- 40
rigged relationship among different media technologies—rather than a fully
integrated system. Right now, the cultural shifts, the legal battles, and the economic consolidations that are fueling media convergence are preceding shifts
in the technological infrastructure. How those various transitions unfold will
determine the balance of power in the next media era.

The American media environment is now being shaped by two seemingly
contradictory trends: on the one hand, new media technologies have lowered

---

[18]Mizuko Ito, "Mobile Phones, Japanese Youth and the Re-placement of the Social Contract," in Rich Ling and Per Petersen (eds.), *Mobile Communications: Re-Negotiation of the
Social Sphere* (forthcoming). http://www.itofisher.com/mito/archives/mobileyouth.pdf.

[19]For a useful illustration of this point, see Henry Jenkins, "Love Online," in Henry Jenkins (ed.), *Fans, Gamers, and Bloggers* (New York: New York University Press, 2005).

production and distribution costs, expanded the range of available delivery channels, and enabled consumers to archive, annotate, appropriate, and recirculate media content in powerful new ways. At the same time, there has been alarming concentration of the ownership of mainstream commercial media, with a small handful of multinational media conglomerates dominating all sectors of the entertainment industry. No one seems capable of describing both sets of changes at the same time, let alone show how they impact each other. Some fear that media are out of control, others that it is too controlled. Some see a world without gatekeepers, others a world where gatekeepers have unprecedented power. Again, the truth lies somewhere in between.

Another snapshot: People around the world are affixing stickers showing yellow arrows (http://global.yellowarrow.net) alongside public monuments and factories, beneath highway overpasses, onto lamp posts. The arrows provide numbers others can call to access recorded voice messages — personal annotations on our shared urban landscape. They use it to share a beautiful vista or criticize an irresponsible company. And increasingly, companies are co-opting the system to leave their own advertising pitches.

Convergence, as we can see, is both a top-down corporate-driven process and a bottom-up consumer-driven process. Corporate convergence coexists with grassroots convergence. Media companies are learning how to accelerate the flow of media content across delivery channels to expand revenue opportunities, broaden markets, and reinforce viewer commitments. Consumers are learning how to use these different media technologies to bring the flow of media more fully under their control and to interact with other consumers. The promises of this new media environment raise expectations of a freer flow of ideas and content. Inspired by those ideals, consumers are fighting for the right to participate more fully in their culture. Sometimes, corporate and grassroots convergence reinforce each other, creating closer, more rewarding relations between media producers and consumers. Sometimes, these two forces are at war and those struggles will redefine the face of American popular culture.

Convergence requires media companies to rethink old assumptions about what it means to consume media, assumptions that shape both programming and marketing decisions. If old consumers were assumed to be passive, the new consumers are active. If old consumers were predictable and stayed where you told them to stay, then new consumers are migratory, showing a declining loyalty to networks or media. If old consumers were isolated individuals, the new consumers are more socially connected. If the work of media consumers was once silent and invisible, the new consumers are now noisy and public.

Media producers are responding to these newly empowered consumers in contradictory ways, sometimes encouraging change, sometimes resisting what they see as renegade behavior. And consumers, in turn, are perplexed by what they see as mixed signals about how much and what kinds of participation they can enjoy.

As they undergo this transition, the media companies are not behaving in a monolithic fashion; often, different divisions of the same company are pursuing radically different strategies, reflecting their uncertainty about how to proceed. On the one hand, convergence represents an expanded opportunity for media conglomerates, since content that succeeds in one sector can spread across other platforms. On the other, convergence represents a risk since most of the media fear a fragmentation or erosion of their markets. Each time they move a viewer from television to the Internet, say, there is a risk that the consumer may not return.

Industry insiders use the term "extension" to refer to their efforts to expand the potential markets by moving content across different delivery systems, "synergy" to refer to the economic opportunities represented by their ability to own and control all of those manifestations, and "franchise" to refer to their coordinated effort to brand and market fictional content under these new conditions. Extension, synergy, and franchising are pushing media industries to embrace convergence.

You are now entering convergence culture. It is not a surprise that we are not yet ready to cope with its complexities and contradictions. We need to find ways to negotiate the changes taking place. No one group can set the terms. No one group can control access and participation.

Don't expect the uncertainties surrounding convergence to be resolved anytime soon. We are entering an era of prolonged transition and transformation in the way media operate. Convergence describes the process by which we will sort through these options. There will be no magical black box that puts everything in order again. Media producers will only find their way through their current problems by renegotiating their relationship with their consumers. Audiences, empowered by these new technologies, occupying a space at the intersection between old and new media, are demanding the right to participate within the culture. Producers who fail to make their peace with this new participatory culture will face declining goodwill and diminished revenues. The resulting struggles and compromises will define the public culture of the future.

READING THE TEXT

1. Define in your own words what Jenkins means by "convergence culture," and create a list of media examples that would constitute that culture.

2. What contradictions does Jenkins find in convergence culture?

3. Explain how convergence culture is both top down and bottom up.

4. Describe Jenkins's tone, considering the extent to which it may be neutral or biased. How does it affect your response to the concept of convergence culture?

5. In your own words, define what industry insiders mean by "extension," "synergy," and "franchise," and explain how they apply to the new media.

READING THE SIGNS

1. In your journal, reflect on your own experience with the new media. What participatory media do you engage in, and why? If you avoid such media, what are the reasons behind your behavior?

2. Jenkins's claim that "When people take media into their own hands, the results can be wonderfully creative; they can also be bad news for all involved" (para. 39) presents the two outcomes as equally possible. Write an essay in which you support Jenkins's assumption or weigh the outcomes and decide which one is more likely. If you argue the latter position, what tips the balance in favor of the side you choose?

3. **CONNECTING TEXTS**   Write an essay arguing for or against the proposition that "concentration of the ownership of mainstream commercial media" (para. 41) is turning You-Topia into just another way for the corporate world to make money. To develop your ideas, consult Brian Williams's "Enough about You" (p. 472) and Steven Johnson's "It's All about Us" (below).

4. A significant proportion of the videos on YouTube and similar sites consists of copyrighted material. Write an essay in which you support, oppose, or modify the position that ordinary copyright law should apply to the use of such material on YouTube.

5. Since Jenkins wrote the book from which this selection is taken, Facebook and Twitter have joined cell phones and other media as tools of political revolution — for example, in the revolutions against the governments of Egypt, Tunisia, and Libya in 2011. Picking one such revolution, research how social and other media were used, and write an essay that explores the effectiveness of electronic media as a political force.

CELEBRATING YOU

STEVEN JOHNSON

It's All about Us

"If Web 1.0 was organized around pages, Web 2.0 is organized around people" such as online "hobbyists, diarists, [and] armchair pundits," Steven Johnson argues in this opinion piece that originally appeared in the *Time* issue that named "You" Person of the Year in January 2007. Acknowledging the suspicion with which traditional professional journalists and scholars regard such amateur sites as blogs and Wikipedia, Johnson still believes that the democratic opportunities of the Internet offer a chance for ordinary people to converse about the local issues in their lives that the professionals largely ignore. Rather than challenging the experts, the conversations taking place in Web 2.0 are supplementing them, Johnson believes, opening up a vast new discourse where ordinary people themselves are the experts. Steven Johnson is the author of *The Ghost Map* (2006) and *The Invention of Air: A Story of Science, Faith, Revolution, and the Birth of America* (2006).

If Web 1.0 was organized around pages, Web 2.0 is organized around people. And not just those special people who appear on TV screens and in Op-Ed columns. Web 2.0 is made up of ordinary people: hobbyists, diarists, armchair pundits, people adding their voice to the Web's great evolving conversation for the sheer love of it.

Amateurs, in other words. And to a certain extent, how you feel about the broader cultural implications of the Web revolves around the response this permanent amateur hour triggers in you. For some, it has power-to-the-people authenticity. For others, it signals the end of quality and professionalism, as though the history of electronic media turned out to be one long battle between Edward R. Murrow and *America's Funniest Home Videos*, and *Home Videos* won.

I happen to be a great believer in this wave, but there's no avoiding the reality that the shift from pro to am comes at some cost. There is undeniably a vast increase in the sheer quantity of accessibility of pure crap, even when measured against the dregs of the newsstand and the cable spectrum. That decreased signal-to-noise ratio means that filters — search tools, recommendation engines, RSS feeds — become increasingly important to us as a society, and so it's crucial that we have a public discussion about who designs those tools and what values are encoded in them.

If you read through the arguments and Op-Eds over the past few years about the impact of Web amateurism, you'll find that the debate keeps cycling back to two refrains: the impact of blogging on traditional journalism and the impact of Wikipedia on traditional scholarship. In both cases, a trained, institutionally accredited élite has been challenged by what the blogger Glenn Reynolds called an "army of Davids," with much triumphalism, derision, and defensiveness on both sides.

This is a perfectly legitimate debate to have, since bloggers and Wikipe-   5
dians are likely to do some things better than their professional equivalents and some things much worse, and we may as well figure out which is which. The problem with spending so much time hashing out these issues is that it overstates the importance of amateur journalism and encyclopedia authoring in the vast marketplace of ideas that the Web has opened up. The fact is that most user-created content on the Web is not challenging the authority of a traditional expert. It's working in a zone where there are no experts or where the users themselves are the experts.

The most obvious example of this is in the prominence of diary-style pages like those on LiveJournal and MySpace. These people aren't challenging David Brooks or George Will; they're just writing about their lives and the lives of their friends. The overwhelming majority of photographers on Flickr harbor no dream of becoming the next Annie Leibovitz. They just want to share with their extended family the pics they snapped over the holidays.

A few months ago, I helped launch a new service called outside.in that filters and organizes conversations happening online about neighborhoods around the country. Outside.in is a classic Web 2.0 company. We couldn't have built it ten years ago because we are drawing upon the expertise of thousands of amateurs — the "placebloggers" who have emerged in the past few years to write about their neighborhoods and the issues that are most important to the people living in them. They're writing about the mugging last week, the playground that's opening up next week, the overpriced house that finally went off the market, the impact of No Child Left Behind on the local public school. There are thousands of these conversations going on every day on the Web — virtual discussions that are grounded in real places. We've tried to make it easier to find those conversations and add your voice to the mix. But without that extraordinary wave of placeblogging, we'd have nothing to work with. It would be like trying to launch Google back when there were still only a few hundred Web sites.

What's so interesting about those local conversations is that they involve experiences that the experts in traditional media have largely ignored — for good reason. Those experts realize that they can't compete with the real experts: the people who live in these communities and know all the issues — small and large — that shape their daily lives.

There's some irony in that lack of media coverage because the zone of experience that people care the most passionately about — beyond the intimate zone of family life — is the zone of their local community. Every successful neighborhood has always had its mavens and connectors, the true experts of the sidewalk, the playground and the backyard barbecue. But that local knowledge has been limited historically to the personal contact of word-of-mouth. Now, on the Web, it has a megaphone.

READING THE TEXT

1. What is the central difference between Web 1.0 and Web 2.0, according to Johnson?

2. What evidence does Johnson advance to support his belief that user-generated media are largely benign, if not liberating?

3. Why does Johnson believe that online "conversations" create access to information that professional journalists have ignored?

4. Johnson notes that he is a cofounder of a Web 2.0 company, outside.in. How might his relationship to a corporate entity affect his argument?

READING THE SIGNS

1. **CONNECTING TEXTS** Compare and contrast Johnson's and Brian Williams's ("Enough about You," below) discussions of Web 2.0, considering both their characterization of the technology itself and their argument about its cultural consequences. Do you find that they are talking about the same phenomena, or do they have somewhat different focuses?

2. **CONNECTING TEXTS** As Johnson points out, much concern has been raised about the effect of Wikipedia on traditional scholarship, but he feels that such concern is unfounded. Interview at least five writing instructors and/or librarians at your school about their position on Wikipedia. Do they encourage or discourage their students to use it as a resource, and why? Does your school have any policies regarding students' use of Wikipedia? Use your results as the basis of an essay in which you support, oppose, or complicate Johnson's position. You might consult Scott Jaschik's "A Stand against Wikipedia" (p. 66).

3. Write an essay in which you argue whether Web 2.0's challenge to a "trained, institutionally accredited élite" (para. 4) has positive or negative consequences.

BRIAN WILLIAMS
Enough about You

Not everyone is certain that the democratic vistas of the you-centered world of Web 2.0 are entirely beneficial, and in this opinion piece by Brian Williams, which *Time* originally published as a direct counterpoint to Steven Johnson's celebration of Web 2.0, a professional journalist considers what may be lost when everyone is a potential expert and everyone is "talking at once." What is more, Williams worries, with the ability to tailor our media consumption today to only those sources that reflect our already held views, we may be missing out on alternative perspectives "that citizens in an informed democracy need to know." After all, the cover of the *Time* issue in which Williams's selection appeared was a reflective surface intended to resemble a mirror. Brian Williams is the anchor and managing editor of the NBC *Nightly News*.

While the mainstream media were having lunch, members of the audience made other plans. They scattered and are still on the move, part of a massive migration. The dynamic driving it? It's all about you. Me. And all the various forms of the First Person Singular. Americans have decided the most important person in their lives is . . . them, and our culture is now built upon that idea. It's the User-Generated Generation.

For those times when the 900 digital options awaiting us in our set-top cable box can seem limiting and claustrophobic, there's the Web. Once inside, the doors swing open to a treasure trove of video: adults juggling kittens, ill-fated dance moves at wedding receptions, political rants delivered to camera with venom and volume. All of it exists to fill a perceived need. Media executives — some still not sure what *it* is — know only that they want it. And they're willing to pay for it.

The larger dynamic at work is the celebration of self. The implied message is that if it has to do with you, or your life, it's important enough to tell someone. Publish it, record it . . . but for goodness' sake, share it — get it out there so that others can enjoy it. Or not. The assumption is that an audience of strangers will be somehow interested, or at the very worst not offended.

Intimacies that were once whispered into the phone are now announced unabashedly into cell phones as loud running conversations in public places. Diaries once sealed under lock and key are now called blogs and posted daily for all those who care to make the emotional investment.

We've raised a generation of Americans on a mantra of love and the 5 importance of self as taught by brightly colored authority figures with names like Barney and Elmo. On the theory that celebrating only the winners means excluding those who place, show, or simply show up, parents-turned-coaches started awarding trophies — entire bedrooms full — to all those who compete. Today everyone gets celebrated, in part to put an end to the common cruelties of life that so many of us grew up with.

Now the obligatory confession: In an irony of life that I've not yet fully reconciled myself to, I write a daily blog full of intimate details about one of the oldest broadcasts on television. While the media landscape of my youth, with its three television networks, now seems like forced national viewing by comparison, and while I anchor a broadcast that is routinely viewed by an audience of ten million or more, it's nothing like it used to be. We work every bit as hard as our television-news forebears did at gathering, writing, and presenting the day's news but to a smaller audience, from which many have been lured away by a dazzling array of choices and the chance to make their own news.

It is now possible — even common — to go about your day in America and consume only what you wish to see and hear. There are television networks that already agree with your views, iPods that play only music you already know you like, Internet programs ready to filter out all but the news you want to hear.

The problem is that there's a lot of information out there that citizens in an informed democracy *need* to know in our complicated world with U.S. troops on the ground along two major fronts. Millions of Americans have come to regard the act of reading a daily newspaper — on *paper* — as something akin to being dragged by their parents to Colonial Williamsburg. It's a tactile visit to another time . . . flat, one-dimensional, unexciting, emitting a slight whiff of decay. It doesn't refresh. It offers no choice. Hell, it doesn't even move. Worse yet: nowhere does it greet us by name. It's for *everyone*.

Does it endanger what passes for the national conversation if we're all talking at once? What if "talking" means typing on a laptop, but the audience is too distracted to pay attention? The whole notion of "media" is now much more democratic, but what will the effect be on democracy?

The danger just might be that we miss the next great book or the next great idea, or that we fail to meet the next great challenge . . . because we are too busy celebrating ourselves and listening to the same tune we already know by heart.

READING THE TEXT

1. Why does Williams believe that users of the new media are motivated largely by a desire to celebrate the self, and what evidence does he offer to support that belief?

2. Describe Williams's tone. What effect does it, and his "obligatory confession" (para. 6), have on the persuasiveness of his argument?

3. Why does Williams consider people's ability to customize the news and entertainment that they consume to be problematic?

READING THE SIGNS

1. **CONNECTING TEXTS**   Write an essay that proposes your own answer to Williams's concluding question: "The whole notion of 'media' is now much more democratic, but what will the effect be on democracy?" (para. 9). To develop your ideas, consult Henry Jenkins's "Convergence Culture" (p. 455) and Steven Johnson's "It's All about Us" (p. 469).

2. **CONNECTING TEXTS**   In class, form teams and debate the impact of Web 2.0, with one team taking Williams's position and the other adopting the perspective of Steven Johnson ("It's All about Us," p. 469). To develop your ideas, you might consult the Introduction to this chapter.

3. Locate Williams's blog on the Internet and analyze its content. To what extent does it simply share Williams's experiences with broadcast news? Do you see that it may serve any commercial purpose for NBC's *Nightly News*?

4. Write an essay in which you support, refute, or complicate Williams's contention that an overly democratic media environment might cause us to miss important information or a truly great idea or book amidst all the media clutter.

danah boyd

Implications of User Choice: The Cultural Logic of "MySpace or Facebook?"

Once upon a time, everyone was on MySpace. Or almost everyone. Oh, there was Friendster and Facebook, but Facebook was for networking adults and a few Ivy League college students. Then, suddenly, everyone was on Facebook. Well, not everyone, of course, and in this study of the shift from MySpace to Facebook danah boyd explains what happened. Interviewing numerous Facebook users, boyd concludes that a good deal of racial and class snobbery was involved, with Facebook users referring, somewhat shamefacedly, to MySpace as a "ghetto." So maybe the world of social networking isn't really drawing people together after all; it may only be reproducing ancient conflicts and divisions. A social media researcher at Microsoft Research New England and a fellow at Harvard University's Berkman Center for Internet and Society, boyd specializes in the sociology of the Internet.

Many of us have had our lives transformed by technology. And many of us are also enamored of the transformative potential of technology, which has led us to develop technology and become advocates of technological practices. As we become more enveloped in and by technology, it's easy to feel excited about what's going on. Yet we must also be cautious.

The rhetoric around technology often makes it out to be the great equalizer of society, suggesting that technology can in and of itself make the world a better place. Let's ignore the technological determinist overtones for a moment and note that this rhetoric fails to capture the complex ways in which the actual adoption of technology tends to mirror and magnify a whole suite of societal issues.

It is crucial that we begin accounting for how technology actually reveals social stratification and reproduces social divisions. For decades we've assumed that inequality in relation to technology has everything to do with access and that if we fix the access problem, all will be fine. This is the grand narrative of politicized concepts like the digital divide. Yet, increasingly, we're seeing people with similar levels of access engage with technology in very different ways. And we're experiencing a social media landscape in which participation "choice" leads to a digital reproduction of social divisions, which already pervade society.

Rather than staying in the land of the abstract, let's go concrete with a specific case study: the differential adoption of MySpace and Facebook among American teens. I have been doing ethnographic fieldwork on various aspects of social network sites since 2003. Starting in 2005, I began specifically focusing on the social media practices of American high school–age teenagers. During the 2006–2007 school year, I started noticing a trend. In each school, in each part of the country, there were teens who opted for MySpace and teens who opted for Facebook. There were also plenty of teens who used both. At the beginning of the school year, teens were asking "Are you on MySpace? Yes or No?" At the end of the school year, the question had changed to "MySpace or Facebook?"

In analyzing my data, one can reasonably see this as a matter of individual choice in a competitive market. There are plenty of teenagers who will tell you that they are on one or the other as a matter of personal preference having to do with features, functionality, design, and usability. For example, Justin (15, Austin) prefers Facebook because of the unlimited pictures while Anindita (17, Los Angeles) likes that MySpace is "more complex" while "Facebook is just plain white and that's it." 5

Teens will also talk about their perceptions of different sites, about what they think certain affordances mean, or how they perceive the sites in relation to values they hold, such as safety. For example, Cachi (18, Iowa) likes that "Facebook is less competitive than MySpace" while Tara (16, Michigan) thinks that Facebook seems safer.

For all of the technology-specific commentary teens offer, the dominant explanation teens will give to justify their choice has to do with their friends. Simply put, they go where their friends are:

KEVIN (15, Seattle): I'm not big on Facebook; I'm a MySpace guy. I have a Facebook and I have some friends on it, but most of my friends don't check it that often so I don't check it that often.

RED (17, Iowa): I am on Facebook and MySpace. I don't talk to people on MySpace anymore. . . . The only reason I still have my MySpace is because my brother's on there.

In choosing to go where their friends are, teens reproduce preexisting social networks. Yet their choice is not neutral. Teens do not randomly select their friends; they connect with people who are like them. This is the basis of the sociological concept of "homophily," which highlights that "birds of a feather stick together." By the time most teens join MySpace or Facebook, they already know someone who is on the site. They are attracted to the site because of the people there. Thus, the early adopters of the sites and the network effects of adoption fundamentally shaped each site's tenor.

MySpace came out first and quickly attracted urban twenty-somethings. It spread to teenagers through older siblings and cousins as well as those who were attracted to indie rock and hip-hop culture. Facebook started at Harvard and spread to the Ivies before spreading more broadly, first to other colleges, then to companies, then elite high schools, and then the unwashed masses. The first teenagers to hear about Facebook were those connected to the early adopters of Facebook (i.e., the Ivy League–bound). Thus, the desirability of the site spread from people who were heading to college. As the two sites grew, they initially attracted different audiences. But by early 2007, teens were choosing between the sites. And while that choice was driven by friendship, it also reinforced distinctions.

Teens recognize that MySpace and Facebook attracted different populations: 10

KAT (14, Massachusetts): I was the first one of my friends to get a Facebook, and then a lot of people got one afterwards. . . . The people who use MySpace—again, not in a racist way—but are usually more like ghetto and hip-hop rap lovers group. And pretty much everyone else might have a Facebook. But there's some people that aren't that. All the rockers, too, will have a MySpace.

In trying to describe what distinguishes the two groups, Kat chooses words that signal that those on MySpace are from a lower socio-economic background and, most probably, black. This is reinforced both by her apology for the racial connotation of her distinction and also by her reference to a different group of youth defined by music, who are presumably not lumped into the group she marks as "ghetto."

The structure of social relations in the United States is shaped by race, socio-economic status, education, and lifestyle. Given the network-driven adoption of MySpace and Facebook, it is not surprising that the adoption patterns also play out along these lines. What is interesting is what happened when some teens chose to move from MySpace to Facebook.

Social media is faddish. MySpace came first and many teens chose to embrace it. When Facebook came along, plenty of teens adopted it as the "new thing." In doing so, some chose to leave MySpace, while others simply maintained two profiles. Yet Facebook did not simply usurp MySpace. In May 2009—two and a half years after teens began splitting—comScore reported that MySpace and Facebook had roughly equal numbers of unique visitors. In other words, while a shift did occur, not all MySpace users left for Facebook, and not all who joined after both were available opted for the newer site.

Those teens who left were not abstractly driven by fads; they were driven by their social networks. Thus, the shift that took place was also shaped by race, socio-economic status, education, and lifestyle. Here is where the division solidified, marked by social categories and distinctions:

ANASTASIA (17, New York): My school is divided into the "honors kids" (I think that is self-explanatory), the "good not-so-honors kids," "wangstas" (they pretend to be tough and black but when you live in a suburb in Westchester you can't claim much hood), the "latinos/hispanics" (they tend to band together even though they could fit into any other groups), and the "emo kids" (whose lives are allllllways filled with woe). We were all in MySpace with our own little social networks, but when Facebook opened its doors to high schoolers, guess who moved and guess who stayed behind. . . . The first two groups were the first to go and then the "wangstas" split with half of them on Facebook and the rest on MySpace. . . . I shifted with the rest of my school to Facebook and it became the place where the "honors kids" got together and discussed how they were procrastinating over their next AP English essay.

In choosing between the two sites, teens marked one as for "people like me," which suggested that the other was for the "other" people. Teens — and adults — use social categories and labels to identify people with values, tastes, and social positions. As teens chose between MySpace and Facebook, these sites began reflecting the cultural frames of those social categories. Nowhere is this more visible than in the language of those who explicitly chose Facebook over MySpace.

CRAIG (17, California): The higher castes of high school moved to Facebook. It was more cultured, and less cheesy. The lower class usually were content to stick to MySpace. Any high school student who has a Facebook will tell you that MySpace users are more likely to be barely educated and obnoxious. Like Peet's is more cultured than Starbucks, and jazz is more cultured than bubblegum pop, and like Macs are more cultured than PCs, Facebook is of a cooler caliber than MySpace.

Craig's description focuses on a comparison of MySpace and Facebook to a series of lifestyle brands. Taste identification is a way in which people self-segregate. Yet, as with social networks, taste is highly correlated with race, socio-economic status, and education. Social networks also drive taste; people like what their friends like. Thus, in choosing Facebook, teens were both connecting with their friends and identifying with a particular lifestyle brand.

The mere fact that network effects, shaped by homophily, resulted in a self-segregation of teens across two social network sites should not be particularly surprising. Yet it ruptures a well-loved fantasy that the Internet would be a great equalizer in which race and class would no longer matter. Furthermore, it presents new challenges for those seeking to address the costs of social stratification in American society.

Social network sites are not like e-mail, where it doesn't matter if you're on Hotmail or Yahoo (although there are connotations implied, with AOL conveying a different signal than Gmail). These are walled gardens. Those who use MySpace can't communicate with those on Facebook, and vice versa. So choosing to participate in one but not the other introduces a hurdle for communication across social divisions. This is further magnified when educators and politicians and universities and organizations choose to use social network sites to connect with their students/constituents/customers. Choosing one becomes political, because choosing only one means excluding those who opted for the other. Consider, for example, the universities that are doing all of their high school recruiting through Facebook. Or the public officials who use just one platform to reach all constituents, thinking that everyone is or will be present. It's one thing to make this choice to reach a specific demographic; it's another to do so blindly and think that everyone is at the table simply because people like you are.

We cannot expect to suddenly eradicate inequality from society, and it is not surprising that technology reflects persistent social stratification. In raising these issues, I'm not arguing that technology can or should be the great equalizer. Instead, I want us to all recognize that it is not. The technologies that we build are never neutral — they are infused with the values and ideas of the creators and the actions and goals of the users. Network effects of adoption patterns further shape technology. As people begin to identify with specific technologies, they take on specific frames in society and begin to reflect them in everyday life. Understanding that divisions are taking place does not necessarily mean trying to "fix" them; there are perfectly rational explanations for self-segregating. Rather, recognizing social divisions means being conscious of the underlying factors and vigilant in thinking of the implications.

We can ignore the fact that social divisions are taking place, but in doing 20 so we fail to realize that we shape what's unfolding. We are building systems in which social stratification will be reproduced and reenacted even if we do not design it that way. We often launch our systems first to those who are like us; the early adopters who set the norms are baking specific cultural values into our systems. These values can alienate people who are not like us, and the choices we make can thus reinforce social divisions. We are shaping the public dialogue about these technologies and our attitudes reflect our personal structural positions, often at the expense of people who are not like us. Knowing how the technologies we create mirror and shape society is crucial to being an ethical technologist. Even if we don't know how to tackle large societal issues, the least we can do is be conscious of their presence in the environments we create and respect the choices and attitudes of those who aren't like us.

READING THE TEXT

1. How, according to boyd's research, do digital choices reflect existing social divisions?

2. What is the image of MySpace for such young Facebook users as Kat and Anastasia? How do they view the users of Facebook?

3. What does boyd mean by the word "homophily"?

4. In your own words, how are MySpace and Facebook "walled gardens"?

5. What is the social effect of universities' use of Facebook for recruiting purposes but not MySpace, according to boyd?

READING THE SIGNS

1. In your journal discuss why you prefer to use MySpace, Facebook, or another social networking site. What is your view of sites that you do not use? If you do not use a social networking site, discuss why you are not attracted to them.

2. Write an essay in which you support, refute, or complicate boyd's claim that Facebook and MySpace reproduce racial divisions in America.

3. Watch the movie *The Social Network* and write a paper arguing for or against the proposition that the prestige of Facebook's Harvard origins has been a significant cause of its rise in popularity and the decline of MySpace.

4. Conduct a class debate in which you address the proposition that technology "reveals social stratification and reproduces social divisions" (para. 3). To develop your ideas, consult the Introduction to this chapter. Use the debate as a jumping-off point for your own essay that responds to this proposition.

5. Write a comparative essay that analyzes today's Facebook and MySpace. Do the appearances of the sites continue to reflect teenager Craig's opinion that Facebook "was more cultured, and less cheesy" than MySpace (para. 15)?

IAN DALY

Virtual Popularity Isn't Cool — It's Pathetic

It's easy to have lots of friends on the Internet, especially on social networking sites like Facebook. In fact, Facebook goes out of its way to make finding new friends even easier and, bypassing the traditional word for making friends ("befriending"), has made "friending" one of the hottest new verbs in American English. Something of a competitive sport now, friending, in Ian Daly's opinion, has gotten a lot of grown men acting giddy, spending hours online tending their Facebook pages rather than doing their work. This is not a good trend, Daly believes, but he has hopes, based upon the notorious fickleness of high technology fads, that "If you resist, you will be vindicated. Like the popular kids, Facebook will end up living in a trailer — just down the gravel road from Friendster." Ian Daly is a contributing editor at *Details* and a contributing writer at *Wired U.K.* who specializes in popular culture and art.

In a few short years, Facebook has leaked out of the college dormitory like some rare tropical disease and has begun infecting grown men in disturbingly vast numbers. The fastest-growing demographic among Facebook's 64 million users is those over 25. More than half of MySpace's 110 million users are older than 35. The hosts, once infected, exhibit a tendency to "superpoke" each other, hyperventilate over friend counts, and share their thoughts about the latest episode of *The Hills* with hundreds of near strangers — behavior normally associated with teenage girls, not men in the middle of their fourth decade. Somewhere tonight, a man with a successful white-collar career and a family who needs his attention will log on to his MacBook to see who "trout-slapped" him and left him a "zombie hug"—hypnotized by the soft glow of the LCD screen into thinking his online popularity has some kind of bearing on his life.

"I'd say 90 percent of my friends have that silly page, putting 'funny' pictures of themselves half-naked and drunk on them," says Michael Lupo, 26, a marketing director in Manhattan who says he's never given in to their pleas to join them. "There are so many bad attempts at being quasi-famous. These people who have like 10,000 friends? I'm like, 'But they're not your friends—you do realize that. You don't hang out, and you don't know anything about them besides what's on their Facebook page.'"

Sure, it's difficult to resist the allure of a site that everyone with Internet access seems to have embraced with open arms. But that appeal might be worth scrutinizing if the same site causes otherwise judicious adult-male converts to behave like 13-year-old girls.

"There's a sense that you're actually *accomplishing* something when you're on these sites," says Dr. Jerald Block, an Oregon psychologist who studies Internet addiction. But the truth is, other than the adolescent joys of Scrabulous and *Alias* trivia, there aren't too many benefits to this site that can't be realized via e-mail and telephone. Take a good, long look at your friend list and ask yourself how many of these people would meet you for a beer—or how many you would actually *want* to meet for a beer. And did you *really* want to reconnect with that awkward kid from boarding school who drew battle-axes on his Trapper Keeper?

Of course not, but once you decide to join Facebook don't be surprised 5 if you're no longer in control of your self-image. For Michael, a 24-year-old private-equity associate in Chicago who decided to delete his profile, the promise of social status just wasn't enough for him to make that kind of sacrifice.

"You really don't get to control your own identity on the site," he says. "Other people can put pictures of you up there, tag them, write on your 'wall'—and all of a sudden you've got the one 'hilarious' buddy from high school to deal with, who you love but who maybe doesn't realize that you've got *colleagues* looking at your profile."

Forty percent of employers say they'd consider Facebook profiles when screening potential employees, according to a 2006 survey conducted by the University of Dayton (some companies have even rescinded job offers after seeing profiles). And we've all heard the stories about high-profile firings that stemmed from bad photo decisions on MySpace—that weatherman in Roanoke, Virginia, who got canned for posting nude shots of himself stepping out of the shower, or Carmen Kontur-Gronquist, former mayor of Arlington, Oregon, who lost her job after posing in her underwear for her profile (her defense—"That's *my space*; that's why they call it MySpace"—sadly, did not fly). But to object to social-networking wonderlands on these grounds is almost too obvious, the kind of censoriousness that serves only to produce more converts. This is about more than lost productivity and cautionary career tales. What's at stake here is nothing less than the mass infantilization of our culture.

"All my friends said, 'You need to get on there!'" says Lupo. "They're like, 'You can find out what's going on with us any time you want!' I said, 'Well, then I could call you or we can meet up for dinner—you don't need to send me little messages online and *poke* me.' It's too time-consuming. It's like a 24-hour obsession that you have to update and take care of. Why don't I just get a puppy and take it to work with me all day?"

The conviction that you're somehow missing out if you don't buy in— that you'll be left to wander alone in some kind of pre-technological hinter-land—is as misguided as the notion that your ego is tied to the testimonials left on your comment wall. There are far more dignified avenues to regres-sion, and most of these involve actual friends. These sites are the digital equivalents of the high-school cafeteria—except without Rib-b-que Tuesdays. Why the hell would you want to go back?

Rest assured: If you resist, you will be vindicated. Like the popular kids,   10 Facebook will end up living in a trailer—just down the gravel road from Friendster.

READING THE TEXT

1. How have the demographics for social networking sites changed in recent years, according to Daly?

2. How can social networking affect one's job and career?

3. What does Daly mean by saying that "What's at stake here is nothing less than the mass infantilization of our culture" (para. 7)?

4. Characterize Daly's tone in this essay. How does it affect your response to his ideas?

READING THE SIGNS

1. **CONNECTING TEXTS**   Write an essay in which you propose your own definition of "friendship" as it exists on social networking sites. To develop your ideas, read or reread danah boyd's "Implications of User Choice: The Cultural Logic of 'MySpace or Facebook?'" (p. 475).

2. Write an essay supporting or challenging Daly's prediction that "Facebook will end up living in a trailer" (para. 10).

3. Social networking initially attracted young people, as Daly indicates, but increasingly adults are joining them as well. Write an analysis presenting your thesis for why social networking has become so popular with adults. To develop your ideas, interview at least five adults who are fans of such sites.

4. Write an essay in which you evaluate Daly's titular claim that seeking pop-ularity on social networking sites is "pathetic." What value judgments does that word imply, and do you share Daly's attitude?

INTERNATIONAL CENTER FOR MEDIA AND THE PUBLIC AGENDA

Students Addicted to Social Media

It's official: the use of digital technology is addictive, or so concludes a 2010 study by the International Center for Media and the Public Agenda at the University of Maryland. After two hundred University of Maryland students willingly gave up their digital devices for twenty-four hours, journalism professor Susan D. Moeller found them virtually traumatized by the experience. Indeed, as one student wrote, "Texting and IM-ing my friends gives me a constant feeling of comfort. . . . [W]hen I did not have those two luxuries, I felt quite alone and secluded from my life. Although I go to a school with thousands of students, the fact that I was not able to communicate with anyone via technology was almost unbearable." Maybe iPhones should come with a warning from the Surgeon General?

American college students today are addicted to media, describing their feelings when they have to abstain from using media in literally the same terms associated with drug and alcohol addictions: *In withdrawal, Frantically craving, Very anxious, Extremely antsy, Miserable, Jittery, Crazy.*

A new study out today from the International Center for Media & the Public Agenda (ICMPA) at the University of Maryland concludes that most college students are not just unwilling, but functionally unable to be without their media links to the world. "I clearly am addicted and the dependency is sickening," said one student in the study. "I feel like most people these days are in a similar situation, for between having a BlackBerry, a laptop, a television, and an iPod, people have become unable to shed their media skin."

The new ICMPA study, "24 Hours: Unplugged," asked 200 students at the College Park campus to give up all media for 24 hours. After their 24 hours of abstinence, the students were then asked to blog on private class Web sites about their experiences: to report their successes and admit to any failures. The 200 students wrote more than 110,000 words: in aggregate, about the same number of words as a 400-page novel.

Without Digital Ties, Students Feel Unconnected Even to Those Who Are Close By

"We were surprised by how many students admitted that they were 'incredibly addicted' to media," noted the project director Susan D. Moeller, a journalism professor at the University of Maryland and the director of the

International Center for Media and the Public Agenda which conducted the study. "But we noticed that what they wrote at length about was how they hated losing their personal connections. Going without media meant, in their world, going without their friends and family."

"The students did complain about how boring it was to go anywhere and 5 do anything without being plugged into music on their MP3 players," said Moeller. "And many commented that it was almost impossible to avoid the TVs on in the background at all times in their friends' rooms. But what they spoke about in the strongest terms was how their lack of access to text messaging, phone calling, instant messaging, e-mail, and Facebook, meant that they couldn't connect with friends who lived close by, much less those far away."

"Texting and IM-ing my friends gives me a constant feeling of comfort," wrote one student. "When I did not have those two luxuries, I felt quite alone and secluded from my life. Although I go to a school with thousands of students, the fact that I was not able to communicate with anyone via technology was almost unbearable."

The student responses to the assignment showed not just that 18–21-year-old college students are constantly texting and on Facebook — with calling and e-mail distant seconds as ways of staying in touch, especially with friends — but that students' lives are wired together in such ways that opting out of that communication pattern would be tantamount to renouncing a social life.

News: Accessed via Connections with Friends & Family

Very few students in the study reported that they regularly watched news on television or read a local or national newspaper (although a few said they regularly read *The Diamondback*, the University of Maryland student newspaper). They also didn't mention checking mainstream media news sites or listening to radio news while commuting in their cars. Yet student after student demonstrated knowledge of specific news stories. How did they get the information? In a disaggregated way, and not typically from the news outlet that broke or committed resources to a story. "To be entirely honest I am glad I failed the assignment," wrote one student, "because if I hadn't opened my computer when I did I would not have known about the violent earthquake in Chile from an informal blog post on Tumblr."

"Students expressed tremendous anxiety about being cut-off from information," observed Ph.D. student Raymond McCaffrey, a former writer and editor at *The Washington Post*, and a current researcher on the study. "One student said he realized that he suddenly 'had less information than everyone else, whether it be news, class information, scores, or what happened on *Family Guy*.'"

"They care about what is going on among their friends and families and 10 even in the world at large," said McCaffrey. "But most of all they care about being cut off from that instantaneous flow of information that comes from all sides and does not seem tied to any single device or application or news outlet."

That's the real takeaway of this study for journalists: Students showed no significant loyalty to a news program, news personality or even news platform. Students have only a casual relationship to the originators of news, and in fact rarely distinguished between news and more general information.

While many in the journalism profession are committing significant resources to deliver content across media platforms — print, broadcast, online, mobile — the young adults in this study appeared to be generally oblivious to branded news and information. For most of the students reporting in the study, information of all kinds comes in an undifferentiated wave to them via social media. If a bit of information rises to a level of interest, the student will pursue it — but often by following the story via "unconventional" outlets, such as through text messages, their e-mail accounts, Facebook, and Twitter.

Students said that only the most specific or significant news events — for example, a medal event at the Olympics — merited their tuning in to a mainstream outlet. Even news events that students cared about were often accessed via their personal interactions. To learn about the Maryland vs. Virginia Tech basketball game, for example, one student told of "listening to someone narrate the game from a conversation they were having on their own phone" (although he would have preferred watching it on TV) and another student told of calling her father to learn more about the earthquake in Chile.

Study Background

The University of Maryland is a large state university campus, and the class, *JOUR 175: Media Literacy*, that undertook this 24-hour media-free assignment, is a "core course" for the entire student body — which means it enrolls undergraduate students across majors. It is, in short, a class of 200 students, characterized by a diversity of age, race, ethnicity, religion, and nationality. According to the assignment, students had to go media-free for a full day (or had to try to go media-free), but they were allowed to pick which 24 hours in a nine-day period, from February 24–March 4. By coincidence that period saw several major news events, including the earthquake in Chile on February 27, and the close of the Vancouver Olympics on February 28.

According to separately obtained demographic data on the student class,   15
75.6 percent of the students in JOUR 175 self-identify as Caucasian/White, 9.4 percent as Black, 6.3 percent as Asian, 1.6 percent as Latino, 3.1 percent as Mixed Race, and 3.9 percent as Other. Students who self-reported themselves as non-American said they were from China, South Korea, Sri Lanka, and Ethiopia. Women outnumbered men, 55.9 percent to 44.1 percent.

44.1 percent of the class reported that their parents or guardians earned over $100,000 or more; 28.3 percent reported that their parents or guardians earned between $75–$100,000; 22 percent reported coming from a household with an income between $50–75,000; and 5.5 percent reported that their families' income was between $25–50,000.

40.9 percent of the students who responded to the demographic survey reported that they were first-year students, 40.9 percent reported that they were sophomores, 11 percent reported that they were juniors, and 7.1 reported that they were seniors or beyond. Most students reported their ages as between 18–21; the average class age was 19.5.

When asked about what types of media devices they own, 43.3 percent of the students reported that they had a "smart phone" (e.g., a BlackBerry or an iPhone), and 56.7 percent said they did not.

Prof. Susan Moeller led the study research team, and the six teaching assistants for the course acted as researchers/authors, conducting a qualitative content analysis of the student responses. Those six TAs, all PhD students in the Philip Merrill College of Journalism, were: Ms. EunRyung Chong, Mr. Sergei Golitsinski, Ms. Jing Guo, Mr. Raymond McCaffrey, Mr. Andrew Nynka, and Ms. Jessica Roberts.[1]

READING THE TEXT

1. What are the symptoms of addiction to social media, according to the International Center for Media and the Public Agenda study conducted at the University of Maryland?
2. What can journalists learn from this study?
3. What is the primary reason for the use of digital media for the students in this study?
4. In your own words, how can people's reliance on social media be considered an "addiction"?

READING THE SIGNS

1. Write a journal entry in which you reflect upon your own use of text messaging, online social media, and other forms of electronic media. Why do you use such media? Would you consider yourself "addicted"? If you do not use them, or do so rarely, why is that your preference?
2. Conduct a similar experiment in your class, having everyone give up their use of all digital media for 24 hours. Then use your course Web site to blog about your experiences (or discuss them in class). To what extent does your experiment replicate the results of the University of Maryland study? If your results differ, how do you account for that difference?

[1] The study is available online at http://www.withoutmedia.wordpress.com.

3. **CONNECTING TEXTS**   Read Brian Williams's "Enough about You" (p. 472) and, adopting his perspective, write an essay that assesses students' reliance on text messaging and social media as their primary source for news of the world rather than mainstream news sources.

4. **CONNECTING TEXTS**   In "Fast Entertainment and Multitasking in an Always-On World" (p. 142), S. Craig Watkins asks whether media multitasking is "healthy." In an essay, write your own response to his query, using the University of Maryland study as your evidence. To develop your essay, consult as well Ian Daly's "Virtual Popularity Isn't Cool — It's Pathetic" (p. 480).

ZACH WAGGONER

Videogames, Avatars, and Identity

By day a mild-mannered composition instructor at Arizona State University, by night Zach Waggoner is Zach the Chosen One, a hero in the video game world of *Fallout 2*. Or at least that's who he was in 1999. More recently he has become Zach the Wood Elf in *The Elder Scrolls IV: Oblivion*. But aside from confessing to his addiction to video-games, Waggoner is interested in learning just what all this role-playing means for his identity, and in this excerpt from *My Avatar, My Self: Identity in Video Role-Playing Games* (2009) he explores videogame role-playing theory, especially as guided by the work of James Paul Gee. Hang on, things get liminal, with the boundary between a gamer's real world identity and virtual identity getting awfully fuzzy at times. Zach Waggoner is a lecturer in the Arizona State University Writing Programs.

Our connection to the real world is very thin, and our connection with the artificial world is going to be more intimate and satisfying than anything that's come before.
— MARVIN MINSKY, MIT scientist, 1989

We may not want to acknowledge a connection between ourselves and the mechanical world, but to be alive in our time is to be faced with this reflection, like it or not.
— JANET MURRAY, technology theorist, 1997

It is September of 1999. A Thursday night. I should be asleep by now, but I'm not. Tomorrow is a teaching day, and I have to get up early. I roll over, pounding my pillow in frustration. I glance at the digital dock: The smug 11:53 p.m. mocks me. *"Only five hours until you need to get up,"* it seems to say. Dammit, I close my eyes, trying to drift down into sleep. But it's no use:

my mind fills with images of giant geckos and plasma rifles, supermutants and radioactive ghouls. Frantically, I struggle to clear my head. Relax. Just relax. But I can't: I am Zach the Chosen One, and have much on my mind. Should I visit Redding or Reno next? Is my Small Guns skill high enough to help me survive if I'm ambushed in the Wastes? Will I come to regret not freeing the slaves in the Den? Should I have opted for a higher Perception skill when creating Zach, given my penchant for long-distance sniping? I can't stop these thoughts. I am powerless to control my mind. Sighing, I look at the clock once more: 12:17 a.m. What is wrong with me? How can I obsess this much over a videogame? Sure, *Fallout 2* is a great game: terrific story, open-ended gameplay, incredibly deep customization options. But it is still just a game, a fiction. Resigned to a poor night's sleep, I vow never to get this hooked on a virtual world during the middle of a semester ever again. . . .

It is February of 2008. Groaning inwardly, I squint at the pale blue glow of my old nemesis: 1:02 a.m. Not again. Tomorrow is a long day, with committee meetings late in the afternoon after an early spate of classes. I needed to be asleep seventy-five minutes ago. When will I learn? I thought just an hour wouldn't hurt me, but here I am, unable to get that haunting music out of my head. It's triumphal and orchestric: great for inspiring me while grading papers, but lousy as a sleep aid. Plus, I'm reliving my last foray into the Oblivion gate near Kvatch. Those scamps really piss me off, and it is becoming increasingly clear that I'm going to need to improve both my Destruction magic skill and my Marksman skill before I go back in. I might need new armor, too. Zach the Wood Elf just isn't as strong as he needs to be. *The Elder Scrolls IV: Oblivion* is consuming me, piece by mental piece. I can't stop playing, even though the demands of this semester's teaching load are calling for attention. Just one more hour, and I can finish the slaughterfish quest. Just one more hour, and I can buy Zach a new pair of boots. Just one more hour, and I can increase my Alchemy skill three times. Just. One. More. Hour.

Okay, I obviously didn't learn my lesson after spending more than 100 hours playing *Fallout 2*. It's almost a decade later, and I'm still investing copious amounts of time and energy in virtual videogame worlds. *Oblivion* is just my latest addiction. Somehow, video role-playing games (v-RPGs) speak to me, whisper to my soul. It is hard to explain why this happens. At least I can take comfort in knowing that I'm not alone: *Oblivion* has sold more than two million copies worldwide. Massively multiplayer online role-playing games (MMORPGs) like *World of Warcraft* have several million subscribers as well. Videogame revenue now reaches several billion dollars annually in the United States alone (with global figures expected to pass $50 billion in 2009). Clearly, other players enjoy videogames as much as I do. But do other v-RPGers care as much about their avatars as I do about mine? Am I alone in my virtual obsessions, having contracted some sort of virtu-virus or techno-schizophrenia? The words of videogame theorist Arthur Asa Berger, written in 2002, resonate with me, but offer cold comfort: "Playing video games may lead to alienation; this alienation can often lead to a sense of estrangement from oneself . . . what is difficult to know is how being immersed will affect players. Will new video games become a kind of opiate for people who can find an outlet in simulations that seem better than those offered by their real-life experiences?" (107–8). Hmm. Estranged from my self. That doesn't seem to fit how I feel about Zach the Wood Elf. My relationship with my avatar seems more complicated than that. Exactly how I believe it is more compli-cated (for other videogamers as well as myself) and will take some explaining, as videogame technologies offer users interactive and immersive experiences that convey verisimilitude and beyond more with each passing year.

Avatars and Videogames

There have been many landmark achievements in the history of videogames,[1] leading us to where we are now: In 2007, video and computer game software sales exceeded nine billion dollars in the United States. Over 267 million video and computer game units were sold in this country as well (Entertain-ment Software Association). The new medium of videogames is now poised to surpass cinema as the most lucrative entertainment medium the United States has ever known. Why? What is it about videogames that captivates so many users of all ages? Mark Wolf helps us understand this phenomenon by pointing out how truly unique videogames are from their main competi-tors, cinema and television: Videogames are "the first [medium] to combine real-time game play with a navigable, on-screen diegetic space [and] the first to feature avatars and player-controlled surrogates that could influence on-screen events: real-time user interaction in one machine" (11, 5). Here, Wolf suggests that real-time user interactivity within the game space, via avatars, is crucial to videogame popularity and success.

Avatars. It's time I defined and complicated this essential term. What are they, and why are they so important to videogames? Videogame scholars apply the term in several different ways, but the origins of the word are clear. *Avatara*, meaning "descent," is a Sanskrit word that in Hinduism refers to an incarnation, a bodily manifestation, of an immortal being. Hindu gods and goddesses use avatars as necessary when they want to access the physical, mortal world of humanity. However, with the rise of computer technology and the virtual spaces made possible by this technology, the term "avatar" has been applied to videogames with several competing definitions.[2] In the broad-est sense, an avatar is "the user's representative in the virtual universe" (Fili-ciak 89). Chris Crawford describes avatars in a similar way: "virtual constructs that are controlled by human players and function as a means of interacting with other characters" (Berger 33). These definitions combine Wolf's above notions of "avatar" and "player-controlled surrogates" and seem to cover any on-screen representation controlled by the user. Under these definitions, the small "blip" of light in *Spacewar!* representing the user's spaceship would be an avatar. Bob Rehak, using Miroslaw Filiciak's definition, provides a brief

5

history of significant avatar moments in videogames beginning with *Space-war!* He highlights *Pac-Man* as providing the first "alive" avatar: *Pac-Man* is portrayed as an organic creature, rather than a machine. All previous video-games had the user controlling either spaceships or other machines (like the ground-defense turrets of *Space Invaders*); being given control of an organic creature was a new idea. As previously mentioned, *Battlezone* allowed the user to operate from "inside" the avatar (a tank) from a first-person POV. *Myst* also provided a first-person POV, but was revolutionary for its emphasis on spatial exploration over narrative (an important distinction I'll return to later). *Quake* was the first videogame that allowed the user to change the appear-ance of the avatar, offering several different "skins" the user could choose from. Using this simplified definition, avatars have been present since the inception of videogames.

The epigraph from Marvin Minsky states: "Our connection to the real world is very thin, and our connection with the artificial world is going to be more intimate and satisfying than anything that's come before" (161). Filiciak (perhaps influenced by the film *EXistenZ*) adds the following sentiments about the connections between real and artificial worlds: "In the foreseeable future [of videogames, the] differentiation between artificial and real or between out-side and inside will be blurred" (98). When considering these two statements it is difficult to imagine a user's connection to *Pac-Man* (or even *Tomb Raider*'s Lara Croft) as being more "intimate and satisfying" than the interactions with friends at work or at school. So too is it difficult to imagine a user blurring the distinction between videogame play where she is "inside" her *Zaxxon* fighter jet or in control of Dirk the Daring in *Dragon's Lair* and "outside" activities like taking a calculus test or eating dinner at a pizza parlor. What is it about vid-eogames and videogame avatars that lead to the notions espoused by Minsky and Filiciak that speculate on the blurring between real and virtual identities?

To begin to answer this question it is necessary to further refine the defi-nition of "avatar" in relationship to videogames. Athomas Goldberg aids this process by distinguishing between "avatars" and "agents." He defines a vir-tual avatar as any "representations of 'real' people in computer-generated environment[s]" and agents as "any semiautonomous pieces of software that assume some visual embodiment" (161). Distinguishing between virtual avatars and agents is helpful, but Goldberg's definitions are still too vague: *Pac-Man* could be identified as either an avatar (since *Pac-Man* represents the user in the gameworld maze) or an agent (since it is the on-screen embodiment of semiautonomous software). Further refinement in the definition of avatar is needed to avoid this ambiguity, and Laetitia Wilson succeeds in providing it:

> [An avatar is] a virtual, surrogate self that acts as a stand-in for our real-space selves, that represents the user. The cyberspace avatar functions as a locus that is multifarious and polymorphous, displaced from the facticity of our real-space selves. . . . Avatar spaces indisputably involve choice in the creation of one's avatar; there is substantial scope in which to exercise choice and create meaning [within the video game] [2–3].

This notion of creative choice is crucial to not only defining avatars in virtual spaces but also to understanding exactly how users connect with videogames and become immersed within them. Using Wilson's criterion of creative choice, it becomes much easier to distinguish between videogame avatars and agents. Pac-Man cannot be altered in any way by the user. He can only be controlled. His appearance and skills never change throughout the course of the game. This makes Pac-Man an agent. The same holds true for *Spacewar!*'s spaceship, Lara Croft of *Tomb Raider* fame, Mario, of *Super Mario Bros., Frogger, Sonic the Hedgehog, Duke Nukem, Grand Theft Auto: Vice City*'s Tommy Vercetti, and *Perfect Dark*'s Joanna Dark. All of these famous videogame characters are agents, as they can only be controlled by the user, never altered in appearance or skill level.

Users and Avatars: Relationships

In fact, when considering this much more restricted definition for avatars (the necessity for the user to have much creative control over the agent's appearance, skills, and attributes), it becomes clear that most of the controllable characters in videogames are agents rather than avatars. What genre of videogame allows the user to have creative license to construct an avatar, then? To move forward in answering this question I must first go back: in 1997, Janet Murray's landmark *Hamlet on the Holodeck: The Future of Narrative in Cyberspace* was published. In that work, Murray focused on how computer technology would impact the evolution of narrative stories and established many terms and concepts that remain crucial to the theoretical landscape of computer and videogame technology. She acknowledged the importance of cyber-games and of game play in general:

> In games we have a chance to enact our most basic relationship to the world — our desire to prevail over adversity, to survive our inevitable defeats, to shape our environment, to master complexity, and to make our lives fit together like the pieces of a jigsaw puzzle. Like the religious ceremonies of passage by which we mark birth, coming of age, marriage, and death, games are ritual actions allowing us to symbolically enact the patterns that give meaning to our lives [143].

By placing game play as a rite of passage alongside such events as birth, marriage, and death, Murray reveals just how important she believes game play to be in human meaning-making. How exactly can videogames achieve this meaning-making? Earlier in her book, Murray describes her own experiences playing an arcade Western-themed shooter game named *Mad Dog McCree*, which used cinematic video and put a laser pistol in the user's hands to engage in gunfight after gunfight. Murray described the moment she became aware that she was both pacifist mother and cyber gunslinger: "I was conscious of being two very different people. I would not claim that

Mad Dog McCree was a masterful piece of storytelling. But the moment of self-confrontation it provoked, the moment in which I was suddenly aware of an authentic but disquieting side of myself, seems to me to be the mark of a new kind of dramatic experience" (54). Clearly a rich and compelling narrative was not necessary for Murray's experience playing the game to be significant as it forced her to become aware of parts of herself she had been previously unaware of. And *Mad Dog McCree* is a game that provides neither agent nor avatar: the user simply points their laser gun at the video screen, aims, and attempts to hit the targets. If Murray could come to such self-awareness without any avatar present, and if, as Rehak and other scholars suggest, the most crucial relationship in videogames is between user and avatar, then how much more powerful might Murray's experience have been if undertaken through an avatar? How can we characterize the relationships between a user and their avatar in a videogame world?

Several videogame scholars have theorized about the relationship between users and their virtual world avatars; this work reveals much uncertainty about the connection between the two. Katherine Hayles writes, "The avatar both is and is not present, just as the user both is and is not inside the screen" (38). Similarly, Rehak suggests:

> [The avatar's] behavior is tied to the player's through an interface: its literal motion, as well as its figurative triumphs and defeats, result from the player's actions. At the same time, avatars are unequivocally other. Both limited and freed by difference from the player, they can accomplish more than the player alone; they are supernatural ambassadors of agency [106].

Both authors here suggest a relationship between user and avatar that is filled with tension: The avatar is part of the user but at the same time remains separate, and the user makes decisions as to the nature of the avatar but the avatar also exists independent from the user (statically, frozen until the user returns to the game). Marie Ryan also recognizes this tension, but suggests that the user has control over how she relates to her avatar: "Will she be like an actor playing a role, innerly distanciated from her character and simulating emotions she does not really have, or will she experience her character in first-person mode, actually feeling [the emotions] that motivate the character's behavior or that may result from her actions?" (6). Wilson's definition of avatar privileges user choice, and Ryan's question here suggests that the user has complete conscious control over her relationship with her avatar. But when I read about Murray's experience playing *Mad Dog McCree*, or when I read Berger's comparison of videogames to an addictive drug, I am forced to wonder again about the nature of the user/avatar relationship and exactly how much choice the user has in this relationship. In an interview conducted by Celia Pearce, longtime LucasArts game designer Tim Schafer suggested that even as users may have complete control over their avatars in the early stages of a videogame, this relationship may change as the game play continues.

In the beginning, he says, games "have to provide the character with motivation and you have to provide the player with motivation. Because the character will care about things that the player will not necessarily care about" (1). As game play progresses, Schafer hypothesizes that users begin to "ego-invest, they share the motivations of the character" (9). This notion of "ego-investing" is a complicated one and does indeed imply a reciprocal relationship between user and avatar.

Role-Playing Games

The concepts of ego-investing in an avatar and of seeing avatars as ambas- 10
sadors of agency, provoking self-confrontation, are interesting ones. It seems to me that these concepts, used by different theorists to try to explain the relationship between a user and her videogame avatar, are all related to one important concept: identity. How is human identity formed? Can videogame play impact identity formation? These are complex questions. For now, I want to return my focus to avatars, since so many theorists agree that they are crucial to immersive videogame play. In distinguishing between agents and avatars earlier in this essay, I eliminated most videogame genres from having true avatars, since most playable videogame agents are not customizable by the user. And so the question remains: Which videogame genres have true avatars and provide the best opportunities for users to identify with them?

To begin to answer this question, I return to Murray's *Hamlet and the Holodeck* (1997) to highlight her prophetic talents. In this text, Murray made several speculative statements about how videogames in the future would best immerse users and impact them emotionally. Murray's predictions for immersive and emotionally evocative videogames dealt with several different aspects of videogame play. I share all of her prophetic statements here and then discuss their significance and relationship to the current status of avatars and videogame play. To sustain compelling storytelling in an interactive medium like videogames, Murray was convinced that the key was "to invent scripts that are formulaic enough to be easily grasped and responded to but flexible enough to capture a wide range of human behavior" (79). Regarding immersive game worlds, she envisioned the ideal spatial navigation:

> The potential of the labyrinth would seem to lie somewhere between the single-path maze adventure and the underdetermined form of the rhizome, in stories that are goal-driven enough to guide navigation but open-ended enough to allow free exploration and that display a satisfying dramatic structure no matter how the interactor chooses to traverse the space [135].

For Murray, the key to immersive videogames lay in impacting the user emotionally: "We need to find ways of drawing a player so deeply into the situated point of view of a character that a change of position will raise important moral questions" (147). At the end of her text, Murray finally revealed the type of videogame genre she felt would best meet all these criteria as she discussed the virtual world of future videogames:

> Lushly realized places will turn from spectacle experiences to dramatic stages. We will move from the pleasures of immersion and navigational agency to increasingly active and transformational experiences. . . . Unlike a videogame, **a role-playing world** [emphasis mine] should allow each interactor to choose from several ways to go about the task, including bartering as well as fighting. . . .The private pleasures of the digital environment are likely to continue to attract us. Solo play would allow the interactor to explore all the stories within the limits of the world and to play all the parts until they had exhausted all the possibilities of personal imaginative engagement within a nostalgically charged situation. As a domain in which we can actively participate in a responsive environment, **without consequence in the real world** [emphasis mine], the desktop story world may engage our most compelling transformational fantasies [264, 268, 270–71].

All of Murray's predictions have come true, and all of her suggestions have been realized in a particular genre of videogame. Not coincidentally, this is the same genre that allows users to construct true avatars: the video role-playing game (v-RPG).

The History of Role-Playing Games

Of course, v-RPGs owe their origins to table-top role-playing games. *Dungeons & Dragons* (1974), created by Gary Gygax, was the first published table-top RPG. Eddie Dombrower provides a simple beginning definition for role-playing games, whether they be table-top or video: "The player assumes a persona that changes over time. The persona is assigned a range of physical and other attributes that change over time. These attributes also change as a result of the user's actions. The art of playing RPGs lies in mastering the complex relationships" (31) between the avatar and any given game situation. Gygax set *Dungeons & Dragons* (*D & D*) in a vast fantasy world inspired in part by J. R. R. Tolkien's Middle Earth, replete with magic and mythical creatures. Table-top RPGs need one person to perform the role of "dungeon master," who narrates the unfolding story for each individual gaming session, answers the players' questions about the gameworld, and takes on the role of any non-player characters[3] (NPCs) that were encountered during the session. *D & D* was enormously popular, and many additional table-top RPGs set in many additional fantastical worlds were quickly produced.[4] Table-top RPGs were epic open-ended affairs, with vast game worlds that could be expanded via the whims of dungeon masters' imaginations and endless adventuring and questing for the players' avatars. It didn't take long before techno-enthusiasts began to try to replicate the RPG experience virtually, and in 1975 several text-based v-RPGs came out for the PLATO[5] system. In 1980, Richard Garriott created *Akalabeth*, a graphical RPG that used vectoring lines much in the same way *Battlezone* did. Garriott's *Ultima* series, among the most successful v-RPGs of all time, was based on *Akalabeth*, The first v-RPG for a console system was created in 1982, when *Advanced Dungeons & Dragons: Treasure of Tarmin* debuted for the Intellivision. In 2007, v-RPGs remain among the most popular videogames, with MMORPGs such as *Everquest, Ultima Online*, and *World of Warcraft* each having hundreds of thousands of subscribers. However, single-player v-RPGs have been popular as well, with games such as *Final Fantasy X, Baldur's Gate, Knights of the Old Republic, Morrowind, Oblivion*, and *Mass Effect* all boasting strong sales and critical acclaim in recent years. With the continual development of computer technology, each new generation of v-RPG is now able to provide an arguably more immersive experience than table-top RPGs in all of the defining characteristics of the genre: a creative dungeon master (now "performed" by elaborate computer software), NPC interaction, a responsive, detailed environment, quantified assessment and evolution of the avatar's abilities, and a map of the game environment (Mackay 23–24). All of the v-RPGs mentioned here meet Murray's predictive criteria for immersive and emotionally meaningful videogames with open-ended game worlds and stories and most importantly for the purposes of this project, with customizable avatars. Indeed, it is the relationship between the user and their avatar that I explore to examine what identity connections exist. However, in order to study the relationships between the identity of the user and the identity of the avatar, a clear terminological framework is needed. For that framework, I turn to the writings of noted videogame scholar James Paul Gee.

Gee's Virtual, Real-World, and Projective Identities

In *What Video Games Have to Teach Us About Learning and Literacy* and *Why Video Games are Good for Your Soul*, Gee argues that in v-RPGs, three different distinct identities are involved. The first of these is a virtual identity: the avatar that exists in the fictionalized virtual gameworld. Gee provides the example of the half-elf named "Bead Bead" he created for the v-RPG *Arcanum*. The second type Gee calls real-world identity. For Gee, this is the "real-world character" (*What Video Games* 55) that sits down in front of a computer and plays the game. James Gee is a real-world identity: Gee has a physical body that exists (much of the time in Tempe, Arizona). However, Gee points out that each of us have many different "nonvirtual identities" at all times, identifying himself as a "professor, a linguist, an Anglo American, a middle-age male baby boomer, a parent, an avid reader, a former devout Catholic" (55) and so on. These multiple aspects of our identities are accessed by us as necessary as we encounter and react to life stimuli. Given Gee's notion of multiple identities, how does he characterize the interactions between his real-world identity

(James Gee) and his virtual identity (Bead Bead)? Gee describes Bead Bead as a "delicious blend of my doing and not my doing" (54–55) and to explain this he creates his third type of identity, projective identity, which he describes as:

> The kind of person I want Bead Bead to be, the kind of history I want her to have, the kind of person and history I am trying to build in and through her is what I mean by a projective identity. Since these aspirations are my desires for Bead Bead, the projective identity is both mine and hers, and it is a space in which I can transcend both her limitations and my own. . . . In this identity, the stress is on the interface between — the interactions between — the real-world person and the virtual character [56].

Gee's projective identity then is the middle ground between the real-world identity and the virtual identity of the user: the avatar. Like Gee, I too am interested in the relationship between the real-world identity of the user, the virtual identity of the avatar, and the connections and tensions that exist between these two types of identity.

Even though he never uses the word itself, Gee's description of projective identity as the bridge between the real-world and virtual identities suggests that he sees the projective identity as liminal space. Liminality, from the Latin word meaning "threshold," was used by Van Gennep in 1908 as part of his three-step sequence describing rites of passage: separation, liminality, and reincorporation. Liminality, the middle stage, was the phase where one belonged to both and neither of the other two phases: a phase of transition during which normal limits to self-understanding are relaxed thus opening the way to something new. Seeing Gee's projective identity as a type of liminality clarifies the ways other videogame scholars also consider the relationship between user and avatar as intriguing yet problematic space. Rehak discusses avatars and liminality in the following manner:

> Movement back and forth across the border separating self from other might therefore be considered a kind of liminal play. We create avatars to leave our bodies behind, yet take the body with us in the form of codes and assumptions about what does and does not constitute a legitimate interface with reality — virtual or otherwise. . . . The worlds we create — and the avatarial bodies through which we experience them — seem destined to mirror not our wholeness, but our lack of it [123, 124].

Flynn defines a liminal experience in gaming as a "moment of heightened pleasure as the player is briefly suspended between one realm of experience and another" (2). Both of these theoretical descriptions seem consistent with Gee's explanation of projective identity. Even Murray spoke of liminal objects, "located on the threshold between external reality and our own minds" (99). She described this balancing act: "In order to sustain such powerful immersive trances we have to do something inherently paradoxical: We have to keep the virtual world 'real' by keeping it 'not there.' We have to keep it balanced squarely on the enchanted threshold without letting it collapse onto either side" (100). All of these scholars, Gee included, seem convinced that the liminal, threshold space between the user and the videogame avatar is crucial to any identity formation that occurs as the result of v-RPG play. But is there reason to believe that such identity formation is actually occurring? Is there evidence to suggest that the real-world identities of v-RPG users are impacted in meaningful ways by their virtual identities? To find out, I turned my attention to two v-RPGs that I knew had large fan bases devoted to them, and in which I had personally felt strong connections to my own avatars: *The Elder Scrolls III: Morrowind* and *The Elder Scrolls IV: Oblivion.*[6]

Identity in Elderscrolls.com's *Morrowind* and *Oblivion* Forums

Both games are set in the Elder Scrolls fantasy universe[7] and are single-player v-RPGs. *Morrowind* was originally released in 2002 for PCs and the Xbox console system; *Oblivion* came out in 2006 for PCs and the Xbox 360. Both v-RPGs topped many videogame critics' "Game of the Year" lists and remain popular today.[8] This popularity is evidenced by the large number of postings in the *Morrowind* and *Oblivion* forums[9] at Elderscrolls.com, a comprehensive Web site devoted to the Elder Scrolls universe depicted in Bethesda Software's games. It was to these avid *Morrowind* and *Oblivion* gamers in the Elderscrolls.com forums that I turned to begin my examination of just how closely connected users believed their real-world identities were to their virtual identities. Joining the *Morrowind* forum, I posted the following entry: 15

> Is your *Morrowind* identity any less "real" than your real-world identity? If many of us are logging hundreds of hours with our *Morrowind* avatars (a virtual identity), what impact does this have on our "real" identity? In other words, does the time spent in *Morrowind* carry over/impact when you leave that virtual setting? I'm interested in hearing how you see your identities (real, virtual, and the intersection between these two) being impacted/influenced by *Morrowind.* Do you find your virtual *Morrowind* identity to be as "real" in some ways as your non-virtual identity? How does one inform the other?

I also posted a similar question in the *Oblivion* forum. The replies I received to these questions were fascinating as they highlighted what appeared to be a significant, dynamic, yet poorly understood relationship between the users' real-life identities and their virtual identities. Dante Nerevar wrote:

> In many ways I look at my character as me, except for the fact that my skin is not gray. I look at it like this: There are two of me, Nick [real-world identity] and Dante [virtual identity]. When not playing *Morrowind* I am Nick, but when I am I'm a completely different person. When I get lost in a virtual reality it is a good thing. Regardless, some of my characteristics influence Dante's and his influence mine [1].

Here, the user seems to contradict himself, at first stating that his two identities were "completely different" but later admitting to mutual influence between the two. Toastman shows a similar contradiction when he discusses the separation between his real-world identity and his *Morrowind* avatars:

> For me, playing a character in a game is like playing a character in a play or movie. I love getting completely absorbed in a new identity, discovering how he reacts that is different from my reactions. I do things in character that I would never, ever think of doing in real life, [but] for some of my characters I make decisions based on my own values. While the [avatars] are fun to play, they're not me. Sure, maybe they represent subconscious aspects of my personality, but while I may act somewhat differently when I'm with family, or friends, or coworkers, I'm still essentially the same. Any differences are mostly superficial. Even though my own identity can change depending on who I'm with, my *Morrowind* identities are less real to me than my own identity. I know that when the lights go down on the stage, or when I power down my computer, that I will be myself again [1].

Toastman is willing to admit that his real-world identity is constantly shifting given different stimuli, but isn't willing to concede that his virtual identity (which also evolves thanks to Toastman's reactions to stimuli) is as significant as his real-world identity. His last phrase is provocative: if he wasn't himself during his *Morrowind* gameplay, then who was he? Did his avatar have a life of its own? Toastman seems unwilling to concede that the relationship between himself and his avatar might be substantial in any way. Another gamer, Anais, chooses to distance herself from her avatar. In writing about her favorite *Oblivion* avatar, she says, "I find that with my most played Bosmer [an elf] we often have disagreements. She has solutions to problems that wouldn't occur to me. I also have to respect her wishes" (1). Here, she seems to suggest that her Bosmer virtual identity comes up with solutions to problems without any input from Anais' real-world identity. Of course, this is impossible, since the *Morrowind* avatar takes no actions that are not explicitly triggered by the user. These users all seem to be in denial about the connections between themselves and their avatars.

Other *Morrowind* and *Oblivion* gamers seemed much more comfortable acknowledging the reciprocal relationship between their real-world identity and their virtual identity via their avatar. Syronj wrote, "Shaka [the avatar] is an idealized version of what I would look up to in a character: brave and unselfish, whenever possible. I found that I'm not good at playing evil characters in the game. At the same time, I sometimes think the game has made me more likely to take a chance in real life" (1). Syronj credits her virtual experience in *Morrowind* with making her real-world identity braver. Danile also readily admits that her avatars are:

> Mainly how I would like to be in real life. Tough, and not taking any put downs or anything from anyone. But, like me, they are caring and do not hurt anyone if they do not have to. One of my current characters likes to go pearl diving and all the pearls he gets he sells to get money for widows and orphans. It's beyond me to be evil [1].

I can't help but notice in Danile's posting how she seems to unconsciously move from the avatar ("he") to herself ("me"). This was a common phenomenon in many gamers' postings. James Gee himself demonstrated a similar connection to his *Morrowind* avatar Bead when recounting the shame he felt when Bead disrobed at the request of an NPC to obtain information. Gee confesses that he ended up killing that NPC out of rage and shame shortly thereafter. He also admits to having guilt over killing a guard while stealing a weapon out of a museum: "We felt guilty about this murder to the end. Many times we wished we had re-played that part of the game to clear our record" (*Why Video Games* 94). Note Gee's usage of "we" and "our" in this statement; this usage reflects the first-person plurality of his videogame identity. Bob seems to share Danile's identification with her avatar, saying that he does "feel what my [*Oblivion*] characters must be feeling given the person they are and their situation in the game. I try to play according to their world view" (1). Another user blames his virtual-world struggles with addiction on his real-world identity's similar problems, as he admits to having logged over 1,000 hours playing *Morrowind* in a post that reminds me of Berger's statement at the start of this reading. The vrrc writes, "I have spent entire days doing nothing but playing *Morrowind*. Quite literally 18 hours a day, sometimes for several days in a row. I have a very addictive personality . . . which is also why I can't stay off the skooma"[10] (1).

The presence of a liminal projective identity between real-world and virtual identities was perhaps best articulated in these forums by the users named doctor44 and Bloom. Doctor44 acknowledges that his *Oblivion* avatars are really "expressions of myself. They express the darker sides of my personality that are inappropriate to express in the real world — it's a way to keep myself in balance in a safe and secure manner" (1). In describing his current *Morrowind* avatar Boris Karl, Bloom writes:

> It is amazing to me that Boris Karl is not even a level 5 character,[11] yet has walked around the entire circumference of Vvardenfell. He has been killed several times, but never has he been all that interested in leveling up. It's not in his nature. When Boris encounters something that interests Bloom, the two have a tendency to overlap, although I try to resist that . . . I think the middle ground between them (Boris and Bloom) is the arena of exploration and discovery. It is why I love the game as much as I do [1].

Other gamers expressed a similar and somewhat inexplicable fondness for their avatars. Cobb ruminated in the following manner about his *Oblivion* avatar: "I've stuck with the same character right through *Oblivion* — all 1000+ hours! She certainly isn't a 'perfect' character, in fact she's bloody useless — especially once mountain lions start appearing. I dunno, though, she's kind of grown on me even though I'm not sure what I was aiming for in the character creation stage. I've gotten so used to having her around" (1). Cobb's attachment to his female avatar is interesting indeed. Bloom and Cobb aren't alone in deriving pleasure from their Elder Scrolls video-game experiences as the following quote from Ice Troll illustrates: "Some consider *Morrowind* to be better than sex. I think they are exaggerating a bit, but it's pretty close" (1). Ice Troll's comment may well be tongue-in-cheek, but Bloom seems to believe that Boris and Bloom are both the same and different, joined and separate, that Boris has his own "nature" just as Bloom does. This tension between being/not being takes place in liminal space via Gee's projective identity as these replies from die-hard gamers strongly suggest.

Other postings in the *Morrowind* and *Oblivion* forums also suggest that the journey between real-world identity and virtual identity is not always instantaneous: it may take time for some gamers to complete the passage out of their virtual identity. One topical thread contained in both forums illustrated this clearly. It was entitled "You know you've played too much *Morrowind/Oblivion* when. . . ." Each user was invited to share an example that completed this sentence. Brayf provided the following response: "When somebody walks into the room while you're playing, and you try to turn and look at them by moving the mouse" (1). Padalin made the following confession: "When you're mad with a friend and you say 'khajiit has no words for you[12] and that actually happened to me whether you believe me or not" (1). Farterman suggested that "you know you have been playing too much when in REAL life you think of doing something bad that might affect you, and you ask yourself, 'Maybe I should save before I do this'" (1). Lonesniper admits to having real-world nightmares based on *Morrowind*: "When you have dreams about Corprus monsters[13] attacking you in the real world. Guilty" (1). Toast-man posted the following response to this topic thread: "When this happens to you: I was doing the Sanctus Shrine Temple Quest[14] and my housemate came into my room and asked me a question. It took me a few seconds to realize that I could actually talk to him without messing up the pilgrimage" (1). Toastman apparently needed a few seconds to move from his virtual identity to his real-world identity.

All of these postings seem to suggest that the virtual experiences the users had in *Morrowind* and *Oblivion* via their avatars were carrying over into their real-world experiences in certain ways.

But exactly how was this happening? And to what extent does the level of immersive identification with the avatar and gaming world in question dictate the time needed to transition out of a virtual identity? This preliminary examination of *Morrowind* and *Oblivion* gamers using Gee's terminological identity construct led me to some very interesting questions indeed: How do the virtual identities of avatars in v-RPGs get constructed? Using *Morrowind, Oblivion*, and *Fallout 3* as representative examples, what is the relationship between real-world identity, virtual identity, and projective identity in video role-playing games? Before examining data collected specifically from players of these three v-RPGs I need to first provide an overview of the theoretical fields relevant to these questions.

20

NOTES

[1] Many more important games and moments in the history and evolution of videogames exist. For more comprehensive historical coverage, see Dombrower (1998).

[2] The term "avatar" was first used in a virtual context in 1985 in the popular *Ultima* series of video role-playing games. *Ultima IV* (1985) named the player character "Avatar" and later games in the series followed suit. Other early videogames to specifically use the term in-game were *Habitat* (1987) and *Shadowrun* (1989). The term was first used to refer to an online virtual body in Neal Stephenson's 1992 cyberpunk classic *Snow Crash*. These important texts helped to familiarize videogame users and theorists with the term and it has been used with increasing frequency (albeit inconsistently) since the mid-1990s in MUDs, videogames, and to refer to Instant Messenger icons. Another landmark cyberpunk text ought to be mentioned here as well: William Gibson's *Neuromancer*. Released in 1985, the novel engrained the term "cyberspace" into popular consciousness. Gibson's notions of the benefits and risks of cyberspace interaction resonate within much of the scholarship quoted in this study.

[3] In RPG worlds, players create avatars to control and role-play. But many other characters are needed to flesh out the gaming experience and make the RPG world dynamic. For example, the player's avatar might discover a small inn located near the path they are traveling on. Staying at the inn is not free: the innkeeper must be talked to, and the price of lodging ascertained. The innkeeper is not being role-played by the user, but rather by the dungeon master, since the innkeeper is a "static" character whose attributes never change and who will likely never be seen in the RPG again once the avatar leaves the inn and ventures on. Many such non-player characters (NPCs) incorporate an RPG world, usually located in strategic spots to aid the avatar in some manner (such as providing food, shelter, and new equipment) or provide information to help further the current quest or narrative arc.

[4] Among the more popular table-top RPGs that capitalized on *Dungeons & Dragons'* success were *Tunnels and Trolls* (1975), *Traveller* (1977), and *Runequest* (1978).

[5] PLATO (Programmed Logic for Automatic Teaching Operations) was one of the first computer-assisted instruction systems and was created at the University of Illinois.

[6] As you've likely already guessed, I am an avid videogame player. I estimate that I logged over 200 hours playing *Morrowind* and over 100 hours so far in *Oblivion*. I remain fascinated by the large scope of both gameworlds and the open-ended nature of the choices available to the avatars. If one wants to study videogames, one must also play videogames (just as a film critic must watch a film to be able to critique it). All of my gameplay time in *Morrowind* was spent with one avatar, a dark Elf female named Zaara. All of my *Oblivion* experiences have been with a Wood Elf named Zach (who looks suspiciously like me).

[7] Bethesda's *Elder Scrolls* series pioneered open-ended worlds and freeform gameplay, where players could go and do whatever they wanted. The series began in 1994 with the release of *Arena*, continued with *Daggerfall* in 1996, *Morrowind* in 2002, and *Oblivion* in 2006. Each game is popularly known without the Elder Scrolls designation; henceforth in this study I will refer to the games simply as *Morrowind* and *Oblivion*.

[8] Bethesda Softworks Web site (www.bethsoft.com/news/) lists several of the gaming magazines and Web sites that selected *Morrowind* as 2002's best videogame and *Oblivion* as 2006's best videogame. Among them are *Gamespot*, *Gamespy*, *Game Chronicles*, and *USA Today*.

[9] For example, on August 22, 2007, there were 296 different topic threads in the Elderscrolls *Morrowind* forum. Among these were questions related to the game

("What does the Pool of Forgetfulness do?" "Can you become a vampire while carrying vampire dust?"), surveys related to the game ("What is the best weapon in the game?" "What is the worst town or city in the game?"), and threads solely devoted to the statistics and attributes of the users' avatars. Many other types of threads exist as well.

[10]In *Morrowind* and *Oblivion*, skooma is an extremely addictive illegal narcotic, similar to crack cocaine or heroin. Many NPCs in the game will not even speak to the user's avatar if the avatar has skooma in their possession.

[11]As previously noted, part of the appeal of v-RPGs is the ability to customize the avatar, both at the beginning of the game and as the gameplay progresses. The avatar continually gains experience in *Morrowind* by repeatedly using their skills (whether the skills be swinging a sword, casting spells, repairing armor, bartering with NPCs, etc.). When a certain number of skills have been increased, the avatar may then "level up": the user is allowed to choose which primary attributes to strengthen. A level five character indicates very little progression in terms of strengthening the avatar's skills and overall abilities. The maximum level for all attributes and skills is 100.

[12]In the Elder Scrolls universe, the khajiit are a feline-like species: the user's avatar may be khajiit if they wish. Khajiit NPCs encountered in the game will often say, "Khajiit has no words for you" to someone (usually the avatar) they are disgusted by. It is the greatest verbal insult the species can utter.

[13]Corprus is a contagious, incurable disease which distorts the features of the victim and effectively turns them into a mindless zombie. Catching corprus is one of the greatest fears of *Morrowind*'s denizens.

[14]This quest in *Morrowind* can only be completed if the avatar avoids detection by any NPCs on the way to the shrine. This requires stealthy movement and no speaking to any other diegetic characters.

BIBLIOGRAPHY

Berger, Arthur Asa. *Video Games; A Popular Culture Phenomenon*. New Brunswick, NJ: Transaction Publishers, 2002.

Bloom. "Real vs. virtual identity." *Morrowind* general discussion. December 14, 2005. www.elderscrolls.com/forums.

Brayf. "You know you've played too much Morrowind when . . ." *Morrowind* general discussion. December 2, 2005. www.elderscrolls.com/forums.

Cobb. "Real vs. virtual identity." *Oblivion* general discussion. September 2, 2008. www.elderscrolls.com/forums.

Dombrower, Eddie. *Dombrower's Art of Interactive Entertainment Design*. New York: McGraw-Hill, 1998.

Entertainment Software Association. "Top Ten Industry Facts, 2005." 17 May 2006. http://www.theesa.com.

Filiciak, Miroslaw. "Hyperidentities: Postmodern Identity Patterns in Massively Multiplayer Online Role-Playing Games." *The Video Game Theory Reader*. Mark J. P. Wolf and Bernard Perron, eds. New York: Routledge, 2003. 87–102.

Flynn, Bernadette. "Language of Navigation Within Computer Games." *Fine Art Forum* 17, no. 8 (2003). http://www.fineartforum.org/backissues/Vol_17/index.html.

Gee, James Paul. *What Video Games Have to Teach Us About Learning and Literacy*. New York: Palgrave Macmillan, 2004.

Goldberg, Athomas. "Avatars and Agents, or Life Among the Indigenous Peoples of Cyberspace." In *Digital Illusion: Entertaining the Future with High Technology*, edited by Clark Dodsworth Jr., 161–80. New York: Addison-Wesley, 1997.

Hayles, N. Katherine. *How We Became Posthuman: Virtual Bodies in Cybernetics, Literature, and Informatics*. Chicago: University of Chicago Press, 1999.

Ice Troll. "Real vs. virtual identity." *Morrowind* general discussion. December 14, 2005. www.elderscrolls.com/forums.

Lonesniper. "You know you've played too much Morrowind when . . ." *Morrowind* general discussion. December 2, 2005. www.elderscolls.com/forums.

Mackay, Daniel. *The Fantasy Role-Playing Game.* Jefferson, NC: McFarland, 2001.

Murray, Janet H. *Hamlet on the Holodeck: The Future of Narrative in Cyberspace.* New York: Simon and Schuster, 1997.

Padalin. "You know you've played too much Morrowind when . . ." *Morrowind* general discussion. December 2, 2005. www.elderscrolls.com/forums.

Pearce, Celia. "Game Noir: A Conversation with Tim Schafer." *Game Studies* 3, no. 3 (2003). http://www.gamestudies.org.

Rehak, Bob. "Playing at Being: Psychoanalysis and the Avatar." In *The Video Game Theory Reader,* edited by Mark J. P. Wolf and Bernard Perron, 103–27. New York: Routledge, 2003.

Syronj. "Real vs. virtual identity." *Morrowind* general discussion. December 14, 2005. www.elderscrolls.com/forums.

Toastman. "Real vs. virtual identity." *Morrowind* general discussion. December 14, 2005. www.elderscrolls.com/forums.

Wilson, Laetitia. "Interactivity or Interpassivity: A Question of Agency in Digital Play." *Fine Art Forum* 17, no. 8 (2003). http://www.fineartforum.org/Backissues/Vol_17/index.html.

READING THE TEXT

1. How does Waggoner use personal experience to introduce his topic? Is it effective? Why, or why not?

2. According to Waggoner's definition, what is an "avatar"? How does it differ from an "agent"?

3. How does the use of avatars in videogames blur the line "between real and virtual identities," in Waggoner's view?

4. What three identities are involved in role-playing videogames, according to James Paul Gee?

5. What responses did Waggoner get to the questions about videogame identity he posted on the *Morrowind* and *Oblivion* forums?

READING THE SIGNS

1. If you play role-playing videogames, discuss your experiences in a journal entry. Have you created your own avatar? If so, what criteria did you use for its design?

2. Write an essay arguing for or against the proposition that the heavy use of role-playing videogames can blur one's ability to distinguish between fantasy and reality.

3. Interview friends who play role-playing videogames and ask them about their experiences with creating avatars. Which of James Paul Gee's three categories of identity do they fit? How closely linked are their real-world identities

and their virtual identities? Use your results to propose your own answer to Waggoner's question "Can videogame play impact identity formation?"

4. Research the history of role-playing videogames and write an analysis of the sorts of experience that they offer. Are there any patterns to the kinds of games that are most popular? Use your analysis to propose your own argument about why the most popular games earn that status.

5. Drawing upon your own experience playing videogames or that of friends, write an essay that responds to Arthur Asa Berger's query: "Will new videogames become a kind of opiate for people who can find an outlet in simulations that seem better than those offered by their real-life experiences?" (qtd. in para. 3).

A. B. HARRIS

Average Gamers Please Step Forward

Are you an "average gamer"? If you are, you must be a "male head-of-household professional" in your early thirties and "read books or daily newspapers on a regular basis," at least according to the Entertainment Software Association. Sound peculiar? It does to A. B. Harris, who really is an average gamer but who is well aware that, according to common opinion, gamers are mostly over-sexed male adolescents with a penchant for violence. Arguing in this "Speak Out" piece for *Computer Games* that game magazines and gamers themselves are at least partly responsible for their "sordid and seedy" reputation, Harris calls for his fellow average game players to make themselves heard and demonstrate that they are "far more credible and intelligent" than their public image would suggest. Maybe this calls for a new *World of Warcraft* chess-playing character. A. B. Harris is an average reader of *Computer Games*.

According to the Entertainment Software Association, I'm the average gamer. I'm a male head-of-household professional in my early 30s, and I play games almost eight hours a week. I even fit some of the ESA's more obscure data, such as "devoting more than triple the amount of time spent playing games each week to exercising . . . creative endeavors . . . [and] cultural activities," as well as "reading books or daily newspapers on a regular basis." Is this sufficiently average?

How about — hold on to your hats — "exhibit a high level of interest in current events . . . [and] vote in most of the elections for which they are eligible"?

That's me, the ESA's poster child for gaming.

So why is it that, when I attempt a nonpartisan appraisal of my alleged brethren in the gaming populace at large, I feel so different? So alone? Consider the recent next-generation console launches: All across the country myriad gamers queued up outside their favorite big-box retailers, sometimes up to a week in advance. Surely within this dedicated group, I thought to myself, I'd find a generous sampling of the average gamer. But in the amateur, shaky-cam event coverage, I saw not professional early-30s heads of household, but a motley group of Mountain Dew–addicted juveniles who had somehow shirked life's responsibilities for a week-long urban campout. Wondering whether my initial judgment was biased, I watched on, as people in line were briefly interviewed. Unsettling snatches of conversation, tantamount to leet-speak, confirmed my fears — I was certainly not a member of this stratum of the population, be they average gamers or potential eBay sellers.

Dumbfounded, I silently asked where exactly the ESA had gathered its data. Perhaps it was merely pandering to the mainstream press and its portrayal of gaming. But this assertion was promptly nullified, for I knew all too well that the plebeian view of gaming is rife with Hot Coffee–style shenanigans and ghastly tales of game-induced violence. Games are, according to mainstream media and the general public, a sordid and seedy form of entertainment, debauching our youth with sex and violence — which is a far cry from what the ESA suggests.

I therefore shifted my attention away from the mainstream to focus on the gaming press itself. Certainly our industry has a responsibility to represent the average gamer, to be able to define its veritable consumer base? Or so one would think!

But, after scrutinizing game magazine advertisements and fan forums, gamer interviews and reviews, I found no solace in what I discovered. Aside from occasional clever advertisements and infrequent constructive commentary, I found brainless ads and immature journalism. Sex and violence? Check. Tasteless banter? You bet. Shallow visual appeal? All present and accounted for. A sophisticated and insightful manner? Bueller? Bueller?

Years ago, when the videogaming industry was in its infancy, the brainless ads and immature journalism might have been more acceptable, for all young industries have a learning curve. More importantly, the average gamer certainly wasn't the professional, early-30s head of household, but was more likely to be a teenage technology enthusiast that the mainstream would deem a "nerd."

But this is the year 2007, not 1982. Within that quarter-century, this industry has seen an untold degree of technological evolution, surpassing anything before. More than ever, we have seemingly limitless options in the games available to us. We are closer than ever to creating truly virtual worlds that permit us to indulge the desire for personal experiences impossible in real life. And as time goes on, this evolution will assuredly continue unabated.

But some perplexing questions remain: If gaming has evolved to such a 10 great degree, why have the culture surrounding gaming and the mainstream's opinion of that culture remained inert? And if indeed our industry's culture is stagnant or, worse yet, actually devolving, who exactly is to blame? Furthermore, what steps can be taken to rectify the debasement?

I alone can offer no solid answers to the above inquiries. Nor can the gaming magazines, journalists, and marketers; they simply cater to the perceived gamer demographic, the "average" gamer.

And what about the ESA's gamer profile? Although my findings suggest an entirely different profile, I still maintain the ESA in high regard. In fact, I consider their Game Player Data to be a paradigm to which we should all aspire. Dear friends, consider this a call to arms to demonstrate to not only our fellow gamers but also the general public that we are far more credible and intelligent than our perceived demographic suggests. Consider this a plea for us to serve as ambassadors, whether among our own or in foreign company. To maintain our awareness of gaming academia and share this knowledge with non-gamers. To live up to our average gamer profile. As a group of responsible gamers, we can change the mainstream.

READING THE TEXT

1. Summarize the profile of the average gamer, as described by the Entertainment Software Association.

2. According to Harris, what is the mainstream image of gamers?

3. How has advertising contributed to the mainstream image of gamers?

READING THE SIGNS

1. Write a semiotic analysis of a gaming magazine like *Computer Games*, focusing on the image of gamers that the magazine, including its advertising and editorial content, projects. Does the magazine reflect the identity of the "average gamer," as Harris would wish, or of the mainstream stereotype that he decries?

2. If you are an online game player, write a journal entry in which you assess whether you and your acquaintances fit the popular image of a gamer. How might your choice of game sites affect the image that is constructed?

3. The mainstream image of a gamer is male. Visit a fan forum for a game that appeals to women or to both genders, such as *The Sims*, and study the image of gamers it presents. To what extent does it reflect or deviate from the stereotype that Harris describes?

4. **CONNECTING TEXTS**   Harris issues a "call to arms" (para. 12) to fellow gamers, much in the way Gloria Steinem ("Sex, Lies, and Advertising," p. 249) also concludes her selection with an appeal to readers for social and political changes. Study the appeal for change in the two selections. To what extent do you find them effective, and why? In what ways might the intended readership of the selections affect their persuasiveness?

Master Chief Waits in Line

READING THE SIGNS

1. Jim Cush, of Babylon, New York, was photographed waiting in line dressed as Master Chief, the hero of the videogame *Halo 3*, with other fans waiting to buy the game in Manhattan on September 24, 2007. What is your initial reaction to this photograph?

2. What, typically, is the purpose of putting on a costume? What does it allow the wearer to do? In what ways is a gaming avatar, which the user can personalize (such as those in *Second Life*), like a costume?

3. **CONNECTING TEXTS** Cush says he spent several thousand dollars creating his Master Chief outfit; he was not paid by Microsoft to promote the release of the game. What statement does that make about the intersection of commercial culture with personal identity? Speculate on reasons why Cush may have worn this outfit. Would you ever feel so devoted to a product that you would dress as a character derived from it? Why, or why not? You might enrich your analysis by consulting Linda Seger's "Creating the Myth" (p. 386).

4. Consider the meaning of the name "Master Chief" and try to account for the purposes of the parts of the Master Chief outfit. Then consider what associations you can make with the Master Chief costume. What other costumes, outfits, or uniforms does it remind you of? What elements of the human body does it exaggerate? What elements does it hide? To what end?

JONATHAN RAUCH

The Tea Party Online

Though they are inspired by the doings of the eighteenth-century Bostonians who threw English tea into Boston Harbor, the members of the Tea Party movement are not averse to using contemporary technology to advance their cause. In fact, as Jonathan Rauch reports, the Tea Party has been able to transform a decentralized political movement — "The Tea Party began as a network, not an organization, and that is what it mostly remains," Rauch writes — into a national powerhouse largely through its exploitation of the resources of the Internet. The ideological mirror image of MoveOn.org, the Tea Party is yet another signifier of a wired society; whether it will succeed in its goal to change American consciousness is something that Rauch does not predict. A journalist who has worked for the *National Journal* and *The Atlantic*, Rauch has published numerous articles and books, including *Gay Marriage: Why It Is Good for Gays, Good for Straights, and Good for America* (2004) and *Government's End: Why Washington Stopped Working* (2000).

Though headless, the Tea Party movement is not mindless. Its collective brain meets every Monday night.

More than two hundred leaders of local Tea Parties — coordinators, as they usually call themselves — join a conference call organized by an umbrella group called the Tea Party Patriots, the largest national Tea Party organization. Organizers estimate that membership totals about fifteen million.

On one Monday recently, three national coordinators began the session with a rundown on plans for upcoming rallies. The group was polled on whether to hold a second round of house parties throughout the country. A coordinator gave an update on an iPhone app for Tea Partiers who will be going door to door this fall to talk to voters.

The floor was then opened. Rick, from Albuquerque, N.M., asks if the national agenda includes investigating voter-roll irregularities, something his group is concerned about. Mark Meckler, a Tea Party Patriots coordinator and cofounder, weighed in. Newcomers "often don't understand how badly we need you to lead the way," he says. "If this is an area of concern to you," he admonishes, "the way the Tea Party Patriots works is that you guys really lead the organization."

"Essentially what we're doing is crowd-sourcing," says Meckler, whose vocabulary betrays his background as a lawyer specializing in Internet law. "I use the term open-source politics. This is an open-source movement." Every day, anyone and everyone is modifying the code. "The movement as a whole is smart." 5

And, as was apparent in Delaware, the movement is gaining power. Christine O'Donnell's upset victory in the Republican primary for the U.S. Senate, coming on the heels of insurgent candidates backed by the Tea Party winning in GOP Senate primaries in Alaska, Kentucky, Nevada, and Utah, has made the Tea Party movement a force.

The question now is whether a grassroots movement that is, by design, leaderless can sustain itself after this election cycle.

In American politics, radical decentralization has never been tried on so large a scale. Tea Party activists believe that their hivelike structure is their signal innovation and secret weapon, the key to outlasting and outmaneuvering traditional political organizations and interest groups. They intend to rewrite the rule book for political organizing, turning decades of established practice upside down. If they succeed, or even half succeed, the Tea Party's most important legacy may be organizational, not political.

From Washington's who's-in-charge-here perspective, the Tea Party model seems downright bizarre. Perplexed journalists keep looking for the movement's leaders, which is like asking to meet the boss of the Internet. Baffled politicians and lobbyists can't find anyone to negotiate with.

"There's such a uniqueness to every one of these groups, just as there's an individuality to every person," says Dawn Wildman, a national coordinator based in San Diego. "It has this bizarre organic flow, a little bit like lava. It heats up in some places and catches on fire; it moves more slowly in other places." 10

Lava is a pretty good analogy. Ask the activists to characterize their organizational structure, however, and usually they will say it is a starfish.

The Starfish and the Spider, a business book by Ori Brafman and Rod A. Beckstrom, was published in 2006 to no attention at all in the political world. The subtitle, however, explains its relevance to the Tea Party model: "The Unstoppable Power of Leaderless Organizations."

Traditional thinking, the book contends, holds that hierarchies are most efficient at getting things done. Hierarchies, such as corporations, have leaders who can make decisions and set priorities and chains of command to hold everyone accountable. This type of system has a central command, like a spider's brain. Like the spider, it dies if you thump it on the head.

The rise of the Internet and other forms of instantaneous, interpersonal interaction, however, has broken the spider monopoly, Brafman and Beckstrom argue. Radically decentralized networks — everything from illicit music-sharing systems to Wikipedia — can direct resources and adapt ("mutate") far faster than corporations can. "The absence of structure, leadership, and formal organization, once considered a weakness, has become a major asset," the authors write. "Seemingly chaotic groups have challenged and defeated established institutions. The rules of the game have changed."

In decentralized networks, knowledge and power are distributed throughout the system. As a result, the network is impervious to decapitation. No foolish or self-serving boss can wreck it, because it has no boss. 15

Fragmentation, the bane of traditional organizations, actually makes the network stronger. It is like a starfish: Cut off an arm, and it grows (in some species) into a new starfish. Result: two starfish, where before there was just one.

"We're a starfish organization," says Scott Boston, the Tea Party Patriots' educational coordinator, and a rare paid staffer.

Will it work?

Answering the skeptics, Tea Partiers point out that bygone efforts at radical decentralization lacked Internet-age networking and communications technologies — without which, of course, the Tea Party movement could not have arisen in the first place. The Tea Party Patriots' very existence suggests that something new is afoot. One coordinator notes that Facebook alone allows the movement to communicate with up to two million people simultaneously.

Listening to Tea Partiers talk about their ambitions, one hears echoes of leftist movements. Raise consciousness. Change hearts, not just votes. Attack corruption in society, not just on Capitol Hill. In America, right-wing movements have tended to focus on taking over politics, left-wing ones on changing the culture. Like its leftist precursors, the Tea Party Patriots thinks of itself as a social movement, not a political one.

Centerless swarms are bad at deal-making practical politics. But they may   20
be pretty good at cultural reform. In any case, the experiment begins.

READING THE TEXT

1. What does Tea Party cofounder Mark Meckler mean by calling the Tea Party an "open-source movement" (para. 5)?

2. How does the Tea Party's power structure differ from the traditional Washington, D.C., power structure?

3. According to Rauch, how is the Tea Party like a starfish? How does it differ from a spider?

4. What echoes of the rhetoric of leftist movements does Rauch hear in Tea Party discussions?

READING THE SIGNS

1. The Tea Party claims to be an independent movement, but all of its candidates in the 2010 elections ran within the Republican Party. Write an essay arguing for or against the proposition that the Tea Party represents an ideological wing of the Republican Party rather than an independent political organization.

2. Write an essay in which you analyze the extent to which Wikipedia is indeed analogous to a "starfish" organization, as Rauch suggests.

3. According to Rauch, "the Tea Party Patriots thinks of itself as a social movement, not a political movement." Write an essay in which you define the

kind of "social movement" the Tea Party might be, focusing on its use of the Internet to promote its cause.

4. **CONNECTING TEXTS**   In "Implications of User Choice: The Cultural Logic of 'My-Space or Facebook?'" (p. 475), danah boyd discusses how social networking sites tend to replicate, not challenge, the social status quo. Read or reread her essay, and using it as a critical framework assess the assumption that the Tea Party can "rewrite the rule book for political organizing" (para. 8) through the use of social media.

AMERICAN PARADOX

Culture, Conflict, and Contradiction in the U.S.A.

Be Stupid

You've probably seen the ads: Images of young men and women doing something that looks rather, well, stupid—getting sat on by an elephant, attacking a tiger, lighting a bonfire while wearing nothing but briefs, getting their heads stuck in a mailbox, stashing one girlfriend under the bed to make room for the other girlfriend, and did we mention having sex? Lots of sex. The ads are for Diesel clothing and accessories, and they combine elements of the Gap's James Dean [et. al.] Wore Khakis series, Levi's Go Forth campaign, and the Abercrombie and Fitch catalogs that essentially promise that if you purchase their clothes you will have plenty of entertaining opportunities to take them off.

The Diesel Be Stupid campaign is a textbook case of the many contradictions within American culture and the ways that they can lead both to **commodification** and conflict. Why would we be concerned with such contradictions in this book, which emphasizes how **signs** so permeate our shared culture that we tend to take them for granted? As we've discussed in the general Introduction, when analyzing popular culture, to arrive at a meaningful interpretation (as opposed to an obvious one), you should consider the **mythologies** that underlie our cultural preferences, the deep-seated beliefs that tell us that X idea or image makes sense or is attractive or funny, or that Y idea is wrong, ugly, or dull. And America's mythologies can be remarkably contradictory. Now, in nations that have a unicultural heritage, the dominant social mythologies tend to erase conflicts and contradictions (though they may exist underground, especially in totalitarian states). But, thanks to

513

Exploring the Signs of American Contradictions

The Janet Jackson–Justin Timberlake "wardrobe malfunction" during the 2004 Super Bowl half-time show led to heightened sensitivity to supposedly offensive episodes in the media, with increased FCC monitoring of programming and with Congress increasing fines for indecency. In your journal, explore the consequences of these responses. Do you regard them as a contradiction between the need to protect audiences, especially children, on the one hand, and the constitutional guarantee of freedom of speech, on the other?

America's complex **multicultural**, multipolitical, and democratic history, it's not surprising that our nation's most fundamental beliefs so often appear bifurcated, with one belief system challenging another, leading to the endless rancor and debate that is not allowed in some countries.

Thus, to interpret the contradictions to be found in the Diesel Be Stupid campaign it would be useful first to look at the broader American cultural context within which the Diesel ads signify. Since the contradictions that divide Americans are most apparent in our political system, we'll begin there.

What's Red and Blue and Mad All Over?

In 2000, America split right down the middle in a presidential election in which the candidate who won the popular vote lost the election by one vote in the Electoral College. At the time, maps showing the states that leaned Republican color-coded them red, while color-coding the states that went Democratic blue, and since then it has been common to refer to the political and cultural differences that divide the country as "red state" (roughly the South, the Midwest, and the noncoastal West) and "blue state" (the East Coast north of Virginia, the Old Northwest states, and the West Coast). Although these terms run the risk of overgeneralization, red and blue states do tend to take different sides in relation to America's ideological contradictions, and with the recent rise of the so-called Tea Party movement, this division has been accentuated. Given the cultural as well as political implications of what is in effect a growing conflict within American society, a survey of some of these contradictions can be illuminating.

Puritanism vs. the Sexual Revolution. Prior to the sexual revolution of the 1960s–1970s, puritanism was the dominant code in American attitudes toward human sexuality. We inherit this ideology from the Puritans themselves, who founded the Massachusetts Bay Colony in the 1620s. Deeply repressive of any expression of sexuality, puritanism in America had become so striking by the nineteenth century that British visitors began to joke about finding the legs of American pianos draped in woolen stockings to avoid the exposure of a bare leg. It was this puritanical streak that caused the notorious filming of Elvis Presley from the waist up when he first performed on *The Ed Sullivan Show* in the 1950s (broadcasters objected to the King's vigorous pelvic gyrations). And it prompted a cultural backlash against such early rock 'n' rollers as Chuck Berry (arrested on a Mann Act violation), Little Richard (who performed in drag), and Jerry Lee Lewis (who married his thirteen-year-old cousin) that led to the popularization of squeaky-clean performers like Pat Boone and Debbie Reynolds.

But in the wake of the "Summer of Love" in 1967, a sexual revolution swept America, a revolution that divides red state and blue state attitudes to this day. This transformation is especially apparent in our popular culture, and is one reason why red staters tend to despise and mistrust the entertainment industry. An America that once judicially banned James Joyce's classic novel *Ulysses* because it contained a brothel scene, a soliloquy on oral sex, and the "F" word now can transform a classic children's story like *The Cat in the Hat* into a movie filled with off-color humor. Prime-time TV programs like *Desperate Housewives* (which staged its own sexually revealing NFL stunt in 2004 on behalf of some free publicity) turn the asexual suburbs of the classic sitcoms upside down, while in the aftermath of such early, and racy, reality TV hits as *The Real World* and *Temptation Island* we now have *Jersey Shore*.

Populism vs. Elitism. Described in detail in one of this chapter's readings, "Masters of Desire," this contradiction concerns our tendency to embrace cultural populism and social elitism simultaneously. That is to say, Americans at once value the democratic society "of the people, by the people, and for the people" that Abraham Lincoln so eloquently described in the Gettysburg Address, while at the same time we embrace an American dream that urges us to rise above the crowd to achieve elite status, power, and wealth. Thus, in the eighteenth century, a French-born American writer named Michel-Guillaume-Jean de Crevècoeur could celebrate an American society that, unlike aristocratic Europe, did not contain large gaps between rich and poor (or so he claimed), but at the same time, Americans today can turn the television show *The Apprentice*, which stars a billionaire who got his start by inheriting millions, into a hit, and subscribe to a magazine like *Fortune*, whose primary purpose is to let us know who really has the bucks.

Those who hold red state opinions tend to be populist in their point of view, regarding themselves as "Heartland" Americans and accusing coastal blue staters of cultural as well as economic "elitism." Thus, they tend to be hostile to both New York City, which is the financial services capital of the nation, and Los Angeles, which is the entertainment capital, preferring small town and rural America.

Individualism vs. Conformity. America's tradition of self-reliant individualism runs side by side with a tendency toward conformity that prompts us to be just like everybody else. Thus, where Ralph Waldo Emerson and Henry

David Thoreau propounded the virtues of self-reliance and marching to the beat of a different drummer, and Americans to this day tend to mistrust centralized governmental institutions that limit personal freedom, America is also the country that in the McCarthyite 1950s compelled its citizens to conform to a middle-class standard of conduct and appearance, looking askance at the odd individual who happened to grow a beard or refused to wear a business suit, and threatening him with an accusation of being a communist. And even today in small-town America, individuals can experience enormous social pressures to join the same churches as their neighbors and, generally, to live the same sort of lives.

Social Responsibility vs. Libertarianism. It is in this country's politics and economy that we see the conflict between American altruism, which led to Social Security, Medicare, and federal and state welfare programs, and the libertarianism that draws Americans to the novels of Ayn Rand. We like to think of ourselves as a caring, charitable people, but we hate paying taxes. We like social services, but we don't like to make personal sacrifices to pay for them. If you happen to attend a public college, you know about this contradiction firsthand: Your tuition is probably rising because the people of your state will not pay higher taxes to support higher education, conveniently placing the burden on you.

Materialism vs. Spirituality. On a more personal level, America's materialistic adoration of money and possessions often clashes with its commitment to religion and spirituality. The same land that attracted John Smith to Jamestown in 1607 in search of instant and easy wealth also attracted the Pilgrims in 1620 in search of religious freedom, along with Puritans in search of a place to build a theocratic "city on a hill." The most consumer-oriented society in history, America is also a place where some 80 percent of the population claims to be religious. Perhaps nothing better exemplifies this contradiction than the American Christmas, which combines the rituals of Christianity with the rituals of rampant consumerism. Every year we hear complaints about this, but no one does anything about it—which is perhaps just as well because, with a quarter of the nation's retail sales taking place during the Christmas season, the economy would collapse if anything actually happened to change it.

Equality vs. Inequality. Last but by no means least, there is the contradiction between America's grand declaration of universal human freedom and equality in the Declaration of Independence and its racial history, which has witnessed institutionalized African slavery, the destruction of indigenous peoples, and the general marginalization of nonwhite Americans. This is a contradiction and not an exception. That it coexists with a genuine history of promoting freedom and equality does not erase its painful existence, nor does it reduce its continuing potential to divide rather than unite us.

When we look at red state vs. blue state values, we find that the red states tend to lean toward sexual puritanism, socioeconomic populism, self-reliant libertarianism, and religiosity (many such states belong to the so-called Bible Belt, for example). And while the matter is explosively con-troversial, the fact remains that every state in the former Confederacy was registered in the red column in the election that launched the whole dichotomy in the first place, which is something that cannot be ignored in a consideration of the racial attitudes of red state politics. On the flip side, blue states tend to be more sexually liberated, are the sites of economic power, are more prone to support social spending, are more secular, and are more racially diverse than red states. Of course, within every state there is a mixture of both sets of values, but this too leads to conflict rather than consensus in states like California, where representatives of each set of values cannot work together in the legislature, just as major legislation in Washington, D.C., can be accomplished only by super majorities to over-come partisan filibustering.

The Tea Party

The presidential election in 2008 temporarily suggested that perhaps the divi-sion between red state and blue state values was on the mend, with a num-ber of traditional red states voting for Barack Obama. But the emergence of the so-called Tea Party movement in 2009–2010 indicates otherwise. Self-consciously populist in orientation, the Tea Party continues the populist tra-dition of opposition to financial and cultural elites (Sarah Palin regards Tea Party members as "Real Americans," as opposed to the, presumably, "unreal" Americans on the coasts), leveling much of its resentment against the finan-cial services industry and the federal bailout that was inaugurated to prevent its collapse. Reviving something of the tradition of Jacksonian democracy, the anti-tax Tea Party also has become a rallying ground for opposition to the tradition of Franklin Delano Roosevelt, making many of the same accusa-tions against current governmental social spending programs that were made against Roosevelt in the 1930s.

Discussing the Signs of American Contradictions

In class, discuss the results of the 2008 presidential and 2010 midterm elections. Do you find in the results a fundamental divide between the values and political positions of the so-called blue and red states? If students hail from different states, compare the political climates in your home states; if most of the class comes from one state, consider whether your state has an internal red-blue divide. If you see differ-ences in political attitudes, what are they, and who is aligned with which positions?

Proponents of the Tea Party view themselves as being in opposition to both of the major political parties in America, insisting upon their independence from either the Republicans or the Democrats. Such a stand might indicate that the Tea Party is actually offering a way around the old conflicts and contradictions and blazing a path toward a new synthesis to replace the old antitheses. But the fact that, at least to date, every Tea Party–endorsed candidate who has made a run for office has done so from within the Republican party, making a challenge to that party on the basis of a clearly announced demand for an ideological movement to the right, indicates that rather than leading to synthesis the Tea Party is only intensifying the antithesis between liberal and conservative politics in America. Occupying not a middle ground but a position on the ideological frontier, the Tea Party is a signifier of an intensification of the red state/blue state divide, not a mediation.

Conservative, populist, individualistic, and libertarian, the Tea Party has also been unable to mediate the racial controversies that roil America's op-

A family attends a Tea Party rally.

positional politics today, highlighting the ideological wedge that has been driven into the conflict-laden landscape of American politics. This wedge is quite visible within popular culture, especially in the competition between Fox News (with such affiliates as Rush Limbaugh and Glenn Beck) and programs like *The Daily Show* and *The Colbert Report*. (This conflict assumed dramatic propositions when Glenn Beck and Jon Stewart held competing political rallies in Washington, D.C., in 2010.)

Hostile to the point of belligerency, the competing infotainment sources mirror deep social divisions that can ultimately be traced to many of the contradictions we have just surveyed. When Americans no longer get their news from the same sources (once, everyone, regardless of party affiliation, tuned in to the same network news sources, which attempted to avoid taking partisan positions) but instead get their information pre-filtered to suit already-taken political positions, the conflict only grows. Public debate and discourse becomes mere ranting and invective in a culture of contradiction rather than consensus.

Be Really Stupid

We're now ready to look more closely at the Diesel Be Stupid campaign. With its uninhibited appeal to sexuality, it is very much a blue state affair, rejecting the old puritan traditions on behalf of the sexual revolution. But beyond its obvious sexual appeal, it is very much worth a deeper semiotic analysis to identify the conflicting mythologies that shape it.

First, we have to make clear that being "stupid" in the Diesel ads doesn't really mean being stupid; it means being daring or independent, creative or rebellious. Being stupid is the new "marching to the beat of a different drummer," as if "Henry David Thoreau Wore Khakis." And that highlights the first contradiction we can see in the Diesel ads: American culture is simultaneously highly conformist and individualistic. We cherish Thoreau — he chose to live alone and on his own terms at Walden Pond — even as we live in a society of mass consumption wherein we buy the same mass-produced products and follow the same fashions. Such a contradiction, lived out by most Americans without realizing it, is what made possible ad campaigns like Reebok's Let U be U series, which said, in effect, "you can express your unique individuality by wearing a pair of mass-produced sneakers that are identical to millions of other sneakers being worn by millions of other people who are expressing their uniqueness by wearing the same shoes that you do." And it is exactly the same logic at work in the Diesel campaign: If you buy the company's mass-produced clothing and accessories, you will be just like the daring, creative, independent, rebellious, and sexy models in the ads. These ads are designed to appeal to millions who are supposed to conclude that if they buy the stuff that you are buying, they will all be arch-individualists, just like you. Which adds up to everybody. Being the same. Good for Diesel's bottom line. Not much in the spirit of Thoreau, however.

For other contradictions in the Diesel ads, let's look at one of their favorite taglines: "Smart May Have the Brains, But Stupid Has the Balls." Of course, since this tagline most often accompanies the image of a semi-naked young woman, it isn't meant literally. It really means "is gutsy," "has moxie," "nerve," or even "chutzpah." But it is still a line designed to appeal to Americans, who have a long and contradictory attitude toward intelligence. Think of Washington Irving's story "The Legend of Sleepy Hollow." A weak but intelligent schoolteacher (Ichabod Crane) is pitted against a strong but rather brutal fellow named Brom Bones in the competition for a woman's affection. Brom Bones gets the girl after either murdering Ichabod or terrorizing him into fleeing the territory one Halloween night, and it is the highly physical Mr. Bones who is most likely to appeal to Irving's American audience, which has always been rather ambivalent about sheer intellect. Physical strength and courage are the stuff of athletes and the pioneers (Levi's Go Forth campaign uses Walt Whitman's poem "O Pioneers!" as a verbal backdrop), both perennial American favorites. But intellectuals (who are called names like "egghead" or "pointy head," or whatnot) are rarely culture heroes. (The one major exception here was the German-born physicist Albert Einstein, who became a popular cultural icon in spite of his own personal disassociation from mass culture.) When brainy folk are culture heroes, they are often people like Thomas Edison, who was a hands-on, applied scientist, an inventor of useful and profitable products, not an abstract philosopher.

And yet, America is also the place that established universal education — especially higher education — as a national right, and that today most often rewards those who have used their brains to become doctors, lawyers, and business executives, rather than their brawn. A contradiction indeed. The same country that has made a college degree, if not a post-graduate degree, practically a necessity for anyone hoping to have an upper-middle-class career is also a country that thinks that smart people are just a little too smart by half.

And that takes us back to the Be Stupid campaign that tells us being smart seems, well, stupid, and being stupid means being very cool.

We can see other contradictions. The Be Stupid campaign is clearly marked as being for a youth market, and with its open exploitation of American contradictions, it accordingly exploits a history of youth rebellion. Because the history of a cultural product can lead us to its semiotic significance, let's look back to the 1940s and 1950s Beat generation. Led by such iconic figures as Jack Kerouac, Allen Ginsberg, and William Burroughs, the Beats provided models of nonconformist rebellion against America's middle-class, consumerist values for the Baby Boomers who would turn the Beats' small-scale movement into a mass cultural revolution in the 1960s. In every generation since (punk, post-punk, alternative, grunge, indie, and so forth), rejection of bourgeois values has been a hallmark of American youth culture, wherein words like "corporate culture" are dirty words.

But as Thomas Frank points out (see his essay "Commodify Your Dissent" in Chapter 1), this imperative to rebel has for a long time been a mainstay of corporate advertising. An ad campaign like Diesel's seeks to sell products as symbols of rebellion by associating the gear with edgy, attitude-laden images of youthful freedom and independence. Frank calls this pattern the "commodification of dissent," that is, the turning of rebelliousness itself into a commodity you can purchase by buying the products that are associated with anticorporate, dissenting values. That's what Diesel wants its target market to think: By buying Diesel's products, you are expressing your rejection of corporate values and culture. Consume to protest consumption. And thereby make the Diesel corporation very happy.

Isn't that just a little, well, stupid?

Be Exploitative

Let's look at one last contradiction Diesel presents. A good many of its ads feature sexy female models in one state or another of undress. That's a tried and true attention-getter, but it isn't only trying to attract the male gaze. It is also aimed at women, and it is saying that if you want to express your daring, your creativity, your independence, do something like flash a CCTV camera, or get yourself trapped under your boyfriend's bed in your underwear while he, um, entertains another girlfriend, or photograph your private parts while wearing a bikini as a lion looks on hungrily in the background. Such actions will prove that you "have balls." Or "stories" to tell. Or whatever.

A number of these images come close to being soft porn, and in so doing exemplify the American contradiction between capitalistic materialism and puritan spirituality. These two characteristics coexist in a constant uneasy cultural tension that occasionally explodes when someone crosses the line, as Calvin Klein did a few years ago when he used erotic images of little children

---

Reading the Signs of American Contradictions on the Net

Despite the explosion in the number of media outlets in the last decade, critics have charged that the increased consolidation of media has in fact homogenized the mass media, with Americans paradoxically now having a narrower range of options available to them. Does the Internet — an environment that allows for blogs, chat rooms, discussion forums, and the like — manage to cut through this paradox? Or, with the rise of powerhouses like Amazon.com, Google, and eBay, do you see signs of corporate control threatening the much-heralded democratic freedom that the Internet offers?

in an ad campaign that was squelched after massive public protest, or in the notorious halftime show featuring Janet Jackson and Justin Timberlake at Super Bowl XXXVII.

The fact that the Be Stupid ads appear in teen magazines raises a related contradiction. It didn't bother Shakespeare's audience that Romeo and Juliet were fourteen years old, but in America sexual activity among minors (that is, under eighteen years of age) is quite literally a crime. Even the dissemination and possession of images of unclothed minors is a criminal offense. (Indeed, at a time when some teenage girls have been prosecuted for sexting, the Be Stupid campaign had better be certain that its models are over eighteen years of age.) Yet here is Diesel essentially telling its audience, which includes underaged minors, that one very cool way to express their individuality, creativity, and daring is to have sex. Why is Diesel doing this and how is the company getting away with it?

In four words: Because it sells products. For most of American history, the essentially puritan tradition of repressing teen sexuality trumped the capitalistic tradition of the profit motive, and ads exploiting teen sexuality were either forbidden outright or protested (the latter was the case with the Calvin Klein campaign featuring a very sexy teenage Brooke Shields in the 1970s). But in recent years the profit motive is winning out. This difference, exemplified by the Be Stupid campaign, marks a shift in American culture from its spiritual to its material side, a change indicating the triumph of what cultural analyst Jeremy Rifkin has called **hypercapitalism** — which can be defined as a society in which the values of capitalism overwhelm all other values — or, as we like to put it — as capitalism on steroids. It is within the context of hypercapitalism that clothing manufacturers sell tween fashions to twelve-year-old girls that might have embarrassed a prostitute just a generation ago, or beauty contests are held for six-year-olds like the now long-deceased child model JonBenét Ramsey.

This takes us to our final cultural signifier: In a hypercapitalistic environment, money becomes the preeminent measure of value. The Be Stupid campaign presents a blue state version of this attitude, commodifying the sexual revolution on behalf of profits. But when we consider the Tea Party's foundational opposition to taxation we find a red state equivalent, with a libertarian belief in the superiority of private property rights trumping all other social values.

Which just might be the greatest paradox of them all.

The Readings

David Brooks begins our survey of American contradictions with an ultimately optimistic exploration of the cultural divide that has made the terms "red America" and "blue America" household words. Barbara Ehrenreich follows with a trenchant analysis of the kinds of predicaments that good old

American optimism can get us into, while Jack Solomon's semiotic explora-tion of American advertising highlights the contradiction between Ameri-can populism and elitism at the heart of the American dream. Phyllis M. Japp and Debra K. Japp next survey the cultural contradictions inherent in America's search for "the good life," a quest that is simultaneously mate-rialistic and spiritual as Americans seek simplicity through consumption via the "voluntary simplicity" movement. Mariah Burton Nelson's essay on the predicament of women athletes points out the cultural contradictions that women must negotiate when they enter into the world of competitive sport. Randall Kennedy follows with an analysis of racial profiling, one of the legacies of America's contradictory racial history. Alfred Lubrano then offers a personal reflection on what it was like to move from working-class commonality to the Ivy League elite. Daniel Mackay offers an analysis of the mythological contradictions to be found within the *Star Wars* saga, and Richard Corliss explores an emerging rapprochement between evangelicism and entertainment. Murray Milner Jr. concludes the chapter with an analy-sis of how the cultural contradictions within capitalism lead to the hedonis-tic ethos of "bourgeois bohemians."

DAVID BROOKS
One Nation, Slightly Divisible

Red is red, and blue is blue, and never the twain shall meet — or so one might conclude after presidential elections in which the American electorate divided decisively between so-called red states and blue states. Shortly after the 2000 election, which first introduced the red state–blue state division, David Brooks went on the road (he didn't have to go far) to see whether Americans were so hopelessly culturally divided after all. He found that, while red America may have fewer Starbucks and Pottery Barn outlets than does blue America, the feared divide may not go so deep after all. Brooks is a columnist for the *New York Times* and a commentator on *The News-Hour with Jim Lehrer*. This selection was first published in 2001 in the *Atlantic Monthly*. He is the author of *Bobos in Paradise: The New Upper Class and How They Got There* (2000) and *On Paradise Drive: How We Live Now (and Always Have) in the Future Tense* (2004).

Sixty-five miles from where I am writing this sentence is a place with no Starbucks, no Pottery Barn, no Borders or Barnes & Noble. No blue *New York Times* delivery bags dot the driveways on Sunday mornings. In this place people don't complain that Woody Allen isn't as funny as he used to be, because they never thought he was funny. In this place you can go to a year's worth of dinner parties without hearing anyone quote an aperçu he first heard on *Charlie Rose*. The people here don't buy those little rear-window stickers when they go to a summer-vacation spot so that they can drive around with "MV" decals the rest of the year; for the most part they don't even go to Martha's Vineyard.

The place I'm talking about goes by different names. Some call it America. Others call it Middle America. It has also come to be known as Red America, in reference to the maps that were produced on the night of the 2000 presidential election. People in Blue America, which is my part of America, tend to live around big cities on the coasts. People in Red America tend to live on farms or in small towns or small cities far away from the coasts. Things are different there.

Everything that people in my neighborhood do without motors, the people in Red America do with motors. We sail; they powerboat. We cross-country ski; they snowmobile. We hike; they drive ATVs. We have vineyard tours; they have tractor pulls. When it comes to yard work, they have rider mowers; we have illegal aliens.

Different sorts of institutions dominate life in these two places. In Red America churches are everywhere. In Blue America Thai restaurants are everywhere. In Red America they have QVC, the Pro Bowlers Tour, and hunting.

In Blue America we have NPR, Doris Kearns Goodwin, and socially conscious investing. In Red America the Walmarts are massive, with parking lots the size of state parks. In Blue America the stores are small but the markups are big. You'll rarely see a Christmas store in Blue America, but in Red America, even in July, you'll come upon stores selling fake Christmas trees, wreath-decorated napkins, Rudolph the Red-Nosed Reindeer collectible thimbles and spoons, and little snow-covered villages.

We in the coastal metro Blue areas read more books and attend more plays than the people in the Red heartland. We're more sophisticated and cosmopolitan — just ask us about our alumni trips to China or Provence, or our interest in Buddhism. But don't ask us, please, what life in Red America is like. We don't know. We don't know who Tim LaHaye and Jerry B. Jenkins are, even though the novels they have cowritten have sold about forty million copies over the past few years. We don't know what James Dobson says on his radio program, which is listened to by millions. We don't know about Reba or Travis. We don't know what happens in mega-churches on Wednesday evenings, and some of us couldn't tell you the difference between a fundamentalist and an evangelical, let alone describe what it means to be a Pentecostal. Very few of us know what goes on in Branson, Missouri, even though it has seven million visitors a year, or could name even five NASCAR drivers, although stock-car races are the best-attended sporting events in the country. We don't know how to shoot or clean a rifle. We can't tell a military officer's rank by looking at his insignia. We don't know what soy beans look like when they're growing in a field.

All we know, or all we think we know, about Red America is that millions and millions of its people live quietly underneath flight patterns, many of them are racist and homophobic, and when you see them at highway rest stops, they're often really fat and their clothes are too tight.

And apparently we don't want to know any more than that. One can barely find any books at Amazon.com about what it is like to live in small-town America — or, at least, any books written by normal people who grew up in small towns, liked them, and stayed there. The few books that do exist were written either by people who left the heartland because they hated it (Bill Bryson's *The Lost Continent*, for example) or by urbanites who moved to Red America as part of some life-simplification plan (*Moving to a Small Town: A Guidebook for Moving from Urban to Rural America*; National Geographic's *Guide to Small Town Escapes*). Apparently no publishers or members of the Blue book-buying public are curious about Red America as seen through Red America's eyes.

Crossing the Meatloaf Line

Over the past several months, my interest piqued by those stark blocks of color on the election-night maps, I have every now and then left my home in Montgomery County, Maryland, and driven sixty-five miles northwest to Franklin County, in south-central Pennsylvania. Montgomery County is one of the steaming-hot centers of the great espresso machine that is Blue America. It is just over the border from northwestern Washington, D.C., and it is full of upper-middle-class towns inhabited by lawyers, doctors, stockbrokers, and establishment journalists like me — towns like Chevy Chase, Potomac, and Bethesda (where I live). Its central artery is a burgeoning high-tech corridor with a multitude of sparkling new office parks housing technology companies such as United Information Systems and Sybase, and pioneering biotech firms such as Celera Genomics and Human Genome Sciences. When I drive to Franklin County, I take Route 270. After about forty-five minutes I pass a Cracker Barrel — Red America condensed into chain-restaurant form. I've crossed the Meatloaf Line; from here on there will be a lot fewer sun-dried-tomato concoctions on restaurant menus and a lot more meatloaf platters.

Franklin County is Red America. It's a rural county, about twenty-five miles west of Gettysburg, and it includes the towns of Waynesboro, Chambersburg, and Mercersburg. It was originally settled by the Scotch-Irish, and has plenty of Brethren and Mennonites along with a fast-growing population of evangelicals. The joke that Pennsylvanians tell about their state is that it has Philadelphia on one end, Pittsburgh on the other, and Alabama in the middle. Franklin County is in the Alabama part. It strikes me as I drive there that even though I am going north across the Mason-Dixon line, I feel as if I were going south. The local culture owes more to Nashville, Houston, and Daytona than to Washington, Philadelphia, or New York.

I shuttled back and forth between Franklin and Montgomery Counties   10 because the cultural differences between the two places are great, though the geographic distance is small. The two places are not perfect microcosms of Red and Blue America. The part of Montgomery County I am here describing is largely the Caucasian part. Moreover, Franklin County is in a Red part of a Blue state: overall, Pennsylvania went for Gore. And I went to Franklin County aware that there are tremendous differences within Red America, just as there are within Blue. Franklin County is quite different from, say, Scottsdale, Arizona, just as Bethesda is quite different from Oakland, California.

Nonetheless, the contrasts between the two counties leap out, and they are broadly suggestive of the sorts of contrasts that can be seen nationwide. When Blue America talks about social changes that convulsed society, it tends to mean the 1960s rise of the counterculture and feminism. When Red America talks about changes that convulsed society, it tends to mean World War II, which shook up old town establishments and led to a great surge of industry.

Red America makes social distinctions that Blue America doesn't. For example, in Franklin County there seems to be a distinction between those fiercely independent people who live in the hills and people who live in the valleys. I got a hint of the distinct and, to me, exotic hill culture when a hill dweller asked me why I thought hunting for squirrel and rabbit had gone out of fashion. I thought maybe it was just more fun to hunt something bigger. But he said, "McDonald's. It's cheaper to get a hamburger at McDonald's than to go out and get it yourself."

There also seems to be an important distinction between men who work outdoors and men who work indoors. The outdoor guys wear faded black T-shirts they once picked up at a Lynyrd Skynyrd concert and wrecked jeans that appear to be washed faithfully at least once a year. They've got wraparound NASCAR sunglasses, maybe a NAPA auto parts cap, and hair cut in a short wedge up front but flowing down over their shoulders in the back — a cut that is known as a mullet, which is sort of a cross between Van Halen's style and Kenny Rogers's, and is the ugliest hairdo since every hairdo in the seventies. The outdoor guys are heavily accessorized, and their accessories are meant to show how hard they work, so they will often have a gigantic wad of keys hanging from a belt loop, a tape measure strapped to the belt, a pocket knife on a string tucked into the front pants pocket, and a pager or a cell phone affixed to the hip, presumably in case some power lines go down somewhere and need emergency repair. Outdoor guys have a thing against sleeves. They work so hard that they've got to keep their arm muscles unencumbered and their armpit hair fully ventilated, so they either buy their shirts sleeveless or rip the sleeves off their T-shirts first thing, leaving bits of fringe hanging over their BAD TO THE BONE tattoos.

The guys who work indoors can't project this rugged proletarian image. It's simply not that romantic to be a bank-loan officer or a shift manager at the local distribution center. So the indoor guys adopt a look that a smart-ass, sneering Blue American might call Bible-academy casual — maybe Haggar slacks, which they bought at a dry-goods store best known for its appliance department, and a short-sleeved white Van Heusen shirt from the Bon-Ton. Their image projects not "I work hard" but "I'm a devoted family man." A lot of indoor guys have a sensitive New Age demeanor. When they talk about the days their kids were born, their eyes take on a soft Garth Brooks expression, and they tear up. They exaggerate how sinful they were before they were born again. On Saturdays they are patio masters, barbecuing on their gas grills in full Father's Day–apron regalia.

At first I thought the indoor guys were the faithful, reliable ones: the ones 15 who did well in school, whereas the outdoor guys were druggies. But after talking with several preachers in Franklin County, I learned that it's not that simple. Sometimes the guys who look like bikers are the most devoted community-service volunteers and church attendees.

The kinds of distinctions we make in Blue America are different. In my world the easiest way to categorize people is by headroom needs. People who went to business school or law school like a lot of headroom. They buy humongous sport-utility vehicles that practically have cathedral ceilings over the front seats. They live in homes the size of country clubs, with soaring entry atriums so high that they could practically fly a kite when they come through the front door. These big-headroom people tend to be predators: their jobs have them negotiating and competing all day. They spend small fortunes on dry cleaning. They grow animated when talking about how much they love their BlackBerries. They fill their enormous wall space with huge professional family portraits — Mom and Dad with their perfect kids (dressed in light-blue Oxford shirts) laughing happily in an orchard somewhere.

Small-headroom people tend to have been liberal-arts majors, and they have liberal-arts jobs. They get passive-aggressive pleasure from demonstrating how modest and environmentally sensitive their living containers are. They hate people with SUVs, and feel virtuous driving around in their low-ceilinged little Hondas, which often display a RANDOM ACTS OF KINDNESS bumper sticker or one bearing an image of a fish with legs, along with the word "Darwin," just to show how intellectually superior to fundamentalist Christians they are.

Some of the biggest differences between Red and Blue America show up on statistical tables. Ethnic diversity is one. In Montgomery County 60 percent of the population is white, 15 percent is black, 12 percent is Hispanic, and 11 percent is Asian. In Franklin County 95 percent of the population is white. White people work the gas-station pumps and the 7-Eleven counters. (This is something one doesn't often see in my part of the country.) Although the nation is growing more diverse, it's doing so only in certain spots. According to an analysis of the 2000 census by Bill Frey, a demographer at the Milken Institute, well over half the counties in America are still at least 85 percent white.

Another big thing is that, according to 1990 census data, in Franklin County only 12 percent of the adults have college degrees and only 69 percent have high school diplomas. In Montgomery County 50 percent of the adults have college degrees and 91 percent have high school diplomas. The education gap extends to the children. At Walt Whitman High School, a public school in Bethesda, the average SAT scores are 601 verbal and 622 math, whereas the national average is 506 verbal and 514 math. In Franklin County, where people are quite proud of their schools, the average SAT scores at, for example, the Waynesboro area high school are 495 verbal and 480 math. More and more kids in Franklin County are going on to college, but it is hard to believe that their prospects will be as bright as those of the kids in Montgomery County and the rest of upscale Blue America.

Because the information age rewards education with money, it's not 20 surprising that Montgomery County is much richer than Franklin County. According to some estimates, in Montgomery County 51 percent of households have annual incomes above $75,000, and the average household income is $100,365. In Franklin County only 16 percent of households have incomes above $75,000, and the average is $51,872.

A major employer in Montgomery County is the National Institutes of Health, which grows like a scientific boomtown in Bethesda. A major economic engine in Franklin County is the interstate highway Route 81. Trucking companies have gotten sick of fighting the congestion on Route 95, which runs up the Blue corridor along the northeast coast, so they move their stuff along 81, farther inland. Several new distribution centers have been built along 81 in Franklin County, and some of the workers who were laid off when their factories closed, several years ago, are now settling for $8.00 or $9.00 an hour loading boxes.

The two counties vote differently, of course—the differences, on a nationwide scale, were what led to those red-and-blue maps. Like upscale areas everywhere, from Silicon Valley to Chicago's North Shore to suburban Connecticut, Montgomery County supported the Democratic ticket in last year's presidential election, by a margin of 63 percent to 34 percent. Meanwhile, like almost all of rural America, Franklin County went Republican, by 67 percent to 30 percent.

However, other voting patterns sometimes obscure the Red-Blue cultural divide. For example, minority voters all over the country overwhelmingly supported the Democratic ticket last November. But—in many respects, at least—blacks and Hispanics in Red America are more traditionalist than blacks and Hispanics in Blue America, just as their white counterparts are. For example, the Pew Research Center for the People and the Press, in Washington, D.C., recently found that 45 percent of minority members in Red states agree with the statement "AIDS might be God's punishment for immoral sexual behavior," but only 31 percent of minority members in Blue states do. Similarly, 40 percent of minorities in Red states believe that school boards should have the right to fire homosexual teachers, but only 21 percent of minorities in Blue states do.

From Cracks to a Chasm?

These differences are so many and so stark that they lead to some pretty troubling questions: Are Americans any longer a common people? Do we have one national conversation and one national culture? Are we loyal to the same institutions and the same values? How do people on one side of the divide regard those on the other?

I went to Franklin County because I wanted to get a sense of how deep   25 the divide really is, to see how people there live, and to gauge how different their lives are from those in my part of America. I spoke with ministers, journalists, teachers, community leaders, and pretty much anyone I ran across. I consulted with pollsters, demographers, and market-research firms.

Toward the end of my project the World Trade Center and the Pentagon were attacked. This put a new slant on my little investigation. In the days immediately following September 11 the evidence seemed clear that despite our differences, we are still a united people. American flags flew everywhere in Franklin County and in Montgomery County. Patriotism surged. Pollsters started to measure Americans' reactions to the events. Whatever questions they asked, the replies were near unanimous. Do you support a military response against terror? More than four fifths of Americans said yes. Do you support a military response even if it means thousands of U.S. casualties? More than three fifths said yes. There were no significant variations across geographic or demographic lines.

A sweeping feeling of solidarity was noticeable in every neighborhood, school, and workplace. Headlines blared, A NATION UNITED and UNITED STATES. An attack had been made on the very epicenter of Blue America — downtown Manhattan. And in a flash all the jokes about and seeming hostility toward New Yorkers vanished, to be replaced by an outpouring of respect, support, and love. The old hostility came to seem merely a sort of sibling rivalry, which means nothing when the family itself is under threat.

But very soon there were hints that the solidarity was fraying. A few stray notes of dissent were sounded in the organs of Blue America. Susan Sontag wrote a sour piece in *The New Yorker* about how depressing it was to see what she considered to be a simplistically pro-American reaction to the attacks. At rallies on college campuses across the country speakers pointed out that America had been bombing other countries for years, and turnabout was fair play. On one NPR talk show I heard numerous callers express unease about what they saw as a crude us-versus-them mentality behind President Bush's rhetoric. Katha Pollitt wrote in *The Nation* that she would not permit her daughter to hang the American flag from the living-room window, because, she felt, it "stands for jingoism and vengeance and war." And there was evidence that among those with less-strident voices, too, differences were beginning to show. Polls revealed that people without a college education were far more confident than people with a college education that the military could defeat the terrorists. People in the South were far more eager than people in the rest of the country for an American counterattack to begin.

It started to seem likely that these cracks would widen once the American response got under way, when the focus would be not on firemen and rescue workers but on the Marines, the CIA, and the special-operations forces. If the war was protracted, the cracks could widen into a chasm, as they did during Vietnam. Red America, the home of patriotism and military service (there's a big military-recruitment center in downtown Chambersburg), would undoubtedly support the war effort, but would Blue America (there's a big gourmet dog bakery in downtown Bethesda) decide that a crude military response would only deepen animosities and make things worse?

A Cafeteria Nation

These differences in sensibility don't in themselves mean that America has become a fundamentally divided nation. As the sociologist Seymour Martin Lipset pointed out in *The First New Nation* (1963), achievement and equality are the two rival themes running throughout American history. Most people, most places, and most epochs have tried to intertwine them in some way. 30

Moreover, after bouncing between Montgomery and Franklin Counties, I became convinced that a lot of our fear that America is split into rival camps arises from mistaken notions of how society is shaped. Some of us still carry the old Marxist categories in our heads. We think that society is like a layer cake, with the upper class on top. And, like Marx, we tend to assume that wherever there is class division there is conflict. Or else we have a sort of *Crossfire* model in our heads: Where would people we meet sit if they were guests on that show?

But traveling back and forth between the two counties was not like crossing from one rival camp to another. It was like crossing a high school cafeteria. Remember high school? There were nerds, jocks, punks, bikers, techies, druggies, God Squadders, drama geeks, poets, and Dungeons & Dragons weirdoes. All these cliques were part of the same school: they had different sensibilities; sometimes they knew very little about the people in the other cliques; but the jocks knew there would always be nerds, and the nerds knew there would always be jocks. That's just the way life is.

And that's the way America is. We are not a divided nation. We are a cafeteria nation. We form cliques (call them communities, or market segments, or whatever), and when they get too big, we form subcliques. Some people even get together in churches that are "nondenominational" or in political groups that are "independent." These are cliques built around the supposed rejection of cliques.

We live our lives by migrating through the many different cliques associated with the activities we enjoy and the goals we have set for ourselves. Our freedom comes in the interstices; we can choose which set of standards to live by, and when.

We should remember that there is generally some distance between 35 cliques—a buffer zone that separates one set of aspirations from another. People who are happy within their cliques feel no great compulsion to go out and reform other cliques. The jocks don't try to change the nerds. David Rawley, [a] Greencastle minister . . . , has been to New York City only once in his life. "I was happy to get back home," he told me. "It's a planet I'm a little scared of. I have no desire to go back."

What unites the two Americas, then, is our mutual commitment to this way of life—to the idea that a person is not bound by his class, or by the religion of his fathers, but is free to build a plurality of connections for himself. We are participants in the same striving process, the same experimental journey. . . .

READING THE TEXT

1. Summarize in your own words the typical characteristics of red and blue America, as Brooks presents them.

2. What does Brooks mean by saying that, in blue America, "the easiest way to categorize people is by headroom needs" (para. 16)?

3. What ethnic and economic patterns does Brooks see in red and blue America?

4. How did the September 11 attacks affect Brooks's view of the two Americas?

READING THE SIGNS

1. In class, form groups and debate whether Brooks could be accused of stereotyping Americans and whether he is identifying a fundamental contradiction in American culture.

2. Would Brooks characterize your community as red or blue? Provide specific details to demonstrate your position. If you believe your community escapes Brooks's dichotomy, explain why.

3. Brooks wrote this article in 2001. To what extent does the red/blue divide still exist after the 2008 presidential election? If you believe that it remains, has the divide become larger or smaller? In what ways does the advent of the Tea Party affect Brooks's argument? You might analyze media coverage of that and subsequent elections for evidence that supports your position.

4. **CONNECTING TEXTS**   In an analytic essay, write your own response to Brooks's question "Are Americans any longer a common people?" (para. 24). To develop your ideas, you might consult the Introduction to Chapter 7, "American Makeover: Constructing Identity in the Age of Entertainment" (p. 615).

BARBARA EHRENREICH
Bright-Sided

Americans are optimists. One of America's greatest strengths, this optimism has enabled us to take great risks and dare great things. But as Barbara Ehrenreich points out in this excerpt from *Bright-Sided: How the Relentless Promotion of Positive Thinking Has Undermined America* (2009), this optimism can also make Americans reckless, as when investors, bankers, and home buyers between 2001 and 2006 bet on eternally increasing home values, an overly rosy gamble that led to the Great Recession. And then there was the best-selling book *The Secret* (2006), which told Americans that all they had to do was think positively and everything they ever desired could be theirs. Not wanting to cast a cloud on America's sunny disposition, Ehrenreich nevertheless believes that America could be a better, indeed happier, place, if it can only "recover from the mass delusion that is positive thinking." A major figure in American social analysis, Barbara Ehrenreich has published many books, including *This Land Is Their Land:*

Reports from a Divided Nation (2009), *Bait and Switch: The (Futile) Pursuit of the American Dream* (2006), *Nickel and Dimed: On (Not) Getting By in America* (2001), and *The Worst Years of Our Lives: Irreverent Notes from a Decade of Greed* (1990).

Americans are a "positive" people. This is our reputation as well as our self-image. We smile a lot and are often baffled when people from other cultures do not return the favor. In the well-worn stereotype, we are upbeat, cheerful, optimistic, and shallow, while foreigners are likely to be subtle, world-weary, and possibly decadent. American expatriate writers like Henry James and James Baldwin wrestled with and occasionally reinforced this stereotype, which I once encountered in the 1980s in the form of a remark by Soviet émigré poet Joseph Brodsky to the effect that the problem with Americans is that they have "never known suffering." (Apparently he didn't know who had invented the blues.) Whether we Americans see it as an embarrassment or a point of pride, being positive — in affect, in mood, in outlook — seems to be engrained in our national character.

Who would be churlish or disaffected enough to challenge these happy features of the American personality? Take the business of positive "affect," which refers to the mood we display to others through our smiles, our greetings, our professions of confidence and optimism. Scientists have found that the mere act of smiling can generate positive feelings within us, at least if the smile is not forced. In addition, good feelings, as expressed through our words and smiles, seem to be contagious: "Smile and the world smiles with you." Surely the world would be a better, happier place if we all greeted one another warmly and stopped to coax smiles from babies — if only through the well-known social psychological mechanism of "mood contagion." Recent studies show that happy feelings flit easily through social networks, so that one person's good fortune can brighten the day even for only distantly connected others.[1]

Furthermore, psychologists today agree that positive feelings like gratitude, contentment, and self-confidence can actually lengthen our lives and improve our health. Some of these claims are exaggerated, as we shall see, though positive feelings hardly need to be justified, like exercise or vitamin supplements, as part of a healthy lifestyle. People who report having positive feelings are more likely to participate in a rich social life, and vice versa, and social connectedness turns out to be an important defense against depression, which is a known risk factor for many physical illnesses. At the risk of redundancy or even tautology, we can say that on many levels, individual and social, it is *good* to be "positive," certainly better than being withdrawn, aggrieved, or chronically sad.

---

[1] "Happiness Is 'Infectious' in Network of Friends: Collective — Not Just Individual — Phenomenon," *ScienceDaily,* Dec. 5, 2008, http://www.sciencedaily.com/releases/2008/12/081205094506.htm.

So I take it as a sign of progress that, in just the last decade or so, econo-mists have begun to show an interest in using happiness rather than just the gross national product as a measure of an economy's success. Happiness is, of course, a slippery thing to measure or define. Philosophers have debated what it is for centuries, and even if we were to define it simply as a greater frequency of positive feelings than negative ones, when we ask people if they are happy we are asking them to arrive at some sort of average over many moods and moments. Maybe I was upset earlier in the day but then was cheered up by a bit of good news, so what am I really? In one well-known psychological experiment, subjects were asked to answer a questionnaire on life satisfaction — but only after they had performed the apparently irrelevant task of photocopying a sheet of paper for the experimenter. For a randomly chosen half of the subjects, a dime had been left for them to find on the copy machine. As two economists summarize the results, "Reported satisfaction with life was raised substantially, by the discovery of the coin on the copy machine — clearly not an income effect."[2]

In addition to the problems of measurement, there are cultural differ- 5 ences in how happiness is regarded and whether it is even seen as a virtue. Some cultures, like our own, value the positive affect that seems to signal internal happiness; others are more impressed by seriousness, self-sacrifice, or a quiet willingness to cooperate. However hard to pin down, though, hap-piness is somehow a more pertinent metric for well-being, from a humanistic perspective, than the buzz of transactions that constitute the GDP.

Surprisingly, when psychologists undertake to measure the relative hap-piness of nations, they routinely find that Americans are not, even in pros-perous times and despite our vaunted positivity, very happy at all. A recent meta-analysis of over a hundred studies of self-reported happiness world-wide found Americans ranking only twenty-third, surpassed by the Dutch, the Danes, the Malaysians, the Bahamians, the Austrians, and even the sup-posedly dour Finns.[3] In another potential sign of relative distress, Americans account for two-thirds of the global market for antidepressants, which happen also to be the most commonly prescribed drugs in the United States. To my knowledge, no one knows how antidepressant use affects people's responses to happiness surveys: Do respondents report being happy because the drugs make them feel happy or do they report being unhappy because they know they are dependent on drugs to make them feel better? Without our heavy use of antidepressants, Americans would likely rank far lower in the happi-ness rankings than we currently do.

When economists attempt to rank nations more objectively in terms of "well-being," taking into account such factors as health, environmental

[2]Daniel Kahneman and Alan B. Krueger, "Developments in the Measurement of Subjec-tive Well-Being," *Journal of Economic Perspectives* 20 (2006): 3–24.

[3]"Psychologist Produces the First-Ever 'World Map of Happiness,'" *ScienceDaily*, Nov. 14, 2006, http://www.sciencedaily.com/releases/2006/11/061113093726.htm.

sustainability, and the possibility of upward mobility, the United States does even more poorly than it does when only the subjective state of "happiness" is measured. The Happy Planet Index, to give just one example, locates us at 150th among the world's nations.[4]

How can we be so surpassingly "positive" in self-image and stereotype without being the world's happiest and best-off people? The answer, I think, is that positivity is not so much our condition or our mood as it is part of our ideology—the way we explain the world and think we ought to function within it. That ideology is "positive thinking," by which we usually mean two things. One is the generic content of positive thinking—that is, the positive thought itself—which can be summarized as: Things are pretty good right now, at least if you are willing to see silver linings, make lemonade out of lemons, etc., and things are going to get a whole lot better. This is optimism, and it is not the same as hope. Hope is an emotion, a yearning, the experience of which is not entirely within our control. Optimism is a cognitive stance, a conscious expectation, which presumably anyone can develop through practice.

The second thing we mean by "positive thinking" is this practice, or discipline, of trying to think in a positive way. There is, we are told, a practical reason for undertaking this effort: Positive thinking supposedly not only makes us feel optimistic but actually makes happy outcomes more likely. If you expect things to get better, they will. How can the mere process of thinking do this? In the rational explanation that many psychologists would offer today, optimism improves health, personal efficacy, confidence, and resilience, making it easier for us to accomplish our goals. A far less rational theory also runs rampant in American ideology—the idea that our thoughts can, in some mysterious way, directly affect the physical world. Negative thoughts somehow produce negative outcomes, while positive thoughts realize themselves in the form of health, prosperity, and success. For both rational and mystical reasons, then, the effort of positive thinking is said to be well worth our time and attention, whether this means reading the relevant books, attending seminars and speeches that offer the appropriate mental training, or just doing the solitary work of concentration on desired outcomes—a better job, an attractive mate, world peace.

There is an anxiety, as you can see, right here in the heart of American positive thinking. If the generic "positive thought" is correct and things are really getting better, if the arc of the universe tends toward happiness and abundance, then why bother with the mental effort of positive thinking? Obviously, because we do not fully believe that things will get better on their own. The practice of positive thinking is an effort to pump up this belief in the face of much contradictory evidence. Those who set themselves up as instructors in the discipline of positive thinking—coaches, preachers, and gurus of various sorts—have described this effort with terms like "self-hypnosis," "mind

10

---

[4]http://rankingamerica.wordpress.com/2009/01/11/the-us-ranks-150th-in-planet-happiness/, Jan. 11, 2009.

control," and "thought control." In other words, it requires deliberate self-deception, including a constant effort to repress or block out unpleasant possibilities and "negative" thoughts. The truly self-confident, or those who have in some way made their peace with the world and their destiny within it, do not need to expend effort censoring or otherwise controlling their thoughts. Positive thinking may be a quintessentially American activity, associated in our minds with both individual and national success, but it is driven by a terrible insecurity.

Americans did not start out as positive thinkers — at least the promotion of unwarranted optimism and methods to achieve it did not really find articulation and organized form until several decades after the founding of the republic. In the Declaration of Independence, the founding fathers pledged to one another "our lives, our fortunes, and our sacred honor." They knew that they had no certainty of winning a war for independence and that they were taking a mortal risk. Just the act of signing the declaration made them all traitors to the crown, and treason was a crime punishable by execution. Many of them did go on to lose their lives, loved ones, and fortunes in the war. The point is, they fought anyway. There is a vast difference between positive thinking and existential courage.

Systematic positive thinking began, in the nineteenth century, among a diverse and fascinating collection of philosophers, mystics, lay healers, and middle-class women. By the twentieth century, though, it had gone mainstream, gaining purchase within such powerful belief systems as nationalism and also doing its best to make itself indispensable to capitalism. We don't usually talk about American nationalism, but it is a mark of how deep it runs that we apply the word "nationalism" to Serbs, Russians, and others, while believing ourselves to possess a uniquely superior version called "patriotism." A central tenet of American nationalism has been the belief that the United States is "the greatest nation on earth" — more dynamic, democratic, and prosperous than any other nation, as well as technologically superior. Major religious leaders, especially on the Christian right, buttress this conceit with the notion that Americans are God's chosen people and that America is the designated leader of the world — an idea that seemed to find vivid reinforcement in the fall of Communism and our emergence as the world's "lone superpower." That acute British observer Godfrey Hodgson has written that the American sense of exceptionalism, which once was "idealistic and generous, if somewhat solipsistic," has become "harder, more hubristic." Paul Krugman responded to the prevailing smugness in a 1998 essay entitled "American the Boastful," warning that "if pride goeth before a fall, the United States has one heck of a come-uppance in store."[5]

But of course it takes the effort of positive thinking to imagine that America is the "best" or the "greatest." Militarily, yes, we are the mightiest

[5]Godfrey Hodgson, *The Myth of American Exceptionalism* (New Haven: Yale University Press, 2009), 113; Paul Krugman, "America the Boastful," *Foreign Affairs*, May–June 1998.

nation on earth. But on many other fronts, the American score is dismal, and was dismal even before the economic downturn that began in 2007. Our children routinely turn out to be more ignorant of basic subjects like math and geography than their counterparts in other industrialized nations. They are also more likely to die in infancy or grow up in poverty. Almost everyone acknowledges that our health care system is "broken" and our physical infrastructure crumbling. We have lost so much of our edge in science and technology that American companies have even begun to outsource their research and development efforts. Worse, some of the measures by which we do lead the world should inspire embarrassment rather than pride: We have the highest percentage of our population incarcerated, and the greatest level of inequality in wealth and income. We are plagued by gun violence and racked by personal debt.

While positive thinking has reinforced and found reinforcement in American national pride, it has also entered into a kind of symbiotic relationship with American capitalism. There is no natural, innate affinity between capitalism and positive thinking. In fact, one of the classics of sociology, Max Weber's *Protestant Ethic and the Spirit of Capitalism,* makes a still impressive case for capitalism's roots in the grim and punitive outlook of Calvinist Protestantism, which required people to defer gratification and resist all pleasurable temptations in favor of hard work and the accumulation of wealth.

But if early capitalism was inhospitable to positive thinking, "late" capitalism, or consumer capitalism, is far more congenial, depending as it does on the individual's hunger for *more* and the firm's imperative of *growth*. The   15 consumer culture encourages individuals to want more — cars, larger homes, television sets, cell phones, gadgets of all kinds — and positive thinking is ready at hand to tell them they deserve more and can have it if they really want it and are willing to make the effort to get it. Meanwhile, in a competitive business world, the companies that manufacture these goods and provide the paychecks that purchase them have no alternative but to grow. If you don't steadily increase market share and profits, you risk being driven out of business or swallowed by a larger enterprise. Perpetual growth, whether of a particular company or an entire economy, is of course an absurdity, but positive thinking makes it seem possible, if not ordained.

In addition, positive thinking has made itself useful as an apology for the crueler aspects of the market economy. If optimism is the key to material success, and if you can achieve an optimistic outlook through the discipline of positive thinking, then there is no excuse for failure. The flip side of positivity is thus a harsh insistence on personal responsibility: If your business fails or your job is eliminated, it must be because you didn't try hard enough, didn't believe firmly enough in the inevitability of your success. As the economy has brought more layoffs and financial turbulence to the middle class, the promoters of positive thinking have increasingly emphasized this negative judgment: to be disappointed, resentful, or downcast is to be a "victim" and a "whiner."

But positive thinking is not only a water carrier for the business world, excusing its excesses and masking its follies. The promotion of positive thinking has become a minor industry in its own right, producing an endless flow of books, DVDs, and other products; providing employment for tens of thousands of "life coaches," "executive coaches," and motivational speakers, as well as for the growing cadre of professional psychologists who seek to train them. No doubt the growing financial insecurity of the middle class contributes to the demand for these products and services, but I hesitate to attribute the commercial success of positive thinking to any particular economic trend or twist of the business cycle. America has historically offered space for all sorts of sects, cults, faith healers, and purveyors of snake oil, and those that are profitable, like positive thinking, tend to flourish.

At the turn of the twenty-first century, American optimism seemed to reach a manic crescendo. In his final State of the Union address in 2000, Bill Clinton struck a triumphal note, proclaiming that "never before has our nation enjoyed, at once, so much prosperity and social progress with so little internal crisis and so few external threats." But compared with his successor, Clinton seemed almost morose. George W. Bush had been a cheerleader in prep school, and cheerleading — a distinctly American innovation — could be considered the athletically inclined ancestor of so much of the coaching and "motivating" that has gone into the propagation of positive thinking. He took the presidency as an opportunity to continue in that line of work, defining his job as that of inspiring confidence, dispelling doubts, and pumping up the national spirit of self-congratulation. If he repeatedly laid claim to a single adjective, it was "optimistic." On the occasion of his sixtieth birthday, he told reporters he was "optimistic" about a variety of foreign policy challenges, offering as an overview, "I'm optimistic that all problems will be solved." Nor did he brook any doubts or hesitations among his close advisers. According to Bob Woodward, Condoleezza Rice failed to express some of her worries because, she said, "the president almost demanded optimism. He didn't like pessimism, hand-wringing or doubt."[6]

Then things began to go wrong, which is not in itself unusual but was a possibility excluded by America's official belief that things are good and getting better. There was the dot-com bust that began a few months after Clinton's declaration of unprecedented prosperity in his final State of the Union address, then the terrorist attack of September 11, 2001. Furthermore, things began to go wrong in a way that suggested that positive thinking might not guarantee success after all, that it might in fact dim our ability to fend off real threats. In her remarkable book, *Never Saw It Coming: Cultural Challenges to Envisioning the Worst*, sociologist Karen Cerulo recounts a number of ways that the habit of positive thinking, or what she calls optimistic bias, undermined preparedness and invited disaster. She quotes *Newsweek* reporters Michael Hirsch and Michael Isikoff, for example, in their conclusion that "a whole summer of missed clues, taken together, seemed to presage the terrible September of 2001."[7] There had already been a terrorist attack on the World Trade Center in 1993; there were ample warnings, in the summer of 2001, about a possible attack by airplane, and flight schools reported suspicious students like the one who wanted to learn how to "fly a plane but didn't care about landing and takeoff." The fact that no one — the FBI, the INS, Bush, or Rice — heeded these disturbing cues was later attributed to a "failure of imagination." But actually there was plenty of imagination at work — imagining an invulnerable nation and an ever-booming economy — there was simply no ability or inclination to imagine the worst.

A similar reckless optimism pervaded the American invasion of Iraq. Warnings about possible Iraqi resistance were swept aside by leaders who promised a "cakewalk" and envisioned cheering locals greeting our troops with flowers. Likewise, Hurricane Katrina was not exactly an unanticipated disaster. In 2002, the New Orleans *Times-Picayune* ran a Pulitzer Prize–winning series warning that the city's levees could not protect it against the storm surge brought on by a category 4 or 5 hurricane. In 2001, *Scientific American* had issued a similar warning about the city's vulnerability.[8] Even when the hurricane struck and levees broke, no alarm bells went off in

[6]2000 State of the Union Address, Jan. 27, 2000, http://www.washingtonpost.com/wp-srv/politics/special/states/docs/sou00.htm; Geoff Elliott, "Dubya's 60th Takes the Cake," *Weekend Australian*, July 8, 2006; Woodward, quoting Rice, *Meet the Press* transcript, Dec. 21, 2008, http://today.msnbc.msn.com/id/28337897/.

[7]Quoted in Karen A. Cerulo, *Never Saw It Coming: Cultural Challenges to Envisioning the Worst* (Chicago: University of Chicago Press, 2006), 18.

[8]Cerulo, *Never Saw It Coming*, 239.

Washington, and when a New Orleans FEMA official sent a panicky e-mail to FEMA director Michael Brown, alerting him to the rising number of deaths and a shortage of food in the drowning city, he was told that Brown would need an hour to eat his dinner in a Baton Rouge restaurant.[9] Criminal negligence or another "failure of imagination"? The truth is that Americans had been working hard for decades to school themselves in the techniques of positive thinking, and these included the reflexive capacity for dismissing disturbing news.

The biggest "come-uppance," to use Krugman's term, has so far been the financial meltdown of 2007 and the ensuing economic crisis. By the late first decade of the twenty-first century, positive thinking had become ubiquitous and virtually unchallenged in American culture. It was promoted on some of the most widely watched talk shows, like *Larry King Live* and the *Oprah Winfrey Show*; it was the stuff of runaway best sellers like the 2006 book *The Secret*; it had been adopted as the theology of America's most successful evangelical preachers; it found a place in medicine as a potential adjuvant to the treatment of almost any disease. It had even penetrated the academy in the form of the new discipline of "positive psychology," offering courses teaching students to pump up their optimism and nurture their positive feelings. And its reach was growing global, first in the Anglophone countries and soon in the rising economies of China, South Korea, and India.

But nowhere did it find a warmer welcome than in American business, which is, of course, also global business. To the extent that positive thinking had become a business itself, business was its principal client, eagerly consuming the good news that all things are possible through an effort of mind. This was a useful message for employees, who by the turn of the twenty-first century were being required to work longer hours for fewer benefits and diminishing job security. But it was also a liberating ideology for top-level executives. What was the point in agonizing over balance sheets and tedious analyses of risks—and why bother worrying about dizzying levels of debt and exposure to potential defaults—when all good things come to those who are optimistic enough to expect them?

I do not write this in a spirit of sourness or personal disappointment of any kind, nor do I have any romantic attachment to suffering as a source of insight or virtue. On the contrary, I would like to see more smiles, more laughter, more hugs, more happiness and, better yet, joy. In my own vision of utopia, there is not only more comfort, and security for everyone—better jobs, health care, and so forth—there are also more parties, festivities, and opportunities for dancing in the streets. Once our basic material needs are met—in my utopia, anyway—life becomes a perpetual celebration in which everyone has a talent to contribute. But we cannot levitate ourselves into that blessed condition by wishing it. We need to brace ourselves for a struggle against terrifying obstacles, both of our own making and imposed by the natural

---

[9]Hope Yen, "Death in Streets Took a Back Seat to Dinner," *Seattle Times*, Oct. 25, 2005.

world. And the first step is to recover from the mass delusion that is positive thinking.

READING THE TEXT

1. What contradictions have psychological studies found between Americans' valuing of happiness and well-being and their actual state of happiness?

2. When did positive thinking begin to be a cultural trait of Americans, according to Ehrenreich?

3. What is the relationship, in Ehrenreich's view, between positive thinking and capitalism?

4. How, according to Ehrenreich, has positive thinking contributed to recent and current American problems and catastrophes?

5. Examine Ehrenreich's rhetorical strategies. Why does she outline, early in her essay, the reasons that a positive attitude can be helpful? What effect does that discussion have on your response to her essay?

READING THE SIGNS

1. **CONNECTING TEXTS**   Read or reread John Verdant's "The Ables vs. the Binges" (p. 152), and write an argumentative essay in which you demonstrate which family is in fact happy and positive. If you do not believe that either family can be considered in these terms, explain why.

2. Conduct a class debate over the proposition that positive thinking led Americans, especially politicians, to be naïvely optimistic in not anticipating recent national crises despite plenty of warning signs. You might focus on the September 11, 2001, terrorist attacks, the civic disaster wrought on New Orleans by Hurricane Katrina in 2005, or the still ongoing financial meltdown triggered by loose lending practices predicated on the assumption that housing values would only increase.

3. **CONNECTING TEXTS**   Read or reread Laurence Shames's "The More Factor" (p. 90). Adopting Ehrenreich's argument about Americans' predilection for positive thinking, write an essay in which you explain why "the hunger for more," as Shames puts it, is so prevalent in American culture.

4. **CONNECTING TEXTS**   Read or reread Neal Gabler's "The Social Networks" (p. 355), and write an essay in which you argue whether the ever-present friendships and sense of close community that Gabler identifies in some TV shows reflect the sort of positive thinking that Ehrenreich describes. Be sure to base your argument on a close reading of at least one show that Gabler mentions.

5. Read Rhonda Byrne's *The Secret* and write an analysis of how it reflects the American cult of positive thinking. Alternatively, do such an analysis of one of the many in the series of *Chicken Soup for the Soul* books.

JACK SOLOMON

Masters of Desire: The Culture of American Advertising

When the background music in a TV or radio automobile commercial is classical, you can be pretty certain that the ad is pitching a Lexus or a Mercedes. When it's country western, it's probably for Dodge or Chevy. English accents are popular in Jaguar ads, while a good western twang sure helps move pickup trucks. Whenever advertisers make use of status-oriented or common-folk-oriented cultural cues, they are playing on one of America's most fundamental contradictions, as Jack Solomon explains in this cultural analysis of American advertising. The contradiction is between the simultaneous desire for social superiority (elitism) and social equality (populism) that lies at the heart of the American dream. And one way or another, it offers a good way to pitch a product. Solomon, a professor of English at California State University, Northridge, is the author of *The Signs of Our Time* (1988), from which this selection is taken, and *Discourse and Reference in the Nuclear Age* (1988). He is also coeditor with Sonia Maasik of both *California Dreams and Realities* (2005) and this textbook.

Amongst democratic nations, men easily attain a certain equality of condition; but they can never attain as much as they desire.

— ALEXIS DE TOCQUEVILLE

On May 10, 1831, a young French aristocrat named Alexis de Tocqueville arrived in New York City at the start of what would become one of the most famous visits to America in our history. He had come to observe firsthand the institutions of the freest, most egalitarian society of the age, but what he found was a paradox. For behind America's mythic promise of equal opportunity, Tocqueville discovered a desire for *unequal* social rewards, a ferocious competition for privilege and distinction. As he wrote in his monumental study, *Democracy in America*:

When all privileges of birth and fortune are abolished, when all professions are accessible to all, and a man's own energies may place him at the top of any one of them, an easy and unbounded career seems open to his ambition. . . . But this is an erroneous notion, which is corrected by daily experience. [For when] men are nearly alike, and all follow the same track, it is very difficult for any one individual to walk quick and cleave a way through the same throng which surrounds and presses him.

Yet walking quick and cleaving a way is precisely what Americans dream of. We Americans dream of rising above the crowd, of attaining a social summit beyond the reach of ordinary citizens. And therein lies the paradox.

The American dream, in other words, has two faces: the one communally egalitarian and the other competitively elitist. This contradiction is no accident; it is fundamental to the structure of American society. Even as America's great myth of equality celebrates the virtues of mom, apple pie, and the girl or boy next door, it also lures us to achieve social distinction, to rise above the crowd and bask alone in the glory. This land is your land and this land is my land, Woody Guthrie's populist anthem tells us, but we keep trying to increase the "my" at the expense of the "your." Rather than fostering contentment, the American dream breeds desire, a longing for a greater share of the pie. It is as if our society were a vast high-school football game, with the bulk of the participants noisily rooting in the stands while, deep down, each of them is wishing he or she could be the star quarterback or head cheerleader.

For the semiotician, the contradictory nature of the American myth of equality is nowhere written so clearly as in the signs that American advertisers use to manipulate us into buying their wares. "Manipulate" is the word here, not "persuade"; for advertising campaigns are not sources of product information, they are exercises in behavior modification. Appealing to our subconscious emotions rather than to our conscious intellects, advertisements are designed to exploit the discontentments fostered by the American dream, the constant desire for social success and the material rewards that accompany it. America's consumer economy runs on desire, and advertising stokes the engines by transforming common objects — from peanut butter to political candidates — into signs of all the things that Americans covet most.

But by semiotically reading the signs that advertising agencies manufacture to stimulate consumption, we can plot the precise state of desire in the audiences to which they are addressed. Let's look at a representative sample of ads and what they say about the emotional climate of the country and the fast-changing trends of American life. Because ours is a highly diverse, pluralistic society, various advertisements may say different things depending on their intended audiences, but in every case they say something about America, about the status of our hopes, fears, desires, and beliefs.

We'll begin with two ad campaigns conducted by the same company that 5 bear out Alexis de Tocqueville's observations about the contradictory nature of American society: General Motors' campaigns for its Cadillac and Chevrolet lines. First, consider an early magazine ad for the Cadillac Allanté. Appearing as a full-color, four-page insert in *Time*, the ad seems to say "I'm special — and so is this car" even before we've begun to read it. Rather than being printed on the ordinary, flimsy pages of the magazine, the Allanté spread appears on glossy coated stock. The unwritten message here is that an extraordinary car deserves an extraordinary advertisement, and that both car and ad are aimed at an extraordinary consumer, or at least one who wishes to appear extraordinary compared to his more ordinary fellow citizens.

Ads of this kind work by creating symbolic associations between their product and what is most coveted by the consumers to whom they are addressed. It is significant, then, that this ad insists that the Allanté is virtually an Italian rather than an American car, an automobile, as its copy runs, "Conceived and Commissioned by America's Luxury Car Leader — Cadillac" but "Designed and Handcrafted by Europe's Renowned Design Leader — Pininfarina, SpA, of Turin, Italy." This is not simply a piece of product information, it's a sign of the prestige that European luxury cars enjoy in today's automotive marketplace. Once the luxury car of choice for America's status drivers, Cadillac has fallen far behind its European competitors in the race for the prestige market. So the Allanté essentially represents Cadillac's decision, after years of resisting the trend toward European cars, to introduce its own European import — whose high cost is clearly printed on the last page of the ad. . . .

American companies manufacture status symbols because American consumers want them. As Alexis de Tocqueville recognized a century and a half ago, the competitive nature of democratic societies breeds a desire for social distinction, a yearning to rise above the crowd. But given the fact that those who do make it to the top in socially mobile societies have often risen from the lower ranks, they still look like everyone else. In the socially immobile societies of aristocratic Europe, generations of fixed social conditions produced subtle class signals. The accent of one's voice, the shape of one's nose, or even the set of one's chin immediately communicated social status. Aside from the nasal bray and uptilted head of the Boston Brahmin, Americans do not have any native sets of personal status signals. If it weren't for his Mercedes-Benz and Manhattan townhouse, the parvenu Wall Street millionaire often couldn't be distinguished from the man who tailors his suits. Hence, the demand for status symbols, for the objects that mark one off as a social success, is particularly strong in democratic nations — stronger even than in aristocratic societies, where the aristocrat so often looks and sounds different from everyone else.

Status symbols, then, are signs that identify their possessors' place in a social hierarchy, markers of rank and prestige. We can all think of any number of status symbols — Rolls-Royces, Beverly Hills mansions, even shar-pei puppies (whose rareness and expense has rocketed them beyond Russian wolfhounds as status pets and has even inspired whole lines of wrinkle-faced stuffed toys) — but how do we know that something *is* a status symbol? The explanation is quite simple: When an object (or puppy!) either costs a lot of money or requires influential connections to possess, anyone who possesses it must also possess the necessary means and influence to acquire it. The object itself really doesn't matter, since it ultimately disappears behind the presumed social potency of its owner. Semiotically, what matters is the signal it sends, its value as a sign of power. One traditional sign of social distinction is owning a country estate and enjoying the peace and privacy that attend it. Advertisements for Mercedes-Benz, Jaguar, and Audi automobiles thus frequently feature drivers motoring quietly along a country road, presumably on their way to or from their country houses.

Advertisers have been quick to exploit the status signals that belong to body language as well. As Hegel observed in the early nineteenth century, it is an ancient aristocratic prerogative to be seen by the lower orders without having to look at them in return. Tilting his chin high in the air and gazing down at the world under hooded eyelids, the aristocrat invites observation while refusing to look back. We can find such a pose exploited in an advertisement for Cadillac Seville in which we see an elegantly dressed woman out for a drive with her husband in their new Cadillac. If we look closely at the woman's body language, we can see her glance inwardly with a satisfied smile on her face but not outward toward the camera that represents our gaze. She is glad to be seen by us in her Seville, but she isn't interested in looking at *us*!

Ads that are aimed at a broader market take the opposite approach. If the 10
American dream encourages the desire to "arrive," to vault above the mass, it also fosters a desire to be popular, to "belong." Populist commercials accordingly transform products into signs of belonging, utilizing such common icons as country music, small-town life, family picnics, and farmyards. All of these icons are incorporated in GM's Heartbeat of America campaign for its Chevrolet line. Unlike the Seville commercial, the faces in the Chevy ads look straight at us and smile. Dress is casual; the mood upbeat. Quick camera cuts take us from rustic to suburban to urban scenes, creating an American montage filmed from sea to shining sea. We all "belong" in a Chevy.

Where price alone doesn't determine the market for a product, advertisers can go either way. Both Johnnie Walker and Jack Daniel's are better-grade whiskies, but where a Johnnie Walker ad appeals to the buyer who wants a mark of aristocratic distinction in his liquor, a Jack Daniel's ad emphasizes the down-home, egalitarian folksiness of its product. Johnnie Walker associates itself with such conventional status symbols as sable coats, Rolls-Royces, and black gold; Jack Daniel's gives us a Good Ol' Boy in overalls. In fact, Jack Daniel's Good Ol' Boy is an icon of backwoods independence, recalling the days of the moonshiner and the Whisky Rebellion of 1794. Evoking emotions quite at odds with those stimulated in Johnnie Walker ads, the advertisers of Jack Daniel's have chosen to transform their product into a sign of America's populist tradition. The fact that both ads successfully sell whisky is itself a sign of the dual nature of the American dream. . . .

Populist advertising is particularly effective in the face of foreign competition. When Americans feel threatened from the outside, they tend to circle the wagons and temporarily forget their class differences. In the face of the Japanese automotive "invasion," Chrysler runs populist commercials in which Lee Iacocca joins the simple folk who buy his cars as the jingle "Born in America" blares in the background. Seeking to capitalize on the popularity of Bruce Springsteen's *Born in the USA* album, these ads gloss over Springsteen's ironic lyrics in a vast display of flag-waving. Chevrolet's Heartbeat of America campaign attempts to woo American motorists away from Japanese automobiles by appealing to their patriotic sentiments.

The patriotic iconography of these campaigns also reflects the general cultural mood of the early to mid-1980s. After a period of national anguish in the wake of the Vietnam War and the Iran hostage crisis, America went on a patriotic binge. American athletic triumphs in the Lake Placid and Los Angeles Olympics introduced a sporting tone into the national celebration, often making international affairs appear like one great Olympiad in which America was always going for the gold. In response, advertisers began to do their own flag-waving.

The mood of advertising during this period was definitely upbeat. Even deodorant commercials, which traditionally work on our self-doubts and fears of social rejection, jumped on the bandwagon. In the guilty sixties, we had ads like the Ice Blue Secret campaign with its connotations of guilt and shame. In the feel-good Reagan eighties, Sure deodorant commercials featured images of triumphant Americans throwing up their arms in victory to reveal—no wet marks! Deodorant commercials once had the moral echo of Nathaniel Hawthorne's guilt-ridden *The Scarlet Letter*; in the early eighties they had all the moral subtlety of *Rocky IV*, reflecting the emotions of a Vietnam-weary nation eager to embrace the imagery of America Triumphant. . . .

Live the Fantasy

By reading the signs of American advertising, we can conclude that America is a nation of fantasizers, often preferring the sign to the substance and easily enthralled by a veritable Fantasy Island of commercial illusions. Critics of Madison Avenue often complain that advertisers create consumer desire, but semioticians don't think the situation is that simple. Advertisers may give shape to consumer fantasies, but they need raw material to work with, the subconscious dreams and desires of the marketplace. As long as these desires remain unconscious, advertisers will be able to exploit them. But by bringing the fantasies to the surface, you can free yourself from advertising's often hypnotic grasp.

I can think of no company that has more successfully seized upon the subconscious fantasies of the American marketplace—indeed the world marketplace—than McDonald's. By no means the first nor the only hamburger chain in the United States, McDonald's emerged victorious in the "burger wars" by transforming hamburgers into signs of all that was desirable in American life. Other chains like Wendy's, Burger King, and Jack-In-The-Box continue to advertise and sell widely, but no company approaches McDonald's transformation of itself into a symbol of American culture.

McDonald's success can be traced to the precision of its advertising. Instead of broadcasting a single "one-size-fits-all" campaign at a time, McDonald's pitches its burgers simultaneously at different age groups, different classes, even different races (Budweiser beer, incidentally, has succeeded in the same way). For children, there is the Ronald McDonald campaign, which presents a fantasy world that has little to do with hamburgers in any rational sense but a great deal to do with the emotional desires of kids. Ronald McDonald and his friends are signs that recall the Muppets, *Sesame Street*, the circus, toys, storybook illustrations, even *Alice in Wonderland*. Such signs do not signify hamburgers. Rather, they are displayed in order to prompt in the child's mind an automatic association of fantasy, fun, and McDonald's.

The same approach is taken in ads aimed at older audiences — teens, adults, and senior citizens. In the teen-oriented ads we may catch a fleeting glimpse of a hamburger or two, but what we are really shown is a teenage fantasy: groups of hip and happy adolescents singing, dancing, and cavorting together. Fearing loneliness more than anything else, adolescents quickly respond to the group appeal of such commercials. "Eat a Big Mac," these ads say, "and you won't be stuck home alone on Saturday night."

To appeal to an older and more sophisticated audience no longer so afraid of not belonging and more concerned with finding a place to go out to at night, McDonald's has designed the elaborate "Mac Tonight" commercials, which have for their backdrop a nightlit urban skyline and at their center a cabaret pianist with a moon-shaped head, a glad manner, and Blues Brothers shades. Such signs prompt an association of McDonald's with nightclubs and urban sophistication, persuading us that McDonald's is a place not only for breakfast or lunch but for dinner too, as if it were a popular off-Broadway nightspot, a place to see and be seen. Even the parody of Kurt Weill's "Mack the Knife" theme song that Mac the Pianist performs is a sign, a subtle signal to the sophisticated hamburger eater able to recognize the origin of the tune in Bertolt Brecht's *Threepenny Opera*.

For yet older customers, McDonald's has designed a commercial around 20 the fact that it employs a large number of retirees and seniors. In one such ad, we see an elderly man leaving his pretty little cottage early in the morning to start work as "the new kid" at McDonald's, and then we watch him during his first day on the job. Of course he is a great success, outdoing everyone else with his energy and efficiency, and he returns home in the evening to a loving wife and a happy home. One would almost think that the ad was a kind of moving "help wanted" sign (indeed, McDonald's *was* hiring elderly employees at the time), but it's really just directed at consumers. Older viewers can see themselves wanted and appreciated in the ad — and perhaps be distracted from the rationally uncomfortable fact that many senior citizens take such jobs because of financial need and thus may be unlikely to own the sort of home that one sees in the commercial. But realism isn't the point here. This is fantasyland, a dream world promising instant gratification no matter what the facts of the matter may be.

Practically the only fantasy that McDonald's doesn't exploit is the fantasy of sex. This is understandable, given McDonald's desire to present itself as a family restaurant. But everywhere else, sexual fantasies, which have always had an important place in American advertising, are beginning to dominate the advertising scene. You expect sexual come-ons in ads for perfume or cosmetics or jewelry — after all, that's what they're selling — but for room deodorizers? In a magazine ad for Claire Burke home fragrances, for example, we see a well-dressed couple cavorting about their bedroom in what looks like a cheery preparation for sadomasochistic exercises. Jordache and Calvin Klein pitch blue jeans as props for teenage sexuality. The phallic appeal of automobiles, traditionally an implicit feature in automotive advertising, becomes quite explicit in a Dodge commercial that shifts back and forth from shots of a young man in an automobile to teasing glimpses of a woman — his date — as she dresses in her apartment.

The very language of today's advertisements is charged with sexuality. Products in the more innocent fifties were "new and improved," but everything in the eighties is "hot!" — as in "hot woman," or sexual heat. Cars are "hot." Movies are "hot." An ad for Valvoline pulses to the rhythm of a "heat wave, burning in my car." Sneakers get red hot in a magazine ad for Travel Fox athletic shoes in which we see male and female figures, clad only in Travel Fox shoes, apparently in the act of copulation — an ad that earned one of *Adweek*'s annual "badvertising" awards for shoddy advertising.

The sexual explicitness of contemporary advertising is a sign not so much of American sexual fantasies as of the lengths to which advertisers will go to get attention. Sex never fails as an attention-getter, and in a particularly competitive, and expensive, era for American marketing, advertisers like to bet on a sure thing. Ad people refer to the proliferation of TV, radio, newspaper, magazine, and billboard ads as "clutter," and nothing cuts through the clutter like sex.

By showing the flesh, advertisers work on the deepest, most coercive human emotions of all. Much sexual coercion in advertising, however, is a sign of a desperate need to make certain that clients are getting their money's worth. The appearance of advertisements that refer directly to the prefabricated fantasies of Hollywood is a sign of a different sort of desperation: a desperation for ideas. With the rapid turnover of advertising campaigns mandated by the need to cut through the "clutter," advertisers may be hard pressed for new ad concepts, and so they are more and more frequently turning to already-established models. In the early 1980s, for instance, Pepsi-Cola ran a series of ads broadly alluding to Steven Spielberg's *E.T.* In one such ad, we see a young boy, who, like the hero of *E.T.*, witnesses an extraterrestrial visit. The boy is led to a soft-drink machine where he pauses to drink a can of Pepsi as the spaceship he's spotted flies off into the universe. The relationship between the ad and the movie, accordingly, is a parasitical one, with the ad taking its life from the creative body of the film. . . .

Madison Avenue has also framed ad campaigns around the cultural prestige of high-tech machinery. This is especially the case with sports cars, whose high-tech appeal is so powerful that some people apparently fantasize about *being* sports cars. At least, this is the conclusion one might draw from a Porsche commercial that asked its audience, "If you were a car, what kind of car would you be?" As a candy-red Porsche speeds along a rain-slick forest road, the ad's voice-over describes all the specifications you'd want to have if you *were* a sports car. "If you were a car," the commercial concludes, "you'd be a Porsche."

In his essay "Car Commercials and *Miami Vice*," Todd Gitlin explains the semiotic appeal of such ads as those in the Porsche campaign. Aired at the height of what may be called America's "myth of the entrepreneur," these commercials were aimed at young corporate managers who imaginatively identified with the "lone wolf" image of a Porsche speeding through the woods. Gitlin points out that such images cater to the fantasies of faceless corporate men who dream of entrepreneurial glory, of striking out on their own like John DeLorean and telling the boss to take his job and shove it. But as DeLorean's spectacular failure demonstrates, the life of the entrepreneur can be extremely risky. So rather than having to go it alone and take the risks that accompany entrepreneurial independence, the young executive can substitute fantasy for reality by climbing into his Porsche — or at least that's what Porsche's advertisers wanted him to believe.

But there is more at work in the Porsche ads than the fantasies of corporate America. Ever since Arthur C. Clarke and Stanley Kubrick teamed up to present us with HAL 9000, the demented computer of *2001: A Space Odyssey*, the American imagination has been obsessed with the melding of man and machine. First there was television's *Six Million Dollar Man*, and then movieland's *Star Wars*, *Blade Runner*, and *Robocop*, fantasy visions of a future dominated by machines. Androids haunt our imaginations as machines seize the initiative. *Time* magazine's "Man of the Year" for 1982 was a computer. Robot-built automobiles appeal to drivers who spend their days in front of computer screens — perhaps designing robots. When so much power and prestige is being given to high-tech machines, wouldn't you rather be a Porsche?

In short, the Porsche campaign is a sign of a new mythology that is emerging before our eyes, a myth of the machine, which is replacing the myth of the human. The iconic figure of the little tramp caught up in the cogs of industrial production in Charlie Chaplin's *Modern Times* signified a humanistic revulsion to the age of the machine. Human beings, such icons said, were superior to machines. Human values should come first in the moral order of things. But as Edith Milton suggests in her essay "The Track of the Mutant," we are now coming to believe that machines are superior to human beings, that mechanical nature is superior to human nature. Rather than being threatened by machines, we long to merge with them. *The Six Million Dollar Man* is one iconic figure in the new mythology; Harrison Ford's sexual coupling with an android is another. In such an age it should come as little wonder that computer-synthesized Max Headroom should be a commercial spokesman for Coca-Cola, or that Federal Express should design a series of TV ads featuring mechanical-looking human beings revolving around strange and powerful machines.

Fear and Trembling in the Marketplace

While advertisers play on and reflect back at us our fantasies about every-thing from fighter pilots to robots, they also play on darker imaginings. If dream and desire can be exploited in the quest for sales, so can nightmare and fear.

The nightmare equivalent of America's populist desire to "belong," for example, is the fear of not belonging, of social rejection, of being different. Advertisements for dandruff shampoos, mouthwashes, deodorants, and laun-dry detergents ("Ring around the Collar!") accordingly exploit such fears, bul-lying us into consumption. Although ads of this type were still around in the 1980s, they were particularly common in the fifties and early sixties, reflect-ing a society still reeling from the witch-hunts of the McCarthy years. When any sort of social eccentricity or difference could result in a public denuncia-tion and the loss of one's job or even liberty, Americans were keen to con-form and be like everyone else. No one wanted to be "guilty" of smelling bad or of having a dirty collar.

"Guilt" ads characteristically work by creating narrative situations in which someone is "accused" of some social "transgression," pronounced guilty, and then offered the sponsor's product as a means of returning to "innocence." Such ads, in essence, are parodies of ancient religious rituals of guilt and atonement, whereby sinning humanity is offered salvation through the agency of priest and church. In the world of advertising, a product takes the place of the priest, but the logic of the situation is quite similar.

In commercials for Wisk detergent, for example, we witness the drama of a hapless housewife and her husband as they are mocked by the jeering voices of children shouting "Ring around the Collar!" "Oh, those dirty rings!" the housewife groans in despair. It's as if she and her husband were being stoned by an angry crowd. But there's hope, there's help, there's Wisk. Cleansing her soul of sin as well as her husband's, the housewife launders his shirts with Wisk, and behold, his collars are clean. Product salvation is only as far as the supermarket. . . .

If guilt looks backward in time to past transgressions, fear, like desire, faces forward, trembling before the future. In the late 1980s, a new kind of fear commercial appeared, one whose narrative played on the worries of young corporate managers struggling up the ladder of success. Represent-ing the nightmare equivalent of the elitist desire to "arrive," ads of this sort created images of failure, storylines of corporate defeat. In one ad for Apple computers, for example, a group of junior executives sits around a table with the boss as he asks each executive how long it will take his or her department to complete some publishing jobs. "Two or three days," answers one nervous executive. "A week, on overtime," a tight-lipped woman responds. But one young up-and-comer can have everything ready tomorrow, today, or yester-day, because his department uses a Macintosh desktop publishing system. Guess who'll get the next promotion?

For other markets, there are other fears. If McDonald's presents senior citizens with bright fantasies of being useful and appreciated beyond retirement, companies like Secure Horizons dramatize senior citizens' fears of being caught short by a major illness. Running its ads in the wake of budgetary cuts in the Medicare system, Secure Horizons designed a series of commercials featuring a pleasant old man named Harry — who looks and sounds rather like Carroll O'Connor — who tells us the story of the scare he got during his wife's recent illness. Fearing that next time Medicare won't cover the bills, he has purchased supplemental health insurance from Secure Horizons and now securely tends his roof-top garden. . . .

The Future of an Illusion

There are some signs in the advertising world that Americans are getting fed 35
up with fantasy advertisements and want to hear some straight talk. Weary
of extravagant product claims and irrelevant associations, consumers trained
by years of advertising to distrust what they hear seem to be developing an
immunity to commercials. At least, this is the semiotic message I read in the
"new realism" advertisements of the eighties, ads that attempt to convince
you that what you're seeing is the real thing, that the ad is giving you the
straight dope, not advertising hype.

You can recognize the "new realism" by its camera techniques. The
lighting is usually subdued to give the ad the effect of being filmed without
studio lighting or special filters. The scene looks gray, as if the blinds were
drawn. The camera shots are jerky and off-angle, often zooming in for sudden and unflattering close-ups, as if the cameraman were an amateur with
a home video recorder. In a "realistic" ad for AT&T, for example, we are
treated to a monologue by a plump stockbroker — his plumpness intended
as a sign that he's for real and not just another actor — who tells us about the
problems he's had with his phone system (not AT&T's) as the camera jerks
around, generally filming him from below as if the cameraman couldn't
quite fit his equipment into the crammed office and had to film the scene on
his knees. "This is no fancy advertisement," the ad tries to convince us, "this
is sincere."

An ad for Miller draft beer tries the same approach, re-creating the effect
of an amateur videotape of a wedding celebration. Camera shots shift suddenly from group to group. The picture jumps. Bodies are poorly framed. The
color is washed out. Like the beer it is pushing, the ad is supposed to strike us
as being "as real as it gets."

Such ads reflect a desire for reality in the marketplace, a weariness with
Madison Avenue illusions. But there's no illusion like the illusion of reality.
Every special technique that advertisers use to create their "reality effects"
is, in fact, more unrealistic than the techniques of "illusory" ads. The world,
in reality, doesn't jump around when you look at it. It doesn't appear in

subdued gray tones. Our eyes don't have zoom lenses, and we don't look at things with our heads cocked to one side. The irony of the "new realism" is that it is more unrealistic, more artificial, than the ordinary run of television advertising.

But don't expect any truly realistic ads in the future, because a realistic advertisement is a contradiction in terms. The logic of advertising is entirely semiotic: It substitutes signs for things, framed visions of consumer desire for the thing itself. The success of modern advertising, its penetration into every corner of American life, reflects a culture that has itself chosen illusion over reality. At a time when political candidates all have professional image-makers attached to their staffs, and the president of the United States can be an actor who once sold shirt collars, all the cultural signs are pointing to more illusions in our lives rather than fewer — a fecund breeding ground for the world of the advertiser.

READING THE TEXT

1. Describe in your own words the paradox of the American dream, as Solomon sees it.

2. In Solomon's view, why do status symbols work particularly well in manipulating American consumers?

3. What is a "guilt" ad (para. 33), according to Solomon, and how does it affect consumers?

4. Why, in Solomon's view, has McDonald's been so successful in its ad campaigns?

5. What relationship does Solomon find between the "new realism" (para. 38) of some ads and the paradoxes of the American dream?

READING THE SIGNS

1. **CONNECTING TEXTS**   The American political scene has changed since the late 1980s, when this essay was first published. In an analytic essay, argue whether you believe the contradiction between populism and elitism that Solomon describes still affects American advertising and media. Be sure to discuss specific media examples. To develop your ideas, you might consult Thomas Frank's "Commodify Your Dissent" (p. 163).

2. **CONNECTING TEXTS**   Read or reread David Brooks's "One Nation, Slightly Divisible" (p. 524). In an essay, argue whether you find a correlation between the red-state/blue-state dichotomy that he describes and Solomon's populist-elitist paradox. Be sure to support your position with specific examples from the media or consumer culture.

3. Bring to class a general-interest magazine such as *Time*, and in small groups study the advertising. Do the ads tend to have an elitist or popular appeal? What relationship do you see between the appeal you identify and the magazine's target readership? Present your group's findings to the class.

4. In class, brainstorm a list of status symbols common in advertising today. Then discuss what groups they appeal to and why. Can you detect any patterns based on gender, ethnicity, or age?

5. Visit your college library, and locate an issue of a popular magazine from earlier decades, such as the 1930s or 1940s. Then write an essay in which you compare and contrast the advertising found in that early issue with that in a current issue of the same publication. What similarities and differences do you find in the myths underlying the advertising, and what is their significance?

PHYLLIS M. JAPP AND DEBRA K. JAPP

Purification through Simplification: Nature, the Good Life, and Consumer Culture

One of the greatest paradoxes of American culture is its simultaneous devotion to rampant consumerism and its celebration of rural simplicity as the ideal model for "the Good Life." And as Phyllis M. Japp and Debra K. Japp argue in this reading, these two contradictory impulses come together in the "voluntary simplicity movement." Selecting the Home and Garden network's reality TV series *The Good Life* as an apt expression of the movement and subjecting it to an in-depth rhetorical analysis, they find a similar theme in each episode — people "who have left highly paid, highly stressed jobs in the city and relocated to a more natural environment to live a simpler and therefore better life" — with a similar outcome: "Voluntary simplicity . . . appears to reinforce dictates of simple living while wrapped firmly within commodity culture, defining it primarily as a psychological search for self-actualization in which nature becomes a resource for purchase." Phyllis M. Japp is a professor emerita in the Department of Communication Studies at the University of Nebraska-Lincoln, and is the coeditor, with Mark Meister, of *Enviropop: Studies in Environmental Rhetoric and Popular Culture* (2002), from which this essay is taken. Debra K. Japp is a professor of communications studies at St. Cloud State University.

The search for the good life is a major theme in human societies, from Aristotle to the present. In its current incarnation in late twentieth century America, the term represents dual and contradictory visions. Since the beginning of the nation, two major myths of the good life have developed simultaneously. The first is the belief in happiness and fulfillment through technology, the availability and acquisition of wealth and possessions, upward social mobility, and political influence. Existing alongside and countering this mythos has been the belief that happiness and fulfillment are found in a life of simplicity, one with the minimum of possessions, a life that does not seek wealth or influence but finds joy in connection to nature and service to others. As Shi (1985) notes, "From colonial days, the image of America as a spiritual commonwealth and a republic of virtue has survived alongside the more tantalizing vision of America as a cornucopia of economic opportunities and consumer delights" (p. 277). If these are the two poles in the definition of the good life, there have been many variations over the years, as each era has engaged the tension between having less and having more.

In times of prosperity and unchecked consumption, when it seems as if the "more is better" mentality has gained complete control, a growing sense of unease and guilt seems to draw the "less is more" rhetoric into focus and odes to a simpler mode of life appear.

In popular culture, the opposing visions of the good life are integrated into advertising, entertainment, and popular literature. For example, a Sears advertising campaign informs consumers that Sears stands ready to supply the "good life at a great price, guaranteed" as we view clothing, appliances, and other commodities supposedly essential to the quality of life. Alternately, the state of Nebraska's advertising slogan is "Nebraska — The Good Life," invoking visions of endless sky and bountiful prairies, a place where life is simple and nature revered. Note that however contradictory these visions are in many respects, nature in some form is necessary to their fulfillment. In the first version, nature must provide the resources utilized to manufacture the endless list of commodities now necessary to living the good life, the SUVs and fuel to run them, the lumber for bigger and bigger homes, the land that can be converted to golf courses and resorts where one can vacation in style. In the second version, nature is a spiritual and psychological resource, a retreat from the frantic pace of urban life, a reassurance in the healing powers of the earth. . . .

If the "more is better" mythos uses nature as raw material to develop and maintain the commodities necessary for the good life, the "less is more" mythos finds the real meaning of life in the human connection to natural environments. Nature plays a central role in this vision of life. Shi (1985) observes: "Contact with nature, whether the virgin wilderness, the plowed field, or the Arcadian retreat, meant turning away from the artificiality of modern civilization to more abiding realities. God and goodness always seemed more accessible in the woods than in the city. Moreover, the countryside offered fresh air and a stimulus to strenuous activity" (p. 195). And Kenneth Burke (1984b) concurs: "The most basic support of all, the Earth, is perhaps the deepest source of reestablishment for bewildered sophisticates who, having lost all sense of a moral fountainhead, would restore themselves by contact with the 'telluric'" (1984b, p. 205).

While simple living has been a consistent theme since the beginning of   5
the republic, it remains an abstraction that can be shaped to fit a variety of
conditions and purposes. As Shi (1985) notes, "the precise meaning of the
simple life has never been fixed"; rather, it has always been represented by "a
shifting cluster of ideas, sentiments, and activities" (p. 3). Staple ingredients
in the traditional recipe have included "a hostility toward luxury and a suspicion of riches, a reverence for nature and a preference for rural over urban
ways of life and work, a desire for personal self-reliance through frugality
and diligence, a nostalgia for the past and a skepticism toward the claims of
modernity, conscientious rather than conspicuous consumption, and an aesthetic taste for the plain and functional" (Shi, 1985, p. 3). Thus the concept
survives as both an "enduring myth" and as "an actual way of living" for at
least a few citizens in each era (Shi, 1985, p. 279). In a technologically oriented commodity culture, we argue, this longstanding tradition of frugal living
is transformed by an inescapable dependence on, and embrace of, products
and services that have come to be defined as necessities of life. The reverence
for nature is transformed into consumption as well, as the natural environment becomes yet another commodity, to be owned or appropriated as part
of the simple lifestyle. Thus the rhetoric of simple living is inescapably infiltrated with the attitudes and orientations of consumption.

Burke and Environmental Rhetoric

Kenneth Burke looms as an important figure in many works on environmental rhetoric. He is well suited to be the patron theorist of environmental criticism for several reasons. First, Burke lived the life of an environmentalist,
rejecting a life revolving around commodities for one closely in touch with
the earth, the seasons, the rhythms of nature. Burks (1991) notes that Burke
"seems to have despised consumerism and capitalism's promotion of it
throughout his adult life" (p. 224). His lifestyle (Burke called himself an "agro-
bohemian" with "Garden of Eden plumbing") testified to his rejection of consumer values and his need for engagement with nature (Burks, 1991, p. 224).
Second, the environment is a theme that runs through his writings. Examples
of the barnyard, the wren, the hapless fish with a faulty orientation, references to walking down the road, gardening, and the weather not only permeate his work but provided him inspiration to develop his critical perspective.
Third, Burke's theory of symbolic action, his "tools" for deconstructing rhetoric, is ideal for discovering nuances in cultural artifacts. These tools are especially useful for the investigation of popular culture, for it is clear that what
we desire, buy, eat, and wear, and where and how we choose to live are symbolic responses that articulate, support, and/or challenge the power structures
of cultural institutions.

While Burke makes a number of specific references to the good life, the
concept implicitly pervades his thought and energizes much of his terminology.

Indeed, one could argue that a subtext of Burke's corpus could be the search for the good life, with attendant warnings about those motivational patterns that placed such in peril. Writing in the 1930s, Burke was traumatized by the Depression, by economic threats to the quality of life. By the 1960s he feared that nuclear war, the technology of destruction, could destroy all that we valued in life. He increasingly believed that environmental pollution, exacerbated and excused by consumer culture, stood poised to destroy any hope of a good life lived in tune with nature. Although he personally chose a life of simplicity, he was aware that the accumulation of possessions was the definition that most citizens embraced. Thus what is examined here, the cultural tension between the simple life of "less" and the commodified life of "more," is a tension also evident in Burke from *Counterstatement* (1968) to his last essays.

"Voluntary Simplicity": A Variation on *The Good Life*

A recent trend in contemporary popular culture is often termed "voluntary simplicity." This current variation on the theme of simple living is described in how-to books, films, television programming, and magazines. A recent bibliography of over 160 recent books, posted on a simple living Web site, includes such titles as *Circle of Simplicity: Return to the Good Life, 101 Ways to Simplify Your Life, Six Weeks to a Simpler Life Style*, and *Skills for Simple Living*. Two simple living magazines have been recently launched, *Real Simple* and *Simplycity*. As *USA Today* observes in reviewing the magazines, "The simple life now comes with instructions" (Horovitz, 2000, p. 1A). Certainly there is much variation evident within this theme. Some advocate a complete lifestyle change and rejection of consumer values; others seek to downsize and de-stress within present circumstances. For still others, simplicity is a stylistic trend that determines which new home décor to purchase and what sort of vacation to take.

The vast amount of self-help literature surrounding this movement calls to mind Burke's (1973b) assertion that the people who consume such literature often have no intention of actually doing what is advocated. Reading is not the *prelude to*, but the *substitute for*, action; vicarious, armchair experience is less threatening than facing the decisions necessary for change (1973b, pp. 298–299). Certainly the widespread popularity of simple living ideas seems to have made little difference in the consumption styles of most of the population.

The theme of voluntary simplicity holds an especially powerful appeal for middle-class professionals torn between the need for more and the need for less as they try to manage the complexity of their lives. As with most calls for change, however, the desire for simple, painless maxims drives this massive quantity of literature. Irony abounds as self-styled experts in simplicity write books, circulate newspapers and magazines, develop Web sites, and

10

travel the country presenting symposiums, consuming fuel and resources in the process, thereby reinforcing the importance of money, space, mobility, and other non-simple practices. The irony is reinforced as the media technology that has developed around the desire for wealth, that is the proliferation of materials, seminars, books, and guides advising people how to get rich, is now employed to help people simplify their lives. In the case study to follow, the television program *The Good Life* depends upon a complex media organization and a profusion of technology, including the equipment required to film a television series, although such is carefully kept out of camera range, rendering invisible its intrusion on the pristine natural settings in which the program is usually filmed.

Equally ironic is that this effort at simplicity must be *voluntary*, the result of a choice to renounce affluence and artificiality. The poor, who live lives of enforced rather than voluntary simplicity, are deprived of the moral value of such lives, voluntary simplicity being the prerogative of those "free to choose their standard of living" rather than the sordid poverty of those on the lower socioeconomic rungs of the hierarchy (Shi, 1985, p. 7). "Selective indulgence" is the theme of much of the current literature. As MonDesire (2000) notes, "The nostalgic urge for a simple life by and large emanates from people who've never had to duck a landlord on the first of the month, never had to wait in the rain for a packed city bus that rides on by, never had to slide the money for a half-gallon of milk under the narrow slot in a grocery store's bullet-proof window" (p. 19A).

Overall, the simple life appears dictated by personal needs and is framed almost entirely in the desire for fulfillment and personal growth. Converts do not renounce consumerism for religious reasons, for political dedication, or as a result of an environmental conscience. The quest is personal not political; secular rather than religious; self- instead of other-centered. As defined by the oxymoronic *Simple Life Corporation*, the concept means a journey, an awakening to self and one's inner needs, the removal of things that distract one from "finding" oneself, including not only possessions but activities, relationships, and duties. A *Cathy* cartoon strip neatly sums up the ironies. The script reads: "The simple life: Discard the day planner, disconnect call waiting, unplug the TV, cancel all subscriptions, say 'no' to invitations, clear closets and cupboards of everything but the bare essentials, and travel to a cool, quiet place that inspires possibility. The Mall" (Guisewrite, 2000).

HGTV's *The Good Life*

A variety of texts could be used to exemplify the rhetoric of voluntary simplicity, for example, Internet Web sites, books, advice columns, sermons, and instructional seminars, for it is the interaction of these aspects of popular culture that constructs and supports the ideologies of simple living. For this essay, a Home and Garden network (HGTV) half-hour series entitled *The*

Good Life was chosen and the analysis included more than twenty episodes aired over a period of two years. Although the stories vary — there are former lawyers, professors, journalists, models, executives, importers, even oil riggers — they are all variations on a theme. All articulate a core vision of what it means to live the good life. The stories, in fact, are strikingly similar despite the assurance that the good life is different for every individual. In these dramatic presentations the cultural drama of "less is more" plays out against its counter, "more is better." The stories are introduced as examples of people ("people just like you and me" the narrator assures us) who have left highly paid, highly stressed jobs in the city and relocated to a more natural environment to live a simpler and therefore better life. The verbal and visual dramas provide standard, mutually reinforcing formulas as viewers follow the stories of people who have changed their lives, following their dreams to the good life. Although viewers experience visual and verbal dramas simultaneously, in this chapter visual and verbal dramas are each considered first as a separate domain of meaning, and then considered together to point out how each complements the other as they construct the meanings of *The Good Life*.

The Verbal Drama of *The Good Life*

The verbal drama of *The Good Life* is a classic example of Burke's dramatistic process of guilt, repentance, and redemption. This well-known cycle of cleansing, drawn from religious rhetoric, is appropriated by Burke as a critical strategy for understanding how both social and personal change takes place symbolically. In this drama, conflicts of motives construct hierarchies, which in turn create various sorts of guilt. These shortcomings, when recognized, require change or redemption. Burke argues this process as fundamental to human communication. Thus in any situation, a critic can profitably look for the guilt, that is, the shortcoming, inadequacy, inconsistency, need for closure, that is the impetus for communicating. In the inevitable socioeconomic hierarchies, those with more are guilty of their excesses, those with less, of their lack of prestige or attainments; and each must seek to be redeemed via explanation and justification. In any social structure characterized by hierarchies, says Burke (1966), "Those 'Up' are guilty of not being 'Down,' those 'Down' are certainly guilty of not being 'Up'" (1966, p. 15). These are not necessarily conscious emotions or explicit rhetorical strategies but are inherent motives or "patterns of action" that drive explanations, justifications, comparisons, identifications, divisions. In *The Good Life*, these implicit motives become an explicit motif or narrative form.

　　The Good Life features such salvation stories as its fundamental script. Participants guilty of the sin of overwork at high-stress professions and refugees from frantic urban lifestyles repent of their erring ways and seek redemption. Nature is, as we will see, the primary agency of purification. Thus each episode of *The Good Life* turns on a conversion experience, as overworked suburbanites discover that something is missing in their lives and embrace change. At the root of their desires is a need for purification, through nature, from the guilt of consumerism. They repent, turn from their current way of life, and become new people, born again to a supposedly simpler existence, closer to nature, and implicitly, closer to God. Edye Ellis, the host and guru of the program, serves as an evangelist for this lifestyle change, exhorting others to follow in the footsteps of those whose conversion story was featured in this week's program. As with the self-help genre that infuses this portrayal, there is the "before and after" theme characteristic of any narrative of change (weight loss, addiction recovery, relational renewal, or political or religious conversions, to mention a few examples). The story each week follows the standard form of conversion testimony, from guilt to repentance to redemption.

Establishing guilt. The narrative begins with attention to the pathology of the participants' old way of life, by implication a "bad life." They describe their former lives as filled with stress, complexity, urban crowding, and long daily commutes, as they recount long hours on the job, mourn their disconnect from nature, and describe familial relationships in peril. The resulting self-diagnosis is described as a loss of self, identity, and meaning. They are no longer satisfied with the success they sought, the prestige gained, or the possessions accumulated by climbing the ladder to the top of their professions. "There must be something better" is the mantra of these seeking souls. For example, a former university dean tells of the day he discovered that he "had everything he wanted but didn't want anything he had" and vowed to quit his job and change his life.

Evincing repentance. The conversion always involves *risk* as well as renunciation. Penitents must pay the price by taking an economic or social risk, giving up something, either something *actual* (e.g., a high salary, social prestige) or *potential* (e.g., the chance for advancement). The "no pain, no gain" formula is reminiscent of the stories of risk-taking in pursuit of wealth. The definitions of risk, however, are comfortingly middle class, attractive to those who know they can somehow recover what may be lost. Thus they risk investing their savings in a business, in a move from a familiar location, by leaving their circle of friends, by choosing to live in a smaller space, or by making do with fewer possessions in their quest for something better. Although there is an attempt to maintain suspense, risk remains little more than a minor and temporary challenge to their middle-class values and identities. For example, a former journalist risks his savings to open a bakery in a small town, a Texas landscaper invests his life savings to convert a rural hotel to a bed-and-breakfast, a Chicago lawyer abandons his practice to open a restaurant.

Seeking redemption. Once willingness to risk is established, the redemptive moment of the narrative occurs, a turning point of almost mystical quality. Some penitents drive down a country road and find at the end a location where they are "meant to be." Or they may discover a small town and feel instantly as if they were born there. Almost always this redemptive moment involves some contact with the earth, or with nature in some form. This mystical moment is also a pivotal point at which penitents can surrender and embrace the salvation of the good life or draw back from the risk and remain doomed to its alternative. Following the muse involves, above all, the search for a location where a good life is possible. Few manage the conversion without some physical move, most frequently from urban to rural, large town to small town.

Thus, communion with nature is essential to the good life, whether from a cabin in the woods, a farm, the rural charm of a small town, or even a tranquil garden in a suburban backyard. Also essential to the conversion experience is a new occupation compatible with the conversion values. Work in some form is essential; few remain idle. Entrepreneurship is especially attractive, satisfying the yearning to be one's own boss, control one's own time. Artistry is likewise a key to the good life (writing, crafting, achieving creative fulfillment, and frequently making money from the endeavor). The new occupation or avocation often requires some contact with the earth, from growing one's own food to using natural products to make beautiful and artistic creations.

A constant redemptive theme is the search for ideal relationships, for [20] people with whom one can live the good life. Some converts bring intact families in need of renewal via simplicity; some seek change because of broken relationships and look for new, like-minded friends and/or life partners. Problems in previous relationships are linked to the values and practices of the old life (to date we have seen no programs about those whose relationships have broken up as a result of converting to the simple life). The search for self is paramount, however. As the old life is stripped away, as old locations, occupations, and relationships are replaced, the unique authentic self of the convert is revealed, hidden below the artificiality of the old life. The needs that were ignored in the complexity of urban professional life can now thrive and grow. Hidden skills and talents are uncovered: a professor discovers he is an artist, a former model becomes a world-class chef, others find amazing abilities to sculpt, create music, take prize-winning photographs.

Bearing witness. The final turn of the salvation drama is the evangelical responsibility of the convert. All participants devoutly affirm that they are now living the good life, lives of "deep fulfillment" as one declares. To a person, they express no regrets or nostalgia for the life left behind. The gains are far greater than the losses, the satisfaction worth the risk. They encourage others to make the same choice, again emphasizing choice and reinforcing the voluntary nature of their life change. The host completes the narrative with an altar call for conversion as she addresses viewers directly: "You too can have the good life." Like these inspiring stories, renewal begins "one step at a time."

Nature's role as commodity is evident in the consumerist attitude of selecting and owning an appropriate natural setting or backdrop for living the simple life. Control of life choices remains central; the stories turn on the volunteerist motive. The centrality of voluntary choice is significant. It implies that what has been surrendered can, if desired, be reappropriated. Participants stress they could have continued, even succeeded, in their former circumstances but chose to change their lives, always for personal and relational reasons. Thus choice implies a way out if the rigors of simple living are too great and smoothes a path back into the former lifestyle. The factors that support the ability to choose simplicity (money, education, social class) are also the very attributes necessary to success in a consumer society; thus these important qualities remain the property of the individual, to be played out as desires dictate. The sense of entitlement or ownership of nature as well as the implicit dependence on the attributes of consumerism continue to reinforce the orientations of the "old life," undermining the claims of conversion to simplicity.

The Visual Drama of *The Good Life*

In this analysis of the visual drama of *The Good Life*, another dimension of Burke's dramatism is used, focusing on how various elements are presented visually as the substance or grounding of the good life. Burke's pentad is built upon the concept of substance, the symbolically constructed foundation or basis on which various aspects of the drama are played out. Burke (1973a) identifies five major orientations that compel the human drama—scene, act, agent, agency, and purpose (1973a, pp. 21–23). Humans use symbol systems to constitute their situations and contexts, their identities and differences, their shared pasts and futures, their needs, goals, desires. In the process, they construct compelling explanations of the human condition—narratives of human agency, of the constraining power of natural conditions, of being bound or liberated by ideas, of individual desire or cooperative action that overpowers restraints. Burke (1973a) argues that these orientations and the tensions among them, e.g. the struggle between the power of will (agent) and the power of situation (scene), are necessary to any wellrounded explanation of "what people are doing and why they are doing it" (1973a, p. xv). This perspective seems ideal for exploring the visual drama of *The Good Life* because of the overwhelming visual power of the physical settings as the essence or substance of the good life. We concentrate on the primacy of the scenic in the visualizations of the good life but the other terms are ever-present and inevitably accessed in understandings of the visual drama presented in the program.

Nature as scene. The visual drama powerfully constructs the scenic dimension of the good life, both the foundational substance that grounds this life and the context, that is, the physical spaces or places in which the good life can be lived. Nature is a major component of both the grounding and the setting of a good life. But this scene is not raw and unruly nature. It is a nature ordered, controlled, and structured into the perfect setting for the values and qualities of the good life. This nature of pristine mountains, meadows, streams, and oceans is a nature without heat, humidity, drought, cold, damp, mosquitoes, snakes, storms, or blight. Thus the camera pans over beautiful views, bountiful gardens, wildlife, forests, landscaped lawns, even occasional swimming pools and guest houses. Nature here is a visual feast, with shots carefully chosen to exclude power lines, cellular towers, jet contrails, litter, dams, encroaching urbanization, highways, and other visual blights from human development. Likewise the cameras, trucks, and other equipment necessary to filming are carefully kept out of camera range, as noted above, ignoring the irony that their presence destroys the very tranquility they are attempting to capture.

As the scene of the good life is visualized, it is done in true Burkean fash- 25 ion by referencing what it "is not" in order to substantiate what it "is." Shots of the "old life" of stress and complexity, pollution and gridlock, are juxtaposed with those of the "new life." Nature thus is instantiated as both the substance that generates the good life and the setting or scene in which such a life is possible. (Of course, by implication, the scenes of the old life become places where a good life is not possible.)

Style as scene. There is another component to the scene, however, overlapping and extending the emphasis on nature. If the good life is grounded in nature, it is also rooted in the stylistic, an element necessary to separate the middle-class good life from the inadvertent and unavoidable simplicity of poverty and lower-class existence. Burke (1984b) defines style as a moral dimension of symbolizing that involves doing or being "right," that is, appropriate to the situation. It is "an elaborate set of prescriptions and proscriptions for 'doing the right thing' . . . a complex schema of what-goes-with-what carried through all the subtleties of manner and attitudes" (1984b, pp. 268–269). Those scenes and agents imbued with style determine the "correct" use of commodities. While most folks dress themselves, set their tables, and decorate their homes, to do so with style requires a knowledge of the nuances of social correctness as well as a flair for originality within the bounds of appropriateness. Thus style is an option for those with money and good taste, setting them apart from those who must take whatever is available at a price they can afford.

In *The Good Life*, nature as chief commodity must be stylized, made appropriate to the scene. Just as the natural beauty of the outdoors is configured into an aesthetic backdrop for the good life, the interiors of the simple but tasteful abodes are charmingly decorated with arts, crafts, and fabrics that utilize nature in elegant and artistic ways. Edye Ellis, the host of the program and the Martha Stewart of simple living, provides an enduring aura of taste, elegance, and aesthetic appeal. Cameras linger on Edye as she poses with flower arrangements, room decor, gardens, beautiful views, and tasteful accessories that embed style into the substance of the good life.

"Doing" nature with style: Constructing agents. Thus, these two components, nature and style, combine to produce the grounding for the good life. The scene, however, requires agents appropriate to that scene, generated by and imbued with its qualities. As Burke (1973a) explains: "It is a principle

of drama that the nature of acts and agents should be consistent with the nature of the scene" (1973a, p. 3). As the verbal narrative stresses, converts to the good life must experience a rebirth, a reawakening of appreciation for nature and their own artistic abilities. The visual drama chronicles this rebirth. We see photos of the subjects as children, growing up, engaging as adults in the "bad life," juxtaposed with shots of new converts enjoying the good life. The visual connection between "what I was and what I am" constructs a new identity forged by their identification with the scene.

As noted above, converts to the good life almost always discover hidden artistic talents that can only now be developed. Abilities to paint, sculpt, photograph, decorate, or do crafts emerge as if by magic, as the substance of the good life draws these forth from participants. They thus possess the necessary style to be appropriate agents in the good life drama, style being a latent quality called forth by their participation in the scene. We often see participants actually constructing, physically and metaphorically, their placement in the new location. Often at the end of the program, the camera integrates agent and scene, as it lingers on converts engaged in the daily routines of the good life, for example, walking in the woods or by a lake, taking in a natural panorama from a deck, working in the garden, creating artistic objects from natural products, tastefully decorating their homes, or taking photographs of nature. The visual message is: "This is the good life and we now belong here, we have grown from and are now situated in this place, like the mountains and trees that surround us."

The snake in the garden: Commodity as agency. The visual drama has another component, however, one that challenges and ultimately overpowers the Edenic visions of the good life, infusing both scene and agent with the values of commodity culture—advertising. According to Burke (1973a), agency is the manner or means by which action is possible (1973a, p. xv). Advertising thus is implicitly the agency or means by which a good life is possible. As with all television programming, advertising is a vital ingredient of the program, and becomes part of the visual flow of meaning. The viewer can validly assume that the products advertised are by implication those necessary for, or at least compatible with, the good life. Television programming constructs a flow of meaning, evoking "subtle associations between aspects of the show and the commodity" presented in the commercials (Budd, Craig, & Steinman, 1999, pp. 153–154). Thus as visuals of Nature are juxtaposed with repeated ads for luxury automobiles, vacation cruises, and investment opportunities, the program implicitly argues that expensive commodities, consumed with style, are essential to the good life. In fact, these commodities and the wealth they imply are instantiated as the agency or means through which the good life is attained, making this a life framed by, surrounded by, and energized by consumer culture.

Style therefore is the essential quality that links nature and consumer culture. Living with nature appropriately requires style, just as style requires appreciation of the finest commodities that only money can purchase. The good life, then, uses consumption (with style) as agency to bridge the fundamental disjunction that has always rested at the heart of this culture's vision of the good life, the term that connects the "less is more" and "more is better" versions of the good life. As visualized in this program, the good life apparently means being able to drive up to your rural abode in your new Lexus, booking a Caribbean cruise from your rustic living room when you need a break from simplicity, and taking it for granted that you have a right to consume both nature and commodities as long as you do it with style.

Interaction of the Visual and Verbal Dramas of *The Good Life*

Obviously the verbal and visual dramas are interdependent, both needed to define the good life. If one considers the verbal narrative the dominant narrative — and that is only because our tools for dealing with words are more familiar — the visual narrative reduces and expands, abstracts and concretizes the verbal. Together the verbal and the visual dramas reside in the tensions between stability and change. If the verbal drama is the story of change, of agential choice shaping, molding, creating the desired environments for one's salvation, the visual drama privileges scenic power, as stable, enduring nature embraces the prodigal, restores those who dwell therein to the timeless serenity of the universe. The incompleteness of each makes space for the other; in their contradictions lies satisfactory completion.

The verbal drama of choice includes no admission that the lifestyle of consumption being renounced bears any responsibility for misuse of nature. The visual narrative presents a static, ever-stable natural beauty, for example, pristine mountains, streams, and meadows unaffected by human excess and mismanagement. As noted, nature is visual artwork, purchased and now possessed via the risks taken. In no sense is it an active entity. This visualization of nature energizes the verbal, temporal drama of human quest. The eternal ever-present backdrop of nature becomes an object of desire in the temporal formula, placed back in eternal timelessness at the end. Each narrative (spatial and temporal) supports and constrains the other. The visual reduces nature to an aesthetic that complements the verbal drama's definition of nature as a choice of lifestyle, implying that a beautiful environment exists to satisfy human desires but failing to assign any responsibility for preserving that environment.

HGTV's *The Good Life* is one example, among many, of current visions of simple living. It is particularly striking because it embeds so many values in one compact package and presents so many seemingly oppositional ideas in a coherent verbal and visual narrative; this version of the good life provides vicarious atonement, offers the chance to reform without serious sacrifice. Its pathology is that it allows no serious economic, social, or environmental issues to emerge. It reduces complex, potentially tragic consequences of policies and practices to matters of individual preference, stylistic choices, aesthetic visions. Here the good life is about following one's own dream, discovering one's inner self. It is individualized as the freedom to "do what I want, when I want," as a number of participants observe. There are no stories of failure, no acknowledgment of social responsibility, no sympathy for those who cannot choose. It maintains the myth of infinite possibility for all, defining simplicity not as a moral alternative or environmental necessity but as a trendy lifestyle, allowing the viewer to forget that only the fortunate few can choose to leave a mess they have helped to create and maintain for a flight to rural, unspoiled areas.

By implication, the good life takes place in select localities, in rural, 35 sparsely populated, attractive, and relatively unspoiled places such as the slopes of the Rockies, the foothills of the Appalachians, the ocean, lakefront, or bayou, in quaint New England towns, in other rural and unspoiled beauty spots of the nation. The visual component strengthens the aesthetic and grounds it in nature in ways the verbal cannot. Most examples presented in *The Good Life* require money, influence, and taste as the converts attempt to create a lifestyle of elegance and beauty in a new setting. Great emphasis is placed on improving communication in families and relationships; nature is the mystique that makes this possible. The work ethic is retained but relocated to include contact with nature. Each episode ends with an altar call, "You too can have the good life."

Thus, the good life utilizes natural environments as a stage-set for a lifestyle that continues to valorize commodity culture. Nature, in fact, is the foremost commodity; in order to live the good life it must be purchased, modified, and controlled. Nature and simplicity must be managed with the same skills and dedication that former professional careers were managed. As Burke (1973b) observes, the vision of the good life was built around the

> ideal of the "live-wire" salesman, with culture taken to mean the maximum purchase of manufactured commodities. . . . Out of books, out of delightful moments in one's personal life, out of sporadic voyages, out of *vacational* experiences as distinct from *vocational* ones, people got visions of a noncompetitive structure of living, a "good life" involving gentle surroundings, adequate physical outlets, the pursuit of knowledge, etc., and the very slogans of the commercial ethic assured them that they were "entitled" to all this. (1973b, p. 248)

Conclusion

Voluntary simplicity in 2002, then, appears to reinforce the dictates of simple living while wrapped firmly within commodity culture, defining it primarily as a psychological search for self-actualization in which nature becomes a resource for purchase. It calls us not to change our ways but to dabble in self-fulfillment, while continuing on our present course of overconsumption and self-indulgence. By reducing the issues to individual conversion experiences, there is no need for national repentance, for a brake on conspicuous and wasteful consumption of resources. As this example illustrates, the simple life discourse is framed in and contained by assumptions and connections to consumption. It is constructed in the language of a consumer society. It is not a call for change but a powerful endorsement of the status quo. The cultural myth of success, the "divine right" to consume the world's resources, the unwillingness to acknowledge that the environment is not merely a backdrop or stage-set for our consumption of goods and enactment of trendy lifestyles, makes many current odes to simplicity, the "less is more" narratives, merely alternate versions of the "more is better" stories.

One program from one genre of popular culture—television entertainment—says little except when, as with *The Good Life*, its assumptions and expectations are deeply embedded in American culture. The program draws from and reinforces the powers of consumerism and the inevitable subsuming of environmental concerns to consumerist values. When these same assumptions, expectations, and values are evident across various genres of popular culture, they become an uncritical and unconscious dimension of our cultural reality. Popular culture thus implicitly assures us that we are entitled to a good life, whether one of economic complexity or voluntary simplicity, and offers us nature for sale, an environment to be purchased and used in the search for personal fulfillment.

REFERENCES

Budd, M., Craig, S., & Steinman, C. (1999). *Consuming environments: Television and commercial culture.* New Brunswick, NJ: Rutgers University Press.

Burke, K. (1966). *Language as symbolic action.* Berkeley, CA: University of California Press.

Burke, K. (1968). *Counterstatement.* Berkeley, CA: University of California Press.

Burke, K. (1970). *Rhetoric of religion.* 2nd ed. Berkeley, CA: University of California Press.

Burke, K. (1973a). *Grammar of motives.* 2nd ed. Berkeley, CA: University of California Press.

Burke, K. (1973b). *Philosophy of literary form.* 3rd ed. Berkeley, CA: University of California Press.

Burke, K. (1984a). *Attitudes toward history.* 4th ed. Berkeley, CA: University of California Press.

Burke, K. (1984b). *Permanence and change.* 4th ed. Berkeley, CA: University of California Press.

Burks, D. (1991). Kenneth Burke: The agro-bohemian "Marxoid." *Communication Studies, 42,* 219–233.

Dudgeon, C. (Executive Producer). *The Good Life.* Knoxville, TN: Home and Garden Television (HGTV). Retrieved from http://www.hgtv.com

Guisewite, C. (2000, June 24). Cathy Cartoon. *Omaha World Herald.*

Horovitz, B. (2000, June 1). Simplesells: Chic back-to-basics explosion carries hefty load of irony. *USA Today,* p. 1A +.

MonDesire, D. (2000, June 9). How hard should we strive for simple life? *USA Today,* p. I9A.

Shi, D. E. (1985). *The simple life: Plain living and high thinking in American culture.* New York, NY: Oxford.

What is the Simple Life? (2000, July 5). *Simple Life Corporation.* Retrieved from http://members.aol.com/simplfe/spirit.html

READING THE TEXT

1. What are the two major myths of the good life in American culture, according to the authors? And what contradictory belief do Americans hold that counter the two major myths?

2. Summarize in your own words rhetorician Kenneth Burke's theory of symbolic action and how it applies to *The Good Life*.

3. How does American popular culture reflect, or mediate, the contradictory tendencies in Americans' views of the good life?

4. What is the "voluntary simplicity movement," and how is it represented in the HGTV program *The Good Life*?

5. What are the "visual" and "verbal" dramas of *The Good Life*?

READING THE SIGNS

1. Visit a site such as TVrage.com or Hulu that archives TV programs, and watch a later episode of *The Good Life*. In an essay, analyze the narrative the episode tells about the featured participant. To what extent does it conform to the salvation formula that Japp and Japp claim is typical of the show? If it deviates, how does it do so and what alternative narrative is created for the participant?

2. Analyze a magazine such as *Real Simple* or a TV program such as *Simple Living*. To what extent does your subject "reinforce the dictates of simple living while wrapped firmly within commodity culture" (para. 37)?

3. Read Jon Krakauer's *Into the Wild*, which narrates the ultimately fatal journey of Chris McCandless into the Alaska wilderness, and write an essay that analyzes the protagonist's experiment with "voluntary simplicity." To what extent does McCandless engage in a genuine rejection of material culture and embrace of nature or, as some critics have noted, does he turn living in nature into something of a self-indulgent competitive sport?

4. **CONNECTING TEXTS** Write an analysis of the contradictions you find in green marketing campaigns that present the possession of consumer goods as ways to achieve the simple life. To develop your ideas, consult Julia Corbett, "A Faint Green Sell: Advertising and the Natural World" (p. 227) and Alan Foljambe, "Car Advertising—Dominating Nature" (p. 246).

5. **CONNECTING TEXTS** Compare and contrast Japp and Japp's critique of the voluntary simplicity movement's use of nature with Thomas Frank's analysis of the countercultural pose of much current advertising (see "Commodify Your Dissent," p. 163). In what ways do the authors see nature and countercultural beliefs as being coopted by consumer culture?

6. When describing the convention of "style as scene," the authors claim that "While most folks dress themselves, set their tables, and decorate their homes, to do so with style requires a knowledge of the nuances of social correctness as well as a flair for originality within the bounds of appropriateness" (para. 26). Analyze an issue of *Martha Stewart Living*. To what extent does the publication replicate the authors' indictment of media that simply present a visual drama of the good life?

"Leave Area Clean"

READING THE SIGNS

1. What contradictory impulses does this image bring to mind? Is litter an inevitable by-product of our consumption-oriented society?

2. The Web site www.stoplittering.com, featuring the slogan "Just Pick It Up," suggests that the problem of litter can be solved if everyone stopped to clean up a few pieces of litter each day. Do you think this idea might work? Would you be willing to give it a try? Can you think of a more effective method of preventing the kind of litter seen in this image? What are some trade-offs with your method? What, in your opinion, should be the penalty for littering?

MARIAH BURTON NELSON

I Won. I'm Sorry.

Athletic competition, when you come right down to it, is about winning, which is no problem for men, whose gender codes tell them that aggression and domination are admirable male traits. But "how can you win, if you're female?" Mariah Burton Nelson asks, when the same gender codes insist that women must be "feminine," "not aggressive, not victorious." And so women athletes, even when they do win, go out of their way to signal their femininity by dolling themselves up and smiling a lot. Beauty and vulnerability seem to be as important to today's female athlete as brawn and gold medals, Nelson complains, paradoxically contradicting the apparent feminist gains that women athletes have made in recent years. A former Stanford University and professional basketball player, Nelson is the author of six books, including *We Are All Athletes* (2002) and *Making Money on the Sidelines* (2008). She is executive director of the American Association for Physical Activity and Recreation. This piece originally appeared in *SELF* magazine.

When Sylvia Plath's husband, Ted Hughes, published his first book of poems, Sylvia wrote to her mother: "I am so happy that HIS book is accepted FIRST. It will make it so much easier for me when mine is accepted. . . ."

After Sylvia killed herself, her mother published a collection of Sylvia's letters. In her explanatory notes, Aurelia Plath commented that from the time she was very young, Sylvia "catered to the male of any age so as to bolster his sense of superiority." In seventh grade, Aurelia Plath noted, Sylvia was pleased to finish second in a spelling contest. "It was nicer, she felt, to have a boy first."

How many women still collude in the myth of male superiority, believing it's "nicer" when boys and men finish first? How many of us achieve but only in a lesser, smaller, feminine way, a manner consciously or unconsciously designed to be as nonthreatening as possible?

Since I'm tall, women often talk to me about height. Short women tell me, "I've always wanted to be tall—but not as tall as you!" I find this amusing, but also curious. Why not? Why not be six-two?

Tall women tell me that they won't wear heels because they don't want   5
to appear taller than their husbands or boyfriends, even by an inch. What are these women telling me—and their male companions? Why do women regulate their height in relation to men's height? Why is it still rare to see a woman who is taller than her husband?

Women want to be tall enough to feel elegant and attractive, like models. They want to feel respected and looked up to. But they don't want to be so tall that their height threatens men. They want to win—to achieve, to reach new heights—but without exceeding male heights.

How can you win, if you're female? Can you just do it? No. You have to play the femininity game. Femininity by definition is not large, not imposing, not competitive. Feminine women are not ruthless, not aggressive, not victorious. It's not feminine to have a killer instinct, to want with all your heart and soul to win—neither tennis matches nor elected office nor feminist victories such as abortion rights. It's not feminine to know exactly what you want, then go for it.

Femininity is about appearing beautiful and vulnerable and small. It's about winning male approval.

One downhill skier who asked not to be identified told me the following story: "I love male approval. Most women skiers do. We talk about it often. There's only one thing more satisfying than one of the top male skiers saying, 'Wow, you are a great skier. You rip. You're awesome.'

"But it's so fun leaving 99 percent of the world's guys in the dust—oops,"   10
she laughs. "I try not to gloat. I've learned something: If I kick guys' butts and lord it over them, they don't like me. If, however, I kick guys' butts then act 'like a girl,' there is no problem. And I do mean girl, not woman. Nonthreatening."

Femininity is also about accommodating men, allowing them to feel bigger than and stronger than and superior to women, not emasculated by them. Femininity is unhealthy, obviously. It would be unhealthy for men to act passive, dainty, obsessed with their physical appearance, and dedicated to bolstering the sense of superiority in the other gender, so it's unhealthy for women too. These days, some women are redefining femininity as strong, as athletic, as however a female happens to be, so that "feminine" becomes synonymous with "female." Other women reject both feminine and masculine terms and stereotypes, selecting from the entire range of human behaviors instead of limiting themselves to the "gender-appropriate" ones. These women smile only when they're happy, act angry when they're angry, dress how they want to. They cling to their self-respect and dignity like a life raft.

But most female winners play the femininity game to some extent, using femininity as a defense, a shield against accusations such as bitch, man-hater, lesbian. Feminine behavior and attire mitigate against the affront of female victory, soften the hard edges of winning. Women who want to win without losing male approval temper their victories with beauty, with softness, with smallness, with smiles.

In the fifties, at each of the Amateur Athletic Union's women's basketball championships, one of the players was crowned a beauty queen. (This still happens at Russian women's ice hockey tournaments.) Athletes in the All-American Girls Baseball League of the forties and fifties slid into base wearing skirts. In 1979, professional basketball players with the California Dreams were sent to John Robert Powers' charm school. Ed Temple, the legendary coach of the Tennessee State Tigerbelles, the team that produced

Serena Williams at Wimbledon.

Wilma Rudolph, Wyomia Tyus, Willye White, Madeline Manning, and count-less other champions, enforced a dress code and stressed that his athletes should be "young ladies first, track girls second."

Makeup, jewelry, dress, and demeanor were often dictated by the male   15
coaches and owners in these leagues, but to some extent the players played along, understanding the trade-off: in order to be "allowed" to compete, they had to demonstrate that they were, despite their "masculine" strivings, real ("feminine") women.

Today, both men and women wear earrings, notes Felshin, "but the media is still selling heterosexism and 'feminine' beauty. And if you listen carefully, in almost every interview" female athletes still express apologetic behavior through feminine dress, behavior, and values.

Florence Griffith-Joyner, Gail Devers, and other track stars of this mod-ern era dedicate considerable attention to portraying a feminine appearance. Basketball star Lisa Leslie has received more attention for being a model than for leading the Americans to Olympic victory. Steffi Graf posed in bikinis for the 1997 *Sports Illustrated* swimsuit issue. In a Sears commercial, Olympic basketball players apply lipstick, paint their toenails, rock babies, lounge in bed, and pose and dance in their underwear. Lisa Leslie says, "Everybody's allowed to be themselves. Me, for example, I'm very feminine."

In an Avon commercial, Jackie Joyner Kersee is shown running on a beach while the camera lingers on her buttocks and breasts. She tells us that she can bench-press 150 pounds and brags that she can jump farther than "all but 128 men." Then she says: "And I have red toenails." Words flash on the screen: "Just another Avon lady." Graf, Mary Pierce, Monica Seles, and Mary Jo Fernandez have all played in dresses. They are "so much more comfort-able" than skirts, Fernandez explained. "You don't have to worry about the shirt coming up or the skirt being too tight. It's cooler, and it's so feminine."

"When I put on a dress I feel different—more feminine, more elegant, more ladylike—and that's nice," added Australia's Nicole Bradtke: "We're in a sport where we're throwing ourselves around, so it's a real asset to the game to be able to look pretty at the same time."

Athletes have become gorgeous, flirtatious, elegant, angelic, darling—and   20
the skating commentators' favorite term: "vulnerable." Some think this is good news: proof that femininity and sports are compatible. "There doesn't have to be such a complete division between 'You're beautiful and sexy' and 'you're athletic and strong,'" says Linda Hanley, a pro beach volleyball player who also appeared in a bikini in the 1997 *Sports Illustrated* swimsuit issue.

Athletes and advertisers reassure viewers that women who compete are still willing to play the femininity game, to be cheerleaders. Don't worry about us, the commercials imply. We're winners but we'll still look pretty for you. We're acting in ways that only men used to act but we'll still act how you want women to act. We're not threatening. We're not lesbians. We're not ugly, not bad marriage material. We're strong but feminine. Linguists note that the word "but" negates the part of the sentence that precedes it.

There are some recent examples of the media emphasizing female power in an unambiguous way. "Women Muscle In," the *New York Times Magazine* proclaimed in a headline. The *Washington Post* wrote, "At Olympics, Women Show Their Strength." And a new genre of commercials protests that female athletes are NOT cheerleaders, and don't have to be. Olympic and pro basketball star Dawn Staley says in a Nike commercial that she plays basketball "for the competitiveness" of it. "I need some place to release it. It just builds up, and sports is a great outlet for it. I started out playing with the guys. I wasn't always accepted. You get criticized, like: 'You need to be in the kitchen. Go put on a skirt.' I just got mad and angry and went out to show them that I belong here as much as they do."

Other commercials tell us that women can compete like conquerors. A Nike ad called "Wolves" shows girls leaping and spiking volleyballs while a voice says, "They are not sisters. They are not classmates. They are not friends. They are not even the girls' team. They are a pack of wolves. Tend to your sheep." Though the athletes look serious, the message sounds absurd. When I show this commercial to audiences, they laugh. Still, the images do depict the power of the volleyball players: their intensity, their ability to pound the ball almost through the floor. The script gives the players (and viewers) permission not to be ladylike, not to worry about whether their toenails are red.

But in an American Basketball League commercial, the Philadelphia Rage's female basketball players are playing rough; their bodies collide. Maurice Chevalier sings, "Thank heaven for little girls." The tag line: "Thank heaven, they're on our side."

Doesn't all this talk about girls and ladies simply focus our attention on 25 femaleness, femininity, and ladylike behavior? The lady issue is always there in the equation: something to redefine, to rebel against. It's always present, like sneakers, so every time you hear the word *athlete* you also hear the word *lady* — or feminine, or unfeminine. It reminds me of a beer magazine ad from the eighties that featured a photo of Olympic track star Valerie Brisco-Hooks. "Funny, she doesn't look like the weaker sex," said the print. You could see her impressive muscles. Clearly the intent of the ad was to contrast an old stereotype with the reality of female strength and ability. But Brisco-Hooks was seated, her legs twisted pretzel style, arms covering her chest. But in that position, Brisco-Hooks didn't look very strong or able. In the line, "Funny, she doesn't look like the weaker sex," the most eye-catching words are funny, look, weaker, and sex. Looking at the pretzel that is Valerie, you begin to think that she looks funny. You think about weakness. And you think about sex.

When she was young, Nancy Kerrigan wanted to play ice hockey with her older brothers. Her mother told her, "You're a girl. Do girl things."

Figure skating is a girl thing. Athletes in sequins and "sheer illusion sleeves" glide and dance, their tiny skirts flapping in the breeze. They achieve, but without touching or pushing anyone else. They win, but without visible signs of sweat. They compete, but not directly. Their success is measured not by confrontation with an opponent, nor even by a clock or a scoreboard. Rather, they are judged as beauty contestants are judged: by a panel of people who interpret the success of the routines. Prettiness is mandatory. Petite and groomed and gracious, figure skaters—like cheerleaders, gymnasts, and aerobic dancers—camouflage their competitiveness with niceness and prettiness until it no longer seems male or aggressive or unseemly.

The most popular sport for high school and college women is basketball. More than a million fans shelled out an average of $15 per ticket in 1997, the inaugural summer of the Women's National Basketball Association. But the most televised women's sport is figure skating. In 1995 revenue from skating shows and competitions topped six hundred million dollars. In the seven months between October 1996 and March 1997, ABC, CBS, NBC, Fox, ESPN, TBS, and USA dedicated 162.5 hours of programming to figure skating, half of it in prime time. Kerrigan earns up to three hundred thousand dollars for a single performance.

Nearly 75 percent of the viewers of televised skating are women. The average age is between twenty-five and forty-five years old, with a household income of more than fifty thousand dollars. What are these women watching? What are they seeing? What's the appeal?

Like golf, tennis, and gymnastics, figure skating is an individual sport favored by white people from the upper classes. The skaters wear cosmetics, frozen smiles, and revealing dresses. Behind the scenes they lift weights and sweat like any serious athlete, but figure skating seems more dance than sport, more grace than guts, more art than athleticism. Figure skating allows women to compete like champions while dressed like cheerleaders.

In women's figure skating, smiling is part of "artistic expression." In the final round, if the competitors are of equal merit, artistry weighs more heavily than technique. Midori Ito, the best jumper in the history of women's skating, explained a weak showing at the 1995 world championships this way: "I wasn't 100 percent satisfied. . . . I probably wasn't smiling enough."

The media portray female figure skaters as "little girl dancers" or "fairy tale princesses" (NBC commentator John Tesh); as "elegant" (Dick Button); as "little angels" (Peggy Fleming); as "ice beauties" and "ladies who lutz" (*People* magazine). Commentators frame skaters as small, young, and decorative creatures, not superwomen but fairy-tale figments of someone's imagination.

After Kerrigan was assaulted by a member of Tonya Harding's entourage, she was featured on a *Sports Illustrated* cover crying "Why me?" When she recovered to win a silver medal at the Olympics that year, she became "America's sweetheart" and rich to boot. But the princess turned pumpkin shortly after midnight, as soon as the ball was over and she stopped smiling and started speaking. Growing impatient during the Olympic medal ceremony while everyone waited for Baiul, Kerrigan grumbled, "Oh, give me a break, she's just going to cry out there again. What's the difference?"

What were Kerrigan's crimes? She felt too old to cavort with cartoon characters. Isn't she? She expressed anger and disappointment — even bitterness and bad sportsmanship — about losing the gold. But wasn't she supposed to want to win? What happens to baseball players who, disappointed about a loss, hit each other or spit on umpires? What happens to basketball players and football players and hockey players who fight? Men can't tumble from a princess palace because we don't expect them to be princesses in the first place, only athletes.

Americans fell out of love with Kerrigan not because they couldn't adore 35 an athlete who lacked grace in defeat, but because they couldn't adore a female athlete who lacked grace in defeat.

Female politicians, lawyers, and businesswomen of all ethnic groups also play the femininity game. Like tennis players in short dresses, working women seem to believe it's an asset to look pretty (but not too pretty) while throwing themselves around. The female apologetic is alive and well in corporate boardrooms, where women say "I'm sorry, maybe someone else already stated this idea, but . . ." and smile while they say it.

When Newt Gingrich's mother revealed on television that Newt had referred to Hillary Clinton as a bitch, how did Hillary respond? She donned a pink suit and met with female reporters to ask how she could "soften her image." She seemed to think that her competitiveness was the problem and femininity the solution.

So if you want to be a winner and you're female, you'll feel pressured to play by special female rules. Like men, you'll have to be smart and industrious, but in addition you'll have to be "like women": kind, nurturing, accommodating, nonthreatening, placating, pretty, and small. You'll have to smile. And not act angry. And wear skirts. Nail polish and makeup help, too.

READING THE TEXT

1. Summarize in your own words the contradictory messages about appropriate gender behavior that women athletes must contend with, according to Nelson.

2. Nelson begins her article with an anecdote about poet Sylvia Plath. How does this opening frame her argument about women in sports?

3. What is the "femininity game" (para. 7), in Nelson's view, and how do the media perpetuate it?

4. What sports are coded as "feminine," according to Nelson, and why?

READING THE SIGNS

1. Watch a women's sports event on television, such as an LPGA match, analyzing the behavior and appearance of the athletes. Use your observations as evidence in an essay in which you assess the validity of Nelson's claims about the contradictory gender role behaviors of female athletes.

2. If you are a female athlete, write a journal entry exploring whether you feel pressure to act feminine and your responses to that pressure. If you are not a female athlete, reflect on the behavior and appearance of women athletes on your campus. Do you see signs that they are affected by the femininity game?

3. Obtain a copy of a magazine that focuses on women's sports, such as *Sports Illustrated Women*, or visit an online magazine such as sportsister.com or womensportreport.com. Analyze the articles and the ads in the magazine, noting models' and athletes' clothing, physical appearance, and speech patterns. Using Nelson's argument as a critical framework, write an essay in which you analyze whether the magazine perpetuates traditional gender roles or presents sports as an avenue for female empowerment.

4. Interview women athletes on your campus and ask them whether they feel pressured by the femininity game. Have they faced derogatory or stereotypical accusations simply because they are athletes? Do they feel pressure to be physically attractive or charming? Do you see any correlation between an athlete's sport and her responses? Use your observations as the basis of an argument about the influence of traditional gender roles on women's sports at your school.

RANDALL KENNEDY
Blind Spot

Racial profiling has been a hot-button issue in recent years, eliciting such sardonic condemnations as the claim that for many Americans it has become a crime to be caught "driving while black." Randall Kennedy, a professor of law at Harvard Law School, enters the controversy here from an unusual angle, finding a fundamental contradiction in the positions of both supporters and opponents of racial profiling. With supporters of racial profiling asserting the rights of the community over those of the individual, while at the same time endorsing the rights of the individual over those of the community when it comes to affirmative action, and opponents of racial profiling doing just the reverse, it is time, Kennedy suggests, for both sides to listen to what the other has to say. Kennedy is the author of *Race, Crime, and the Law* (1997), *Nigger: The Strange Career of a Troublesome Word* (2002), *Interracial Intimacies: Sex, Marriage, Identity, and Adoption* (2003), and *Sellout: The Politics of Racial Betrayal* (2008). This selection originally appeared in the April 2002 issue of the *Atlantic*.

What is one to think about "racial profiling"? Confusion abounds about what the term even means. It should be defined as the policy or practice of using race as a factor in selecting whom to place under special surveillance: if police officers at an airport decide to search Passenger A because he is twenty-five to forty years old, bought a first-class ticket with cash, is flying cross-country, and is apparently of Arab ancestry, Passenger A has been subjected to racial profiling. But officials often prefer to define racial profiling as being based *solely* on race; and in doing so they are often seeking to preserve their authority to act against a person *partly* on the basis of race. Civil rights activists, too, often define racial profiling as solely race-based; but their aim is to arouse their followers and to portray law-enforcement officials in as menacing a light as possible.

The problem with defining racial profiling in the narrow manner of these strange bedfellows is that doing so obfuscates the real issue confronting Americans. Exceedingly few police officers, airport screeners, or other authorities charged with the task of foiling or apprehending criminals act solely on the basis of race. Many, however, act on the basis of intuition, using race along with other indicators (sex, age, patterns of past conduct) as a guide. The difficult question, then, is not whether the authorities ought to be allowed to act against individuals on the basis of race alone; almost everyone would disapprove of that. The difficult question is whether they ought to be allowed to use race *at all* in schemes of surveillance. If, indeed, it is used, the action amounts to racial discrimination. The extent of the discrimination may be relatively small when race is only one factor among many, but even a little racial discrimination should require lots of justification.

The key argument in favor of racial profiling, essentially, is that taking race into account enables the authorities to screen carefully and at less expense those sectors of the population that are more likely than others to contain the criminals for whom officials are searching. Proponents of this theory stress that resources for surveillance are scarce, that the dangers to be avoided are grave, and that reducing these dangers helps everyone — including, sometimes especially, those in the groups subjected to special scrutiny. Proponents also assert that it makes good sense to consider whiteness if the search is for Ku Klux Klan assassins, blackness if the search is for drug couriers in certain locales, and Arab nationality or ethnicity if the search is for agents of al-Qaeda.

Some commentators embrace this position as if it were unassailable, but under U.S. law racial discrimination backed by state power is presumptively illicit. This means that supporters of racial profiling carry a heavy burden of persuasion. Opponents rightly argue, however, that not much rigorous empirical proof supports the idea of racial profiling as an effective tool of law enforcement. Opponents rightly contend, also, that alternatives to racial profiling have not been much studied or pursued. Stressing that racial profiling generates clear harm (for example, the fear, resentment, and alienation felt by innocent people in the profiled group), opponents of racial profiling

Which man looks guilty? If you picked the man on the right, you're wrong.

Wrong for judging people based on the color of their skin. Because if you

look closely, you'll see they're the same man. Unfortunately, racial stereo-

typing like this happens every day. On America's highways, police stop drivers

based on their skin color rather than for the way they are driving. For example,

in Florida 80% of those stopped and searched were black and Hispanic,

while they constituted only 5% of all drivers. These humiliating and illegal

searches are violations of the Constitution and must be fought. Help us defend

your rights. Support the ACLU. www.aclu.org **american civil liberties union**

Which man looks guilty?

sensibly question whether compromising our hard-earned principle of anti-discrimination is worth merely speculative gains in overall security.

A notable feature of this conflict is that champions of each position fre- 5 quently embrace rhetoric, attitudes, and value systems that are completely at odds with those they adopt when confronting another controversial instance of racial discrimination — namely, affirmative action. Vocal supporters of racial profiling who trumpet the urgency of communal needs when discussing law enforcement all of a sudden become fanatical individualists when condemning affirmative action in college admissions and the labor market. Supporters of profiling, who are willing to impose what amounts to a racial tax on profiled groups, denounce as betrayals of "color blindness" programs that require racial diversity. A similar turnabout can be seen on the part of many of those who support affirmative action. Impatient with talk of communal needs in assessing racial profiling, they very often have no difficulty with subordinating the interests of individual white candidates to the purported good of the whole. Opposed to race consciousness in policing, they demand race consciousness in deciding whom to admit to college or select for a job.

The racial-profiling controversy — like the conflict over affirmative action — will not end soon. For one thing, in both cases many of the contestants are animated by decent but contending sentiments. Although exasperating, this is actually good for our society; and it would be even better if participants in the debates acknowledged the simple truth that their adversaries have something useful to say.

READING THE TEXT

1. Summarize in your own words the contradiction Kennedy finds in the controversies over racial profiling and affirmative action.

2. Why does Kennedy say that definitions of racial profiling are marked by "confusion" (para. 1)?

3. Why does Kennedy call opponents and supporters of racial profiling "strange bedfellows" (para. 2)?

4. Why do you think Kennedy finds "the decent but contending sentiments" at the heart of the racial profiling controversy to be "good for our society" (para. 6)?

READING THE SIGNS

1. Kennedy finds a contradiction between opposing racial profiling and promoting affirmative action. Write an essay in which you support, refute, or modify his stance.

2. Write a journal entry in which you reflect on an experience in which you believe you were singled out because of your appearance, ethnicity, gender, or other physically obvious characteristic. How did you respond at the time, and would you respond the same way today? Alternatively, write about a friend who had such an experience.

3. Write an essay in which you explore the relative claims of the rights of the individual and the rights of the community in modern American culture. To what extent do those claims reflect a fundamental contradiction in American social ideology?

4. **CONNECTING TEXTS**   In the debates over both racial profiling and affirmative action, the discussions tend to presume that determining ethnic identity is a simple matter. Read or review Jack Lopez's "Of Cholos and Surfers" (p. 654), Nell Bernstein's "Goin' Gangsta, Choosin' Cholita" (p. 661), and Melissa Algranati's "Being an Other" (p. 667), and write an essay in which you explore the implications that mixed-race backgrounds and cultural practices such as claiming may have for these debates.

ALFRED LUBRANO

The Shock of Education: How College Corrupts

One of America's most fundamental contradictions lies at the heart of the American dream itself. That is, America's promise of social mobility compels those who begin at the bottom to leave behind their origins in order to succeed, which entails giving up a part of oneself and leaving one's home behind. It can be a wrenching transition, and in this reflection on what it means to achieve the dream, Alfred Lubrano describes the strain of moving between two worlds, relating both his own experiences moving from working-class Brooklyn to an Ivy League school and those of other working-class "straddlers" who moved into the middle class. The son of a bricklayer, Lubrano is a journalist and National Public Radio commentator. He is the author of *Limbo: Blue-Collar Roots, White-Collar Dreams* (2004), from which this selection is taken.

College is where the Great Change begins. People start to question the blue-collar take on the world. Status dissonance, the sociologists call it. Questions arise: Are the guys accurate in saying people from such-and-such a race are really so bad? Was Mom right when she said nice girls don't put out? Suddenly, college opens up a world of ideas — a life of the mind — abstract and intangible. The core blue-collar values and goals — loyalty to family and friends, making money, marrying, and procreating — are supplanted by stuff you never talked about at home: personal fulfillment, societal obligation, the pursuit of knowledge for knowledge's sake, and on and on. One world opens and widens; another shrinks.

There's an excitement and a sadness to that. The child, say Sennett and Cobb, is deserting his past, betraying the parents he is rising above, an unavoidable result when you're trying to accomplish more with your life than merely earning a paycheck.[1] So much will change between parent and child, and between peers, in the college years. "Every bit of learning takes you farther from your parents," says Southwest Texas State University history professor Gregg Andrews, himself a Straddler. "I say this to all my freshmen to start preparing them." The best predictor of whether you're going to have problems with your family is the distance between your education and your parents', Jake Ryan says. You may soon find yourself with nothing to talk to your folks or friends about.

This is the dark part of the American story, the kind of thing we work to hide. Mobility means discomfort, because so much has to change; one can't allow for the satisfactions of stasis: You prick yourself and move, digging spurs into your own hide to get going, forcing yourself to forget the comforts of the barn. In this country, we speak grandly of this metamorphosis, never stopping to consider that for many class travelers with passports stamped for new territory, the trip is nothing less than a bridge burning.

Fighting Self-Doubt

When Columbia plucked me out of working-class Brooklyn, I was sure they had made a mistake, and I remained convinced of that throughout most of my time there. My high school was a gigantic (4,500 students) factory; we literally had gridlock in the halls between classes, kids belly to back between history and English class. A teacher once told me that if every one of the reliable corps of truant students actually decided to show up to class one day, the school could not hold us all. (We were unofficially nicknamed "the Italian Army." When our football guys played nearby New Utrecht, which boasted an equivalent ethnic demographic, kids dubbed the game the "Lasagna Bowl.") Lafayette High School roiled with restless boys and girls on their way to jobs in their parents' unions or to secretaries' desks. How could you move from that to an elite college?

At night, at home, the difference in the Columbia experiences my father and I were having was becoming more evident. The family still came together for dinner, despite our disparate days. We talked about general stuff, and I learned to self-censor. I'd seen how ideas could be upsetting, especially when wielded by a smarmy freshman who barely knew what he was talking about. No one wanted to hear how the world worked from some kid who was first learning to use his brain; it was as unsettling as riding in a car with a new driver. When he taught a course on Marx, Sackrey said he used to tell his students just before Thanksgiving break not to talk about "this stuff at the dinner table" or they'd mess up the holiday. Me mimicking

[1] Richard Sennett and Jonathan Cobb, *The Hidden Injuries of Class* (New York: Alfred A. Knopf, 1972), 131.

my professors' thoughts on race, on people's struggle for equality, or on politics didn't add to the conviviality of the one nice hour in our day. So I learned to shut up.

After dinner, my father would flip on the TV in the living room. My mom would grab a book and join him. And I'd go looking for a quiet spot to study. In his autobiography, *Hunger of Memory: The Education of Richard Rodriguez*, the brilliant Mexican-American Straddler, writer, and PBS commentator invokes British social scientist Richard Hoggart's "scholarship boys," finding pieces of himself in them. Working-class kids trying to advance in life, the scholarship boys learned to withdraw from the warm noise of the gathered family to isolate themselves with their books.[2] (Read primarily as a memoir of ethnicity and — most famously — an anti-affirmative action tract, the book is more genuinely a dissertation on class. At a sidewalk café in San Francisco, Rodriguez himself tells me how often his book is miscatalogued.) Up from the immigrant working class, Rodriguez says in our interview, the scholarship boy finds himself moving between two antithetical places: home and school. With the family, there is intimacy and emotion. At school, one learns to live with "lonely reason." Home life is in the now, Rodriguez says; school life exists on an altogether different plane, calm and reflective, with an eye toward the future.

The scholarship boy must learn to distance himself from the family circle in order to succeed academically, Rodriguez tells me. By doing this, he slowly loses his family. There's a brutality to education, he says, a rough and terrible disconnect. Rodriguez says he despised his parents' "shabbiness," their inability to speak English. "I hated that they didn't know what I was learning," he says. He thought of D. H. Lawrence's *Sons and Lovers*, and of Paul Morel, the coal miner's son. Lawrence is a model for Rodriguez, in a way. Rodriguez remembers the scene in which the son watches his father pick up his schoolbooks, his rough hands fingering the volumes that are the instruments separating the two men. Books were establishing a disharmony between the classroom and Rodriguez's house. Preoccupation with language and reading is an effeminacy not easily understood by workers. "It sears your soul to finally decide to talk like your teacher and not your father," Rodriguez says. "I'm not talking about anything less than the grammar of the heart."

Myself, I studied in the kitchen near the dishwasher because its white noise drowned out the television. As long as the wash cycle ran, I could not hear Mr. T and the A-Team win the day. I did not begrudge my father his one indulgence; there wasn't much else that could relax him. He was not a drinker. TV drained away the tumult and hazard of his Columbia day. My own room was too close to the living room. My brother's small room was too crowded for both of us to study in. You never went in your parents' bedroom without them

[2]Richard Rodriguez, *Hunger of Memory: The Education of Richard Rodriguez* (New York: Bantam Books, 1983), 46. Rodriguez himself quotes from Richard Hoggart, *The Uses of Literacy* (London: Chatto and Windus, 1957), chap. 10.

in it, inviting you. When the dishes were clean and the kitchen again too quiet to beat back the living room noise, I'd go downstairs to my grandparents' apartment. If they were both watching the same TV show on the first floor, then the basement was free. Here was profound and almost disquieting silence. I could hear the house's systems rumble and shake: water whooshing through pipes, the oil burner powering on and off, and the refrigerator humming with a loud efficiency. Down in the immaculate redwood-paneled kitchen/living room, which sometimes still smelled of the sausages and peppers my grandfather may have made that night (my grandparents cooked and ate in their basement, something that never seemed unusual to us), I was ninety minutes from my school and two floors below my family in a new place, underscoring my distance from anything known, heightening my sense of isolation — my limbo status. I read Homer, Shakespeare, and Molière down there. I wrote a paper on landscape imagery in Dante's *Inferno*. In my self-pitying, melodramatic teenager's mind, I thought I had been banished to a new, lonely rung of hell that Dante hadn't contemplated.

By 11 p.m., I'd go back upstairs. My mother would be in bed, my father asleep on his chair. I'd turn off the TV, which awakened my dad. He'd walk off to bed, and I'd study for a couple more hours. His alarm would go off before 5 a.m., and he'd already be at Columbia by the time I woke up at 6:30. That's how our Ivy League days ended and began. When my father was done with Columbia, he moved on to another job site. When I was done with Columbia, I was someone else. I'd say I got the better deal. But then, my father would tell you, that was always the plan. . . .

Macbeth and Other Foolishness

Middle-class kids are groomed for another life. They understand, says Patrick Finn, why reading *Macbeth* in high school could be important years down the road. Working-class kids see no such connection, understand no future life for which digesting Shakespeare might be of value. Very much in the now, working-class people are concerned with immediate needs. And bookish kids are seen as weak.

Various education studies have shown that schools help reinforce class. 10 Teachers treat the working class and the well-to-do differently, this work demonstrates, with the blue-collar kids getting less attention and respect. It's no secret, education experts insist, that schools in poorer areas tend to employ teachers who are less well-trained. In these schools, the curriculum is test-based and uncreative. Children are taught, essentially, to obey and fill in blanks. By fourth grade, many of the children are bored and alienated; nothing in school connects to their culture. Beyond that, many working-class children are resistant to schooling and uncooperative with teachers, experts say. They feel pressure from other working-class friends to not participate and are told that being educated is effeminate and irrelevant. Educators have long understood that minority children have these problems, says Finn. But they rarely understand or see that working-class white kids have similar difficulties. "So we're missing a whole bunch of people getting screwed by the education systems," he says.

In our conversations, Finn explains that language is a key to class. In a working-class home where conformity is the norm, all opinions are dictated by group consensus, by what the class says is so. There's one way to do everything, there's one way to look at the world. Since all opinions are shared, there's never a need to explain thought and behavior. You talk less. Language in such a home, Finn says, is implicit.

Things are different in a middle-class home. There, parents are more willing to take the time to explain to little Janey why it's not such a good idea to pour chocolate sauce on the dog. If Janey challenges a rule of the house, she's spoken to like an adult, or at least not like a plebe at some military school. (Working-class homes are, in fact, very much like the military, with parents barking orders, Straddlers tell me. It's that conformity thing again.) There is a variety of opinions in middle-class homes, which are more collaborative than conformist, Finn says. Middle-class people have a multiviewed take on the world. In such a home, where one needs to express numerous ideas and opinions, language is by necessity explicit.

When it's time to go to school, the trouble starts. The language of school — of the teachers and the books — is explicit. A child from a working-class home is at a huge disadvantage, Finn says, because he's used to a narrower world of expression and a smaller vocabulary of thought. It's little wonder that kids from working-class homes have lower reading scores and do less well on SATs than middle-class kids, Finn says.

In high school, my parents got me a tutor for the math part of the SATs, to bolster a lackluster PSAT score. That sort of thing happens all the time in middle-class neighborhoods. But we were setting precedent among our kind. Most kids I knew from the community were not taking the SATs, let alone worrying about their scores. If you're from the middle class, you do not feel out of place preparing for college. Parents and peers help groom you, encourage you, and delight in your progress. Of course, when you get to freshman year, the adjustments can be hard on anyone, middle-class and working-class kids alike. But imagine going through freshman orientation if your parents are ambivalent — or hostile — about your being there, and your friends aren't clear about what you're doing.

It was like that for my friend Rita Giordano, forty-five, also a journalist, 15 also from Brooklyn. Her world, like mine, was populated by people who thought going from 60th to 65th Streets was a long journey. So when Rita took sojourns into Greenwich Village by herself on Saturday mornings as a teenager, she made sure not to tell any of her friends. It was too oddball to have to explain. And she'd always come back in time to go shopping with everyone. She couldn't figure out why she responded to the artsy vibe of the Village; she was just aware that there were things going on beyond the neighborhood. When it came time for college, she picked Syracuse University because it was far away, a new world to explore. That bothered her friends, and she'd have to explain herself to them on trips back home. "What do you do up there?" they asked her. "Don't you get homesick?" Suddenly, things felt awkward among childhood friends who had always been able to talk. "It was confusing to come home and see people thinking that you're not doing what they're doing, which meant you're rejecting them," said Rita, a diminutive, sensitive woman with large, brown eyes. " 'Don't they see it's still me?' I wondered. I started feeling like, how do I coexist in these two worlds, college and home? I mean, I could talk to my girlfriends about what color gowns their bridesmaids would wear at their fantasy weddings. But things like ambition and existential questions about where you fit in the world and how you make your mark — we just didn't go there."

And to make matters more complicated, there was a guy. Rita's decision to go to Syracuse didn't sit well with the boyfriend who was probably always going to remain working class. "In true Brooklyn fashion, he and his friends decided one night they were going to drive four hundred miles to Syracuse to bring me back, or whatever. But on the way up, they totaled the car and my boyfriend broke his leg. He never got up there, and after that, the idea of him bringing me to my senses dissipated."

Another Straddler, Loretta Stec, had a similar problem with a blue-collar lover left behind. Loretta, a slender thirty-nine-year-old English professor at San Francisco State University with delicate features and brown hair, needed to leave the commotion of drugs and friends' abortions and the repressed religious world of Perth Amboy, New Jersey, for the calm life of the mind offered by Boston College. The only problem was Barry. When Loretta was seventeen, she and Barry, an older construction worker, would ride motorcycles in toxic waste dumps. He was wild and fine — what every working-class girl would want. But Loretta knew life had to get better than Perth Amboy, so she went off to Boston. Barry and she still got together, though. They even worked on the same taping crew at a construction site during the summer between Loretta's freshman and sophomore years. But the differences between them were growing. All the guys on the job — Barry included — thought it was weird that Loretta would read the *New York Times* during lunch breaks. "What's with that chick?" people asked.

By the time Loretta returned to Boston for her second year, she knew she was in a far different place than Barry. The working class was not for her. Hanging around with this guy and doing construction forever — it sounded awful. "I was upwardly mobile, and I was not going to work on a construction crew anymore," Loretta says. She tried to break it off, but Barry roared up I-95 in a borrowed car to change her mind. Loretta lived in an old Victorian with middle-class roommates who had never met anyone like Barry. When he showed up with a barking Doberman in tow, she recalled he was screaming like Stanley Kowalski in *A Streetcar Named Desire* that he wanted Loretta back. The women became terrified. Loretta was able to calm first Barry, then her roommates. Afterward, the couple went to listen to some music. In a little place on campus, a guitar trio started performing a Rolling Stones song. Suddenly, Barry turned to Loretta and began scream-singing about wild horses not being able to drag him from her, really loud, trying to get her to see his resolve. "People were wondering who was this guy, what's his deal?" Loretta says. "It pointed out the clash between my new world and the old. You don't do stuff like that. It was embarrassing, upsetting, and confusing. I didn't want to hurt him. But I knew it wasn't going to work for me." They walked around campus, fighting about things coming to an end. At some point, she recalls, Barry noticed that a college student with a nicer car than his — Loretta can't remember exactly what it was — had parked behind his car, blocking him. Already ramped up, Barry had a fit and smashed a headlight of the fancy machine with a rock. There Loretta was, a hundred feet from her campus Victorian, newly ensconced in a clean world of erudition and scholarship, far from the violence and swamps of central Jersey. Her bad-boy beau, once so appealing, was raving and breathing hard, trying to pull her away from the books, back down the turnpike to the working class.

"That was really the end of it," Loretta says. "I couldn't have a guy around who was going to act like that. He was wild and crazy and I was trying to make my way." Barry relented, and left Loretta alone. They lost touch, and Loretta later learned that Barry had died, the cause of death unknown to her. It was such a shock. . . .

READING THE TEXT

1. What is your response to Lubrano's title, and why do you think he chose it for his essay?

2. Summarize in your own words the difference between Lubrano's high school and college experiences.

3. What does Richard Rodriguez mean by saying "There's a brutality to education" (para. 6)?

4. Why did Lubrano avoid discussing his Columbia University experiences with his family?

5. How does childrearing differ in blue-collar and in middle-class families, in Lubrano's view? What evidence does he advance to support his claims?

READING THE SIGNS

1. In your journal, reflect on the effects — positive or negative — that attending college may have had on your relationship with your family and high school friends. How do you account for any changes that may have occurred?

2. In an argumentative essay, support, challenge, or complicate Gregg Andrews's statement that "Every bit of learning takes you further from your parents" (para. 1).

3. Write a synthesis of the personal tales of Lubrano, Loretta Stec, and Rita Giordano. Then use your synthesis as the basis of an essay in which you explain how their collective experiences combine to demonstrate Lubrano's position that "for many class travelers with passports stamped for new territory, the trip is nothing less than a bridge burning" (para. 2).

4. Interview students from both blue-collar and middle- or upper-class backgrounds about the effect that attending college has had on their relationship with their family and high school friends. Use your findings to support your assessment of Lubrano's position that college can create divisions between blue-collar students and their families but that it tends not to have that effect on other classes.

DANIEL MACKAY
The Magic of the Anti-Myth

In 1997, the Smithsonian's National Air and Space Museum assembled an elaborate exhibition entitled "*Star Wars*: The Magic of Myth." Packed with artifacts from one of America's favorite cinematic sagas, the exhibition, as Daniel Mackay notes in this detailed analysis, is part of a widespread tendency to treat the *Star Wars* films as, in Andrew Gordon's words, "'a new mythology which can satisfy the emotional needs of both children and adults.'" Acknowledging the well-known influence of the work of Joseph Campbell on writer and director George Lucas, Mackay is skeptical nevertheless about such claims, arguing that there is a profound contradiction at work here. While the story of *Star Wars* tells us that "we *cannot* rely on technology to save us . . . the films require the latest technological advances in sound and picture-recording technology in order to be told." In the end, Mackay concludes, "The *Star Wars* films are an anti-mythological message contained within a form — the films — that is very much a product of our contemporary — scientific and capitalist — mythology." Daniel Mackay is the author of *The Fantasy Role-Playing Game: A New Performing Art* (2001).

"*Star Wars*: The Magic of Myth" is the Smithsonian's National Air and Space Museum's latest effort to increase the jet stream of visitors passing through its glass doors. It is an exhibition of original production models, props, costumes, and characters used in the first three *Star Wars* features: *A New Hope* (1977), *The Empire Strikes Back* (1980), and *Return of the Jedi* (1983). During this exhibit, visitors behold C-3PO, R2-D2, Chewbacca, Yoda, the Wampa, Jabba's court (complete with Sy Snootles and Salacious B. Crumb), Boba Fett, Wicket, Admiral Ackbar, Darth Vader, a storm trooper and Imperial royal guard, a Jawa and Tusken Raider, and the costumes of Han, Luke, Lando, and Leia. Also included is a fleet of models and vehicles used in the films: a life-size speeder bike with a scout trooper in the saddle, a fifteen-foot-long Mon Calamari transport, the prop of Han Solo frozen in carbonite, an AT-AT, and, a Millennium Falcon, measuring two and a half feet in diameter, built for *Return of the Jedi*, complete with carbon-scorched armor, melted shielding, and (thanks to the merry pranksters at Industrial Light and Magic) a tiny "Champion" spark-plug sticker worn like a license plate across its bow.

Covering the walls are a plethora of original previsualization sketches, storyboards, and paintings, the majority of which were rendered by the conceptual artist for the trilogy, Ralph McQuarrie. The storyboards contain sketches of what each shot in question was intended to look like, along with a breakdown of other elements that would have to be composited into the shot. Visitors may be surprised at how closely the special effects team at ILM followed these sketches. In *Return of the Jedi*'s final space battle, some shots required up to sixty different elements; it was the storyboard that allowed the ILM cameramen to keep track of these dizzyingly complicated effects.

The effect of displaying the storyboards — which were followed so closely that they almost look like sketches done *after* the film was shot — alongside McQuarrie's paintings, many of which feature settings and scenarios that never made it to the final script stage, incites an endless string of "what-ifs" inside the mind of the visitor. McQuarrie's industrially polished paintings, always dramatic and epic in scope, depict scratched concepts for a Darth Vader Castle, in which the Emperor would appear to Vader in *Empire*. Also hanging on the walls of the exhibit is a painting of a Rebel base set in a grassland version of Monument Valley that was in an early draft of *Jedi*. A pyramid-covered landscape is the setting for another painting, this one of an archaic technological Imperial City slightly reminiscent of the Los Angeles of the future in Ridley Scott's *Blade Runner* (1982). This concept painting would be revisited for the special edition of *Jedi* (1997), in which we are finally treated to a brief glimpse of Coruscant, the Imperial planet/city, during the revised conclusion. Finally, most interesting of all, there are early concept paintings for a duel between Luke Skywalker and Darth Vader in the volcanic bowels of the Emperor's Throne Room, set on a planet pitted with molten lava lakes that stretch out into the infernal horizon.

The exhibit reveals the craftsmanship that went into the making of another world: from deliberately frayed Tatooine-worn desert robes to the knotted and clumped strings of yak hair that make Chewbacca look as if he could bust out of his glass cage and pilot one of the museum's V-2 rockets to some Wookie planet far, far away. For those who dressed up as Princess Leia for Halloween, or Han Solo, Darth Vader, or the cackling Emperor, here is their chance to see how far off they were when struggling to assemble some approximation of what they remembered the characters to be wearing in the film. The illusion these artifacts made when assembled in the films themselves, unified by John Williams's unforgettable score, was more than the sum of its parts, but those parts remain well-crafted icons resonant within the imagination of millions of Americans. The focus of the exhibit is on the art and craftsmanship of the visual designers of the film, and it is in this area that curator Mary Henderson and exhibition designer Linda King focused their talents and produced a rich, evocative presentation.

The great theme of the exhibit is that *Star Wars* is not just an awesome 5 spectacle — an immersive and overwhelming image that transports the visitor to another time and place for a period of two hours. No, visitors are instructed that these films have cultural capital; they are relevant to a "timeless" audience because of their mythological themes. Considering *Star Wars* as if it were a modern mythology is an approach that harkens back to the rhetoric around the film during its initial release. At the time, writer/director George Lucas told an interviewer, "I wanted to do a modern fairy tale, a myth" (Zito 1978:13). Film critics, journalists, and scholars picked up on George Lucas's pastiche of American popular culture (which includes everything from Disney's versions of European fairy tales, pulp science-fiction stories and serials, Westerns, and Akira Kurosawa's Japanese samurai epics) and wrote articles like Andrew Gordon's "*Star Wars:* A Myth for Our Time," in which Gordon writes: "In the absence of any shared contemporary myths, Lucas has constructed out of the usable past, out of bits of American pop culture, a new mythology which can satisfy the emotional needs of both children and adults" (1978:315).

The triumph of this point of view came in 1987 when Joseph Campbell, architect of the seminal works on mythology *The Hero with a Thousand Faces* (1949) and the four-volume *Masks of God* (1959–1968), was filmed at Lucas's own Skywalker Ranch in a series of conversations with telejournalist Bill Moyers. In these conversations, which were eventually released on PBS as the successful series *Moyers: Joseph Campbell and the Power of Myth*, Moyers seems to take every opportunity he can to ask Campbell to comment on the mythic themes in *Star Wars*. Campbell, who had never even seen the films until Lucas invited him and his wife over for a private screening of all three films (Campbell 1990:216), courteously obliged Moyers and used *Star Wars* examples when expounding upon the meaning of certain reoccurring mythic archetypes and themes: "*Star Wars* is not a simple morality play, it has to do with the powers of life as they are either fulfilled or broken and suppressed through the action of man" (Campbell. 1991:145).

Exhibit curator Henderson reiterates this idea of *Star Wars* as mythology in the beautifully designed companion book to the Smithsonian exhibit. The 214-page book follows the same format as the exhibit: twenty-five mythic themes (in the exhibit there are sixteen descriptive plaques) that "reveal classical mythology themes and motifs that are woven throughout the trilogy" (1997). Each such theme is given its own subheading and then elucidated in a near word-for-word reiteration of Campbell's observations on the "monomyth," a term coined by James Joyce and adapted by Campbell in order to articulate the archetypal pattern of the heroic quest described in *The Hero with a Thousand Faces*. Themes such as the hero's "Call to Adventure," "Refusal of the Call," the "Dark Road of Trials," and the hero's journey "Into the Belly of the Beast" are first introduced and then used as analytic tools in order to reveal the structure, meaning, and themes of the three *Star Wars* movies.

There is nothing particularly novel about such an approach. Not only have critics been alluding to the mythic themes in *Star Wars* for over twenty years,* but Lucas himself has said that he deliberately set out to fabricate a fairy tale using Joseph Campbell's idea of the monomyth:

> I set out to write a children's film, and I had an idea of doing a modern fairy tale.... I started working, started doing research, started writing, and a year went by. I wrote many drafts of this work and then I stumbled across *The Hero with a Thousand Faces*.... And I said, "This is it." After reading more of Joe's books I began to understand how I could do this. When that happened to me I realized how important the contribution that Joe had made to me was. I had read these books and said, Here is a lifetime of scholarship, a life of work that is distilled down into a few books that I can read in a few months that enable me to move forward with what I am trying to do and give me focus to my work. It was a great feat and very important. It's possible that if I had not run across him I would still be writing *Star Wars* today [Campbell 1990:180].

For Mary Henderson, Andrew Gordon, and other critics, to identify where Lucas used Campbell's observations is one thing, but to proceed to claim that this pattern has "transformed *Star Wars* itself into myth," as Henderson claims (1997:7), or that the popularity of the films is *because* "of the connections the films make with the collective and personal unconscious of the viewers," as Charles Champlin suggests in *George Lucas: The Creative Impulse* (1997:96), is to obscure from whence comes the authority — "the

---

*In addition to works cited in this paper, see: Roger Copeland. 1977. "When Films Quote Films, They Create a New Mythology," *The New York Times* 25 September:D1; Richard Grenier. 1980. "Celebrating Defeat," *Commentary* #70.2:58–62; Aljean Harmetz. 1983. "George Lucas: Burden of Dreams," *American Film* June:36; Anne Lancashire. 1981. "Complex Design in *The Empire Strikes Back*," *Film Criticism* #5.3 (Spring):38–52; Anne Lancashire. 1984. "Once More with Feeling," *Film Criticism* #8.2 (Winter):55–66; "Tarot and *Star Wars*," *Mythlore* #76 (Spring 1994):27–31; Todd H. Sammons. 1987. "*Return of the Jedi*: Epic Graffiti," *Science-fiction Studies* #43, v.14.3 (November):355–371; David Wyatt. 1982. "*Star Wars* and the Productions of Time," *Virginia Quarterly Review* #58:600–615; Dennis Wood. 1978. "Growing Up Among the Stars," *Literature/Film Quarterly* #6:327–341.

Force" — behind *Star Wars*. The authority behind the *Star Wars* story is not a universal mythic faculty within the human psyche, it is Joseph Campbell. Campbell was like a disembodied Obi-Wan Kenobi whispering his esoteric teachings into the receptive ear of Lu[ke]cas, his apt pupil. Bringing Campbell in front of the television cameras to explicate the mythic themes in *Star Wars* (*his* mythic themes, the ones he universalized and identified nearly forty years before, which Lucas then used as a blueprint for the films), thereby validating the "universality" of the films, is itself a supreme sleight-of-hand trick worthy of the wizards at Industrial Light and Magic.

The phenomenal popularity of *Star Wars*, a story based on Campbell's monomyth, has been used as a vindication of the universality of Campbell's work; the truth, however, is less mysterious and seductive. *Star Wars* is an exciting spectacle movie, thoughtfully conceived, well crafted, and featuring astonishing special effects thanks to innovations like the Dykstraflex Camera and the Electronic Motion Control System, which, when used in concert with the creations of the film's crack model-building team, achieved the convincing illusion of immersing the audience in another world.

Like the blockbuster *Jaws* (1975) two years previous, *Star Wars* was   10 released at a time when the audience demographic was ideally suited for the mass appeal of a film like *Star Wars*. Created by baby boomers as their version of the ultimate child's space fantasy — the perfection of what films like the *Flash Gordon* series (1936–1940) and *Forbidden Planet* (1956) promised them in their childhood — *Star Wars* was eminently appealing to the new generation of parents (the largest number of new parents ever in America's history), who could think of nothing better to entertain their children with than that which had once entertained them.

As for those parents — the twenty- to thirty-something boomers — *Star Wars* was a palliative on many levels. By 1977 the hippie youth movement had failed to meet its own meteoric expectations throughout the cultural and political field of Cold War America. The Vietnam War had dragged on into the 1970s and had only come to a dissatisfying conclusion at the very time when Nixon was being driven from office in disgrace. The hopes many staked on rock and roll as a rallying point were dashed as Woodstock faded into the nightmare at Altamont Speedway (as shown in the concert movie *Gimme Shelter*, which, coincidentally enough, George Lucas was a cameraman for) as well as the premature deaths of many of that movement's heroes (Jimmie Hendrix, 1970; Janis Joplin, 1970; and Jim Morrison, 1971). The United States, still in the midst of the never-ending Cold War, suffered economic recession due to two oil shocks during the 1970s. Families and neighborhoods were affected as businesses closed or relocated, more often than not out of the city and into the suburbs. All this left many Americans exasperated and exhausted as their security, pride, and hope for the future were threatened.

Star Wars made people feel better. It gave them an opportunity to celebrate victory through a clear and unambiguous polarization of moral and political forces (the good and the bad) to which the 1977-dominant baby boom generation had been conditioned to respond (the 1950s Red scare, cowboy and Indian serials on the Saturday-afternoon matinee screen, Matt Dillon and *The Lone Ranger* cantering through black-and-white pixelated Dodge Cities, Tombstones, Amarillos, and other desert prairie towns as vacant and relaxed as the newborn American suburb). The unambiguous contexts in which the baby boomers were raised were frustrated and complicated during the 1960s and 1970s. They were, however, joyfully reaffirmed (in fantasy if not in fact) through *Star Wars* and its contemporary forms of fantasy participation: everything from the punk relocation back to a 1950s-styled arena of contest (us and them, "never mind those bollucks"), a *Dungeons & Dragons* form of role-playing game morality in which "lawful good" characters slay "chaotic evil" orcs, and professional wrestling, wherein the production of comfortable dichotomies takes the form of Hulk Hogan vs. The Iron Sheik.

Robert G. Collins, in "*Star Wars*: The Pastiche of Myth and the Yearning for a Past Future," may choose to gloss over this demographic foundation for *Star Wars*' force in America's collective psyche, asserting instead that "*Star Wars* confronts us as the first omnibus work of generalized myth in the film medium" (1977:2), but what he and writers of his ilk have failed to grasp, and what Campbell himself observes, is that there is no "generalized myth." All mythology is grounded in the particulars of a society and culture, in a people's way of life, in the *praxis* — the practice — of living in a specific time and place.

Nevertheless, Henderson's *Star Wars: The Magic of Myth* may not be misguided in its effort to identify Arthurian, Christian, Zen Buddhist, and whatever other mythological themes, archetypes, or tropes are to be found in *Star Wars*. Of course, the themes are going to be there because Lucas deliberately drew from this material in writing *Star Wars*. A work like Henderson's can, therefore, prove useful in gaining a deeper appreciation for Lucas's deliberate attempt to appropriate patterns and themes from Campbell's observations (which stress the similarity — universality? — of mythic themes by citing specific ritual practices or stories when they correspond to his idea of the monomyth). At the Smithsonian exhibit, it is interesting to read the exhibit plaque that explains how the mythological "Belly of the Beast" motif (drawn from *The Hero with a Thousand Faces*) is used as the setting for transformative events in the lives of the characters in *The Empire Strikes Back*. The plaque notes that Darth Vader only begins to show his weakness and eventual fallibility once he emerges from his cocoon-like meditation chamber. Vader does this first through appearing unhelmeted for a brief moment, so that we see his bald, scarred, old-man's head, and second, through immediately leaving his chamber and bowing before the Emperor, revealing for the first time that Vader is a servant to a higher master. Similarly, it is in the belly of the giant space slug that Han and Leia's romance finally blossoms into a kiss. Finally, it is in the dank, womblike swamp cave of the planet Dagobah where Luke confronts a vision of Darth Vader as a dark shadow of himself. These observations can enrich one's appreciation of the film. However, it can hardly be used as evidence that such a mythic theme is universal simply because *Star Wars* used it. Nor does it move *Star Wars* itself any closer to being a myth. Observations that suggest *Star Wars* and its artifacts have achieved the status of mythology are misguided. Even more than that, they malign the idea of mythology and its relevance for a community of people. The message of *Star Wars*, when viewed in the context of the society from which it comes, is that of a modern-day anti-myth.

In *Masks of God* (a work referred to much less often than *The Hero with a Thousand Faces*, but a work that nevertheless represents the author at the height of his literary powers), Campbell identifies four functions of mythology. The first function is to instill within the person a sense of awe and beauty at the magnitude, wonder, and plurality (both physical and spiritual) of the universe. The second function is to explain why the world is the way it is: why the sky is blue, why snakes do not have legs, and so forth (such stories are called etiologic tales) — it establishes the cosmology of the world for a people. The third function teaches people how to live a model life despite all manner of circumstances — it enforces a moral order. Finally, the fourth function of mythology, what Campbell identifies as its most important, "is to foster the centering and unfolding of the individual in integrity, in accord with" oneself, one's culture, the universe, and the "awesome ultimate mystery which is both beyond himself and all things" (1968:4–6). Campbell generally asserted that, in our society, science has picked up the explanation of the cosmos (the second function); art, the awe and beauty of the universe, as well as the instilling of a moral order (the first and third functions); and that, in the wake of the collapse of our ancestral mythology, nothing has yet stepped in to satisfy the fourth function — how one lives in accord with the rest of the universe — which is bound up with ritual: therefore we get random acts of violence, surreptitious gang activities, and other evidences of an unbridled, chaotic world filled with unbridled, chaotic men and women (Campbell 1991:82).

The experience of watching *Star Wars* is an experience of an overwhelming "imaginary." The famous opening shot of *Star Wars*, in which an Imperial Star Destroyer cruises over the audience's head, exhausts one even before the story begins. Richard Edlund knew that shot would determine how audiences would respond to the film's subsequent special effects. It is the longest special effects shot in the film, and it was shot five times until Edlund was certain that he had it right. The shot lures the viewer into the imaginary world of the film. The Smithsonian exhibit and accompanying book try to configure the three films' six hours of the imaginary into the sphere of the symbolic. They do this through language — a necessity for symbolic systems — such as the sixteen plaques spaced throughout the exhibit, which recontextualize the artifacts from the film into a symbolic code Campbell derived from his study of the world's mythology (primarily Hindu, Buddhist, Christian, Islamic, American Indian, Egyptian, prehistorical shamanism, and Zoroastrian religions), artists (Arthurian poets, Richard Wagner, Walt Whitman, T.S. Eliot, Robinson Jeffers,

15

Pablo Picasso, Thomas Mann, and, especially, James Joyce), and philosophers (Immanuel Kant, Arthur Schopenhauer, Friedrich Nietzsche, Sigmund Freud, Carl Jung, D. T. Suzuki, Mircea Eliade, and Martin Buber).

This endeavor, while not arbitrary, is misguided in that it attempts — using Campbell as a kind of superego father figure—to structure the audience's experience of the imaginary in the film into a symbolic code. They use the term "mythology" for this symbolic order. However, from a look at how Campbell's four functions of mythology are fulfilled in America today it is clear that society's efficacious mythology is not the story of the movement of heroic archetypes through a liminal field, as Campbell identifies in the foundational text of the exhibit, *The Hero with a Thousand Faces*. Rather, our contemporary mythology is the story of the manufacture of the "individual" from recombined bits of archived information (Critical Art Ensemble 1994). Our mythology is the electronic archiving of quantified individuality according to scientific methods, and an implementation of this process in order to serve the capitalism upon which our economy is based. "Our atrocity," writes Baudrillard, "is exactly inverse of that of the former centuries. It is to efface blood and cruelty by objectivity" (1983:1).

A pioneering work in the field of ethnography, Arnold Van Gennep's *Rites of Passage* (1908), upon which Campbell based many of his observations, identified a three-phase sequence of events during mythological rituals (Campbell's fourth function of mythology could be called the ritual function):

> Separation from the Community→
> Liminal Stage→
> Reincorporation into the Community

When watching a movie, the viewer is separated from his community, displaced in a darkened theater. For the two-hour duration of the film, the audience is in a liminal state, inhabiting the imaginary. Performance studies theorist Richard Schechner might call this state one of double negativity: The viewer is both *not there* in the theater (for he or she is lost in the image) and *not not there* in the theater (for surely a body sits in the darkened room) (1985:123).

However, with *Star Wars*, Van Gennep's third stage is never achieved. When the last credits roll, John Williams's score ceases, and the lights go on, the viewer returns to the community, but he or she is not reincorporated into the community after such a liminal experience, The liminal experience of the film has no avenue into which it can be reincorporated into *praxis* — daily experience. *Star Wars*–as–image fails in an essential mythological function: It can take you "out there," but it cannot take you back. And, in taking the viewer "out there" to a galaxy far, far away, it is really doing nothing more than stranding the audience in a liminal stage in which they are excluded from the larger non–*Star Wars* community. The film is a two-hour liminal experience that excites the passions and nerves of the audience. Leaving the theater all worked up but with no obvious direction in which to apply (reincorporate) this energy, the viewer may quell this tension by returning to the queue wrapped around the theater in order to watch it again. What other way is there of doing something with this experience of having watched the film? Its life as video or DVD is guaranteed — the *form* guarantees a successful market performance. So the viewer returns to the theater line or video store or the Smithsonian National Air and Space Museum. Here, inside the museum that deigns to honor scientific man's most lauded achievements in air and space exploration, the *Star Wars* phenomenon plays into the scientific rhetoric and capitalist ideology that shapes our contemporary mythology. Though it does so with mythological motifs that Henderson, Gordon, Collins, and Champlin may not suspect.

Star Wars cannot reincorporate its viewers back into the community [20] with an impartation of any kind of efficacious knowledge, as the mythological rites of passage that Van Gennep writes about do, because the experience of watching *Star Wars* is not corporeal — it is imaginary, a body (as French philosophers Deleuze and Guattari would say) without organs. The Critical Art Ensemble observes that "If the BwO [Body without Organs] is conceived of as appearance of self contained in screenal space, it is nearly supernatural to think that the BwO can possess the flesh and walk the earth" (1994:7–8). This near-supernatural process is a moment of possible weakness, they continue, because it subjects the imaginary to the limits of the real, but it is also a moment of amplification for the spectacle. The *Star Wars* exhibition is an example of the celebrity of objecthood. During the press conference before the event's unveiling, it was announced that Chewbacca, R2-D2, C-3PO, and Darth Vader were in the exhibit, and that George Lucas would be conducting interviews "next to Chewbacca." In a film in which masks and costumes very often *are* the characters, the public display of the costumes is equivalent to the "flesh possession" of the spectacle of the image.

Marshall Blonsky relates that Malraux identified the function of museums as ripping the work from the "setting of its age," and the museologist "must institutionalize the rip-away" (1996:2). Henderson and her associates have ripped the elements of *Star Wars* from their imaginary context, have displayed them to the public, hungry for the "assurances of the pre-electronic order," and have, in so doing, both strengthened the spectacle of the film itself by presenting its elements apart from the spectacle, thereby amplifying the value of that spectacle, and written a symbolic code to contextualize the *Star Wars* image, institutionalizing that symbolic code through its public presentation in the National Air and Space Museum, and, having done so, introduced an ideological subtext into a nostalgic process (and even pilgrimage) for two generations: the baby boomers and their children.

Establishing an exhibition of the artifacts of a film would, merely by its intent, be an example of the Critical Art Ensemble's physical avatar of the electronic world. However, by ordering the exhibition according to a symbolic code — the monomyth of Campbell — the Smithsonian exhibit determines the context in which two generations of viewers experience the physical avatar — the celebrityhood — of the film. In the *Star Wars* exhibit the "nearly supernatural" Body without Organs has been incarnated in the flesh and made to "walk the earth," or at least the National Air and Space Museum's second floor. The pervading sense that something is lost or hidden within the subtext of *Star Wars* is what sustains the exhibit, which purports to reveal the hidden mythological underpinnings of the film. The audience's desire to rediscover itself in the image of the film compels the viewer to become a pilgrim, to travel to the exhibit, where the fading image of the film is both recontextualized into a symbolic code and is finally reified from out of the electronic ether of the imaginary. Part of the film is materialized, but at the same time, what is not materialized — the experience of watching the film (complete with John Williams's score)—is made that much more untouchable.

The exhibit, trying to promote the idea that *Star Wars* is a mythology, is engaging in an ideological attempt to change the phenomenological experience of the film. Through an attribution of *Star Wars* as mythology, the Smithsonian is attempting to raise its cultural worth and importance. They are, of course, obligated to do this because their reason for creating a *Star Wars* exhibit — to exploit its extraordinary popularity in order to increase the museum's revenue — would never fly as the sole means of justifying the inclusion of artifacts from a space fantasy movie in a museum devoted to humankind's real efforts to explore space. Therefore, they must increase the cultural worth of their object before they use that object (as a sort of Hope Diamond on display behind museum glass) to increase their economic worth.

The message and themes of *Star Wars* are decidedly nonscientific: the story tells us to follow our hearts, to rely on intuition and not technological devices. The story tells us not to rely on technology to save us, that, in fact, we *cannot* rely on technology to save us. Yet the films require the latest technological advances in sound and picture-recording technology in order to be told: George Lucas waited twelve years before beginning his new trilogy of *Star Wars* prequels, waiting for computer imaging technology to catch up with his imagination.

The *Star Wars* message is, in fact, an anti-mythological message, pre- 25 cisely because its message about the human spirit is assembled from the remnants of the old mythologies — mythologies that no longer carry weight in the way we live our lives today — and runs perpendicular to the scientific capitalism mythology of our day. The *Star Wars* films are an anti-mythological message contained within a form — the films — that is very much a product of our contemporary — scientific and capitalist — mythology. How appropriate, then, that the Smithsonian has chosen to exhibit the anti-mythological artifacts of the films inside its temple to the real mythological artifacts of our day: the airplanes, rockets, and space stations of scientists reaching to walk the sky and sail the stars. In the exhibit "*Star Wars*: The Magic of Myth," as in the films, an anti-mythological message is contained inside a very contemporary mythological format. That *Star Wars* does this in a form so palatable to our way of seeing and living perhaps makes that pill a little easier to swallow. Let us just hope that its form does not anesthetize us to its, thankfully, anti-mythological themes.

BIBLIOGRAPHY

Baudrillard, Jean. 1983. "What Are You Doing after the Orgy?" *Traverses* (29 October).
Blonsky, Marshall. 1996. Untitled evaluation of the future of online museology. 1–12.
Campbell, Joseph. 1990. *The Hero's Journey: The World of Joseph Campbell*. New York: Harper.
———. 1968. *Masks of God, Volume 4: Creative Mythology*. New York: Viking.
———, with Bill Moyers. 1991 [1988]. *The Power of Myth*. New York: Doubleday.
Champlin, Charles. 1997. *George Lucas: The Creative Impulse; Lucasfilm's First Twenty-Five Years*. New York: Abrams.
Collins, Robert G. 1977. "*Star Wars*: The Pastiche of Myth and the Yearning for a Past Future." *Journal of Popular Culture* 11:1–10.
Critical Art Ensemble. 1994. *The Electronic Disturbance*. Brooklyn: Autonomedia.
Gordon, Andrew. 1978. "*Star Wars*: A Myth for Our Time." *Literature/Film Quarterly* 6:314–326.
Henderson, Mary. 1997. *Star Wars: The Magic of Myth*. New York: Bantam.
Schechner, Richard. 1985. *Between Theater and Anthropology*. Philadelphia: U of Pennsylvania P.
Zito, Stephen. 1978. "George Lucas Goes Far Out." *American Film* (April):13.

READING THE TEXT

1. What sorts of details from the *Stars Wars* saga were included in the Smithsonian's National Air and Space Museum exhibition, and how did they shape visitors' responses to it?

2. What is the "great theme of the exhibit" (para. 5), according to Mackay?

3. What does Mackay mean by saying that *Star Wars* "was a palliative on many levels" (para. 11) when it was released in 1977?

4. Summarize in your own words the role that Joseph Campbell's work played in creating the mythology behind *Star Wars*.

5. Why does Mackay argue that *Star Wars* contradicts its mythological pretensions with an "anti-mythological message"?

READING THE SIGNS

1. Write an essay in which you support, qualify, or contest Mackay's central claim that "Observations that suggest *Star Wars* and its artifacts have achieved the status of mythology are misguided" (para. 14). To develop your ideas, view at least one of the *Star Wars* films and use details from it as evidence for your argument.

2. Research the ways in which the *Star Wars* franchise has been commodified (from action figure toys to costumes to uses in advertising campaigns for just about every imaginable product), and write an essay on how consumerism has engulfed the spiritual mythology of the *Star Wars* saga.

3. Mackay suggests that the National Air and Space Museum's presentation of *Star Wars* as mythology was motivated, at least in part, by economic considerations. Research the museum's exhibitions during the last five years. How many, if any, seem to reflect similar motivations, and how? Use your research as the basis of an essay in which you argue whether the museum has departed from its mission "to honor scientific man's most lauded achievements in air and space exploration" (para. 19).

4. **CONNECTING TEXTS**   Using Linda Seger's "Creating the Myth" (p. 386) as a critical framework, write a critique of Mackay's argument that the *Star Wars* saga presents an anti-mythological message, not a mythological one. Be sure to ground your essay in an examination of the movie itself.

RICHARD CORLISS

The Gospel According to Spider-Man

"For decades, America has embraced a baffling contradiction," Richard Corliss writes in this *Time* analysis published in 2004. "The majority of its people are churchgoing Christians, many of them evangelical. Yet its mainstream pop culture . . . is secular at best, often raw and irreligious." As often happens in the strange dialectics of history, however, antitheses can come to meet in a new synthesis, as they do in America when a religious pastor can offer a sermon entitled "*Catwoman*: Discovering My True Identity." As Corliss reports, this melding of religion and pop culture is no isolated event, and with the growing Christian rock music and Christian film industries, we can expect to see more such weddings of onetime antagonists in the future. A senior writer for *Time*, Corliss is also the author of *Talking Pictures* and *Greta Garbo* (both 1974).

The Congregation for today's service of the Journey, "a casual, contemporary, Christian church," fills the Promenade, a theater on upper Broadway in New York City. The Sunday-morning faithful—a few hundred strong—have come to hear the Journey's laid-back pastor, Nelson Searcy, give them the word. The word made film. Searcy, 32, who in jeans and a goatee looks like a way less Mephistophelian Charlie Sheen, is about to deliver the last of the church's eight-part God on Film series. The topic? "*Catwoman*: Discovering My True Identity."

Searcy points to a large screen at his right that shows other comic-book heroes with multiple identities. In his sermon, he alludes only vaguely to the

Catwoman myth and gives the impression that he (like most other Americans) hasn't seen the Halle Berry version. But Searcy knows that a person tormented by questions of image and identity can find encouragement in the message of Genesis 1:27: "So God created people in his own image." That biblical quotation is projected on the screen, which also features an icon of a smiling cartoon Catwoman sporting purple tights, a feather boa, and a whip.

For decades, America has embraced a baffling contradiction. The majority of its people are churchgoing Christians, many of them evangelical. Yet its mainstream pop culture, especially film, is secular at best, often raw and irreligious. In many movies, piety is for wimps, and the clergy are depicted as oafs and predators. It's hard to see those two vibrant strains of society ever coexisting, learning from each other.

Yet the two are not only meeting; they're also sitting down and breaking bread together. The unearthly success of Mel Gibson's *The Passion of the Christ* helped movie execs recognize that fervent Christians, who spend hundreds of millions of dollars on religious books and music, are worth courting. Publicists hired by studios feed sermon ideas based on new movies to ministers. Meanwhile, Christians are increasingly borrowing from movies to drive home theological lessons. Clergy of all denominations have commandeered pulpits, publishing houses, and especially Web sites to spread the gospel of cinevangelism.

What's the biblical import of, say, *Spider-Man*? "Peter Parker gives us   5 all a chance to be heroic," says Erwin McManus, pastor of Mosaic, a Baptist-affiliated church in Los Angeles. "The problem is, we keep looking for radioactive spiders, but really it's God who changes us." What's the big idea behind *The Village*, according to the Web site movieministry.com? "Perfect love drives out fear." Behind *The Notebook*? "God can step in where science cannot." And, gulp, *Anchorman*? "What is love?" If your minister floated those notions recently, it may be because movieministry.com provides homilies for Sunday sermons. The Web site is a kind of Holy Ghostwriter.

By splicing Matthew and Mark with Ebert and Roeper, ministers can open a window to biblical teachings and a door to the very demographic that Hollywood studios know how to reach: young people.

"Film, especially for those under 35, is the medium through which we get our primary stories, our myths, our read on reality," says Robert K. Johnston, professor of theology and culture at the Fuller Theological Seminary and the author of the newly published *Finding God in the Movies: 33 Films of Reel Faith*. It was members of that generation, says Johnston, who "even if they loved God, were simply not going to church. Clergy are realizing that unless we reorient how we talk about our faith, we will lose the next generation." He sees movies as modern parables that connect to an audience that seeks not reason but emotional relevance. "As the culture has moved from a modern to a postmodern era, we have moved from wanting to understand truth rationally to understanding truth as it's embedded in story," he says.

The cinevangelists would say that the churches' appropriation of pop culture is nothing new. "Jesus also used stories," Johnston says. "In his day, parables were the equivalent of movies." Marc Newman, who runs movieministry .com, traces pop proselytizing back to the Apostle Paul. "In Acts there's a Scripture describing how he came to the Areopagus, the marketplace in Athens where people exchanged ideas. Paul speaks to the men of Athens and refers to their poets and their prophets. He used the things they knew as a way to reach out with the Gospel."

If Paul could cite Greek poets to the Greeks, then today's proselytizers will bring the church to moviegoers and, they hope, vice versa. "Today, with DVDs and the VCR, all of us can engage a movie text," Johnston says. "When a person in a worship congregation refers to *The Shawshank Redemption*, either people have seen it or they can rent it." In addition, 3,000-screen bookings and saturation marketing guarantee that a film that opens Friday will have been seen or at least talked about by Sunday morning.

Some conservative clergy prefer using the Bible, not *Bruce Almighty*, as   10 the text for a sermon. "It's not my cup of tea," says Jerry Falwell of movie-inspired sermons. But progressive Christians love plumbing the subtexts of comedies, satires, and action movies. Now, says Ted Baehr of movieguide .org, "a church group can highlight biblical teachings by using anything from *Dodgeball* to *Saved!* to *Kill Bill*."

Baehr, who grew up in Hollywood (his father was ranger Bob Allen in cowboy serials of the '30s), has put his Columbia University Film School education to use by giving a Christian take on current movies. "We try to teach people media wisdom. If Christians didn't believe in communications, they wouldn't believe that in the beginning was the Word and the Word was God and the Word has a salutary effect within society."

But movies? From the beginning, they were considered, in the words of Catholic doctrine, an occasion of sin. The Catholic Legion of Decency was more notable for proscribing movies than promoting them. Some of the sterner Christian sects forbade filmgoing. And that was when Hollywood still produced religious films, from uplifting tales of jolly priests (Bing Crosby in *Going My Way*) and selfless sisters (Audrey Hepburn in *The Nun's Story*) to outright miracle plays like *The Song of Bernadette*, with Jennifer Jones as a French girl who had a vision at Lourdes.

By the '70s, the religious film had virtually disappeared. Today, *The Passion* aside, the genre exists only in niche markets: Mormon films (Ryan Little's *Saints and Soldiers*, Richard Dutcher's *God's Army*), well crafted and proudly square; and Rapture movies (*The Moment After*, *Caught in the Rapture*), which announce a personal and earthly apocalypse. Both types of film usually fly under the radar of studios, critics, and audiences.

Rarely, a Christian message is implicated in a Hollywood film. Steven Spielberg's *Close Encounters of the Third Kind*, in which an ordinary guy sees the light and travels far to make contact with extraterrestrials, was conceived by its original screenwriter, Paul Schrader, as Saul's transforming journey to become the Apostle Paul. *The Matrix* (the first one, not the sequels) was manna to hermeneuticians. In a recent Museum of Modern Art film series called "The Hidden God: Film and Faith," *Groundhog Day*, the Bill Murray comedy about a man who relives the same day over and over, was cited as a profound statement of faith, either Buddhist (rebirth), Jewish (acceptance), or Christian (redemption).

In the broadest sense, movies are getting more religious. According 15 to Baehr, only one film in 1985 (*The Trip to Bountiful*) had "positive Christian content," compared with 69 in 2003 (including *Finding Nemo*, *Spy Kids 3D*, and *Master and Commander*). Of course, it all depends on what counts as Christian and who's doing the counting. What's irrefutable is the growing number of theocentric movie Web sites, most recently a sophisticated one launched in February by the magazine *Christianity Today*.

The clergy may see all this as a revival; Hollywood sees it as a customer bonanza. New Line Cinema reaches out to Christian groups with films — like *Secondhand Lions*, about a boy living with his two codgerly, kindly uncles — whose themes might resonate. Says Russell Schwartz, New Line's president of domestic marketing: "The thing about all special-interest groups — Christian, Jewish, whatever — is that they have to discover something relevant to their experience." Some studio bosses go further. Baehr says he talked with a mogul who told him, "We want to be seen as Christian friendly. We realize there's a big church audience out there, and we need to reach them."

"It's a vast, untapped market," says Jonathan Bock, a former sitcom writer (*Hangin' with Mr. Cooper*), whose Grace Hill Media helps sell Hollywood films to Christian tastemakers. He pitches media outlets like *Catholic Digest* and *The 700 Club* and has created sermons and Bible-study guides and marketed such movies as *The Lord of the Rings*, *Signs*, *The Rookie*, and, yes, *Elf*. "The ground was softened before *The Passion*," says Bock. "There are hundreds of Christian critics and Jewish writers and ministers who are writing about films." And millions of the faithful who see them. A July 2004 study by George Barna, the Gallup of born-again religion, shows that Christian evangelicals are among the most frequent moviegoers. "Being a Christian used to mean you didn't go to Hollywood movies," says David Bruce, who runs the Web site hollywoodjesus.com. "Now it is seen as a missionary activity."

All this could just be the church's appropriation of Hollywood salesmanship: luring audiences with promises of a movie and some good talk, as the Journey's Searcy offered. Finding a Christian message in secular films like *Catwoman* and *Spider-Man* could be either a delusion or, as Jeffrey Overstreet, a critic for *Christianity Today* says, "a way of affirming that God's truth is inescapable and can be found even in the stories of people who don't believe in him."

Hollywood doesn't necessarily want to make Christian movies. It wants to make movies Christians think are Christian. Moviemakers are happy to be the money changers in the temple, even as preachers are thrilled that a discussion of — what, *Harold & Kumar Go to White Castle*? — can guarantee a full house on Sunday.

READING THE TEXT

1. What is the effect on the reader of Corliss's opening description of pastor Nelson Searcy's sermon entitled "*Catwoman*: Discovering My True Identity"?

2. Describe in your own words the contradiction in American culture that Corliss identifies.

3. Why do some ministers find religious dimensions in *Spider-Man*, in Corliss's view?

4. What conflicts does Corliss see in the religious attitudes toward popular culture?

5. How does Corliss use the history of popular culture to explain the current tendency of religion to engage with popular culture?

READING THE SIGNS

1. Write an essay in which you support, refute, or complicate Corliss's contention that films like *Spider-Man* enable religious groups to "open a window to biblical teachings and a door to the very demographic that Hollywood studios know how to reach: young people" (para. 6).

2. Taking Corliss's article into account, write your own explanation of the response to *The Passion of the Christ*, which was supported by many Christian groups and opposed by some Christian and Jewish groups. Alternatively, interpret the response to another film or TV program that includes a religious dimension.

3. Adopt the perspective of pastor Nelson Searcy, and write a response to Corliss's claim that Christian evangelicals' view of moviegoing as a "missionary activity . . . could just be the church's appropriation of Hollywood salesmanship" (paras. 17–18).

4. Write an argumentative response to Corliss's assertion that "Hollywood doesn't necessarily want to make Christian movies. It wants to make movies Christians think are Christian" (para. 19).

5. Visit www.movieministry.com and assess the validity of Corliss's belief that "the Web site is a kind of Holy Ghostwriter" (para. 5).

MURRAY MILNER JR.

Freaks, Geeks, and Cool Kids

While America has become a consumer culture, it has not entirely abandoned the tradition of the Protestant work ethic: the view that hard-working productivity is both a social and a personal good. The result is a paradoxical cultural synthesis within which, as Murray Milner Jr. puts it, "the social ideal becomes the person who both works hard and plays hard." In practice, Milner argues, this ideal is exemplified in youth by the high school "preppie," and in adulthood by the "bourgeois bohemian," both of whom work hard to attain a status that will enable them to become lavish consumers. Thus hedonism meets asceticism, a cultural contradiction that carries a possible threat: America's "exhortation to self-indulgence needed to maintain consumption potentially undercuts the self-discipline and commitment to work needed for efficient production." Milner is professor emeritus of sociology at the University of Virginia and senior fellow at the Institute for Advanced Studies in Culture. His books include *The Illusion of Equality: The Effects of Educational Opportunity on Inequality and Conflict* (1972); *Status and Sacredness: A General Theory of Status Relations* (1994), and *Freaks, Geeks, and Cool Kids: American Teenagers, Schools, and the Culture of Consumption* (2004), from which this selection is taken.

From Abstract Desire to Patriotic Consumption

The centrality of consumption and its near sacral status became clear following the terrorism of September 11, 2001, which killed nearly 3,000 people at the World Trade Center, the Pentagon, and the airline crash in Pennsylvania. Following this event a variety of public figures claimed that it was patriotic for individuals to spend money in order to stimulate the economy. Supposedly people had a duty to buy more, even if the events they experienced caused them to focus on personal, family, and political concerns rather than economic ones. An article appeared in the nationally circulated daily paper *USA Today* reporting on these exhortations to a new form of patriotism. Entitled, "Shoppers splurge for their country," it notes that Americans have long had numerous rationales for shopping. "But just weeks after the terrorist attacks that shook the nation, we are suddenly home to a new breed: the militant shopper. . . . It's the consumer, traveler, or executive who is buying stuff right now, not just because he or she needs it, but also because the economy does." Several prominent politicians, including President George W. Bush, publicly made expensive purchases and urged others to do likewise. Getting back to normal was equated — or at least strongly linked to — shopping and spending. The article concluded, "And who can name one thing that's more intrinsically American than to buy something?"[1] This new version of social responsibility seemed to be a collective version of that old ironic quip, "When the going gets tough, the tough go shopping."

 There was some dissent from this line of thought by a few intellectuals, but there was no visible public disapproval, much less any sense of moral outrage. While many might disagree that the essence of being an American is buying things, it is perfectly acceptable to suggest that this is the case, even in a time of national tragedy and mourning. In short, consumption has become an end in itself. We now have a moral duty, not only to be hard-working producers, but also to be fast-spending consumers. With only a little hyperbole it can be said that consumption has consumed life.

The Cultural Contradictions of Capitalism

The emphasis on our roles as consumers, at the expense of other social roles, has contributed to a form of abstract desire and patriotic profligacy. Quite aside from what this has done to our inner selves and our interpersonal relationships, it also has led to a form of hedonism that has implications for the operation of the core institution of capitalist society, the market economy.

THE PROBLEM

In recent years Robert Putnam and others have drawn considerable attention to the decline of social capital: people's neglect of their roles as citizens in voluntary associations and non-economic interpersonal networks that constitute "civil society."[2] Others have pointed to the costs of the decline of marriage and family relationships.[3] The problem of consumer capitalism, however, is not only the pride of place given to producing and consuming—at the expense of other social roles. There is also a key tension between the roles of producer and consumer. Daniel Bell, renowned sociologist and once an editor of *Fortune*, refers to this as the cultural contradiction of capitalism.[4] His book argues that there is increasingly a conflict between the discipline and asceticism needed for efficient production and the hedonism and self-indulgence needed to maintain levels of consumption and market demand. Many have commented on this thesis. David Bosworth, an English professor and scholar of popular culture, gives his version of this argument:

> We live in a philosophy/economy that has long proceeded through separation and division, which has divided the classes, the sexes, and now the generations to enhance its own authority and multiply profits. So we shouldn't be shocked to discover that even that most valued of reifications, the Single Self, was also divided for exploitation. There was to be a Producing Self, and there was to be a Consuming Self; one set of ideal behaviors for behind the desk; another, and nearly opposite, for browsing in the mall. Each person was supposed to labor like a Calvinist and spend like an Epicurean.[5]

In less critical and more conventional terminology, the social ideal becomes the person who both works hard and plays hard. This has become a virtual philosophy of life among the professional and managerial classes. To be effective, ideologies must be sustained over time. How is such an ideology inculcated in the next generation?

THE SOLUTION: PREPPIES

I want to suggest that high school status systems are a key social mechanism 5 for creating selves who incorporate these two roles. In modern high schools it is the prep who attempts to embody these two ideals. Preppies may or may not care about learning and ideas, but they are concerned about getting decent grades. They generally conform to adult expectations — at least enough to avoid being labeled a loser. They may not be like Weber's ascetic Calvinists, but they develop moderate amounts of self-discipline. The most successful students are often very disciplined and work exceedingly hard. But if they want to avoid being labeled a brain, or even worse a nerd, they must also learn how to "have a good time." This cannot be simply a private experience, such as appreciating fine art or beautiful scenery, though to show some knowledge and appreciation of these can be a subsidiary asset. One's commitment to a hedonistic good time must be publicly displayed. This is one of the reasons that partying is such a central feature of prep life. It provides an opportunity to publicly display your willingness and ability to "let go," to "go wild," to "get bombed." But this form of hedonism must be limited to weekends and special events if it is not to incapacitate the producing self. Hence, an additional type of self-indulgence is needed for "everyday," something that can be regularly combined with self-discipline. This takes the form of purchasing and displaying good quality fashionable clothes, cars, and other publicly visible status symbols. But these items must communicate both self-indulgence and self-discipline; hence, the expensive designer shirt — with the buttoned-down collar; the dress that is sexy and elegant — but not cheap in either the literal or figurative sense. In short, becoming a preppie is an effective way to learn to manage the two key roles required to be successful in a consumer capitalist society. Perhaps more important than the individual effects are the collective ones; the result is a substantial population of selves committed to the key requirements of a consumer society: high production and high consumption.

The cross pressures of meeting these two sets of role requirements is even more intense for adolescents — because high school preps must hide both their ambition and their hedonism, and to be openly preoccupied about doing well in school is to be labeled a brain or a nerd. But if ambition and self-discipline must be hidden from peers, hedonism must be hidden from adults. Purchasing and consuming alcohol — not to speak of drugs — is illegal for teenagers. They are expected and even encouraged to look and act sexy, but exhorted to refrain from sex. Even if everyone knows what is going on, it must not be made explicit. To do so would risk having parents restrict their activities or cut their allowances. They may lose the good opinion of teachers, who will write the all-important letters of recommendation during the college admissions process. Therefore, young people in general and preps in particular must learn to be less than candid. At times they are obliged to engage in outright deception and lying. When such behavior becomes routine — as it is in most high schools — it is hardly surprising that some students become systematically dishonest and deceitful. Even more significant, it encourages a form of cynicism. For many students this becomes not merely an attitude, but an ideology — a public pose that is regularly displayed in the presence of one's friends and peers. The enormous popularity of the animated television programs *Beavis and Butthead* and *South Park* is an indicator of the prevalence of this mindset. Cynicism toward those in authority and one another is a central element of their content. These programs may reinforce such cynicism, but they are much more likely to be a reflection of this outlook rather than its cause. For some, cynicism becomes a worldview that is carried into adulthood. In its weaker form, cynicism is not the core of the cynic's worldview, but its close complements, irony and sarcasm, are abundant in his style of communicating.[6] These attitudes and styles are further reflected in the disillusionment of younger cohorts with politics and their low rates of voting. At the very least it becomes fashionable to express such indifference and cynicism about politicians and politics.

Students who embrace some version of being "alternative" — whether punk, goth, hippy, or some other variant — are in part rejecting the hypocrisy that they perceive as inherent in the preppy lifestyle. In various ways they are more open about their hedonism. "Normals" are those who are unwilling or unable to both work hard and play hard to the degree that is characteristic of preppies. The various forms of "losers" are those who are undisciplined about both their work and play. They fail to get their schoolwork done and they play in ways that get them into serious trouble with their parents, the school, or the police.

The preppy lifestyle can also be seen in a more positive light. Preppies can be understood as the young people who are learning to deal with the complexities and moral ambiguities of the postmodern adult world. Hypocrisy can be seen as realism — as tact, discretion, and prudence. Young people with these attributes can be seen as having the sophistication needed to be the future leaders of our society.

But whether a negative or a positive interpretation is given to the preppy lifestyle, the key point is that it is not a world unto itself. Rather it is a diminutive version of the lifestyle of the managerial and professional classes of the adult world. More generally, the structure of high school status systems is not simply a transitory stage — a period of hormones and immaturity — unrelated to the adult world. For all of the separation from and contrast with the adult world, there are important parallels between the lives of teenagers and adults. These parallels both reflect and help create some of the key realities of the adult world in consumer capitalism.[7]

THE OUTCOME: BOURGEOIS BOHEMIANS

Many see alternating disciplined hard work and a genuine enjoyment of the good life as a high social accomplishment, a new, more balanced, and creative culture. This ethos is the hallmark of the educated managerial and professional classes. This is the central theme of David Brooks's *Bobos in Paradise: The New Upper Class and How They Got There*.[8] "Bobo" is the contraction of *bourgeois* and *bohemian*; such an amalgamated lifestyle is characteristic of the educated classes at the beginning of the twenty-first century. The social ideal is to be both a thoughtful, educated, disciplined professional and to maintain the bohemian appreciation of sensuality, the avant-garde, and egalitarianism. Bobos believe in individual freedom and choice. They also believe in social responsibility and strong communities. The style of Brooks's book is often ironic and playful; at points it seems superficial. For example he quips, "To calculate a person's status [in Bobo culture], you take his net worth and multiply it by his antimaterialistic attitudes."[9] Yet, this sometimes-flippant style is a way of communicating the irony, modesty, and pragmatism that he sees as characteristic of this worldview. This is a much more serious and thoughtful analysis than its mode of presentation sometimes suggests. He captures well many of the characteristics of the managerial and professional classes.

Brooks's description, however, suggests a very insular, even provincial social existence — not too different from the largely self-contained world of high school status groups. This bright, hardworking, environmentally concerned, and emotionally sensitive upper class has limited, and seemingly superficial, connections with the lives of less talented and less privileged people. The thirty-one million Americans who officially live in poverty, not to speak of the eighty-five percent of the world's population with less than one-tenth of U.S. income levels, are largely invisible in this account.[10] This insulation of the Bobo milieu from other classes and cultures is a serious shortcoming in Brooks's view of social reality, and probably in the world-view of the classes he describes.[11]

American culture in general and Bobo culture in particular is certainly envied and copied around the world. Unquestionably, it has had a profound impact in shaping a global culture for the middle and upper classes of the world. But is it the "paradise" Brooks claims? Or is this socially structured oblivion? Of course, Brooks and all Bobos are not ignorant of those below them or of the wider world. Yet, Brooks's characterization of Bobos captures well what might be called a "cosmopolitan provincialism." It is not a provincialism rooted in a lack of knowledge, or even a lack of concern; their politics may very well be informed and support efforts to reduce poverty and inequality. Rather, it involves seeing little connection between the poverty of others and their own style of life. This form of oblivion helps to explain why members of this class (and those who try to copy them) are shocked and mystified by resentments expressed in the Oklahoma City bombing, the killings at Columbine High School, and the destruction of the World Trade Center.[12] Following the terrorism of September 11, 2001, comments by many people — especially Bobos, who are often the people that make comments in the public media — claimed that "their world" or even "the world" would "never be the same." These events were indeed awful and tragic. Compared to events experienced by many people around the world, however, the consequences of

September 11 were quite limited in terms of the number of people affected, the aggregate suffering experienced, and the sense of security people have. Americans in general and Bobos in particular had joined "the real world."[13]

The Future: Who Do We Want to Be?

As we have seen, Brooks thinks that a combination of the bourgeois work ethic and the bohemian enjoyment of life are a kind of paradise. Many more people affirm the legitimacy of this way of life, though they would not identify it with a heavenly kingdom. Though adult rhetoric often criticizes materialism and hedonism, adult behaviors regularly affirm these values. But even if one accepts the legitimacy of this worldview and lifestyle, it is not how most contemporary young people will live their lives. First, the data seem to indicate that fewer and fewer adolescents even aspire to being preps. (Preps joined by a few brilliant nerds and weirdos are the main source of Bobos.) Whatever the virtues of the preppy lifestyle in preparing young people for success in the adult world, the majority of contemporary high school students find it unappealing or unavailable. Perhaps various kinds of school reform will convince young Americans to undergo the process of becoming work-hard producers and play-hard consumers; citizens who eschew grand visions of the future and are content to seek pragmatic solutions to concrete problems. Even if this should occur there is another problem. As September 11, 2001, so tragically showed, significant segments of the billions of people from less developed regions of the world are unlikely to leave our paradise of pragmatism undisturbed.[14]

Our educational system plays a central role, not just in giving people technical skills, but also in molding their desires and ambitions. Life with one's peers, in and out of the classroom, powerfully shapes people's worldviews and personalities. The peer status system is central to this process. Currently that status system is an integral part of consumer capitalism; learning to consume is one of the most important lessons taught in our high schools. The question we need to face is whether this is the kind of education we want to give our children and the kind of people we want them to become. The answer to that question will be determined, in large measure, by how adults choose to organize their own lives.

A reminder is appropriate. Like all stories, my account has been selective. [15] Some people do live rather banal lives centered on the most crass forms of status seeking and consumerism. Yet, the concrete lives of most individuals are more complex. Many students are not simply preps, brains, weirdos, or whatever. Most adults see themselves as trying to be good employees, parents, and citizens — not simply compulsive achievers and hedonistic consumers. Most of us resist being categorized in any simple way; subjectively our lives feel more complex; the differences between others and ourselves seem subtler; and our motivations for adopting a particular lifestyle are many-faceted.

The arguments I have proposed do not capture the complicated motivations and myriad pressures that we sense shape our personal lives. That is not what they are intended to do. Their purpose is to point to processes and relationships that we tend to overlook, ignore, or repress as we go about living our day-to-day lives. The goal is to highlight things on the collective level that indirectly shape our individual lives — and to point out how our own interests and behaviors significantly contribute to this latent but ever more prevalent collective reality.

Maintaining high levels of consumption has become crucial to the economic prosperity of advanced capitalist societies, which can legitimately be characterized as consumer capitalism. Changes in fashion and more generally the desire to acquire status symbols have become central to maintaining high levels of consumption and economic demand. High school status systems play an important role in socializing people to be concerned about their status and more specifically the way this status is displayed through the acquisition of consumer commodities. "Learning to consume," not "learning to labor," is the central lesson taught in American high schools.

While most adults complain about teenagers' preoccupation with status and status symbols, adults support the basic institutions that encourage these adolescent behaviors because in certain important respects the grown-ups benefit from the existing social arrangements. Many businesses have become very self-conscious of how their economic interests are linked to the status preoccupations of adolescents. They have developed extensive marketing campaigns to encourage the preoccupations of both young people and adults with status, consumption, and the associated ideals of youthfulness, self-indulgence, and hedonism. Consumption now consumes much of life.

According to some analyses this produces a cultural contradiction within capitalism: The new exhortation to self-indulgence needed to maintain consumption potentially undercuts the self-discipline and commitment to work needed for efficient production. One partial remedy was to train people at a relatively early age to both work hard and play hard, to see their core identities as being linked to both production and consumption. The lifestyle of high school preppies incorporates both of these ideals. Being a preppy requires a level of deception that often produces cynicism. For this and other reasons the cultural dominance of the preppy lifestyle within high schools has declined and a more complex form of pluralism has emerged within many schools. In the adult world intellectuals have articulated explicit moral rationales for preppy-like behavior by adults. The emphasis is on a pragmatism that combines a bourgeois work ethic with bohemian hedonism, a strong commitment to disciplined production, and guiltless consumption. Whatever the moral legitimacy of this vision for people in an advanced consumer economy, the resentment of the billions of people around the world, who either reject such an ideal or see little possibility in sharing its fruits, raises the question of whether this insular subculture can be sustained as a *world*view.

NOTES

[1]The article by Bruce Horowitz in *USA Today*, October 3, 2001, included the following passages:

> Even cheerleader-in-chief President Bush jumped onto the buying-as-patriotism bandwagon last week and Tuesday when he urged Americans to take to the skies. He also suggested that folks go to Disney World. Several big-shot politicians, and one former president, have recently been doing some high-profile shopping in New York City. Immediately after New York Mayor Rudy Giuliani urged New Yorkers to go out and spend money, former president Bill Clinton bought $342.79 worth of gifts for children of victims at the NBA Store in midtown Manhattan.
>
> Over the weekend, governors and mayors from several states flew to New York to do some very public consumption. They chowed down at the Carnegie Deli. They spent hundreds of dollars at Macy's. Several took in a Broadway performance of *The Lion King*.
>
> The rationale: Shopping has become a patriotic duty, and an economic necessity. The simplest way to make sure the terrorists don't have a nice day: Buy something. No matter if it's dinner at Sardi's, a sweater at Bloomie's or a round-trip ticket to Las Vegas. The economy needs it — or so the thinking goes.

[2]Putnam (2000), *Bowling Alone*.
[3]For example, Nock (1998), *Marriage in Men's Lives*.
[4]Bell (1975), *The Cultural Contradictions of Capitalism*.
[5]Bosworth (1996), *The Georgia Review*, 451.
[6]An example of this is the popularity of humorist Andy Borowitz, especially among well-educated young adults. He is a former president of the *Harvard Lampoon*, his writing appears in the pages of *The New Yorker*, the *New York Times, Vanity Fair, TV Guide*, and at Newsweek.com. He is a regular guest on CNN's *American Morning* and commentator for National Public Radio's *Weekend Edition*. The following is his satirical essay entitled, "Let's Give Thanks: A Thanksgiving List," Borowitzreport.com, published November 26, 2002:

> I'm thankful to the producers of *Stuart Little 2*, for making a film that seems to have greatly reduced the chances of a *Stuart Little 3*.
>
> I'm thankful to the executives of VH1 for pulling the plug on the reality show *Liza and David*, since a program about Liza Minnelli's marriage couldn't really be considered a reality show.
>
> I'm thankful for the emergence of a public figure who finally justifies our trust — the Anaheim Angels' Rally Monkey.
>
> I'm thankful for the scientists at the Coca-Cola Company, who turned mankind's long-elusive dream of a diet vanilla cola beverage into a reality.
>
> I'm thankful to Mr. and Mrs. Blix for naming their son Hans, because I think Hans Blix is just about the coolest name I've ever heard.
>
> I'm thankful to CBS for airing the *Victoria's Secret Fashion Show*, although I secretly fear that Fruit-of-the-Loom will demand equal time.
>
> I'm thankful for the urgent news alert crawl on CNN, which informed me that Rosie O'Donnell had taken her name off her magazine.
>
> I'm thankful for Kelly Ripa, who continues to be our nation's best defense against the return of Kathie Lee Gifford.
>
> I'm thankful to J.-Lo and Ben Affleck for announcing their engagement, since the suspense was killing me.
>
> I'm thankful to Michael Jackson for making all of my parenting look perfect.
>
> I'm thankful for Winona Ryder, who showed that security measures seem to be working in at least one place in this country — Saks Fifth Avenue.

> I'm thankful for whoever came up with the term "perp walk."
> And finally, I'm thankful for how the election turned out — on *The West Wing*.

It needs to be kept in mind that this essay focuses on a holiday that historically has centered on a genuine expression of thankfulness and the reaffirmation of traditional values; it was one of the least cynical occasions in the year. Note how the focus of the essay is on the banalities of the media and contemporary popular culture. My point is not to criticize this essay, but to use it as an illustration of the rise of cynicism as a common and perhaps even a dominant mode of expression.

[7]Lamont's (2000) *The Dignity of Working Men*, especially 108–109, study of working-class men shows striking similarities between the criticisms that working-class men express toward those in the middle and upper classes and the criticisms that are expressed by high school students toward preppies. For example, workingmen often complain that members of the "upper half" are "two-faced," "engage in too much politicking," are "unreal" like "Barbie and Ken people." As "normals" and "alternatives" in high schools often reject grades and popularity as measures of self-worth, working-class men often reject economic and occupational ambition and success as the primary measures of moral worth. They frequently invoke other criteria that emphasize straight-forwardness and thoughtfulness toward others. In contrast, "[F]ewer New York professionals and managers expressed alternative definitions of success, and most measured freedom by consumption, for instance, by being able to buy a house in a good neighborhood or to take off regularly for a weekend of skiing in Vermont." See Lamont's (2000) *The Dignity of Working Men*, 116. In sum, working-class men's image of managers and professionals often parallels non-preppy students' perceptions of their preppy peers. While the behaviors and perceptions of adults are obviously shaped by more than their high school experience, it seems highly likely that these patterns are linked.

[8]Brooks (2000), *Bobos in Paradise*. Brooks's argument is another version in a long line of theories of the "new class," though he does not connect his analysis to this tradition. See Dahrendorf (1959), *Class and Class Conflict*; Bell (1973), *The Coming of Regular Post-Industrial Society*; and Gouldner (1979), *The Future of Intellectuals*, for a sampling of earlier versions of new class theory. See Brint (1994), *In an Age of Experts*, for a critique and specification of such arguments.

[9]Brooks (2000), *Bobos in Paradise*, 50.

[10]These figures are from U.S. Bureau of the Census estimates for 2000 and World Bank estimates for 1999. In the low- and middle-income countries, which contain 85 percent of the world's population, the per capita national income is $1,240, compared to $31,910 for the U.S., which contains 4.7 percent of the world's population. Even if one uses the "purchasing price parity" figures, which take into account differences in cost of living in different countries, the figures are $3,610 for the low- and middle-income countries and $31,910 for the U.S. Of those within most of the low- and middle-income countries, 25 percent are below the World Bank poverty line of earning less than $1.08 per day. Source: http:// www.worldbank.org/ data/wdi2001 /pdfs/tabl_l.pdf; http://www.worldbank.org/research/povmonitor/index.htm and http:// www.census.gov/prod/2001pubs/p60-214.pdf; November 5, 2001.

[11]There is also the question of whether the educated professionals and managers that compose most of the subculture Brooks describes are the "upper class." It could be argued that they are largely the employees of those who control large concentrations of property. Brooks's description includes people in this category, but it seems clear that most of those who compose the class have human and cultural capital, but do not own significant amounts of property. See the works of William Domhoff for an alternative view.

[12]For a brief, eloquent characterization of this resentment, see Pamuk (2001), "The Anger of the Damned."

[13]In the year 2000 alone there were forty armed conflicts in thirty-five countries. [An armed conflict is defined as a political conflict involving armed combat by the

military forces of at least one state (or one or more armed factions seeking to gain control of all or part of the state), and in which at least 1,000 people have been killed during the fighting.] As of December 31, 2000, the U.S. Committee for Refugees estimated that there were 14,500,000 refugees throughout the world. In 2001 there were more than fifty major natural disasters. One of these, an earthquake in India, killed nearly 19,000 people and left 600,000 homeless. This is not to suggest that events of September 11, 2001, were not horrible, but only that the rest of the world regularly suffers even greater natural and human-made disasters. Source: http://www.infoplease.com /ipa/A0878269.html, accessed July 2, 2002.

14Let me briefly discuss two problems which are beyond the scope of the present analysis, but which my conclusions point to. The billions of poor people around the world are likely to demand a significantly greater share of the world's resources and power. Worldwide income inequality has increased over a long period of time. This trend may have moderated, but currently about 70 percent of the income inequality in the world is due to differences between countries, not to differences within countries. See Firebaugh (2000), "Between-Nation Income Inequality," for a relatively conservative view of the extent and trend in international inequality. This structure of between-nation inequality means that, on average, being born into a poor (or rich) country has much more to do with your economic opportunities than anything you can do to improve your lot within that setting. The global media are making people increasingly conscious of this at the same time it is raising their desires for goods and services. In the political realm, it is obvious that with the collapse of the Soviet Union in 1989, military power became much more unequal, with the U.S. being the only world power. Moreover, whatever the justification, the U.S. invasion of Afghanistan and the two invasions of Iraq significantly raised fears and hostility toward the U.S. in both the developing and the developed worlds. American supremacy in the areas of communication and culture production also increased. In countless villages without running water, people are well acquainted with American television programs and advertising logos. Many embrace American culture and consumerism, but many — sometimes the same people — fear and resent our spreading cultural dominance and the closely related consumerism. September 11 showed the lengths to which a relatively small group of fanatics were willing to go to express their resentments. Even when they admire and envy many things about the U.S., literally billions of people see American society, its government, and its culture, as a threat, and even an enemy. It is unlikely that any amount of military might or homeland security can protect Americans from such resentments.

The strategy of economic development and world trade via free markets holds out the hope that our consumerism can become sufficiently available to those in the rest of the world that their resentments can be alleviated. Yet, even assuming that this occurs, it leaves unanswered another increasingly pressing question. What would be the ecological consequences of spreading anything approximating American consumption patterns to the rest of the world? Even with the most optimistic of assumptions it is difficult to imagine how such a world economy could be sustained without dire consequences for the natural environment. Obviously, these issues are beyond the scope of this book and hinge on much more than the nature of peer status systems in high schools. My point is that high school status systems and their link to consumerism potentially contribute to even broader processes that are of fundamental importance.

READING THE TEXT

1. How did American consumerism become especially highlighted after the September 11, 2001, terrorist attacks, according to Milner?

2. Summarize in your own words Daniel Bell's notion of "the cultural contradiction of capitalism" (para. 4).

3. How do preppies resolve the cultural contradiction of capitalism, in Milner's view?

4. How does the cultural contradiction of capitalism lead to the emergence of "bourgeois bohemians" (para. 10)?

READING THE SIGNS

1. Describe in your journal your own desires for your future. Were you once a "preppie"? Might you become a "bourgeois bohemian"? What is your attitude toward such categories?

2. In an essay, support, refute, or complicate Milner's claim that "'Learning to consume,' not 'learning to labor,' is the central lesson taught in American high schools" (para. 16).

3. Milner suggests the self-indulgence manifested by both preppies and bourgeois bohemians is fundamentally at odds with notions of an informed citizenry concerned about the public good. Write an essay in which you defend, oppose, or complicate the proposition that this conflict is fundamental to the American psyche. To develop your ideas, read or reread the Introduction to this chapter.

4. **CONNECTING TEXTS**   Read or reread John Verdant's "The Ables vs. the Binges" (p. 152). Adopting Milner's article as a critical framework, analyze the two families that the article describes. To what extent is each family "committed to the key requirements of a consumer society: high production and high consumption" (para. 5)?

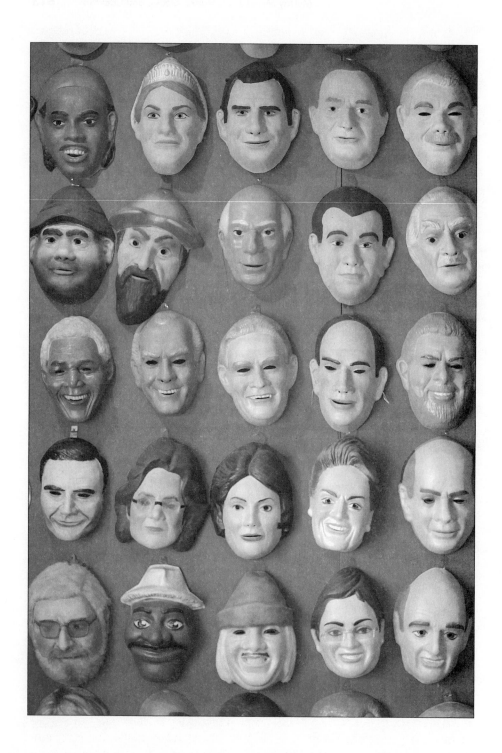

AMERICAN MAKEOVER

Constructing Identity in the Age of Entertainment

Avatar

In 2009 a movie about a man who chooses to become a member of an extra-terrestrial species became the most profitable film in history.

In the same year, a movie about a man who is involuntarily transformed into an alien species became one of the most talked about films of the year and was nominated for four Academy Awards.

And in the beginning of that same year, a Coca-Cola commercial broadcast during the Super Bowl featured an urban landscape filled with people being transformed into the kinds of avatars that are commonly chosen for online gaming and social networking sites.

It's almost as if people are tired of being people.

Or, to put it more precisely, what *Avatar*, *District 9*, Coca-Cola, and a host of other popular cultural signifiers appear to be telling us is that people are eager to try on new identities, new ways of determining who, and even what, they are. The traditional identifiers — nation, religion, race, class, gender, and even, apparently, species — are evidently getting tired. It isn't that they are no longer relevant (indeed, in many ways they are more potent than ever before), but the indicators are that Americans (especially younger Americans) would prefer to have some more choices.

For example, even as ever increasing numbers of Americans are abandoning the mainline religious denominations of their parents (especially mainline Protestantism) to choose spiritual identities of their own, so too are an increasing number experimenting with the **gender codes** that tradition-ally govern sexual and social behavior. Racial identity, too, is becoming more fluid, with more and more people adopting "mixed race" identities, a choice that the 2010 census allowed by letting people check off more than one race or to fill in their own racial identification. And even the sense of national identity is changing, from a monocultural melting pot identity to a **multiculturally** diverse one.

None of these changes has been absolute, and all have raised political and social controversy. Even mentioning them can inspire debate. And that isn't really very surprising, because your identity, your sense of who you are, is probably the most intimately personal element in your whole outlook on life. This is especially true in individualistic societies like America's, whose **mythologies** maintain that identity is a matter of individual, not societal, determination.

It is quite a different matter in traditional societies where personal identity may be a construct of the state, the tribe, the clan, the family, or a combination thereof. In such societies, the likelihood is that you will make a living the way your parents did, reside in the place your parents lived, remain in the social caste in which you were born, and be strictly bound by rules governing gender roles and behaviors. Even the ancient Athenians, who are widely credited for developing the ethos of individualism, defined individuals in terms of their relationships to the state, the *polis*, at large. In Athens, who you were had a great deal to do with the social role you performed in society, whether that be musician, carpenter, physician, or warrior.

Such societies can look rather strange from an American perspective, where personal identity has always been more flexible. As a whole, Americans resent the state as a determiner of identity, a resentment that is piquantly reflected in the Bob Seger classic "I Feel Like a Number," preferring instead the sense, as enshrined within the American dream, that you can be whatever you want to be. Though sentimental about the family, Americans expect to go their separate ways as they grow up and move out, with college often serving as a place not only for education but as a site for individual development as well: a transition from one's childhood identity as

Exploring the Signs of Gender

In your journal, explore the expectations about gender roles that you grew up with. What gender norms were you taught by your family or the media, either overtly or implicitly? Have you ever had any conflicts with your parents over "natural" gender roles? If so, how did you resolve them? Do you think your gender-related expectations today are the same as those you had when you were a child?

part of a family to a maturity in which newly hatched adults create their own families.

But even in America, identity is never really *simply* a matter of individual choice. Rather, identity is a dynamic interplay between individual desire and social determination, something at once internal and external. We cannot entirely escape the external categories that help define who we are (we can't really change species at all, of course, though a woman did become rather notorious several years ago for using plastic surgery in an attempt to make herself look like a cat), but we can experiment with them.

Who Are You?

There is a mysterious moment in J. R. R. Tolkien's *The Lord of the Rings* when the hobbit Frodo Baggins, moved to a sense of wonder by the stories told by Tom Bombadil, asks Tom just who he is. Tom's answer is evasive: "Who are you, alone, yourself, and nameless?" he replies. Indeed, at that level we are all pretty mysterious, our identities incommunicable to anyone else. The fact that we often take our social *roles* as markers of personal identity can confuse the matter even further, for we also identify ourselves as sons, daughters, sisters, brothers, students, and even by the work we do. So asking yourself "Who am I?" is a very complicated question.

Part of you, it might be added, comes simply from your own unique DNA, but your identity doesn't stop there, because a large part of you also is shaped from your many experiences in life. Your *social class*, for example, will influence what life experiences you may (or may not) have, and these experiences will play a strong role in shaping your consciousness and sense of self. Your *race*, too, will have a powerful effect, because, rightly or wrongly, the way people treat you is affected by your ethnicity, and how you are treated has a role in how your identity gets shaped. And your **gender**, too, will have profound effects on your experience and identity.

It is easy to forget the ways in which our identities begin to be constructed in childhood, and all societies have their ways of influencing that process. Such institutions as family, church, and education play a large role in telling you who you are and what you should expect of life. But in an entertainment culture like that of contemporary America, popular culture has emerged as a major shaper of individual identity and desire.

Just think of all those children's television programs you may have begun watching even before you could walk or talk. America's children spend hours in front of television sets (which are called "the great pacifier"), watching programs whose plots and characters subtly communicate how to behave in society, from appropriate gender roles (think of the difference between the Bratz and Dora the Explorer) to appropriate professional identities (consider Bob the Builder). At the same time children are being exposed to all that television, they are absorbing a great deal of advertising. These ads are carefully constructed not only to shape you as a consumer when you grow up but also to "brand" you as a consumer of the products that you see advertised, in the expectation of a lifetime of brand loyalty.

The entertainments you enjoy in your youth can also have a powerful effect on your sense of identity. Your favorite music and clothing fashions are not only personal forms of expression but **signs** of belonging to the various youth cohorts who share your tastes. From Indie to Hip-Hop, Emo to Metal, Skater to Surfer, and on and on, popular cultural movements provide American youth with ways of identifying themselves to, and bonding with, others. In a sense, using popular cultural signs as badges of your identity can be considered a form of stereotyping, but if we are the ones adopting the signs, the process doesn't seem to bear the negative connotations we usually ascribe to the word "stereotyping."

But what if we are not so in control? At the same time that culture presents us with images that we might embrace as our own, it also categorizes us in ways that we may not choose for ourselves. This is especially true when it comes to racial identity, and sometimes individuals may seek to strike back, creating their own categories of racial identification. Consider the case of the late Michael Jackson.

Neverland

Perhaps Michael Jackson simply wanted to be Peter Pan.

That's one theory, anyway, explaining the ranch at Neverland, the procession of children, some of the plastic surgery.

But then there was the question of his changing skin color. Long before his death, this was a matter of much speculation and controversy, with Jackson's many fans insisting that it was due to a case of vitiligo, but his plastic surgeries and his choice of straight-hair wigs in his later years Europeanized his appearance as well. Many of his fans saw this as an expression of Jackson's desire to transcend racial distinctions, while others thought he was trying to become white. Whatever his motivations were in the end, the controversies surrounding Jackson's physical changes demonstrate that while attitudes toward racial identification are changing, race is still a particularly powerful category of American identity.

The representation of race in American entertainment is a striking case in point. African Americans, Asians Americans, Native Americans, and Latin Americans — as well as such non-Anglo-Saxon Europeans as Italians and Eastern Europeans — have endured long histories of stereotyping in American popular culture, and the problem has by no means disappeared in more modern times. Complaints about the character Jar Jar Binks in the *Star Wars* saga, for example, were based upon a perception of stereotyping, and even *Avatar*, with its sympathetic depiction of a nonwhite society under siege by white invaders, has been compared to *Dances with Wolves* as yet another example of a stereotypical story in which a group of nonwhites need to turn to a white

---

Discussing the Signs of Race

Demographers predict that, by the middle of the twenty-first century, America will no longer have any racial or ethnic majority population. In class, discuss what effects this may have on Americans' sense of this country's history, culture, and identity.

---

hero to lead them. (In the same vein, complaints were made about the movie *The Last Airbender* for changing the originally Asian savior figure to a European, and about the casting of a white actor as *Prince of Persia*.) At the same time, the diversity, or lack thereof, of racial representation in prime-time TV continues to be a matter of controversy and complaint.

But while the representation of race in popular culture is still a politically sensitive topic, certain changes in racial identity itself are altering the landscape. With increasing numbers of Americans identifying themselves as being of mixed race (indeed, while President Barack Obama chose to identify himself as "Black, African Am or Negro" on his 2010 census form, he could have chosen mixed race as well), the traditional racial categories are in a certain state of flux today. Constructing himself as a liminal figure on the boundary between blackness and whiteness, the late Michael Jackson could serve as a dramatic signifier of what lies ahead.

Gender Codes

Like race, your gender, too, is a category of identification, but there is a difference between your biological identity as a male or female and the **gender codes** that determine just how men and women are supposed to behave. A culturally constructed system that defines and dictates the appropriate roles and behaviors for men and women in society, a gender code tells you how to conduct yourself as a man or woman. *Boys don't cry, girls do; girls wear makeup, boys don't; boys are aggressive, girls are passive; boys play sports, girls are cheerleaders.* The list is long, and until recently, you ignored it at the risk of social ridicule or ostracization.

Consider the advertising campaign for Axe grooming products. In essence, Axe is a perfume, but the traditional gender codes specify that perfume is for women, so it has a name associated with such masculine-coded traits as violence and aggression (Axe, BRUT) in order to make the product appear manly. Ads for Axe accordingly have featured a swarm of passionate women running frantically toward a beach where a single man stands dousing himself in Axe fragrance, reinforcing the gender-coded belief that an unmarried man should "score" as often as possible (a woman who behaves in the same way can be called all kinds of unpleasant names).

But a decades-long challenge to traditional gender codes, led particularly by the women's movement, has destabilized the ground upon which gender codes stand, arguing that the codes are not the result of some sort of natural or biological destiny but are instead politically motivated cultural constructions. One of the results of this challenge has been a widespread deconstruction of the traditional gender codes, with individuals picking and choosing for themselves what gender means to them. Products aimed at metrosexuals, for example, eschew the sorts of codes that guide the Axe campaigns, depicting men choosing fragrances and other body-related products without all the frantic attempts to associate the product with hypermasculine images and symbols. The well-known Dove Campaign for Real Beauty, for its part, has attempted to modify the demands on beauty that traditionally are placed upon women, but while the campaign does feature more ordinary looking models than do other beauty products ads, it does not abandon the focus on beauty that the traditional code assigns to women — and, it might also be pointed out, the same company that constructed the Dove campaign is also behind the Axe line of products.

Which suggests that maybe things haven't changed so much after all.

Postfeminist or Third Wave?

For its part, the tendency of American popular culture today to tell American girls and women that their primary identities lie in their ability to be sexually attractive to men through endless images of eroticized female bodies presents a particular challenge to cultural theory. For, given the attempts of the feminist movement to challenge and counteract such messages, which are part of what journalist Ariel Levy has called "raunch culture," the current era might seem to be more postfeminist than feminist when it comes to female identity in America. That is, we may have left the goals of feminism behind and reverted to the most conservative of gender-coded prescriptions.

But it may not be that simple, because it is also the case that traditional gender codes insist that female sexuality must be tightly controlled by male masters, whereas for many women who embrace what is often called third wave feminism, the confident display of their sexuality is actually empowering rather than degrading, a taking charge rather than a knuckling under — an attitude that was behind the immense popularity, among women, of the TV hit *Sex and the City*. Thus, third wave feminists regard themselves as representing an evolution within the feminist movement itself, not a movement away from it, arguing that being proud of her body and using it to get what she wants is part of a woman's empowerment and a valid identity choice. More traditional second wave feminists are not persuaded by this argument and may point out that, by focusing their attention on their bodies rather than their minds, women are in some danger of subjecting themselves to the tyranny of a youth-worshipping culture that will reject them once they are past the peak of their sexually appealing years. It is no accident that the vast majority of the images of women we see in popular culture are of very young women. There are a lot more Betty Boops than Betty Whites.

Be Whatever You Want to Be, or Not Be

In the game *World of Warcraft* you can choose from among the following player identities: Dwarves, Gnomes, Humans, Night Elves, Draenei, Orcs, Tauren, Trolls, Undead and Blood Elves (http://www.worldofwarcraft.com/info/ races/). And every year, the comic book convention Comic-Con International grows larger and larger, packed with fans dressed up in their favorite fantasy superhero or extraterrestrial attire. This ability to pretend to be someone, or something, else is an especial attraction of the Internet, which, due to the peculiar circumstances of its technology, enables people to socialize with others in elaborate identity-shifting disguises. Like an ongoing costume party or carnival, the Internet offers a profound intervention in the history of human interaction, allowing its users to put on and remove identities like the clothing they choose to wear every morning.

Of course, not everyone chooses to play act. On Facebook, people generally play themselves, although they may well exaggerate (or create) some attractive features and ignore less attractive ones. But as the Super Bowl ad for Coca-Cola referred to earlier in this introduction demonstrates, a great many people assume many different kinds of online avatars, online identities that they may occupy for considerable portions of their waking lives.

The cultural effects of the carnival-like spaces of the Internet are still too new to be clear. But some patterns are evident. First, while the Internet most certainly creates communities, its offer of disguise and/or anonymity to its users also unleashes some of our most antisocial tendencies. Just read the comments that follow YouTube videos, or Yahoo! news stories, or really just about anything on the Net. You will find the same aggression, vile language,

Reading Identity on the Net

Many Internet sites are devoted to the culture of a particular ethnicity, gender, or cultural subgroup. Visit several such sites and survey the breadth of information available within them. Is there any information that you wish would appear on the Net but could not find? Do you find any material problematic?

Science fiction fans wear elaborate costumes at the annual Comic-Con convention.

flame wars, hate, and hostility, no matter what the topic being commented upon happens to be. This "keyboard courage" is made possible by the anonymity that the Internet confers upon its users, who feel emboldened to say things that they would not say face-to-face because nonvirtual society has ways of policing itself that the Internet does not (for example, a lot of rude comments on the Internet would get their posters punched out if said in person; others would get them fired).

Paradoxically, then, the Internet offers to its users a kind of *non-identity* in its offer of anonymity. And since identification is also a form of social control (think of your driver's license: It is your ID, and without it you cannot drive your car or board a commercial airplane), the outbursts that fill the Net are signifiers not only of all the conflict that there is in this world but also of a resentment of the restrictions that come with social identity. Such a resentment bears a close relation to that fundamental American **mythology** of individualism that can be found at work so often in American culture, for it is our individualism that guides our cherishing of our freedom. The possibility of escaping identity, of having a non-identity, offers an immense freedom — even if that freedom is only expressed as a license to rant in public.

The Supermarket of IDs

But let's look again at your ability to choose from a host of identities in *World of Warcraft*. Significantly, they aren't free: You have to pay to play, and you have to pay extra if you want to change sides from, say, the Alliance to the

Horde. And nothing on the Internet is really free, either. The price you pay for a Facebook account, for example, lies in the site's usage of your personal information. The price you pay on YouTube or Yahoo! (or whatever) lies in the advertising that appears when you access the site, which it is hoped you will pay attention to (just as with commercial television).

And then, whether you actually purchase your identity, as on *World of Warcraft*, or merely treat it as something that can be put on and taken off at will, identity itself is becoming a commodity in America. This can be very disturbing to members of a society in which individualism is so highly valued, but one of the profoundest effects of our consumer culture is the way in which it shapes our sense of self, of who we are. Although an appeal to individualism is commonly employed to stimulate mass consumption ("Reeboks Let U Be U"), the fact is that in our consumer society identity, too, is for sale.

Which means that as individualistic as we think our identities to be, there is another social **mythology** at work as well in the shaping of who we are: the ideology of consumer capitalism. From the cradle, you have been shaped as a consumer by a nonstop barrage of advertising, and often when you think you are expressing your most idiosyncratic individuality you may find that you are doing so through the purchase of something. The advantage to the state here is profound: With over two-thirds of the American economy dependent upon consumption, America needs consumers, and so it constructs its citizens accordingly.

And so we come full circle to what it really means to live in a consumer society and why the study and understanding of popular culture, so much of which is involved with consumption, is so important. Though one American tradition, a **mythology** that goes back to the roots of this nation, clings desperately to a sense of individualism within a mass society, another more recent development — the advent of consumerism — is taking that all away, telling us that we are what we buy. And if that worries you, just look online: Plenty of vendors are out there ready to sell you a tee shirt that reads "I'm Not a Number." The shirt refers to a popular television program.

The Prisoner.

The Readings

This chapter looks at the construction of identity in America, beginning with Michael Omi's survey of how race works as an identifier in popular American culture. Stuart Buck follows with an analysis of the controversial issue of "acting white," arguing that it does exist and tracing its social effects. The excerpt that follows is from Angeline F. Price's Web site, which she devotes to describing the stereotyped images of "white trash" that are disseminated through the American popular media. Next, Jack Lopez offers a personal memoir of what it is like to be a wannabe surfer in the Mexican American community of East Los Angeles, while Jim Whitmer and Nell Bernstein photographically and journalistically report on the phenomenon of "claiming" — white teens choosing to identify themselves with nonwhite ethnic groups. Melissa Algranati offers a college student's perspective on what it's like to be a Puerto Rican–Egyptian–American Jew in a country that demands clear ethnic identifications. In a paired set of readings, Aaron Devor analyzes gender roles and the ways in which men and women manipulate the signs by which we traditionally communicate our gender identity, while Deborah Blum suggests that biology *does* play a role in gender identity and that we can best understand the gender gap by looking at both the cultural and the physiological determinants of human behavior. Kevin Jennings is next with a personal memoir that chronicles his struggles with growing up gay in conflict with the traditional construction of male heterosexual identity, and Andrew Sullivan concludes the chapter with an essay on how American attitudes are evolving from a tendency to identify homosexuality as an "activity" to a legal redefinition by which homosexuals are seen as individuals within a minority group identifiable "along the lines of gender or race."

MICHAEL OMI

In Living Color: Race and American Culture

Though many like to think that racism in America is a thing of the past, Michael Omi argues that racism is a pervasive feature in our lives, one that is both overt and inferential. Using race as a sign by which we judge a person's character, inferential racism invokes deep-rooted stereotypes, and as Omi shows in his survey of American film, television, and music, our popular culture is hardly immune from such stereotyping. Indeed, when ostensibly "progressive" programs like *Saturday Night Live* can win the National Ethnic Coalition of Organizations' "Platinum Pit Award" for racist stereotyping in television, and shock jocks such as Howard Stern command big audiences and salaries, one can see popular culture has a way to go before it becomes colorblind. The author of *Racial Formation in the United States: From the 1960s to the 1980s* (with Howard Winant, 1986, 1994), Omi is a professor of comparative ethnic studies at the University of California, Berkeley. His most recent project is a survey of antiracist organizations and initiatives.

In February 1987, Assistant Attorney General William Bradford Reynolds, the nation's chief civil rights enforcer, declared that the recent death of a black man in Howard Beach, New York, and the Ku Klux Klan attack on civil rights marchers in Forsyth County, Georgia, were "isolated" racial incidences. He emphasized that the places where racial conflict could potentially flare up were "far fewer now than ever before in our history," and concluded that such a diminishment of racism stood as "a powerful testament to how far we have come in the civil rights struggle."[1]

Events in the months following his remarks raise the question as to whether we have come quite so far. They suggest that dramatic instances of racial tension and violence merely constitute the surface manifestations of a deeper racial organization of American society—a system of inequality which has shaped, and in turn been shaped by, our popular culture.

In March, the NAACP released a report on blacks in the record industry entitled "The Discordant Sound of Music." It found that despite the revenues generated by black performers, blacks remain "grossly underrepresented" in the business, marketing, and A&R (Artists and Repertoire) departments of major record labels. In addition, few blacks are employed as managers, agents, concert promoters, distributors, and retailers. The report concluded that:

[1] Reynolds's remarks were made at a conference on equal opportunity held by the bar association in Orlando, Florida. *The San Francisco Chronicle* (7 February 1987). Print.

The record industry is overwhelmingly segregated and discrimination is rampant. No other industry in America so openly classifies its operations on a racial basis. At every level of the industry, beginning with the separation of black artists into a special category, barriers exist that severely limit opportunities for blacks.[2]

racism still here

Decades after the passage of civil rights legislation and the affirmation of the principle of "equal opportunity," patterns of racial segregation and exclusion, it seems, continue to characterize the production of popular music.

The enduring logic of Jim Crow is also present in professional sports. In April, Al Campanis, vice president of player personnel for the Los Angeles Dodgers, explained to Ted Koppel on ABC's *Nightline* about the paucity of blacks in baseball front offices and as managers. "I truly believe," Campanis said, "that [blacks] may not have some of the necessities to be, let's say, a field manager or perhaps a general manager." When pressed for a reason, Campanis offered an explanation which had little to do with the structure of opportunity or institutional discrimination within professional sports:

> [W]hy are black men or black people not good swimmers? Because they don't have the buoyancy. . . . They are gifted with great musculature and various other things. They're fleet of foot. And this is why there are a lot of black major league ballplayers. Now as far as having the background to become club presidents, or presidents of a bank, I don't know.[3]

Black exclusion from the front office, therefore, was justified on the basis of biological "difference."

The issue of race, of course, is not confined to the institutional arrangements   5 of popular culture production. Since popular culture deals with the symbolic realm of social life, the images which it creates, represents, and disseminates contribute to the overall racial climate. They become the subject of analysis and political scrutiny. In August, the National Ethnic Coalition of Organizations bestowed the "Golden Pit Awards" on television programs, commercials, and movies that were deemed offensive to racial and ethnic groups. *Saturday Night Live*, regarded by many media critics as a politically "progressive" show, was singled out for the "Platinum Pit Award" for its comedy skit "Ching Chang" which depicted a Chinese storeowner and his family in a derogatory manner.[4]

These examples highlight the *overt* manifestations of racism in popular culture — institutional forms of discrimination which keep racial minorities out of the production and organization of popular culture, and the crude racial

---

[2]Economic Development Department of the NAACP, "The Discordant Sound of Music (A Report on the Record Industry)," (Baltimore, Maryland: The NAACP, 1987), pp. 16–17. Print.

[3]Campanis's remarks on *Nightline* were reprinted in *The San Francisco Chronicle* (April 9, 1987). Print.

[4]Ellen Wulfhorst, "TV Stereotyping: It's the 'Pits,'" *The San Francisco Chronicle* (August 24, 1987). Print.

caricatures by which these groups are portrayed. Yet racism in popular culture is often conveyed in a variety of implicit, and at times invisible, ways. Political theorist Stuart Hall makes an important distinction between overt racism, the elaboration of an explicitly racist argument, policy, or view, and *inferential* racism which refers to "those apparently naturalized representations of events and situations relating to race, whether 'factual' or 'fictional,' which have racist premises and propositions inscribed in them as a set of *unquestioned assumptions.*" He argues that inferential racism is more widespread, common, and indeed insidious since "it is largely *invisible* even to those who formulate the world in its terms."[5]

Race itself is a slippery social concept which is paradoxically both "obvious" and "invisible." In our society, one of the first things we notice about people when we encounter them (along with their sex/gender) is their *race.* We utilize race to provide clues about *who* a person is and *how* we should relate to her/him. Our perception of race determines our "presentation of *self,*" distinctions in status, and appropriate modes of conduct in daily and institutional life. This process is often unconscious; we tend to operate off of an unexamined set of *racial beliefs.*

Racial beliefs account for and explain variations in "human nature." Differences in skin color and other obvious physical characteristics supposedly provide visible clues to more substantive differences lurking underneath. Among other qualities, temperament, sexuality, intelligence, and artistic and athletic ability are presumed to be fixed and discernible from the palpable mark of race. Such diverse questions as our confidence and trust in others (as salespeople, neighbors, media figures); our sexual preferences and romantic images; our tastes in music, film, dance, or sports; indeed our very ways of walking and talking are ineluctably shaped by notions of race.

Ideas about race, therefore, have become "common sense"—a way of comprehending, explaining, and acting in the world. This is made painfully obvious when someone disrupts our common sense understandings. An encounter with someone who is, for example, racially "mixed" or of a racial/ethnic group we are unfamiliar with becomes a source of discomfort for us, and momentarily creates a crisis of racial meaning. We also become disoriented when people do not act "black," "Latino," or indeed "white." The content of such stereotypes reveals a series of unsubstantiated beliefs about who these groups are, what they are like, and how they behave.

The existence of such racial consciousness should hardly be surprising.   10 Even prior to the inception of the republic, the United States was a society shaped by racial conflict. The establishment of the Southern plantation economy, Western expansion, and the emergence of the labor movement, among other significant historical developments, have all involved conflicts over

[5]Stuart Hall, "The Whites of Their Eyes: Racist Ideologies and the Media," in George Bridges and Rosalind Brunt, eds., *Silver Linings* (London: Lawrence and Wishart, 1981), pp. 36–37. Print.

the definition and nature of the *color line*. The historical results have been distinct and different groups have encountered unique forms of racial oppression — Native Americans faced genocide, blacks were subjected to slavery, Mexicans were invaded and colonized, and Asians faced exclusion. What is common to the experiences of these groups is that their particular "fate" was linked to historically specific ideas about the significance and meaning of race.[6] Whites defined them as separate "species," ones inferior to Northern European cultural stocks, and thereby rationalized the conditions of their subordination in the economy, in political life, and in the realm of culture.

A crucial dimension of racial oppression in the United States is the elaboration of an ideology of difference or "otherness." This involves defining "us" (i.e., white Americans) in opposition to "them," an important task when distinct racial groups are first encountered, or in historically specific periods where preexisting racial boundaries are threatened or crumbling.

Political struggles over the very definition of who an "American" is illustrate this process. The Naturalization Law of 1790 declared that only free *white* immigrants could qualify, reflecting the initial desire among Congress to create and maintain a racially homogeneous society. The extension of eligibility to all racial groups has been a long and protracted process. Japanese, for example, were finally eligible to become naturalized citizens after the passage of the Walter-McCarran Act of 1952. The ideological residue of these restrictions in naturalization and citizenship laws is the equation within popular parlance of the term "American" with "white," while other "Americans" are described as black, Mexican, "Oriental," etc.

Popular culture has been an important realm within which racial ideologies have been created, reproduced, and sustained. Such ideologies provide a framework of symbols, concepts, and images through which we understand, interpret, and represent aspects of our "racial" existence.

Race has often formed the central themes of American popular culture. Historian W. L. Rose notes that it is a "curious coincidence" that four of the "most popular reading-viewing events in all American history" have in some manner dealt with race, specifically black/white relations in the south.[7] Harriet Beecher Stowe's *Uncle Tom's Cabin*, Thomas Ryan Dixon's *The Clansman* (the inspiration for D. W. Griffith's *The Birth of a Nation*), Margaret Mitchell's *Gone with the Wind* (as a book and film), and Alex Haley's *Roots* (as a book and television miniseries) each appeared at a critical juncture in American race relations and helped to shape new understandings of race.

Emerging social definitions of race and the "real American" were reflected in American popular culture of the nineteenth century. Racial and ethnic stereotypes were shaped and reinforced in the newspapers, magazines, and

[6]For an excellent survey of racial beliefs see Thomas F. Gossett, *Race: The History of an Idea in America* (New York: Shocken, 1965). Print.

[7]W. L. Rose, *Race and Religion in American Historical Fiction: Four Episodes in Popular Culture* (Oxford: Clarendon, 1979). Print.

pulp fiction of the period. But the evolution and ever-increasing sophistication of visual mass communications throughout the twentieth century provided, and continue to provide, the most dramatic means by which racial images are generated and reproduced.

Film and television have been notorious in disseminating images of racial minorities which establish for audiences what these groups look like, how they behave, and, in essence, "who they are." The power of the media lies not only in their ability to reflect the dominant racial ideology, but in their capacity to shape that ideology in the first place. D. W. Griffith's aforementioned epic *Birth of a Nation*, a sympathetic treatment of the rise of the Ku Klux Klan during Reconstruction, helped to generate, consolidate, and "nationalize" images of blacks which had been more disparate (more regionally specific, for example) prior to the film's appearance.[8]

In television and film, the necessity to define characters in the briefest and most condensed manner has led to the perpetuation of racial caricatures, as racial stereotypes serve as shorthand for scriptwriters, directors, and actors. Television's tendency to address the "lowest common denominator" in order to render programs "familiar" to an enormous and diverse audience leads it regularly to assign and reassign racial characteristics to particular groups, both minority and majority.

Many of the earliest American films deal with racial and ethnic "difference." The large influx of "new immigrants" at the turn of the century led to a proliferation of negative images of Jews, Italians, and Irish which were assimilated and adapted by such films as Thomas Edison's *Cohen's Advertising Scheme* (1904). Based on an old vaudeville routine, the film featured a scheming Jewish merchant, aggressively hawking his wares. Though stereotypes of these groups persist to this day,[9] by the 1940s many of the earlier ethnic stereotypes had disappeared from Hollywood. But, as historian Michael Winston observes, the "outsiders" of the 1890s remained: "the ever-popular Indian of the Westerns; the inscrutable or sinister Oriental; the sly, but colorful Mexican; and the clowning or submissive Negro."[10]

In many respects the "Western" as a genre has been paradigmatic in establishing images of racial minorities in film and television. The classic scenario involves the encircled wagon train or surrounded fort from which whites bravely fight off fierce bands of Native American Indians. The point of reference and viewer identification lies with those huddled within the

[8]Melanie Martindale-Sikes, "Nationalizing 'Nigger' Imagery through *Birth of a Nation*," paper prepared for the 73rd Annual Meeting of the American Sociological Association (September 4–8, 1978) in San Francisco.

[9]For a discussion of Italian, Irish, Jewish, Slavic, and German stereotypes in film, see Randall M. Miller, ed., *The Kaleidoscopic Lens: How Hollywood Views Ethnic Groups* (Englewood, N.J.: Jerome S. Ozer, 1980). Print.

[10]Michael R. Winston, "Racial Consciousness and the Evolution of Mass Communications in the United States," *Daedalus*, vol. III, No. 4 (Fall 1982). Print.

circle—the representatives of "civilization" who valiantly attempt to ward off the forces of barbarism. In the classic Western, as writer Tom Engelhardt observes, "the viewer is forced behind the barrel of a repeating rifle and it is from that position, through its gun sights, that he receives a picture history of Western colonialism and imperialism."[11]

Westerns have indeed become the prototype for European and American 20 excursions throughout the Third World. The cast of characters may change, but the story remains the same. The "humanity" of whites is contrasted with the brutality and treachery of nonwhites; brave (i.e., white) souls are pitted against the merciless hordes in conflicts ranging from Indians against the British Lancers to Zulus against the Boers. What Stuart Hall refers to as the imperializing "white eye" provides the framework for these films, lurking outside the frame and yet seeing and positioning everything within; it is "the unmarked position from which . . . 'observations' are made and from which, alone, they make sense."[12]

Our "common sense" assumptions about race and racial minorities in the United States are both generated and reflected in the stereotypes presented by the visual media. In the crudest sense, it could be said that such stereotypes underscore white "superiority" by reinforcing the traits, habits, and predispositions of nonwhites which demonstrate their "inferiority." Yet a more careful assessment of racial stereotypes reveals intriguing trends and seemingly contradictory themes.

While all racial minorities have been portrayed as "less than human," there are significant differences in the images of different groups. Specific racial minority groups, in spite of their often interchangeable presence in films steeped in the "Western" paradigm, have distinct and often unique qualities assigned to them. Latinos are portrayed as being prone toward violent outbursts of anger; blacks as physically strong, but dim-witted; while Asians are seen as sneaky and cunningly evil. Such differences are crucial to observe and analyze. Race in the United States is not reducible to black/white relations. These differences are significant for a broader understanding of the patterns of race in America, and the unique experience of specific racial minority groups.

It is somewhat ironic that *real* differences which exist within a racially defined minority group are minimized, distorted, or obliterated by the media. "All Asians look alike," the saying goes, and indeed there has been little or no attention given to the vast differences which exist between, say, the Chinese and Japanese with respect to food, dress, language, and culture. This blurring within popular culture has given us supposedly Chinese characters who wear kimonos; it is also the reason why the fast-food restaurant McDonald's can offer "Shanghai McNuggets" with teriyaki sauce. Other groups suffer a similar

---

[11]Tom Engelhardt, "Ambush at Kamikaze Pass," in Emma Gee, ed., *Counterpoint: Perspectives on Asian America* (Los Angeles: Asian American Studies Center, UCLA, 1976), p. 270. Print.

[12]Hall, "Whites of Their Eyes," p. 38. Print.

fate. Professor Gretchen Bataille and Charles Silet find the cinematic Native American of the Northeast wearing the clothing of the Plains Indians, while living in the dwellings of Southwestern tribes:

> The movie men did what thousands of years of social evolution could not do, even what the threat of the encroaching white man could not do; Hollywood produced the homogenized Native American, devoid of tribal characteristics or regional differences.[13]

The need to paint in broad racial strokes has thus rendered "internal" differences invisible. This has been exacerbated by the tendency for screenwriters to "invent" mythical Asian, Latin American, and African countries. Ostensibly done to avoid offending particular nations and peoples, such a subterfuge reinforces the notion that all the countries and cultures of a specific region are the same. European countries retain their distinctiveness, while the Third World is presented as one homogeneous mass riddled with poverty and governed by ruthless and corrupt regimes.

While rendering specific groups in a monolithic fashion, the popular cultural imagination simultaneously reveals a compelling need to distinguish and articulate "bad" and "good" variants of particular racial groups and individuals. Thus each stereotypic image is filled with contradictions: The bloodthirsty Indian is tempered with the image of the noble savage; the *bandido* exists along with the loyal sidekick; and Fu Manchu is offset by Charlie Chan. The existence of such contradictions, however, does not negate the one-dimensionality of these images, nor does it challenge the explicit subservient role of racial minorities. Even the "good" person of color usually exists as a foil in novels and films to underscore the intelligence, courage, and virility of the white male hero.

Another important, perhaps central, dimension of racial minority stereo- 25 types is sex/gender differentiation. The connection between race and sex has traditionally been an explosive and controversial one. For most of American history, sexual and marital relations between whites and nonwhites were forbidden by social custom and by legal restrictions. It was not until 1967, for example, that the U.S. Supreme Court ruled that antimiscegenation laws were unconstitutional. Beginning in the 1920s, the notorious Hays Office, Hollywood's attempt at self-censorship, prohibited scenes and subjects which dealt with miscegenation. The prohibition, however, was not evenly applied in practice. White men could seduce racial minority women, but white women were not to be romantically or sexually linked to racial minority men.

Women of color were sometimes treated as exotic sex objects. The sultry Latin temptress — such as Dolores Del Rio and Lupe Velez — invariably had boyfriends who were white North Americans; their Latino suitors were portrayed as being unable to keep up with the Anglo-American competition. From Mary Pickford as Cho-Cho San in *Madame Butterfly* (1915) to Nancy

[13]Gretchen Bataille and Charles Silet, "The Entertaining Anachronism: Indians in American Film," in Randall M. Miller, ed., *Kaleidoscopic Lens*, p. 40. Print.

Kwan in *The World of Suzie Wong* (1961), Asian women have often been seen as the gracious "geisha girl" or the prostitute with a "heart of gold," willing to do anything to please her man.

By contrast, Asian men, whether cast in the role of villain, servant, sidekick, or kung fu master, are seen as asexual or, at least, romantically undesirable. As Asian American studies professor Elaine Kim notes, even a hero such as Bruce Lee played characters whose "single-minded focus on perfecting his fighting skills precludes all other interests, including an interest in women, friendship, or a social life."[14]

The shifting trajectory of black images over time reveals an interesting dynamic with respect to sex and gender. The black male characters in *The Birth of a Nation* were clearly presented as sexual threats to "white womanhood." For decades afterward, however, Hollywood consciously avoided portraying black men as assertive or sexually aggressive in order to minimize controversy. Black men were instead cast as comic, harmless, and nonthreatening figures exemplified by such stars as Bill "Bojangles" Robinson, Stepin Fetchit, and Eddie "Rochester" Anderson. Black women, by contrast, were divided into two broad character types based on color categories. Dark black women such as Hattie McDaniel and Louise Beavers were cast as "dowdy, frumpy, dumpy, overweight mammy figures"; while those "close to the white ideal," such as Lena Horne and Dorothy Dandridge, became "Hollywood's treasured mulattoes" in roles emphasizing the tragedy of being of mixed blood.[15]

It was not until the early 1970s that tough, aggressive, sexually assertive black characters, both male and female, appeared. The "blaxploitation" films of the period provided new heroes (e.g., *Shaft*, *Superfly*, *Coffy*, and *Cleopatra Jones*) in sharp contrast to the submissive and subservient images of the past. Unfortunately, most of these films were shoddy productions which did little to create more enduring "positive" images of blacks, either male or female.

In contemporary television and film, there is a tendency to present and 30 equate racial minority groups and individuals with specific social problems. Blacks are associated with drugs and urban crime, Latinos with "illegal" immigration, while Native Americans cope with alcoholism and tribal conflicts. Rarely do we see racial minorities "out of character," in situations removed from the stereotypic arenas in which scriptwriters have traditionally embedded them. Nearly the only time we see young Asians and Latinos of either sex, for example, is when they are members of youth gangs, as *Boulevard Nights* (1979), *Year of the Dragon* (1985), and countless TV cop shows can attest to.

Racial minority actors have continually bemoaned the fact that the roles assigned them on stage and screen are often one-dimensional and imbued with stereotypic assumptions. In theater, the movement toward "blind casting"

[14]Elaine Kim, "Asian Americans and American Popular Culture," in Hyung-Chan Kim, ed., *Dictionary of Asian American History* (New York: Greenwood, 1986), p. 107. Print.
[15]Donald Bogle, "A Familiar Plot (A Look at the History of Blacks in American Movies)," *The Crisis*, Vol. 90, No. 1 (January 1983), p. 15. Print.

(i.e., casting actors for roles without regard to race) is a progressive step, but it remains to be seen whether large numbers of audiences can suspend their "beliefs" and deal with a Latino King Lear or an Asian Stanley Kowalski. By contrast, white actors are allowed to play anybody. Though the use of white actors to play blacks in "black face" is clearly unacceptable in the contemporary period, white actors continue to portray Asian, Latino, and Native American characters on stage and screen.

Scores of Charlie Chan films, for example, have been made with white leads (the last one was the 1981 *Charlie Chan and the Curse of the Dragon Queen*). Roland Winters, who played Chan in six features, was once asked to explain the logic of casting a white man in the role of Charlie Chan: "The only thing I can think of is, if you want to cast a homosexual in a show, and you get a homosexual, it'll be awful. It won't be funny . . . and maybe there's something there."[16]

Such a comment reveals an interesting aspect about myth and reality in popular culture. Michael Winston argues that stereotypic images in the visual media were not originally conceived as representations of reality, nor were they initially understood to be "real" by audiences. They were, he suggests, ways of "coding and rationalizing" the racial hierarchy and interracial behavior. Over time, however, "a complex interactive relationship between myth and reality developed, so that images originally understood to be unreal, through constant repetition began to *seem* real."[17]

Such a process consolidated, among other things, our "common sense" understandings of what we think various groups should look like. Such presumptions have led to tragicomical results. Latinos auditioning for a role in a television soap opera, for example, did not fit the Hollywood image of "real Mexicans" and had their faces bronzed with powder before filming because they looked too white. Model Aurora Garza said, "I'm a real Mexican and very dark anyway. I'm even darker right now because I have a tan. But they kept wanting to make my face darker and darker."[18]

Historically in Hollywood, the fact of having "dark skin" made an actor or 35 actress potentially adaptable for numerous "racial" roles. Actress Lupe Velez once commented that she had portrayed "Chinese, Eskimos, Japs, squaws, Hindus, Swedes, Malays, and Japanese."[19] Dorothy Dandridge, who was the first black woman teamed romantically with white actors, presented a quandary for studio executives who weren't sure what race and nationality to make her. They debated whether she should be a "foreigner," an island girl, or a West Indian.[20] Ironically, what they refused to entertain as a possibility was to present her as what she really was, a black American woman.

---

[16]Frank Chin, "Confessions of the Chinatown Cowboy," *Bulletin of Concerned Asian Scholars*, Vol. 4, No. 3 (Fall 1972). Print.

[17]Winston, "Racial Consciousness," p. 176. Print.

[18]*The San Francisco Chronicle* (September 21, 1984). Print.

[19]Quoted in Allen L. Woll, "Bandits and Lovers: Hispanic Images in American Film," in Miller, ed., *Kaleidoscopic Lens*, p. 60. Print.

[20]Bogle, "Familiar Plot," p. 17.

The importance of race in popular culture is not restricted to the visual media. In popular music, race and race consciousness have defined, and continue to define, formats, musical communities, and tastes. In the mid-1950s, the secretary of the North Alabama White Citizens Council declared that "Rock and roll is a means of pulling the white man down to the level of the Negro."[21] While rock may no longer be popularly regarded as a racially subversive musical form, the very genres of contemporary popular music remain, in essence, thinly veiled racial categories. "R & B" (Rhythm and Blues) and "soul" music are clearly references to *black* music, while Country & Western or heavy metal music are viewed, in the popular imagination, as *white* music. Black performers who want to break out of this artistic ghettoization must "cross over," a contemporary form of "passing" in which their music is seen as acceptable to white audiences.

The airwaves themselves are segregated. The designation "urban contemporary" is merely radio lingo for a "black" musical format. Such categorization affects playlists, advertising accounts, and shares of the listening market. On cable television, black music videos rarely receive airplay on MTV, but are confined instead to the more marginal BET (Black Entertainment Television) network.

In spite of such segregation, many performing artists have been able to garner a racially diverse group of fans. And yet, racially integrated concert audiences are extremely rare. Curiously, this "perverse phenomenon" of racially homogeneous crowds takes place despite the color of the performer. Lionel Richie's concert audiences, for example, are virtually all-white, while Teena Marie's are all-black.[22]

Racial symbols and images are omnipresent in popular culture. Commonplace household objects such as cookie jars, salt and pepper shakers, and ashtrays have frequently been designed and fashioned in the form of racial caricatures. Sociologist Steve Dublin in an analysis of these objects found that former tasks of domestic service were symbolically transferred onto these commodities.[23] An Aunt Jemima–type character, for example, is used to hold a roll of paper towels, her outstretched hands supporting the item to be dispensed. "Sprinkle Plenty," a sprinkle bottle in the shape of an Asian man, was used to wet clothes in preparation for ironing. Simple commodities, the household implements which help us perform everyday tasks, may reveal, therefore, a deep structure of racial meaning.

A crucial dimension for discerning the meaning of particular stereotypes and images is the *situation context* for the creation and consumption of popular culture. For example, the setting in which "racist" jokes are told determines 40

[21]Dave Marsh and Kevin Stein, *The Book of Rock Lists* (New York: Dell, 1981), p. 8. Print.

[22]*Rock & Roll Confidential*, No. 44 (February 1987), p. 2. Print.

[23]Steven C. Dublin, "Symbolic Slavery: Black Representations in Popular Culture," *Social Problems*, Vol. 34, No. 2 (April 1987). Print.

the function of humor. Jokes about blacks where the teller and audience are black constitute a form of self-awareness; they allow blacks to cope and "take the edge off" of oppressive aspects of the social order which they commonly confront. The meaning of these same jokes, however, is dramatically transformed when told across the "color line." If a white, or even black, person tells these jokes to a white audience, it will, despite its "purely" humorous intent, serve to reinforce stereotypes and rationalize the existing relations of racial inequality.

Concepts of race and racial images are both overt and implicit within popular culture — the organization of cultural production, the products themselves, and the manner in which they are consumed are deeply structured by race. Particular racial meanings, stereotypes, and myths can change, but the presence of a *system* of racial meanings and stereotypes, of racial ideology, seems to be an enduring aspect of American popular culture.

The era of Reaganism and the overall rightward drift of American politics and culture has added a new twist to the question of racial images and meanings. Increasingly, the problem for racial minorities is not that of misportrayal, but of "invisibility." Instead of celebrating racial and cultural diversity, we are witnessing an attempt by the right to define, once again, who the "real" American is, and what "correct" American values, mores, and political beliefs are. In such a context, racial minorities are no longer the focus of sustained media attention; when they do appear, they are cast as colored versions of essentially "white" characters.

The possibilities for change — for transforming racial stereotypes and challenging institutional inequities — nonetheless exist. Historically, strategies have involved the mobilization of political pressure against an offending institution(s). In the late 1950s, for instance, "Nigger Hair" tobacco changed its name to "Bigger Hare" due to concerted NAACP pressure on the manufacturer. In the early 1970s, Asian American community groups successfully fought NBC's attempt to resurrect Charlie Chan as a television series with white actor Ross Martin. Amidst the furor generated by Al Campanis's remarks cited at the beginning of this essay, Jesse Jackson suggested that a boycott of major league games be initiated in order to push for a restructuring of hiring and promotion practices.

Partially in response to such action, Baseball Commissioner Peter Ueberroth announced plans in June 1987 to help put more racial minorities in management roles. "The challenge we have," Ueberroth said, "is to manage change without losing tradition."[24] The problem with respect to the issue of race and popular culture, however, is that the *tradition* itself may need to be thoroughly examined, its "common sense" assumptions unearthed and challenged, and its racial images contested and transformed.

[24]*The San Francisco Chronicle* (June 13, 1987). Print.

READING THE TEXT

1. Describe in your own words the difference between "overt racism" and "inferential racism" (para. 6).

2. Why, according to Omi, is popular culture so powerful in shaping America's attitudes toward race?

3. What relationship does Omi see between gender and racial stereotypes?

4. How did race relations change in America during the 1980s, in Omi's view?

READING THE SIGNS

1. In class, brainstorm stereotypes, both positive and negative, attributed to specific racial groups. Then discuss the possible sources of these stereotypes. In what ways have they been perpetuated in popular culture, including film, TV, advertising, music, and consumer products? What does your discussion reveal about popular culture's influence on our most basic ways of seeing the world?

2. Watch *Malcolm X* or another film that addresses race relations, such as *Mi Familia*. Using Omi's essay as your critical framework, write an essay in which you explore how this film may reflect or redefine American attitudes toward racial identity and race relations.

3. Study an issue of a magazine targeted to a specific ethnic readership, such as *Ebony* or *Hyphen*, analyzing both its articles and advertising. Then write an essay in which you explore the extent to which the magazine accurately reflects that ethnicity or, in Omi's words, appeals to readers as "colored versions of essentially 'white' characters" (para. 42).

4. **CONNECTING TEXTS** Omi claims that "In contemporary television and film, there is a tendency to present and equate racial minority groups and individuals with specific social problems" (para. 30). In class, brainstorm films and TV shows that have characters that are ethnic minorities; pick one example and watch it. Does Omi's claim apply to that example, or does it demonstrate different patterns of racial representation? To develop your ideas, you might consult Roland Laird's "*The Boondocks*: Carrying On the Tradition of Subversive Black Comedy" (p. 359).

5. **CONNECTING TEXTS** Read or reread Mitu Sengupta's "Race Relations Light Years from Earth" (p. 412). Using the categories of "overt" and "inferential" racism as Omi describes them, write your own analysis of the race relations in *Avatar*.

STUART BUCK

Acting White

At the 2004 Democratic Convention, then-Senator Barack Obama, while speaking on the need to improve inner-city education, remarked that "children can't achieve unless we raise their expectations and eradicate the slander that says that a black youth with a book is acting white." Whether such a slander really exists among African American students has been a matter of much debate and controversy, but Stuart Buck, in this excerpt from his book *Acting White: The Ironic Legacy of Desegregation* (2010), wants to go beyond the debate to analyze "*where* that criticism came from in the first place." His provocative thesis is that the "acting white" criticism is an ironic legacy of desegregation, which, he argues "was often implemented in a way that was devastating to black communities." Subjecting the "acting white" phenomenon to a historical and sociological analysis, Buck explains how the well-intentioned policies of desegregation eventually led to such a reversal of intention. A graduate of Harvard Law School, Stuart Buck is a research associate at the University of Arkansas department of education reform.

"Go into any inner-city neighborhood," Barack Obama said in his address to the Democratic National Convention in 2004, "and folks will tell you that government alone can't teach kids to learn. They know that parents have to parent, that children can't achieve unless we raise their expectations and eradicate the slander that says a black youth with a book is acting white." Michelle Obama, according to a May 2009 report in *Newsweek*, "described the ridicule she faced from neighborhood kids for 'acting white' when she got good grades" as a child.

The Obamas are far from alone in their observations. Many people in recent years — most famously, Bill Cosby — have pointed out that black children often seem to think of schoolwork as a "white" activity. Anecdotal evidence abounds in newspaper articles and on the Internet. One black valedictorian in Virginia, for example, told a newspaper that "as I've gone through my whole school career, people have called me white because I've made good grades and didn't conform to the stereotype."

Along with these reports in the popular press, scholars have had a contentious debate about "acting white" for some twenty years now. On one side, many academic studies have shown that some black children think of doing schoolwork as "acting white," and a study by Roland Fryer — a black Harvard economist — shows that black children nationwide become less popular if their grade-point average rises above 3.5.

On the other side, a few studies have purported to disprove "acting white." But these studies are flawed: they rely on limited anecdotal evidence or on black children's reports of their own popularity (which could be inflated by the perfectly natural desire to brag). Moreover, it is implausible that the "acting white" criticism would not affect children's ability to achieve at high levels in school. We are all less likely to throw ourselves wholeheartedly into anything that might bring the ridicule or even the slight disapproval of our peers. This is true of choosing an occupation or a university, a neighborhood to live in, what clothes to wear, whether or not to take up golf, or countless other examples. Black schoolchildren are surely not immune to such a universal human trait.

The "acting white" thesis is controversial, of course, because of the fear 5 that it lets the rest of us off the hook too easily — that suburban whites will, perhaps regretfully, write off the urban black population as uneducable. But people who are inclined to ignore the problems of poor blacks will always be able to come up with an excuse to do so, regardless of what the scholarly community says. Another perceived problem is that the "acting white" thesis seems to blame black children themselves for failing to achieve in school, rather than blaming only external factors such as poverty, racism, and inadequate schools. No one denies that these other factors have a strong effect on academic achievement, but poverty and inadequate schools cannot be the whole story. There is an achievement gap between black students and white students even in studies that compare children in the same schools, with the same household incomes and family backgrounds. *Something else* has to be a contributing factor as well, and an obvious candidate is the attitude that people have toward education.

So much for the current state of the "acting white" debate. . . . For all of the back and forth on "acting white," few scholars have stopped to consider *where* that criticism came from in the first place.

"Acting white" has been discussed so often in the popular press that it no longer comes as a surprise. *But it should.* If we look at the historical record, there is no evidence that black schoolchildren back in the days of slavery or Jim Crow accused a studious schoolmate of "acting white." To the contrary, *white* people occasionally accused educated blacks of trying to be white. As historian Leon Litwack points out, nineteenth-century whites sometimes "equated black success with 'uppityness,' 'impudence,' 'getting out of place,' and pretensions toward racial equality. 'He think he white' was the expression whites sometimes used to convey that suspicion, or 'He is too smart,' 'He wants to be white and act like white people,' and 'He think he somebody.' "[1] A Northerner who had moved to Georgia after the Civil War noted that "in the days of Slavery, the masters ridiculed the negroes' efforts to use good language, and become like the whites."[2] In the 1960s, a black plaintiff in a North Carolina desegregation case testified that she had received threatening telephone calls, many of which "asked me was I trying to get white."[3]

Yet today, the "acting white" criticism that was once occasionally used by racist whites has been adopted by some black schoolchildren. . . . What happened between the nineteenth century and today?

The answer, I believe, springs from the complex history of desegregation. Although desegregation arose from noble and necessary impulses, and although desegregation was to the overall benefit of the nation, it was often implemented in a way that was devastating to black communities. It destroyed black schools, reduced the numbers of black principals and teachers who could serve as role models, and brought many black schoolchildren into daily contact with whites who made school a strange and uncomfortable environment that was viewed as quintessentially "white."

Numerous scholars and commentators have observed that the "acting 10 white" criticism arose during the 1960s — precisely the time when desegregation actually happened. Indeed, many black people recall that they were first accused of "acting white" or "trying to be white" during the desegregation experience. For example, Bernice McNair Barnett, who teaches at the University of Illinois at Urbana-Champaign, recalls that she was "isolated and cut off from the world of my former Black peers (who saw my school desegregation choice as 'trying to be White') as well as my new White peers (who were both hate-filled bullies and otherwise good-hearted but silent bystanders)." As Beverly Daniel Tatum — the president of Spelman College — points out, "An oppositional identity that disdains academic achievement has not always been a characteristic of Black adolescent peer groups. It seems to be a post-desegregation phenomenon."[4]

All of this occurred in part because desegregation undermined one of the traditional centers of the black community: the school. In the segregated schools, black children had consistently seen other blacks succeeding in the academic world. The authority figures and role models — that is, the teachers and principals — were virtually always black. And the best students in black schools were black as well.

This ended with desegregation. Many black schools disappeared altogether: school boards all across the South closed or demolished black schools in pursuit of desegregation (or occasionally kept the school open while changing its name and status, so as to erase its historical connection to the black community). After desegregation, many black children were taught by white teachers who disliked them, did not care about their success, underestimated their capabilities, or — at the opposite extreme — coddled them out of guilt. Even when the white teachers did everything right, the black schoolchildren still, for the first time, faced the possibility of seeing "school" as a place where success equaled seeking the approval of whites.

Black schoolchildren, now dispersed into formerly all-white schools, suddenly had to deal with unfriendly classmates on a day-to-day basis. School was no longer a place where black children could avoid interacting with racist people. As John McWhorter points out, the "demise of segregation" helped "pave the way for the 'acting white' charge. With the closing of black schools after desegregation orders, black students began going to school with white ones in larger numbers than ever before, which meant that whites were available for black students to model themselves against."[5]

Many desegregated schools made greater use of academic "tracking," which kept most of the better-prepared white students in a separate class from the black students. This too reinforced the message that "academic achievement is the province of whites." By contrast, as Beverly Daniel Tatum explains, "in the context of a segregated school, it was a given that the high achieving students would all be Black. Academic achievement did not have to mean separation from one's Black peers."[6]

Thus, as Harvard economist Roland Fryer points out, one's attitude toward education can now function as a *racial signal*. A black student who is too eager in class may be seen as trying to curry favor with the mostly white teachers. And where the advanced classes or academic clubs are predominantly white, the black student who takes advanced classes or joins an academic club is seen as having preferred the company of whites over blacks. In other words, just by the fact that desegregation brought black and white students into contact with one another, it became possible for either blacks *or* whites to view the other race as outsiders in the school environment, and to start punishing children who spent too much time crossing the boundary lines between races.

There is nothing unusual in this: Humans are tribal creatures. It is a universal human trait for group members to expect loyalty to the group, whether the "group" involves employees of a particular corporation; Democrats or Republicans; literally thousands of religious sects and denominations; citizens of a particular country, state, or town; fans of the Yankees or any other sports team; or a nearly infinite range of groups based on all sorts of characteristics. It was an ironic byproduct of desegregation that this universal human expectation — "be loyal to our group, or else" — showed up in schools.

Some people might rationally wonder whether I oppose desegregation. Why else would I take the time to highlight problems with desegregation rather than focus on some other aspect of education?

I believe strongly in integration as a moral ideal. The message that I intend to convey is *not* that desegregation was a bad idea, *not* that the people who pursued desegregation were foolish or misguided, *not* that desegregation is something that we should consider reversing. Desegregation was unquestionably the right thing to do, and it benefited many black Americans by bringing them into the mainstream of American society.

At the same time, nothing in life is free. Anything that is valuable and worth achieving comes at a price. Intellectual honesty obligates us to weigh — and consider how to mitigate — the costs imposed by our preferred policies, rather than sweeping the problems under the rug. The costs of desegregation included the destruction of black institutions, the trauma experienced by some black children, and the overall effect on black attitudes toward education. While the benefits of desegregation outweigh the costs, this essay is not intended to focus on the benefits (which are amply discussed elsewhere). Rather, it is intended to consider how the costs arose and whether we might reduce or eliminate them.

My argument will be controversial in some circles, if only because I say [20] that "acting white" exists and should be taken seriously. To some people, it is borderline racist to suggest that any cultural factors might contribute to the fact that black students lag far behind white students. What's more, if you say that some black students think of studiousness as "acting white," it is as if you have accused black students of bizarre and nonsensical behavior. These critics appear to believe that "acting white" must be downplayed or denied at all costs, because if it did exist, it would be an inexcusable form of stupidity.

As it happens, I think that those critics are wrong all the way around. They are wrong in claiming that "acting white" is a myth. But they are also wrong assuming that "acting white" is nonsensical and inexcusable behavior. Indeed, I would *defend* the "acting white" criticism as entirely normal.

To be sure, *normal* does not mean *beneficial*. Rather, it is normal in the sense that eating too much sugar is normal — it is behavior that arises from deeply rooted and commonplace desires that made sense throughout our history, but that, unfortunately, can be destructive if given full rein today.

Thus, in order to have an idea how the "acting white" criticism might be reduced, we need to understand the powerful psychological forces that generate it in the first place.

Humans Are Tribal

What do I mean by saying that the "acting white" criticism is "normal"?

Human beings are usually tribal. We like to associate with people who are [25] similar to ourselves. As Gordon Allport says in his classic work *The Nature of Prejudice*, "Everywhere on earth we find a condition of separateness among groups."[7] Thus, we have the proverb, "Birds of a feather flock together." Sociologists call this tendency "homophily," from the Greek "homo" (or "same") and "phileo" (or "friendship"). Homophily is particularly strong in the area of race: Sociologists have found "strong homophily on race and ethnicity in a wide array of relationships, ranging from the most intimate bonds of marriage and confiding, to the more limited ties of schoolmate friendships and work relations, to the limited networks of discussion about a particular topic, to the mere fact of appearing in public together or 'knowing about' someone else."[8] Indeed, scientists are beginning to trace homophily to specific areas of the brain.[9]

Not only do we humans associate with others who are like ourselves; we also tend to pit our own group in competition against other groups. The entire history of the world shows that people of different races and nationalities are often hostile toward one another, even over cultural or ethnic differences that are completely imperceptible to outsiders.[10] This shows up at the earliest age: As Judith Rich Harris points out, "Babies around the world begin to show a wariness of strangers at around six months of age."[11]

Examples abound from every possible aspect of life. Fans of one sports team cordially (or not so cordially) despise the fans of the opposing team. Fans of alternative rock music roll their eyes at the thought that anyone still listens to Bon Jovi. Gourmet cooks and organic gardeners pity the rest of us for eating at McDonald's. Avant-garde artists sneer at Norman Rockwell paintings. American Baptists dislike the more fundamentalist Southern Baptists. Managers versus union workers; waiters versus diners; Southerners versus Yankees; people who shop at Nordstrom's versus people who shop at Gap versus people who get their clothes on sale at K-Mart; Hummer drivers versus Prius drivers; chess club members versus cheerleaders. We love to bask in the feeling that our own little coterie is different from everyone else.

In fact, the human drive to categorize is so strong that people will differentiate themselves from another group even based on very slight differences that have no rational basis at all. There is a large social psychology literature on this phenomenon, stretching back several decades.

In one experiment, for example, Henri Tajfel and two colleagues had ninety-six children rate their favorites from several pairs of pictures that were supposedly drawn by other children in one of two schools: the Red School and the Blue School. They then told the children that "we have found something quite amazing: about half of you preferred pictures from the Red School and about half preferred pictures from the Blue School." This wasn't actually true; it was just a way of getting the children to believe that they were part of a group that had chosen similar pictures.

The researchers then gave the children little cards with pairs of numbers, and had the children take turns assigning money to the "Blue" group and the "Red" group by choosing one of the options on the cards. For example, one of the cards had these three choices: three coins for your group and four for the other group; two coins for each group; or one coin for your group and zero coins for the other. Thus, the first option would lead to the maximum payoff for both groups, while the last option would allow your own group to have more money than the other group. The researchers discovered that the children showed a large preference for the latter result—giving your own group the advantage, even if it effectively cost money to do so. This showed the "ease" with which "discriminatory social acts" can be "triggered in children as young as seven years of age."[12]

Similarly, the mere act of dressing people in white versus red coats causes them to dislike each other more. In one experiment, two groups of people had to complete tasks such as devising a plan to rehabilitate a juvenile delinquent and coming up with an advertising slogan for toothpaste. People liked their own group more than the other group, even when the two groups were being graded together. They had an even stronger preference for their own group when the two groups were graded competitively, and the strongest preference for their own group occurred when one group was made to wear white coats and the other wore red coats.[13]

In another pair of similar experiments, Tajfel and his colleagues were able to get a group of teenagers to engage in "deliberate discriminatory behavior" in awarding money to themselves and another group of teenagers, even though they thought that the groups had been chosen based on a fairly meaningless characteristic (that is, in one experiment, the groups were told that they had been chosen based on whether members had overestimated or underestimated the number of dots on a piece of paper; in the other experiment, groups were told that they had been chosen based on their own preference for Klee versus Kandinsky). Amazingly, the groups showed discriminatory behavior even though the groups were *completely anonymous* — no one knew who else was in his own "group."[14]

As Tajfel and Michael Billig said, "it seems that the mere mention of 'groups' by the experimenters was sufficient to produce strong intergroup discrimination."[15]

How Group Interactions Cause "Acting White"

So we divide ourselves into groups. What of it?

Groups often enforce the boundaries between themselves and another group — especially one that appears threatening — by demanding that same-group members comply with the right social norms.[16] If you belong to a group of hardcore punk rockers who think that mainstream music has sold out to corporate interests, and you start waxing eloquent about your love for *American Idol* or Britney Spears, you are in for some skepticism. If you show up to the typical university faculty meeting wearing a cowboy hat and carrying a rifle, expect some odd stares. If you attend a revival at a Pentecostal church wearing a perfectly modest swimsuit, people will not approve.

Why? Because by the way that you act, talk, and dress, you are *signaling* something to other people.[17] By doing something that is contrary to the group's typical behavior, you are signaling that you do not care about the group's opinion, and ultimately that you do not care about belonging to the group. The theory of signaling, as Eric Posner points out, "shows why schoolchildren and the rest of us devote so much energy and worry to what always seem in the grand scheme of things to be trivial — clothes, hygiene, appearance, manners, forms of speech, and all the other attributes which, because of their salience, present opportunities for others to discriminate against us."[18]

Just as groups tend to be wary of other groups, they dislike group members who flout group norms and signal that they would rather resemble another group. *More so*, in fact: People usually resent a dissenting member of their own group even more than a complete outsider. Heretics are more of a threat than nonbelievers. The nonbeliever merely shows that there are people who never believed in your religion in the first place, while the heretic is trying to undermine and even ditch your religion altogether.

The same is true in the racial context. As Posner observes, the reason that blacks have traditionally despised "Uncle Toms" is because they "submitted

35

more readily to white racism," and "special venom is directed to the insider who breaks ranks and treats outsiders with respect."[19]

How do group norms play out in schools? In integrated schools, the two relevant groups are blacks and whites (other ethnicities exist, of course, but they are not the subject here). As we know from the studies of social psychologists, even if children were *randomly* assigned to be "black" or "white," you would expect to see group competition or animosity emerge. But children are obviously not randomly assigned. Instead, they arrive at the middle or high school having lived their entire lives as either black or white, and the middle school years are the first time when children truly become aware of racial issues.

Why "acting white"? What is the signal being sent there? Why would other black students resent this signal? 40

For hundreds of years, blacks were forced into a position of subservience to white people—most dramatically in the case of slavery, but also in the years of legally mandated segregation and Jim Crow laws. As a result, the black community in America has tended to be of two minds toward the white community. On the one hand, whites were viewed as the oppressors, as the slave owners, as the privileged. On the other hand, whites were often envied for their superior wealth, clothes, education, station in society, and innumerable other advantages. This created a deep and historic antagonism toward those blacks who sought to advance their own privilege by associating with oppressive whites, such as "house slaves" or "Uncle Toms."[20]

The same antagonism was present at the time of desegregation, and it lingers to some extent today. An integrated school can often appear to black students to be controlled by whites, or to be run in a way that benefits white students. Thus, the black student who tries to curry favor with the white authorities is seen as saying, "I'm better than you."

Indeed, in one of the earliest scholarly accounts of "acting white," one of the poorer black students was remarkably frank about how he viewed the more accomplished black students in his class: "There're just a few of these Uncle Toms at school, these are the goody-goody guys. Maybe I say this, though, because they're doing a little bit better than I am. And maybe I'm a little bit ashamed of myself because I'm not doing as good as they are in school, and I'm jealous. Maybe that's why I think of them as Uncle Toms."[21] Similarly, another poor black student said, "Well, the type of Negro that joins that type of thing [a certain club] are Negroes who look down on other Negroes anyway, and conform to the white ways. . . . Their idea is to get a good education and try to be as white as possible. They're what we call 'white Negroes.'"[22] The same sentiments are expressed today, as can be seen in a story from Cincinnati: "Since she began achieving high grades as a freshman three years ago, the Mount Auburn teen has endured a stream of verbal harassment from some of her African American peers. 'It was always, "Why are you trying to be white? Are you trying to be better than us?"' Carrie says."[23]

The fear of trying to be "better" than your peers could cause an "acting white" effect even *without* express peer pressure. As Ronald Ferguson of Harvard points out, "Students who have the skills to perform at high levels sometimes hold back [voluntarily] because their friends are struggling and they want to fit in. . . . Consider two friends walking on the street, urgently en route to an important destination. The slower walker is not in good physical condition. He does not appear to be able to keep up if the friend who is more fit were to accelerate. A decision by the faster friend to hold back in this situation — to keep walking slowly — would seem completely reasonable based on feelings of empathy and social attachment. Active peer pressure, stigmas, or stereotypes are not required for such voluntary inclinations toward accommodation to operate."[24] In other words, "acting white" is just another way in which people change their behavior so as to send the right signal to their friends.

"Acting white" is strongest by far in schools that are most evenly balanced and integrated — with neither huge white majorities nor huge black majorities. This is consistent with Martin Patchen's finding (in a large study of desegregation in Indianapolis) that in schools where blacks were a tiny minority, they got along well with whites, as they had no other choice. Similarly, where blacks were an overwhelming majority, they also got along with whites, because they felt comfortable and didn't have to worry about "possible rejection or domination by whites." But race relations (as well as academic achievement) were the worst in well-integrated schools, where there were substantial numbers of both blacks and whites. Why was this? Because this was where blacks "often felt disliked and unwelcome," but also had enough of a critical mass to form a "separate 'black society.' "[25] Another study similarly found that "at the extremes of the racial composition dimension (our one virtually all-black school and the most highly-white schools)" blacks were more likely to identify themselves as "students" than "in the more racially-balanced schools."[26]

The same thing, incidentally, is true of religion. In looking at a wide variety of countries around the world, economists at Harvard have found that religious strife tends to be highest when around half the country is religious. It's at that point that there are struggles for dominance. When a religion already is overwhelmingly dominant, the people in that religion feel more comfortable and can afford to be a bit more tolerant; when a religion is an overwhelming minority, its adherents realize that their best option is to play nice.[27]

In short, when we feel that we are part of a beleaguered group that is caught in a struggle for dominance, it becomes all the more important to stick together as a group and to punish group members who seem disloyal. That is what the "acting white" charge does. It is a perfectly normal human reaction, akin to the group solidarity felt by all types of minority groups (whether involving religion, sexual orientation, or anything else).

Even if my suggestions are unavailing, anyone who wants to address the achievement gap in America should carefully consider cultural factors. More importantly, we should all be aware that policies carried out with the best of intentions and goals may nonetheless have unintended consequences that can partly unravel the good we hope to do.

NOTES

[1] Leon F. Litwack, *Trouble in Mind: Black Southerners in the Age of Jim Crow* (New York: Knopf, 1998), p. 154.

[2] Charles Stearns, *The Black Man of the South and the Rebels; or, the Characteristics of the Former, and the Recent Outrages of the Latter* (New York: American News, 1872; reprint, New York: Kraus, 1969), p. 484.

[3] Molly McDonough, "Making Brown Real: A North Carolina Family Fought Threats and Intimidation After Suing to Integrate Schools," *ABA Journal* 90 (2004): 45

[4] Beverly Daniel Tatum, *Why Are All the Black Kids Sitting Together in the Cafeteria?* (New York: Basic, 1997), pp. 64–65.

[5] John McWhorter, *Winning the Race: Beyond the Crisis in Black America* (New York: Gotham, 2006), p. 268.

[6] Tatum, *"Why Are All the Black Kids Sitting Together in the Cafeteria?"* pp. 64–65. I did not come across Tatum's passage until a year or so after conceiving the idea for this book.

[7] Gordon Allport, *The Nature of Prejudice* (Boston: Beacon, 1954), p. 17.

[8] Miller McPherson, Lynn Smith-Lovin, and James Cook, "Birds of a Feather: Homophily in Social Networks," *Annual Review of Sociology* 27 (2001): 420.

[9] Jason P. Mitchell, C. Neil Macrae, and Mahzarin R. Banaji, "Dissociable Medial Prefrontal Contributions to Judgments of Similar and Dissimilar Others," *Neuron* 50 (18 May 2006): 655–63.

[10] An interesting paper on this subject is Timur Kuran, "Ethnic Norms and Their Transformation Through Reputational Cascades," *Journal of Legal Studies* 27 (1998): 623–59.

[11] Judith Rich Harris, *No Two Alike: Human Nature and Human Individuality* (New York: W. W. Norton, 2006), p. 157.

[12] Graham M. Vaughan, Henri Tajfel, and Jennifer Williams, "Bias in Reward Allocation in an Intergroup and an Interpersonal Context," *Social Psychology Quarterly* 44, no. 1 (1981): 37–42. Henri Tajfel and his colleagues found a similar result in J. C. Turner, R. J. Brown, and H. Tajfel, "Social Comparison and Group Interest in Ingroup Favouritism," *European Journal of Social Psychology* 9 (1979): 187–204. See also Henri Tajfel, "Experiments in Intergroup Discrimination," *Scientific American* 223 (1970): 96–102.

[13] See Stephen Worchel, Danny Axsom, Frances Ferris, Gary Samaha, and Susan Schweizer, "Determinants of the Effect of Intergroup Cooperation on Intergroup Attraction," *Journal of Conflict Resolution* 22, no. 3 (1978): 429–39. For more examples, see Naomi Ellemers, Cathy van Dyck, Steve Hinkle, and Annelieke Jacobs, "Intergroup Differentiation in Social Context: Identity Needs Versus Audience Constraints," *Social Psychology Quarterly* 63, no. 1 (2000): 60–74; Thomas E. Ford and George R. Tonander, "The Role of Differentiation between Groups and Social Identity in Stereotype Formation," *Social Psychology Quarterly* 61, no. 4 (1998): 372–84. On the other hand, some researchers have been able to reduce the amount of intergroup discrimination in such experiments by "priming" people to think about concepts such as "equality" or "fairness" (this is done by giving them a list of thirty words to remember, ten of which are words related to fairness); Guido Hertel and Norbert L. Kerr, "Priming In-Group Favoritism: The Impact of Normative Scripts in the Minimal Group Paradigm," *Journal of Experimental Social Psychology* 37 (2001): 316–24.

14See Henri Tajfel, M. G. Billig, and R. P. Bundy, "Social Categorization and Inter-group Behaviour," *European Journal of Social Psychology* I, no. 2 (1971): 149–77.

15Michael Billig and Henri Tajfel, "Social Categorization and Similarity in Inter-group Behaviour," *European Journal of Social Psychology* 3 (1973): 27–52.

16See Carmen G. Arroyo and Edward Zigler, "Racial Identity, Academic Achievement, and the Psychological Well-Being of Economically Disadvantaged Adolescents," *Journal of Personality and Social Psychology* 69, no. 5 (1995): 903–14.

17For a sophisticated mathematical analysis of how "acting white" is an example of signaling, see David Austen-Smith and Roland G. Fryer, Jr., "An Economic Analysis of 'Acting White,'" *Quarterly Journal of Economics* 102, no. 2 (2005): 551–83.

18Eric Posner, *Law and Social Norms* (Cambridge: Harvard University Press, 2000), p. 25.

19Posner, *Law and Social Norms*, p. 141.

20See, e.g., Thomas L. Webber, *Deep Like the Rivers* (New York: Norton), pp. 233–34; John U. Ogbu, "Collective Identity and the Burden of 'Acting White' in Black History, Community, and Education," *Urban Review* 36, no. 1 (2004): 1–35.

21Frank A. Petroni, Ernest A. Hirsch, and C. Lillian Petroni, *2, 4, 6, 8: When You Gonna Integrate?* (New York: Behavioral, 1970), p.173.

22Petroni, Hirsch, and Petroni, *2, 4, 6, 8*, p. 44.

23Curnutte, "For Some Black Students, Failing Is Safer."

24Ronald F. Ferguson, "A Diagnostic Analysis of Black-White GPA Disparities in Shaker Heights, Ohio." In *Brookings Papers on Educational Policy 2001*, ed. Diane Ravitch (Washington, D.C.: Brookings Institution Press, 2001).

25Martin Patchen, *Black-White Contact in Schools: Its Social and Academic Effects* (West Lafayette, Ind.: Purdue University Press, 1982), pp. 141–47. At least two other studies also found that race relations were worst in desegregated schools where the races were roughly balanced. See Janet Ward Schofield and H. Andrew Sagar, "Desegregation, School Practices, and Student Race Relations," in *The Consequences of School Desegregation*, ed. Christine H. Rossell and Willis D. Hawley (Philadelphia: Temple University Press, 1983), pp. 70–71.

26Barry Wellman, "I Am a Student," *Sociology of Education* 44, no. 4 (1971): 422–37.

27See Edward L. Glaeser, Giacomo A. M. Ponzetto, and Jesse M. Shapiro, "Strategic Extremism: Why Republicans and Democrats Divide on Religious Values," *Quarterly Journal of Economics* 120, no. 4 (2004): 1283–1330.

READING THE TEXT

1. Define in your own words what "acting white" means and why the concept is controversial.

2. According to Buck, how did desegregation change the racial dynamics in education, especially for African American students? How did it lead to the "acting white" phenomenon?

3. According to Buck, what does economist Roland Fryer mean by saying that "one's attitude toward education can now function as a *racial signal*" (para. 15)?

4. As Buck acknowledges, his contention that "acting white" exists can be considered "borderline racist" (para. 20). What rhetorical strategies does he use to allay his readers' temptation to so label his argument? Do you find them effective? Why, or why not?

5. What does the sociological term "homophily" (para. 25) mean, and how does Buck use it to explain that the "acting white" criticism is "normal"?

Reading the Signs

1. In your journal, reflect on the race relations in your high school. To what extent did they reflect the pattern that race relations are most problematic in well-integrated schools, but less so in schools that are dominated by one ethnicity?

2. Write an argumentative essay in which you support, refute, or complicate Buck's central thesis that desegregation has had unintended, ironically damaging effects on African American students.

3. **CONNECTING TEXTS**   Compare and contrast the "acting white" phenomenon with "claiming" (see Nell Bernstein's "Goin' Gangsta, Choosin' Cholita," p. 661). Use your observations as evidence in an essay about the importance of race in formulating a sense of personal identity.

4. In an essay, evaluate the persuasiveness of Buck's argument about the existence of the "acting white" phenomenon, focusing on his use of historical and scholarly evidence.

ANGELINE F. PRICE
Working Class Whites

Over the years, American popular culture has worked — not always successfully and sometimes fitfully — to rid itself of the racial stereotyping that has so marred its history. But one group of Americans, Angeline F. Price believes, has not benefited from this repudiation of negative stereotyping: working-class whites, especially those in the South. So Price has set up a Web site to analyze and document the ways in which "white trash" continue to be subject to distortion and disrespect in the mass media. We present here a selection from that site, the rest of which can be viewed at http://xroads .virginia.edu/ ∼ MA97/price/intro.htm. Price is a marketing consultant in Seattle.

"One class gets the sugar and the other gets the shit" (Fussell, 25), and in American society the "other" is invariably poverty stricken and powerless. Classism is at the core of the problem. The hatred of the poor is an evil secret of America, hidden by the ingrained myths of "liberty and justice for all." Americans are taught to believe in a classless, equal opportunity society. Yet, the facts of poverty, illiteracy, and ignorance are hard to ignore, and the reality is that some people have advantages over other people depending on which family they are born into. Therefore, when wealthy people confront the poor, a sense of guilt and superiority merge into the reactionary fear that has manifested itself as racism and classism through the centuries. Sut Lovingood, an anti-hero of Southwestern humor, may have put it best when he said of the genteel class, "they are powerful feard ove low things, low ways, an' low pepil" (Cook, 8).

The working class white has always been an ideal candidate for this role in society, and mainstream society has revealed their fright. As Jim Goad explains in his *Redneck Manifesto*, the "redneck" stereotype is especially fitting because it fills all the scapegoat requirements: biological differences — inbred, less intelligent, unattractive; geographic and regional differences — trailer parks, rural South, hillbilly; economic differences — poor, sick, lazy, dirty; cultural differences — fundamentalist, superstitious, loud, kin networks; and moral differences — trashy, racist, violent (Goad, 76).

Representations of working class whites in the popular media are responsible for the dissemination of "white trash" as well as "good country folk" stereotypes in society. The working class white, placed in these two distinct roles, serves as a personified id and superego for the collective psyche of America, particularly of middle and upper class whites.

The "white trash" portrayal represents the little devil on one shoulder — embodying racism, ignorance, violence, filth, and base desires. He operates outside of societal boundaries with an emphasis on the "id's" instinct and primalism. The "good country folk" portrayal represents the little angel on the other side — embodying simplicity, loyalty, faith in religion and humanity, and a connection to family and community. This "superego" maintains moral absolutes in a world where such ideals no longer belong.

Society has not chosen one to be the representative model, but instead 5 *uses* (and I mean that in the harshest sense) this dichotomy to fulfill its own desires on either end of the spectrum. As "id," the working class white is burdened with all the crimes and guilt of the white race over time. This allows the audience to feel justifiable hatred toward a group which they can demonize and thereby release guilt and aggression onto — while hating what is worst within themselves. As "superego," the working class white is used to nostalgize and idealize the desire for a simpler life, thus enabling the audience to reassure itself of qualities they hope are best within themselves in a kind, moral world. These images reappear over time and in many forms of media. They are considered for their impact on public perception and treatment of working class whites.

Modern day experience with white trash stereotypes is, as with most modern cultural phenomena, disseminated through movies and television. The images society has created fall into two conflicting categories. Most often the working class white is a whisky-drinking, abusive, violently racist, uneducated, macho, close-minded, dirty, fat, insensitive, monster-truck-show-watching hunter who is better laughed at than associated with. Yet in rare instances, one

This 1964 photo shows an unemployed Appalachian miner with his family.

encounters the poor white as honest, hard-working, honorable, simple, loyal, God-fearing, and patriotic. And here exists the dichotomy of white trash versus good country folk.

American society has used the working class white to alternately allay its fear of faltering morality or to bolster its confidence in the correctness of the modern lifestyle. Examples of this tendency occur in the typecasting of working class whites in television series as well as film. Stemming from the disillusionment of Vietnam, Watergate, and other corruptions of the time, we can trace a movement of "good country folk" in the television shows of the seventies. Programs like *The Andy Griffith Show* and *The Waltons* provided a simple, honest way of life that appealed to viewers as an escape from the cynicism and the loss of moral absolutes that was becoming prevalent in society. Once again, America turned to the South as the appropriate setting for such nostalgia.

At around the same time, we also have popular Southern sitcoms like *The Dukes of Hazzard* and *The Beverly Hillbillies* playing on the more typical stereotype of uneducated, criminal (Duke brothers' constant battles with the corrupt Boss Hogg) characters with substandard eating habits and speech patterns. We also find sexy yet innocent women protected by their families with Daisy and Ellie May. *The Beverly Hillbillies* proves that even when poor whites

The television show *The Beverly Hillbillies,*
about a poor Ozark family that strikes it
rich and moves to Beverly Hills, ran from
1962 to 1971.

stumble upon money, they retain their low class ways, and are useful only
for the purposes of humor. *The Dukes of Hazzard* gives a solid continuation
of redneck stereotypes, tempered with the idea that the Dukes are "never
meanin' no harm" as the theme song implies.

The use of violence in film and writing is often a hallmark of social passion. During the 1930s there was a movement to expose the brutality of the
lives of working class whites. Yet often the attempts to give aid were actually
forms of condescension and control. That is commonly the effect of the literature and case studies of the time. John Ford's film adaptation of *The Grapes
of Wrath* is the strongest example of dignified poor white media portrayal.
Henry Fonda and Jane Darwell, echoing the themes of Southern agrarianism,
are rural saints attacked by the forces of modern, capitalistic society.

In recent years, the popularity of poor white imagery has come in two   10
forms. One is the simple, idiotic portrayal in the humorous sketches of Jeff
Foxworthy (a middle to upper class actor — not a redneck) and the brass
unorthodoxy of Roseanne, or the dark and perverse killer in movies like
Deliverance or *Sling Blade.* Though the complex and human character in *Sling
Blade* is much easier to accept than the sodomizing mountain man in *Deliverance*, both characters portray a warped sense of morality that is equated to
their Southern, poor white upbringing. The father of the killer in *Sling Blade*
is shown surrounded by religious iconography, and he and his wife blatantly
use religion to justify their horrific treatment of the child and the murder
of an unwanted baby that is born to them. The depth of ignorance necessary to explain the characters' behavior is only fitting in the environment of

John Steinbeck's novel *The Grapes of Wrath* (1939) was made into a movie starring Henry Fonda.

the poor white. Filled with domestic violence and dark secrets, the Southern small town setting ensures that such events would not take place in any other context.

Deliverance may be the most well-known and damaging film centered around poor whites, in this case "hillbillies." *Deliverance* embodies all the fear of urban modern America concerning what is most primitive and dangerous in the character of man. The conflict is between modern mainstream capitalist America and the lurking potential of evil in mankind . . . an evil which has been left behind to remain only in those mountaineers most remote and ignorant of civilization. In the film, urban macho man takes on the raw brutality of nature and its inhabitants with no respect and pays the price. The punishment is one of male on male rape by the embodiment of poor white trash, confirming mainstream America's fear of the poverty-stricken savage.

The view from inside the working class is much more complex. The working class white is operating off his own cultural, family, and individual biases; yet coupled with these are the pervasive, historically assumed ideas that violence, racism, and fundamentalism are somehow inherent in his class. Even if one becomes aware of the layers of identification applied to oneself, and most people do not, a battle against your own heritage is difficult at best, and usually impossible. The class to which we are born, in which our family circulates and our formative years are spent, is the guiding principle with which we view other groups and their cultural beliefs within our life experience.

Films that show poor whites as violent people who attack wealthy citified whites allow the rich to justify their treatment of "white trash" by portraying the poor whites as racist, criminal, and uneducated. This allows other typically marginalized groups to join upper class whites against the "white trash." This justifies upper class stereotyping of poor whites and serves to aid in relieving upper class white guilt over treatment of "others" in the past.

The hatred and condescension of the poor seems to be the last available method of prejudice in our society. Just as Americans have made an effort to educate, understand, and alter the treatment of marginalized groups and alternate cultures within our society, we have held on to poor whites as a group to demean. Making assumptions about groups of any sort on societal and biased definitions is flawed in any situation. As with other groups, there must be an effort taken to use an open mind and individual code to ascribe merit to those in our world.

WORKS CITED

Cook, Sylvia Jenkins. *From Tobacco Road to Route 66: The Southern Poor in Fiction*. Chapel Hill: University of North Carolina, 1976. Print.
Fussell, Paul. *Class*. New York: Simon & Schuster, 1983. Print.
Goad, Jim. *The Redneck Manifesto*. New York: Simon & Schuster, 1997. Print.

READING THE TEXT

1. Explain in your own words Price's definitions of "white trash" and "good country folk."
2. What is the logic behind Price's analogies between white trash and the id and good country folk and the superego?
3. Summarize in your own words the evolution of cinematic depictions of poor whites from the 1970s to more recent years.
4. What does Price mean by saying that "a battle against your own heritage is difficult at best, and usually impossible" (para. 12)?

READING THE SIGNS

1. Watch a recent movie that has working-class white characters and analyze it according to the stereotypes that Price describes. Do you find depictions of "white trash" or "good country folk," or do the characters have traits that Price does not discuss?
2. At your school's media library, watch an episode of one of the TV shows Price mentions, such as *The Dukes of Hazzard* or *The Beverly Hillbillies*, or watch one of the films that she describes. Then write your own analysis of its portrayal of the characters. Is the portrayal hostile or affectionate toward working-class white characters?
3. Write a reflective essay in which you respond to Price's assertion that "the hatred and condescension of the poor seems to be the last available method

of prejudice in our society" (para. 14). Support your essay with references to current popular entertainment.

4. In class, discuss why the "white trash" stereotype persists, even in an age of heightened sensitivity about racial stereotyping. Use the discussion as the springboard for an essay in which you propose your own explanation for this phenomenon.

5. **CONNECTING TEXTS**   Compare and contrast Price's argument about the way class is depicted in media with that of Michael Parenti ("Class and Virtue," p. 421). How do you account for any differences you may discern?

JACK LOPEZ
Of Cholos and Surfers

If you want to be a surfer, L.A.'s the place to be, but things can get complicated if you come from East Los Angeles, which is not only miles from the beach but is also the home turf for many a cholo street gangster who may not look kindly on a Mexican American kid carrying a copy of *Surfer Quarterly* and wearing Bermuda shorts. This is exactly what happened to Jack Lopez as he tells it in this memoir of growing up Latino in the 1960s — but not to worry, the beach and the barrio are not mutually exclusive, and, in the end, Lopez was able to have "the best of both worlds." A professor of English at California State University, Northridge, Lopez has published the memoir *Cholos & Surfers: A Latino Family Album* (1998), the story collection *Snapping Lines* (2001), and the novel *In the Break* (2006).

The only store around that had this new magazine was a Food Giant on Vermont Avenue, just off Imperial. *Surfer Quarterly*, it was then called. Now it's *Surfer Magazine* and they've celebrated their thirtieth anniversary. Sheldon made the discovery by chance when he'd gone shopping with his mother, who needed something found only at Food Giant. Normally we didn't go that far east to shop; we went west toward Crenshaw, to the nicer part of town.

We all wanted to be surfers, in fact called ourselves surfers even though we never made it to the beach, though it was less than ten miles away. One of the ways you could become a surfer was to own an issue of *Surfer Quarterly*. Since there had been only one prior issue, I was hot to get the new one. To be a surfer you also had to wear baggy shorts, large Penney's Towncraft

T-shirts, and go barefoot, no matter how much the hot sidewalks burned your soles.

That summer in the early sixties I was doing all sorts of odd jobs around the house for my parents: weeding, painting the eaves, babysitting during the daytime. I was earning money so that I could buy Lenny Muelich's surfboard, another way to be a surfer. It was a Velzy-Jacobs, ten feet six inches long, twenty-four inches wide, and it had the coolest red oval decal. Lenny was my across-the-street neighbor, two years older than I, the kid who'd taught me the facts of life, the kid who'd taught me how to wrestle, the kid who'd played army with me when we were children, still playing in the dirt.

Now we no longer saw much of each other, though he still looked out for me. A strange thing happened to Lenny the previous school year. He grew. Like the Green Giant or something. He was over six feet tall and the older guys would let him hang out with them. So Lenny had become sort of a hood, wearing huge Sir Guy wool shirts, baggy khaki pants with the cuffs rolled, and French-toed black shoes. He drank wine, even getting drunk in the daytime with his hoodlum friends. Lenny was now respected, feared, even, by some of the parents, and no longer needed or desired to own a surfboard — he was going in the opposite direction. There were two distinct paths in my neighborhood: hood or surfer.

I was entering junior high school in a month, and my best friends were 5 Sheldon Cohen and Tom Gheridelli. They lived by Morningside Heights, and their fathers were the only ones to work, and their houses were more expensive than mine, and they'd both been surfers before I'd aspired toward such a life. Sheldon and Tom wore their hair long, constantly cranking their heads back to keep their bangs out of their eyes. They were thirteen years old. I was twelve. My parents wouldn't let hair grow over my ears no matter how much I argued with them. But I was the one buying a surfboard. Lenny was holding it for me. My parents would match any money I saved over the summer.

Yet *Surfer Quarterly* was more tangible since it only cost one dollar. Lenny's Velzy-Jacobs was forty-five dollars, quite a large sum for the time. The issue then became one of how to obtain the object of desire. The Food Giant on Vermont was reachable by bike, but I was no longer allowed to ride up there. Not since my older brother had gone to the Southside Theatre one Saturday and had seen a boy get knifed because he wasn't colored. Vermont was a tough area, though some of the kids I went to school with lived up there and they weren't any different from us. Yet none of them wished to be surfers, I don't think.

What was needed was for me to include my father in the negotiation. I wasn't allowed to ride my bike to Vermont, I reasoned with him. Therefore, he should drive me. He agreed with me and that was that. Except I had to wait until the following Friday when he didn't have to work.

My father was a printer by trade. He worked the graveyard shift. I watched my younger brother and sister during the day (my older brother, who was fifteen years old, was around in case anything of consequence should arise, but we mostly left him alone) until my mother returned from work — Reaganomics had hit my family decades before the rest of the country. Watching my younger sister and brother consisted of keeping them quiet so my father could sleep.

In the late afternoons I'd go to Sportsman's Park, where I'd virtually grown up. I made the all-stars in baseball, basketball, and football. Our first opponent on the path to the city championships was always Will Rogers Park in Watts. Sheldon and Tom and I had been on the same teams. Sometimes I'd see them in the afternoons before we'd all have to return home for dinner. We'd pore over Sheldon's issue of *Surfer* while sitting in the bleachers next to the baseball diamond. If it was too hot we'd go in the wading pool, though we were getting too old for that scene, since mostly women and kids used it.

When Friday afternoon arrived and my father had showered and my   10
mother had returned from work, I reminded my father of our agreement. We drove the neighborhood streets up to Vermont, passing Washington High School, Normandie Avenue, Woodcrest Elementary School, and so on. We spoke mostly of me. Was I looking forward to attending Henry Clay Junior High? Would I still be in accelerated classes? My teachers and the principal had talked with my parents about my skipping a grade but my parents said no.

Just as my father had exhausted his repertoire of school questions, we arrived at the Food Giant. After parking in the back lot, we entered the store and made for the liquor section, where the magazines were housed. I stood in front of the rack, butterflies of expectation overtaking my stomach while my father bought himself some beer. I knew immediately when I found the magazine. It looked like a square of water was floating in the air. An ocean-blue cover of a huge wave completely engulfing a surfer with the headline BANZAI PIPELINE. I held the magazine with great reverence, as if I were holding something of spiritual value, which it was.

"Is that it?" my father asked. He held a quart of Hamm's in each hand, his Friday night allotment.

"Yes." I beamed.

At the counter my father took the magazine from me, leafing through it much too casually, I thought. I could see the bulging veins in his powerful forearms, and saw too the solid bumps that were his biceps.

"Looks like a crazy thing to do," he said, finally placing the magazine on the   15
counter next to the beer. My father, the practical provider, the person whose closet was pristine for lack of clothes — although the ones he did own were stylish, yet not expensive. This was why he drank beer from quart bottles — it was cheaper that way. I know now how difficult it must have been raising four children on the hourly wages my parents made.

The man at the counter rang up the purchases, stopping for a moment to look at the *Surfer*. He smiled.

"*¿Eres mexicano?*" my father asked him.

"*Sí, ¿cómo no?*" the man answered.

Then my father and the store clerk began poking fun at my magazine in Spanish, nothing too mean, but ranking it as silly adolescent nonsense.

When we got back in the car I asked my father why he always asked 20 certain people if they were Mexican. He only asked men who obviously were, thus knowing in advance their answers. He shrugged his shoulders and said he didn't know. It was a way of initiating conversation, he said. Well, it was embarrassing for me, I told him. Because I held the magazine in my lap, I let my father off the hook. It was more important that I give it a quick thumb-through as we drove home. The *Surfer* was far more interesting for me as a twelve-year-old than larger issues of race.

I spent the entire Friday evening holed up in my room, poring over the magazine, not even interested in eating popcorn or watching *77 Sunset Strip*, our familial Friday-night ritual. By the next morning I had almost memorized every photo caption and their sequence. I spoke with Sheldon on the phone and he and Tom were meeting me later at Sportsman's Park. I did my chores in a self-absorbed trance, waiting for the time when I could share my treasure with my friends. My mother made me eat lunch before I was finally able to leave.

Walking the long walk along Western Avenue toward Century and glancing at the photos in the magazine, I didn't pay attention to the cholo whom I passed on the sidewalk. I should have been more aware, but was too preoccupied. So there I was, in a street confrontation before I knew what had happened.

"You a surfer?" he said with disdain. He said it the way you start to say *chocolate*. *Ch*, like in *choc — churfer*. But that didn't quite capture it, either.

I stopped and turned to face him. He wore a wool watch cap pulled down onto his eyebrows, a long Sir Guy wool shirt with the top button buttoned and all the rest unbuttoned, khaki pants so long they were frayed at the bottoms and so baggy I couldn't see his shoes. I wore Bermuda shorts and a large Towncraft T-shirt. I was barefoot. My parents wouldn't let hair grow over my ears. Cholo meets surfer. Not a good thing. As he clenched his fists I saw a black cross tattooed onto the fleshy part of his hand.

His question was *not* like my father's. My father, I now sensed, wanted a 25 common bond upon which to get closer to strangers. This guy was Mexican American, and he wanted to fight me because I wore the outfit of a surfer.

I rolled the magazine in a futile attempt to hide it, but the cholo viewed this action as an escalation with a perceived weapon. It wasn't that I was overly afraid of him, though fear can work to your advantage if used correctly. I was big for my age, athletic, and had been in many fights. The problem was this: I was hurrying off to see my friends, to share something important with them, walking on a summer day, and I didn't feel like rolling on the ground with some stranger because *he'd* decided we must do so. Why did he get to dictate when or where you would fight? There was another consideration, one more utilitarian: Who knew what sort of weapons he had under all that baggy clothing? A rattail comb, at the least. More likely a knife, because in those days guns weren't that common.

At Woodcrest Elementary School there was a recently arrived Dutch Indonesian immigrant population. One of the most vicious fights I had ever seen was the one when Victor VerHagen fought his own cousin. And the toughest fight I'd ever been in was against Julio, something during a baseball game. There must be some element of self-loathing that propels us to fight those of our own ethnicity with a particular ferocity.

Just before the cholo was going to initiate the fight, I said, "I'm Mexican." American of Mexican descent, actually.

He seemed unable to process this new information. How could someone be Mexican and dress like a surfer? He looked at me again, this time seeing beyond the clothes I wore. He nodded slightly.

This revelation, this recognition verbalized, molded me in the years to 30 come. A surfer with a peeled nose and a Karmann Ghia with surf racks driving down Whittier Boulevard in East L.A. to visit my grandparents. The charmed life of a surfer in the midst of cholos.

When I began attending junior high school, there was a boy nicknamed Niño, who limped around the school yard one day. I discovered the reason for his limp when I went to the bathroom and he had a rifle pointed at boys and was taking their money. I fell in love with a girl named Shirley Pelland, the younger sister of a local surfboard maker. I saw her in her brother's shop after school, but she had no idea I loved her. That fall the gang escalation in my neighborhood became so pronounced my parents decided to move. We sold our house very quickly and moved to Huntington Beach, and none of us could sleep at night for the quiet. We were surrounded by cornfields and strawberry fields and tomato fields. As a bribe for our sudden move my parents chipped in much more than matching funds so I could buy Lenny Muelich's surfboard. I almost drowned in the big waves of a late-autumn south swell, the first time I went out on the Velzy-Jacobs. But later, after I'd surfed for a few years, I expertly rode the waves next to the pier, surfing with new friends.

But I've got ahead of myself. I must return to the cholo who is about to attack. But there isn't any more to tell about the incident. We didn't fight that summer's day over thirty years ago. In fact, I never fought another of my own race and don't know if this was a conscious decision or if circumstances dictated it. As luck would have it, I fought only a few more times during my adolescence and did so only when attacked.

My father's question, which he'd asked numerous people so long ago, taught me these things: The reason he had to ask was because he and my mother had left the safe confines of their Boyle Heights upbringing. They had thrust themselves and their children into what was called at the time the melting pot of Los Angeles. They bought the post–World War II American dream of assimilation. I was a pioneer in the sociological sense that I had no distinct ethnic piece of geography on which my pride and honor depended. Cast adrift in the city streets. Something gained, something lost. I couldn't return to my ethnic neighborhood, but I could be a surfer. And I didn't have to fight for ethnic pride over my city street. The neighborhood kids did, however, stick together, though this was not based upon race. It was a necessity. The older guys would step forward to protect the younger ones. That was how it was done.

The most important thing I learned was that I could do just about anything I wished, within reason. I could be a surfer, if I chose, and even cholos would respect my decision. During my adolescence I went to my grandparents' house for all the holidays. They lived in East Los Angeles. When I was old enough to drive I went on my own, sometimes with a girlfriend. I was able to observe my Los Angeles Mexican heritage, taking a date to the *placita* for Easter service and then having lunch at Olvera Street. An Orange County girl who had no idea this part of Los Angeles existed. I was lucky; I got the best of both worlds.

READING THE TEXT

1. What symbolic significance did being a surfer have for Lopez and his friends?
2. How did Lopez's attitude toward his Mexican heritage compare with that of his father, and how do you explain any difference?
3. Why does the cholo object to Lopez's surfer clothing?
4. How did Lopez eventually reconcile his surfer and his Mexican American identities?
5. Characterize Lopez's tone and persona in this selection. How do they affect your response as a reader?

READING THE SIGNS

1. In your journal, write your own account of how, in your childhood, you developed a sense of ethnic identity. Use Lopez's article as a model that pinpoints concrete, specific events as being significant.
2. **CONNECTING TEXTS** Compare and contrast Lopez's development of a sense of ethnic identity with that of Melissa Algranati ("Being an Other," p. 667). How can you account for any differences you might see?
3. A generational gap separated Lopez's and his father's attitudes toward assimilation. Interview several friends, preferably of different ethnicities, and their parents about their sense of ethnic identity. Write an essay in which you explore the extent to which one's age can influence one's attitudes toward ethnicity.
4. In class, discuss the extent to which your community is characterized by a "distinct ethnic piece of geography" (para. 33). Do people of different ethnicities interact frequently? Or do people tend to associate primarily with those of the same background? Use your discussion as the basis of an essay in which you evaluate the race relations in your community, taking care to suggest causes for the patterns that you see.
5. **CONNECTING TEXTS** Adopting Lopez's perspective on race relations, write a response to Stuart Buck's description of the "acting white" phenomenon ("Acting White," p. 637).

JIM WHITMER
Four Teens

READING THE SIGNS

1. Describe Whitmer's photograph. What is taking place? How would you characterize the attitudes of the four youths in this photo? Examine them one by one. You might comment on their facial and body expressions, for instance.

2. What do you think is the relationship among these four youths? What evidence do you have for your answers? Assume that the photographer has deliberately placed each subject in the photograph. Speculate on the motives of his placement and the effect he has achieved.

3. How would you characterize the clothing, hair, and jewelry — the styles — of the figures in the photo? That is, what do their styles say about them? Would you be willing to adopt their styles? Why or why not?

NELL BERNSTEIN

Goin' Gangsta, Choosin' Cholita

> Ever wonder about wannabes — white suburban teenagers who dress and act like nonwhite inner-city gangsters? In this report on the phenomenon of "claiming," Nell Bernstein probes some of the feelings and motives of teens who are "goin' gangsta" or "choosin' cholita" — kids who try on a racial identity not their own. Their reasons may surprise you. Bernstein is a journalist who has published in *Glamour, Woman's Day, Salon,* and *Mother Jones.* She is also the author of *All Alone in the World: Children of the Incarcerated* (2005).

Her lipstick is dark, the lip liner even darker, nearly black. In baggy pants, a blue plaid Pendleton, her bangs pulled back tight off her forehead, fifteen-year-old April is a perfect cholita, a Mexican gangsta girl.

But April Miller is Anglo. "And I don't like it!" she complains. "I'd rather be Mexican."

April's father wanders into the family room of their home in San Leandro, California, a suburb near Oakland. "Hey, cholita," he teases. "Go get a suntan. We'll put you in a barrio and see how much you like it."

A large, sandy-haired man with "April" tattooed on one arm and "Kelly" — the name of his older daughter — on the other, Miller spent twenty-one years working in a San Leandro glass factory that shut down and moved to Mexico a couple of years ago. He recently got a job in another factory, but he expects NAFTA to swallow that one, too.

"Sooner or later we'll all get nailed," he says. "Just another stab in the 5 back of the American middle class."

Later, April gets her revenge: "Hey, Mr. White Man's Last Stand," she teases. "Wait till you see how well I manage my welfare check. You'll be asking me for money."

A once almost exclusively white, now increasingly Latin and black working-class suburb, San Leandro borders on predominantly black East Oakland. For decades, the boundary was strictly policed and practically impermeable. In 1970 April Miller's hometown was 97 percent white. By 1990 San Leandro was 65 percent white, 6 percent black, 15 percent Hispanic, and 13 percent Asian or Pacific Islander. With minorities moving into suburbs in growing numbers and cities becoming ever more diverse, the boundary between city and suburb is dissolving, and suburban teenagers are changing with the times.

In April's bedroom, her past and present selves lie in layers, the pink walls of girlhood almost obscured, Guns N' Roses and Pearl Jam posters overlaid by rappers Paris and Ice Cube. "I don't have a big enough attitude to be a black girl," says April, explaining her current choice of ethnic identification.

What matters is that she thinks the choice is hers. For April and her friends, identity is not a matter of where you come from, what you were born into, what color your skin is. It's what you wear, the music you listen to, the words you use — everything to which you pledge allegiance, no matter how fleetingly.

The hybridization of American teens has become talk show fodder, with "wiggers" — white kids who dress and talk "black" — appearing on TV in full gangsta regalia. In Indiana a group of white high school girls raised a national stir when they triggered an imitation race war at their virtually all-white high school last fall simply by dressing "black."

In many parts of the country, it's television and radio, not neighbors, that introduce teens to the allure of ethnic difference. But in California, which demographers predict will be the first state with no racial majority by the year 2000, the influences are more immediate. The California public schools are the most diverse in the country: 42 percent white, 36 percent Hispanic, 9 percent black, 8 percent Asian.

Sometimes young people fight over their differences. Students at virtually any school in the Bay Area can recount the details of at least one "race riot" in which a conflict between individuals escalated into a battle between their clans. More often, though, teens would rather join than fight. Adolescence, after all, is the period when you're most inclined to mimic the power closest at hand, from stealing your older sister's clothes to copying the ruling clique at school.

White skaters and Mexican would-be gangbangers listen to gangsta rap and call each other "nigga" as a term of endearment; white girls sometimes affect Spanish accents; blonde cheerleaders claim Cherokee ancestors.

"Claiming" is the central concept here. A Vietnamese teen in Hayward, another Oakland suburb, "claims" Oakland — and by implication blackness — because he lived there as a child. A law-abiding white kid "claims" a Mexican gang he says he hangs with. A brown-skinned girl with a Mexican father and a white mother "claims" her Mexican side, while her fair-skinned sister "claims" white. The word comes up over and over, as if identity were territory, the self a kind of turf.

At a restaurant in a minimall in Hayward, Nicole Huffstutler, thirteen, sits with her friends and describes herself as "Indian, German, French, Welsh, and, um . . . American": "If somebody says anything like 'Yeah, you're just a peckerwood,' I'll walk up and I'll say 'white pride!' 'Cause I'm proud of my race, and I wouldn't wanna be any other race."

"Claiming" white has become a matter of principle for Heather, too, who says she's "sick of the majority looking at us like we're less than them." (Hayward schools were 51 percent white in 1990, down from 77 percent in 1980, and whites are now the minority in many schools.)

Asked if she knows that nonwhites have not traditionally been referred to as "the majority" in America, Heather gets exasperated: "I hear that all the time, every day. They say, 'Well, you guys controlled us for many years, and it's time for us to control you.' Every day."

When Jennifer Vargas — a small, brown-skinned girl in purple jeans who quietly eats her salad while Heather talks — softly announces that she's "mostly Mexican," she gets in trouble with her friends.

"No, you're not!" scolds Heather.

"I'm mostly Indian and Mexican," Jennifer continues flatly. "I'm very   20
little . . . I'm mostly . . ."

"Your mom's white!" Nicole reminds her sharply. "She has blond hair."

"That's what I mean," Nicole adds. "People think that white is a bad thing. They think that white is a bad race. So she's trying to claim more Mexican than white."

"I have very little white in me," Jennifer repeats. "I have mostly my dad's side, 'cause I look like him and stuff. And most of my friends think that me and my brother and sister aren't related, 'cause they look more like my mom."

"But you guys are all the same race, you just look different," Nicole insists. She stops eating and frowns. "OK, you're half and half each what your parents have. So you're equal as your brother and sister, you just look different. And you should be proud of what you are — every little piece and bit of what you are. Even if you were Afghan or whatever, you should be proud of it."

Will Mosley, Heather's seventeen-year-old brother, says he and his friends listen   25
to rap groups like Compton's Most Wanted, NWA, and Above the Law because they "sing about life" — that is, what happens in Oakland, Los Angeles, anyplace but where Will is sitting today, an empty Round Table Pizza in a minimall.

"No matter what race you are," Will says, "if you live like we do, then that's the kind of music you like."

And how do they live?

"We don't live bad or anything," Will admits. "We live in a pretty good neighborhood, there's no violence or crime. I was just . . . we're just city people, I guess."

Will and his friend Adolfo Garcia, sixteen, say they've outgrown trying to be something they're not. "When I was eleven or twelve," Will says, "I thought I was becoming a big gangsta and stuff. Because I liked that music, and thought it was the coolest, I wanted to become that. I wore big clothes, like you wear in jail. But then I kind of woke up. I looked at myself and thought, 'Who am I trying to be?'"

They may have outgrown blatant mimicry, but Will and his friends remain   30
convinced that they can live in a suburban tract house with a well-kept lawn on a tree-lined street in "not a bad neighborhood" and still call themselves "city" people on the basis of musical tastes. "City" for these young people means crime, graffiti, drugs. The kids are law-abiding, but these activities connote what Will admiringly calls "action." With pride in his voice, Will predicts that "in a couple of years, Hayward will be like Oakland. It's starting to get

more known, because of crime and things. I think it'll be bigger, more things happening, more crime, more graffiti, stealing cars."

"That's good," chimes in fifteen-year-old Matt Jenkins, whose new beeper — an item that once connoted gangsta chic but now means little more than an active social life — goes off periodically. "More fun."

The three young men imagine with disdain life in a gangsta-free zone. "Too bland, too boring," Adolfo says. "You have to have something going on. You can't just have everyday life."

"Mowing your lawn," Matt sneers.

"Like Beaver Cleaver's house," Adolfo adds. "It's too clean out here."

Not only white kids believe that identity is a matter of choice or taste,   35
or that the power of "claiming" can transcend ethnicity. The Manor Park Locos — a group of mostly Mexican Americans who hang out in San Leandro's Manor Park — say they descend from the Manor Lords, tough white guys who ruled the neighborhood a generation ago.

They "are like our . . . uncles and dads, the older generation," says Jesse Martinez, fourteen. "We're what they were when they were around, except we're Mexican."

"There's three generations," says Oso, Jesse's younger brother. "There's Manor Lords, Manor Park Locos, and Manor Park Pee Wees." The Pee Wees consist mainly of the Locos' younger brothers, eager kids who circle the older boys on bikes and brag about "punking people."

Unlike Will Mosley, the Locos find little glamour in city life. They survey the changing suburban landscape and see not "action" or "more fun" but frightening decline. Though most of them are not yet eighteen, the Locos are already nostalgic, longing for a Beaver Cleaver past that white kids who mimic them would scoff at.

Walking through nearly empty Manor Park, with its eucalyptus stands, its softball diamond and tennis courts, Jesse's friend Alex, the only Asian in the group, waves his arms in a gesture of futility. "A few years ago, every bench was filled," he says. "Now no one comes here. I guess it's because of everything that's going on. My parents paid a lot for this house, and I want it to be nice for them. I just hope this doesn't turn into Oakland."

Glancing across the park at April Miller's street, Jesse says he knows what   40
the white cholitas are about. "It's not a racial thing," he explains. "It's just all the most popular people out here are Mexican. We're just the gangstas that everyone knows. I guess those girls wanna be known."

Not every young Californian embraces the new racial hybridism. Andrea Jones, twenty, an African American who grew up in the Bay Area suburbs of Union City and Hayward, is unimpressed by what she sees mainly as shallow mimicry. "It's full of posers out here," she says. "When *Boyz N the Hood* came out on video, it was sold out for weeks. The boys all wanna be black, the girls all wanna be Mexican. It's the glamour."

Driving down the quiet, shaded streets of her old neighborhood in Union City, Andrea spots two white preteen boys in Raiders jackets and hugely baggy pants strutting erratically down the empty sidewalk. "Look at them," she says. "Dislocated."

She knows why. "In a lot of these schools out here, it's hard being white," she says. "I don't think these kids were prepared for the backlash that is going on, all the pride now in people of color's ethnicity, and our boldness with it. They have nothing like that, no identity, nothing they can say they're proud of.

"So they latch onto their great-grandmother who's a Cherokee, or they take on the most stereotypical aspects of being black or Mexican. It's beautiful to appreciate different aspects of other people's culture — that's like the dream of what the twenty-first century should be. But to garnish yourself with pop culture stereotypes just to blend — that's really sad."

Roland Krevocheza, eighteen, graduated last year from Arroyo High   45
School in San Leandro. He is Mexican on his mother's side, Eastern European on his father's. In the new hierarchies, it may be mixed kids like Roland who have the hardest time finding their place, even as their numbers grow. (One in five marriages in California is between people of different races.) They can always be called "wannabes," no matter what they claim.

"I'll state all my nationalities," Roland says. But he takes a greater interest in his father's side, his Ukrainian, Romanian, and Czech ancestors. "It's more unique," he explains. "Mexican culture is all around me. We eat Mexican food all the time, I hear stories from my grandmother. I see the low-riders and stuff. I'm already part of it. I'm not trying to be; I am."

His darker-skinned brother "says he's not proud to be white," Roland adds. "He calls me 'Mr. Nazi.'" In the room the two share, the American flags and the reproduction of the Bill of Rights are Roland's; the Public Enemy poster belongs to his brother.

Roland has good reason to mistrust gangsta attitudes. In his junior year in high school, he was one of several Arroyo students who were beaten up outside the school at lunchtime by a group of Samoans who came in cars from Oakland. Roland wound up with a split lip, a concussion, and a broken tailbone. Later he was told that the assault was "gang-related" — that the Samoans were beating up anyone wearing red.

"Rappers, I don't like them," Roland says. "I think they're a bad influence on kids. It makes kids think they're all tough and bad."

Those who, like Roland, dismiss the gangsta and cholo styles as affecta-   50
tions can point to the fact that several companies market overpriced knockoffs of "ghetto wear" targeted at teens.

But there's also something going on out here that transcends adolescent faddishness and pop culture exoticism. When white kids call their parents "racist" for nagging them about their baggy pants; when they learn Spanish to talk to their boyfriends; when Mexican American boys feel themselves descended in spirit from white "uncles"; when children of mixed marriages insist that they are whatever race they say they are, all of them are more than just confused.

They're inching toward what Andrea Jones calls "the dream of what the twenty-first century should be." In the ever-more diverse communities of

Northern California, they're also facing the complicated reality of what their twenty-first century will be.

Meanwhile, in the living room of the Miller family's San Leandro home, the argument continues unabated. "You don't know what you are," April's father has told her more than once. But she just keeps on telling him he doesn't know what time it is.

READING THE TEXT

1. How do teens like April Miller define their identity, according to Bernstein?
2. Describe in your own words what "claiming" (para. 14) an ethnic identity means and why so many teens are tempted to do so.
3. What relationship does Bernstein see between claiming and mass media?
4. What does being white mean to many of the kids who claim a nonwhite identity?
5. What does the city signify to the young people whom Bernstein describes?

READING THE SIGNS

1. In class, stage a conversation between April Miller and her father on her adoption of a Mexican identity, with April defending her choice and her father repudiating it.
2. Write an essay in which you support, challenge, or modify Andrea Jones's assumption that it is media-generated "glamour" (para. 41) that prompts young people to claim a new ethnic identity. Be sure to base your argument on the evidence of specific pop culture personalities.
3. Write an argumentative essay in which you explain whether the claiming fad is an expression of racial tolerance or racial stereotyping.
4. **CONNECTING TEXTS**   Bernstein describes teens claiming the identities of ethnic minorities, but she provides few instances of claiming a white identity. In an essay, propose your own explanation for this pattern. To develop your ideas, you might consult Angeline F. Price's "Working Class Whites" (p. 648).
5. **CONNECTING TEXTS**   Assuming the perspective of Jack Lopez ("Of Cholos and Surfers," p. 654), write an analysis of the social and cultural pressures that prompt these teens to "claim" an ethnicity. Do they desire to have "the best of both worlds," as Lopez does, or are other forces at work?

MELISSA ALGRANATI

Being an Other

In a country as obsessed with racial identification as America is, Melissa Algranati poses a dilemma. As she puts it, "there are not too many Puerto Rican, Egyptian Jews out there," so the only category left for her on the census form is "other." In this personal essay, Algranati tells the story of how she came to be an "other," a saga of two immigrant families from different continents who eventually came together in a "marriage that only a country like America could create." Algranati is a graduate of the State University of New York at Binghamton and has a master's degree from Columbia University. She is a staff writer for www.studio2b.org.

Throughout my whole life, people have mistaken me for other ethnic backgrounds rather than for what I really am. I learned at a young age that there are not too many Puerto Rican, Egyptian Jews out there. For most of my life I have been living in two worlds, and at the same time I have been living in neither. When I was young I did not realize that I was unique, because my family brought me up with a healthy balance of Puerto Rican and Sephardic customs. It was not until I took the standardized PSAT exam that I was confronted with the question: "Who am I?" I remember the feeling of confusion as I struggled to find the right answer. I was faced with a bad multiple-choice question in which there was only supposed to be one right answer, but more than one answer seemed to be correct. I did not understand how a country built on the concept of diversity could forget about its most diverse group, inter-ethnic children. I felt lost in a world of classification. The only way for me to take pride in who I am was to proclaim myself as an other, yet that leaves out so much. As a product of a marriage only a country like America could create, I would now try to help people understand what it is like to be a member of the most underrepresented group in the country, the "others."

My father, Jacques Algranati, was born in Alexandria, Egypt. As a Sephardic Jew, my father was a minority in a predominantly Arab world. Although in the minority, socially my father was a member of the upper middle class and lived a very comfortable life. As a result of strong French influence in the Middle Eastern Jewish world, my father attended a French private school. Since Arabic was the language of the lower class, the Algranati family spoke French as their first language. My whole family is polyglot, speaking languages from the traditional Sephardic tongue of Ladino to Turkish and Greek. My grandfather spoke seven languages. Basically, my father grew up in a close-knit Sephardic community surrounded by family and friends.

However, in 1960 my father's world came to a halt when he was faced with persecution on an institutional level. As a result of the Egyptian-Israeli conflict, in 1956 an edict was issued forcing all foreign-born citizens and Jews out of Egypt. Although my father was a native-born citizen of the country, because of a very strong anti-Jewish sentiment, his citizenship meant nothing. So in 1960 when my family got their exit visas, as Jews had done since the time of the Inquisition, they packed up and left the country as one large family group.

Unable to take many possessions or much money with them, my father's family, like many Egyptian Jews, immigrated to France. They proceeded to France because they had family who were able to sponsor them. Also, once in France my family hoped to be able to receive a visa to America much sooner, since French immigration quotas to the United States were much higher than those in Egypt. Once in France my family relied on the generosity of a Jewish organization, the United Jewish Appeal. For nine months my father lived in a hotel sponsored by the United Jewish Appeal and attended French school until the family was granted a visa to the United States.

Since my father's oldest brother came to the United States first with his wife, they were able to sponsor the rest of the family's passage over. The Algranati family eventually settled in Forest Hills, Queens. Like most immigrants, my family settled in a neighborhood filled with immigrants of the same background. Once in the United States, my father rejoined many of his old friends from Egypt, since most Egyptian Jewish refugees followed a similar immigration path. At the age of fourteen my father and his group of friends were once again forced to adjust to life in a new country, but this time they had to learn a new language in order to survive. Like many of his friends, my father was forced to leave the comforts and luxuries of his world for the hardships of a new world. But as he eloquently puts it, once his family and friends were forced to leave, there was really nothing to stay for.

Like my father, my mother is also an immigrant; however, my parents come from very different parts of the world. Born in Maniti, Puerto Rico, my mom spent the first five years of her life in a small town outside of San Juan. Since my grandfather had attended private school in the United States when he was younger, he was relatively proficient in English. Like many immigrants, my grandfather came to the United States first, in order to help establish the family. After securing a job and an apartment, he sent for my grandmother, and three weeks later my mother and her fourteen-year-old sister came.

Puerto Ricans are different from many other people who come to this country, in the sense that legally they are not considered immigrants. Because Puerto Rico is a commonwealth of the United States, Puerto Ricans are granted automatic U.S. citizenship. So unlike most, from the day my mother and her family stepped on U.S. soil they were considered citizens. The only problem was that the difference in language and social status led "real" Americans not to consider them citizens.

As a result of this unique status, my mother faced many hardships in this new country. From the day my mother entered first grade, her process of Americanization had begun. Her identity was transformed. She went from being Maria Louisa Pinto to becoming Mary L. Pinto. Not only was my mother given a new name when she began school, but a new language was forced upon her as well. Confronted by an Irish teacher, Mrs. Walsh, who was determined to Americanize her, my mother began her uphill battle with the English language. Even until this day my mother recalls her traumatic experience when she learned how to pronounce the word "run":

"Repeat after me, run."

"Rrrrrrrrrun."   10

"No, Mary, run."

"Rrrrrrrrrun."

No matter how hard my mother tried she could not stop rolling her "r's." After several similar exchanges Mrs. Walsh, with a look of anger on her face, grabbed my mother's cheeks in her hand and squeezed as she repeated in a stern voice, "RUN!" Suffice it to say my mother learned how to speak English without a Spanish accent. It was because of these experiences that my mother made sure the only language spoken in the house or to me and my sister was English. My parents never wanted their children to experience the pain my mother went through just to learn how to say the word "run."

My mother was confronted with discrimination not only from American society but also from her community. While in the United States, my mother lived in a predominantly Spanish community. On first coming to this country her family lived in a tenement in the Bronx. At the age of twelve my mother was once more uprooted and moved to the projects on the Lower East Side. As one of the first families in a predominantly Jewish building, it was a step up for her family.

It was not her environment that posed the biggest conflict for her; it was   15
her appearance. My mother is what people call a "white Hispanic." With her blond hair and blue eyes my mother was taken for everything but a Puerto Rican. Once my mother perfected her English, no one suspected her ethnicity unless she told them. Since she was raised to be above the ghetto, never picking up typical "Hispanic mannerisms," she was able to exist in American society with very little difficulty. Because of a very strong and protective mother and the positive influence and assistance received from the Henry Street Settlement, my mother was able to escape the ghetto. As a result of organizations like Henry Street, my mother was given opportunities such as fresh air camps and jobs in good areas of the city, where she was able to rise above the drugs, alcohol, and violence that consumed so many of her peers.

As a result of her appearance and her upbringing, my mother left her people and the ghetto to enter American society. It was here as an attractive "white" female that my mother and father's two very different worlds merged. My parents, both working on Wall Street at the time, were introduced by a mutual friend. Since both had developed a rather liberal view, the differences in their backgrounds did not seem to be a major factor. After a year of dating my parents decided to get engaged.

Although they were from two different worlds, their engagement seemed to bring them together. Growing up in the midst of the Jewish community of the Lower East Side, my mother was constantly influenced by the beauty of Judaism. Therefore, since my mother never had much connection with Catholicism and had never been baptized, she decided to convert to Judaism and raise her children as Jews. The beauty of the conversion was that no one in my father's family forced her to convert; they accepted her whether she converted or not. As for my mother's family, they too had no real objections to the wedding or conversion. To them the only thing that mattered was that my father was a nice guy who made my mom happy. The most amusing part of the union of these two different families came when they tried to communicate. My father's family is descended from Spanish Jewry where many of them spoke an old Castilian-style Spanish, while my mother's family spoke a very modern Caribbean-style Spanish. To watch them try to communicate in any language other than English was like watching a session of the United Nations.

It was this new world, that of Puerto Rican Jewry, my parents created for me and my sister, Danielle. Resembling both my parents, having my mother's coloring with my father's features, I have often been mistaken for various ethnicities. Possessing light hair and blue eyes, I am generally perceived as the "all-American" girl. Occasionally I have been mistaken for Italian since my last name, Algranati, although Sephardic, has a very Italian flair to it. I have basically lived a chameleon-like existence for most of my life.

As a result of my "otherness," I have gained "acceptance" in many different crowds. From this acceptance I have learned the harsh reality behind my "otherness." I will never forget the time I learned about how the parents of one of my Asian friends perceived me. From very early on, I gained acceptance with the parents of one of my Korean friends. Not only did they respect me as a person and a student, but her father even went so far as to consider me like "one of his daughters." I will always remember how I felt when I heard they made one of their daughters cancel a party because she had invited Hispanics. Even when my friend pointed out that I, the one they loved, was Hispanic they refused to accept it. Even today to them, I will always be Jewish and not Puerto Rican because to them it is unacceptable to "love" a Puerto Rican.

Regardless of community, Jewish or Puerto Rican, I am always confronted 20 by bigots. Often I am forced to sit in silence while friends utter in ignorance stereotypical responses like: "It was probably some spic who stole it," or "You're just like a Jew, always cheap."

For the past three years I have worked on the Lower East Side of Manhattan at the Henry Street Settlement. Basically my mother wanted me to support the organization that helped her get out of the ghetto. Unlike when my mother was there, the population is mostly black and Hispanic. So one day during work I had one of my fellow workers say to me "that is such a collegian white thing to say." I responded by saying that his assumption was only partially correct and asked him if he considered Puerto Rican to be white.

Of course he doubted I was any part Hispanic until he met my cousin who "looks" Puerto Rican. At times like these I really feel for my mother, because I know how it feels not to be recognized by society for who you are.

Throughout my life I do not think I have really felt completely a part of any group. I have gone through phases of hanging out with different crowds trying in a sense to find myself. Basically, I have kept my life diverse by attending both Catholic-sponsored camps and Hebrew school at the same time. Similar to my parents, my main goal is to live within American society. I choose my battles carefully. By being diverse I have learned that in a society that is obsessed with classification the only way I will find my place is within myself. Unfortunately, society has not come to terms with a fast-growing population, the "others." Therefore when asked the infamous question: "Who are you?" I respond with a smile, "a Puerto Rican Egyptian Jew." Contrary to what society may think, I know that I am somebody.

READING THE TEXT

1. Summarize in your own words why Algranati feels like one of the "others" (para. 1).
2. How did the childhood experiences of Algranati's parents differ?
3. How does physical appearance affect strangers' perceptions of ethnic identity, according to Algranati?
4. Why does Algranati say she has never "really felt completely a part of any group" (para. 22)?

READING THE SIGNS

1. In your journal, reflect on your answer to the question "Who am I?"
2. Write an essay in which you defend or oppose the practice of asking individuals to identify their ethnicity in official documents such as census forms and school applications.
3. Algranati's background includes racial, cultural, and religious differences. Write an essay explaining how you would identify yourself if you were in her shoes.
4. **CONNECTING TEXTS** Do you think Algranati would be sympathetic or hostile toward people who "try on" different ethnic identities? Writing as if you were Algranati, write a letter to one of the teens who claims a new ethnic identity in Nell Bernstein's "Goin' Gangsta, Choosin' Cholita" (p. 661).
5. In class, brainstorm names of biracial actors, musicians, politicians, or models. Then discuss the extent to which the mass media presume that people neatly fit ethnic categories. What is the effect of such a presumption?

AARON DEVOR

Gender Role Behaviors and Attitudes

"Boys will be boys, and girls will be girls": few of our cultural mythologies seem as natural as this one. But in this exploration of the gender signals that traditionally tell what a "boy" or "girl" is supposed to look and act like, Aaron Devor shows how these signals are not "natural" at all but instead are cultural constructs. While the classic cues of masculinity—aggressive posture, self-confidence, a tough appearance—and the traditional signs of femininity—gentleness, passivity, strong nurturing instincts—are often considered "normal," Devor explains that they are by no means biological or psychological necessities. Indeed, he suggests, they can be richly mixed and varied, or to paraphrase the old Kinks song "Lola," "Boys can be girls and girls can be boys." Devor is dean of social sciences at the University of Victoria and author of *Gender Blending: Confronting the Limits of Duality* (1989), from which this selection is excerpted, and *FTM: Female-to-Male Transsexuals in Society* (1997).

Gender Role Behaviors and Attitudes

The clusters of social definitions used to identify persons by gender are collectively known as "femininity" and "masculinity." Masculine characteristics are used to identify persons as males, while feminine ones are used as signifiers for femaleness. People use femininity or masculinity to claim and communicate their membership in their assigned, or chosen, sex or gender. Others recognize our sex or gender more on the basis of these characteristics than on the basis of sex characteristics, which are usually largely covered by clothing in daily life.

These two clusters of attributes are most commonly seen as mirror images of one another with masculinity usually characterized by dominance and aggression, and femininity by passivity and submission. A more even-handed description of the social qualities subsumed by femininity and masculinity might be to label masculinity as generally concerned with egoistic dominance and femininity as striving for cooperation or communion.[1] Characterizing femininity and masculinity in such a way does not portray the two

---

[1] Eleanor Maccoby, *Social Development: Psychological Growth and the Parent-Child Relationship* (New York: Harcourt, 1980), p. 217. Egoistic dominance is a striving for superior rewards for oneself or a competitive striving to reduce the rewards for one's competitors even if such action will not increase one's own rewards. Persons who are motivated by desires for egoistic dominance not only wish the best for themselves but also wish to diminish the advantages of others whom they may perceive as competing with them.

clusters of characteristics as being in a hierarchical relationship to one another but rather as being two different approaches to the same question, that question being centrally concerned with the goals, means, and use of power. Such an alternative conception of gender roles captures the hierarchical and competitive masculine thirst for power, which can, but need not, lead to aggression, and the feminine quest for harmony and communal well-being, which can, but need not, result in passivity and dependence.

Many activities and modes of expression are recognized by most members of society as feminine. Any of these can be, and often are, displayed by persons of either gender. In some cases, cross-gender behaviors are ignored by observers, and therefore do not compromise the integrity of a person's gender display. In other cases, they are labeled as inappropriate gender role behaviors. Although these behaviors are closely linked to sexual status in the minds and experiences of most people, research shows that dominant persons of either gender tend to use influence tactics and verbal styles usually associated with men and masculinity, while subordinate persons, of either gender, tend to use those considered to be the province of women.[2] Thus it seems likely that many aspects of masculinity and femininity are the result, rather than the cause, of status inequalities.

Popular conceptions of femininity and masculinity instead revolve around hierarchical appraisals of the "natural" roles of males and females. Members of both genders are believed to share many of the same human characteristics, although in different relative proportions; both males and females are popularly thought to be able to do many of the same things, but most activities are divided into suitable and unsuitable categories for each gender class. Persons who perform the activities considered appropriate for another gender will be expected to perform them poorly; if they succeed adequately, or even well, at their endeavors, they may be rewarded with ridicule or scorn for blurring the gender dividing line.

The patriarchal gender schema currently in use in mainstream North American society reserves highly valued attributes for males and actively supports the high evaluation of any characteristics which might inadvertently become associated with maleness. The ideology underlying the schema postulates that the cultural superiority of males is a natural outgrowth of the innate predisposition of males toward aggression and dominance, which is assumed to flow inevitably from evolutionary and biological sources. Female attributes are likewise postulated to find their source in innate predispositions acquired in the evolution of the species. Feminine characteristics are thought to be intrinsic to the female facility for childbirth and breastfeeding. Hence, it is popularly believed that the social position of females is biologically mandated to

[2]Judith Howard, Philip Blumstein, and Pepper Schwartz, "Sex, Power, and Influence Tactics in Intimate Relationships," *Journal of Personality and Social Psychology* 51 (1986), pp. 102–9; Peter Kollock, Philip Blumstein, and Pepper Schwartz, "Sex and Power in Interaction: Conversational Privileges and Duties," *American Sociological Review* 50 (1985), pp. 34–46.

be intertwined with the care of children and a "natural" dependency on men for the maintenance of mother-child units. Thus the goals of femininity and, by implication, of all biological females are presumed to revolve around heterosexuality and maternity.[3]

Femininity, according to this traditional formulation, "would result in warm and continued relationships with men, a sense of maternity, interest in caring for children, and the capacity to work productively and continuously in female occupations."[4] This recipe translates into a vast number of proscriptions and prescriptions. Warm and continued relations with men and an interest in maternity require that females be heterosexually oriented. A heterosexual orientation requires women to dress, move, speak, and act in ways that men will find attractive. As patriarchy has reserved active expressions of power as a masculine attribute, femininity must be expressed through modes of dress, movement, speech, and action which communicate weakness, dependency, ineffectualness, availability for sexual or emotional service, and sensitivity to the needs of others.

Some, but not all, of these modes of interrelation also serve the demands of maternity and many female job ghettos. In many cases, though, femininity is not particularly useful in maternity or employment. Both mothers and workers often need to be strong, independent, and effectual in order to do their jobs well. Thus femininity, as a role, is best suited to satisfying a masculine vision of heterosexual attractiveness.

Body postures and demeanors which communicate subordinate status and vulnerability to trespass through a message of "no threat" make people appear to be feminine. They demonstrate subordination through a minimizing of spatial use: People appear feminine when they keep their arms closer to their bodies, their legs closer together, and their torsos and heads less vertical than do masculine-looking individuals. People also look feminine when they point their toes inward and use their hands in small or childlike gestures. Other people also tend to stand closer to people they see as feminine, often invading their personal space, while people who make frequent appeasement gestures, such as smiling, also give the appearance of femininity. Perhaps as an outgrowth of a subordinate status and the need to avoid conflict with more socially powerful people, women tend to excel over men at the ability to correctly interpret, and effectively display, nonverbal communication cues.[5]

---

[3]Nancy Chodorow, *The Reproduction of Mothering: Psychoanalysis and the Sociology of Gender* (Berkeley: U of California P, 1978), p. 134.

[4]Jon K. Meyer and John E. Hoopes, "The Gender Dysphoria Syndromes: A Position Statement on So-Called 'Transsexualism,'" *Plastic and Reconstructive Surgery* 54 (Oct. 1974), pp. 444–51.

[5]Erving Goffman, *Gender Advertisements* (New York: Harper, 1976); Judith A. Hall, *Non-Verbal Sex Differences: Communication Accuracy and Expressive Style* (Baltimore: Johns Hopkins UP, 1984); Nancy M. Henley, *Body Politics: Power, Sex and Non-Verbal Communication* (Englewood Cliffs, N.J.: Prentice, 1979); Marianne Wex, *"Let's Take Back Our Space": "Female" and "Male" Body Language as a Result of Patriarchal Structures* (Berlin: Frauenliteraturverlag Hermine Fees, 1979).

Rearing children is work typically done by women, but not always.

Speech characterized by inflections, intonations, and phrases that convey nonaggression and subordinate status also make a speaker appear more feminine. Subordinate speakers who use more polite expressions and ask more questions in conversation seem more feminine. Speech characterized by sounds of higher frequencies are often interpreted by listeners as feminine, childlike, and ineffectual.[6] Feminine styles of dress likewise display subordinate status through greater restriction of the free movement of the body, greater exposure of the bare skin, and an emphasis on sexual characteristics. The more gender distinct the dress, the more this is the case.

Masculinity, like femininity, can be demonstrated through a wide variety 10 of cues. Pleck has argued that it is commonly expressed in North American society through the attainment of some level of proficiency at some, or all, of the following four main attitudes of masculinity. Persons who display success and high status in their social group, who exhibit "a manly air of toughness, confidence, and self-reliance" and "the aura of aggression, violence, and daring," and who conscientiously avoid anything associated with femininity are seen as exuding masculinity.[7] These requirements reflect the patriarchal ideology that masculinity results from an excess of testosterone, the assumption being that androgens supply a natural impetus toward aggression, which in turn impels males toward achievement and success. This vision of masculinity also reflects the ideological stance that ideal maleness (masculinity) must remain untainted by female (feminine) pollutants.

[6]Karen L. Adams, "Sexism and the English Language: The Linguistic Implications of Being a Woman," in *Women: A Feminist Perspective*, 3rd ed., ed. Jo Freeman (Palo Alto, Calif.: Mayfield, 1984), pp. 478–91; Hall, pp. 37, 130–37.

[7]Joseph H. Pleck, *The Myth of Masculinity* (Cambridge, Mass.: MIT P, 1981), p. 139.

Masculinity, then, requires of its actors that they organize themselves and their society in a hierarchical manner so as to be able to explicitly quantify the achievement of success. The achievement of high status in one's social group requires competitive and aggressive behavior from those who wish to obtain it. Competition which is motivated by a goal of individual achievement, or egoistic dominance, also requires of its participants a degree of emotional insensitivity to feelings of hurt and loss in defeated others, and a measure of emotional insularity to protect oneself from becoming vulnerable to manipulation by others. Such values lead those who subscribe to them to view feminine persons as "born losers" and to strive to eliminate any similarities to feminine people from their own personalities. In patriarchally organized societies, masculine values become the ideological structure of the society as a whole. Masculinity thus becomes "innately" valuable and femininity serves a contrapuntal function to delineate and magnify the hierarchical dominance of masculinity.

Body postures, speech patterns, and styles of dress which demonstrate and support the assumption of dominance and authority convey an impression of masculinity. Typical masculine body postures tend to be expansive and aggressive. People who hold their arms and hands in positions away from their bodies, and who stand, sit, or lie with their legs apart — thus maximizing the amount of space that they physically occupy — appear most physically masculine. Persons who communicate an air of authority or a readiness for aggression by standing erect and moving forcefully also tend to appear more masculine. Movements that are abrupt and stiff, communicating force and threat rather than flexibility and cooperation, make an actor look masculine. Masculinity can also be conveyed by stern or serious facial expressions that suggest minimal receptivity to the influence of others, a characteristic which is an important element in the attainment and maintenance of egoistic dominance.[8]

Speech and dress which likewise demonstrate or claim superior status are also seen as characteristically masculine behavior patterns. Masculine speech patterns display a tendency toward expansiveness similar to that found in masculine body postures. People who attempt to control the direction of conversations seem more masculine. Those who tend to speak more loudly, use less polite and more assertive forms, and tend to interrupt the conversations of others more often also communicate masculinity to others. Styles of dress which emphasize the size of upper body musculature, allow freedom of movement, and encourage an illusion of physical power and a look of easy physicality all suggest masculinity. Such appearances of strength and readiness to action serve to create or enhance an aura of aggressiveness and intimidation central to an appearance of masculinity. Expansive postures and gestures combine with these qualities to insinuate that a position of secure dominance is a masculine one.

Gender role characteristics reflect the ideological contentions underlying the dominant gender schema in North American society. That schema leads

[8]Goffman; Hall; Henley; Wex.

us to believe that female and male behaviors are the result of socially directed hormonal instructions which specify that females will want to have children and will therefore find themselves relatively helpless and dependent on males for support and protection. The schema claims that males are innately aggressive and competitive and therefore will dominate over females. The social hegemony of this ideology ensures that we are all raised to practice gender roles which will confirm this vision of the nature of the sexes. Fortunately, our training to gender roles is neither complete nor uniform. As a result, it is possible to point to multitudinous exceptions to, and variations on, these themes. Biological evidence is equivocal about the source of gender roles; psychological androgyny is a widely accepted concept. It seems most likely that gender roles are the result of systematic power imbalances based on gender discrimination.[9]

READING THE TEXT

1. List the characteristics that Devor describes as being traditional conceptions of "masculinity" and "femininity" (para. 1).

2. What relationship does Devor see between characteristics that are considered masculine and feminine?

3. How does Devor explain the cultural belief in the "superiority" (para. 5) of males?

4. How, in Devor's view, do speech and dress communicate gender roles?

READING THE SIGNS

1. In small same-sex groups, brainstorm lists of traits that you consider to be masculine and feminine, and then have each group write its list on the board. Compare the lists produced by male and female groups. What patterns of differences or similarities do you see? To what extent do the traits presume a heterosexual orientation? How do you account for your results?

2. Study the speech patterns, styles of dress, and other nonverbal cues communicated by your friends during a social occasion, such as a party, trying not to reveal that you are observing them for an assignment. Then write an essay in which you analyze these cues used by your friends. To what extent do your friends enact the traditional gender codes Devor describes?

3. **CONNECTING TEXTS** Study a popular magazine such as *Vanity Fair, Rolling Stone,* or *Maxim* for advertisements depicting men and women interacting with each other. Then write an essay in which you interpret the body postures of the models, using Devor's selection as your framework for analysis. How do males and females typically stand? To what extent

[9]Howard, Blumstein, and Schwartz; Kollock, Blumstein, and Schwartz.

do the models enact stereotypically masculine or feminine stances? To develop your essay, consult Steve Craig's "Men's Men and Women's Women" (p. 187).

4. **CONNECTING TEXTS** Devor argues that female fashion traditionally has restricted body movement while male styles of dress commonly allow freedom of movement. In class, discuss whether this claim is still true today, being sure to consider a range of clothing types (such as athletic wear, corporate dress, party fashion, and so forth). To develop your ideas, consult Mariah Burton Nelson's "I Won. I'm Sorry." (p. 569).

DEBORAH BLUM

The Gender Blur: Where Does Biology End and Society Take Over?

There's an old argument over whether nature or nurture is more important in determining human behavior. Nowhere is this argument more intense than in gender studies, where proponents of the social construction of gender identities are currently exploring the many ways in which our upbringing shapes our behavior. But after watching her two-year-old son emphatically choose to play only with carnivorous dinosaur toys and disdainfully reject the "wimpy" vegetarian variety, Deborah Blum decided that nurture couldn't be all that there was to it. Exploring the role of biology in the determination of human behavior, Blum argues that both nature and nurture have to be taken into account if we are to understand gender differences. A Pulitzer Prize–winning professor of journalism at the University of Wisconsin at Madison, Blum is the author of several books, including *Sex on the Brain: The Biological Differences between Men and Women* (1997), *Ghost Hunters: William James and the Search for Scientific Proof of Life after Death* (2006), and *The Prisoner's Handbook: Murder and the Birth of Forensic Medicine in Jazz Age New York* (2010).

I was raised in one of those university-based, liberal elite families that politicians like to ridicule. In my childhood, every human being—regardless of gender—was exactly alike under the skin, and I mean exactly, barring his or her different opportunities. My parents wasted no opportunity to bring this point home. One Christmas, I received a Barbie doll and a softball glove. Another brought a green enamel stove, which baked tiny cakes by the heat of a lightbulb, and also a set of steel-tipped darts and competition-quality dartboard. Did I mention the year of the chemistry set and the ballerina doll?

It wasn't until I became a parent—I should say, a parent of two boys—that I realized I had been fed a line and swallowed it like a sucker (barring the part about opportunities, which I still believe). This dawned on me during my older son's dinosaur phase, which began when he was about two-and-a-half. Oh, he loved dinosaurs, all right, but only the blood-swilling carnivores. Plant-eaters were wimps and losers, and he refused to wear a T-shirt marred by a picture of a stegosaur. I looked down at him one day, as he was snarling around my feet and doing his toddler best to gnaw off my right leg, and I thought: This goes a lot deeper than culture.

Raising children tends to bring on this kind of politically incorrect reaction. Another friend came to the same conclusion watching a son determinedly bite his breakfast toast into the shape of a pistol he hoped would blow away—or at least terrify—his younger brother. Once you get past the guilt part—Did I do this? Should I have bought him that plastic allosaur with the oversized teeth?—such revelations can lead you to consider the far more interesting field of gender biology, where the questions take a different shape: Does love of carnage begin in culture or genetics, and which drives which? Do the gender roles of our culture reflect an underlying biology, and, in turn, does the way we behave influence that biology?

The point I'm leading up to—through the example of my son's innocent love of predatory dinosaurs—is actually one of the most straightforward in this debate. One of the reasons we're so fascinated by childhood behaviors is that, as the old saying goes, the child becomes the man (or woman, of course). Most girls don't spend their preschool years snarling around the house and pretending to chew off their companion's legs. And they—mostly—don't grow up to be as aggressive as men. Do the ways that we amplify those early differences in childhood shape the adults we become? Absolutely. But it's worth exploring the starting place—the faint signal that somehow gets amplified.

"There's plenty of room in society to influence sex differences," says 5 Marc Breedlove, a behavioral endocrinologist at the University of California at Berkeley and a pioneer in defining how hormones can help build sexually different nervous systems. "Yes, we're born with predispositions, but it's society that amplifies them, exaggerates them. I believe that—except for the sex differences in aggression. Those [differences] are too massive to be explained simply by society."

Aggression does allow a straightforward look at the issue. Consider the following statistics: Crime reports in both the United States and Europe record between ten and fifteen robberies committed by men for every one by a woman. At one point, people argued that this was explained by size difference. Women weren't big enough to intimidate, but that would change, they predicted, with the availability of compact weapons. But just as little girls don't routinely make weapons out of toast, women—even criminal ones—don't seem drawn to weaponry in the same way that men are. Almost twice as many male thieves and robbers use guns as their female counterparts do.

Or you can look at more personal crimes: domestic partner murders. Three-fourths of men use guns in those killings; 50 percent of women do. Here's more from the domestic front: In conflicts in which a woman killed a man, he tended to be the one who had started the fight — in 51.8 percent of the cases, to be exact. When the man was the killer, he again was the likely first aggressor, and by an even more dramatic margin. In fights in which women died, they had started the argument only 12.5 percent of the time.

Enough. You can parade endless similar statistics but the point is this: Males are more aggressive, not just among humans but among almost all species on earth. Male chimpanzees, for instance, declare war on neighboring troops, and one of their strategies is a warning strike: They kill females and infants to terrorize and intimidate. In terms of simple, reproductive genetics, it's an advantage of males to be aggressive: You can muscle your way into dominance, winning more sexual encounters, more offspring, more genetic future. For the female — especially in a species like ours, with time for just one successful pregnancy a year — what's the genetic advantage in brawling?

Thus the issue becomes not whether there is a biologically influenced sex difference in aggression — the answer being a solid, technical "You betcha" — but rather how rigid that difference is. The best science, in my opinion, tends to align with basic common sense. We all know that there are extraordinarily gentle men and murderous women. Sex differences are always generalizations: they refer to a behavior, with some evolutionary rationale behind it. They never define, entirely, an individual. And that fact alone should tell us that there's always — even in the most biologically dominated traits — some flexibility, an instinctive ability to respond, for better and worse, to the world around us.

This is true even with physical characteristics that we've often assumed ₁₀ are nailed down by genetics. Scientists now believe height, for instance, is only about 90 percent heritable. A person's genes might code for a six-foot-tall body, but malnutrition could literally cut that short. And there's also some evidence, in girls anyway, that children with stressful childhoods tend to become shorter adults. So while some factors are predetermined, there's evidence that the prototypical male/female body design can be readily altered.

It's a given that humans, like most other species — bananas, spiders, sharks, ducks, any rabbit you pull out of a hat — rely on two sexes for reproduction. So basic is that requirement that we have chromosomes whose primary purpose is to deliver the genes that order up a male or a female. All other chromosomes are numbered, but we label the sex chromosomes with the letters X and Y. We get one each from our mother and our father, and the basic combinations are these: XX makes female, XY makes male.

There are two important — and little known — points about these chromosomal matches. One is that even with this apparently precise system, there's nothing precise—or guaranteed—about the physical construction of male and female. The other point makes that possible. It appears that sex doesn't matter in the early stages of embryonic development. We are unisex at the point of conception.

If you examine an embryo at about six weeks, you see that it has the ability to develop in either direction. The fledgling embryo has two sets of ducts—Wolffian for male, Muellerian for female—an either/or structure, held in readiness for further development. If testosterone and other androgens are released by hormone-producing cells, then the Wolffian ducts develop into the channel that connects penis to testes, and the female ducts wither away.

Without testosterone, the embryo takes on a female form; the male ducts vanish and the Muellerian ducts expand into oviducts, uterus, and vagina. In other words, in humans, anyways (the opposite is true in birds), the female is the default sex. Back in the 1950s, the famed biologist Alfred Jost showed that if you castrate a male rabbit fetus, choking off testosterone, you produce a completely feminized rabbit.

We don't do these experiments in humans—for obvious reasons—but 15 there are naturally occurring instances that prove the same point. For instance: In the fetal testes are a group of cells, called Leydig cells, that make testosterone. In rare cases, the fetus doesn't make enough of these cells (a defect known as Leydig cell hypoplasia). In this circumstance we see the limited power of the XY chromosome. These boys have the right chromosomes and the right genes to be boys; they just don't grow a penis. Obstetricians and parents often think they see a baby girl, and these children are routinely raised as daughters. Usually, the "mistake" is caught about the time of puberty, when menstruation doesn't start. A doctor's examination shows the child to be internally male; there are usually small testes, often tucked within the abdomen. As the researchers put it, if the condition had been known from the beginning, "the sisters would have been born as brothers."

Just to emphasize how tricky all this body-building can get, there's a peculiar genetic defect that seems to be clustered by heredity in a small group of villages in the Dominican Republic. The result of the defect is a failure to produce an enzyme that concentrates testosterone, specifically for building the genitals. One obscure little enzyme only, but here's what happens without it: You get a boy with undescended testes and a penis so short and stubby that it resembles an oversized clitoris.

In the mountain villages of this Caribbean nation, people are used to it. The children are usually raised as "conditional" girls. At puberty, the secondary tide of androgens rises and is apparently enough to finish the construction project. The scrotum suddenly descends, the phallus grows, and the child develops a distinctly male body—narrow hips, muscular build, and even slight beard growth. At that point, the family shifts the child over from daughter to son. The dresses are thrown out. He begins to wear male clothes and starts dating girls. People in the Dominican Republic are so familiar with this condition that there's a colloquial name for it: *guevedoces*, meaning "eggs (or testes) at twelve."

It's the comfort level with this slip-slide of sexual identity that's so remarkable and, I imagine, so comforting to the children involved. I'm positive that the sexual transition of these children is less traumatic than the abrupt awareness of the "sisters who would have been brothers." There's a message of tolerance there, well worth repeating, and there are some other key lessons, too.

These defects are rare and don't alter the basic male-female division of our species. They do emphasize how fragile those divisions can be. Biology allows flexibility, room to change, to vary and grow. With that comes room for error as well. That it's possible to live with these genetic defects, that they don't merely kill us off, is a reminder that we, male and female alike, exist on a continuum of biological possibilities that can overlap and sustain either sex.

Marc Breedlove points out that the most difficult task may be separating how the brain responds to hormones from how the brain responds to the results of hormones. Which brings us back, briefly, below the belt: In this context, the penis is just a result, the product of androgens at work before birth. "And after birth," says Breedlove, "virtually everyone who interacts with that individual will note that he has a penis, and will, in many instances, behave differently than if the individual was a female."

Do the ways that we amplify physical and behavioral differences in childhood shape who we become as adults? Absolutely. But to understand that, you have to understand the differences themselves — their beginning and the very real biochemistry that may lie behind them.

Here is a good place to focus on testosterone — a hormone that is both well-studied and generally underrated. First, however, I want to acknowledge that there are many other hormones and neurotransmitters that appear to influence behavior. Preliminary work shows that fetal boys are a little more active than fetal girls. It's pretty difficult to argue socialization at that point. There's a strong suspicion that testosterone may create the difference.

And there are a couple of relevant animal models to emphasize the point. Back in the 1960s, Robert Goy, a psychologist at the University of Wisconsin at Madison, first documented that young male monkeys play much more roughly than young females. Goy went on to show that if you manipulate testosterone level — raising it in females, damping it down in males — you can reverse those effects, creating sweet little male monkeys and rowdy young females.

Is testosterone the only factor at work here? I don't think so. But clearly we can argue a strong influence, and, interestingly, studies have found that girls with congenital adrenal hypoplasia — who run high in testosterone — tend to be far more fascinated by trucks and toy weaponry than most little girls are. They lean toward rough-and-tumble play, too. As it turns out, the strongest influence on this "abnormal" behavior is not parental disapproval, but the company of other little girls, who tone them down and direct them toward more routine girl games.

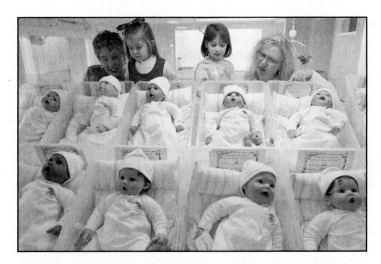

Girls and moms check out an American Girl doll fashion show in Staten Island, New York.

And that reinforces an early point: If there is indeed a biology to sex dif- 25 ferences, we amplify it. At some point — when it is still up for debate — we gain a sense of our gender, and with it a sense of "gender-appropriate" behavior.

Some scientists argue for some evidence of gender awareness in infancy, perhaps by the age of twelve months. The consensus seems to be that full-blown "I'm a girl" or "I'm a boy" instincts arrive between the ages of two and three. Research shows that if a family operates in a very traditional, Beaver Cleaver kind of environment, filled with awareness of and association with "proper" gender behaviors, the "boys do trucks, girls do dolls" attitude seems to come very early. If a child grows up in a less traditional family, with an emphasis on partnership and sharing — "We all do the dishes, Joshua" — children maintain a more flexible sense of gender roles until about age six.

In this period, too, relationships between boys and girls tend to fall into remarkably strict lines. Interviews with children find that three-year-olds say that about half their friendships are with the opposite sex. By the age of five, that drops to 20 percent. By seven, almost no boys or girls have, or will admit to having, best friends of the opposite sex. They still hang out on the same playground, play on the same soccer teams. They may be friendly, but the real friendships tend to be boy-to-boy or girl-to-girl.

There's some interesting science that suggests that the space between boys and girls is a normal part of development; there are periods during which children may thrive and learn from hanging out with peers of the same sex. Do we, as parents, as a culture at large, reinforce such separations? Is the pope Catholic? One of my favorite studies looked at little boys who asked for toys. If they asked for a heavily armed action figure, they got the soldier about 70 percent of the time. If they asked for a "girl" toy, like a baby doll or a Barbie, their parents purchased it maybe 40 percent of the time. Name a child who won't figure out how to work *that* system.

How does all this fit together — toys and testosterone, biology and behavior, the development of the child into the adult, the way that men and women relate to one another?

Let me make a cautious statement about testosterone: It not only has 30 some body-building functions, it influences some behaviors as well. Let's make that a little less cautious: These behaviors include rowdy play, sex drive, competitiveness, and an in-your-face attitude. Males tend to have a higher baseline of testosterone than females — in our species, about seven to ten times as much — and therefore you would predict (correctly, I think) that all of those behaviors would be more generally found in men than in women.

But testosterone is also one of my favorite examples of how responsive biology is, how attuned it is to the way we live our lives. Testosterone, it turns out, rises in response to competition and threat. In the days of our ancestors, this might have been hand-to-hand combat or high-risk hunting endeavors. Today, scientists have measured testosterone rise in athletes preparing for a game, in chess players awaiting a match, in spectators following a soccer competition.

If a person — or even just a person's favored team — wins, testosterone continues to rise. It falls with a loss. (This also makes sense in an evolutionary perspective. If one was being clobbered with a club, it would be extremely unhelpful to have a hormone urging one to battle on.) Testosterone also rises in the competitive world of dating, settles down with a stable and supportive relationship, climbs again if the relationship starts to falter.

It's been known for years that men in high-stress professions — say, police work or corporate law — have higher testosterone levels than men in the ministry. It turns out that women in the same kind of strong-attitude professions have higher testosterone than women who choose to stay home. What I like about this is the chicken-or-egg aspect. If you argue that testosterone influenced the behavior of those women, which came first? Did they have high testosterone and choose the law? Or did they choose the law, and the competitive environment ratcheted them up on the androgen scale? Or could both be at work?

And, returning to children for a moment, there's an ongoing study by Pennsylvania researchers, tracking that question in adolescent girls, who are being encouraged by their parents to engage in competitive activities that were once for boys only. As they do so, the researchers are monitoring, regularly, two hormones: testosterone and cortisol, a stress hormone. Will these hormones rise in response to this new, more traditionally male environment? What if more girls choose the competitive path; more boys choose the other? Will female testosterone levels rise, male levels fall? Will that wonderful, unpredictable, flexible biology that we've been given allow a shift, so that one day, we will literally be far more alike?

We may not have answers to all those questions, but we can ask them, 35 and we can expect that the answers will come someday, because science clearly shows us that such possibilities exist. In this most important sense, sex differences offer us a paradox. It is only through exploring and understanding what makes us different that we can begin to understand what binds us together.

READING THE TEXT

1. What effect do Blum's opening personal anecdotes have on the persuasiveness of her argument?

2. What evidence does Blum offer to support her contention that males are naturally more aggressive than females?

3. How does testosterone affect human behavior, according to Blum's research?

4. In Blum's view, how do the cultural choices that humans make, such as engaging in sports or other competitive activities, affect hormone balances?

READING THE SIGNS

1. In your journal, reflect on the way your upbringing shaped your sense of appropriate gender behavior.

2. **CONNECTING TEXTS** Blum's selection challenges the common cultural studies position that gender behavior is socially constructed. Write an essay in which you defend, qualify, or reject Blum's point of view. To develop your ideas, consult Aaron Devor's "Gender Role Behaviors and Attitudes" (p. 672), Kevin Jennings's "American Dreams" (p. 686), and Andrew Sullivan's "My Big Fat Straight Wedding" (p. 691).

3. Write an essay describing how you would raise a boy to counteract his tendencies to aggressive behavior.

4. Visit the library and investigate recent research on the possible genetic basis for homosexuality. Then write an essay in which you extend Blum's argument for the biological basis of gendered behavior to sexual orientation.

KEVIN JENNINGS
American Dreams

When Ellen DeGeneres became the first television star to come out of the closet on prime-time TV, gay men and lesbians around the country celebrated what appeared to be a major step forward for one of America's most marginalized communities. But the firestorm of protest that also attended Ellen's coming-out equally demonstrated just how far homosexuals have to go before winning full acceptance into American society. In this personal narrative (first published in 1994) of what it means to grow up gay in America, Kevin Jennings reveals the torment endured by a child forced to conceal his differ-ence from everyone around him, especially his own parents. With years of self-denial and one suicide attempt behind him, Jennings shows how he eventually came to accept himself as he is and in so doing achieved his own version of the American dream. Jennings is founder of the Gay, Lesbian, and Straight Education Network (GLSEN) and author (with Pat Shapiro) of *Always My Child: A Parent's Guide to Understanding Your Gay, Lesbian, Bisexual, Transgendered, or Ques-tioning Son or Daughter* (2003). His most recent book is *Mama's Boy, Preacher's Son: A Memoir* (2006). He is the assistant deputy secretary for the Office of Safe and Drug-Free Schools at the U.S. Department of Education.

When I was little, I honestly thought I would grow up to be the president. After all, I lived in a land of opportunity where anyone, with enough determination and hard work, could aspire to the highest office in the land. I planned to live out the American Dream.

I realized, however, that something was amiss from an early age. I grew up in the rural community of Lewisville, North Carolina, just outside the city of Winston-Salem. As you might guess from the city's name, Winston-Salem, Winston-Salem makes its living from the tobacco industry: It was cigarettes that propelled local conglomerate RJR-Nabisco to its status as one of the world's largest multinational corporations. Somehow this rising tide of pros-perity never lapped at our doors, and the Jennings family was a bitter family indeed. Poor whites descended from Confederate veterans, we eagerly sought out scapegoats for our inexplicable failure to "make it" in the land of opportu-nity. My uncles and cousins joined the Ku Klux Klan, while my father, a fun-damentalist minister, used religion to excuse his prejudices — against blacks, against Jews, against Catholics, against Yankees, against Communists and lib-erals (basically the same thing, as far as he was concerned), and, of course, against gays. Somehow the golden rule of "Do unto others as you would have them do unto you" never made it into his gospel. Instead, I remember church services filled with outbursts of paranoia, as we were warned about the evils of those whom we (incorrectly) held responsible for our very real oppression. I grew up believing that there was a Communist plot undermining our nation, a Jewish conspiracy controlling the banks and the media, and that black men — whom I unselfconsciously referred to as "niggers" — spent their days plotting to rape white women. In case this seems like a history lesson on the Stone Age, please consider that I was born in 1963 and graduated from high school in 1981. Hardly the ancient past!

My father's profession as a traveling minister never left much money for luxuries like college tuition. Nevertheless, my mother was determined that I, her last chance, was going to make good on the Dream that had been denied to her and to my four older siblings — that one of her children would be the first member of our extended family ever to go to college. Not that it was going to be easy: my father died when I was eight, and my mother went to work at McDonald's (the only job she could get with her limited credentials). Every penny was watched carefully; dinner was often leftover quarter-pounders that she didn't have to pay for. I'm the only person I know who sees the Golden Arches, takes a bite, and thinks, "Mmm, just like Mom used to make!"

Throughout high school, I was determined to make it, determined to show my mother — and myself — that the American Dream really could come true.

Seniors march for gay rights.

I worked hard and got ahead, earning a scholarship to Harvard after I had remade myself into the image of what I was told a successful person was like. Little did I realize at that point the price I was paying to fit in.

The first thing to go was any sign of my Southern heritage. As I came   5 into contact with mainstream America, through high school "gifted and talented" programs and, later, at college in Massachusetts, I began to realize that we Southerners were different. Our home-cooked meals — grits, turnip greens, red-eye gravy — never seemed to show up in frozen dinners, and if a character on television spoke with a Southern accent, that immediately identified him or her as stupid or as comic relief. As the lesbian writer Blanche Boyd put it:

> When television programs appeared, a dreadful truth came clear to me: Southerners were not normal people. We did not sound like normal people . . . [and] what we chose to talk about seemed peculiarly different also. I began to realize we were hicks. Television took away my faith in my surroundings. I didn't want to be a hick. I decided to go North, where people talked fast, walked fast, and acted cool. I practiced talking like the people on television. . . . I became desperate to leave the South.

Like Blanche Boyd, I deliberately erased my accent and aped the false monotone of television newscasters. I never invited college friends home to North Carolina for fear they might meet my family and realize they were worthless, ignorant hicks — which is how I'd come to view those whom I loved. I applied to colleges on the sole criterion that they not be in the South. I ran as far from Lewisville, North Carolina, as I could.

But there were some things about myself I could not escape from or change, no matter how hard I tried — among them the fact that I am gay.

I had always known I was gay, even before I had heard the word or knew what it meant. I remember that at age six or seven, the "adult" magazines that so fascinated my older brothers simply didn't interest me at all, and I somehow knew that I'd better hide this feeling from them. As I grew older and began to understand what my feelings meant, I recoiled in horror from myself. After all, my religious upbringing as a Southern Baptist had taught me that gay people were twisted perverts destined for a lifetime of eternal damnation.

Being as set as I was on achieving the American Dream, I was not about to accept the fact that I was gay. Here is where I paid the heaviest price for my Dream. I pursued what I thought was "normal" with a vengeance in high school, determined that, if the spirit was weak, the flesh would be more willing at the prospect of heterosexuality. I dated every girl I could literally get my hands on, earning a well-deserved reputation as a jerk who tried to see how far he could get on the first date. I attacked anyone who suggested that gay people might be entitled to some rights, too, and was the biggest teller of fag jokes at Radford High. But what I really hated was myself, and this I couldn't escape from, no matter how drunk or stoned I got, which I was doing on an almost daily basis by senior year.

That was also the year I fell in love for the first time, with another boy in my class. It turned out he was gay, too, and we made love one night in late May. I woke up the next morning and realized that it was true — I really was a fag after all. I spent that day trying to figure out how I was going to live the American Dream, which seemed impossible if I was homosexual. By nightfall I decided it *was* impossible, and without my Dream I couldn't see a reason why I'd want to be alive at all. I went to my family's medicine cabinet, took the new bottle of aspirin out, and proceeded to wash down 140 pills with a glass of gin. I remember the exact number — 140 — because I figured I could only get down about ten at one swallow, so I carefully counted out fourteen little stacks before I began. Thanks to a friend who got to me in time, I didn't die that night. My story has a happy ending — but a lot of them don't. Those moments of desperation helped me understand why one out of every three gay teens tries to commit suicide.

At Harvard, the most important lessons I learned had little to do with Latin   10
American or European history, which were my majors. Instead, I learned the importance of taking control of my own destiny. I met a great professor who taught me that as long as I stayed in the closet, I was accepting the idea that there was something wrong with me, something that I needed to hide. After all, as my favorite bisexual, Eleanor Roosevelt, once said, "No one can make you feel inferior without your consent." By staying closeted, I was consenting to my own inferiority. I realized that for years, I had let a Dream — a beautiful, seductive, but ultimately false Dream — rule my life. I had agreed to pay its price, which was the rejection of my family, my culture, and eventually myself. I came to understand that the costs of the Dream far outweighed its rewards. I learned that true freedom would be mine only when I was able to make my own decisions about what I wanted out of life instead of accepting those thrust upon me by the Dream. Since I made that realization, I have followed my own path instead of the one I had been taught was "right" all my life.

Once I started down this new path, I began to make some discoveries about the society in which I was raised, and about its notions of right and wrong. I began to ask many questions, and the answers to these questions were not always pleasant. Why, for example, did my mother always earn less than men who did the same exact work? Why did I learn as a child that to cheat someone was to "Jew" them? Why was my brother ostracized when he fell in love with and later married a black woman? Why did everyone in my family work so hard and yet have so little? I realized that these inequalities were part of the game, the rules of which were such that gays, blacks, poor people, women, and many others would always lose to the wealthy white heterosexual Christian men who have won the Presidency forty-two out of forty-two times. Those odds — 100 percent — are pretty good ones to bet on. No, I discovered that true freedom could not be achieved by a Dream that calls on us to give up who we are in order to fit in and become "worthy" of power. Holding power means little if women have to become masculine "iron ladies" to get it, if Jews have to "Americanize" their names, if blacks have to learn to speak so-called Standard English (though we never acknowl-edge *whose* standard it is), or if gays and lesbians have to hide what every-one else gets to celebrate — the loves of their lives.

Real freedom will be ours when the people around us — and when we ourselves — accept that we, too, are "real" Americans, and that we shouldn't have to change to meet anyone else's standards. In 1924, at age twenty-two, the gay African American poet Langston Hughes said it best, in his poem "I, Too":

> Tomorrow,
> I'll be at the table
> When company comes.
> Nobody'll dare
> Say to me,
> "Eat in the kitchen,"
> Then.
> Besides,
> They'll see how beautiful I am
> And be ashamed —
> I, too, am America.

By coming out as a gay man and demanding my freedom, I realize that I have done the most American thing of all. And while I have come a long way since the days when I dreamed of living in the White House, I have discov-ered that what I'm fighting for now is the very thing I thought I'd be fighting for if I ever became President — "liberty and justice for all."

READING THE TEXT

1. According to Jennings, how did his Southern upbringing influence his goals for the future?

2. Why did Jennings feel he had to eschew his Southern heritage?

3. In what ways did Jennings deny to himself his sexual orientation, and why did he do so?

4. In your own words, trace the evolution of Jennings's understanding of the American dream as he grew up.

5. What is the relationship between the excerpt from Langston Hughes's "I, Too" and Jennings's story?

READING THE SIGNS

1. In your journal, write your own account of how you responded to norma-tive gender codes as a high school student. To what extent did you feel pressure to conform or to renounce traditional expectations — or to do both?

2. Jennings describes his early attempts to deny his sexual orientation. In class, discuss how other minority or underprivileged groups — ethnic

minorities, women, the disabled — sometimes try to erase their identity. What social and cultural forces motivate such self-denial? Use the discussion as a springboard for an essay in which you explore why one might be motivated to do so.

3. In class, brainstorm two lists: films or TV shows that reinforce heterosexuality as normative and those that present homosexuality positively. Then compare your lists. What conclusions do you draw about popular culture's influence on American gender codes?

4. **CONNECTING TEXTS**   Compare and contrast Jennings's arrival at a confident sense of identity with that of Melissa Algranati ("Being an Other," p. 667). How do you explain any differences you observe?

ANDREW SULLIVAN
My Big Fat Straight Wedding

"What if gays were straight?" Andrew Sullivan asks in this essay on gay marriage that first appeared in *The Atlantic* in 2008. Though the question sounds odd, it is at the heart of the legal battle over the right of homosexuals to marry. The key point lies in treating gays as individuals rather than as people engaged in certain activities, and once that shift is made, "the question becomes a matter of how we treat a minority with an involuntary, defining characteristic along the lines of gender or race" — which is to say, like any other American citizen. A senior editor for *The New Republic* and columnist at *The Atlantic*, Andrew Sullivan is the author of numerous books, including *Same Sex Marriage: Pro and Con* (2004) and *Virtually Normal* (1996).

What if gays were straight?

The question is absurd — gays are defined as not straight, right? — yet increasingly central to the debate over civil-marriage rights. Here is how California's Supreme Court put it in a key passage in its now-famous May 15 ruling that gay couples in California must be granted the right to marry, with no qualifications or euphemisms:

> These core substantive rights include, most fundamentally, the opportunity of an individual to establish — with the person with whom the individual has chosen to share his or her life — an *officially recognized and protected family* possessing mutual rights and responsibilities and entitled to the same respect and dignity accorded a union traditionally designated as marriage.

What's notable here is the starting point of the discussion: an "individual." The individual citizen posited by the court is defined as prior to his or her sexual orientation. He or she exists as a person before he or she exists as straight or gay. And the right under discussion is defined as "the opportunity of an individual" to choose another "person" to "establish a family" in which reproduction and children are not necessary. And so the distinction between gay and straight is essentially abolished. For all the debate about the law in this decision, the debate about the terms under discussion has been close to nonexistent. And yet in many ways, these terms are at the core of the decision, and are the reason why it is such a watershed. The ruling, and the language it uses, represents the removal of the premise of the last generation in favor of a premise accepted as a given by the next.

The premise used to be that homosexuality was an activity, that gays were people who chose to behave badly; or, if they weren't choosing to behave badly, were nonetheless suffering from a form of sickness or, in the words of the Vatican, an "objective disorder." And so the question of whether to permit the acts and activities of such disordered individuals was a legitimate area of legislation and regulation. But when gays are seen as the same as straights — as individuals; as normal, well-adjusted, human individuals — the argument changes altogether. The question becomes a matter of how we treat a minority with an involuntary, defining characteristic along the lines of gender or race. And when a generation came of age that did not merely grasp this intellectually, but knew it from their own lives and friends and family members, then the logic for full equality became irresistible.

This transformation in understanding happened organically. It began with 5 the sexual revolution in the 1970s, and then came crashing into countless previously unaware families, as their sons and uncles and fathers died in vast numbers from AIDS in the 1980s and 1990s. It emerged as younger generations came out earlier and earlier, and as their peers came to see gay people as fellows and siblings, rather than as denizens of some distant and alien subculture. It happened as lesbian couples became parents and as gay soldiers challenged the discrimination against them. And it percolated up through the popular culture — from *Will & Grace* and *Ellen* to almost every reality show since *The Real World*.

What California's court did, then, was not to recognize a new right to same-sex marriage. It was to acknowledge an emergent cultural consensus. And once that consensus had been accepted, the denial of the right to marry became, for many, a constitutional outrage. The right to marry, after all, is, as the court put it, "one of the basic, inalienable civil rights guaranteed to an individual." Its denial was necessarily an outrage — and not merely an anomaly — because the right to marry has such deep and inalienable status in American constitutional law.

The political theorist Hannah Arendt, addressing the debate over miscegenation laws during the civil-rights movement of the 1950s, put it clearly enough:

The right to marry whoever one wishes is an elementary human right compared to which "the right to attend an integrated school, the right to sit where one pleases on a bus, the right to go into any hotel or recreation area or place of amusement, regardless of one's skin or color or race" are minor indeed. Even political rights, like the right to vote, and nearly all other rights enumerated in the Constitution, are secondary to the inalienable human rights to "life, liberty and the pursuit of happiness" proclaimed in the Declaration of Independence; and to this category the right to home and marriage unquestionably belongs.

Note that Arendt put the right to marry before even the right to vote. And this is how many gay people of the next generation see it. Born into straight families and reared to see homosexuality as a form of difference, not disability, they naturally wonder why they would be excluded from the integral institution of their own families' lives and history. They see this exclusion as unimaginable — as unimaginable as straight people would if they were told that they could not legally marry someone of their choosing. No other institution has an equivalent power to include people in their own familial narrative or civic history as deeply or as powerfully as civil marriage does. And the next generation see themselves as people first and gay second.

Born in a different era, I reached that conclusion through more pain and fear and self-loathing than my twenty-something fellow homosexuals do today. But it was always clear to me nonetheless. It just never fully came home to me until I too got married.

It happened first when we told our families and friends of our intentions. 10 Suddenly, they had a vocabulary to describe and understand our relationship. I was no longer my partner's "friend" or "boyfriend"; I was his fiancé. Suddenly, everyone involved themselves in our love. They asked how I had proposed; they inquired when the wedding would be; my straight friends made jokes about marriage that simply included me as one of them. At that first post-engagement Christmas with my in-laws, I felt something shift. They had always been welcoming and supportive. But now I was family. I felt an end — a sudden, fateful end — to an emotional displacement I had experienced since childhood.

The wedding occurred last August in Massachusetts in front of a small group of family and close friends. And in that group, I suddenly realized, it was the heterosexuals who knew what to do, who guided the gay couple and our friends into the rituals and rites of family. Ours was not, we realized, a different institution, after all, and we were not different kinds of people. In the doing of it, it was the same as my sister's wedding and we were the same as my sister and brother-in-law. The strange, bewildering emotions of the moment, the cake and reception, the distracted children and weeping mothers, the morning's butterflies and the night's drunkenness: this was not a gay marriage; it was a marriage.

And our families instantly and for the first time since our early childhood became not just institutions in which we were included, but institutions that we too owned and perpetuated. My sister spoke of her marriage as if it were interchangeable with my own, and my niece and nephew had no qualms in referring to my husband as their new uncle. The embossed invitations and the floral bouquets and the fear of fluffing our vows: in these tiny, bonding gestures of integration, we all came to see an alienating distinction become a unifying difference.

It was a moment that shifted a sense of our own identity within our psyches and even our souls. Once this happens, the law eventually follows. In California this spring, it did.

READING THE TEXT

1. What popular cultural phenomenon is Sullivan's title alluding to, and how does the allusion affect your response to his essay?

2. What significance does Sullivan see in a California Supreme Court ruling that begins a discussion by referring to "an individual" (para. 3)?

3. In your own words, summarize the historical changes that led to what Sullivan calls "an emergent cultural consensus" that supports same-sex marriage.

4. Often writers start an essay with a personal narrative or anecdote, but Sullivan chooses to lead up to the discussion of his own gay marriage. Why do you think he adopts that organization?

5. How did marriage affect Sullivan's sense of his own identity?

READING THE SIGNS

1. In class, brainstorm different patterns of family structure — two parents, single-parent, extended family, unmarried adults without children, and so forth — thinking about families of friends and acquaintances. Use your discussion as a springboard for an essay in which you propose your own definition of family.

2. Form teams in class and debate Sullivan's claim that there is an "emergent cultural consensus" (para. 6) supporting same-sex marriage. Use the debate as a brainstorming session in preparation for your own essay arguing whether you think Sullivan's reading of the current cultural climate is accurate.

3. Watch *The Kids Are All Right* (2010), and write an essay analyzing the relationship between the two lesbian protagonists, Nic and Jules. To what extent does the film portray their marriage the way Sullivan describes his: "this was not a gay marriage; it was a marriage" (para. 11)?

4. Research the current status of attempts to legalize same-sex marriages, and use your findings as the basis of an argument supporting or opposing such unions.

GLOSSARY

abduction (n.)   A form of logical inference, first proposed by Charles Sanders Peirce, by which one seeks the most likely explanatory hypothesis or cause for a phenomenon. For example, the most likely explanation for the fact that in teen horror movies the first victims of the murderous monster are the cheerleader and the football player is that the majority of the teen audience enjoys the imaginative revenge of seeing snooty high school types done in.

archetype (n.)   A recurring character type or plot pattern found in literature, mythology, and popular culture. Sea monsters like Jonah's whale and Moby Dick are archetypes, as are stories that involve long sea journeys or descents into the underworld.

canon (n.)   Books or works that are considered essential to a literary tradition, as the plays of Shakespeare are part of the canon of English literature.

class (n.)   A group of related objects or people. Those who share the same economic status in a society are said to be of the same social class: for example, working class, middle class, upper class. Members of a social class tend to share the same interests and political viewpoints.

code (n.)   A system of **signs** or values that assigns meanings to the elements that belong to it. Thus, a traffic code defines a red light as a "stop" signal and a green light as a "go," while a fashion code determines whether an article of clothing is stylish. To *decode* a system is to figure out its meanings, as in interpreting the tattooing and body-piercing fads.

commodification (n.)   The transforming of an abstraction or behavior into a product for sale. For example, selling mass-produced hamburgers as an expression of rule-breaking defiance and individualism. See also **hypercapitalism**.

connotation (n.)   The meaning suggested by a word, as opposed to its objective reference, or **denotation**. Thus, the word *flag* might connote (or suggest) feelings of patriotism, while it literally denotes (or refers to) a pennant-like object.

consumption (n.)   The use of products and services, as opposed to their production. A *consumer culture* is one that consumes more than it produces. As a consumer culture, for example, America uses more goods such as computers and stereos than it manufactures, which results in a trade deficit with those *producer cultures* (such as China) with which America trades.

context (n.)   The environment in which a **sign** can be interpreted. In the context of a college classroom, for example, tee shirts, jeans, and sneakers are interpreted as ordinary casual dress. Wearing the same outfit in the context of a job interview at an investment bank would be interpreted as meaning that you're not serious about wanting the job.

cultural studies (n.)   The academic study of ordinary, everyday culture rather than **high culture**. See also **culture**; **culture industry**; **mass culture**; **popular culture**.

culture (n.)   The overall system of values and traditions shared by a group of people. Not exactly synonymous with *society*, which can include numerous cultures within its boundaries, a culture encompasses the worldviews of those who belong to it. Thus, the United States, which is a multicultural society, includes the differing worldviews of people of African, Asian, Native American, and European descent. See also **cultural studies**; **culture industry**; **high culture**; **mass culture**; **popular culture**.

culture industry (n.)   The commercial forces behind the production of **mass culture** or entertainment. See also **cultural studies**; **culture**; **high culture**; **mass culture**; **popular culture**.

denotation (n.)   The particular object or class of objects to which a word refers. Contrast with **connotation**.

discourse (n.)   The words, concepts, and presuppositions that constitute the knowledge and understanding of a particular community, often academic or professional.

dominant culture (n.)   The group within a **multicultural** society whose traditions, values, and beliefs are held to be normative, as the European tradition is the dominant culture in the United States.

Eurocentric (adj.)   Related to a worldview founded on the traditions and history of European culture, usually at the expense of non-European cultures.

function (n.)   The utility of an object, as opposed to its cultural meaning. Spandex or Lycra shorts, for example, have a functional value for cyclists because they're lightweight and aerodynamic. On the other hand, such shorts are a general fashion item for both men and women because of

their cultural meaning, not their function. Many noncyclists wear spandex to project an image of hard-bodied fitness, sexiness, or just plain
trendiness, for instance.

gender (n.)   One's sexual identity and the roles that follow from it, as determined by the norms of one's culture rather than by biology or genetics. The assumption that women should be foremost in the nurturing of
children is a gender norm; the fact that only women can give birth is a
biological phenomenon.

high culture (n.)   The products of the elite arts, including classical music, literature, drama, opera, painting, and sculpture. See also **cultural studies**;
culture; **culture industry**; **mass culture**; **popular culture**.

hypercapitalism (n.)   Introduced by Jeremy Rifkin, hyercapitalism refers to
a society in which the values of capitalism, especially the profit motive
and the commodification of experience, have come to override all other
values.

icon (n.), **iconic** (adj.)   In **semiotics**, a **sign** that visibly resembles its refer-
ent, as a photograph looks like the thing it represents. More broadly, an
icon is someone (often a celebrity) who enjoys a commanding or representative place in popular culture. Michael Jackson and Madonna are
music video icons. Contrast with **symbol**.

ideology (n.)   The beliefs, interests, and values that determine one's interpretations or judgments and that are often associated with one's social
class. For example, in the ideology of modern business, a business is
designed to produce profits, not social benefits.

image (n.)   Literally, a pictorial representation; more generally, the identity
that one projects to others through such things as clothing, grooming,
speech, and behavior.

mass culture (n.)   A subset of **popular culture** that includes the popular
entertainments that are commercially produced for widespread consumption. See also **cultural studies**; **culture**; **culture industry**; **high
culture**.

mass media (n. pl.)   The means of communication, often controlled by the
culture industry, that include newspapers, popular magazines, radio,
television, film, and the Internet.

multiculturalism (n.), **multicultural** (adj.)   In American education, the
movement to incorporate the traditions, history, and beliefs of the United
States' non-European cultures into a traditionally *monocultural*
(or single-culture) curriculum dominated by European thought and history.

mythology (n.)   The overall framework of values and beliefs incorporated
in a given cultural system or worldview. Any given belief within such
a structure — like the belief that "a woman's place is in the home" — is
called a *myth*.

overdetermination (n.)   Originally a term from Freudian psychoanalytic
theory to describe the multiple causes of a psychological affect, overdetermination more generally describes the multiplicity of possible

causes for any social phenomenon. Combined with abductive reasoning, overdetermination is a key element in **semiotic** interpretation. See also **abduction**.

politics (n.)   Essentially, the practice of promoting one's interests in a competitive social environment. Not restricted to electioneering; there may be office politics, classroom politics, academic politics, and sexual politics.

popular culture (n.)   That segment of a **culture** that incorporates the activities of everyday life, including the consumption of consumer goods and the production and enjoyment of mass-produced entertainments. See also **cultural studies**; **culture industry**; **high culture**; **mass culture**.

postmodernism (n.), **postmodern** (adj.)   The worldview behind contemporary literature, art, music, architecture, and philosophy that rejects traditional attempts to make meaning out of human history and experience. For the *postmodern* artist, art does not attempt to create new explanatory myths or **symbols** but rather recycles or repeats existing images, as does the art of Andy Warhol.

proxemics (n.)   The study of human uses of space in interactions with other humans, including body language, facial expression, distance between subjects, gestures, and so on.

semiotics (n.)   In short, the study of **signs**. Synonymous with *semiology*, semiotics is concerned with both the theory and practice of interpreting linguistic, cultural, and behavioral sign systems. One who practices *semiotic analysis* is called a *semiotician* or *semiologist*.

sign (n.)   Anything that bears a meaning. Words, objects, images, and forms of behavior are all signs whose meanings are determined by the particular **codes**, or **systems**, in which they appear.

symbol (n.), **symbolic** (adj.)   A **sign**, according to semiotician Charles Sanders Peirce, whose significance is arbitrary. The meaning of the word *bear*, for example, is arbitrarily determined by those who use it. Contrast with **icon**.

system (n.)   The **code**, or network, within which a **sign** functions and so achieves its meaning through its associational and differential relations with other signs. The English language is a sign system, as is a fashion code.

text (n.)   A complex of **signs**, which may be linguistic, imagistic, behavioral, and/or musical, that can be read or interpreted.

Acknowledgments (continued from page iv)

"The Ables vs. the Binges" (originally titled "Two Families, Compared") from http://verdant.net /families.htm. Reprinted by permission of John Verdant, http://verdant.net.

Melissa Algranati, "Being an Other" from *Becoming American, Becoming Ethnic: College Students Explore Their Roots*, ed. by Thomas Dublin. Copyright © 1996 by Melissa Algranati. Reprinted by permission of the author.

Drake Bennett, "Guiding Lights: How Soap Operas Could Save the World" published in the *Boston Globe*, May 5, 2010. Copyright © 2010 Boston Globe. All rights reserved. Used by permission and protected by the Copyright Laws of the United States. The printing, copying, redistribution, or retransmission of this Content without express written permission is prohibited. [Digital use requires link to *Boston Globe* Web site.]

Nell Bernstein, "Goin' Gangsta, Choosin' Cholita." Copyright © 1995 by Nell Bernstein. First published in *Utne Reader*, March/April 1995. Reprinted by permission of the author.

Deborah Blum, "The Gender Blur: Where Does Biology End and Society Take Over?" from *Utne Reader*, Sept./Oct. 1998. Copyright © 1998 by Deborah Blum. Reprinted by permission of International Creative Management, Inc.

danah boyd, "Implications of User Choice: The Cultural Logic of 'MySpace or Facebook?'" from interactions.acm.org, Vol. 16, Issue 6, Nov./Dec. 2009. Reprinted by permission of the author. http://interactions.acm.org/content/?p=1302

David Brooks, "One Nation, Slightly Divisible" from *The Atlantic*, Dec. 2001. Copyright © 2001 by David Brooks. Reprinted by permission of the author.

Stuart Buck, excerpts from *Acting White*, Copyright © 2010 Yale University. Reprinted by permission of Yale University Press.

Patti S. Caravello, "Judging Quality on the Web" by Patti Schifter Caravello, UCLA Research Library. Reprinted with permission.

Andrea Chang, "Teen 'Haulers' Become a Fashion Force" from the *Los Angeles Times*, Aug. 1, 2010. Copyright © 2010 Los Angeles Times. Reprinted with permission.

Julia B. Corbett, "A Faint Green Sell: Advertising and the Natural World" from *Enviropop: Studies in Environmental Rhetoric and Popular Cultures*, eds. Mark Meister & Phyllis M. Japp, pp. 81–94. Copyright © 2002 by Mark Meister and Phyllis M. Japp. Reproduced with permission of ABC-CLIO, LLC.

Richard Corliss, "The Gospel According to *Spider-Man*" from *Time*, August 9, 2004. Copyright © 2004 by Time Inc. *Time* is a registered trademark of Time Inc. Reprinted by permission. All rights reserved.

Steve Craig, "Men's Men and Women's Women: How TV Commercials Portray Gender to Different Audiences" from *Issues and Effects of Mass Communication: Other Voices* by Steve Craig. Reprinted by permission of the author.

Ian Daly, "Virtual Popularity Isn't Cool — It's Pathetic," originally published on Details.com. Reprinted by permission of the publisher. Copyright © 2008 Condé Nast. All rights reserved.

David Denby, "High-School Confidential: Notes on Teen Movies" published in *The New Yorker*, May 31, 1999. Copyright © 1999 by David Denby. Reprinted by permission of the author.

Mark Dery, "Dawn of the Dead Mall" from *ChangeObserver* online. Reprinted by permission of the author with grateful acknowledgment to Julie Lasky, editor.

Aaron Devor, "Gender Role Behaviors and Attitudes" from *Gender Blending: Confronting the Limits of Duality* by Aaron Devor. Copyright © 1989 by Indiana University Press. Reprinted with permission of Indiana University Press.

Minette E. Drumwright and Patrick E. Murphy, from "How Advertising Practitioners View Ethics: Moral Muteness, Moral Myopia, and Moral Imagination" from *Journal of Advertising*, Vol. 33, No. 2 (Summer 2004): 7–22. Copyright © 2004 by American Academy of Advertising. Reprinted with permission of M.E. Sharpe, Inc. All Rights Reserved. Not for reproduction without permission.

Umberto Eco, "Casblanca, or, The Clichés are Having a Ball" published in Italian as "*Casablanca o la rinascita degli Dei*" from *Dalla periferia dell'impero* by Umberto Eco, copyright © R.C.S. Libri S.A., Milan. Used by permission of RCS Libri.

Jack Lopez, "Of Cholos & Surfers" in *California Dreaming: Myths of the Golden Land*. Copyright © 1998 by Jack Lopez. Reprinted by permission of the author.

Alfred Lubrano, "The Shock of Education: How College Corrupts" in *Limbo: Blue-Collar Roots, White-Collar Dreams*. Copyright © 2004 by Alfred Lubrano. Reprinted with permission of John Wiley & Sons, Inc.

Daniel Mackay, "*Star Wars*: The Magic of Anti-Myth" by Daniel Mackay from *Performing the Force: Essays on Immersion into Science Fiction, Fantasy and Horror Environments*, ed. by Kurt Lancaster and Tom Mikotowicz (2001). Reprinted by permission of the author.

Carol Matheson, "*The Simpsons*, Hyper-Irony, and the Meaning of Life" in The Simpsons *and Philosophy*, edited by William Irwin, Mark T. Conrad, and Aeon J. Skoble. Copyright © 2001 by Open Court Publishing Company. Reprinted by permission of Open Court Publishing Company, a division of Carus Publishing Company, Chicago, IL.

Andy Medhurst, "Batman, Deviance, and Camp" from *The Many Lives of Batman*, ed. by Roberta E. Pearson and Eilliam Uricchio (Routledge 1991). Reprinted by permission.

Murray Milner Jr., from *Freaks, Geeks and Cool Kids: American Teenagers, Schools and the Culture of Consumption*. Copyright © 2004. Used by permission of Routledge c/o Taylor & Francis via the Copyright Clearance Center.

Mariah Burton Nelson, "I Won. I'm Sorry." was originally published in *Self* Magazine, 1998. Reprinted with permission of the author.

Anne Norton, excerpts from *Republic of Signs*. Copyright © 1993 by the University of Chicago. Reprinted by permission of the University of Chicago Press.

Tammy Oler, "Making Geek Chic" from *Bitch Magazine* online, Nov. 12, 2010. Reprinted by permission of the author.

Michael Omi, "In Living Color: Race and American Culture" from *Cultural Politics in Contemporary America*, ed. by Ian Angus and Sut Jhally. Copyright © 1989 by Michael Omi. Reprinted by permission of the author.

Michael Parenti, "Class and Virtue" From *Make-Believe Media: The Politics of Entertainment*, 1st ed., by Michael Parenti. Copyright © 1992 by Wadsworth. Reprinted with permission of Wadsworth, a part of Cengage Learning, Inc. Reproduced by permission. www.cengage.com/permissions

Jennifer L. Pozner, "Dove's 'Real Beauty' Backlash" from *Bitch: Feminist Response to Pop Culture*, Issue 30, Fall 2005. Copyright © 2005. Reprinted by permission of the author.

Angeline Price, "Working Class Whites" is reprinted by permission of the author.

Francine Prose, "Voting Democracy Off the Island: Reality TV and the Republican Ethos," Copyright © 2004. First appeared in *Harper's Magazine*. Reprinted with permission of the Denise Shannon Literary Agency. All rights reserved.

Jonathan Rauch, "The Tea Party Online" is reprinted with permission from *National Journal* online, Sept. 17, 2010. Copyright © 2011 by National Journal Group, Inc. All rights reserved.

Robert B. Ray, excerpts from "Formal and Thematic Paradigms" from *A Certain Tendency of the Hollywood Cinema 1930–1980*. Copyright © 1985 Princeton University Press. Reprinted by permission of Princeton University Press.

Bob Samuels, "*Inception* as Deception: A Future Look at Our Everyday Reality" (2010) is reprinted by permission of the author.

Hirsh Sawhney, "An Idiot's Guide to India" by Hirsh Sawhney from *The Guardian* online. Reprinted by permission of the publisher. Copyright © 2009 Guardian News & Media Ltd.

Eric Schlosser, "Kid Kustomers" from *Fast Food Nation: The Dark Side of the All-American Meal* by Eric Schlosser. Copyright © 2001 by Eric Schlosser. Reprinted by permission of Houghton Mifflin Company. All rights reserved.

Linda Seger, "Creating the Myth" from *Making a Good Script Great*. Copyright © 1987 by Linda Seger. Reprinted by permission of the author.

Mitu Sengupta, "Race Relations Light Years from Earth" from Ryeberg.com, Feb. 1, 2010. Reprinted by permission of the author.

ART CREDITS

Page 3: Deborah Voight, Richard Drew/Associated Press

Page 5: Bill Monroe, Associated Press

Page 6: Barbie MP3 player, Mark Lannihan/Associated Press

Page 12: *Leave it to Beaver* television still, © ABC/The Kobal Collection

Page 16: *Dracula*, 1931, Universal Pictures/Photofest

Page 17: *The Twilight Saga: New Moon*, 2009, Summit Entertainment/Photofest

Page 35: Lee straight leg stretch jeans ad, The Advertising Archive

Page 80: Prada store in desert, Daniel Hsu

Page 83: Levi's rugged jeans ad, The Advertising Archive

Page 100: NikeTown store, © Cathy Melloan Resources/PhotoEdit

Page 117: Credit Card Barbie, © Richard Hutchings/PhotoEdit

Page 170: "Mind if I smoke?" billboard, © Theo Anderson/Aurora Photos

Page 176: Home Shopping Network, © Jeff Greenberg/PhotoEdit

Page 181: Public Domain

Page 185: The VALS2 paradigm, Stategic Business Insight

Page 220: Dove's "Real Beauty" campaign, Narn Y. Hun/Associated Press

Page 224: Frosted Flakes plus Yoda, © Bill Freeman/PhotoEdit

Page 251 Gloria Steinem and Patricia Carbine, Angel Franco/New York Times Co./Getty Images

Color Insert: Emmelie, Natural Perfumer/Everyone is a Star ad, Courtesy of Nike, Inc, Target, and Emmelie Brunetti

Color Insert: The New Celica Action Package. Look Fast ad, Courtesy of Toyota and Eric Hameister

Color Insert: Braun, Wear Your Face ad, Courtesy of The Procter & Gamble Company

Color Insert: Ignoring Global Warming Won't Make It Go Away ad, Courtesy of the World Wildlife Fund

Color Insert: You Sang ad, Courtesy of Levi's®

Color Insert: Journey to the Ends of the Earth ad, Courtesy of GoRVing

Color Insert: Teenagers ad, AdCouncil

Page 270: *I Love Lucy* film still, CBS Photo Archive/Hulton Archive/Getty Images

Page 285: Stephen Colbert, Jason DeCrow/Associated Press

Page 289: Cast of *Survivor*, CBS/Landov

Page 195: "You're Fired." Donald Trump on ad for *The Apprentice*, © Nancy Kaszerman/ZUMA/Corbis

Page 297: Dr. Melfi and Tony Soprano, © HBO/The Kobal Collection

Page 324: *Mad Men*, Season 1, 2007, AMC/Photofest

Page 329: *Glee*, Season 1, 2009, Fox Broadcasting/Photofest

Page 364: Hollywood sign, © Robert Landau/Corbis

Page 367: Oscar Statues, © Gunnar Kullenberg

Page 371: *The Dark Knight poster*, © Warner Bros./Courtesy Everett Collection

Page 373: Jack Nicholson as the Joker, Photofest

Page 373: Heath Ledger as the Joker, Photographer Stephen Vaughn/Warner Bros./Photofest

Page 379: The "outlaw hero," Davy Crockett, portrayed by Fess Parker, The Kobal Collection

Page 388: *Star Wars* (1977), Photofest

Page 398: Anna May Wong, Photofest

Page 399: Michelle Yeoh in *Tomorrow Never Dies* (1997), Photofest

Page 409: Michael Clarke Duncan in *The Green Mile* (1999), Warner Brothers/Photofest

Page 414: *Avatar*, Twentieth Century Fox Film Corporation/Photofest

Page 434: John Travolta and Samuel L. Jackson in *Pulp Fiction*, Photofest

Page 437: *Reservoir Dogs* movie poster, © Miramax/courtesy Everett Collection

Page 444: *Time* Magazine "You" Person of the Year cover, *Time* Magazine, December 25, 2006/January 1, 2007 © 2007 Time Inc. Used under license.

Page 456: Ignacio's collage surprisingly appeared in CNN coverage of anti-American protests, © Reuters/Corbis

Page 459: Microsoft researchers Larry Zitnick and Richard Hughes demonstrating "Lincoln," Justin Sullivan/Associated Press

Page 507: Master Chief waits in line, AP Photo/Stuart Ramson/Xbox

Page 512: National Unemployment Rate Rises To 9.8 Percent, Scott Olson/Getty Images

Page 518: "Don't Tread on Me" protesters, Jason Andrew/Getty Images

Page 537: Stack of books, Gaye Gerard/Getty Images

Page 568: Garbage under "leave area clean" sign, Corbis

Page 571: Serena Williams at Wimbledon, AP Photo/Alastair Grant

Page 578: "Which man looks guilty?" ACLU ad, Courtesy of American Civil Liberties Union

Page 614: Masks, AP Photo/Felipe Dana

Page 622: Comic-Con International, AP Photo/Denis Poroy

Page 650: 1964 photo: unemployed miner and his family, John Dominis/Time & Life Pictures/ Getty Images

Page 651: *Beverly Hillbillies*, CBS Photo Archive/Getty Images

Page 652: Henry Fonda in *The Grapes of Wrath* (1939), 20th Century Fox /The Kobal Collection

Page 660: Four Teens, © Jim Whitmer/Stock Boston

Page 675: "Rearing children is a work typically done by women, but not always" Geoff Manasse/ Aurora Photos

Page 683: "Girls and moms check out an American Girl doll fashion show in Staten Island, New York." © Joel Gordon

Page 687: © Jeff Greenberg/The Image Works

Page 693: Two bride figurines on wedding cake, CBS Photo Archive/Getty Images

INDEX OF AUTHORS AND TITLES